THATCHER'S BRITAIN

Also by Richard Vinen

A HISTORY IN FRAGMENTS
THE UNFREE FRENCH

THATCHER'S BRITAIN

The Politics and Social Upheaval of the Thatcher Era

Richard Vinen

**SIMON &
SCHUSTER**

London · New York · Sydney · Toronto

A CBS COMPANY

First published in Great Britain by Simon & Schuster UK Ltd, 2009
A CBS COMPANY

1 3 5 7 9 10 8 6 4 2

Simon & Schuster UK Ltd
1st Floor
222 Gray's Inn Road
London
WC1X 8HB

www.simonsays.co.uk

Simon & Schuster Australia
Sydney

A CIP catalogue for this book is available
from the British Library.

ISBN: 978-1-84737-175-1

Typeset in Baskerville by Ellipsis Books Limited, Glasgow

Printed and bound in Great Britain by CPI Mackays, Chatham, ME5 8TD

For Emma

CONTENTS

ACKNOWLEDGEMENTS

I am grateful to Andrew Wylie for selling this book and to Andrew Gordon for buying it. After Andrew Gordon moved on, Mike Jones and Rory Scarfe adopted my literary orphan and brought it up as though it was their own. Only authors know what a difference a good copy-editor makes and Bela Cunha is the best. She handled my manuscript with an impressive mix of rigour and good humour.

The first draft of this book was written in Houston, Texas. Houston is Thatcher's kind of town; she went there on her first visit to the United States in 1967 and returned to the meeting of the G7 a few months before she resigned as prime minister. Houston's appeal was not immediately apparent to me, and the fact that I grew to appreciate the city's charms owes much to the friendship of Sarah Fishman and Daniel Cohen. I am also grateful to Martin Wiener, whose influence is discussed in chapter 8, for arranging for me to enjoy the status of visiting scholar at Rice University. I also owe much to my students and colleagues at King's College, particularly Laura Clayton and Paul Readman.

All historians of modern Britain owe a debt to the Margaret Thatcher Foundation, which is making an extraordinary range of sources available on the web. I am particularly grateful to Chris Collins of the Foundation for his advice on a number of points.

Karl French read a draft of this book and made many helpful suggestions. Three professors also took time out from their own busy schedules to read my work and comment on it from their different perspectives. My father, Joe Vinen, represents that strand of the British establishment which shifted from the Labour Party to the SDP in 1981 and from *The Times* to the *Independent* in 1986. John Ramsden is a veteran streetfighter for Conservatism as well as being a distinguished historian of the party. Miles Taylor claims never to have voted; he belongs to that curious group of British historians who became post-Marxists without ever having been Marxists. All three of them were generous with their time and very perceptive in their comments.

My mother, Susan, and my sister, Katie, provided much practical and emotional support. Alison Henwood read my work, did her best to make me understand the workings of capitalism, and undertook more than her fair share of childcare whilst I was writing. I am, however, grateful to Alison for many things that are more important than any book and, most of all, for our children: Emma and Alexander.

INTRODUCTION

I remember where I was when it began. On the morning of 4 May 1979 I was in an 'O' level Latin class. Our teacher put a transistor radio on his desk and turned it on so that we could hear the speech that Margaret Thatcher read out from notes jotted on the back of a card as she entered 10 Downing Street:

> I would just like to remember some words of Saint Francis of Assisi which I think are just particularly apt at the moment. 'Where there is discord, may we bring harmony. Where there is error, may we bring truth. Where there is doubt, may we bring faith. And where there is despair, may we bring hope.'

My school was in Solihull, the second safest Conservative seat in the country,* and the whole place was pulsating with excitement at the Conservative election victory – all the same, I think that most of my classmates thought that the speech was pretty mad.

I remember with equal clarity where I was when it ended. I was walking down a back street near Euston station on 28 November 1990. I looked up and saw a sign that someone had placed against an office window. It said: 'She's gone.' Anyone seeing it that day would have known that Margaret Thatcher had resigned as prime minister.

It is not just self-indulgence that makes me begin this book with

* Just after Sutton Coldfield.

personal reminiscence. There was something about Margaret Thatcher's premiership that cut deeply into the personal lives of many British people. In 1985 psychiatrists produced an interesting piece of research that illustrated this. Generally, patients suffering from dementia forget things about the present whilst remembering things that are more permanent. For most of the post-war period, for example, many demented people knew that Queen Elizabeth II was the monarch but could not remember who was the prime minister. Under Thatcher things changed: 'Mrs Thatcher has given an item of knowledge to demented patients that they would otherwise have lacked: she reaches those parts of the brain other prime ministers could not reach.'[1]

References to Margaret Thatcher suffuse British culture. The head of drama commissioning at the BBC remarked in 2005: 'the Eighties and Nineties are the new Victorian drama. Contemporary writers are now looking to this era and Thatcher's influence is huge.'[2] Speeches delivered in her strange, unnaturally deep voice, the product of careful coaching by her advisers, are used, often incongruously juxtaposed with the music of Frankie Goes to Hollywood, as a soundtrack to television programmes about the 1980s. Her phrases – 'The Lady's not for turning' or 'There is no such thing as Society' – are quoted, though the first of these was coined by someone else and the second is usually quoted out of context. She features in films and plays. She has walk-on parts in novels such as Alan Hollinghurst's *The Line of Beauty* (2004).* There has even been a musical produced about her career.

This intense focus on Thatcher as a personality, or as a legend, has gone with a declining interest in what her government actually did. The most widely cited works on 'Thatcherism' – those by Gamble, Jacques, Jenkins (Peter), Jessop, Kavanagh, Riddell, Skidelsky and Young[3] – were written before Thatcher's resignation.

---

* It is said that Thatcher herself was told of Hollinghurst's novel but misheard the title as 'The Line of Duty', which suggests a different kind of book.

Stuart Hall's influential article was published whilst Thatcher was still leader of the opposition.[4] Much was written by journalists, political scientists or left-wing activists, whose interest in Thatcherism was associated with a desire to devise strategies against it. Most of these people moved on to new interests when Thatcher fell. Even the emphasis on the extent to which Thatcherism's legacy has endured goes, curiously, with a tendency to downplay its importance – Margaret Thatcher is often now presented as though her main historical function was to serve as John the Baptist for Tony Blair.

There has also been a persistent tension in writing about the 1980s between an interest in Thatcher and an interest in Thatcherism. Academic writers, especially those of the Left, felt uncomfortable with the personalization of analysis – uncomfortable too, perhaps, with the ways in which attention to the character of Margaret Thatcher could slide into sexism. In his article of January 1979, Stuart Hall used 'Thatcherism' six times and referred to 'Mrs Thatcher' only once. Discussion of the Thatcher government amongst the wider population always laid a heavier emphasis on Margaret Thatcher the woman. Striking miners were said 'universally' to use the Rider Haggardesque term 'she' for the prime minister.[5] Tory canvassers got so used to hearing the phrase 'that bloody woman' that functionaries in Central Office devised the acronym 'TBW' – until an unkind interviewer enlightened her, Mrs Thatcher herself thought that the letters stood for the name of a television station.[6] Most of all, there was a cloyingly fake intimacy in the way in which the name 'Maggie' entered general circulation. Demonstrators shouted 'Maggie, Maggie, Maggie, out, out, out.' Long-suffering audiences at Tory conferences were induced to sing the excruciating 'Hello Maggie' to the tune of 'Hello Dolly'. An excited Norwegian commentator celebrated his country's defeat of the England football team in 1981 by shouting into the microphone: 'Can you hear me Maggie Thatcher? Your boys took a hell of a beating tonight.'

The focus of my own book is on Thatcherism as a project rather than Thatcher as a person. My feeling is that John Campbell's biography of Margaret Thatcher has probably taken us as close to understanding the woman as we are ever likely to get – perhaps closer than she (a person with little taste for introspection) ever got herself.[7] Having said this, I think that the word 'Thatcherism' itself became the centre of a debate that sometimes obscured more than it revealed. Many scholars,[8] and at least one of Thatcher's own ministers,[9] assume that the term was invented by the sociologist Stuart Hall in January 1979. However, as time went on, many writers became uncomfortable with the word and, as was often the case with debates of the 1980s, the two sides of the political spectrum expressed themselves in remarkably similar ways. On the Right, T. E. Utley wrote that 'Thatcherism' was a 'monstrous invention'[10] that made the government seem more original than it really was. On the Left, Bob Jessop complained that his fellow Marxists had created a 'monstrous monolith' by presenting Thatcherism as a coherent phenomenon,[11] overemphasizing the importance of ideology and downplaying the role of division, conjuncture and disagreement.

In fact, the word 'Thatcherism' was quite widely used before January 1979 – Thatcher used it, in a flippant aside, in March 1975.[12] The mere fact that the term came into general use suggests a recognition that Margaret Thatcher was associated with something novel and distinctive. However, using the word 'Thatcherism' did not imply some platonic absolute of ideological purity that marked a complete break with everything that had gone before it. One should not assume that displays of pragmatism reveal Thatcherism to be somehow 'false' because it had failed to live up to abstract ideas that existed in the pamphlets of the Institute of Economic Affairs or the mind of Alfred Sherman. Thatcherism was always about power, and it is the nature of power to adjust to circumstances.

The aims of my account are modest ones. I am aware that, as this book goes to press, I will for the first time be teaching students who were born after Margaret Thatcher resigned. I think there is a need for an account of this period that is designed for people who have no personal memories of it. I have tried to explain who the *dramatis personae* were, what they stood for, and to answer the simplest of questions: what happened next?

My account is more *événementiel* than most books on the Thatcher government. When Margaret Thatcher was still leader of the opposition, one of her advisers talked of the need to develop 'event-led communication'.[13] It seems to me that events such as the 1981 budget, the Falklands War or the miners' strike probably did more to communicate Thatcherism than the speeches of Sir Keith Joseph. I have stressed the difference between the Conservative Party in opposition from 1975 to 1979 and the party in government – as well as the differences between its various governments. Even my thematic chapters (notably that on Europe) are designed largely to show how thinking on particular issues evolved over time.

I have tried to strike a middle way between the very personalized biographical approaches that revolve around anecdotal details of 'Maggie' and the bloodlessly theoretical approaches that revolve around concepts such as 'relative autonomy of the state' or 'hegemony'. I have tried to give attention to the characters of people other than Thatcher and, in particular, to restore her ministers to the story. Thatcher's flamboyant style sometimes overshadowed that of her colleagues – one writer talked of 'a tyrant surrounded by pygmies'. A number of Thatcher's personal advisers or backbench supporters – Gardiner, Sherman and Mount – have also implied that the serious decisions were taken around Thatcher's kitchen table rather than in formal meetings of the cabinet. My own feeling is that Thatcherism makes more sense if it is examined in large measure through ministers. Studied in purely abstract terms, it is sometimes hard to pin down *what* Thatcherism was. It is, however, relatively easy to identify *who*, on the Conservative front bench, were Thatcherites. Few would, I think, deny this title to Howe, Lawson, Nott, Ridley and Tebbit.

Ministers are crucial figures when it comes to seeing how the ideas dreamt up in think tanks were converted into policy.

There is one character in this story who was not a minister under Thatcher and never, indeed, a member of the Conservative Party during her leadership of it. I have given considerable attention to Enoch Powell. I should stress that the most important part of the chapter title 'Thatcherism before Thatcher?' is the question mark, and that my own answer to the question would be 'no'. Having said that, Powell does seem to me to be a uniquely important figure in the history of British Conservatism. He thought about many of the matters that concerned Thatcherites and he expressed his conclusions with a degree of clarity and force that they rarely achieved. He also thought about issues – 'Englishness', the end of Empire, Ulster – about which most Thatcherites were revealingly silent. Tory ministers regarded him with a mixture of admiration, exasperation and fear. If Thatcherism is to be understood in terms of intellectual history, Powell is vastly more important than any number of Austrian philosophers, American economists or earnest young men at the Adam Smith Institute. Powell is also important because he was a practising politician even if not, judged in conventional terms, a successful one. He understood the realities of power and, for this reason, was often the most eloquent commentator on the differences between Thatcherism and his own 'purer' vision of politics.

I think that I differ most sharply from other recent historians in terms of the historical context in which I seek to place Thatcher. David Cannadine, Peter Clarke and Ewen Green[14] – came to look at Thatcherism after having worked on earlier periods of British history. Not surprisingly, they were very exercised by the occasional references of Thatcherites to the nineteenth century or to 'Victorian values'; one of them even believed that he had invented this phrase.[15] I am sceptical about all this. I do not believe that Thatcherism seriously sought to make itself the heir to nineteenth-century liberalism, and I think that the occasional references by Thatcherite ministers to Gladstonianism probably had more to do with electoral strategy at a time when the Liberal/Social Democrat alliance was doing well in the polls than with serious thought about the nineteenth century.

I am also sceptical about interpretations that lay much emphasis on thinking in the immediate aftermath of the Second World War or on rejection of the 'post-war consensus'. In many ways, I see Thatcher as the defender of the post-war consensus (especially in the form in which it was expressed during the 1950s) against the 'progressive consensus' of the late 1960s and early 1970s (see chapter 1). Thatcher herself, and some of her ministers, made much of Friedrich Hayek's *The Road to Serfdom* (first published in 1945), which had sought to defend the free market against 'socialists of all parties'. It is not, however, clear that Thatcher herself read this book until quite late in her career.[16] I suspect that this work merely provided a convenient philosophical polish on things that Thatcherites wanted to do for reasons that had little to do with Hayek's thinking. When Norman Tebbit was interviewed in 1986, he referred to the writings of 'Fred what's his name'; only when an official from Central Office stepped in did it become clear that he was referring to Hayek.[17] Green presents Richard Law, the Conservative MP whose *Return from Utopia* (1951) defended free-market Conservatism against the encroaching state, as a kind of proto-Thatcherite,[18] but I doubt whether many people, other than historians who are concerned with Thatcherism's intellectual ancestry, have ever paid much attention to his book. It is unclear whether any minister in the Thatcher government had heard of Law at the time they held power.[19]

I see Thatcherism as rooted in a specific time – it emerged out of debates on national decline, trade union power and economic modernization during the 1970s and it ceased to be relevant when those issues became less pressing. If I was forced to give precise dates for a 'Thatcher era', then I would suggest 1968–88. The period stretched from Thatcher's 'What's wrong with Politics?'

speech, which can be seen, though only in retrospect, as the first sign that Thatcher represented a distinctive political vision, until her Bruges speech of 1988, which can be seen as the first sign that Thatcherism was beginning to break up.

There are writers, of whom the most prominent is Simon Jenkins,[20] who see Thatcherism as having a life beyond Thatcher's resignation in 1990 and who, in particular, are interested in the way that Thatcher laid the foundations of New Labour. Obviously, Thatcher changed Britain in ways that mean that we all now live with her legacy. However, Thatcherism cannot be understood unless we recognize the remoteness of the recent past. Thatcher came to power less than twenty-five years after the end of the Second World War. Almost half the members of her first cabinet had fought in that war – three of them had been wounded;* four had been decorated for gallantry.† This compares to Margaret Thatcher's immediate successor as prime minister, who had grown up since the Second World War, or to his two successors, both men born after 1945. Tony Blair's first government in 1997 did not contain a single minister who had ever worn military uniform. Thatcher's world was dominated by the Cold War. For the whole of her premiership, there really were weapons of mass destruction pointed at London. This coloured not just her attitude to the Soviet Union but her attitude to Europe (especially West Germany), the United States, trade unions in Britain and Britain's status in the world. The political map changed almost beyond recognition as the Soviet Union reformed during the late 1980s; inability to adjust to these changes partly explains why Thatcherism became less successful during this period. The economy in the early 1980s was different from the economy of the early twenty-first century in ways that cannot be captured with mere statistics. As I lectured on Thatcherism in 2008, I looked at the rows of tiny, garishly coloured

* Hailsham, Joseph and Soames. Maude was a prisoner of war.
† Carrington, Pym, Soames and Whitelaw.

mobile phones that my students had laid out on the desks in front of them and I recalled how, when I myself was a student, the *Spectator* had run a series of articles devoted to the difficulty of getting the nationalized Post Office to install a new phone line in the magazine's offices.

This book is designed to be dispassionate. I was very much opposed to the Thatcher government when it was in power (or, at least, I often said I was – it is sobering to realize how hard I find it to recapture my own real feelings), and I have never been seriously tempted to vote Conservative. However, I have often felt exasperated by the partisan nature of writing on this subject and particularly by the sneering tone many authors adopt with regard to Margaret Thatcher herself.

Many French historians have managed to write interesting and sympathetic books about de Gaulle and his regime, even when they themselves had opposed him during his life. I feel that it is time British historians attempt to do the same for Margaret Thatcher. I have tried to avoid posing the Sellar and Yeatmanish question of whether or not Thatcher was a 'good thing'. However, it does seem to me that a little humility on this matter is in order from those of us who denounced Thatcher when she was in power. Many of us claimed repeatedly that the government's policies were so obviously wrong-headed that they were bound to bring some signal disaster. We should now have the grace to recognize that the signal disaster never arrived and that, at least in its own terms, the government was often – though not always – successful.

Perhaps I should finish the introduction by marking out the limits of this book. This is very largely about what Maurice Cowling, a historian sometimes seen as having been involved in the transformation of Conservative thought during the 1970s, labelled as 'high politics'. I have made three quite long excursions outside the high politics of the Tory party. One of these involves the Labour Party and the Social Democratic Party in the early 1980s, one of them involves the Falklands War and one of them involves the miners' strike of 1984–5. I think that all three were particularly important for the Thatcher government. I also think that analysts of Thatcherism have sometimes been too prone to treat all three as though they were acts of God. The electoral collapse of the Labour Party, British victory in the South Atlantic and the poor tactics of Arthur Scargill are invoked as evidence that Margaret Thatcher was 'lucky'. Thatcher clearly was lucky (no one would survive as prime minister for ten years unless they had some spectacular good fortune). But there was more to it than luck. Sometimes, the failure of Thatcher's enemies had deeper causes, often related to the social changes that had brought Thatcher to power in the first place; sometimes, it was due, to a greater extent than the government's critics have cared to concede, to skilful management by Thatcher and her colleagues.

Having said all this, I have not tried to write a social history of Britain in the 1980s. I have not, for example, attempted any serious research on whether British people during this decade were increasingly likely to define themselves in terms of consumption rather than work. I have discussed questions such as 'why did many British coal miners return to work before their union authorized them to do so during the strike of 1984–5?'; 'why did people buy their council houses?' or, for that matter, 'why did they vote Conservative?' on the basis of information that is already in the public domain.

Equally, this is not a history of the world from 1975 to 1990. Thatcher existed in an international context. Her positions on many issues, not just those directly relating to the Soviet Union, were born of the Cold War. Her political demise was in many ways associated with the fact that reform in the Soviet Union shot away the foundations of her political world. It would be possible to write a different kind of history that presented Thatcherism as one element in a global transition and which attempted to discern the extent to which changes in Britain were effects or causes of a change that brought down Soviet Communism and strengthened capitalism in most of the world. On the whole, my interests have been confined to looking at the extent to which British politics were influenced by events in the wider world. I have not attempted to say how far British policy influenced those wider events or, for that matter, to say very much about the extent to which Thatcherism might have been part of a wider pattern. Looking at the international context can be useful on one very simple level: it cuts Britain down to size. Thatcher led the British Conservative Party from 1975 to 1990. During these years, China saw all the extraordinary upheaval that lay between the death of Chairman Mao and the aftermath of the Tiananmen Square massacre. The year Thatcher became leader of the Conservative Party was also the year Vaclav Havel wrote his open letter to the president of Czechoslovakia – a brave and, as it seemed at the time, hopeless gesture of defiance against authoritarianism. In 1990 Havel, himself now president of the Czechoslovakia, dined in Downing Street. Between 1975 and 1990, Chile went from the worst years of state-sponsored murder to being, more or less, a democracy. All this reminds us that the Anglocentric obsession with Thatcherism as a 'revolution' needs to be judged against countries where politics really could be a matter of life and death.

Chapter 1

THATCHER BEFORE THATCHERISM, 1925–75

There is . . . the sheer romance of it, which will remain alive for generations of readers in the wider world who may know little of late twentieth-century British politics and care even less. A woman from the provincial lower-middle class, without family connections, oratorical skills, intellectual standing or factional backing of any sort, established herself as leader of a great party which had represented hierarchy, social stratification and male dominance.

Alfred Sherman (adviser to Margaret Thatcher)[1]

I seem to have done very little in thirty years.

Margaret Thatcher, March 1956[2]

Margaret Thatcher did not share the fascination with her petit-bourgeois origins that was felt by so many of her admirers and enemies. The volume of her memoirs dealing with her time in Downing Street was published before that dealing with her life up to 1979. No doubt this was partly due to decisions taken by publishers and literary agents, but the order also reflects a feeling that Margaret Thatcher's early life made sense only when seen through the prism of her later career. Thatcher herself seems to have found the young Margaret Roberts to be an inscrutable figure. In her autobiography she thanks her 'memoirs team' for their skill in unearthing 'all the multifarious files where little bits of modern lives are written down and stored away[3] – as though her researchers had discovered a person previously unfamiliar to the adult Margaret Thatcher.

During her early years in parliament, Margaret Thatcher was usually seen as a typical Conservative lady. Her clothes, voice, pearls and general air of strained formality seemed to belong to the world of the garden party and the summer fête. An American diplomat who met her in 1973 described her as 'an almost archetypical, slightly to the Right-of-center Tory whose views are strongly influenced by her own middle-class background and experience'. It was clear that 'middle class' in this context meant 'upper-middle class' – the meeting had taken place over lunch at the Connaught Hotel.[4]

When she ran for the leadership of the Conservative Party in 1975, Thatcher's campaign team paraded her humble origins precisely because these origins seemed to run against the popularly held view of their candidate. One member of that campaign team – George Gardiner MP – subsequently published a biography of Margaret Thatcher.[5] It was one of the first full-length biographies; it was also, at least for a long time, the last book that was written by an author who had full access to Margaret Thatcher and to other members of her family.[6] Gardiner portrayed Margaret Roberts as the hard-working daughter of a Methodist grocer from the Lincolnshire town of Grantham. Grantham was almost turned into a brand name by Thatcher's associates. Thatcher's son was to name the enterprise at the centre of his business operations after his mother's birthplace.[7] But Margaret Thatcher rarely went back after she left home at the age of eighteen. Many of her ministers had, or at least affected to have, a visceral attachment to the area in which they had been born. Thatcher was never really happy anywhere except central London – for all her allegedly 'suburban' qualities, she regarded the retirement home that she and her husband briefly owned in Dulwich as being too remote.

Subsequent discussion of Thatcher was to make so much of the vices, or virtues, that she had allegedly acquired from her upbringing that it is sometimes hard to dig the real experience out from under the weight of subsequent mythology. Thatcher did not mention either her mother or her sister in her *Who's Who* entry. This provoked one Labour MP to build a psycho biography around Thatcher's alleged abnormality in this respect.[8] But Thatcher's memoirs contain a convincing account of her grief at her mother's death. Equally, most historians have underlined Thatcher's close relations with her father and the extent to which his example inspired her subsequent career. However, the precise details of Thatcher's relations with her father were rewritten in successive accounts. In one interview she expressed pleasure at the fact that her father had lived to see her on the government front bench.[9] In fact, as she recalls in her memoirs, he had died several months before she entered the cabinet.

Margaret Roberts was born in 1925. She was the second daughter of Beatrice, a seamstress who had run her own business before marriage, and Alfred, a tall good-looking man whose one indulgence seems to have been smoking, and who had been excluded from military service during the Great War on account of his poor eyesight. Alfred Roberts became manager of a grocery, and he saved enough money to buy his own shop in 1919. He was a devout Methodist and a well-known lay preacher. He was also a local politician. He had been a Liberal and was elected to Grantham Town Council as an Independent, though he seems to have been recognized as a functional Conservative by the time he became Mayor of Grantham in 1945. Certainly the Labour Party, which took control of Grantham Town Council in 1952, saw him as an opponent and ended his career as an alderman.

As John Campbell has shown, presenting the Roberts family as simply belonging to the 'provincial lower-middle class' ignores some important details. For one thing, Alfred Roberts was a good deal more prosperous by the 1930s than the average shopkeeper; he eventually bought two shops and employed several people. The gap between him and his neighbours was all the more marked because the Roberts family did not strictly speaking live in Grantham but in Little Gonerby, a working-class area built around a brewery. Alfred Roberts' political career also brought him into contact with other local notables – some of rather patrician background. The notion of Alfred Roberts as a sturdy exponent of free enterprise is also slightly misleading. His shop was a sub-post office and consequently, in a small way, an agency of the state.[10]

Margaret was a bright child and her father, who regretted his own lack of schooling, devoted great effort to her education. He sent her to the state elementary school in Huntingtower Road, which was said to be better than the school that was nearer to her house. In 1936 Margaret won a place at Kesteven and Grantham Girls' Grammar School. Grammar schools were to play an important part in Thatcherite mythology, but Thatcher did not belong to the post-war generation of grammar school children who enjoyed free places courtesy of the Butler Education Act (1944). She went to grammar school in an age when parents were still required to pay, though the fees were more modest than they would have been at a private school. KGGGS took some girls from quite humble backgrounds on scholarships, but Thatcher was privileged by the standards of the school, and of Grantham more generally. She was always well dressed and, perhaps the result of being a grocer's daughter at a time of rationing, better fed than most of her contemporaries.[11]

A girls' grammar school in the late 1930s was a good place to be educated. It was one of the few institutions in which young women could escape from male condescension. No one seems to have suggested that Margaret Roberts should study subjects 'appropriate for a girl' or to have objected to her decision to specialize in science. Economic depression had driven bright graduates who needed secure jobs into the teaching profession. Male casualties in the First World War had increased the number of spinsters who, like Muriel Sparks's Miss Jean Brodie, lived their lives through the girls whom they taught, and girls' schools, unlike those for boys, did not lose their youngest teachers to the armed forces during the Second World War.

In 1943 Margaret Roberts left home to read chemistry at Somerville College, Oxford. Oxford has educated twenty-five British prime ministers, including all the graduate prime ministers who took office in the second half of the twentieth century. Thatcher was not, however, the usual Oxford undergraduate. She was a woman in a male-dominated institution. She was a scientist in a university notable for its emphasis on the arts. Most of all, her university career began at a time when a large proportion of her male contemporaries were away fighting in the war. Her Oxford was one of black-outs and rationing rather than balls and punting.

Margaret Roberts was not a well-known Oxford figure. The only important political friend she made at Oxford was Edward Boyle, who was later to be her boss when she was a junior minister at the Department of Education in the 1960s and with whom she was to remain on good terms in spite of their differences. Julian Critchley, who came up to Oxford in the early 1950s, recalls: 'The talk . . . was of great men who had just gone down, Robin Day, Peter Kirk, Jeremy Thorpe and Ken Tynan. Shirley Caitlin, later Williams, was talked of as Britain's first woman Prime Minister. No one mentioned Margaret Roberts.'[12]

Thatcher's relationship with Oxford was notoriously difficult.[13] The university refused to grant Margaret Thatcher an honorary degree (a distinction conferred on all previous Oxonian prime ministers). When she became prime minister, dons made much of her apparently mediocre academic record; her former tutor insisted that Margaret Roberts had been an unremarkable student. Thatcher's intellectual attainments generally were to be a subject of much discussion for the rest of her career. Her enemies derided her as a philistine of vulgar tastes who was interested only in knowledge that had some economic utility. There was much amusement when she told an interviewer that she was 'rereading Frederick Forsyth's *The Fourth Protocol*'.[14] Even her closest associates often implied that there was something deficient, or at least strange, in her intellect or education.'[15]

Yet occasionally we see glimpses of a very different kind of mind at work in Margaret Thatcher. She knew a great deal of poetry and had a special affection for Kipling, an unfashionable taste that she shared with George Orwell and Antonio Gramsci. She could be deeply affected by books such as Solzhenitsyn's *The Gulag Archipelago* or Harold Bloom's *The Closing of the American Mind*.[16] She disliked the poems of T. S. Eliot (the mere willingness to express dislike suggests that poetry mattered to her), but Anthony Powell overheard her talking about Helen Gardner's study of *The Four Quartets*.[17] Her interest in science was not purely utilitarian. She took pride in Britain's record of scientific achievement (particularly the number of Nobel prizes that its citizens had won) and, as secretary of state for science and education, she defended 'blue skies research'. Thatcher sometimes expressed disdain for 'intellectuals',[18] but she had a high, perhaps excessive, regard for 'first-class minds'.

Margaret Thatcher's last year at Oxford coincided with the return of the generation of men who had fought in the war. Almost the first political association she joined after graduating was called the '39 to 45' club. Throughout her career, Thatcher was to come up against men who had had 'a good war'. Especially when she was accused of having 'usurped' patriotism during the Falklands War of 1982, her opponents were to make much of her comparatively inactive role during the Second World War. David Ennals, a Labour MP who opposed British intervention in the Falklands and who perhaps anticipated the fact that he was to be swept away in the Conservative landslide of 1983, pointedly reminded her that he had been 'storming up the beaches of Normandy' in the summer of 1944.

In the 1940s and 1950s the war pervaded politics in ways that made it all the more difficult for a woman who wanted to have a political career. Candidates campaigned in uniform and evoked their experiences of war at every opportunity.[19] Thatcher's first experience of elections came when she supported Squadron Leader Worth in Grantham in 1945. Her own attempts to become a candidate for a winnable Conservative seat brought her into competition with a succession of decorated heroes. At Beckenham her rivals included Major Ian Fraser MC. At Hemel Hempstead she lost out to Lieutenant Colonel Allason. At Finchley the two other names on the shortlist from which Thatcher finally emerged victorious were, respectively, a holder of the Military Cross and a former member of the Special Operations Executive.

How did Margaret Thatcher herself look back on the war and how did it shape her politics? Sharp-eyed observers noted that Thatcher's references to the Second World War tended to concentrate on one year of the conflict: 1940.[20] Time and again, Margaret Thatcher was to refer to Dunkirk, the Battle of Britain and, most of all, our 'finest hour', a phrase that Churchill had used in a speech of 18 June 1940.[21] This focus on one year and, more particularly, on the months between May and September might be explained in all sorts of ways. It focused attention on a war that had been fought by a small group of men under the leadership of Winston Churchill and centred on the south of England. It avoided much reference to the large-scale industrial mobilization that came later in the war. It emphasized Britain 'alone'. In spite of her Atlanticist sympathies, Thatcher made little reference to the American role in the war. The Soviet Union was even more conspicuous by its absence – indeed the focus of her speeches on the early part of the war sometimes went with an emphasis on the fates of Finland[22] and Poland,[23] both countries that raised embarrassing questions about Soviet behaviour.

Thatcher's 'memory' of the Second World War was, like many aspects of her public personality, partly constructed by other people.

Some of the 'Churchillian' references that so annoyed Thatcher's enemies had, in fact, been inserted into her speeches by advisers and ghostwriters.[24] The most systematic attempt to separate the 'good' war of Churchillian patriotism from the 'bad' war of increasing state power was made by Nigel Lawson.[25] Some of Thatcher's opponents also developed their own particular interpretation of the Second World War. They emphasized mass mobilization, working-class participation and plans for a new social order that were drawn up in 1943 and 1944. The phrase 'people's war', coined by the eccentric Communist soldier Tom Wintringham, was used frequently by the Left during the 1980s. Wintringham became an object of interest partly because his ideas could be used to attack the defence policy of the Thatcher government.[26]

The notion that Thatcher herself tried to rewrite the history of British participation in the Second World War to suit her political project is unfair. In public, she spoke respectfully of wartime projects for a new social order; indeed she was ostentatiously respectful towards the memory of the wartime leaders of the Labour Party, partly because she found it useful to contrast them with the supposedly lesser men who led the party later. She even occasionally spoke in terms that seemed very close to those who talked of a 'people's war'.[27]

It is true, however, that Thatcher focused most on the exploits of airmen and soldiers in 1940, rather than the more large-scale mobilization that came later. It is also true that this focus seems to have reflected the perception of the war that the young Margaret Roberts had at the time, as well as the more deliberately constructed view that Margaret Thatcher and her advisers found it useful to deploy in the 1980s. The two books on the war that struck Margaret Roberts most were the biography of Ronald Cartland, published by his sister Barbara, and the autobiography of Richard Hillary;[28] she was to say that the latter had affected her more than any other book she had ever read. Ronald Cartland was a soldier and anti-Munich Tory MP, who was killed in action during the retreat to

Dunkirk.[29] Richard Hillary was a Spitfire pilot who was shot down and badly injured during the Battle of Britain.

Thatcher's perception of the war was different from that of most ruling-class Englishmen of her generation, the kind of men who were to dominate her first government in 1979. Such men had usually served in the war. Most of them had fought, not during the 'finest hour' of 1940, but during the bloody campaigns in southern Italy and Normandy. Thatcher's war was relatively simple: it pitted Britain against Germany, and right against wrong. Most serving soldiers saw something messier and less heroic. They belonged to a large and chaotic army made up mainly of conscripts. In personal terms, they remembered the war as one of squalor, confusion, fear, despair, separation and infidelity, as much as heroism. John Peyton, a Conservative MP who stood against Thatcher in the 1975 leadership contest and was later broken under the Thatcherite juggernaut, wrote:

The Second World War was, for most of those over whom it cast its shadow, by far the greatest event of their lives. It reached down from its cosmic dimensions into their hearts, minds and bodies, and after its fearful passage, left them, as well as the world, changed.[30]

Peyton was captured, whilst hiding in a pigsty, near Dunkirk. He spent the next five years in a German prisoner-of-war camp. It was there that he learned that his fiancée had married another man and that his brother had been killed in the St Nazaire raid.

It is revealing to contrast Thatcher's view of the war with that of Peter Rawlinson, another of the politicians who was to be cast aside when Thatcher became prime minister. Rawlinson was wounded serving with the Irish Guards in North Africa. The shrapnel did not work its way out of his body until thirty years later, and the name of the young guardsman who had been blown apart whilst sitting next to him suddenly came back into his mind when he was writing his memoirs. Rawlinson's war was more ugly and morally ambiguous than Thatcher's. This was apparent in his personal memories of Thatcher's hero Richard Hillary: 'He wanted to join in a part of the gaiety of our youth, but as his had been burned away he would also sneer and scratch at us. We probably deserved it, but we had the grace to understand and to tolerate the savagery of the wounded man.'[31]

What was Margaret Roberts to do when she graduated? She rejected the obvious careers for a woman graduate of her class. She did not want to teach and she did not want to be a civil servant. Instead she went into industry and was hired as a research chemist by BX Plastics in Colchester. Here she was disappointed by the tedium of repeating simple tests. Moving to work at Allied Lyons a few years later took her to London, which was useful for her political career, and gave her slightly more scope for real research. It was still, however, not the kind of job that she wanted. For all her enthusiasm for business in principle, Thatcher was to make little of her own brief career in British industry; the cv that she prepared when she was a parliamentary candidate, and her *Who's Who* entry when she was elected to parliament, merely alluded to her having spent several years engaged in 'chemical research'.

Margaret Roberts also began the long haul that would eventually get her into parliament, a desire that she later claimed to have conceived quite suddenly in 1945 or 1946, as a result of a brief discussion of politics after a dance. It is hard to recapture now what an astonishing ambition this was. There were only twenty-four women MPs in the 1945 parliament. Being a Conservative woman Member of Parliament was particularly difficult. Of 618 Conservative candidates in the 1945 election, fourteen were women, and only one of these was elected. Most Conservative MPs were still public school men from upper-middle-class families. The Conservative Party was keen to recruit parliamentary candidates from a wider social base and constituency associations were no longer allowed to ask candidates to pay all of their election expenses.

In spite of this, it was considered difficult to live on an MP's salary and consequently a political career was easiest for those who had a private income or who had a job, which being a research chemist was conspicuously not, that could be undertaken alongside parliamentary duties.

In 1949 Margaret Roberts was selected as a Conservative candidate for Dartford. As the local papers pointed out, she was the youngest woman Conservative candidate in the country. However, selection by the Dartford Conservative Association was hardly a political triumph. In spite of the fact that Dartford was a safe Labour seat, some party notables resented the selection of a woman. The Conservative MP for a neighbouring constituency wrote that he had been asked why 'a young girl of 23, Miss Margaret Robertson [sic], had been selected as Candidate for Dartford? Could not they have got some prominent business man?'[32]

The barriers that an unmarried woman with no money or contacts faced in getting a Conservative seat can be highlighted by looking at how easy some men found things. John Wells, an old Etonian who had had a 'good war', beat her to selection for a seat in Maidstone. His parliamentary career was notable mainly for his interest in inland waterways and horticulture. He came close to achieving political fame only during the brief period when he considered joining the Social Democratic Party and resigning his seat to allow Roy Jenkins to fight a by-election.[33] Paul Channon, later to be described as a 'lightweight' by Thatcher and to serve as an undistinguished minister in her government, had been chosen, whilst still an undergraduate at Christ Church, to fight a safe Tory seat once held by his father. James Prior, another of her future ministers, described how a casual acquaintance whom he met whilst driving his tractor back from the fields asked whether he would like to stand for the Tories in Lowestoft.[34]

Margaret Roberts's political prospects were transformed by Denis Thatcher – a man ten years her senior who had served in the

Second World War. Denis Thatcher had very right-wing views on most matters – though he did not share his wife's support for the death penalty. His family seems, at least by the standards of the Home Counties middle class, to have been faintly bohemian, and he had contracted a brief wartime marriage.[35] In the 1980s Denis Thatcher was to tell a friend that he was a cavalier whilst his wife was a roundhead.[36] The couple met in 1950 and were married in December 1951. By all accounts the marriage was happy. It also transformed Margaret Roberts in material ways. She was now able to abandon chemistry and devote all her time to reading for the Bar, a more fitting occupation for a would-be Tory candidate. Denis was a wealthy man and on his way to being a millionaire by the time he sold the family business to Burmah Oil in the mid-1960s. Until she began to cash in on the fruits of her fame on the international lecture circuit in the 1990s, Margaret Thatcher's money came from her husband. In the 1980s she told the daughter of a friend: 'Marriages are made in heaven, but it is better if the money is made on earth.'[37]

In view of the frequency with which historians have evoked the influence of her father on Margaret Thatcher, it is worth noting that she married a man who could hardly have been more different from Alderman Roberts. Her father had been, in a minor way, a public figure; her husband was careful to avoid any public statements at all once his wife embarked on her political career. Her father was a Methodist; her husband belonged to the Church of England, and, after marriage in a Wesleyan chapel, the couple began to practise a low-Church Anglicanism – Thatcher was not one of the three Tory MPs elected in 1959 who declared themselves to be Methodists. Her father had left school at thirteen to earn his own living; her husband had attended a minor public school (Mill Hill) and inherited the family business. Her father was a teetotaler who occasionally played bowls; her husband was a hard-drinking ex-soldier who spent his weekends refereeing rugby matches.

Marriage and the Bar provided Margaret Thatcher with the

basis on which to build a new political career. After having briefly withdrawn her name from the list of potential Conservative candidates, she began to look for a winnable parliamentary seat. Even with the advantages conferred by a rich husband, being selected for such a seat was not easy. Selection committees repeatedly asked her who would look after her young children. In a more subtle way, her social origins also counted against her. Anyone leafing through the *Who's Who* entries of candidates who were chosen ahead of Margaret Thatcher will notice some recurring patterns – 'the Carlton', 'country pursuits', 'Eton'.

It took Margaret Thatcher ten years of hard work to get into parliament,[38] but her persistence was rewarded in 1958, when she was selected as Conservative candidate for Finchley in North London. Her victory was narrow – she beat the last of her rivals by 46 votes to 43 – and, unusually, a 'handful' of members refused to observe the convention that the successful candidate should be given a unanimous vote of support at the end of the process.[39] The scale of Thatcher's achievement in getting selected for a safe Conservative seat can be illustrated by looking at her predecessor. Sir John Crowder, who had held the seat since 1935, was a Lloyd's underwriter who had been educated at Eton and Christ Church and served with the Household Cavalry during the Second World War. On being told that the shortlist for his succession contained both Thatcher and Peter Oppenheim, he said: 'We've got to choose between a bloody Jew and a bloody woman.'[40]

Thatcher held Finchley for the Conservatives, with a majority of 16,000, in 1959, and she was to do so again in every election, until she entered the House of Lords in 1992. It was a good springboard for an ambitious Conservative. Thatcher held her seat comfortably through three Labour victories in general elections so that her parliamentary career was never disturbed by the need to find a new seat – indeed she was one of only three Conservative MPs elected in 1959 who managed to hold exactly the same seats through the general elections and boundary changes of the next three decades.*

What was it like to be one of the twenty-five women MPs in the 1959 parliament? In her memoirs, Margaret Thatcher recalls the boisterous atmosphere of the House and the fact that women were effectively excluded from the smoking room, in which political deals were often hatched. However, she also insists that she felt unalloyed pleasure in her new role, that parliamentarians judged colleagues on their abilities, and that prejudice against women was less insidious than it had been in industry or at the Bar. Her parliamentary colleagues remember her arrival in parliament as being less comfortable. Peter Rawlinson first met Margaret Thatcher at a meeting of Conservative lawyers in the House of Commons. He recalled the occasion thus:

> She spoke even then . . . with a vehemence rather too exaggerated for the subject and, I noticed, with an irritating emphasis on the wrong word, a habit she has never wholly lost. It was obvious that her 'contribution' had been designed merely to attract attention. She had of course attracted notice from every man in the room before she had ever opened her mouth. But that was not the kind of notice which she sought.[41]

Thatcher had recognized privately that some of the opposition to her candidature in Finchley had come from 'anti-woman' prejudice'.[42] Her attitude to the disadvantages under which women laboured was hard to read. Interviewed by the *Daily Express* in 1960, she said that she would send her daughter to university, rather than 'to finish abroad', and talked at length about the education and career appropriate for a woman. However, she also stressed the centrality of marriage for women and the importance of 'domestic arts'.[43] Some biographers argue that Thatcher's position

---

* The others were Sir John Farr and Nicholas Ridley.

on the rights of women changed as her career advanced – that, as time went on, she became less keen to ensure that other women had the advantages that she had enjoyed.[44] It is certainly true that Thatcher could be hypocritical. In later years she sometimes claimed that she had not worked when her children were young when she had, in fact, filled in the application to take her Bar exams when she was still in the maternity ward. It was not, however, just that Thatcher's position changed; rather that the whole nature of discussion around women's rights changed with the rise of feminism in the late 1960s and 1970s. Thatcher was emphatic that she was not a 'feminist',[45] and she often spoke of what she described as 'women's lib' with some disdain.[46] Addressing a group of children during a television programme in 1982, she said:

> I think most of us got to our own position in life without Women's Lib and we got here, not by saying 'you've got to have more women doing so and so' but saying 'look, we've got the qualifications, why shouldn't we have just as much a chance as a man?' And you'll find that so many male bastions were conquered that way, whereas Women's Lib, I think, has been rather strident, concentrated on things which don't really matter and, dare I say it, being rather unfeminine. Don't you think that? What do the girls think, don't you think Women's Lib is sometimes like that?[47]

The truth was that Margaret Thatcher's sex, which had been a disadvantage when she was trying to get into parliament, was probably an advantage once she was in it, at least unless and until she tried to obtain one of the major offices of state. From 1959 until her entry into the cabinet in 1970, she benefited from the need for token women in certain kinds of position and from the attention that was given to someone relatively young and attractive.

For most of her time in parliament, Thatcher was a loyal party woman. She had promised the electors of Dartford in 1950 that she would vote according to her conscience and not the party line.[48] In fact, she voted against a Conservative three-line whip only once in her entire Commons' career, when she supported birching for young criminals. In any case, Thatcher's period as an ordinary backbench MP was comparatively short. She was appointed as parliamentary secretary to the Ministry of Pensions and National Insurance in October 1961 and she shadowed this department after the Conservative defeat in the general election of 1964. She worked through two further shadow posts: first at Housing and Land, from October 1965, and then as deputy to the shadow chancellor, Iain Macleod, from April 1966. She joined the shadow cabinet in October 1967 with responsibility for fuel and then took the transport brief in November 1968. In October 1969 she became shadow education minister. She was seen as effective and competent in the House of Commons. Education was a 'woman's job', but her post at Pensions and as deputy to Macleod had given her the opportunity to demonstrate a grasp of technical financial matters. The Labour MP Denis Healey had first been told of Thatcher by his colleague Charlie Pannell, who acted as her 'pair' and had a high opinion of her abilities. At first, Healey could not see anything special in the new MP, but, by the late 1960s, he had come to regard her with grudging admiration.[49]

What did Margaret Thatcher believe in during the 1960s? In the 1980s some historians talked about a post-war 'consensus' that revolved around the welfare state,[50] and the parallel lines on which the Conservative chancellor, R. A. Butler, and his Labour shadow, Hugh Gaitskell, had supposedly developed their economic policies. Interest in this phenomenon was sharpened by the frequency with which Thatcher herself denounced 'consensus'. Some of the fiercer Thatcherite ministers – Norman Tebbit[51] and Nicholas Ridley[52] – were particularly bitter in their attacks on Harold Macmillan. Thatcher's own relation with Macmillan was an interesting one. He was prime minister during her first four years in parliament, and gave her her first government office. In her memoirs, Thatcher talked of being 'uneasy with the general direction in which we

seemed to be going' during the Macmillan government.[53] Macmillan's
parliamentary private secretary listed Thatcher as one of four junior
ministers who did not give the prime minister unqualified support.[54]
If, however, Thatcher was dissatisfied with Macmillan, then she
kept it quiet for a long time. Until at least 1979, she continued to
praise Macmillan in extravagant terms. In one of the first interviews
she gave as party leader, Thatcher suggested that Macmillan was
a particularly important model for her.[55] She insisted that he was
a visionary and the single twentieth-century politician that she
admired the most – more, apparently, even than Churchill.[56]

Thatcherite dislike of Macmillan probably had as much to do
with things that he said during the 1980s as with things that he
had done during the 1960s. 'The Great Macmillan Speech' – with
its evocation of Edwardian England, the tragedy of the First World
War, the horrors of the Great Depression and the possibilities of
new technology – had been a well-recognized and much parodied
institution since the early 1970s. During the 1980s Macmillan
injected it with new notes of sexism and snobbery (economic policy
was evoked with references to nannies, family silver and the Brigade
of Guards) to make his speech into an anti-Thatcher weapon. He
ostentatiously supported her opponents in the cabinet and devoted
his maiden speech in the House of Lords to attacking government
economic policy. He republished *The Middle Way. Theories of a Mixed
Economy* – a book he had first brought out in 1938 when under
the influence of John Maynard Keynes.

There was, however, an irony in all this. Macmillan the elder
statesman of the 1980s recalled himself as the young soldier of
1916 or the middle-aged parliamentary radical of 1938, but glossed
over the small matter of his years as prime minister. He had, in
fact, been a tough political operator, a vigorous defender of the
free market and a bitter enemy of the Labour Party. It is true that
Macmillan did not try to humble the unions or reduce state spending
in the way that Margaret Thatcher's government was to do. But
this was partly because he lived in different times – Thatcher

wistfully remarked that Macmillan had presided over 'golden years', in which public spending had consumed only around 34 per cent of gross domestic product (it consumed around 42 per cent in 1984),[57] and in which inflation had seemed 'worrying' when it rose to 4.5 per cent.[58] It is interesting to ask how Macmillan would have behaved if he had still been an active politician when Britain began to face the problems of the 1970s. There is evidence that, in private, he anticipated some of the measures that Thatcher was to take (see chapter 7).

Thatcher's view of the post-war period was more subtle than that of some of her supporters. She usually used the word 'consensus' to describe a style of politics rather than to denounce particular politicians or policies. She was careful not to condemn the whole direction of British social policy since 1945; indeed, she sometimes confounded her opponents by citing with approval the documents that had influenced the immediate post-war period – the Beveridge Report of 1942 and the White Paper on Full Employment of 1944.[59] There was only one occasion on which she applied 'consensus' specifically to the three post-war decades of British history, and even then she was careful to note change across the period.[60]

Throughout the 1950s and 1960s some had campaigned against what they saw as the betrayal of free-market economics by all the major parties. Particularly important in this campaign was the Institute of Economic Affairs (IEA). The IEA was founded in 1955 by Antony Fisher, an entrepreneur who derived his fortune from battery chickens and his ideas from Friedrich Hayek.[61] Fisher recruited two economists – Arthur Seldon and Ralph Harris. The IEA was not a party political organization – the Liberal MP Oliver Smedley was closely involved in it and Seldon was, at least for most of the 1950s, a Liberal. The institute operated by publishing papers and organizing discussions, and it aimed to focus economic thinking on specific practical problems.

Some free-market Conservative MPs remained unsure about

whether Thatcher was really 'one of us' on economic grounds until well into the 1970s.[62] Others regarded her as an ally, but one of uncertain value. When sounded out by Arthur Seldon about Margaret Thatcher in 1969, Geoffrey Howe wrote:

> I am not at all sure about Margaret. Many of her economic prejudices are certainly sound. But she is inclined to be rather too dogmatic for my liking on sensitive issues like education and might actually retard the cause by over-simplification. We should certainly be able to hope for something better from her – but I suspect that she will need to be exposed to the humanizing side of your character as much as to the pure welfare-market-monger. There is much scope for her to be influenced between triumph and disaster.[63]

The speech that Thatcher delivered to the Conservative Political Centre in October 1968 has attracted much interest from historians of Thatcherism because of its reference to controlling the money supply.[64] This was, however, a rather unusual expression of views on Thatcher's part; perhaps the only occasion in her life when she sought to tackle broad questions of political philosophy without having recourse to speechwriters. Parts of the speech seemed to allude to the critique of Heathite 'technocracy' that was being advanced at the time by Angus Maude and Enoch Powell. However, this was hardly mainstream Thatcherism – she would never again hint that economic growth might not be a good thing. Nor did the speech have a great impact on perceptions of Thatcher's position: a *Times* interview in the following year was to conclude that 'she is no supporter of the Angus Maude wing of the Tory party'.[65]

The post-war political consensus was not just, perhaps not mainly, about economics. The single most important thing on which there was cross-party agreement during the 1950s was foreign policy.[66] In this area, Thatcher was an emphatic defender of consensus. She shared the belief that Britain should remain a great power.

In pursuit of this status, she believed in a British nuclear bomb and in the maintenance of the Anglo-American 'special relationship' – she was later to claim that Macmillan's greatest achievement was his reconstruction of this relationship after Suez.[67] Thatcher also shared the belief widespread in the 1960s that the state had a duty to strengthen the family. She voted in favour of legislation to legalize homosexuality and abortion but she did so precisely because, like most other politicians of the time, she thought that this legislation would address 'anomalies' and 'special cases' rather than establish an alternative morality.

On social matters, as much as economic ones, the important point about the 'progressive consensus' was that it progressed. Sometimes, indeed, it might be argued that Thatcher was a defender of the 'post-war consensus' (i.e. that established in the late 1940s) against the 'progressive consensus' of the late 1960s. This was visible on two issues that Thatcher was most identified with. The first was crime and punishment. The *Sun* noted in 1970 that 'On issues . . . traditionally close to the hearts of Tory women, she [Thatcher] is unhysterically, but firmly, in the law-and-order camp.' Thatcher favoured the restoration of the death penalty (though she wanted its use to be relatively sparing) and regretted that bringing back corporal punishment for young offenders was no longer realistic.[68] Thatcher was entirely consistent on support for the death penalty (her Liberal opponent in Finchley believed that it was her only strong conviction),[69] but her views, which would have seemed unexceptional for a Conservative parliamentary candidate in 1950, had begun to seem right-of-centre for a Conservative frontbencher in 1970.

The other matter that preoccupied Thatcher at the end of the 1960s was education, the subject on which she spoke for the opposition. She was contemptuous of radicalism on university campuses – though less exercised by this than her friend Sir Keith Joseph. More significant was the subject that began to dominate educational debate in the late 1960s: comprehensive schools. Since the Second World War, British schoolchildren had been divided, usually at the age of eleven, into the academically able, who went to grammar schools, and the majority, who went mainly to secondary modern schools. In the 1960s local authorities began to convert all schools into 'comprehensives'. Grammar schools were, in fact, very much a feature of the post-war consensus. It was, after all, success in exams that had given the men in Whitehall their notorious conviction that 'they knew best', and the 1944 Education Act, which gave birth to the post-war grammar school system, had been drawn up under the aegis of the arch consensualist R. A. Butler.

Thatcher defended grammar schools, though her position was, as was often the case, more nuanced than her later pronouncements, or those of her admirers, might suggest. She had expressed reservations about comprehensive schools ever since she had been a parliamentary candidate in Finchley, but she had also stressed that 'there was room for experiment . . . It may be, she said, that comprehensive schools turned out to be wonderful.'[70] When she became shadow minister for education, the *Financial Times* believed that: 'On the vexed issue of comprehensive schools, Mrs Thatcher's position is moderate.'[71] Thatcher never suggested that changes that had already taken place should be reversed, or even that the transformation of schools into comprehensives could be stopped. Her aim seems mainly to have been to retain a few 'top tier grammar schools within a national system of mostly comprehensive education'.[72] A couple of years later she was to compare the relationship of direct grant schools (the grandest kind of grammar school) to state schools with the relationship between Paris fashion houses and Marks and Spencer (a remark that probably says something about her much vaunted admiration for M&S as well as her attitude to education).[73]

In 1970 the Conservatives won the election and Thatcher entered the cabinet for the first time, as secretary of state for education. The prime minister who made the appointment was Edward Heath. Like Thatcher, Heath had been born into a relatively humble background and educated at grammar school and Oxford. Service in the Second World War, which he finished with the rank of lieutenant colonel, gave him a belief in teamwork, efficiency and loyalty. It also gave him, as it gave his friend Denis Healey and his enemy Enoch Powell, a strange honorary membership of the English upper-middle class – he drew his status from the pips on his shoulder rather than his background or wealth. After working as news editor of the *Church Times* and as a merchant banker (it says much about how his world differed from that of the Thatcherites of the 1980s that the first of these jobs was more highly paid and demanding than the second), Heath became a Tory MP in 1950 and made his mark as a successful whip, enforcing discipline on the other ranks after Suez. In 1965 Heath became leader of the party – the first one to be elected by Tory MPs rather than chosen by informal consultations amongst grandees. It was an astonishing achievement for a man of his origins – he succeeded a straight run of three Etonians.[74]

Thatcher voted for Heath in the leadership election, after Sir Keith Joseph told her 'Ted has a passion to get Britain right,' and she served loyally in his government. In spite of this, many came to talk as though Thatcherism was almost defined by opposition to the policies of her predecessor as Tory leader. Some of the tension between the two was personal, but some of it came also from the belief that Heath had, in fact, been elected to pursue radical free-market policies but had effected a 'U turn' and abandoned them. Thatcher's remark to the Conservative Party conference of 1980 – 'You turn if you want to. The Lady's not for turning' – was seen as an implicit rebuke to Heath.

Denunciation of Heath by free-market Conservatives revolved particularly around the conference for members of the shadow cabinet held at the Selsdon Park Hotel in 1970. The conference was designed to prepare the manifesto for the coming election and also, in the eyes of the Conservative apparatchiks, to ensure that frontbenchers actually understood the policies that the party had adopted in the previous few years.[75] The transcript of the meeting suggests that discussion amongst the shadow ministers was, in fact, rather disjointed and that the general thread of policy was often lost. The most revealing comments were those of Iain Macleod who tried to inject some sense of realism into the meeting: 'Absurd to go into details of administration now . . . All we need is the decision en principe.' Macleod's words might almost have served as Heath's epitaph.[76]

Selsdon was, however, important to some people who did not attend the meeting. One of these was the Labour prime minister Harold Wilson, who coined the phrase 'Selsdon Man' to sum up 'the atavistic desire to reverse the course of twenty-five years of social revolution'. Selsdon, or perhaps Wilson's jibe about it, caught the imagination of some Tories. Nicholas Ridley, who felt slighted by the fact that Heath had removed him from a junior ministry in an economic department, founded the Selsdon Group in September 1973, ostensibly to defend the principles on which the Conservatives had been elected. Thatcher never joined it, and probably never really shared its view about what Selsdon had meant. A private briefing by the Conservative Research Department before she confronted a television interviewer in 1977 anticipated that there would be: 'Questions on the Selsdon Conference, what role Mrs Thatcher played and the final shape of the Selsdon policies. (Albeit that Selsdon itself is vastly exaggerated in Labour mythology.)'[77] However, when she became leader of the Conservative Party, Labour MPs asked whether her own economic policies would make her a 'Selsdon Woman' and, like many phrases that were originally intended as insults, this one was eventually adopted by Thatcher herself.

Heath undoubtedly did change course in certain respects during his four years in office. Having initially pledged to avoid intervention in industry, the government provided money for companies that were in difficulty and in 1972 institutionalized such support with the Industry Act. It was also in 1972 that the chancellor Anthony

Barber sought to head off the prospect of rising unemployment with a budget that made borrowing cheaper. This provoked a boom in property prices, quickly followed by a train of bankruptcies and bank failures. It also provoked the resignation from the Central Policy Review Staff of Alan Walters, later to be Thatcher's personal economic adviser. Finally, in a bid to damp down inflation, partly caused by its own loose monetary policy, the government broke a manifesto commitment not to introduce controls over prices and incomes. After experimenting with voluntary agreements, it enforced a succession of statutory controls which seemed to illustrate all the absurdities of a managed economy. Geoffrey Howe, who became commissioner for prices and incomes, claimed that only some quick and discreet negotiations by his civil servants prevented the vicar of Trumpington from being prosecuted for raising the rates that he charged for brass rubbing in his church.[78]

Blaming Heath for changing course is, though, to miss the point. He was never a political fundamentalist. He thought of himself as a pragmatist and regarded adjustments to circumstances as natural. He saw the free market as a means to an end – that end being the modernization of Britain with a special view to making the economy fit for entry into the European Economic Community. Getting into Europe was, in fact, Heath's most cherished ambition and one that he achieved in 1973. In addition to this, the circumstances to which Heath had to adjust were uniquely difficult. Inflation came from the increased union militancy and consequent wage claims that had begun in the late 1960s. There was also a sharp increase in the oil price after the Arab–Israeli War of 1973. Heath's advisers had anticipated that prices might rise to six dollars a barrel or even to nine dollars, a possibility that they described as a 'crisis'. They actually rose to forty dollars.

A series of setbacks undermined the government. Iain Macleod, the chancellor of the exchequer, died unexpectedly in 1970. He had had the very qualities – charm, shrewdness, cynicism and an eye for electoral advantage – that Heath lacked, and it is possible that he might have been the one man capable of saving Heath from himself. Britain became locked in international disputes, the very triviality of which seemed to underline the decline of its power. Iceland declared that British ships would not be allowed to fish within 200 miles of its shores – thus forcing the Admiralty to admit that its aircraft carriers and nuclear submarines could not actually assure the freedom of the seas for British ships. The Ugandan dictator Idi Amin expelled people of Indian descent from his country. Ministers, including Margaret Thatcher, recognized that they were legally and morally obliged to take these refugees in. Doing so, however, damaged the government in the eyes of some Conservatives.

Heath also faced two more serious general problems. The first involved labour relations. The government had come to power with a pledge to introduce an Industrial Relations Act, which eventually came into force in early 1972. The aim of the act was to encourage unions to register with the state and to make agreements between unions and employers enforceable in special industrial courts. But it was introduced at a bad time, when labour militancy was rising, and suffered from a problem that ministers had not anticipated – unions simply refused to register under the legislation (the TUC expelled unions that did so) and effectively dared employers to take them to court. Far from bringing peace to industrial relations, the Heath government had to deal with a succession of disputes. In particular, the miners' strikes of 1972 and 1974 generated a visible sense of failure – the first caused power cuts and the second forced the government to introduce a three-day working week. The legislation allowing British governments to introduce a state of emergency has been on the statute book since 1920. It has only been used eleven times and five of these occurred between 1970 and 1974.

Above all, the Heath government faced problems in Northern Ireland. Ever since the 1920s much power in the province had been devolved to the Ulster parliament at Stormont. The province was dominated by the Unionist Party, which represented Protestant interests. In the late 1960s Catholics began to protest at the ways in which they were excluded from political power, and both sides took up arms to defend their interests. In 1969 there had been thirteen political murders in Ulster; in 1972, the *annus horribilis* for Heath in almost every way, there were 467 – the largest number of violent deaths in the province's history. The government tried to counter this threat with a succession of expedients – sending troops in to maintain order (and, initially, to protect the Catholic population), introducing internment without trial and conducting secret negotiations with leaders of the IRA – most of which made things worse.

Ulster was a particularly awkward issue for a Conservative leader because the Ulster Unionists had traditionally been allied to the Conservative Party on the mainland and because Ulster Unionist MPs at Westminister had taken the Conservative whip.[79] During the 'Troubles', this began to change. Unionism's leaders were now more plebeian and more radical. The Reverend Ian Paisley was the most flamboyant of the movement's new leaders. The tone of the new Unionism became more violent and its style – anti-European, self-consciously archaic, shot through with religious imagery – was far removed from Heathism.

In 1972 the British government suspended the Stormont parliament altogether and introduced direct rule in Ulster. The following year it organized negotiations amongst Ulster parties at that great centre of Heathite technocracy – the Sunningdale Civil Service College. At Sunningdale, the government imposed a 'power-sharing executive' that would have responsibility for some of the government of Northern Ireland. Far from being a solution, the Sunningdale agreement radicalized Ulster Unionism. Official and unofficial Unionists against Sunningdale fought the February 1974 election under a combined ticket which meant that only one of the twelve MPs returned by Ulster supported the agreement. This played a direct role in Heath's political demise.

After his general election defeat of February 1974, Heath was
keenly interested in a parliamentary deal that might keep him in
power. This meant talking to other political parties and particularly
to the Liberals and the Ulster Unionists. Seven of the eleven Ulster
Unionists who had been returned to Westminster still nominally
took the Conservative whip in the House of Commons – though
they had not in fact given much support to the government since
March 1972. Heath hoped that they would continue to vote with
his government on issues other than Ulster. The Unionists hoped
that Heath would abandon Sunningdale in return for their support.
In practice, however, Heath and his advisers found it hard to
separate the Official Unionists from their more radical allies – it
is difficult anyway to imagine how anyone could have built a political
coalition that included the Liberal leader Jeremy Thorpe (pro-
Sunningdale and about to be prosecuted for conspiracy to murder
his male lover) and Ian Paisley (anti-Sunningdale and committed
to 'save Ulster from sodomy').[80]

Problems in Northern Ireland sapped the energy of the
government, and contributed to a general sense that its approach
was not working. Ministers associated with law enforcement or the
army were now obliged to spend their whole lives in the company
of armed police officers. Politics on the mainland and in Northern
Ireland intersected in awkward ways. The miners' strike of 1972
began just after British paratroopers had killed thirteen unarmed
Catholic demonstrators on 'Bloody Sunday', and direct rule was
announced just before the budget of March 1972. The mood of
crisis that developed in Ulster spilled over into discussion of problems
on the mainland. A report to the cabinet cited a Midlands MP
who had warned that calling out troops in the coalfields would
'make a Londonderry out of every colliery'.[81]

Ministers and civil servants discussed industrial relations in
apocalyptic tones – they were agitated by information from the
security services about Communist infiltration of the National
Union of Mineworkers – though the leader of the union, Joe

Gormley, who led two successful strikes, was conspicuously non-Communist and may even have been an MI5 informant. In the aftermath of the 1972 miners' strike, a note to (or perhaps even by) the prime minister suggested: 'The use of violence to achieve social or political ends must increase as society becomes more complex, the vulnerable areas become more numerous, the methods of attack more sophisticated.' The letter added: 'The social revolution need not be destructive – although a growing number of people begin to think that it will have to be.'[82] Someone, presumably Heath, scribbled on this letter 'powerful: learn the lessons for . . .'

The Heath government was ill-equipped to deal with the crises of the early 1970s. Unforeseeable circumstances pose especially awkward problems for a government that presents itself, as Heath's did, as characterized by its capacity to plan the future. Heath was right to claim that his government came to power in 1970 with more detailed projects for action than any previous government. This was part of the problem, and he was probably more damaged by those projects for a new order in industrial relations which he tried to implement, than by those, for a more liberal economic order, which he abandoned. Heath's emphasis on rational discussion, modernization and planning made the chaos of the early 1970s seem all the more humiliating. In 1972 the machinery of government broke down in a very literal sense – during power cuts, senior civil servants sat in candle-lit offices, unable to get documents typed or photocopied.

Heath's corporatism – his desire to establish complicated mechanisms for negotiation between employers, unions and government – also made his problems worse. His government, in conspicuous contrast to Thatcher's, could not simply claim not to be responsible for strikes or negotiations. Heath had problems with both sides of industry. He made assiduous efforts to stay close to organized business – his secretary of state for industry, John Davies, had previously been head of the Confederation of British Industry.

However, this did not produce a smooth managerialism. On the contrary, Heath was often shocked by the political incompetence of business leaders (including Davies), and the Conservative election campaign of February 1974 was damaged when the new head of the CBI (William Campbell Adamson) casually remarked that business did not really regard the government's policies on industrial relations with much favour.

Heath was bad at managing crisis. His fantasies about a 'technocratic' and 'apolitical' approach to government were really suited to France (the country that both fascinated and repelled Heath) rather than Britain. He placed great faith in civil servants, but men who were good at writing elegant reports proved strikingly bad at taking quick and unpleasant decisions. Far from being a detached purveyor of cool advice, William Armstrong (the cabinet secretary, who had won a place in Heath's heart by playing piano duets with him) became obsessed by the belief that Britain was on the verge of Communist revolution and eventually, after having had a nervous breakdown (which caused him to hide under his desk), had to be sent to the West Indies to recuperate.

The Conservatives needed someone who could rally support for their policies, but Heath was not the man for the job. In spite, or because, of his humble origins, he seemed patrician and his interests – classical music and yachting – did not suggest the common touch. He spoke badly when addressing a large audience and on television. The slogan of his 1966 manifesto had been 'action not words' and Heath's greatest weakness was, indeed, a failure to appreciate the importance of words. It is significant that his only memorable phrase – his description of Lonrho as the 'unacceptable face of capitalism' – came from his having mixed up 'face' and 'facet'. Despairingly his aides made a list of jargon that the prime minister should avoid: 'regressive, relativities, anomalies, unified tax system, productivity, threshold agreement, deflation, realignment'.[83]

The end of Heath's premiership came in February 1974. Against the advice of many colleagues, Heath called an election in an attempt to strengthen his hand in dealing with the miners' strike. He was unlucky in almost every respect during the election – even the weather was bad. In spite of it all, the Tories got more votes than Labour, but the Labour Party had 301 seats against the Conservatives' 297. After his attempts to stay in office with the support of smaller parties failed, Heath resigned on 4 March.[84]

Heath's failure was a precondition of Thatcher's success in a very direct way – it is hard to imagine that she would ever have become leader of the Conservative Party if Heath had been elected for a second term. The Heath government came to provide some Thatcherites with a convenient epitome of everything that they opposed. Heath himself was an ideal enemy for Thatcher (almost as good as General Galtieri or Arthur Scargill). The venom of his attacks on her rallied her supporters whilst his own gloomy unclubability prevented him from rallying her opponents. Most of all, though, Heath laid the way for Thatcher in a more complicated fashion. He shared much of her diagnosis about what was wrong with Britain – economic decline, politicized trade unions. His failure seemed to discredit his own particular approach to those problems and this explains the fact that many of the Conservatives who had been close to Heath in the early 1970s were willing to support Margaret Thatcher's more dramatic radicalism ten years later. John Nott, a minister under both Heath and Thatcher, wrote: 'Perhaps Margaret Thatcher owes her election victory in 1979 to the appalling mess left behind in 1974 by a Tory Cabinet – of which she was a member.'[85] Arthur Scargill, a leader of the miners' union which broke Heath and was later to be broken by Thatcher, remarked in 1981:

I think there are enormous differences between this Government and the Heath administration in terms of their application of Conservative policy. It's true that the working class movement learned a lot of lessons from 1970–74 but the ruling class learnt a lot of lessons as well.[86]

If Thatcher benefited from the Heath government in the long run, however, it was certainly not obvious in the early 1970s just how great those benefits would be for her personally. It was taken for granted that Thatcher was a competent minister but one whose sex would impose sharp limits on her career. Sir Gerald Nabarro, a right-wing Tory MP, wrote in 1973:

> Thatcher will probably go a good deal further without reaching the top. She is not prime ministerial material, but I suppose, conceivably, she might find her way into the Treasury . . . if a brave enough Prime Minister could be found to appoint her Chancellor of the Exchequer.[87]

Chapter 2

THATCHERISM BEFORE THATCHER?
ENOCH POWELL

I don't think he'd fit into Mrs Thatcher's Shadow Cabinet.
He's just too powerful for the poor lady.
> Mary Wills, working-class 'Powellite' from Ealing,
> interviewed mid 1970s[1]

[One of her] remarkable characteristics, which stamps
her as a superb politician, is her ability to put up with
things and go along with them, even though she doesn't
agree with them, until the time comes when they can
be dealt with. Now, not possessing that quality myself –
having the loquacity which always impels me to say: 'I
don't agree' – I admire this.
> Enoch Powell on Margaret Thatcher, 1989[2]

In strict academic logic the Right Hon. Gentleman is
right. In everything else he is wrong.
> Margaret Thatcher to Enoch Powell, 1981[3]

Does Enoch Powell belong in a book about Thatcher at all?
Thatcher was not one of the fifteen MPs who voted for
Enoch Powell when he stood for the leadership of the Conservative
Party in 1965. Powell would not have considered voting for Margaret
Thatcher as leader of the Conservative Party – he said that the

party would never stand for 'those hats and that accent'[4] – but, in any case, the question never arose because Powell had left the party by the time that Thatcher became its leader, and he never returned to it. Powell's support for Edward Heath in the 1970 election probably helped the Conservatives to win that election, and his advice to his supporters that they vote Labour in February 1974 probably contributed to Heath's defeat. In both these acts, he might have played an indirect and unintentional role in furthering Margaret Thatcher's career. However, Powell had little influence on the electoral politics of the British mainland after this, and he did not support Margaret Thatcher's party in the 1979 election: he described the result as 'grim'.

A historian of any aspect of post-war British history faces the dilemma of where to put Enoch Powell. His capacity for the striking expression of extraordinary opinions always commanded attention, but his eccentricity means that it is almost impossible to fit him comfortably into any wider movement. He spoke in terms that suggested a superhuman concern for rigour and logic (a journalist jibbed that he was 'lucid to the point of incomprehensibility'[5]), but these qualities were allied to a sense that politics should be informed by feelings that could not be rationally articulated.[6] He valued 'myth' and 'hallucination' and seemed at times to feel that there was something admirable about a rational man who based his life on things that a rational man would know to be untrue. One of the funniest passages in his writing concerns the 'simple faith' of Alec Douglas-Home. Without saying so in so many words, Powell hints that faith can be no great virtue in someone who is too stupid to see how implausible the tenets of Christianity are in the first place.[7]

Powell managed to combine an obsessive air of consistency with a capacity for the volte face. He changed his position dramatically on some of the issues that dominated his political career (Empire, Europe and race). He voted for three different political parties at various times but sometimes did so for reasons that were diametrically opposed to the stated policies of those parties. He was haunted by the death of a close friend during the war and sometimes expressed regret that he himself had not been given the chance to die in action: his whole career was suffused by fascination with the suicidal frontal attack.[8] Powell was always interested in matters of clinical insanity. As minister of health in the early 1960s, he worked hard to shut down Victorian mental hospitals ('the asylums which our forefathers built with such immense solidity to express the notions of their day')[9] and, in a characteristically eccentric moment, he persuaded the Queen's dressmaker to design new uniforms for the staff at Broadmoor. Anyone who studies his career must sometimes wonder whether Powell was not, to quote words that he used in his most notorious speech, 'literally mad'.

For all his eccentricity, however, it would be impossible to understand the political Right in late twentieth-century Britain without understanding something about Enoch Powell. Its whole style – from Roger Scruton's taste for hunting to Michael Portillo's affection for Wagner – owed much to Powell. He had a remarkable capacity for intimidating his fellow Tories. As prime minister, Harold Macmillan had the seating of the cabinet rearranged so that he could avoid Powell's stare, which, he claimed, made him feel like 'one of the more disreputable Popes being eyed by Savonarola'.[10] During the 1970 election, Heath's aides were tormented by anxiety about what Powell might say and one of them believed that the turning point of the whole campaign came on the day (15 June) that Heath said that he would take no more questions from journalists on the subject.[11] In the 1980s, when he was a backbench member of a small party with no hope of holding office again, Powell's long shadow could still darken the Conservative front bench. Ministers quoted his occasional expressions of approval with an almost childlike pleasure,[12] and they were frightened of his denunciation. One of them recalled: 'He was the only adversary in the House of Commons who ever seriously worried me . . .

Powell, by his appearance, voice and choice of words, radiated an authority which I had no immediate resources to match.'[13]

There were more specific links between Thatcher and Powell. Powell was seen as the purveyor of an ideology at a time when the Conservative Party still prided itself on being 'unideological': Iain Macleod first identified the phenomenon of 'Powellism' in 1965. Many of Thatcher's ministers – Geoffrey Howe, John Biffen, Nicholas Ridley, John Nott and Ian Gow – were, or had been, disciples of Powell. Some saw him as the political ancestor of Thatcher. Anthony Howard asked Powell in 1983 whether Thatcherism was 'Powellism by other means'.[14] Cecil Parkinson believed that Thatcher had succeeded Powell in a very direct way and that she had been invited to join the Economic Dining Club (an important free-market pressure group in the Conservative Party) to replace Powell when he left the party in 1974.[15] John Nott argued that the government in which he served from 1979 to 1982 was really 'Powellite' rather than Thatcherite.[16] Powell even provided Thatcherism with much of its language. When Keith Joseph talked of the 'ratchet effect' of socialism, or when Thatcher talked about subversion from 'enemies within',[17] they were, consciously or not, quoting Powell.

Most of all, however, Powell is worth studying alongside Thatcher precisely because of the *differences* between two outlooks that sometimes seemed superficially similar. Powell questioned every orthodoxy and took every argument up to, and sometimes beyond, its logical conclusion. Comparing him with Thatcher and her allies highlights the extent to which the success of her government was based on pragmatism and tactical flexibility. Thatcher is often seen as the enemy of the 'post-war consensus', but looking at Powell illustrates how many aspects of this consensus – Anglo-American alliance, a British nuclear bomb, the emphasis on great power status and on 'reversing decline' – she defended.

Even in purely personal terms, the contrast between Powell and Thatcher is revealing. Thatcher is interesting only because of her political career, and her life before she was elected to parliament was uneventful. Powell would have been an extraordinary and interesting man even if he had never entered politics.[18] He was born, the only child of two schoolteachers, in Birmingham in 1912. His brilliant career as a classical scholar took him through King Edward's Grammar School and Trinity College Cambridge to be professor of Greek at the University of Sydney, but he returned to England in 1939 to join up as a private in the Warwickshire Regiment. His military career was as meteoric as his academic one and Powell could have been a general if he had been willing to stay in the army for just another year or two. By the time he was thirty-four, the age at which Thatcher was first elected to parliament, he had already set two records – as the youngest professor in the British Empire and as the only man to hold every rank between that of private and brigadier in the British army during the Second World War. He was a published poet and could have been a professional clarinetist. As an essayist and reviewer, he could be as interesting on, say, the films of Jacques Tati or the travel writing of Wilfred Thesiger as he was on politics or history. Richard Ingrams was probably joking when he offered Powell the editorship of *Private Eye* (though with Ingrams, as with Powell, it is sometimes hard to tell) but, in fact, Powell was probably the only man in England who could have sustained the magazine's mix of paranoid denunciation and surreal humour.

Powell is now remembered mainly for a speech he made in April 1968 in Birmingham denouncing coloured immigration. Because of Powell's reference to the Tiber 'foaming with much blood', this became known as the 'rivers of blood' speech and it probably attracted more attention than any other statement in that whole tumultuous year. The British establishment was horrified by Powell's apparent racism, and Edward Heath sacked Powell from the Conservative shadow cabinet, thus ending his front-bench career. However, the mail that poured into Conservative Central Office was overwhelmingly favourable to Powell. He had struck a chord amongst part of the white working class – dockers and porters from Smithfield market marched in his support. For the next few years, polls showed that Powell was one of the most popular politicians in the country – sometimes more popular than the official leader of his party.

The 'rivers of blood' speech anticipated and influenced Thatcherism. Members of Thatcher's shadow cabinet repeatedly referred to the importance of 'immigration' as an electoral issue and Thatcher's remarks about the native population of Britain feeling 'rather swamped' were seen as an attempt to exploit public feeling on this issue (see chapter 4). Left-wing commentators sometimes saw Thatcher's 'authoritarian populism' as being an extension of Powell's.

However, the similarities between Thatcher and Powell can be overstated. For one thing, Thatcherites only ever saw immigration as one issue amongst many, while Powell, for a time at least, saw it as the most important issue in British politics. Some Thatcherites seem to have been interested in it because they saw it as a means of mobilizing electoral support for economic policies which might otherwise be unpopular, rather than because they saw it as a matter of central importance in itself. Thatcher's version of populism involved reference to the need for more severe repression of crime, particularly the restoration of the death penalty. Powell made little of crime and opposed the death penalty.

Furthermore, the key to Powell's populism was that it involved a form of politics that spilled out of the conventional party structures – it is significant that he admired Charles de Gaulle, who operated above parties and outside parliament. Though he always described himself as a Tory, Powell was not a conventional member of the Conservative Party. He had voted Labour in 1945, to 'punish' the Conservative Party for Munich, and his appeal after 1968 was largely to people who were not Conservatives. Powell himself voted Labour again in February 1974 (this time in an attempt to obtain British withdrawal from the European Economic Community).

Later in the same year, he joined the Official Ulster Unionists and was elected to represent a constituency in Northern Ireland. And, though Powell adored the House of Commons and was a fanatical defender of the rights of parliament, he talked, with reference to both Europe and immigration, of matters that were so important that they could be decided only 'by the Nation itself'.

Thatcher, by contrast, never countenanced politics that spilt out of ordinary party structures. Her populism was a means to strengthen an existing party rather than to sweep it away. Her response to the 'rivers of blood' was to insist on the importance of the House of Commons: 'I hope Enoch will put his views before the parliamentary forum.'[19] More generally, Thatcher's relations with Powell after April 1968 were marked by the very quality that he most lacked: prudence. She knew how hostile the Conservative front bench was to Powell and understood the damage that could be done by association with him. She told an American diplomat in 1973 that 'John Biffen had once had a great future, but he was now ruined because he had made himself a disciple of Powell.'[20] But, if Thatcher was nervous of being associated with Powell, she was also nervous of being too clearly distanced from him. Association with Powell would damage an ambitious Conservative in the eyes of the party leadership; hostility to him could damage them in the eyes of the party's rank and file – David Hunt had difficulty in being selected to fight a safe Conservative seat after he attacked Enoch Powell at the party conference. Thatcher had a particularly awkward balance to strike: her own constituency association contained a number of Powellites,[21] but also a number of Jews. Powell was not anti-Semitic, but many Jews detected a whiff of late Weimar in his pronouncements and the reaction that they aroused. There was a studied ambiguity in Thatcher's public references to Powell.[22] Her speech to the Conservative Political Centre in 1968 contained an odd allusion to 'Enoch' as an exponent of planning – a reference that might be read as mocking or affectionate, or both.

Relations between Powell and Thatcher were made easier by the fact that Powell joined the Official Ulster Unionists shortly before Thatcher became leader of the Conservatives. In the article that first gave currency to the word 'Powellism', Iain Macleod wrote: 'I am a fellow traveller, but sometimes I leave Powell's train a few stations down the line, before it reaches, and sometimes crashes into, the terminal buffers.'[23] Powell's departure from the Conservative Party made it easier for his admirers in that party to be 'fellow travellers' without risking the crash into the buffers. Had he remained in the party, then Thatcher would have had to deal with some of his extraordinary outbursts. Sooner or later, the party would almost certainly have had to withdraw the whip from Powell. Had he joined a party that opposed the Conservatives, then equally Thatcher might have been expected to produce clear denunciations of Powell's views. As it was, however, Powell belonged to a party that no longer took the Conservative whip but also one that was not in direct competition with Conservative candidates (because the major parties of the mainland did not run candidates in Ulster). Thatcher could maintain a stance of benign neutrality towards Powell. When young Conservatives asked her to pledge that he would never be brought back to the Conservative front bench, Thatcher was able to reply that: 'Mr Powell is not even a member of the Party. He is an Ulster Unionist and we have no Conservative Party in Ulster. I really am not likely to have as a member of the Shadow Cabinet a person who is not even a member of the Party.'[24]

The emphasis on the post-1968 Powell as anti-immigrant populist is somewhat deceptive for anyone who wants to understand the links between Powellism and Thatcherism. Powell's support in the parliamentary Conservative Party was very different from his support in Dudley or Smithfield market. Indeed the Thatcherite Tory MPs who admired Powell most were often those who admired his attitudes to immigration least.[25] Geoffrey Howe was to become the staunchest opponent of racial inequality on the Conservative front bench: he had co-authored the Bow Group's pamphlet on 'Coloured People in Great Britain' in 1952.[26] In 1968 John Nott was one of just sixty-two MPs (seventeen of them Conservatives) who voted against the second reading of the Commonwealth Immigration Bill, which took British passports away from Kenyan Asians.

For men such as Howe and Nott, 'Powellism' meant primarily a certain attitude to economics. Powell had been one of three treasury ministers to resign from Macmillan's government in 1958 in protest at increased public spending. After 1963 he was a vociferous opponent of all forms of state intervention in the economy. He opposed nationalization, economic planning, high public spending, exchange controls and any government policy on prices or incomes. Increasingly, he argued that the sole economic duty of government lay in control of the money supply. His particular style of economic thinking fitted in with his propensity for absolutes and with a tendency to invest all possible matters of political importance into a single issue. A government that controlled the money supply and its own spending could thus be freed of concern for all other economic matters. Indeed, Powell argued that the operations of the free market would free government from the need to interfere in many matters that were not directly related to economics. It was, for example, unnecessary for the government to legislate against sexual discrimination by employers, who had an economic interest in hiring the best candidate: 'Everyone is entitled to conduct his own business to his own disadvantage; but those who do so are destined to be in a small and disappearing minority.'[27] Powell's admiration for capitalism did not necessarily imply admiration for capitalists. He had little time for the Heathite cult of the manager ('this new model army of gentlemen who know best') or for the Thatcherite cult of the entrepreneur. It was the market itself that Powell admired. He saw it as something natural and organic that contrasted with the artificial creations of the modern state, and he celebrated it in tones of romantic nationalism: 'The collective wisdom and collective will of the nation resides not in any little Whitehall clique but in the whole mass of the people – expressing [itself] through all the complex nervous systems of the market.'[28]

The journalist Samuel Brittan, an early exponent of monetarist economics and the half-brother of one of Thatcher's ministers, suggested in the late 1960s that Powell had 'read almost no economics' and that this fact accounted both for his ability to 'go to the heart of economic problems' and for the sometimes simplistic quality of his solutions.[29] There was an element of truth in this allegation. Most political defences of free-market economics were heavily encumbered with jargon, theory and algebra. What set Powell apart was simplicity. At a time when almost no one dared to defend the unfettered operation of the free market, Powell said that he often got down on his knees in church and thanked God for capitalism. On the fringes of the 1968 Conservative Party conference, he presented an alternative budget showing how income tax might be reduced to just over 20 per cent. He explained economics in terms of striking metaphors, often drawn from the cinema. He likened the experience of an incomes policy to that of being repeatedly made to watch a pornographic film: 'is it necessary to stay in our seats through another, and yet another performance?'[30] He described floating exchange rates in terms taken from *Those Magnificent Men in Their Flying Machines*: 'We'll go up tiddly pom; we'll go down tiddly pom.'

An emphasis on economics can, however, be as deceptive as an emphasis on race in understanding Powellism. Powell also spent much of his time thinking about Britain's place in the world. It was here that he stood most sharply apart from the 'post-war consensus' and here that Thatcher was most clearly part of that consensus. If the British governing classes agreed about just one thing in the years after 1945, that thing was that Britain ought to remain a 'great power'. It was thought indelicate of the American secretary of state to suggest that the loss of Empire might have called this role into question. Britain's power was seen to rest on the possession of the nuclear bomb, its 'special relationship' with the United States and its capacity to maintain a military presence 'east of Suez'. Like most Conservatives, Thatcher supported all of these things – indeed the American alliance and British nuclear weapons were to be crucial features of her political position during the 1980s.

Powell was different. He had served in India during the war and it was India that brought him into politics. He saw a British political career as a route to becoming viceroy – though he conceived this ambition at a time when any private who had bothered to stay awake in his political education classes could have told him that British rule in India was finished. After a few years denying reality – according to one story he lectured Churchill on how many divisions he would need to reconquer the subcontinent – Powell accepted that India was gone. For him, this changed everything. Britain could no longer, and should no longer, be a world power. Powell turned against the stationing of British troops east of Suez. He also always disliked nuclear weapons and, by the 1980s, he had come to denounce Britain's status as a nuclear power. Much to the amusement of the cognoscenti of Conservative politics, he managed to cloud both these positions in Jesuitical ambiguity when he was Conservative spokesman on defence during the 1960s.

Most of all, attitudes to the Atlantic alliance illustrated the gulf between Powell and other Conservatives. From the moment that he first met American officials in North Africa in 1943 until his death in 1998, Powell had his own special relationship with America. It was one of pathological hatred. Indeed this was the most consistent theme in his politics – though his consistency was not particularly logical because a man who had first come to dislike America on account of its alleged efforts to dissolve the British Empire had no reason to maintain his hostility beyond the point at which he recognized that the Empire was finished. In any case, Powell's anti-Americanism went way beyond the bounds of logic. In 1945 he seems seriously to have believed that Britain would soon be obliged to fight the United States and to do so in alliance with the Soviet Union. He planned to go to Latin America 'for reconnaissance purposes' in the backyard of his country's enemy.[31] Powell never shared the Cold War fervour that made many Conservatives look to Washington (the American capital, for Powell, was a byword for the problems of racial mixing rather than for moral leadership). In 1978 Powell wrote that the 'portentous moralizing' of Solzhenitsyn, the exiled Russian writer whose denunciations of Soviet tyranny were much admired by Thatcher, was 'a bore and an irritation'.[32] During the 1980s, hostility to America was reflected in his complaints about the subordination of British foreign policy to that of America and, more strikingly, in his assertion that the Americans were conspiring, for their own strategic reasons, to evict the British from Ireland.

Powell's insistence that Britain was no longer a great power intertwined with his thinking about other things in ways that also underlined how different Powellism was from Thatcherism. The first of these was economic decline. Almost the whole of the British establishment began to be obsessed by Britain's economic decline relative to other countries – particularly those of continental western Europe – from the late 1950s. The obsession reached its peak in the 1970s. The promise to 'reverse decline' was an important part of both Heath's and Thatcher's political project. In both cases, such a reversal was seen as important partly because it would allow Britain to play its 'natural' role as a world power. Powell was the most articulate critic of British 'declinism'. He believed that it was based on a deceptive historical comparison (with Britain at the apogee of her relative prosperity in the Victorian era) and a deceptive geographical comparison, with continental western Europe. 'Why? [he asked] compare Britain with France and Germany rather than America or Canada' (whose performance in the 1970s was less impressive) or, for that matter, with 'China or Peru'. He was sceptical about the value of the graphs and tables that permeated so many documents on Britain's state in the 1970s

– 'To be happy it is not necessary to beat the statistical record all comers.'[33] As a true free marketeer, he disliked the idea that it was for the state to establish what level of production was desirable and, unlike many who thought themselves free marketeers, Powell recognized that the most important human desires might not be economic ones: 'But this question of growth brings us near to whatever real meaning can be attached to the idea of a "strong" economy. Ultimately, that idea is subjective – it has to do with what people feel and what people want. The only rational meaning of a "strong" economy is one where people put their efforts and resources to the use which gives them what they consider the greatest satisfaction.'[34]

Powell's view of Britain's role in the world was also tied to his view of what 'Englishness' should mean at home. Most British politicians saw decolonization in coolly rational terms. Emotion was usually injected only by nationalists in Asia and Africa or by sentimental right-wingers who sought to defend the Empire. Powell managed to portray decolonization as a romantic adventure for the British themselves: 'our generation is one which comes home again from years of distant wandering. We discover affinities with earlier generations of English, generations before the "expansion of England", who felt no country but this to be their own.'[35] Powell wanted the end of Empire to mark a clear break with Britain's recent past. He despised the constitutional fudges that allowed the Empire to be transmuted into the Commonwealth – he claimed that the most important speech of his political life involved denouncing the insertion of an 's' after the word 'realm' in the 1953 Royal Titles Bill. Powell became an English equivalent of the French royalist thinker Charles Maurras – trying to defend the *ancien régime* of Church, aristocracy and monarchy, after his own countrymen had forgotten what these things meant. Powell never tried to hide his own origins. He always spoke with a Midlands accent and revelled in his plebeian tastes – his wife made him promise that he would never ask her to cook tripe. However, he regarded the rituals and ranks of the English ruling class with the same scrupulous respect that he had, as a young officer in India, displayed towards the Hindu caste system. When Alec Douglas-Home renounced his peerage in order to become leader of the Conservative Party, many intelligent Conservatives were shocked because they saw Home's appointment as undemocratic or simply because they believed that he was not a good candidate for the job. Only Powell thought that renouncing a peerage was wrong because being the fourteenth earl was itself an important position with inalienable rights and responsibilities.

The struggle against modernization brought Powell up against the whole current of the post-war Conservative Party – a party that was obsessed with forms of modernization that Powell saw as destroying the real genius of England. Powell's most bitter antagonist in this respect was Edward Heath, but Margaret Thatcher was a kind of modernizer too and some of her dealings with Powell in the 1980s revealed how little she understood of his Toryism. Thatcher could not, in particular, understand why Powell, who had no male heir, refused to accept a life peerage after he lost his seat in the Commons in the general election of 1987.

Powell's preoccupation with a certain variety of Englishness accounts for a view of politics that laid a heavy emphasis on sovereignty, and this ties in with the two issues that separated him from the Conservative Party: Ulster and Europe. Powell believed strongly in the Union of England and Ulster – his belief in the integration of Ulster into British political structures was, in some ways, a more absolutist position than the support for Home Rule espoused by more traditional Unionists. Powell's views on this matter were also more absolutist than those of Thatcher – who combined vague professions of belief in Unionism with a half-hearted search for constitutional expedients that might solve the province's problems. Ulster was to be the single issue on which Thatcher and Powell were to clash most strongly (see chapter 9). After Thatcher signed the Anglo-Irish agreement of

1985, Powell told her the penalty for treachery was to fall into public contempt.

On Europe, Powell was initially favourable to Britain's entry into the Common Market – partly because he saw it as a means of promoting free trade and partly because he relished something that seemed to undermine Britain's pretensions to being a world power. In 1969 Powell changed his mind. The resignation of de Gaulle, whom he admired, seems to have precipitated this change. Almost any other politician would have regarded the exit of a notably anti-British statesman from the European scene as making things easier. Perhaps Powell had hoped that de Gaulle would turn the Common Market into a looser and less political federation or perhaps he found de Gaulle's Anglophobia easier to bear than the condescension that younger French politicians displayed to Britain. Whatever the reason, from then on Powell insisted that Britain's entry into the EEC would involve an unforgivable renunciation of the rights of the British parliament. Eventually Europe was to bring Powell and Thatcher back together. Powell welcomed what he saw as the *souverainisme* of Thatcher's 1988 Bruges speech. This reconciliation on Thatcher's political deathbed should not, however, disguise the fact that the Conservative Party was – for most of the period after 1969 and most of the period during which Thatcher led it – the most pro-European of the major British political parties.

Some of Powell's admirers liked to imply that Thatcherism was really Powellism in power. Thatcher and Powell would probably both have recognized that this was a contradiction in terms. If Thatcherism meant anything, it meant power. Thatcher held office, in the government or her party, for most of the time that she was a member of parliament. She only once voted against a three-line whip and she imposed firm discipline on her own party when she was leader. She never resigned from any position and was emotionally broken when she was finally forced out of office.

Powell, by contrast, was one of nature's refuseniks. He voted against the government 115 times between 1970 and 1974, more than any other Conservative MP. He refused office twice, resigned once and forced his party leader into sacking him once. Nicholas Ridley, one of his greatest admirers, conceded in December 1968: 'he is probably an awkward colleague in any administration because if he is not resigning, he is probably threatening to resign'.[36] He was in the cabinet only for a couple of years and, though he enjoyed administration, he seemed to think that ministerial office had a corrupting effect on its holders. His attitude to office-holding is illustrated by his extraordinary position in the Official Ulster Unionists. Joining the party ensured that he would never again hold ministerial office at Westminster; insisting on full integration into the political structures of the mainland ensured that he would never hold office in a devolved Ulster government at Stormont.

In 1959, shortly after he had resigned from the government but at a time when the Tories seemed safely ensconced in power for years to come, Powell wrote an essay in the *Political Quarterly* on 'opposition'. He argued that an opposition 'must have a categorical imperative: "Do this, and this alone, if you would be saved." There must be a great simple, central theme, branching into all fields and subjects of debates.'[37] By this definition, Powell was a great oppositionist. He could always find some single great theme to which all other issues should be subordinated. Thatcher, by contrast, could never afford such political fundamentalism. She wanted power and knew that government meant the continuous juggling and balancing of different issues. In 1988 Thatcher commented that Enoch Powell 'commanded influence without power' and drew an interesting comparison between him and David Owen (another MP from outside the Conservative Party who was sometimes admired by Thatcherites): 'when you have been in Government you know that it is not a question of right or wrong − it is often a question of shades of grey'.[38]

Powell came to recognize that Thatcher's capacity to wait, compromise and tolerate ambiguity were useful qualities, and ones that he conspicuously lacked. Nevertheless he could never entirely tame the urge for political self-destruction that lay at the heart of his own character. On 16 November 1990, when her hostility to Europe had isolated her in her own party and when she faced a challenge for the leadership from Michael Heseltine, Powell wrote a letter to Norman Tebbit, the effective manager of Thatcher's leadership campaign, in which he offered to do anything that he could to defend Thatcher against her opponents in her own party.[39] Worldly Conservatives must have realized that Powell's support was a sure sign that Thatcher was finished.

Chapter 3

BECOMING LEADER

It wasn't an election. It was an assumption.
Norman St John-Stevas on Thatcher becoming leader
of the Conservative Party (1975)[1]

After 1975 it suited some Conservatives to describe the Thatcher leadership as the product of an almost supernatural process. The party made much of loyalty to the leaders and, for this reason, never liked to discuss the means by which they were chosen or deposed. There was also a slightly forced gallantry in the way that senior Tories talked about Margaret Thatcher. No one wanted to admit that a respectable woman had been involved in anything so sordid as an internal party conflict. All the same, Thatcher did come to power through an election and one that left many of her colleagues feeling uncomfortable. Norman St John-Stevas had been a loyal supporter of Edward Heath who also had good personal relations with Margaret Thatcher. In the 1975 contest for the leadership of the Conservative Party, he had voted for Heath in the first round but then voted for Thatcher in the second round after Heath's withdrawal. For all his talk of 'assumptions' St John-Stevas illustrated the complicated mixture of personal and political calculations that lay behind the decisions of so many people (including many who did not like Thatcher or who did not believe that she could win) to cast their votes for the successful candidate in the second round.

In 1973 Thatcher's star had seemed to be in decline. Even the tiny minority of well-informed people who had once thought that she might one day lead a government had begun to think that they had probably been wrong. The American ambassador wrote in May 1973: 'Once touted as a potential first woman Prime Minister; it is most doubtful that she could, or does, realistically expect to lead her party.'[2] A group of sympathetic journalists at the *Spectator* magazine thought that she looked tired and that she seemed not to have the stomach for a future fight. The defeat of the government in the February 1974 election did not offer her any obvious opportunity. She had, after all, been a member of a government that was now seen to have failed.

In the middle of 1974 Heath undertook a U-turn in electoral tactics to match the U-turn in policy that he had undertaken in government. He sought to adopt a more emollient tone and began to suggest that the country might benefit from a 'national government'. He promised that, if elected, he would appoint to his cabinet people who were not members of the Conservative Party. This change of policy alienated both sides of his party. Those who favoured a government of national unity suspected that it would, in fact, be most feasible if Heath stepped aside as a potential prime minister; they were taken aback by his refusal to countenance such a possibility. On the other hand, those in the party who most resented the 'betrayal' of the pledges that it had made in the 1970 election were hardly likely to welcome the possibility of a government that was based on consensus between the parties. It is significant that Thatcher and Keith Joseph were the only prominent Tories who avoided reference to a government of national unity during the general election campaign of October 1974.[3] However, Thatcher had still made no open move against Heath; she still held a post in his shadow cabinet and she still campaigned for the party that he led.

Heath's second, and slightly more decisive, defeat in the general election of October 1974 put his own position as party leader in jeopardy. The party had no mechanism by which a serving leader might be challenged. Ten years earlier, a leader who had endured two successive election defeats would probably have been discreetly eased out by party elders, who would almost certainly have chosen William Whitelaw as the natural successor. As it was, Heath established a committee to look into means by which an election for party leader might be conducted. It was agreed that a challenger who collected a certain number of signatures from their parliamentary colleagues could force an election and that this election would take place in two rounds, unless one of the candidates obtained the support of an absolute majority of members of the Conservative Party in the House of Commons in the first round.

Who, however, was to oppose Heath? Senior ministers who had served in his government were reluctant to seem disloyal – Whitelaw, in particular, refused to stand against his leader. Sir Keith Joseph was the obvious standard bearer of the free-market Right. Since the election of February 1974, he had articulated a vision of Conservatism that emphasized the importance of reviving free enterprise and reducing the power of the state. Initially he had conducted his arguments inside the Tory leadership. He had persuaded Heath to let him establish a Centre for Policy Studies to examine the causes of British decline, which, in practice, soon came to mean proselytizing for a new kind of economic policy. In meetings of the shadow cabinet in the summer of 1974, Joseph urged an approach to inflation that would lay greater emphasis on free enterprise and controlling the money supply. Finally, Joseph broke cover in speeches at Upminster (22 June 1974), Leith (8 August) and Preston (5 September). In them he attacked the power of trade unions and excessive levels of public spending. He urged more emphasis on fighting inflation and less on lowering unemployment. The first two speeches – whilst arguing that the whole post-war period had been excessively 'socialist' – focused on attacking the Labour Party. The speech at Preston laid a more explicit emphasis on the specific faults of the Heath government, in which Joseph had so recently served. It contained a particularly striking and wide-ranging passage of self-criticism:

> To us [i.e. the members of the Heath cabinet], as to all post-war governments, sound money may have seemed out-of-date; we were dominated by the fear of unemployment. It was this which made us turn back against our own better judgement and try to spend our way out of unemployment, while relying on incomes policy to damp down the inflationary effects. It is perhaps easy to understand; our post-war boom began under the shadow of the 1930s. We were haunted by the fear of long-term mass unemployment, the grim hopeless dole queues and the towns which died. So we talked ourselves into believing that these gaunt, tight-lipped men in caps and mufflers were round the corner, and tailored our policy to match these imaginary conditions.[4]

Joseph, the son of a wealthy Jewish building magnate, had been born in 1918. After Harrow, he studied law at Oxford and served in the Royal Artillery during the war, in which he was wounded. Returning to Oxford, he was elected to a fellowship of All Souls where, a portent of things to come, he embarked on an ambitious research project, seeking to distinguish between tolerance and indifference, that was never finished.[5] He had some things in common with Enoch Powell and was sometimes described as a 'Powellite'. However, the two men were very different. Powell's comment on Joseph said much about both of them: 'He was always a butterfly, not only in the sense that he had a mind which loved flitting from flower to flower, and sipping honey where honey could be sipped, but he was a butterfly, not a hawk.'[6] In his own eyes, of course, Powell was a hawk: solitary, high-flying, clear-sighted and utterly ruthless when it came to the kill.

Joseph, by contrast, was a sensitive and humble man, who changed his mind repeatedly. Unlike many Tories, Joseph took the writings of economists and social scientists seriously. He had first become interested in the free-market ideas expounded by the Institute of Economic Affairs in 1964 and embraced such ideas with increasing enthusiasm over the next six years. However, after 1970 Joseph went along with Heath's economic policy and proved to be one of his most enthusiastic spending ministers, a fact that Joseph himself stressed with masochistic pride. More significantly, he often seemed to back away from his own conclusions when people argued with him or simply when, as a minister, he was faced with the human consequences of implementing his own logic.

Joseph was not, in fact, a free-market fundamentalist in the manner of Powell. He believed in the 'enterprise' part of 'free enterprise' where Powell believed mainly in the 'free' part. Joseph thought that it might actually be necessary for the state to stimulate such enterprise and particularly that it might be necessary to direct British education along more practical lines, an idea that Powell loathed.

Where Powell saw himself as a prophet in the desert who drew his ideas from solitary reflection, Joseph surrounded himself with advisers. Particularly important among these was Alfred Sherman. Like Joseph, Sherman was a Jew in his mid fifties, and, like Joseph, he was an intellectual of sorts. In almost every other respect the two men were different. Sherman was an autodidact from the East End. He was short, physically unprepossessing and enormously energetic. In many ways, he was a mirror image of the 'polytechnic trots' who were beginning to exercise influence in the Labour Party. He had hung around the fringes of educational institutions (studying chemistry at Chelsea Polytechnic and later taking a course at the London School of Economics); he had fought for the Republicans in the Spanish Civil War and later served with field intelligence in the British army during the Second World War. For most of his life, he scraped a living through schoolteaching, journalism and political lobbying. The only political office he held was that of councillor for Kensington and Chelsea. In politics he moved from youthful Stalinism towards a mixture of free-market economics and defence of 'traditional' moral values.

Sherman had an extraordinary capacity for making enemies. When he died, a right-wing journalist wrote:

> Mean-spirited, spiteful, envious and resentful, he never had a good word to say about anyone else's intellect and overvalued his own. He had moved to the political Right from the millenarian Marxist Left, without abandoning its sectarian habits of mind. He thought that a firing-squad was too good for anyone who disagreed with him . . . [he] was also prey to temper tantrums that would have disgraced an overtired three-year-old.[7]

Sherman was brilliant at devising hurtful phrases – he once said that giving ministers policies was like giving an impotent man a condom. He embraced unpopular causes. He invited Jean-Marie le Pen, the leader of the French Front National, to a fringe meeting of the Conservative Party conference. He spent much of the later part of his career defending Serbian war criminals – his interest in the Serbian cause was probably increased by the fact that his former patron, Margaret Thatcher, was pro-Bosnian.

Relations between Sherman and Joseph sometimes resembled the relations of inverted domination across social classes depicted in Pinter plays. Sherman, the nominal servant, bullied his master mercilessly. His influence increased after Joseph began an autocritique about his own participation in the Heath government – famously, Sherman refused to shake Joseph's hand when the two men met after Joseph's 'betrayal of his principles' in office. Joseph went along with Sherman's criticism of the Heath government, though Joseph hated the personal animosities that such criticism provoked – eventually he scuttled from one office to another (bent under the weight of a briefcase filled with books) as he tried to escape from arguments with his own colleagues.[8]

The Labour Party could not have hoped for a better leader of the opposition than Sir Keith Joseph. He was neurotic and prone to crack under pressure. He had a hopelessly academic approach to policy-making: a Conservative journalist wrote that he was 'inclined when in doubt to call for more paper as looser men will call for more wine'.[9] His political conversion of the mid-1970s related to his own life in ways that might have interested a psychologist. He began to embrace 'family values' at the moment when his own marriage was breaking up, and he talked about the need for strong management at a time when his family company had fallen into difficulty. He had an almost unique gift for picking the wrong cause at the wrong time. Having been a life-long opponent of the death penalty, he seemed to change his mind in response to the Birmingham pub bombings of 1974: the six men convicted of these offences, who would have hanged if the death penalty had been in force, turned out to be innocent. Most of all, he suffered from a catastrophic political weakness – a propensity to see the strength of his opponents' arguments. The result of all this was that he often cut an absurd figure. With characteristic brutality, Sherman described him as the 'antithesis of a leader'.[10] Denis Healey said that he was a mixture of 'Hamlet, Rasputin and Tommy Cooper'.[11] Joseph's cabinet colleagues were only too well aware of his weaknesses. Hailsham recorded the opinion of much of the establishment: 'a silly man and always wrong';[12] 'dotty and lacks moral fibre for office';[13] 'Keith is an albatross: lost 1974 by larger than nec. May bring us down. Clever-silly. Attracts barmies.'[14]

As it turned out, Joseph destroyed his own chances of leading his party before the hard men of the Labour front bench got a chance to put the boot in. On 19 October 1974, he made a speech at Edgbaston in Birmingham. It was designed partly to emphasize that his political vision was not confined to economic matters and thus, perhaps, to illustrate his suitability for the leadership of the Conservative Party.[15]

The speech was a characteristic Joseph performance: impassioned, based on an eclectic range of sources and ranging over a wide variety of subjects, in the course of forty minutes, Joseph cited Rousseau, Orwell, Gladstone and Freud. It was partly inspired by Alfred Sherman's reading of the works of the Italian priest and Christian Democrat politician Luigi Sturzo[16] – anyone other than Sherman, or Joseph, would have asked themselves whether the leader of a party that lasted for three years before being swept away in the fascist revolution was a good model for a practical politician. The speech also owed much to Joseph's own concern about social deprivation, and it drew on information that he had gleaned from the Child Poverty Action Group (a body that was close to the Labour Left). Joseph rode one of his favourite hobby horses (left-wing infiltration of the universities), attacked aspects of the 'permissive society' and paid tribute to Mary Whitehouse (a Christian housewife who had attracted much derision with her campaign against depictions of sex on television). All of this would probably have been fairly uncontroversial. However, towards the end of the speech, Joseph called attention to the dangers 'for the national stock' that he saw in the large numbers of children being born to mothers from the lowest social and educational categories, and suggested that these groups should be encouraged to practise birth control. This was an argument with something to offend everyone. The Left was shocked by its eugenicism; the Right was shocked by the vision of comprehensive schools handing out contraceptives to retarded teenagers.

Joseph was horrified by the reception of his speech and reacted in the worst possible way. He sought to explain himself in a long letter to *The Times*. At the same time he seemed to apologize and to accept that: 'I may have damaged – things in which I rather deeply believed.'[17] These were not the tones of a potential prime minister. Eventually, Joseph decided that he could not be a candidate for leadership of the party. On 21 November, he told Margaret Thatcher of his decision. According to her own account she then said, quite spontaneously: 'if you're not going to stand, I will, because someone who represents our viewpoint *has* to stand.'[18]

How good did Thatcher's chances of beating Heath in the leadership election seem? She had certain advantages. One of these had been given to her by Heath himself. After the election defeat of February 1974, he had moved her from Education to shadow the Department of the Environment. Here she defended a Tory proposal to abolish the rates and to encourage home ownership through an implausibly complicated mechanism by which special tax concessions to building societies would prevent anyone from paying interest of more than 9.5 per cent on their mortgage. Both these proposals would have increased the financial problems of central government, and the second of them would have been seen as absurd by anyone who understood anything of free-market economics. Privately, Thatcher had doubts about both proposals. That she was willing to defend them in public illustrated her willingness to go along with things that she did not believe in for the sake of political expediency. It may also have made her a stronger figure in the Conservative Party. Her new role meant that she assumed a greater prominence in the general election of October 1974 than she had done in any previous election (even the one that had been held just six months previously). For a time it also made her seem to be associated with the most moderate wing of the Conservative Party's debate on economic policy. Paul Johnson wrote in the *New Statesman* that Conservative policy 'oscillates wildly between the lavish spending promises of Mrs Thatcher and the austere Powellism of Keith Joseph'.[19]

After the second of his election defeats, Heath moved Thatcher again to assist the shadow chancellor, Robert Carr. This provided Thatcher with a good platform for a leadership bid. It gave the sense that she had the kind of wide policy experience (particularly with regard to economics) that might be useful for a prime minister, and it allowed her to display her ability to master detail and to concentrate (she continued her work on this brief even when running for leader of the party). Most of all, Thatcher emerged as a performer in the House of Commons. When she attacked wealth tax, the chancellor, Denis Healey, dubbed her the 'Passionaria of privilege'. She replied: 'Some Chancellors are macroeconomic; some are microeconomic. This one is just cheap . . . If he can be Chancellor, anyone can be Chancellor.' The riposte does not seem very impressive when seen in cold print, but it (or perhaps just the fact that a Conservative was willing to stand up to Labour's resident front-bench bully) apparently excited the parliamentary Conservative Party.

Thatcher also benefited from the absence of competition in the first round of the leadership election. William Whitelaw might have won the vote if he had stood in the first round. He was well connected, experienced and popular – though his virtues were probably more visible to those who had served with him in government than to backbench MPs. However, Whitelaw refused to stand against Heath. The only other candidate in the first round of the leadership election was Sir Hugh Fraser. Fraser's background – he was a Scottish aristocrat who had been born in 1918 and served with distinction in the Second World War – was reminiscent of Whitelaw's. Unlike Whitelaw, though, Fraser had no senior ministerial experience, no reputation for 'sound' judgement and no happy family life (his wife was shortly to leave him for Harold Pinter). Fraser might almost have been picked to illustrate the weaknesses of old-style Tories.

Thatcher's support did not come from the front rank of British politics. It seems that almost no one from the shadow cabinet voted for her in the first round of the leadership election. Julian Critchley labelled Thatcher's victory a 'peasants' revolt' of backbenchers. The reality was slightly more complicated. Thatcher's most important supporters were backbench MPs, but they were not just ordinary backbenchers. A few, such as Norman Tebbit, had only recently entered parliament and would, under Thatcher, make considerable reputations. More important than these were men who exercised particular influence but whose careers had been thwarted in ways that left them bitter towards Edward Heath.

The first backbencher whose influence mattered was Edward du Cann. Du Cann had grown up in difficult circumstances (his father abandoned him and his mother) and risen through grammar school and the City. He had been on the Tory front benches briefly during the 1960s but got on badly with Heath. He resented Heath's much-quoted remark that the company Lonrho, of which du Cann was chairman, represented the 'unacceptable face of capitalism'. Du Cann did not hold ministerial office in the 1970s, but he did chair the 1922 Committee of backbench Tory MPs.

As chairman of the 1922 Committee, du Cann, and the 'Milk Street mafia' who met at his City offices, played an important role in precipitating the challenge to Heath and in swinging support behind Thatcher. Du Cann himself was talked of as a potential leader for a time. He said in November 1974 that he would not stand. His decision sprang partly from the reluctance of his wife and partly from the worry that his business activities might become the subject of unwelcome scrutiny – partly too, perhaps, from the fact that being leader of Her Majesty's Opposition is a badly paid job by the standards of the City. Du Cann summoned Margaret and Denis Thatcher to his grand Lord North Street house to tell them of his decision, and to offer her his support for her own candidacy; he likened the Thatchers' manner to that of a couple who had come to be interviewed for a job as 'housekeeper and handyman'. Du Cann's memoirs give the impression that he had not entirely abandoned prime ministerial ambitions and it may be that his support for Thatcher owed something to the assumption that she would not be elected (or not last if she were elected) and would therefore help clear the way for an eventual candidacy of his own.[20]

George Gardiner was similar to du Cann in some respects. He too had grown up as the impoverished child of a single mother and risen up through grammar school. In spite of having taken a first in politics, philosophy and economics at Balliol, he was very self-consciously not a member of the establishment (a word that obsessed him). He had served in the ranks in the Pioneer Corps during national service. He worked as a journalist on provincial newspapers and eventually wrote for the *Daily Express* (no one could have been further away from the style of *The Times* or even the *Daily Telegraph*). He espoused a succession of unfashionable right-wing causes (capital punishment, support for white rule in South Africa). He claimed (perhaps a little too insistently) that he was proud to be a backbencher and had never wanted ministerial office. He vaunted his own lack of scruple – boasting about how he had rigged an election to the Oxford University Conservative Association and, later in life, revelling in the fact that John Major had called him a 'bastard'. Gardiner loathed Heath and was willing to deploy all his dark arts in support of Margaret Thatcher.

Airey Neave – an Etonian barrister – came from a more conventional background for Conservative politicians. He was widely known as the first English officer to have escaped from Colditz Castle. It seemed likely, however, in 1974 that this would remain his sole claim to fame. He had held only minor ministerial office. He believed that Heath, as Conservative chief whip, had told him that his poor health made it impossible for him to hope for further preferment and he seems to have nurtured a bitter dislike of Heath ever since this episode.

In 1974 Neave was willing to back almost any candidate who stood a chance of ejecting Heath from the leadership. Initially, he was part of a group of MPs (organized by Nigel Fisher) who supported du Cann. Fisher was on the Left of the party; he was one of those who believed that the Conservatives should enter a government of national unity, but that such a government would be made easier if Heath himself ceased to be leader, and he had discreetly been seeking to ease Heath out of the leadership ever since the February general election.[21] When du Cann withdrew, Fisher felt that he could not organize Thatcher's campaign; he planned to vote for her against Heath, but reserved the right to support someone else in the second round of the election. Fisher turned the leadership of his group over to Neave, who was a reassuringly unThatcherite figure – his political views and background fitted into the mainstream of the Conservative Party. Neave was also a skilled plotter, one who spent much of his adult life in the shadow lands where Conservative politics meet the secret services. His most successful strategy was to hint to his fellow Conservative MPs that support for the Thatcher candidacy was weak, and that voting for her was therefore a means of damaging Heath and bringing out more serious candidates in the second round of the leadership contest.

Thatcher's candidacy was greatly helped by the behaviour of the opposing camp. Indeed, it is revealing that no one really knew who ran Heath's campaign: the main suspects – Kenneth Baker, Tim Kitson and Peter Walker – all denied that they had been campaign manager.[22] In any case, Heath was an impossibly awkward candidate. His innate sulkiness had been exacerbated by the humiliations of defeat in two general elections and Thatcher's challenge for the leadership. Heath's belated attempts at seduction were so clumsy and blatantly insincere that they probably lost him votes. On 4 February 1975 Margaret Thatcher got 130 votes on the first round of the leadership election, Heath got 119 and Hugh Fraser got 16.

Even to her supporters, Thatcher's success against Heath probably came as a surprise. At this stage, other candidates threw their hats into the ring. Geoffrey Howe represented the free-market wing of Conservativism and might have damaged Thatcher by taking votes that would otherwise have gone to her, but he had a soporific style – his friend Denis Healey famously likened him to a dead sheep – and seemed faintly embarrassed by his own candidacy. William Whitelaw was the single most popular candidate, and the one anointed by Heath, but Heath's support had probably become a liability by this stage and Whitelaw's failure to stand in the first round had come to seem like weakness by the time of the second. John Peyton, an intelligent and interesting person but one whose carefully cultivated reputation as the rudest man in politics was hardly calculated to win his colleagues over, stood, as did Jim Prior. Some believed that Thatcher's campaign team had deliberately encouraged additional candidacies in the second round in order to split the potential anti-Thatcher vote. Margaret Thatcher won 146 votes in the second round – Whitelaw got 79, Prior and Howe both got 19 and John Peyton got 11.

Thatcher's election as leader of the Conservative Party was a triumph. The very improbability of a woman from her background winning such a position helped to create an aura around her that was to last for many years. But there was no certainty that Thatcher would succeed, or even survive, in her new position. Private interviews conducted with Tory MPs many years later suggested that the profile of the average backbencher who voted for Thatcher in the leadership election anticipated certain traits that would later become associated with Thatcherism. Her supporters tended to have constituencies in the south of England rather than the north or Scotland, and they were less likely than the supporters of her opponents to have been educated at the grandest of public schools, especially Eton.[23] However, this hardly constituted a social base for a new kind of politics. In fact, Thatcher's election had little to do with ideology. She had played down many of her beliefs during the campaign. Though she was seen as being on the Right of the party, Thatcher was not clearly identified with economic radicalism – indeed, as has been suggested, her public positions on rates and the subsidization of mortgages in 1974 had made her seem rather loose on matters of public spending. A few MPs, such as Ian Gow, appear to have seen rebellion against Heath in terms of a new emphasis on controlling the money supply, but these men were against Heath rather than for Thatcher. The candidate most associated with economic radicalism in the second round of the leadership election was Geoffrey Howe. Indeed, in some ways, Howe was the Thatcherite candidate in 1975. His campaign was managed by Gow, who was to become Thatcher's famously loyal parliamentary private secretary during the early 1980s, and was supported by Norman Fowler, who had previously urged Keith Joseph to stand. The election often revolved around trivial questions of personal style. Thatcher's opponents in the first round had made much of an interview in which she had allegedly incited old-age pensioners to hoard tinned salmon as a hedge against inflation; Whitelaw's campaign in the second round had been damaged by comic photographs of him pretending to wash dishes at home.

Thatcher had been almost no one's first choice for the leadership, probably not even her own. Many had voted for her either because they disliked Heath or because they regarded him as an electoral liability. Thatcher had come to seem the candidate who stood the best chance of rallying the party after Heath but support for her was very qualified and provisional. Few Conservative MPs would have shed any tears if she had been quietly ousted after a year or two to make way for some more established party figure.

Chapter 4

OPPOSITION, 1975–9

> Well, what are we going to do after she gets in if she gets in?
> Lord Carrington to Lord Hailsham, March 1977[1]

In the mid-1970s, leaders of both parties recognized that old remedies were not working. The oil crisis, the new radicalism of the trade union leaders and Britain's entry into the EEC all shook British politics. Some Conservatives talked in almost apocalyptic terms and saw their own plight as part of a wider international crisis caused by the advance of Communism. The first letter that Margaret Thatcher ever received from Ronald Reagan was sent on what Reagan himself described as a 'dark day' – it was 30 April 1975, the day that Saigon fell to the Vietcong.

Some thought that the British economy was on the verge of collapse. The Americans were particularly contemptuous (perhaps because the plight of the British provided a partial distraction from the problems they themselves were facing). Henry Kissinger told Gerald Ford: 'Britain is a tragedy – it has sunk to begging, borrowing, stealing, until North Sea Oil comes in.'[2] Edmund Dell, chief secretary to the treasury in the Callaghan government, wrote later that 'everyone I know' regarded the autumn of 1976, when the Labour government had to ask the International Monetary Fund for money to prop up sterling, as the 'worst period of their lives'.[3]

However, judging what political consequences might spring from financial crisis was complicated by the fact that there was a gap between feelings amongst the elite and those amongst the mass of the population. The arcane financial negotiations or gloomy prognostications of long-term industrial decline that so obsessed economists and politicians meant little to most British people. For them, the mid-1970s was a time when wages were higher than ever before and when inflation had eaten much of their debt. Opinion polls suggest that quite large numbers of British people look back on the hot summer of 1976 as the *happiest* time of their life. The Queen's Silver Jubilee in 1977 seemed to reflect a nation that was conservative (with a small c), consensual and at ease with itself. A group of Tory MPs, some of whom were to be closely associated with the most radical policies of the Thatcher government in the 1980s, wrote privately that the Jubilee showed the extent of 'national unity' and the desire for 'continuity'.[4]

There was, in any case, little reason to suppose that economic and political upheaval would lead to the election of a Conservative government led by Margaret Thatcher. For much of their time in opposition, the Conservatives were divided, confused and scared. Internal party documents sometimes evoked radical projects only to dismiss them as unrealistic or dangerous. Much discussion amongst shadow ministers revolved around how they should react to what their political opponents were doing, rather than how they should shift the political debate on to their own ground.

The sense of crisis in the British political elite was greatest from the beginning of 1974, when the National Union of Mineworkers seemed to be running the country, until the autumn of 1976, when the International Monetary Fund seemed to be running the country. However, people anticipated all sorts of different potential outcomes of this crisis. Thatcher recognized in September 1975 that the assumptions of post-war British economic policy were being rethought, not just in the Conservative Party, but across the whole political spectrum.[5] Peter Jay, son-in-law of James Callaghan and soon to be appointed British ambassador in Washington, wrote a series of articles in *The Times* in which he suggested that economic crisis might destroy British democracy – a prospect that was taken seriously by a number of economists and political scientists. The paper's more flippant columnists identified a whole genre of such writing, which they christened 'Doomwatch'.[6] Auberon Waugh wrote in the *New Statesman*: 'the party system is finished and the country is crying out, in its timid and furtive way, for a Gaullist constitution administered from the Centre-Left ... [by] Denis Healey.'[7] Waugh may have been mocking his readers, but members of Thatcher's shadow cabinet did have a sneaking admiration for Healey,[8] and did discuss the prospect that they might be drawn into a government of national unity, led by a Labour moderate.

In 1975 Thatcher's personal position was insecure. As secretary of state for education, she had withdrawn free school milk and this had prompted the *Sun* to ask its readers whether she was 'the most unpopular woman in Britain'.[9] For almost her whole time as leader of the opposition, Thatcher's personal poll ratings were below those of the Labour leader. Rank-and-file Conservatives were famous for their loyalty to the party leader, but, at first, this loyalty counted against Thatcher because she was seen as a usurper who had deposed Heath. Thatcher's own entourage feared that she might get a rough ride when she attended her first party conference as leader in the autumn of 1975.[10] Most particularly, they feared that she might be disliked by the middle-aged suburban ladies (people supposedly much like Thatcher herself) who made up an important part of the Conservative Party's membership.

It was probably not until after the 1983 general election, if then, that Thatcher was able to impose obedience on her senior colleagues. Her position was particularly weak before the 1979 general election. A significant group of members of her shadow cabinet were older than her;* almost all of them had more ministerial experience.

* Whitelaw was born in 1918; Joseph in 1918; Maudling in 1917; Pym in 1922; Peyton in 1919; Neave in 1916; Thorneycroft in 1909; Maude in 1912; Atkins in 1922; Havers in 1923; Hailsham in 1907; Carrington in 1919.

Senior Conservatives were knitted into a network of regiments, smart Oxbridge colleges and public schools from which Thatcher was excluded. Most of them lunched or dined regularly at clubs that would not have let a woman across the threshold.

A prime minister has powers of patronage; loyalty can be bought with office. A leader of the opposition, especially a Conservative opposition, is in a more awkward position. A place on the opposition front bench may be less attractive and less lucrative than the other jobs available to prominent Tories: Lord Carrington spent much of the late 1970s flying around the world on behalf of Rio Tinto Zinc. The more patrician shadow ministers were not always assiduous in their attendance: at the shadow cabinet meeting of 11 April 1975, six – Carrington, Thorneycroft, Peyton, Prior, Jenkin and Edwards – were absent.

Finally, Thatcher faced a problem on the other side of the House of Commons. She had been elected leader when the prime minister was Harold Wilson – a man widely despised in Conservative circles, and outside them for that matter, for his shiftiness and interest in short-term political manoeuvres. Thatcher had certain advantages in confronting such a man – though it was generally believed that he got the better of her in their exchanges in the House of Commons.

In the spring of 1976 Wilson resigned unexpectedly and was replaced by James Callaghan. Callaghan was a more difficult opponent for the Conservatives than Wilson. He seemed, as a member of Thatcher's shadow cabinet recalled, 'good, comfortable and conservative'.[11] He came from a Portsmouth naval family (his father had once served on the Royal Yacht), and he had fought the 1945 election in his naval officer's uniform. He had risen up through the union movement without going to university. He was self-consciously not 'clever' (unlike Wilson) and not an intellectual (unlike Healey). He was much given to homely references to music hall songs or to his farm in Sussex. Callaghan had been parliamentary adviser to the Police Federation in the 1950s and

1960s. As home secretary, he had introduced legislation that excluded many black and Asian holders of UK passports from entry into Britain. He had condemned 'permissive morality' and called for a return to traditional values in education.[12] Thatcher recognized in private that Callaghan was 'the Baldwin of modern politics';[13] she was probably the only person on the Conservative front bench who did not consider this to be a compliment.

Callaghan presented particular problems for Margaret Thatcher personally. He was sixty-four (four years older than Wilson) but his age seemed an advantage – where Wilson had looked tired, Callaghan looked wise. Callaghan was the first prime minister in British history to have held all three of the most important ministerial positions (chancellor, foreign secretary and home secretary), and he made much of Thatcher's comparative lack of experience. He responded to Thatcher's attacks in the House of Commons with a studied condescension that made her appear shrill. When she complained about his 'avuncular flannel', Callaghan responded that he had difficulty in imagining her as his niece.

Thatcher's shadow cabinet was primarily made up of people who had served in the Heath government and included all of the men who had stood against her in the second round of the leadership election. The shadow chancellor was Geoffrey Howe, a barrister, educated at Winchester and Trinity Hall Cambridge. He had played an important part in devising new approaches to trade union law and was also associated with Powellite economic views. In retrospect, he looks like one of the most important of Margaret Thatcher's associates. He was shadow chancellor throughout her period as leader of the opposition, chancellor during the first difficult years in government, when he showed a notable doggedness in sticking to unpopular policies, and held senior positions until shortly before Thatcher's own fall. Thatcher's opinion of Howe was, however, not high. She thought him excessively cautious and, perhaps most importantly, there was something about his style that did not suit her. He spoke in a soft voice. For all his clarity of purpose, he valued collegiality (a favourite word of his), was on good terms with his Labour opposite number and regarded his son's involvement in left-wing demonstrations with rueful pride.

Whitelaw was made deputy leader of the Conservative Party. He epitomized everything that Margaret Thatcher was not. He came from a wealthy family with well-established Conservative traditions – his grandfather and great-grandfather had both been Tory MPs. His father, a Scottish squire, had died of wounds received during the First World War. After Winchester and Trinity College Cambridge, Whitelaw had served as an officer in the Scots Guards during the Second World War. He managed to convey the impression that his political career was governed by notions of public service and that he was untainted by any hint of personal ambition; though men entirely without personal ambition do not often become cabinet ministers.

Most surprisingly, Thatcher brought Reginald Maudling back to the Conservative front bench as foreign secretary. Maudling was relatively old and had resigned as home secretary in 1972, when it became clear that one of his business associates was to be prosecuted for corruption. He was an arch pragmatist. Though he resigned from government before Heath's U-turn of 1972, he probably believed in the later policies that Heath then pursued more than any of the ministers who implemented them. Maudling seemed to stand for everything that Thatcher might be expected to react against, and he was notably rude to, and about, Thatcher personally. His appointment may have reflected Thatcher's weak position and consequent need to maintain good relations with parts of the party that did not share her views. It may just have reflected her poor judgement of people. Maudling was a big, extrovert, easy-going man. He had all the qualities that Howe (or Joseph for that matter) lacked. Thatcher seems to have been genuinely impressed by him, and particularly by his much-vaunted 'first-class mind'. Indeed, Thatcher once asked Maudling what he would do if he were chancellor,[14] a remark that must have been interpreted as a snub to the shadow chancellor, whose opinions on any matter outside his immediate area of concern were usually dismissed.

Conservative Party institutions were reformed when Thatcher became leader, but it is hard to argue that these reforms marked a move towards the radical rethinking of policy. Some insiders complained about lack of clarity in any direction at all. Michael Wolff, who had been director of Conservative Party Organization under Edward Heath, was sacked. The chairmanship of the Conservative Research Department (CRD) was transferred from Ian Gilmour to the anti-Heathite Angus Maude. However, Chris Patten was kept as director of the CRD. Patten had been born in 1944 into a lower-middle-class Catholic family and had been educated at Balliol. He had spent almost all his adult life as a functionary of the party or the state. He had begun working for the CRD in 1966, been seconded to the Cabinet Office from 1970 to 1972 and worked as an assistant to Lord Carrington during his tenure as chairman of the party. An unideological figure who had been close to Heath, Patten represented everything that Thatcherites most despised, and some of them came to think of him in terms of visceral disgust.[15] At the time, however, he was a less controversial figure. *The Times* noted that he 'retained the confidence of a variety of Conservatives who do not have confidence in each other'.[16] Thatcher seems to have shared this confidence in him. She kept him in his post until he himself was elected to parliament in 1979.[17] Patten had one great virtue: he had a good feel for electoral politics – it was he who, as chairman of the party, was to be the architect of John Major's unexpected victory in the general election of 1992. Patten asked the one question that Thatcher's less worldly advisers often neglected: 'Will people vote for this?'

Often Thatcherism in the 1970s seemed to come primarily from outside the shadow cabinet, and sometimes it came from outside the Conservative Party. Part of the impetus came from a group of energetic backbenchers. George Gardiner and Norman Tebbit were particularly important in attacking the Labour Party in parliament. In economic terms, the most important member of the group was Nigel Lawson. Lawson came from a wealthy Jewish family. He had been educated at Westminster and Christ Church, where he had been a favoured pupil of Roy Harrod, the keeper of the Keynesian shrine. He had escaped the institutionalized humiliations with which the English upper classes usually teach boys to hide their cleverness; he even managed to spend his national service in command of his own torpedo boat whilst his contemporaries sweated on the parade ground at Catterick. He began working life as a journalist on the *Financial Times* – where young men are encouraged, in the anonymity of the Lex column or the leader articles, to point out where ministers and captains of industry are getting things wrong. After his election as an MP in 1974, he bombarded front-bench colleagues with notes explaining what their economic policy ought to be.

John Hoskyns was probably Thatcher's most significant adviser from outside parliament. Hoskyns had been an army officer before going into business and making a modest fortune in computer software. A Wykehamist who owed his introduction into the inner counsels of the Conservative Party partly to the fact that he had served in the Rifle Brigade with the son of R. A. Butler, Hoskyns was hardly of plebeian origin. But he was, like many of Thatcher's early associates, intensely conscious of his own status as an outsider – after meeting Lord Plowden, the 'mandarins' mandarin', he wrote in his diary: 'It was clear that I was one of the few people he had ever talked to who was not in *Who's Who*.'[18] A patriot who had become obsessed with reversing British decline, Hoskyns was much given to military metaphors and apocalyptic talk of 'saving' the nation – his father had been killed during the desperate fighting to cover the British retreat at Dunkirk in 1940. Hoskyns was a believer in systems and all-encompassing theories and spent a year drawing a huge diagram to illustrate how all aspects of British decline were linked up. He became Thatcher's adviser in 1975, went to work for her full-time in 1977 and continued to advise her during her first two years in office.

Ideas were also developed outside the formal Conservative Party apparatus. Thatcher and her entourage had meetings with monetarist economists – notably Alan Walters, Patrick Minford and Gordon Pepper. Study groups and committees proliferated in and around the party during the late 1970s. It is hard to tell how many of the radical ideas that were thrown around in such bodies were taken seriously by mainstream Conservative politicians, including Thatcher. Chris Patten argued that pluralism and tolerance would prove productive: 'Let a thousand flowers bloom.' John Hoskyns, who would probably have put weed killer on anything planted by Patten, argued that wide-ranging and open debate would provide Tories with 'a sort of intellectual limbering up' that was a conscious alternative to the party 'sailing into office with a cast-iron "plan", which turns out to be inappropriate (as in 1970)'.[19]

Whole new movements were established on the political Right during the 1970s. The National Association for Freedom (NAFF) was founded by the twin brothers Norris and Ross McWhirter (the latter was murdered by the IRA in 1975). Its nominal leader was Viscount de L'Isle, a war hero and former governor general of Australia who had once been a Conservative MP, and the movement's council took in a disparate collection of famous names – including Douglas Bader, the fighter ace, and Winston Churchill, grandson of the great man. Thatcher later claimed that she gave the NAFF 'as much support as I could',[20] and a few of the movement's leaders – such as Nicholas Ridley and Rhodes Boyson – were to become ministers under Thatcher, though it was never formally affiliated to the Conservative Party. The association was particularly concerned to assert the rights of individuals against those of trade unions. It supported legal action by people who had been dismissed for refusing to join trade unions in workplaces governed by the closed shop.

In retrospect, some of those close to Thatcher seem to be fairly eccentric. John Gouriet, Robert Moss and Brian Crozier were members of the NAFF. Gouriet described the trio as Thatcher's 'liege men'. All talked darkly of the threat posed by internal as well as external subversion. Moss, who was partly responsible for Thatcher's 'Iron Lady' speech of January 1976, wrote spy stories. Crozier sometimes seemed to be living such a story[21] – he introduced Thatcher to a network of shadowy agencies, in which right-wing politics, business interests and Western intelligence services overlapped. Thatcher, Carrington (who was sceptical of the whole business), Whitelaw and Joseph sat for a time on a secret 'Shield' committee to study 'security questions' and Crozier hoped to establish a Counter Subversion Executive. None of these activities seem to have had much influence on government policy after Thatcher's election.[22]

The most passionate advocate of a new Conservatism on the front bench was Keith Joseph. He remained as head of the Centre for Policy Studies and Thatcher gave him a roving brief to rethink party policy – she had considered making him shadow chancellor, but been dissuaded from this by Whitelaw. The tone of Joseph's policy proposals was one of agonized uncertainty. He made much of the potential problems raised by every action that he proposed. Chris Patten wearily suggested that 'There must be some advantage in him [Joseph] shifting his argument from the more painful consequences of a different approach to wealth creation, to the reasons for such a new approach and the benefits that would flow from it.'[23] Joseph often backed away from the implications of his own proposals. In one strategy document, he wrote: 'We shall perhaps help if we can really nerve ourselves to remove supplementary benefits for dependents of strikers.'[24] In the subsequent shadow cabinet discussion of his own proposals, however, it seemed that Joseph had failed to nerve himself for this particular challenge: 'Sir Keith referred to the question of strikers' benefits. He wondered whether the Party wished to add yet another to the several controversies which its programme might inevitably involve.'[25]

In common with almost all prominent Tories, Joseph did not believe a new economic policy would be enough to win an election and turn the country around. He made much of matters such as violence on television, immigration and the break-up of the family. He suggested that the death penalty might be an important issue – though it was hard to imagine that this could be made a matter of party policy and though many of the most important Conservative front-bench spokesmen (including Joseph) had usually voted against its reintroduction.

Joseph's attempt to mark a break with the recent past of his own party ran into opposition from his colleagues. The shadow cabinet that met to discuss a paper he had prepared in April 1975 was particularly outspoken: 'I do not agree with one little bit' (Maudling); 'too much misery in Keith's paper' (Raison); 'hairshirts have gone too far' (Atkins). Many members of the shadow cabinet did not believe that the Heath government had been an unqualified failure. They thought that there was a general and irreversible drift to the Left in British politics, and they also pointed out that countries in continental Europe seemed to have successful economies in spite of having pursued some of the policies that Joseph denounced. According to one account, the meeting to discuss Joseph's paper finished with talk of subsidizing 'jobs that would otherwise be lost' and Heseltine's statement: 'This is being done increasingly in the capitalist world.'[26]

Some in the shadow cabinet argued that the real faultline in British politics lay in the Labour Party, rather than between the two parties, and that it was the duty of Conservatives to support Labour moderates against left-wing infiltrators.[27] Thatcher was never tempted by the idea of an alliance with the Right wing of the Labour Party, which would almost certainly have meant the end of her own career as leader. However, some shadow ministers clearly still hankered after a government of national unity – the idea that had been promoted by Heath in 1974. Keith Joseph countered this notion with the argument that a major faultline of

British politics cut across the Conservative Party on issues 'like crime and punishment and immigration'.[28] He recognized that there was a division in the Conservative Party between those whose primary interest lay in getting back into office as soon as possible and those who accepted a long *cure d'opposition* as necessary in order for the party to renew its ideological purity. Joseph foresaw the risk that the Labour Party might be forced to call an early election, before the Conservative Party was ready for office, or that the Labour Party might institute a siege economy and call the Conservative Party into a national government designed to manage the crisis – thus encouraging Conservatives to embrace the controls and heavy state intervention that some of them had flirted with under Heath.

Constitutional reform was widely discussed amongst Conservatives during this period. In a much quoted television lecture of 1976, Lord Hailsham drew attention to the dangers of what he called 'elective dictatorship'. Far from looking for ways to ensure that a future Thatcher government might have the means to effect radical change, many Conservatives were looking for ways to introduce more checks and balances into the British system. Even men who featured prominently in the demonology of the Left – such as the founder of the Special Air Service[29] or the chairman of Rio Tinto Zinc[30] – seem primarily to have seen politics during the mid-1970s as a defensive operation. They talked of the need for a written constitution or for the institution of proportional representation.

Monetarism – a belief in controlling the money supply as a means of controlling inflation – was seen as the most important element in the economic policy of the first Thatcher government. Things seemed less clear in opposition. The very intellectual success of monetarism in the mid-1970s meant that it transcended conventional political divisions. The three most prominent journalists to be associated with the doctrine were Peter Jay (a Labour supporter), Samuel Brittan (the half-brother of Leon

Brittan and a friend of many Conservatives, but a man whose politics revolved around nostalgia for a truly liberal Liberal Party) and William Rees-Mogg (a Tory). Conservatives faced particular problems in 1976. On the one hand, this looked like a moment of opportunity, because the Labour Party's popularity was damaged by economic problems. On the other hand, Callaghan implemented rather monetarist policies, partly under pressure from the IMF.

Monetarism raised awkward questions for Conservatives. It ran against Tory pragmatism as well as against the party's policy in the recent past. In May 1976 Reginald Maudling submitted a paper to the shadow cabinet in which he underlined the benefits of pay control and dismissed the role of controlling the money supply in combating inflation.[31] Defence of monetarism in the shadow cabinet was surprisingly muted. Keith Joseph's most quoted reference to the new economic doctrine during the 1970s came in a speech – 'Monetarism is not enough' – that was, characteristically, designed to draw attention to the limits of the very theories that he was expounding.[32] Geoffrey Howe was in favour of monetarist policies but aware that they were hard to sell to voters. He simply argued that the party should emphasize 'proper management of the money supply (without much attempt to popularize this unintelligible proposition – except by arguing the case against big public spending, and big borrowing by the government and internationally)'.[33]

Divisions over economic policy were in any case not clear-cut in the shadow cabinet. In a memorandum to President Ford, Henry Kissinger described the internal politics of the Conservative Party thus:

Themselves divided on inflation policy between the advocates of statutory wage controls and 'strict monetarists', the Tories clearly are waiting to see if Labor can make a voluntary incomes policy stick with the unions – where the Conservatives failed with a statutory

policy ... Mrs Thatcher has tried to occupy a middle ground,
resulting in a lack of clear public understanding of what exactly
Tory policy is on this vital issue.[34]

The notion of Thatcher occupying the 'middle ground' may in
retrospect seem odd, but it would not seem strange to one whose
only knowledge of her came from reading her remarks when she
was leader of the opposition. Thatcher's economic ideas were
shrouded in ambiguity, which may have reflected both an
uncertainty in her own mind and a desire to avoid taking unpopular
positions. Unlike some of her colleagues, she did not rule out wage
control in all circumstances.[35] Though she had alluded to the money
supply as a cause of inflation as far back as 1968, she rarely came
across as a monetarist in the economic statements that she made
as leader of the opposition.

The conflict between monetarism and wage control intersected
with views on trade unions and economic management more
generally. Advocates of wage control were not 'soft' on other matters.
On the contrary, their views were often tied to fierce anti-unionism.
In his paper attacking monetarism, Maudling wrote:

All economic problems are basically political problems, and politics
are about power. The sole and overwhelming reason why an incomes
policy is needed is to deal with the monopoly power which the
unions now possess and, even more important, are now fully
conscious that they do possess. So long as they continue to wield
power to destroy individual businesses or indeed, complete industries,
and the threat of bringing the entire economy to a halt, any talk
of a return to 'free collective bargaining' or the ... 'free market'
is meaningless. The simple fact is that for years now the unions
have increasingly demanded, with effective menaces, excessive wage
increases which have inevitably led to excessive cost and price
increases. That is what has happened. That, and the other side of
the union coin, their total unwillingness to co-operate in raising

productivity, constitute the 'English disease' which has become the despair of our friends and the bane of sterling.[36]

Monetarism, on the other hand, did not imply a general hostility to 'corporatism'. There was no reason why control of the money supply should not coexist with control (perhaps even statutory control) of wages. Indeed, the European country seen to have practised monetarism most successfully, and which provided a model of economic success for many Conservatives in the 1970s, was West Germany – a country in which both employers and workers were organized into powerful unions and in which the government certainly did take a view about desirable levels of wage settlement. Nigel Lawson, an admirer of German monetary discipline, suggested to Thatcher that the Tories might outflank Labour and the unions by proposing to legislate for the establishment of German-style work's councils.[37]

Geoffrey Howe was keenly aware of the complexities at work here. He was a monetarist and, as it turned out, tougher than most of his colleagues when it came to applying control of the money supply when in office. However, Howe was subtle and cautious in his approach to wage negotiations and trade unions. He did not believe, à la Powell, that the government should just let employers pay their workers anything they liked and then sit back whilst everyone took the consequences. He insisted that he was for a policy for incomes if not an incomes policy.[38] More generally, Howe favoured a recognition that society was composed of organized interests as well as free-floating individuals. This was partly a reflection of his professional background. It would have been a bit rich for a QC at the English Bar to preach the virtues of an unrestricted free market to other people. Furthermore, he had specialized in labour law and drawn his clients from the Welsh valleys – so, unlike some of his colleagues in the shadow cabinet, he actually knew a few trade unionists.[39] Howe drafted a report in 1977 in which he talked of the need for 'concerted action', the pooling of economic advice from many quarters and discussion with the 'major interest groups'. His emphasis was on education and the flow of information rather than binding arrangements, and he wanted to work 'on a basis compatible with existing British institutions'.[40]

In spite of Howe's cautious tone, or perhaps because of it, this was one area of economic policy on which Margaret Thatcher took a clear stand: she hated it, and her denunciation of it seems to have blended into her general propensity to bully her shadow chancellor. She scrawled her objections across his report and, when he replied in characteristically and annoyingly emollient terms, she wrote that she was 'frightened to death' of the proposals.[41] When Howe drafted a speech on trade unions in which he talked of the 'corporate world of an industrial society', Thatcher wrote: 'Should not use this word – it is too close to "corporatism".'[42]

In their attitude to trade unions, as in so much else, the notable thing about the Conservatives was how cautious they were. Many of them were bitter about the way in which the Heath government had been brought down by the miners (for this reason, hostility to unions was not confined to those most identified with Thatcher). However, the downfall of Heath also made Conservatives tread warily in this area. In the autumn of 1977 John Hoskyns and Norman Strauss (another businessman who had become interested in politics) prepared a report entitled 'Stepping Stones', which was to play an important role in the mythology of Thatcherism. Hoskyns and Thatcher both wrote dramatic accounts of a report that was so radical in its insistence that the union issue should be put at the centre of Conservative policy that the chairman of the party tried to have all copies destroyed.[43]

The actual text of the Stepping Stones report seems rather less dramatic. Much of it consisted of a breathlessly urgent statement of the obvious – there was always a touch of the management consultant about Hoskyns. Reactions to the report amongst senior Tories were interesting. There was no simple Right/Left divide in the shadow cabinet. Whitelaw seemed the most enthusiastic supporter of the report; John Davies was its most severe critic. John Biffen – alway sceptical about plans, even planning to abolish plans – was against. Most of all, by this stage, Conservative leaders were preoccupied by the electoral advantage that might be extracted from a trade union policy. For this reason, they were particularly keen to avoid publicizing their internal discussions and to avoid anything that might give the impression of 'splits' in the party. Patten sought, much to the annoyance of the report's authors, to assimilate Stepping Stones into the general thrust of Conservative policy and particularly electoral strategy. Jim Prior, seen by Thatcher, at least in retrospect, as the major obstruction to Tory radicalism on the trade unions, remained shadow minister for employment. Patten argued that new initiatives on the matter were rendered unnecessary by the fact that opinion 'is already moving our way'.

Trade union policy was an area on which Thatcher's advisers and speechwriters seemed to be pitted against the members of her shadow cabinet – Norman Fowler talked of a division between 'Pymites' (i.e. those loyal to Francis Pym, the shadow agriculture minister and a believer in moderation) and 'Shermanites'.[44] Advisers did much to set the tone for Thatcher's pronouncements, but it seemed safe to assume that front-bench spokesmen would define the policy. John Nott wondered whether grandees such as Carrington and Whitelaw had even condescended to register the existence of Sherman and Hoskyns.[45] In 1977 Robert Moss attacked Prior's attitude to the closed shop: 'He appears to be confused about everything except the need to appease the unions by giving them a licence to conscript labour.' Whatever her private opinions, Thatcher allowed it to be thought that she backed Prior.[46] During the 1979 election, Thorneycroft, the chairman of the party, insisted that Thatcher remove an aggressive passage on trade unions from a speech that had been written for her by the journalist Paul Johnson. Thatcher was cross, or at least had become cross by the time that she described the incident in her memoirs, but she tore up the offending pages.[47]

Conservative attitudes to trade unions during the 1970s had much to do with the Tories' attitudes to continental Europe. The Federal Republic of Germany was held up by many Conservatives as a model that Britain would do well to imitate. The phrase 'social market' was taken from the Germans and picked up by the Right of the Conservative Party.[48] Discussion in shadow cabinet was often about how German political models might be rendered into British idioms, and sometimes this meant literally addressing questions of translation. Geoffrey Howe regretted that there was no English word for '*Konzertierte Aktion*'[49] and Reginald Maudling felt that the English language needed an equivalent of 'Erhard's single favourite word "conjuncturpolitik".'[50] Thatcher never liked foreign words (in her more austere moments she even disapproved of 'bourgeois') and, as has been explained, she was suspicious of Conservative interest in 'concerted action'. However, even she recognized that circumstances for cooperation between unions, management and the state were better in Germany, where the extreme Left was weaker, unions were less prone to strike, and labour productivity was higher. Whatever she may have said later, Thatcher's statements in the 1970s reflected a belief that Britain needed to be more like West Germany.

Throughout the late 1970s the Conservatives who were to be most associated with Thatcher's policy during the 1980s were remarkable for their lack of confidence in the possibility of radical change. Economics was the issue that lay at the centre of their thinking, and the issue on which their policies, once in government, were to break most sharply with the past. However, one of the most consistent themes to be found in internal party documents was that the Conservative Party would not win an election on economic policy, certainly not on a Thatcherite one. Scepticism about this was found across the party (from Joseph on its radical wing to Patten on its centrist one); it was expressed by both Howe and Lawson – the two men who were to dominate economic policy-making from 1979 to 1989.

The comparative weakness of Thatcherism in the Conservative Party was reflected in two documents from 1978. The first was apparently drawn up in secret by a small committee chaired by Lord Carrington. It concerned the prospect of confrontation between a future Thatcher government and the trade unions. After talking to senior civil servants, Carrington's committee concluded that 'no government can win these days in the way that Mr Baldwin's Cabinet triumphed during the General Strike of 1926, by maintaining essential supplies and services', and that a Labour government would find it easier than a Tory government to take on the unions .[51]

Perhaps it was not surprising that a committee chaired by Carrington and advised by senior civil servants should produce such a pessimistic view of the chances of breaking with the recent past. More striking was a document on 'themes' drawn up by Angus Maude and others in early 1978. The MPs who drafted the document were mainly backbenchers who had entered parliament fairly recently. Some of them were to be seen later as important figures in the Thatcherite revolution – two of them, Lawson and Tebbit, were to be very important indeed. One might have expected such a group to embrace radical ideas. In fact, their report seems in retrospect astonishingly averse to change or risk.

> We believe people are fed up with change, and with new systems that don't work. There is a deep nostalgia, in part for what is thought of as a comfortable past, but chiefly for a settled, civilized life. Continuity is vital, and that is in tune with a Conservative approach . . . we must be very careful how we handle 'Time for a Change' as a theme . . . Most people (we hope) want what we are seeking – a major change of trend and style of government – but not a great radical upheaval, based on promises of a Brave New World.[52]

The report suggested that patriotism would play well, if delivered with a 'rather special Disraelian panache', as would the independent nuclear deterrent – 'it is humiliating for Britons to rely solely on Yanks, Frogs and Krauts for their survival'. However, the more novel aspects of Conservative policy that had come to the fore since the deposition of Heath were treated in almost dismissive fashion: 'We are not keen on "Freedom" as a great philosophical theme. "Stop messing us about" is much nearer home ... "Capitalism" is not a good word, and we do not think even "Free Enterprise" rings many bells.'

Given that Thatcher and her allies were so conscious of the weakness of their ideas in their own country and their own party, why did Thatcher survive as leader of the party at all, and why did she win the general election of 1979? A great deal of the answer to both questions is luck. Thatcher was lucky in her enemies inside the Conservative Party. When advised by Carrington to praise his successor in public, Heath said: 'Why on earth? I do not think she is any good. I am much better and ought still to be there.'[53] This lack of grace made him less effective as an opponent, and probably eroded the support that he had initially enjoyed amongst rank-and-file party members. At first Reginald Maudling looked like the most dangerous opponent of Thatcher and her ideas in the shadow cabinet. Maudling, however, was a vain, idle man who was prone to have his first drink of the day at ten o'clock in the morning. His interventions against Thatcher were too tactless to rally his colleagues. He was also mired in corruption allegations that surrounded his association with property developers. In 1976 Thatcher was able to sack him from her front bench without having to endure anything more than an exchange of rude words.

Thatcher was also lucky in the behaviour of her opponents on the other side of the House of the Commons. Many commentators argued that the 1979 election was lost by the Labour Party rather than won by the Conservatives. By most measures, the Labour ministers had been successful. They had survived the financial crisis of 1976, they had brought down inflation and contained public spending. In many ways, they (and particularly the chancellor, Denis Healey) had done the very things that Keith Joseph had blamed the Heath government for failing to do. Part of the problem for Labour leaders, however, was the fact that they were competent managers of a crisis rather than inspired purveyors of a new doctrine. Once the Labour Party had lost its belief in Keynesian economics, which it seemed to have done by the autumn of 1976, then it was split between Tony Benn, who espoused more radical government intervention in the economy, and Denis Healey, who seemed to be motivated by an alternating desire to please the International Monetary Fund, with financial stringency, or the British electorate, with generosity.

In his budget of 1978, Healey swung towards generosity, apparently motivated by the belief that an election was imminent. As it turned out, Callaghan did not call an election in the autumn of 1978. The reasons for his delay are a matter of debate and may not have been entirely clear in his own mind; he may just have wanted to cling on to power for a few more months. However, Callaghan had also seen private polls that suggested that the Labour position in the country was not as strong as generally assumed in the autumn of 1978. Equally, he seems to have believed that the medium-term prospects for the economy were relatively good. He had only a small majority in the House of Commons, but he thought that the Liberals and the Nationalist parties from Scotland and Wales would have their own reasons for not wishing to force an election on him. Most of all, he calculated that the enthusiasm of the trade unions for a Labour victory would prevent them from causing too much trouble.[54]

The last of these calculations turned out to be wrong. Two key trade unionists – Hugh Scanlon of the engineers and Jack Jones of the Transport and General Workers Union (TGWU) – had been good at restraining their own supporters, the former helped in this by his own reputation as a left-winger. However, both men retired. Scanlon's replacement was a more 'moderate' figure, Terry Duffy, who consequently lacked authority over his own troops. The new leader of the TGWU, Mostyn Evans, seems simply not to have understood the wider political context in which wage negotiations took place.

Changes in the trade unions mattered to Labour even more than usual in the late 1970s. The party's economic policy revolved around a 'social contract' between government, employers and trade unions, which sought to impose a voluntary limit on pay rises. These arrangements were due to expire in July 1978, but the TUC and the government now came into conflict. The former wanted a return to free collective bargaining; the latter wanted to limit annual pay rises to 5 per cent. The government did not impose its will by law but it did try to enforce limits in the public sector and it did threaten private companies that paid more than 5 per cent that they would be penalized by the loss of government contracts.

In the winter of 1978–9 there was a series of strikes. The first of these was at the Ford Motor works, but more serious for the government's image were those by a variety of municipal employees. The total number of days lost in strikes was relatively small – smaller than it was to be five years later when the Conservative government faced down the miners. However, the strikes were politically damaging for three reasons. First, they were mainly by workers whose activity, or inactivity, had a direct impact on the public. Cancellation of hospital appointments or the sight of uncollected rubbish piled in the streets made an impression that the interruption of industrial production would not have done. Secondly, a hostile press was able to make much of individual incidents that seemed to display particularly cavalier attitudes to the public – the refusal of a few Liverpool gravediggers to bury corpses in February 1979 probably came to loom larger in the mind of the average reader of the *Daily Mail* than, say, the General Strike of 1926. Finally, a large part of Labour's appeal, and especially Callaghan's appeal, had lain in the belief that they would maintain smooth relations with the unions. By the spring of 1979 intimacy with the trade unions had come to seem a weakness rather than a strength. Callaghan was damaged by a small incident that received wide coverage. On 10 January 1979 he returned from an economic conference in Guadeloupe and told an impromptu press conference at Heathrow that most of the world would be surprised by the notion that Britain was in chaos. The *Sun* newspaper gleefully printed the headline 'CRISIS WHAT CRISIS?' alongside a picture of Callaghan's suntanned face.

Even after the strikes, however, Labour's defeat was not inevitable. Most opinion polls showed the Conservative Party ahead during the spring of 1979, but the lead was not a big one. Thatcher's sex introduced an element of unpredictability into the election. Some Tories believed that voters would not countenance a woman prime minister; others believed that a female leader would give them unique appeal to working-class women – particularly, perhaps, to that growing group of women who worked themselves and who were married to Labour-voting men.

As it turned out Margaret Thatcher won the election with a majority of forty-three seats. The electoral swing to Conservatism was sharper in the south of England than in the north. In other respects, the Conservative vote defied expectations. Thatcher's critics and friends alike had laid a heavy emphasis on her appeal to the middle classes – yet the swing to the Conservatives in 1979 came primarily from the working class, and especially the skilled working class. Middle-class voters (or, at least, university graduates) were actually less prone to vote Conservative in 1979 than they had been in the previous election. The heavy emphasis on Margaret Thatcher's appeal to women, and the fears about her possible lack of appeal to men, sat oddly with the fact that the swing to the Conservative Party was higher amongst men than amongst women. Finally, and in conspicuous contrast to the previous election, the swing to the Conservatives was highest amongst young voters (especially, it seems, amongst those aged twenty-five to thirty-four).[55]

The election victory did not simply mark the return of an ordinary Conservative government brought by the ebb and flow of electoral tides. The key to its novelty was Thatcher herself. Opinion polls showed that she was not popular with the electorate, and Conservative strategists had been worried by this. In 1976 Keith Joseph had argued that the leader should adopt a 'national' tone and that she should display 'her warmth and humanity' whilst men like him should do the dirty business of attacking the government.[56] In 1979 it looked as if this strategy had failed. Interviewing her in September 1978, Brian Walden brought out a paradox in Thatcher's public image. On the one hand, she was reluctant to identify herself with specific controversial policies. Yet, on the other hand, her tone was – in some almost indefinable way – new: 'Instead of the reassurance we've come to expect from Conservative leaders, Mrs Thatcher's [speeches] conveyed a sense of imminent danger.'[57] Voters thought that Thatcher was particularly 'divisive'.

None of this means that Thatcher was a liability to her party in 1979. The electoral advantage that a party derives from its leader does not depend on popularity with the whole electorate. Thatcher was regarded with disdain by many traditional Conservatives and with active dislike by many committed Labour supporters. Neither of these groups mattered – because they were both made up of people who were unlikely to change their vote. Thatcher does, however, seem to have appealed to a small but important group of voters – those who had not previously voted Conservative but were willing to consider doing so.

Thatcher's appeal did not depend on identification with particular policies – such identification, particularly in economic matters, was weak. It did depend, in a more complicated way, on the sense that she was identified with certain values, with a kind of moral mood music. This moral mood music was in part the product of a deliberate strategy. Internal party documents often talked about the benefits that the party might derive from an emphasis on non-economic issues. However, the sense of Thatcher's personal identification with particular values was not the result of a deliberate strategy by her entourage. Sometimes it seems to have come about partly by accident; sometimes it was Thatcher's enemies who helped to build her image by the very vehemence of their attacks. A banal speech entitled 'Britain Awake' delivered at Kensington Town Hall on 19 January 1976 caused the Red Army newspaper to label Margaret Thatcher 'The Iron Lady' – a soubriquet that was to be enormously useful to her. Similarly, Thatcher's brief remarks about white Britons feeling 'swamped' by immigrant cultures (delivered during a television interview on January 1978) had not been planned by her advisers – some of them were, in fact, rather shocked by the remarks.[58] None the less, they did exactly what some Conservatives had urged in private for the previous four years – communicated a sense that a Conservative government would be tough on immigration.

The very uproar that greeted some of Thatcher's remarks probably served her party's electoral purposes. It contributed to the sense that she had a dramatically new approach, without forcing her to specify how such an approach might translate into policy. In fact, there was often a disjuncture between image and policy in 1979. Thatcher was seen as tough on defence (though the perceived gap between the parties was smaller than it was to become in 1983), but Conservatives had promised to do nothing more than maintain Labour's rate of increase in spending (privately some of the economic spokesmen jibbed at even that). The Conservatives were seen as tough on immigration though in practice their policies differed little from those of the Callaghan government.[59] They were seen as tough on trade unions though they had in fact refused to go along with the NAFF's campaign to ban the closed shop. They were seen as tough on capital punishment though Thatcher ruled out all the measures (a referendum, deselection of anti-hanging MPs by Tory constituency associations, the application of a whip in a House of Commons vote) that might have made the restoration of the death penalty possible.

If the election of 1979 was a triumph for Thatcher, it was conspicuously not a victory for Thatcherism, as it was to be defined in the following decade. Very few expected the ruthless monetarism of the first Thatcher government or the energetic sale of state assets that marked the second. Well-informed people would have laughed aloud it they had been told that, within a decade, trade union power would be sharply reduced. On the day after the election victory, Thatcher's adviser John Hoskyns wrote in his diary: 'I somehow could not get excited about the victory celebrations because I knew that the chances of the new government achieving anything where so many had failed were small. We might as well get some sleep and conserve our energies.'[60]

Chapter 5

PRIMITIVE POLITICS, 1979-83

Now that the (hundred day?) honeymoon is over, and at least until the fruits of our policies show up (which will not be for some time yet), they will attack us for whatever we do; for 'primitive monetarism' if we continue on our present course and for weakness, U-turns and general Heath/Barber recidivism if we do not. There is no way in which we can avoid being attacked, whatever we do: we must be guided by the reflection that it is better to be attacked for the right policies than for the wrong ones and concentrate on getting our own message across, for which purpose incidentally, 'primitive' language is essential: nothing else will be understood.

Nigel Lawson to Geoffrey Howe, August 1979[1]

O n 5 May 1980 members of the Special Air Service stormed the Iranian embassy in London, in which a number of hostages were being held by armed Iranian dissidents. They blew holes in the wall, abseiled down from the roof and killed all but one of the dissidents. In some ways, this was a turning point in world history. Ever since the 1960s, Western politicians had been haunted by the notion that, to paraphrase Baldwin, 'The guerrilla will always get through.' In 1970 fear of terrorist reprisals had forced the Heath government to release the Palestinian hijacker Leila Khalid and, shortly before the storming of the Iranian embassy by the

SAS, American special forces had botched an attempt to rescue American hostages in Tehran – a failure that almost certainly sealed the fate of President Jimmy Carter and ensured the election of Thatcher's friend Ronald Reagan. Thatcher's government seemed to have acted with a determination and ruthlessness that had not been seen in major Western democracies since 1945. There had always been links between the SAS and the Conservative Party. MPs such as Carol Mather, Stephen Hastings, Fitzroy Maclean (it was Maclean's stepson who led the assault on the Iranian embassy), and Thatcher's own patron, Airey Neave, had served with the regiment. The SAS seemed to epitomize a new mood in British life. The cabinet secretary recalled that Thatcher was the 'nearest thing to Queen Elizabeth at Tilbury' after the operation. As luck would have it, a dinner brought permanent secretaries and the prime minister together on the day after the storming of the embassy: the 'Sir Humphreys' were uncomfortably aware that their own caution was now unfavourably compared with the dynamism of the army.[2] The SAS's subsequent exploits in the Falklands and in Ulster launched a whole new genre of books about 'special forces',[3] and established the regiment's reputation as a Thatcherite praetorian guard. One soldier recalled that the prime minister 'practically had her own bunk at Hereford [the SAS headquarters]'. The founder of the Special Air Service, David Stirling, had once been regarded with embarrassment by senior Conservatives.[4] Thatcher brought him in from the cold – he was knighted in 1990.

The storming of the Iranian embassy mattered so much partly because it was almost the only success that the Thatcher government could claim during its first three years in office. For many, it was the unoccupied burnt-out shell of the Iranian embassy – in which the dope smoke of squatters mingled with the lingering smell of cordite – that symbolized the early Thatcher years more strikingly than any military triumph. Even Thatcher's friends were often at a loss to find anything good to say about her government.

Unemployment increased sharply, as did, at first, inflation. A leading industrialist was quoted as saying that the 'removal of Mrs Thatcher' would be the best thing that could happen to the economy.[5] Young men in several cities rioted during the summer of 1981, and some observers seem seriously to have believed that the whole fabric of British society would collapse. In July 1981 Sir Nicholas Henderson, appointed by Thatcher as British ambassador to Washington and a keen supporter of the Conservative government, wrote in his diary:

> The news at home is unredeemably bad; economic decline, rising unemployment, hunger-strike deaths and violence in Ulster, riots in many towns in England. I find that the hopes I entertained exactly two years ago that we might be going to turn over a new leaf under Maggie have been dashed. Our plight is worse than two years ago because we appear to have tried something new and it has failed.[6]

Henderson would have been even more distressed if he had seen the report from the newly installed American ambassador in London, which was summarized for the president: 'Thatcher has lost her grip on the political rudder . . . With no British leader seeming to have a clear idea of where or how to go, some political turbulence is likely, with adverse effects on the country's reliability as a US ally.'[7]

The great and the good of British public life, including some cabinet ministers, wanted the government to reverse its economic policies. However, the most troubling comments on the government's record came in the form of 'support' by John Kenneth Galbraith, a professor at Harvard and probably the best-known economist in the world at the time. He insisted that Britain was a good place to test new economic thinking because the British rarely translated economic despair into physical violence. He told Geoffrey Howe:

I would not wish at all to discourage the Chancellor from continuing with his monetarist experiment. I would indeed deplore it if he stopped because [Milton] Friedman would then be able to say that the policy would have worked if only he had given it another six months.[8]

Thatcher was lucky to survive this period. Conservative performance in opinion polls was consistently bad and Thatcher's personal rating was lower than that of her party. She was fortunate that her cabinet colleagues did not rebel against her – though their reluctance to move directly against her may have sprung from a belief that the force of circumstances would do their work for them. The very difficulty of the first few years in office became an important part of the Thatcher myth. Lawson had called for 'primitive language' that would differentiate the government from all the complexities and compromises of the Heath period. It was often Thatcher's enemies who provided this language. The violent attacks on Thatcherite economic policy conveyed a sense of high drama and often concealed the extent to which the government had, in reality, compromised. Thatcher's parliamentary private secretary divided the cabinet into 'heroes', who supported Thatcher, and 'reptiles'. Her supporters came to relish their own 'heroism' in having pursued unpopular policies in the face of apparently impossible odds. Thatcher and her closest associates were much given to analogies that drew on the Second World War, and their recollections of this period are peppered with references to Dunkirk, El Alamein, Stalingrad and the Battle of Britain.

Overwhelmingly, Thatcherism, from 1979 until 1982, was discussed in terms of economics. Foreign policy, crime and immigration had all been important to the formation of Thatcher's image before 1979, but it was hard to take the radicalism of opposition into government on these issues – partly because Thatcher's appeal had often depended on tone rather than on particular policies that were different from those of her opponents.

The economy would in any case have forced itself on the attention of any British government during this period. The 1979 election was held at a time when the economy seemed to be in good shape. Inflation, which had been over 20 per cent per year, had been pulled down to 8 per cent. In 1978 the British government had been released from the controls over public spending that the International Monetary Fund had imposed in return for loans in 1976.

The apparent prosperity of the British economy did not last long and merely masked the problems that the new government inherited. Denis Healey, the Labour chancellor, had looked forward to 'sod off day' when he would no longer have the representatives of the IMF looking over his shoulder.[9] He exploited the freedom he gained on this day to increase public spending in 1978. Public finances were less healthy in 1979 than they had been a year earlier. To this was added the effect of public-spending commitments made before the election. The Labour government had appointed a commission, under Professor Hugh Clegg, to look into public-sector pay increases. During the election campaign the Conservatives had felt obliged (against the advice of the shadow Treasury team) to promise that they would honour the Clegg Commission's recommendations. This alone meant an increase in public spending. The Labour government had also promised Britain's NATO allies that they would increase defence spending in real terms by 3 per cent per year for several years and the Conservatives honoured this commitment[10] – it would have been hard to avoid increases in defence spending at a time when international tension had risen sharply. In any case, the Conservatives had spending commitments of their own; they had promised to increase pay for soldiers and policemen.

Even the government's good fortune seemed to come with dark linings inside the silver clouds. High oil prices had undermined the Heath government and done much to precipitate the general economic crisis of the 1970s. However, in the 1960s oil had been discovered in the North Sea. Exploiting it was difficult but, as technology improved and the oil price increased, it became obvious that Britain would eventually become an oil exporter. Some politicians came to look on North Sea oil as the magic potion that would solve every British problem. It would support the pound, provide fresh investment for industry and, so Machiavellian Tories hoped, undermine the power of the National Union of Mineworkers. The Labour minister Edmund Dell wrote that politics in the 1970s had been like a 'game of musical chairs' in which both parties prayed that they would be in office when the oil started to flow.[11] In 1980 Thatcher won this particular game because large-scale British extraction of oil began at almost the same moment that the world oil price, driven up by the Iranian revolution of 1979, reached a new height. In the long term, North Sea oil obviously did help the government – if only by giving it new resources to tax. However, sterling's new status as a petrocurrency – along with the government's emphasis on controlling the money supply and, eventually, the fact that the dollar was weakened by deficit spending under Reagan – meant that the pound rose sharply against other currencies. The managers of industries that depended on exports raged against the effects of oil on the exchange rate. Britain's leading motor manufacturer told the CBI conference that he wished the government would 'leave the bloody stuff in the ground'.

In its bid to balance the books, the new government was driven to some strange expedients. In November 1979 it brought forward by two months the date on which companies exploiting North Sea oil were required to pay £750 million of petroleum revenue tax. In the spring of 1981 Nigel Lawson, the financial secretary to the treasury, met the chairman of the Committee of London Clearing Banks, and suggested that the banks might like to take over a proportion of the government's fixed-rate credit export scheme, i.e. effectively, to subsidize the government. When the chairman refused, the government imposed a 'once and for all' levy of 2.5

per cent of all non-interest-bearing deposits the banks held, thus raising £400 million.[12] Both measures were justified on the grounds that 'peculiar circumstances' (respectively high oil prices and high interest rates) were giving the companies concerned 'windfall profits'. The various measures against windfall profits, extraordinary ones for a government that was ostensibly committed to defend free enterprise, provoked only one, rather half-hearted, resignation by a parliamentary private secretary.[13]

Public spending increased during the first few years of the Thatcher government, driven up partly by the commitments on public sector pay and defence described above, and partly by side-effects of the government's own policies. The need to make nationalized industries more efficient often meant, in the short term, granting them more money for investment. Equally, the sharp rise in unemployment during the early 1980s meant that the social security budget increased. Some of the changes that the first Thatcher government made related to accountancy rather than the actual level of spending. Ever since the 1960s, government departments had calculated their future spending in terms of 'volume' or 'funny money', as it came to be known. Thus, for example, the Ministry of Defence's budget would effectively commit the government to spend 'whatever a destroyer happens to cost in five years' time'. Automatic adjustment to inflation meant that civil servants and contractors had little incentive to cut costs. The government now began to move towards the calculation of future spending in terms of cash to be spent.

One of the government's most difficult tasks was a negative one: it resisted pressure, some of it from Conservative MPs, to impose tariffs or import controls. In the short term, the only market that could easily be 'freed' was that in the national currency itself. On 23 October 1979 the government announced the abolition of exchange controls. If controls had been kept, then the City of London would never have assumed the international role that it did during the 1980s. Economic policy in the 1960s and 1970s had been overshadowed by persistent neurosis about a 'sterling crisis'. The fact that Britain was now an exporter of oil made such a crisis less likely: indeed, a fall in the value of the pound was widely considered to be desirable. All the same, abolishing exchange controls was a risk that, literally, kept the chancellor of the exchequer awake at night. Enthusiasts for the free market were quite often to claim that this was the single most important measure imposed by the first, or perhaps any, Thatcher government.

The word that mattered most for economic debate in the early 1980s was 'monetarism'. Monetarism suggests that there is close relation between inflation and the money supply. The fashion for monetarism owed something to the American Milton Friedman, who had won the Nobel prize for economics in 1976. The links between Friedman and British Conservatives were in fact fairly limited,[14] and many British ministers were not unqualified admirers of his thinking or, indeed, of American monetarism more generally.[15] Friedman did, however, exercise a certain influence over the 'primitive language' of British economic debate. His influence derived mainly from presenting a television programme, *Free to Choose*, in 1980, which may have been broadcast by the BBC in an attempt to make amends for the prominence that they had previously given to Galbraith's more dirigiste approach,[16] and which probably contributed to a public perception that monetarism was just another term for free-market economics.

Monetarism did not necessarily go with any other aspect of right-wing economic policy. It was not always associated with a desire to cut public spending or increase the role of the free market. It could be used as a justification for not having any other sort of economic policy. Enoch Powell had embraced it precisely because he thought that it freed the government from all manner of other economic tinkering. Perhaps the 'purest', and certainly the most Powellite, monetarist in Thatcher's cabinet was John Biffen. However, Biffen could be sceptical about other aspects of Thatcherite economics. After leaving the government, he summed up his position thus: 'I am a monetarist, but I am not a great supply-side Conservative, so I accept higher levels of taxation and public spending than many of my colleagues.'[17]

The word 'monetarism' was bandied around in a fairly cavalier manner. John Hoskyns wrote: 'informed opinion in the country at that stage still seemed to think that "monetarism" was some brutal, possibly slightly mad, celebration of man's basest acquisitive instincts, rather than an important and highly technical body of theory and knowledge, in which the US Federal Reserve and the German Bundesbank had considerable and successful experience, and we had virtually none'.[18] Disarmingly, Hoskyns admitted that his own understanding of monetarist theory was imperfect. After meeting Gordon Pepper, an economist and high priest of one of monetarism's sects, he wrote in his diary: 'Pepper talks so fast and so technically it's really hard to follow.'[19] John Sparrow, a banker who had advised Thatcher since 1977 and whom she was to appoint as head of the Central Policy Review Staff in 1982, said: 'I have never described myself as a monetarist, largely because I have never understood what monetarism as one subject is.'[20] A stockbroker said: 'It is monetarism as a fashion rather than as an economic theory which has gripped the City. We are businessmen and solicitors, not economists, and "controlling the money supply" has the same intuitive appeal today that "priming the pump" had in the heyday of Keynesianism, twenty years ago.'[21] Enoch Powell complained that monetarism had simply become another word for 'government economic policy'.[22] Sometimes it was used as a term of abuse. Denis Healey, who had in fact practised fairly monetarist policies for part of his own term as chancellor of the exchequer, talked of the Thatcherites as being 'sado monetarists' or 'punk monetarists'.

Monetarists were divided about the means by which their insights might be implemented. Gordon Pepper, who had once advised Thatcher, denounced most in the Thatcher government as mere 'political' monetarists who had not fully embraced the creed.

Thatcher talked of some of her colleagues as 'fair-weather' monetarists. Lawson wrote that the civil service contained 'non-believing monetarists' who were willing to implement monetarist theories with a degree of rigour that a believer would not have countenanced. Particularly prominent amongst 'non-believing monetarists' was Sir Douglas Wass of the Treasury.[23] Wass had expressed his own scepticism about monetarism during the 1970s and, as shadow chancellor, Howe had developed some of his own ideas in a lecture that was itself designed partly to reply to some of Wass's public statements.[24] In government, however, Howe found that Wass (perhaps hoping to see the government skewered on its own economic logic) was a loyal executor of policy.

Monetarism was not new. Thatcher had talked about controlling the money supply since 1968 and Joseph had described himself as a monetarist (though stressing that he was not just that) in the 1970s. The more urbane Conservatives, aware of how their party distrusted abstraction, were careful to stress that their own monetarism did not depend on arcane theory – particularly theory that had been expounded in foreign accents. Howe wrote: 'It is a great pity that its [monetarism's] practical, common sense importance has been so confused by arid, theoretical dispute. Certainly the words should never have become a term of political abuse.'[25] Nigel Lawson regarded David Hume as the true founder of monetary theory, and said:

In essence, monetarism is simply a new name for an old maxim, formerly known as the quantity theory of money. So far from being the controversial brainchild of an eccentric American professor, it was – in one form or another – the common belief and shared assumption of politicians and administrators of all political parties throughout the industrialized world for the century and more that preceded the Second World War.

It consists of two basic propositions. The first is that changes in the quantity of money determine, at the end of the day, changes in the general price level; the second is that government is able to determine the quantity of money. In practical terms, this was translated into the twin axioms of the pre-Keynesian consensus: that the primary economic duty of government was to maintain the value of the currency, and that this was to be achieved by not increasing its supply – a constraint which operated quasi-automatically for a country on the gold standard, as Britain was for most of the pre-Keynesian period.[26]

The problem for men such as Howe and Lawson was that common sense is difficult to translate into concrete policy and that the monetary system of Britain in the 1980s was more complicated than it had been at the time when Hume was writing. Nigel Lawson, as financial secretary to the treasury, made much of the Medium Term Financial Strategy, by which the government announced targets for the money supply. In practice, though, government targets for the money supply were rarely met. Simply measuring the money supply was difficult. M0 sought to measure the amount of cash in the economy, M1 (the measure that the Heath government had used) took in some bank accounts, M3 (the most important of the measures used under Thatcher) was a broader category that took in all bank accounts but excluded money held by building societies. All these measures were artificial to some degree; all of them hinged on distinctions that would be subverted by the very changes that the Thatcher government promoted. Who, in 1990, would have based monetary policy on a distinction between banks and building societies?[27] Often government policy in one area created new problems in another. The abolition of exchange rate controls, for example, made the 'Corset', an instrument that had been used to control lending by banks, useless.

Interest rates were the main instrument of British monetary policy. The aim of high interest rates was to deter borrowing and hence to reduce the total amount of money in circulation (purists insisted that interest rates reduced *demand* for, rather than supply of, money). However, the effect of interest rates (for those who believed in them as an instrument of monetary policy at all) was hard to determine. Nigel Lawson recognized that sometimes high nominal interest rates were undermined by high inflation. Sometimes high interest rates might actually cause the money supply, or at least that bit of the money supply which the government measured, to increase: 'The increase in short-term interest rates was itself making bank deposits, a major component of M3, particularly attractive to hold.'[28]

The debates in the Thatcher cabinet were as much between different kinds of monetarist as between monetarists and their opponents. Many around Thatcher disliked high interest rates. John Hoskyns and Alan Walters, Thatcher's economic adviser, were worried that they had created an over-valued currency, which was damaging British industry. They found support from the Swiss economist Jurg Niehans, who argued that it was indeed interest rates, rather than the price of oil, that had pushed the pound so high. Thatcher herself was uncomfortable with high interest rates because of the political damage that they might do by making life expensive for home owners. In opposition, Conservatives had been much exercised by the question of how home owners with mortgages might be protected from the impact of high interest rates[29] – but, apart from the scheme that Margaret Thatcher had briefly defended in 1974 to control mortgage rates, they had not come up with anything. Gordon Pepper argued that a more direct control of the money supply – through 'Monetary Base Control' – would allow interest rates to be lower.[30] Treasury ministers, however, argued that British financial structures were different from those of America and Switzerland where Monetary Base Control had seemed to work. The government found no alternative to high interest rates – though the Treasury eventually backed away from an exclusive emphasis on controlling M3 and came to pay more attention to the value of sterling.

Opposition to government policies reached its peak around the

time of the budget in March 1981. The budget aimed to lower
the Public Sector Borrowing Requirement (PSBR), partly because
Thatcher hoped that this would allow her chancellor to lower
interest rates, and thus to relieve the pressure on industry. Having
failed to cut public spending, the only way in which the chancellor
could hope to cut the PSBR was by raising taxes. Raising taxes in
a recession ran against the whole current of post-war economic
thinking and there was real astonishment when the budget did
this.* There is still debate about the political origins of the 1981
budget – in particular about whether or not its general thrust was
the result of Howe's own initiative or whether it was imposed on
him by Thatcher and Walters.[31] There is also debate about the
economic significance of the budget. Ian Gilmour sees it as 'an
elaborate camouflage for monetarist failure' because an interest in
monetary targets was replaced by an interest in the PSBR.[32] Patrick
Minford sees the budget as marking a shift within monetarism as
the government moved from a pessimistic 'Friedmanite' approach,
which assumed that only real economic pain would lower
inflationary expectations, to a monetarism of 'rational expectations',
which assumed that inflation would come down if the government
was perceived as determined to cut its own spending.[33]

The budget provoked much muttering on the Conservative back
benches – as well as a call for the chancellor's resignation from
the Tory Sir Peter Tapsell. It also produced the single most dramatic
denunciation of government economic policy. Two professors of
economics – Robert Neild and Francis Hahn – drew up a letter
stating:

A) There is no basis in economic theory or supporting
   evidence for the Government's belief that by deflating
   demand they will bring inflation permanently under

* Strictly speaking it did not raise taxes but failed to increase allowances in line
with inflation.

control and thereby induce an automatic recovery in output
and employment;

B) Present policies will deepen the depression, erode the
industrial base of our economy and threaten its social
and political stability;

C) There are alternative policies; and

D) The time has come to reject monetarist policies and
consider urgently which alternative offers the best hope
of sustained recovery.

The letter was then signed by 364 economists, a group that was
drawn together quickly via networks of personal contacts during
the Easter holiday. Signatories included most of those who had
served as chief economic adviser to the Treasury since 1945. They
were drawn from the grandest of universities – fifty-four of them
from Cambridge. The letter did not set out alternative policies to
those of the government; its signatories would not have agreed
about what those policies should be. Some were Keynesians who
believed in counter-cyclical finance, some advocated import controls
and tariffs. Stephen Nickell later admitted that he had not agreed
with everything in the letter but felt government monetary policy
was too tight and that the letter was 'the only game in town'.[34]

Wynne Godley was the most articulate and widely reported of
the government's economic critics. He was professor of applied
economics at the University of Cambridge and had served as a
government adviser after having worked at the Treasury as a young
man. The son of an Irish aristocrat, he had once been a professional
oboist and had married the daughter of the sculptor Jacob Epstein.
His denunciations of government policy – delivered with a pained
manner and in an impeccably upper-middle-class accent – were
sometimes illustrated with references to his brother flying
Swordfishes during the Second World War. His patrician manner
and cultural refinement impressed even – his enemies would have
said *especially* – those who understood nothing of economics.

Godley spoke about the consequences of government economic policy in particularly pessimistic terms. He and Francis Cripps argued that the budget was 'severely disinflationary [and] will cause a hyper slump such as Britain has never seen before'.[35] Godley said that he foresaw 'apocalypse' if government policy was not changed.

The British economy did not collapse. In fact, it began to recover soon after the 1981 budget. This contributed to a Thatcherite mythology of the 1981 budget. It was portrayed as 'the turning point in post-war British economic management': a moment when a small, determined group defied conventional wisdom, held fast against apparently impossible odds and consequently began to reverse decades of economic decline.[36]

The government's critics disputed all of this. They argued that ministers claiming credit for upturns in the economic cycle was as irrational as ministers claiming responsibility for 'a sunny day'.[37] Some of them believed that the economic recovery was 'below trend' and would actually have been more pronounced if the government had pursued different policies. Others attributed recovery to the fact that the government had discreetly abandoned some of its more rigorous policies, and that its monetary policy became increasingly loose as time went on. The storm over the March 1981 budget helped to conceal another important economic turning point, which came during a cabinet meeting on 23 July 1981, when even some of Thatcher's most loyal ministers resisted public spending cuts. All these subtleties were, however, difficult to convey and particularly difficult after such a large number of prominent academics had put their names to such a brief and bald prediction of imminent disaster.

The government and its supporters in the City became increasingly contemptuous of criticism by economists. Those ministers who had read economics at university during the years of Keynesian orthodoxy, such as Nigel Lawson or John Nott (who had studied under the aegis of Robert Neild), felt particular glee at the discomfiture of the professors. One stockbroker derided 'Uncle Wynne Godley and all':

> I can't quite put my finger on it, but somehow they don't seem to have brought off whatever it was that they were trying to achieve. Rather like the Charge of the Light Brigade, they meant well but have ended up as slightly humorous subjects. They formed up in their cloistered courts, mounted on a motley collection of nags, clutching a variety of largely obsolete weapons, blunderbusses, spears and lances, and then weren't quite sure where they were going.[38]

In some ways, attention to the precise details of government economic policy in the 1980s – to the various definitions of the money supply, the various means of controlling it, the various alternative indicators and targets – can be deceptive. As Lawson's reference to the need for 'primitive language' suggested, the government's most important task was often just to communicate an air of resolution and clarity. There was a touch of the tribal war dance in its early economic policies. The aim was to illustrate the government's determination as dramatically as possible. In this sense, government economic policy was remarkably successful. At the end of 1982 most people did not understand the details of government economic policy, and many of those people who did were not very impressed. However, the British people had a general sense of a new kind of economic policy – one that made the government responsible for lowering inflation and absolved it of responsibility for unemployment and, most importantly, one that would be pursued ruthlessly beyond the point at which earlier governments had backed down.

How did debates on economic policy affect the members of the government themselves? Broadly, Thatcher took her opposition front bench into office with her. John Peyton was the only member of her last shadow cabinet who did not serve in her first government.

However, the cabinet still contained a number of people who were sceptical about the government's most radical plans. Journalists divided the cabinet into 'wets' (those who were sceptical about radical policies) and 'dries' (those who were most committed to them). The 'wet'/'dry' division was often talked about in relation to other divisions. The 'wets' were seen as nostalgic for an old-style 'One Nation' Conservatism (though the One Nation group in the party had actually contained many Thatcherites) and for the 'post-war consensus' that had allegedly once existed.

Ministers themselves used the terms 'wet' and 'dry'. Lord Thorneycroft, who had been appointed as chairman of the party partly because Thatcher assumed that his brief association with Enoch Powell in the late 1950s would have made him 'dry', told journalists that he was afflicted with 'rising damp'. Lord Hailsham claimed that he sat in cabinet 'oozing'. The divisions were never, however, clear-cut or simple. Belief in a particular kind of policy did not necessarily go with loyalty to Margaret Thatcher. Whitelaw and Carrington were both on the whole loyal to Thatcher as an individual though they were both 'old-style' Tories rather than ideological radicals. Whitelaw's version of loyalty sometimes involved dissuading Thatcher from giving too much prominence to dries – such as Joseph or Ridley – whom he saw as lacking political sense. Carrington seems to have honoured a tacit deal with Thatcher whereby he was allowed a relatively free hand in the conduct of foreign policy in return for not interfering in domestic policy. Howe and Lawson were 'dry' on economic policy, but not, as it turned out, unconditional in their loyalty to Thatcher.

'Wet' implies ineffectuality and the 'wet'/'dry' division was also often associated with a social division between traditional Conservative grandees and self-made men from humbler backgrounds. By this definition, Sir Ian Gilmour was a typical 'wet'. He was the grandson of an earl and the son of a wealthy stockbroker. He had been educated at Eton and Balliol. He criticized the government's economic policy in a series of 'coded' speeches when he was a minister, and then did so more openly after his dismissal in 1981, but his former colleagues pointed out that he had not protested very often, or very effectively, in cabinet discussion. Other 'wets' fit the bill less neatly. Peter Walker, secretary of state for agriculture in Thatcher's first government, had left grammar school at the age of sixteen and begun his political career as one of the last protégés of the imperialist Leo Amery, which meant that he was, before being converted by Edward Heath, hostile to British membership of the EEC. Walker made his fortune in the City. Slater Walker, in which he was a partner, was famous for squeezing value out of assets – so much that the 'dry' Nigel Lawson had pointed out in the 1970s that most people feared having their companies taken over by it more than they feared nationalization.[39] Walker was also an effective minister, more so than Thatcherite ministers such as Keith Joseph.

In the short term Jim Prior was the most important of the 'wets' because, as secretary of state for employment, he occupied an economic ministry. He played up to his image as a red-faced country squire, but he too was a more complicated figure than he looked at first glance. He had been born into the prosperous middle classes – his father was a country solicitor – and he had been to Charterhouse and Cambridge with the novelist Simon Raven (he is said to have been the model for Peter Morrison in Raven's *Alms for Oblivion* sequence of novels). Prior entered agriculture via a first-class degree in estate management rather than an inherited family farm. His emollient manner disguised a ruthless streak – he maintained amicable relations with trade union leaders, but it was on his advice that the government first acquired the services of Ian MacGregor, the man who was to preside over the breaking of the National Union of Mineworkers.[40]

Michael Heseltine fitted into no category at all. He was a self-made businessman, though one whose 'humble origins' were very relative – only those who looked down from the heights of Eton,

Christ Church and the Grenadiers could imagine that Shrewsbury, Pembroke and the Welsh Guards constituted a plebeian background. He was a ferociously unconsensual politician, and in the 1970s he had almost started a brawl in the House of Commons by waving the Mace at the government benches. His personal relations with Thatcher were bad, he favoured certain kinds of economic intervention (sometimes, admittedly, a kind that amounted to little more than exhortation) and he paraded his concern for the unemployed of Liverpool. On the other hand, Heseltine's emphasis on complicated managerial systems was often better at delivering public spending cuts than the more obviously free-market approaches of his colleagues.

Ministers who disliked the economic policy of the first Thatcher government tried, in retrospect, to explain why they had not opposed it more effectively. Gilmour suggests that individual ministers were too absorbed in their departmental briefs to have time for broad economic discussion – an interpretation that does not work well for Gilmour, whose duties, as lord privy seal and as deputy to Carrington at the Foreign Office, cannot have been terribly onerous. More plausibly, Thatcher succeeded in securing acquiescence for her economic policy by placing the majority of economic ministries in the hands of people who were broadly sympathetic to her aims, by controlling cabinet agendas and by ensuring that key decisions were taken outside meetings of the full cabinet.

Ministers who disliked Thatcher's economic policies ended up grumbling amongst themselves, leaking to the press and hoping for some reversal in Thatcher's fortunes, but they never coordinated any public protest against her. Thatcher was able to pick them off one by one. Gilmour, the one whom she feared least, was sacked in 1981 along with Christopher Soames, Churchill's son-in-law, who, as Thatcher noted, could not have been crosser if he had been sacked by his own housemaid.[41] Prior was manoeuvred out of Employment and sent to Northern Ireland in 1981. Walker, the man who might have done most damage on the back benches, was kept in the cabinet almost to the end of the Thatcher government.

Most importantly, there was no simple Left/Right spectrum on which the Thatcher cabinet can be placed. Even on economics, no position was clearly marked out. In particular, enthusiasm for combating the unions was not confined to those who were 'dry' on monetary policy. Since the 1940s Thatcher had been saying that the trade unions were too powerful. However, it was often non-monetarists who, believing that controlling pay was the key to controlling inflation, were most exercised by union power. Though dissatisfaction with the unions had played an important part in the Conservative election victory of 1979, the party did not come to power with many manifesto commitments on the subject. Once in power, the Conservatives were divided about other new laws. Some in the cabinet believed that James Prior was too soft in his approach to the unions and too reluctant to bring in new laws, but reluctance to legislate was not just a sign of pro-union sympathies or lack of determination. Union legislation was complicated, hard to enforce and sometimes associated with the corporatism of the Heath government. Prior himself believed that less formal means would be more effective in taming union power. There was no single Thatcherite view on the subject. Geoffrey Howe was in favour of legislation – partly because as a lawyer he believed in the usefulness of law, and partly because he thought that giving unions a more clearly defined legal status might make them more responsible. John Nott, by contrast, was sceptical of bringing too much law into an area that ought to be governed by the operation of the free market.

In practice, the laws that the government introduced were limited. The Employment Acts of 1980 and 1982 required ballots to be held over closed shops, provided government funds for trade union ballots, and diminished the legal immunities that unions enjoyed, especially with regard to secondary picketing. The laws were comparatively modest. Unions were not yet required to hold ballots before strikes and there was no attempt to ban the closed shop (rather than to provide compensation for those who might be dismissed as a result of it). Legislation was primarily aimed to allow parties who felt themselves to be aggrieved to sue trade unions – rather than to grant the government itself new powers. Thatcher's own position was complicated. When George Gardiner led a backbench rebellion of fifty or so Conservative MPs who voted for more severe legislation on trade unions, he was given to understand that Thatcher was privately sympathetic to their proposals, as were some of her fiercer ministers.[42] However, as was often the case, Thatcher's understanding of the need to maintain a radical image seems to have gone alongside an understanding of the dangers that might go with too many radical policies – her later governments were to introduce more measures to control the unions (in 1984 and 1988), but these added relatively limited scope to the laws that had first been drawn up by Prior in the early 1980s. Only in 1990 did the government finally make it illegal to refuse employment to non-union members, and thus end the closed shop.[43]

Alongside these measures were general circumstances that shifted the balance of power against the unions. Some ministers believed that rising unemployment was an important part of these circumstances – ensuring that workers who kept their jobs were more nervous of doing anything that might jeopardize them. At first glance, a statistical overview does not lend much support to this theory: the number of strikes rose during the high unemployment of the early 1980s.[44] Probably, in truth, the links between unemployment and labour relations were complicated. To take the most obvious example, the miners' strike of 1984–5 coincided with a period of high unemployment. This did not deter the miners themselves – because they were striking to keep pits open and defend jobs, it probably encouraged them. On the other hand, fear of unemployment may well have deterred workers in other industries (notably steel) from helping the miners.

The most important focus for Conservative thinking about the trade unions was in the nationalized industries, where highly unionized workforces came up against employers who depended on the state to underwrite their wage bill. The Thatcher government was at first remarkably uncertain in its approach to public-sector strikes. The biggest strike of the period was that at British Steel in 1980 – it lasted thirteen weeks, involved 155,000 workers and cost 8 million working days. Some believed that the government had forced the management of British Steel into making a low pay offer. The reality seems to have been more complicated. The strike exposed divisions between the management of the company and the government (Thatcher had already decided, in private, to sack its chairman, Sir Charles Villiers),[45] as well as within the management and within the government. The secretary of state for employment rebuked the chairman of British Steel for having made too low an offer and was in turn rebuked by the prime minister. At least one of Thatcher's advisers believed that the whole strike had been brought about because the management of the company had made an unrealistically low offer and that it had almost had catastrophic consequences: 'If the steel strike had ended in humiliation for the Government, it is quite possible that Thatcher would not now be a household name.'[46] Thatcher was to insist that the steel strike had ended in victory for the government, if not for the management of the company. However, her government was careful to persuade other nationalized industries to avoid strikes – in particular, it provided money for a generous pay settlement to the National Union of Mineworkers in 1981 (see chapter 7).

Not all employers wanted weak trade unions. Large companies often felt that they were most threatened by unofficial strikes, and strikes of any kind were in fact least common in firms where all workers were grouped into a single union. Michael Edwardes, managing director of British Leyland – the single company in Britain that was most notoriously afflicted by strikes – insisted that he wanted 'stronger and fewer unions', so that they would be more reliable interlocutors.[47] In opposition, some Conservative frontbenchers had talked of the need to involve both sides of industry in discussion. In spite of her horror of 'corporatism', Thatcher herself had once insisted that she wanted to transform unions rather than to destroy them. She had seemed to follow the internal politics of the TUC with interest and, for example, to relish 'Hughie Scanlon's' attacks on Clive Jenkins.[48] She had, as late as 1978, invited Conservatives to join their unions. During Thatcher's first years in government, all this was forgotten. Tories regarded bodies that brought them into contact with trade unionists – notably the National Economic and Development Council – with disdain and rarely thought much about trade unions, except when they were forced to do so by strikes.

What of organized business? During the 1970s the Conservative Party had sometimes seemed like the political wing of the Confederation of British Industry (CBI) and, indeed, the former head of the CBI, John Davies, sat on the Conservative front bench for much of this period. Relations took a turn for the worse during the early years of Thatcher's leadership. Donald MacDougall, the economic adviser to the CBI, had previously been one of the Treasury officials behind Heath's loose monetary policies and not surprisingly he suggested that most industrialists were committed to the very economic policies that Thatcherism seemed against.[49] Donations to the Conservative Party had increased when business was scared after the 1974 elections.[50] However, they seem to have dropped off later in the decade – perhaps because the Labour government seemed less threatening or perhaps just because business leaders, used to back-slapping bonhomie, did not take to Margaret Thatcher.[51]

In the early 1980s manufacturing was battered by the recession. Its representatives called for lower interest rates and a lower pound. The chairman of ICI told Thatcher that he was considering moving its operations abroad. Terence Beckett, the head of the CBI, promised his members that he would give the government a 'bare knuckle fight' over their policies. Some of the more radical Thatcherites despised the CBI almost as much as they despised the TUC; they associated it with corporatism and disliked the representation it accorded to the heads of the nationalized industries. When John Hoskyns was approached with the suggestion that he might run the CBI, Alfred Sherman told him that the whole thing should be shut down.[52]

The gulf between industry and the Thatcher government was never as wide as a few well-reported spats made it seem. ICI did not move and Beckett was said, after pressure from his members, to have apologized to Thatcher.[53] Companies continued to make political donations to the Conservative Party and few of them seem to have been tempted to change this, even when the creation of the Social Democratic Party offered them a pro-capitalist alternative – indeed, Tory MPs were deterred from joining the new party by the fear that they might lose lucrative business contacts.[54] Regardless of the effects that government policies on interest rates may have had on their companies, senior executives benefited from cuts in the top rate of income tax – in at least one case, a senior executive gained enough money from this in just two years to pay for the donation that his company had given to the Conservatives during the 1979 election campaign.

Some Conservative politicians had always known that their policies would mean unemployment. Nigel Lawson was one of the few candidates in the October 1974 election who had dared to tell his own constituents the 'harsh truth' that he regarded unemployment as a price worth paying in order to beat inflation.[55] During a private meeting with economists in July 1975, Geoffrey Howe had remarked that the effects of unemployment had to be made 'harsher . . . for those elements of the labour force that were insufficiently mobile' – though he also recognized that these consequences had to be made 'less harsh . . . so that frictional or disinflationary unemployment should be made less unpalatable and likely to cause social strain'.[56] Not even the most radical thinkers, however, anticipated the levels that unemployment actually reached in the 1980s. Keith Joseph had argued in the 1970s that post-war governments had been excessively influenced by the need to avoid a return to the mass unemployment of the 1930s, but he based his arguments on the assumption that the level of post-war unemployment was naturally low. When he talked about the acceptability of increased unemployment, the numbers that he had in mind amounted to hundreds of thousands – not millions.[57] A CBI economist had warned him in the 1970s that monetarist policies might mean over a million unemployed, but Joseph had dismissed this as 'rubbish'.[58]

By late January 1982 unemployment stood, for the first time since the 1930s, at over 3 million. High unemployment under Thatcher proved to be unusually long lasting – its level did not drop much until 1986. This was partly because unemployment is usually a 'lagging indicator', which only declines sometime after a general improvement in the economy. More significantly, it was because economic recovery, when it came, involved less labour-intensive industries and drew 'new' people, such as married women, into work rather than creating jobs for the unemployed.

Unemployment haunted British culture in the early 1980s. Regularly the presenter of the nine o'clock news read out a list of factories closed and jobs lost in each region of the United Kingdom. Ken Livingstone, the left-wing Labour leader of the Greater London Council, arranged for the number of unemployed people to be printed on a banner and hung across County Hall, opposite the Houses of Parliament. Alan Bleasdale's *The Boys from the Blackstuff*, a television series about unemployed Liverpudlians, popularized the phrase 'gissa job'. Reference to unemployment statistics produced some of the most contrived lines in the history of English pop music. The Angelic Upstarts entitled one of their albums *Three Million Voices*; the Birmingham band UB 40 were named after the form used to claim unemployment benefit.

Why did the Thatcher government survive such high levels of unemployment? One answer focuses on the state of the political opposition. In 1979 the Labour Party was bitterly divided. Callaghan, widely blamed for the party's election defeat, was bound to go. The potential leader that the Tories feared most was Denis Healey. Healey was a tough operator. He had been beach master during the allied landings in southern Italy and was on good terms with the military – a fact that some senior officers made ostentatiously clear when they were faced with cuts in defence spending during the early 1980s. Twice in his career he was offered the secretary generalship of NATO. However, Healey had been exhausted by his time in government. His abrupt manner had made him powerful enemies in his own party and he was so concerned to try to obtain the support of the Left of the party that he was cavalier towards his natural supporters on the Right. In 1980 he lost the second round of the leadership contest to Michael Foot.

Foot was old (he had been born in 1913), famously indifferent to his appearance and unworldly. He was prone to talk about his pet interests – the novels of Disraeli, the poetry of Byron and the evils of British foreign policy in the 1930s – at times when his audience might have expected him to address matters of more immediate concern.[59] He was the last Labour leader to be chosen by MPs, but it was not clear that they really wanted him. A few right-wingers had already decided to leave the party and voted for Foot in order to saddle Labour with an unelectable leader; some left-wingers voted for him on the assumption that he would soon step down in favour of Tony Benn.[60] Foot was, as many right-wing Tories recognized in private, an impressive orator, a patriot and a man of principle, but no one thought that he would make a good prime minister. During a television broadcast in 1982, a child asked Thatcher to list three things that she admired about Foot. After having said that he had a journalist's ability to meet a deadline, Thatcher seemed genuinely unable to think of any other admirable quality in the leader of Her Majesty's Opposition.[61]

Foot quickly found himself in an absurd position. He had spent his whole career on the Left of his party. He supported unilateral nuclear disarmament and British withdrawal from the European Community. However, his leadership was destabilized by a new kind of left-winger that had risen up in constituency parties during the 1970s. The activists campaigned to make the decisions of party conference carry more weight and to shift the election of the party leader from Labour MPs to an electoral college that represented trade unionists and party members. They also campaigned to ensure that Labour MPs should be forced to face reselection by their constituency associations. Only eight Labour MPs were deselected, and some of them were being punished for sloth rather than right-wing political opinions, but the fear of losing their parliamentary seat struck terror into the hearts of men who often saw their parliamentary salary as a reward for decades of work in trade unions or the party.

The most important figure for the Left of the Labour Party was Tony Benn. Benn was the son of a Labour minister and, when his older brother was killed in the war, he became heir to a peerage. He managed to renounce his place in the House of Lords, changed his name from Anthony Wedgwood Benn to Tony Benn and progressively reduced his entry in *Who's Who* until it disappeared altogether. Having been a modernizing technocrat in the 1960s, he became increasingly interested in workers' control of industry during the 1970s. He became more left-wing and ostensibly plebeian as his contemporaries became grander and more conservative. Wilson quipped that Benn 'immatured with age'.

Benn provided Labour left-wingers with a figure around whom they could unite. He was not a Marxist – his claim that Marxism was 'one of the world's great religions' was just the kind of thing that no Marxist would have said – but his very lack of concern for the theoretical niceties that often obsessed Marxists made it easier for him to draw together a broad coalition of fashionable left-wing causes – feminism, anti-racism, Irish nationalism and support for nuclear disarmament. By 1978 half of Labour Party members were said to favour Benn as leader of the party. Bennism was also convenient for the Tories. His 'extremism' and combination of privilege and working-class affectation made him an easy target.

Having not competed for the leadership of the Labour Party, Benn then competed against Healey for the deputy leadership, a post that served no purpose except to generate acrimony. Healey won narrowly, though Benn got a large majority of votes from constituency activists. The party became so absorbed in its internal quarrels that its leaders sometimes seemed to have little time to address the electorate. Its campaign in the 1983 election was notoriously inept – partly, it seems, because prominent members of the party had lost all hope that they could win. The Labour manifesto, pulled together at the last moment, was a long, rambling document that was full of promises to all sorts of interest groups. It appeared to pledge the party to the unpopular policy of unilateral nuclear disarmament – though Callaghan openly attacked such a policy and Healey deployed Jesuitical subtlety to try to talk his way around it. The manifesto became known as the 'longest suicide note in history', a phrase usually attributed to Gerald Kaufman but which seems to have been coined by Peter Shore, a man who would, at almost any point other than 1983, have been regarded as being on the Left of the Labour Party.[62] The Tories were so confident that the manifesto would damage Labour that Conservative Party officials bought and distributed 1000 copies.[63]

For all its problems, the Labour Party was ahead of the Conservatives in the polls for a large part of Thatcher's first government. Furthermore, it seemed for a time that Labour's problems might generate an even bigger problem for the Tories. In January 1981 the 'gang of four' former Labour ministers – Roy Jenkins, Shirley Williams, David Owen and Bill Rodgers – issued the 'Limehouse Declaration' calling for a 'realignment' of British politics. Two months later they formed the Social Democratic Party (SDP), which was to work in alliance with the Liberals.

At first the SDP/Liberal alliance was extraordinarily successful. It almost won a by-election in Warrington (a 'safe' Labour seat), and it won by-elections in Crosby and Hillhead (Tory seats). Psephologists had played an important part in the foundation of the new party and, for a time, it seemed that the party attracted support on a scale that almost defied conventional measurement. There was a brief heady moment when polls showed that up to 50 per cent of the electorate would support it. The Tories were particularly vulnerable to the SDP at the height of its success and one projection suggested that the Conservatives might hold just one seat, not Finchley, in a general election.

But the alliance failed to live up to the hopes entertained by its most enthusiastic supporters and in particular it did less damage to the Conservative Party than might have been expected. The SDP had famous leaders and numerous potential supporters, but it lacked that intermediate class of local activists that sustained other parties. Labour MPs who joined the SDP tended to be metropolitan. They were less likely than their colleagues who stayed in the party to have experience in local government, or even to live in their constituency. The SDP had awkward relations with trade unions – the electoral college, which had given considerable power to the unions, was the ostensible reason that the 'gang of four' gave for their breach with Labour. Most SDP MPs and a majority of the party's members supported the Thatcher government's 'anti-union' laws. Ian Gilmour, who was personally and politically close to Roy Jenkins, predicted that the SDP would fail because it was not rooted in 'interests'. The SDP's leaders were good at getting Conservative voters, but hesitant about trying to recruit Conservative MPs. They liked to think of themselves as left-wing and, in any case, they had fewer contacts with the Tories. Only one Conservative, Christopher Brocklebank-Fowler, joined the new party.

The SDP suffered from other problems that became more apparent as time went on. Roy Jenkins, a biographer of Asquith, had good relations with the Liberal leader, David Steel. However, most Liberals in the 1980s were not at all like Asquith. Large numbers of them were interested in causes such as nuclear disarmament, which the leaders of the SDP disliked, or gay liberation, to which they were politely indifferent. 'Grassroots' was a favourite Liberal phrase. Liberals were good at municipal politics and suspicious of the extent to which the SDP was a party of London-based national figures. At local level, Liberal activists were often like Michael Meadowcroft, from Leeds, who sometimes seemed to feel that his politics – like his enthusiasm for trad jazz and real ale – might be spoilt if it ceased to be a pursuit of a minority.

The division of Liberals against the SDP went with a split within the SDP that divided Roy Jenkins from David Owen. The latter, having come up against Liberals in the rough-and-tumble of West Country politics, had mixed feelings about alliance with them.[64] In addition to this, Owen was less enthusiastic than Jenkins about Europe. There was also personal tension between the two men – Bill Rodgers maliciously compared Owen's reactions to Jenkins's successful re-entry into British politics to that of a rebellious adolescent boy who finds that his girlfriend is attracted to his father.[65] Owen and some of his supporters were eventually to split with the other founders of the SDP, over a proposed merger with the Liberal Party, in 1988.

Thatcher was lucky in her dealings with the opposition parties – lucky that she was not forced to call an election at the moment when the SDP was at its peak and lucky in that she finally went to the country at a time when both elements of the opposition were in a bad state and when the Falklands War had strengthened the Tories. Not all of it, however, was luck. There was, for one thing, a structural element in the crisis of the Left. The large, and relatively homogenous, working class that had voted for the Labour Party in the early 1960s simply did not exist any more. The SDP and the hard Left of the Labour Party both drew support from a part of the middle class. The trade unions played an odd role in the Labour Party – it was the Left that voted to give them power in the electoral college and voters often associated union leaders with 'extremists', though some trade union leaders were fighting a rearguard action against left-wing influence in the party.[66]

The political manoeuvres of the early 1980s often showed that Thatcher and her supporters had precisely the quality that their opponents reproached them for lacking: pragmatism. This was particularly visible in the way that the Conservative Party dealt with potential defectors to the SDP. At a time when the Labour Party was riven with paranoia about traitors and threats of deselection, the Tory leaders were subtle. Peter Walker, the leading Cabinet 'wet', was entrusted with persuading disaffected MPs not to leave the party. A number of MPs who had been tempted to defect were later given office in Thatcher governments, though one assumes that their discussions with the SDP were known to Tory whips.

Tory survival also revealed something about the British electorate's real attitude to unemployment. Some observers thought society as a whole would break down in the face of very high unemployment. In the early 1980s there was a succession of riots – in Toxteth (Liverpool), Brixton (south London), Handsworth (Birmingham) and St Paul's (Bristol) – and some (including at least one cabinet minister) assumed that these reflected the failure of the government's economic policy. However, riots seem to have been rooted in responses to aggressive policing and in racial conflict rather than unemployment – though it was true that unemployment was one of the many things that black people resented (over half of people drawing supplementary benefit in Handsworth were from ethnic minorities).[67] Many areas of high unemployment – Yorkshire, Scotland, Newcastle – did not see riots. Attempts to mobilize the unemployed generally failed. The 'People's March for Jobs' of 1981 and 1983 were organized by trade union activists rather than by the unemployed themselves.

In some ways, however, the ubiquity of references to unemployment in British popular culture of the 1980s was deceptive. Everyone knew about it, everyone knew that they ought to care and most people probably did care, but they cared about it in an abstract fashion. A pious concern for the unemployed was expressed in even the most unexpected quarters – one researcher found that almost half the merchant bankers he interviewed said that the government was 'not doing enough' for the unemployed.[68] Regarding unemployment as an 'important issue', however, did not necessarily mean that it was one that had much effect on people's own lives. Voters consistently told researchers that unemployment was a 'more important problem' than inflation. Eventually, pollsters learned to ask a different question: 'Which threatens you and your family most?' Now 49 per cent of people said rising prices whilst only 43 per cent said unemployment.[69]

Unemployment divided the British working class. It was higher in Wales, Scotland, Northern Ireland and the north of England than it was in the south east. It hit certain groups – young men without qualifications, old men who had worked in declining industries, black people – harder than it hit the general population. Those with jobs were consistently optimistic about their chances of keeping them and their economic prospects generally; those without jobs were pessimistic about their chances of regaining the standard of living that they had once enjoyed.[70] Practical expressions of solidarity between the employed and unemployed were rare. Unions had difficulty in persuading their members to donate money to support centres for the unemployed – many of these were reduced to the humiliation of having to take money from the Manpower Services Commission, established by the Thatcher government.[71]

Unemployment benefit in the 1980s was distributed according to clear rules that were applied across the whole country – there was little scope for the local disputes over dole payments that had sometimes aroused the unemployed during the 1930s. Benefit payments were sufficiently low to cut many unemployed people off from the company of those who remained in work, which itself reduced the possibility of working-class solidarity, but they were not so low that they induced the desperation that might have come from the prospect of starvation. Many unemployed people did not vote and a significant minority of those who did voted Conservative. To the chagrin of left-wing sociologists who interviewed them, large numbers of unemployed people accepted government explanations for unemployment[72] – a good example of the successful diffusion of Lawson's 'primitive language'.

Chapter 6

UNEXPECTED VICTORY: THE FALKLANDS

[T]he Falkland Islands. Never heard of them, right? Me neither – at least not until last evening . . . 1,800 British-origin sheepherders, pursuing a peaceful life on some wind-blown specks in the South Atlantic, now targeted by Argentine amphibious assault units – who, in turn, may soon be attacked by the largest naval armada ever to steam out of British ports since Suez? Yes indeed, the whole thing certainly does sound like Gilbert and Sullivan as told to Anthony Trollope by Alistair Cooke.

Diary entry by American diplomat James Rentschler
for early April 1982[1]

It was the very best sort of war: fought at a distance against a second-class enemy and with no fear of retaliation on the homeland. And our servicemen were all regulars. It was a bit like the Boer war but without the Boers.

Julian Critchley (Conservative MP)[2]

There are 780 Falklands Islands of which only two are inhabited. In 1982 they had a population of about 1,800 people, just over half of whom lived in the capital, Port Stanley, on East Falkland, and 600,000 sheep. The islands are 8000 miles from Britain and 400 miles from Argentina, which has claimed sovereignty over them since the nineteenth century.

The Falkland Islands (or Malvinas) mattered deeply to Argentina. Schoolchildren learned about them in their textbooks. There was an annual Malvinas Day and Argentine sovereignty over the islands was asserted in the country's constitution. Every Argentine politician for generations had talked about the need to 'restore' Argentine rule over the islands.

Until Argentine forces invaded them in the spring of 1982, the Falkland Islands meant almost nothing to the British. John Nott, the secretary of state for defence, had to refer to the globe in his office to remind himself where they were. Many British people vaguely assumed that they must be somewhere beyond Shetland, and British sailors were sometimes mystified to learn that the task force sent to liberate the islands would sail south rather than north.

The Falklands had no strategic or economic value – a fact pointed out in an essay by Dr Johnson that had first been published in 1771, and which was unearthed by journalists who, in 1982, were desperate for any information about the islands. Sheep farming was the main means by which Falkland Islanders made their living. Most did not, in fact, own their own land, which belonged in large part to the Falkland Islands Company. Contact with Britain depended on annual visits by an Antarctic exploration ship, *Endurance*. The Falklands were a British dependency, administered by a governor and garrisoned by a force of a hundred or so Royal Marines, some of whom helped to diminish the population by sweeping local girls off their feet and taking them back to the delights of married quarters in Portsmouth or Arbroath. Not all Falkland Islanders had full British citizenship, and legislation the government planned to introduce would have further reduced their rights in this regard. In any case, the British community in Argentina was considerably larger than the population of the Falklands.*

---

* There were about 17,000 British passport holders in Argentina and around 100,000 people of British extraction.

For some years the British government had made discreet, though not very urgent, efforts to extricate itself from the Falklands. Simply giving them to Argentina, however, was complicated by the bitter hostility of the islanders. Nicholas Ridley, a junior minister at the Foreign Office, had conducted negotiations with Argentine officials whilst trying to reassure the islanders that their interests would not be neglected. There was an element of farce in the negotiations: Ridley met his Argentine counterpart whilst pretending to paint watercolours at the Hotel du Lac in Lausanne, and he once minuted that it would be helpful to his cause with the islanders if the Argentinians could be as rude as possible to him during his passage through Buenos Aires. Ridley's tactless candour probably caused more problems than his slightly inept efforts to cover his diplomatic tracks. He told the Argentinians that Britain did not care about the Falklands. He also told the islanders that, if the Argentinians invaded, the British would 'kick them out'. Both these statements were true, but the Argentinians eventually interpreted the claim 'not to care' about the Falklands as meaning that they would face no serious opposition if they invaded; the islanders interpreted the promise to 'kick them out' as meaning that they had infinite licence to obstruct negotiations with Argentina.[3]

The Falklands were not at the front of the minds of British ministers in 1982. Defence policy revolved around the threat of conquest or annihilation posed by the Soviet Union, a threat that seemed to have increased since the late 1970s. The government also had to worry about Northern Ireland and about the Middle East (the Israelis invaded Lebanon in June 1982). Even the small proportion of British intelligence analysts which was concerned with affairs in Latin America worried more about the threat that Guatemala posed to Belize than the threat that Argentina posed to the Falklands.[4]

Matters were made more complicated by politics in Argentina. The country had been under military rule since 1976 and General Leopoldo Galtieri, who had become leader of the junta in December

1981, was trapped by a variety of competing pressures. The government had turned away from the corporatism of the Peronist years, cut public spending and tried to revive the private sector. When these policies seemed not to work, the finance minister had attempted to revive the economy with a 'shock approach' of austerity and cuts in public spending. In purely economic terms, the junta's Argentina had much in common with Thatcher's Britain, a fact that Cecil Parkinson, a junior minister with responsibility for trade, noted during an official visit.[5] Unlike its British counterpart, however, the Argentine government could not afford to sit back and hope that its economic policies would eventually produce results. Economic discontent blended into opposition aroused by the severe repression (ostensibly directed against 'Marxist insurgents') during the late 1970s, when the army had murdered thousands of people. Even the Americans were pressing Argentina to improve its human rights record, and some military leaders seem to have recognized that they needed to prepare for a return to civilian government. However, the army was determined that any liberalization of the political system should not involve awkward questions about the fate of those who had 'disappeared'. Galtieri wanted to extend his tenure as head of the army, which was due to end in November 1982,[6] and to do so he needed to maintain good relations with other powerful military leaders – particularly Jorge Anaya, Argentina's senior admiral. Retaking the Falklands seemed an obvious way in which to win over public opinion and buy the support of the navy.

An intelligent man might have waited to see whether the Falklands could be acquired through negotiation or whether the British defence cuts of 1981 (of which more below) might reduce Britain's capacity to defend the islands. But Galtieri was not an intelligent man, and thirty years of peace-time soldiering and heavy drinking had not sharpened his intellect. In any case, he needed a quick success abroad in order to secure his government at home. On 19 March 1982 an Argentine scrap-metal merchant with a contract to dismantle a disused whaling station landed and planted an Argentine flag on South Georgia, an island 600 miles away from the Falklands that was inhabited only by a few members of an Arctic research station.[7]

On 2 April Argentinians landed on East Falkland itself. They did not mean to start a war and they went to some lengths to avoid causing casualties – though the British garrison inflicted quite heavy casualties on the attackers. The Argentinians shipped the entire garrison back to Britain via Montevideo on the very day that they were captured – hardly something that they would have done had they anticipated that those same soldiers would help retake Port Stanley ten weeks later.

The Argentine assumption that there would be no war over the Falklands was initially shared by many in Britain. The islands were a long way away, and they stood in the middle of a particularly rough part of the Atlantic Ocean. Argentina would find it relatively easy to resupply her garrison and, crucially, to provide air support for her troops. Douglas Hurd, a junior minister at the Foreign Office, probably knew more about the Falklands than any other British politician – his father had been a director of the Falkland Islands Company. Hurd assumed that 'The chances of a successful outcome, through either diplomacy or war, seemed hopeless.'[8] Even after British ships had been sent to the Falklands, military journalists were still laying bets that the fleet would be turned around within a week and that the matter would be settled by negotiation.

The debates in the House of Commons, and the more private discussions amongst Conservative MPs, which took place in the aftermath of the Argentine invasion were so ferocious precisely because it appeared that the Falkland Islands were all but lost. The likely casualties of these debates seemed to be Lord Carrington, the foreign secretary, who was seen to have devoted too little attention to the Falklands and who did indeed resign, John Nott and perhaps even Margaret Thatcher herself. In the Conservative

Party indignation at the loss of the Falklands was greatest amongst those MPs (Winston Churchill, Julian Amery and Alan Clark) who felt nostalgic for an era of British military greatness. There was also much foaming at the mouth on the Labour benches. The Labour leader, Michael Foot, had been a fierce opponent of appeasement during the 1930s, and he now summoned up all his rhetorical fervour to indict the government for giving in to a 'fascist dictator'.

Why did the British fight over the Falklands? One possible answer to this question has the British armed forces rescuing politicians from the consequences of their own folly. On 30 March Admiral Sir Henry Leach, the First Sea Lord and thus the most senior officer in the Royal Navy, came to the House of Commons in full dress uniform. He asked to speak to the prime minister and was eventually shown into her office, where he found her in conversation with John Nott. When the prime minister asked him what could be done, Leach insisted that it would be possible to assemble a fleet that would include the aircraft carriers *Invincible* and *Hermes*, and which could be sent on its way to the Falklands within a few days. Veering off purely military questions (as senior officers were to do frequently in the next few months), he added 'if we do not [recapture the Falklands], if we muck around, if we pussyfoot, if we don't move very fast and are not entirely successful in a very few months' time we shall be living in a different country whose word will count for little'.[9]

The contrast between heroic determination on the part of the admiral and 'pussyfooting' on the part of politicians was made all the more striking by the fact that John Nott had just imposed a round of defence 'cuts' (actually reductions in the rate of increase of spending) that had fallen particularly hard on the navy. Nott, a cabinet 'dry', was motivated partly by the general need to cut public expenditure – the defence budget had been more protected than any other aspect of government spending during the previous three years. He was also influenced by thinking about strategic priorities. The share of British defence spending devoted to the navy had increased ever since 1950, but the value of ships (especially surface ships) was unclear. Some projections of war with the Soviet Union anticipated that fighting would last only for a week before nuclear weapons were used, in which case transatlantic convoys were unlikely to play a large role. Anyway, surface ships were vulnerable to attack from the air or from submarines – a fact that was to be made painfully clear to both the British and Argentine navies during the Falklands War. Britain was about to upgrade its submarine-based Trident nuclear weapons system and the spending for this came from the naval budget, thus reducing money available for surface ships.[10] Finally, in a bid to satisfy Treasury demands for further public-spending cuts, Nott had agreed to sell the aircraft carrier *Invincible*; he seems to have done so partly in the hope that his cabinet colleagues would baulk at such a tangible loss and the sale had still not been completed.[11] The cuts earned Nott the undying enmity of the senior naval officers, who lobbied against him with an enthusiasm that bordered on mutiny. The navy's resentment of Nott's policies was most openly displayed in May 1981 when officers (including the First Sea Lord) were ostentatious in their support for Keith Speed, the navy minister who had been sacked for opposing the cuts.[12]

Retaking the Falkland Islands posed a series of particularly awkward military problems. Simply getting the fleet to the South Atlantic was difficult. Some operations would have been tricky even without the presence of an enemy. Troops had to be moved from one ship to another in order to ensure that excessive numbers were not concentrated on a single vulnerable ship just before the landing. Several helicopters crashed in the course of the campaign; in one of these accidents, twenty-one members of the Special Air Service were killed.

The fleet was vulnerable to missiles, which hit three British ships. The landing on East Falkland took place without the level of air cover that strategists regarded as adequate. To avoid direct encounter with Argentine forces, the landing took place on the western side of East Falkland – away from the main centre of population, and the main concentration of Argentine forces, in Port Stanley. The site of the landing, however, created problems of its own. The original plan to helicopter troops across the island had to be abandoned because so many helicopters had been lost when one of the transport ships was hit by a missile. The result was that heavily laden soldiers had to walk across difficult ground in cold weather before facing their enemy.

Coordination between the different components of the task force was difficult. The operation was primarily a naval one until troops were established on East Falkland, and the senior officer in the South Atlantic was Rear Admiral Sandy Woodward, the commander of the task force. However, lines of command could be blurred. Commodore Michael Clapp (the naval officer responsible for amphibious operations) and Brigadier Julian Thompson (the senior marine with the fleet) were outranked by Woodward but technically answerable to the task force headquarters back in England. General Jeremy Moore commanded troops in the Falklands, but he remained in England until the landing had taken place and, due to a fault in radio systems, was unable to communicate with his subordinates for a crucial period whilst he was on a ship travelling from Ascension Island to the Falklands.

Personal and institutional friction affected the task force. The navy, army and air force all regarded each other with suspicion. The Royal Marines were technically part of the navy but functioned more like part of the army. Fierce rivalry separated them from the Parachute Regiment. When journalists sought to explore how far their reports from the task force would be censored, one of them asked whether they would be allowed to file a story about a fight between a para and a marine in which one of them was killed.[13] When his cautious superior seemed likely to overrule an attack, a lieutenant colonel in the Parachute Regiment said: 'I have waited twenty years for this moment and now some fucking marine goes and cancels it.'

In spite of all this, the British had some advantages. The British navy was used to conducting operations in distant waters and the Royal Marines Commandos were trained for cold weather and amphibious warfare (the Argentinians were notoriously unprepared for the former). British commanders had good information about the Falkland Islands and, in particular, they could draw on the expertise of Major Ewen Southby-Tailyour, a latter-day Erskine Childers who had whiled away time whilst he was stationed in the Falklands preparing a map of the shoreline for the use of his fellow yachtsmen.[14]

Britain was also fortunate in her allies. The administration in the United States was divided in its attitude to the conflict. Some officials with links to Latin America were keen not to break with Argentina, as was Jeane Kirkpatrick, the ferociously anti-Communist American ambassador to the United Nations.[15] Ronald Reagan was initially reluctant to come out in support of either side, and Alexander Haig, the secretary of state, was sent to negotiate in London and Buenos Aires to see whether he could broker a compromise. His efforts failed. However, even as negotiations continued, other sections of the administration provided the British with copies of intelligence reports. Caspar Weinberger, the secretary for defence, was particularly helpful. Most importantly, the Americans granted the British access to the base in Ascension Island, a place that was technically British territory, but which had been leased to the United States.

Britain's staunchest ally was France. The French president, François Mitterrand, wanted the Western alliance to be strong in the face of the Soviet Union and he had no desire to see a member of that alliance humiliated. Furthermore, as a member of a resistance organization, he had been infiltrated into France in February 1944 on board a British torpedo boat (commanded by Jane Birkin's father). He had special reasons to feel grateful to

Britain in general, and the Royal Navy in particular. In the face of strong opposition from his foreign minister, but with the support of his prime minister and defence minister, Mitterrand threw France's weight behind Britain's cause. The French had supplied Exocet missiles to the Argentinians. Mitterrand was warned that further sales of French armaments would be damaged if potential buyers thought that the French had helped the British counter Exocets, but he overruled the objections. Further sales to Argentina were blocked and the paperwork for some missile sales to Peru was carefully lost, in case the Peruvians passed their missiles to Argentina.[16] French pilots went to Scotland so that their British comrades could hone their skills in practice dog-fights against Mirage and Super-Etendard jets, with which the Argentinians were equipped.[17]

France pressed other European countries to support sanctions against Argentina. It also had an important influence in the United Nations – persuading francophone countries in Africa to support, or at least not to oppose, the British position. To most people's surprise, the Soviet Union did not use its veto in the Security Council to prevent a motion condemning Argentine action – a motion that the British were able to use as a justification for their action.

Most of all, however, the British were lucky with their enemy. Galtieri responded so little to attempts to broker a peace that American diplomats concluded that he was drunk. He reinforced the garrison in the Falklands to a counterproductive extent – ensuring that the soldiers ran low on food – but kept back some of his best troops to guard against a possible Chilean attack on the mainland.

After the event, two groups of people made much of how close-run the Falklands War had been. On the one hand, left-wingers who believed that Thatcher had derived an 'unfair' political advantage were keen to stress how 'lucky' she had been.[18] On the other hand, soldiers and, particularly, sailors argued that British

defence spending had been reduced to a dangerous extent and
that the war would probably have had a different result if Argentina
had invaded after the Nott Defence Review had been fully
implemented.

At the time, those involved in planning the expedition had
different views about its chances of success. Shortly before the
landings, the commander of the task force told journalists that he
regarded the odds in favour of British victory as twenty to one.
Privately he seems to have been less sanguine. He wrote:

> Lose *Invincible* and the operation is severely jeopardized. Lose *Hermes*
> [the other aircraft carrier and Woodward's flagship] and the
> operation is over. One unlucky torpedo, bomb or missile hit, or
> even a simple but major accident on board, could do it.[19]

Later Woodward was disconcerted to find that the overall
commanders of the operation back in the UK believed that it
would have been feasible after the loss of an aircraft carrier and,
once troops were safely ashore, that it could probably have worked
without either of them.[20]

In fact, questions about victory or defeat were never really just
matters of military calculation. Britain had the second largest navy
in NATO. It was absurd to imagine that it was incapable of taking
the Falklands; the question was always what price, in terms of
money and casualties, the government was willing to pay to achieve
this aim. James Prior said that he had no faith that the British
people would have continued to support the war if their forces
endured serious casualties – though members of the cabinet had
apparently been warned that they should expect casualties of 'up
to three thousand'.[21] Cecil Parkinson admitted that there was
uncertainly about Thatcher's own emotional reaction to casualties.
Until the sinking of the *Sheffield* destroyer, some were convinced
that she would be unable to countenance sending men to their
deaths.[22]

It was often those with most military experience, and/or knowledge of military history, who felt most nervous about retaking the Falklands. Recollections of the Normandy landings haunted discussion of the operation. Several members of the cabinet had been junior officers during the Second World War and still remembered trying to fight their way off the beaches in June 1944. Lord Hailsham recalled that he had been taught that such operations should never be undertaken without air superiority.[23] Many officers had studied D-Day at Staff College.[24] Max Hastings, the most prominent of the journalists to accompany the task force, was actually writing a book about the Normandy landings as he sailed south on board the *Canberra*.

The humiliation of another maritime expedition, that undertaken to Suez in 1956, was also in the minds of those who decided to invade the Falklands. This was a powerful memory in the Conservative Party and in the armed forces – a number of naval officers who went to the Falklands had previously served in the Suez expedition. John Nott wrote: 'Whitelaw, Lewin [chief of the general staff] and I, in the early stages, thought "Suez, Suez, Suez".'[25]

Both Normandy and Suez were misleading analogies. The former had been undertaken against an unusually numerous, determined and well-dug-in enemy. The Falklands expedition might more usefully have been compared with the easier allied landings in North Africa, Sicily, Salerno and Provence, or even with the commando raids on Dieppe and St Nazaire. As for the Suez expedition, its failure was political rather than military and the political context of the Falklands was quite different since the Americans, who had done so much to undermine Suez, always recognized that the Argentinians were the aggressors in 1982.

Misleading though they may have been in purely military terms, references to Suez and the Second World War contributed to a sense that the Falklands had a special kind of historical significance.

The Second World War was a totem of Britain's lost greatness and Suez was a symbol of its more recent decline. Thatcher seemed to have recaptured the first and reversed the second. She certainly thought of the Falklands in terms derived from the Second World War – though, characteristically, her interests centred on Britain the lone hero of 1940 rather than Britain as an element in the coalition of 1944.

The Falklands War fitted into a certain image of Britain. It was a 'clean' war, in which both sides sought to avoid civilian casualties and respected the rights of prisoners – indeed scrupulous respect for the rules of war meant that the British refused to interrogate captured Argentine officers about the very dirty war that they had conducted against civilians in their own country.[26] British soldiers could afford public scrutiny of their actions in the Falklands in a way that they could not have afforded scrutiny of their actions in Ulster. The war was fought by a small professional force, one of the many respects in which it differed from the Normandy landing. Units of the British armed forces that had particular cultural resonance were deployed. The navy, especially the surface fleet, was associated with all the myths of Nelson and Drake – names that popped up with predictable frequency in 1982. The Falklands struck all sorts of chords amongst those who cared for the Royal Navy. Sandy Woodward belonged to the last generation of British naval officers who had begun their careers as thirteen-year-old cadets at Dartmouth. Admiral Sir Henry Leach bore an especially resonant name. His father, Captain John Leach, had commanded the *Prince of Wales* and gone down with his ship in 1941. Amongst the land forces, regiments that were seen as particularly professional and/or particularly smart were sent to the Falklands. Guardsmen were taken straight from ceremonial duty at Buckingham Palace to the South Atlantic and even a detachment of the Household Cavalry was added to the British force, perhaps on the grounds that officers who had spent most of their adult lives playing polo would have a unique insight into the Argentine mind.

Though few British people had known much about the Falklands before 1982, the rainy, green countryside of the islands – without large towns, a significant immigrant population or any apparent crime – looked British, or, rather, they looked as many conservatively minded Britons liked to imagine their own country to be. The governor of the Falklands insisted that the landscape over which he ruled was 'Herriot country'.[27] Visiting the Falklands, the Conservative MP Alan Clark was moved by the sight of 'jolly fair-haired children [from a nursery school], to be collected by their mums. A completely English scene'[28] (after failing to get into Eton, Clark's own son had been sent to school in Switzerland). Clark believed that the war had been fought 'in obedience to a blood tie' and he cited members of the Parachute Regiment who told him that they felt happier defending 'our people' than 'mucking around in the Third World'.[29]

What long-term effects did the war have? In terms of the British armed forces, the answer is relatively little. Two years after the Argentine surrender, a senior officer from the armoured corps told Hugh McManners, a student at the staff college who had served as a commando in the Falklands, that the war had been a 'sideshow'.[30] British defence policy continued to revolve around tanks, nuclear weapons and preparations to fight the Red Army. The military careers of men who had distinguished themselves in the South Atlantic did not always flourish. McManners left the army to devote his life to journalism and rock music. Southby-Tailyour also resigned and returned to yachts and writing. Even Rear Admiral Woodward never became First Sea Lord, perhaps because his success in the Falklands had removed any inclination that he might ever have had to disguise his view that he was cleverer than his comrades-in-arms.

The war was also a sideshow for most politicians. MPs who fancied themselves as experts on matters military had a good few weeks making portentous speeches and scoring points off ministers.

Having had a 'good' war, however, was no guarantee of future success. Being mistaken for a privy councillor on an RAF flight to Port Stanley in the summer of 1982 was in many ways the high point of Alan Clark's career. The speeches of David Owen attracted much attention during the war, but the long-term effect of his prominence was probably to isolate him further from his colleagues in the Social Democratic Party. During the parliamentary debate that followed the Argentine invasion, Michael Foot had probably seemed the politician most likely to gain from events. Always keen to make trouble for Thatcher, the Tory backbencher Edward du Cann had said that Foot 'speaks for us all'. A year later, after the general election of 1983, Foot looked like the most significant political casualty of the war.

The Falklands was not a Thatcherite war – or, at least, it was not much associated with qualities that had most often been imputed to Thatcher's government in the first three years of its existence. The Falkland Islands themselves did not incarnate the thrusting enterprise that supporters of the government usually praised; a visiting Labour minister in the 1970s had said that the economic prospects of the islands were much like those of the 'Welsh mining valleys'.[31]

The only cabinet minister to speak against the military expedition was John Biffen, a monetarist. Outside the cabinet, Jock Bruce-Gardyne (an arch-monetarist MP and junior minister at the Treasury) was embarrassed by the leak of a letter that he had written to a financial journalist, in which he mocked the whole Falklands adventure.[32] Nicholas Ridley, another 'dry', had been the key figure in negotiations to dispose of the Falklands and was said to have regarded the operation to retake the islands as 'mad'.[33] Fighting the Falklands War meant throwing concern with public spending out of the window. On the advice of Harold Macmillan, Thatcher did not even invite the chancellor of the exchequer to sit in her war cabinet.

Alan Walters, Thatcher's economic adviser, had a genuinely

free-market solution to the crisis. He suggested that a plebiscite should be held and that the Argentinians should be given the chance to offer the islanders a fixed sum of money per head in return for accepting Argentine sovereignty. Walters suggested that the first offer would be £50,000 and that, assuming an initial rebuff, 'Granted the acquisitive obsession of the Argentines, their second bid would be likely to be raised to heights which the Falklanders could hardly refuse.' Walters drafted his plan as the task force sailed south but wisely he did not show it to any senior minister until Christmas 1983.[34]

If it was not a 'Thatcherite war', was the Falklands 'Thatcher's war'? She had no military experience and, though she had been considered 'sound' on defence, she had never taken any interest in the details of military matters. Her vision of British 'greatness' up until 1982 was one that involved British participation in the Western alliance against Communism, not lone British action in pursuit of a purely British aim.

In some ways, the very incongruity of Thatcher's position was her strength. She was the perfect war leader – uncompromising about the end and pretty much indifferent about the means. Thatcher did not share the *Boys' Own* obsession with particular weapons, units and tactics that still gripped many Conservative MPs. Her attitude was summed up in her brisk response to an adviser who worried about finding enough ships to transport British troops – 'The world,' said Thatcher, 'is full of ships.'[35]

During the early stages of the war Alan Clark predicted that Thatcher would be a 'hero' in an 'unassailable' position if she won – and that this was, indeed, the reason why some in her own government hoped that she would lose. Julian Critchley believed that the Falklands marked a new 'imperial' phase in Thatcher's government. Historians generally have suggested that Thatcher was 'rebranded' in the aftermath of the Falklands. The precise form that the rebranding took, however, is open to doubt. One writer suggests that she became 'late imperial' and 'little

Englander' – though these are very different things.[36] The
Falklands is hard to fit into any more general transformation of
Thatcherism. It preceded, and to some extent created, the electoral
victory of 1983, which, in turn, produced a period of economic
liberalization – though, as has been stressed, the Falklands War
itself had nothing to do with free-market economics. It preceded,
though less directly, a period in which Thatcherism came
increasingly to mean opposition to European integration and
looking with favour on the alliance with the United States, but
in the immediate aftermath of the war Thatcher was grateful for
the help of 'our European friends', by which she meant, especially,
the French.

The most obvious political result of victory in the Falklands
was the transformation of Thatcher's position in the Conservative
Party. Up until this point, she had been an oddity: she was a
woman, she came from outside the traditional ruling class and
she had held no great office of state before becoming prime
minister. There was always the risk that she would be deposed
if her party came to see her as an electoral liability and the
greatest threat to her probably came not from those who most
opposed her policies but from those patrician grandees (Whitelaw
and Carrington) who might, in a crisis, decide to put their loyalty
to their party, and their own careers, ahead of loyalty to their
leader.

On the day that Port Stanley fell, all this changed. Enoch Powell
was one of the most self-consciously masculine and military
members of parliament. He was also still regarded by many
Conservatives as the expression of the conscience of their party.
During the early stages of the war, he had reminded Thatcher of
her soubriquet 'Iron Lady' and added: 'In the next week or two
this House, the nation and the Right Hon. Lady herself will learn
of what metal she is made.' After victory in the Falklands, Powell
said:

Is the Right Honourable Lady aware that the report has now been received from the public analyst on a certain substance recently subjected to analysis and that I have obtained a copy of the report? It shows that the substance under test consisted of ferrous matter of the highest quality, and is of exceptional tensile strength, is highly resistant to wear and tear, and may be used with advantage for all national purposes.

Powell's laboured joke delighted Thatcherites. Ian Gow, Thatcher's parliamentary private secretary, had the extract from Hansard framed so that she could hang it on her wall.

The woman with no experience of defence or foreign policy was now a warrior queen. The dinner to celebrate British victory was attended by seventy men (many of them in uniform and weighed down with medals) and one woman. Carrington's career was over; Whitelaw would never be able to challenge Thatcher. In many ways, the Falklands saw the passing from the political stage of the whole generation whose outlook had been moulded by military experience of the Second World War. Nott asked for Cecil Parkinson to be included in the war cabinet precisely because he wanted someone to counterbalance Whitelaw and Pym, both of whom had been junior officers in 1945.[37]

The effect of the Falklands War in the country at large was more difficult to assess. Thatcher talked of the nation having found itself in the South Atlantic. She associated the spirit of the Falklands with a denunciation of trade union militancy (the return of the task force coincided with a rail strike) and with a call for economic revival. Her political opponents were bitter about the exploitation of military victory for internal ends and made much of the ways in which the Falklands allegedly benefited the Tories in the 1983 election.

In fact, less than a third of Conservative candidates referred directly to the Falklands during the 1983 campaign, though many of them made more general remarks about the restoration of

British prestige,[38] and few voters admitted that the Falklands had exercised any influence over them. The point about the electoral significance of the Falklands, however, was precisely that it mattered only when mixed with other ingredients. One of these was defence. The election was fought at a time when tension between the Soviet Union and the West was high and when the Labour Party supported unilateral nuclear disarmament.

Did the Falklands create a new kind of populist patriotism? The *Sun*, a keen supporter of Margaret Thatcher since 1979, presented itself as 'the paper that supports our boys', and Tory MPs attacked the BBC as the representative of an elite that had lost touch with the true national spirit. In fact, the new spirit was more complicated than it looked at first glance. The editor of the *Sun* was involved in battles that pitched him against the other tabloid newspapers (the *Star* had introduced bingo for readers in the spring of 1981, thus launching a new circulation war) as well as against some of the *Sun*'s own journalists and printers, who resented their paper's political stand. Surveys showed that most *Sun* readers were Labour voters and that almost a third of them thought that the *Sun* was a Labour newspaper. The paper's most notorious headline 'GOTCHA!' – printed after a British submarine sunk an Argentine cruiser – was withdrawn in later editions to be replaced by 'DID 1,200 ARGIES DIE?' Many people took a more nuanced view of events than the pronouncements of their representatives suggested. When the chairman of the BBC, George Howard, appeared in front of a committee of MPs, Tories shouted him down, but 57 per cent of Conservative voters thought that attacks on the BBC were unfair.[39]

Curiously, the most important 'Falklands factor' may have worked on the Left. The Communist historian Eric Hobsbawm wrote shortly after the end of the war that it had mobilized a 'public sentiment which could actually be felt' and that 'anyone of the Left who was not aware of this grass roots feeling . . . ought seriously to reconsider his or her capacity to assess politics'.[40] One of the most striking features of the Left's behaviour after 1982, and especially of the Labour Party election campaign in 1983, was precisely the sense of lost confidence on the part of its leaders in their ability to judge the public mood.

Chapter 7

VICTORY FORETOLD: THE MINERS

She planned it very, very clever – you've got to admire her . . . It all fit in, in that ten year from '74 to '84 . . . she was determined that, at *any* cost . . . she wasn't going to be humiliated and defeated the same way Ted Heath was . . . it was all geared up for her to *smash* the National Union of Mineworkers – and by God, it worked. It's hard to say it, but it worked.

Miner, who had been on strike in 1984 and 1985, from Bilsthorpe Colliery, Nottingham[1]

On 5 March 1985 British miners, or at least those who remained loyal to their union, returned to work, a year after they had gone on strike. The executive of the National Union of Mineworkers had agreed to support the return in order to avoid the humiliation that would have been inflicted on the union if miners had simply drifted back to work as and when they could hold out no longer. The miners marched to their pits behind the banners of their union lodges, often accompanied by brass bands. Some trade unionists claimed that the strike had been a success because it had slowed the programme of pit closures put forward by the National Coal Board or simply because the miners had kept their dignity.

No one was fooled. The miners had been crushed. They had gone on strike to prevent pit closures. After a year of grinding poverty, they had got nothing. The National Union of Mineworkers had lost members and money: legal action had rendered it technically bankrupt. The miners were divided. About half of them were working by the time the union finally gave up the fight. After the strike, some men, most of whom had opposed the strike, left the NUM to form the Union of Democratic Miners. The membership of the NUM, which had stood at almost a quarter of a million during the strike, had dropped to fewer than 100,000 by the end of 1987.[2] A small group of miners regarded any return to work as a 'betrayal'. When Arthur Scargill, the president of the NUM, led men from his own Yorkshire pit back to work, they were turned away by pickets from the Kent coalfield, which was still on strike.

The very fact that parts of the Left had invested such symbolic importance in the miners meant that their defeat was all the more resonant. Ever since Margaret Thatcher's election as leader of the Conservative Party, her supporters had feared that union resistance might destroy her economic policies. This fear was laid to rest in March 1985. Norman Tebbit wrote that Thatcher had broken 'not just a strike, but a spell'.[3]

Everyone had always known that conflict between the NUM and a Thatcher government was likely. When Brian Walden interviewed Margaret Thatcher in September 1977, he described, in detail and with a series of cartoon illustrations, strikes by the NUM under a future Conservative government.[4] Some believed that the Tories had returned to office in 1979 with a fully worked-out plan to defeat the NUM. They pointed, in particular, to the report on nationalized industries drawn up by Nicholas Ridley in 1977,[5] which contained a 'confidential annex' on 'countering the political threat' to the government's plans to render the nationalized industries more efficient and financially accountable. The annex anticipated a large public-sector strike. It identified coal as the industry in which this was most likely to happen and laid out tactics by which such a strike might be countered. It anticipated cutting off supplementary benefit to strikers, deploying 'a large mobile squad of police' and encouraging hauliers to hire non-union drivers who might be willing to cross picket lines.

The Ridley report, or at least that part of it which had been leaked, acquired vast importance in the eyes of those who supported the miners' strike of 1984–5.[6] However, it was not much discussed in the inner circles of the Conservative leadership during the years immediately before the miners' strike.[7] The selective leaking of the report, and then the even more selective way in which that leak was discussed and recalled, was deceptive. The report was primarily about questions of management and finance in nationalized industries, rather than about labour relations. Furthermore, the Ridley report was one of a series on nationalized industries, and the ideas expressed in these reports were radical hopes discussed in opposition – no one was sure which parts of them, if any, would be implemented. In any case, Ridley (like other Conservatives) was cautious about confrontation with the unions. He regarded some strikes as unbeatable and thought that in many nationalized industries: 'Since they [the unions] have the nation by the jugular vein, the only feasible option is to pay up.' Indeed, Ridley's most significant recommendation was that the government should set aside money to pay large wage claims. He divided unions into three categories: those (electricity or sewerage) that had the power to bring the country to an immediate halt; those that could inflict serious damage only with a more long-term strike; and those (such as the Post Office or education) to which the government was not particularly vulnerable. Ridley put coal in the second of these categories and anticipated that the government would be able to resist a strike in this sector for 'about six weeks'.[8]

The real significance of the Ridley report was not so much that it provided a novel and specific programme for action, but rather that Ridley, with his characteristic bluntness, set out in writing what many Conservatives were thinking. There was no peculiarly Thatcherite approach to the miners. This was an issue on which there was a consensus across the party. On the one hand, everyone

– including, and perhaps especially, those who had been most loyal to Heath – resented the humiliation of 1974. On the other hand, everyone – including those, such as Keith Joseph or John Biffen, who were seen as most radical – recognized that beating the miners would be difficult. The most pessimistic shadow ministers thought that it might be impossible.[9]

The extent to which all Conservatives shared an approach to the miners is illustrated by Harold Macmillan. He is often presented as the arch appeaser of the miners. His remark that the National Union of Mineworkers was, along with the Vatican and the Brigade of Guards, one of the 'great powers' that no British prime minister could afford to annoy was quoted ad nauseam.*[10] When the government yielded to the miners in February 1981 (see below), John Hoskyns, one of Thatcher's advisers, wrote that the prime minister herself had accepted the 'Macmillan doctrine'.[11]

Private conversations suggested that the Macmillan doctrine was closer to the Thatcherite orthodoxy than its author's public declarations suggested. In January 1974 Alan Clark talked to Macmillan and recorded the exchange thus: 'the miners had to be bought off until North Sea Oil came on stream; that it should not be too difficult to outmanoeuvre Len Murray [general secretary of the TUC]; that McGahey [Communist leader of the Scottish miners] wasn't popular in the TUC; that the real agitator was (*Scrimgeour* was it? – the words came thick and fast and I was transfixed)'.[12] The name that Clark heard as 'Scrimgeour' was presumably Scargill. In short, Macmillan advocated a tactical retreat until a future government might be strong enough to take on the miners, and in the long run he anticipated a confrontation that would involve Scargill as the most important figure on the trade union side.

* With his unfailing instinct for getting the wrong end of every stick, Ian MacGregor, head of the National Coal Board during the strike, attributed this remark to Stanley Baldwin.

Once in power, however, the Thatcher government was in no hurry to take on the miners. Towards the end of 1980, the annual pay negotiations between the miners and the National Coal Board were complicated by two things. First, NCB managers wanted to close those pits that were never likely to make a profit. Secondly, the term of office of Joe Gormley as leader of the NUM was coming to an end. Gormley was a staunch monarchist who wrote newspaper articles on horse racing and who accepted a seat in the House of Lords. His politics were rooted in a view of working-class interests that would have horrified young left-wingers of the early 1980s – he wrote that he wanted a society in which everyone 'would have a Jaguar out front to take him to work and a Mini at the side to take his wife to the shops'.[13]

For all his moderation, Gormley was good at getting wage rises for his members. He had won battles with the Conservative government in 1972 and 1974, and he took on the Thatcher government in early 1981 over wages and pit closures. Ministers discussed their chances of holding out if there was a strike. They knew that stocks of coal were high, but they found that this was not enough. Too much of the coal was stored at the pitheads rather than in the electricity generating stations. There was no guarantee that the coal could be transported if railwaymen supported a miners' strike. The particular kind of coke used for starting up power stations was also in short supply. In February the government backed down. It agreed to make more money available to fund higher wages and a halt to pit closures.

In April 1981 Gormley retired as leader of the NUM. His successor was Arthur Scargill. Scargill was relatively young (born in 1938), earnest and vain. He seemed remote from the beery bonhomie of British trade unionism – or, for that matter, from the brusque melancholy of Mick McGahey, whose own chances of leading the NUM had been undermined by the manoeuvres of Joe Gormley. Amongst those who worked most closely with him, Scargill's strange 'mixture of ruthlessness and sensitivity' aroused an exasperated affection.[14] In the wider Labour movement, though, his arrogance annoyed even those – such as Eric Heffer – on the hard Left.[15] Tabloid newspapers and Tory politicians implied that Scargill could not really represent his working-class members. Miners seem to have felt differently. Scargill got almost three quarters of the vote in a large turnout. There were few trade union leaders who had a clearer electoral mandate than him.

Was Scargill a revolutionary? He had been a Communist in his youth and he talked about the tactics of revolution when he was interviewed by the *New Left Review*.[16] Some Conservative ministers made much of his Marxism.[17] However, Scargill had broken with the Communist Party in 1962. The NUM took money from Soviet miners and from the trade unions of Soviet-controlled Afghanistan during the strike of 1984–5, but there is no evidence that it did much in return. Furthermore, the Soviet Union conspicuously failed to do the one thing that might have helped the NUM during its strike – prevent the export of Polish coal to Britain.

Scargill's most marked characteristic was his parochialism. His roots were in Yorkshire, where he had spent his whole life. He felt uneasy when he was obliged to leave his home ground, and he sometimes claimed that he had rejected a place at grammar school because he did not want to go to school in a different town. On being elected president of the NUM, he moved the headquarters of the union from London to Sheffield. Far from looking ahead to some future revolution, Scargill often seemed to be looking back to his own youth. He was obsessed by a single incident in 1972, when he and a group of flying pickets had succeeded in forcing the closure of a coke depot in Saltley in Birmingham. He was to claim in 1981 that this was: 'The greatest victory of the working class, certainly in my lifetime.'[18]

If Scargill was looking to the past, the government was looking to the future. It regarded the settlement of February 1981 with the miners as a tactical withdrawal rather than a defeat, and from then on it began to prepare for a future conflict with the miners.

Discussions about beating a future miners' strike (which had involved politicians, civil servants and outside advisers from the very moment that Thatcher arrived in Downing Street) acquired a new urgency.[19] David Howell, who, as secretary of state for energy, had presided over the settlement with the miners and who was described by Gormley as 'wet behind the ears',[20] was replaced by Nigel Lawson. Lawson built up stocks of coal at power stations and increased the use of oil in electricity generation. He also made special arrangements, so secret that they were hidden from his own cabinet colleagues, to transport vital chemicals into power stations by helicopter. Against protests from his own constituents, he insisted that a new 'super pit' was opened in the Vale of Belvoir, thus helping to make the Nottinghamshire coalfield more productive and Nottinghamshire miners more secure than their colleagues elsewhere.[21]

In June 1983 Lawson was made chancellor and was replaced as secretary of state for energy by Peter Walker. Thatcher says that she wanted Walker to preside over a future miners' strike because he had shown himself a 'tough negotiator' in dealings with the EEC – an odd claim since the government ostentatiously refused to play any direct part in negotiations during the miners' strike – and because he was a 'good communicator', who might be expected to influence public opinion.[22] Perhaps Thatcher's private thinking was more complicated. Walker's willingness to oppose her economic policies in cabinet must have impressed on her the fact that he was a man who did not scare easily. Besides, it made sense to associate a cabinet 'wet' with the government's strategy: it meant that a rebellion within the cabinet was less likely and that someone relatively dispensable could be sacked if things went wrong.

Other appointments also seemed to pave the way for a strike. Nicholas Ridley, who had written the much-discussed plan of 1977, was appointed secretary of state for transport in 1983, and thus made responsible for getting coal from pits to power stations. The Central Electricity Generating Board was obviously going to be important in any future coal strike. Nigel Lawson had no confidence in its head, Glyn England. This was partly because England had been appointed by Tony Benn in 1977 and was a supporter of the Labour Party (he was soon to join the Social Democratic Party). More importantly, perhaps, it was because England resented being obliged to waste money on maintaining large stocks of coal.

England was replaced by Sir Walter Marshall. Marshall was a physicist, who had run the Atomic Energy Authority. In the government's eyes, he was made attractive by the fact that he had quarrelled with Benn over the benefits of nuclear energy. His style also commended itself. He was an extraordinary man from a humble background who had taken a Ph.D. at Birmingham University at the age of twenty-two. His almost incomprehensible accent and manner set him apart from the establishment men who usually ran nationalized industries. He relished dramatic gestures and was unafraid of confrontation. His character was illustrated by the fact that he once arranged for a train to be crashed at full speed: ostensibly this spectacular and expensive experiment was designed to show that the containers in which nuclear waste was transported were hard to break. Marshall's greatest failing, as Lawson admitted, was an almost complete lack of interest in, or knowledge of, finance. His appointment showed how ordinary business considerations were subordinated to the need to defeat a coming coal strike.[23]

The most awkward appointment of all was that of the chairman of the National Coal Board. Edward Heath had appointed Derek Ezra to the post in 1971. He was a member of the Liberal Party and the epitome of post-war corporatism, and had worked in the mining industry ever since leaving the army in 1945. He was close to Joe Gormley – the two men sometimes went away for weekend retreats together – and the NCB was known in Whitehall as the 'Derek and Joe show'. Ezra stood for everything the Thatcher government disliked. Ministers blamed him for the defeat of the Tory government in 1974, and they suspected that he had not been sorry to see the government back down in February 1981.

It was clear that Ezra would not be reappointed when his contract expired at the end of 1982.[24] In the short term, Ezra's deputy Norman Siddall got the job, but Siddall, for medical reasons, was unwilling to stay on beyond the autumn of 1983. Lawson believed that the chairmanship of the NCB was the 'most political' position in British industry and would have liked to appoint a politician to it. He considered Roy Mason, a Labour MP who had attracted much admiration amongst Conservatives for his vigorous policies when Northern Ireland secretary and who had, perhaps more importantly, crossed swords with Scargill when the Left had tried to deselect Mason as Labour candidate for Barnsley.[25]

In the end, the candidate chosen was Ian MacGregor, who had been born and raised in Scotland but had enjoyed a successful business career in the United States. He had kept in touch with business in Britain – serving as deputy chairman of British Leyland and then becoming chairman of British Steel. In spite of his experiences in British business, however, his overall attitude remained rooted in the American climate of free enterprise, in which unions could be crushed or circumvented – he once casually mentioned to a Tory minister that a strike in Wyoming, 'so far as he knew', was still going on.[26]

Like Scargill, MacGregor had a great capacity for self-dramatization and, sometimes, for self-deceit. He repeatedly referred to his confrontation with the miners in terms of 'war', 'storm troopers', 'Rommel' and the 'Gestapo'.[27] Characteristic of him was his attempt to suggest in his autobiography that Peter Walker had lost his nerve and tried to impose a compromise settlement on the NCB during the closing weeks of the strike – a claim that seems to have been the exact reverse of the truth. MacGregor exasperated almost all who worked with him – he was nearly as unpopular with industrialists as Scargill was with trade unionists.[28] Senior managers at the NCB were driven to despair.

MacGregor's term of office began in September 1983. The appointment was seen by the NUM as a provocation. Scargill was increasingly vocal in his public claims that the Coal Board had a 'hit list' of pits which were due to close. However, the NUM constitution required a 55 per cent majority in any ballot to authorize a national strike. Scargill held strike ballots three times on pay and/or pit closures in 1982 and 1983. Every time, he failed to secure the majority he needed – on the first occasion, the case for a strike was undermined by an article Joe Gormley had written in the *Daily Express* urging the miners not to strike. From Christmas 1983, however, leaders of both the NUM and NCB seem to have known that a strike was on the way.[29]

In early 1984 MacGregor agreed with the government that the Coal Board must reduce its deficit. This meant closing pits. MacGregor talked to his area directors – characteristically he referred to them as 'field commanders'.[30] The toughest of them – in Scotland, South Wales and the North East – resisted a sudden new pit closure in their area, which might disturb their relations with the unions and their own carefully laid plans. George Hayes in South Yorkshire was less assured and more willing to go along with orders he was given in London. On 1 March 1984 Hayes told a meeting of union representatives that the Cortonwood pit was to close. The announcement came as a surprise. Strictly speaking, Hayes had not followed the agreed formal procedures for the announcement of pit closures. There were still reserves of coal left at the pit and, indeed, miners had been transferred to it within the previous few weeks. Miners across South Yorkshire walked out in protest over the closure of Cortonwood, and they were followed by miners in Scotland.

At a meeting between the NCB and the unions on 6 March, MacGregor outlined the need for further cuts in spending, and Scargill deduced from this that the board intended to close about twenty pits. The national executive of the NUM now invoked rule 41 of their constitution, which allowed individual areas within the NUM's federal structure to call their men out on strike. Scargill rejected calls for a national ballot and, instead, convened a national delegate conference. This conference duly decided to support the strike – though it also changed the union's constitution so that the threshold for authorizing strike action, if a ballot were to be held, was lowered from 55 per cent to 50 per cent.

Members of the government had been waiting for the strike for years, but they had not anticipated that it would begin under terms that were so favourable to them. Spring was the worst time for the miners to go on strike – because they would have to hold out for at least six months before they could hope for the fuel demands of winter to begin to bite. Furthermore, government plans had anticipated a complete halt in coal production. As it turned out a significant minority of miners worked throughout the strike. The NUM was a federation of regional bodies and, though there was no national ballot, a number of regions did hold ballots at local level, and most of these decided against the strike.[31] In a few areas almost all miners kept working throughout the strike. In Leicestershire there were just thirty strikers; in south Derbyshire there were seventeen.[32] Particularly important were the Nottingham miners. Some of them struck but most worked through the strike. They had political traditions that separated them from miners elsewhere in the country, and their jobs seemed safer than those of their colleagues elsewhere. They voted against a strike in a local ballot and subsequently for the most part stayed at work.

The absence of a national ballot weakened the position of the NUM executive. It made it difficult for leaders of the Labour Party and other unions to defend the strike. It made it easier for Nottinghamshire miners and their allies to argue that the strike was illicit.[33] Ministers were, in fact, far from sure that a national ballot would not favour a strike. However, the NUM executive was trapped by its own rhetoric. Once Scargill and his allies had talked of not letting miners 'be voted out of jobs', it was hard for them to hold a ballot without appearing to have given in; the fact that so much Conservative legislation revolved around encouraging ballots exacerbated this position.

The government insisted that the coal strike was a matter between the NCB and the NUM. This policy of 'non-intervention', however, turned out to mean an extraordinary amount of activity. A cabinet sub-committee was established encompassing Whitelaw (responsible for 'civil emergencies'), Walker, Brittan (the home secretary), Lawson, Tebbit (then minister at the Department of Trade and Industry but also, as former secretary of state for employment, responsible for much of the legislation that might be used against unions), King (secretary of state for employment) and Ridley.

The government's first task was to prevent the use of the very union legislation that it had just enacted. MacGregor wanted to sue the NUM under laws designed to prevent secondary picketing.[34] Walker believed that doing so would bring the striking miners sympathy from other workers, not least their own colleagues in Nottinghamshire.[35] He won the argument and the NCB suspended its action – subsequently other chairmen of nationalized industries were also discreetly discouraged from using laws against secondary picketing.[36] Thatcher and Tebbit were both later to claim rather ungraciously that the strike might have been 'won' earlier if 'Thatcher's laws' had been used.

The alternative to using civil law against secondary picketing was to use criminal law against individual pickets. Trying to stop men from working with violence, or the threat of violence, was an offence. In the strikes of 1972 and 1974 this had not been a particularly important issue: the NUM itself tried to avoid physical violence and the police had been less concerned to protect the right to cross picket lines; at Saltley in 1972 the police had lent Scargill their public address system so that he could tell his men that they had won. In 1984, though, striking miners faced the fact that large numbers of workers, including some of their own colleagues, intended to go to work, and that the authorities were determined to protect their right to do so. Some picket lines became violent – though the miners themselves often distinguished between pushing against the police lines, which they regarded as legitimate, and throwing bricks, which they resorted to only when they believed that the police had broken some unspoken compact by mounting baton charges.

For all their preparations, ministers were not confident that the strike would fail. There was no real agreement about how long coal stocks would last. Tebbit believed that they would run out by January 1985; the Central Electricity Generating Board thought that it could hold out until at least November of that year. Walker deliberately avoided making promises that there would be no power cuts until he was sure that the promises could be kept.

When Walker's assurance that the lights would stay on finally came, in January 1985, its effect on the morale of the strikers was powerful precisely because Scargill had repeatedly claimed that power cuts were imminent. The tactics of the miners came to seem desperate and undignified – miners' support groups urged their members to switch on electrical appliances at six every evening, in the hope of causing a power surge that would shut down the national grid. Scargill's personal involvement distorted the miners' tactics in other ways too. In particular, he diverted pickets to the Orgreave coke plant. He seems to have done this partly because he was hoping to relive the triumph that he had enjoyed at Saltley in 1972, and partly because he had been jostled by police on the picket line at Orgreave. At one point, there were 10,000 pickets, about 7 per cent of all striking miners, at Orgreave, a place that did not, in fact, have great strategic significance.[37]

The NUM organized the strike under increasingly difficult conditions. The NCB did not use recent trade union legislation against the NUM, but other companies that had been damaged by the secondary picketing of the miners eventually did go to court, as did miners who objected to the strike. The first sued under laws designed to prevent secondary picketing and the latter argued that the union's constitution required a ballot before launching a strike. The NUM was declared in contempt of court, and, when it failed to pay a fine, its assets were sequestered.

Other trade unions might have helped the NUM. Railwaymen, steelworkers, dockers and electricians could have impeded the movement of coal, or its use in factories and power stations. The National Association of Colliery Overseers and Deputies, which was responsible for the supervision of pit safety, might have shut down all coal mining in Britain. Twice – once when dockers walked out in July and once when pit deputies seemed on the verge of striking in September – it seemed that a sympathetic strike by other workers might stop the production or movement of coal. The fact that the strike never spread to involve workers who were not members of the NUM was partly the result of skilful concessions by the government. The NCB's attempt to force pit deputies to cross NUM picket lines was abandoned when it seemed that this might provoke all deputies into striking. Railwaymen were given a deliberately generous pay settlement to keep them happy during the miners' strike.

The miners and their would-be allies also fell victim to wider changes in industry. The National Dock Labour Scheme imposed rigid restrictions on the ways that ships could be loaded or unloaded, but important ports – Dover and Felixstowe – were outside this scheme. Besides, increasing amounts of freight were transported in containers that were relatively easy to load and unload. Much freight was also moved by lorry, and lorry drivers – men who worked on their own and in some cases owned their own trucks – did not fit neatly into a traditional working-class culture. Lorry drivers were important in breaking a succession of strikes during the 1980s and their willingness to transport coal in 1984 and 1985 was crucial. The two unions representing electricians were recognized by the government as the one group who almost certainly had the power to bring the country to a halt, but electricians often gained from the very technological change that damaged workers in old-fashioned heavy industry. The electricians' unions were on the Right of the labour movement and had been the object of much solicitous attention from the government.

Steelworkers ought to have been natural allies of the miners. Bill Sirs, leader of the Iron and Steel Trades Confederation, knew that miners, railwayworkers and steelmen (the Triple Alliance) were all members of the 'old' working class, increasingly marginalized in a union movement that was becoming dominated by white-collar workers.[38] However, the steelworkers had lived through their own bruising strike of 1980. Now they wanted to protect their industry and in particular to prevent the closure of one or more of the large steel plants at Scunthorpe (in Yorkshire), Ravenscraig (in Scotland) or Llanwern (in Wales). A blast furnace is damaged if it is allowed to go cold. The steelmen were sometimes able to arrange special deals with the NUM that would allow enough coal in to keep the furnaces operating, but such deals became increasingly difficult as time went on and, as ever, Scargill proved particularly awkward. When the NUM sought to extend the strike by preventing the movement of iron ore by rail, a move that would have cost jobs in the steel industry, Bill Sirs said that he was not willing to allow his industry to be sacrificed on the 'altar of the coal strike'.

For someone who was believed to be a revolutionary, Scargill was remarkably bad at maintaining relations with workers outside his own industry. The NUM did not ask the TUC for help until September 1984. The alliance of coal, steel and rail unions had hinged partly around personal friendship between Joe Gormley, Bill Sirs and Sid Weighell (of the National Union of Railwaymen). Weighell's replacement by Jimmy Knapp and Gormley's replacement by Scargill made things more difficult. Scargill sometimes seemed to go out of his way to antagonize his fellow trade unionists. He had said before the strike that his men would 'throw lorries in the ditch' if transport workers tried to get past picket lines. During the strike itself, Scargill wrote to Bill Sirs: 'The fact that you have acquiesced in the use of scab labour is something that will be on your conscience for the rest of your life. You are a disgrace to the very concept of the Triple Alliance and all that it was supposed to do.'

The attitude of other unions to the miners' strike was not just a function of crude economic self-interest. Workers in other industries felt sympathy for the miners, but they were disturbed by the NUM's refusal to hold a strike ballot and also by violence on picket lines – especially after a taxi driver, David Wilkey, was killed by a concrete block that pickets dropped on his car as he drove a miner to work in Wales.

The National Association of Local Government Officers (NALGO) illustrates the complexities of the union movement at the time of the miners' strike. Early in the strike, the union expressed support for the miners and gave £10,000 of its own funds to the NUM. However, five NALGO branches withheld subscriptions in protest at the donation, and, in August 1984, 200 branches challenged their union's financial support for the miners. They were not numerous enough to force a ballot on the matter, but the union's leaders were sufficiently impressed by the opposition to stage a discreet retreat: they gave no further money to the miners.[39]

Sometimes it seemed that the violence associated with the miners' strike might spill into the trade union movement itself. When Norman Willis, the leader of the TUC, condemned 'violence from either side' at a rally of miners in Wales, someone lowered a noose so that it hung menacingly above his head. When John Lyons, of the electricians' union, attended the TUC conference in the autumn of 1984, he took a bodyguard in case he was attacked by miners or their supporters.[40] Even miners who supported the strike sometimes came to blows with each other. Mick McGahey, the deputy leader of the NUM, was loyal to Scargill – even though McGahey's own comrades in the Communist Party had their doubts about the strategy of the strike. In March 1984, however, McGahey was beaten up, apparently by men who regarded his willingness to countenance a return to work as a 'betrayal'.

Once it had become obvious that the miners would not bring the country to a halt, how was the strike to end? Much was made of the need for negotiation and for 'face-saving formulae'. Ministers, however, did not want to save Arthur Scargill's face. They feared that the NUM would make almost any deal appear to be a victory for the miners, and they were concerned that any settlement should involve the acceptance of the 'right to manage' in the coal industry – many ministers privately believed that the NUM itself had effectively run many pits before the strike. Restoring 'the right to manage', however, raised questions about whose power was being restored. The truth was that ministers despised NCB managers – regarding them as too close to their own workers, too keen on subsidy and craven in the face of the NUM.

From the government's point of view, the strike was about circumventing the power of management as much as crushing that of the union. The appointment of MacGregor was calculated to disrupt management traditions at the NCB; he was almost obsessively hostile to Hobart House (the NCB's headquarters in London). The government did not entirely trust MacGregor himself, though. Throughout the strike, ministers pressured him to adjust his tactics – particularly when it came to public relations – and, according to Walker, the cabinet even discussed dismissing MacGregor during the strike.[41] Towards the end of the strike, Peter Walker heard that MacGregor was talking to the leaders of the TUC about terms on which the strike might be ended. Walker was keen that no agreement should be reached that might be presented as even a partial victory for the NUM. He wrote to MacGregor in strong terms.[42]

The ideal solution for the government was simply that miners should return to work with no agreement. Throughout the strike, some miners kept working, and the numbers increased as workers lost faith in their leadership or in the chance of gaining anything. Statistics about working miners became an important part of the propaganda war that was conducted between the two sides. NCB officials, scornful of the government's claims, sent out spoof Christmas cards at the end of 1984 that alluded to the game of 'New Faces' that was being played as colliery managers sought to identify miners who had returned to work. Thatcher claimed that February 1985 was the crucial month in which, for the first time, there were more working miners than strikers. The NCB's private figures suggest that the majority of miners were back at work on 1 March 1985 – just days before the NUM finally called the strike off.[43]

Who represented the working miners? A Nottinghamshire miner, Chris Butcher, known as 'silver birch', met journalists from time to time. David Hart, an old Etonian, apparently close to MacGregor though not to Peter Walker, who had made and lost a fortune in property development and who lived in a suite at Claridge's, attempted to coordinate actions amongst working miners.[44] The official leaders of the NUM in Nottinghamshire – Ray Chadburn and Henry Richardson – supported the strike, though they also asked for a ballot. During the strike, Nottingham miners began to eject pro-strike officials and replace them with men who were working. Roy Lynk was the most important of the new leaders and, after the strike ended, he became general secretary of the newly formed Union of Democratic Miners.

There was never – for all the rhetoric – a clear-cut division between 'scabs' and strikers. Nottinghamshire miners observed the go-slow (that had begun in 1983) throughout the strike. Some of them stopped work in March 1984 and returned to work only when their own area balloted against a strike; others insisted that they would have gone on strike if a national ballot had favoured one, and even that they personally would have voted for a strike in such a ballot. Equally, quite large numbers of men went on strike but then returned to work before March 1985. In some areas that had observed the strike, the return to work acquired a momentum of its own. Early on, men had feared ostracism if they crossed picket lines. However, the weight of social pressure began to shift as more men returned. Those who were back at work spread rumours of reprisals that might be taken against men who stayed out. The belief that anyone who was away from work for twelve months would have to undergo a medical examination before they could go underground again was especially influential – many middle-aged men, who had spent years breathing coal dust, knew that they did not stand much chance of being passed fit.[45]

The actions of men who worked in areas where the strike was solid are hard to explain. Their enemies accused them of selfishness, but many men's pursuit of 'material advantage' earned them years of ostracism and fear. Some left their mines or the industry when the striking miners returned. One striker suggested that men who risked such penalties must be mentally retarded.[46] Some men broke the strike in ways that seem deliberately perverse. In Staffordshire pits most strikers had returned to work by November 1984. A pro-NUM account of the strike suggested that those who had always been lukewarm in their support for the strike generally went to work in the buses provided by the Coal Board. However, men who had once been 'hardline' chose to walk in, thus exposing themselves to abuse from pickets: 'a symbol of guilt that amounted to self-inflicted punishment'.[47] At Cortonwood, where the strike had begun, four men returned to work just twenty-four hours before the official strike ended.[48] It is hardly likely that men who had stayed out for a whole year could not face one more day without pay. Did they want to display their contempt for the union when they finally realized that all the suffering of the past twelve months had been for nothing? Did they want to prove, perhaps only to themselves, that it was not fear of the picket line that had kept them out?

The strike was riven with hypocrisy on all sides. Coal Board managers wanted to see Scargill defeated, but they often also hoped that the government would provide further subsidies to keep pits open. Ministers pretended that the strike was a matter for management when they were, in fact, giving orders to the chairman of the NCB. Trade union leaders pretended that they wanted the miners to win, though privately many of them loathed Scargill and believed that he was damaging the labour movement. One senior civil servant claimed: 'I remember being told by one union leader that, if we did not destroy Scargill, he would never forgive us.'[49] Eric Hammond, of the electricians, was the only trade union leader to condemn the NUM executive during the strike itself – at the Labour Party conference of 1984 he said that the miners were 'lions led by donkeys' – but other trade unionists, notably Gavin Laird of the engineers and David Basnett of the General and Municipal Workers Union, were widely known to be hostile.[50] Leaders of the Labour Party such as Roy Hattersley, and even Tony Benn, supported the miners in public long after they had conceded in private that the strike was bound to fail.[51]

The return to work involved all sorts of uncomfortable deceptions. Pickets had talked a language of solidarity and uncompromising determination. They had said that they would never work with 'scabs', and that they would hold out for the rights of their comrades who had been dismissed for offences committed during the strike, but sacked men were not reinstated and no one in the enclosed and dangerous conditions of a pit could afford to refuse all dealings with men who had broken the strike. Anyway, the division between striker and 'scab' cut across communities and families in awkward ways. One woman in South Yorkshire was particularly vehement in her denunciation of men who had broken the strike. Her male relatives sometimes left the room when she talked about the matter – they could not bring themselves to tell her that her own son had gone back to the pit in February.[52]

The position of strikers was sometimes oddest of all. They and their supporters insisted that they were striking to 'protect their children's jobs', but how many people really wanted their sons to become miners? How many men, for that matter, wanted to be miners themselves? Interviews conducted with miners and their families by sympathetic historians and journalists suggest that on a personal level strikers were often motivated by the desire to escape the pits. Men who had worked in the industry since they left school, and who were used to going underground every morning, were suddenly able to travel and to spend all day in the open air – for all the well reported violence, picket lines were safer places than coal mines. One Yorkshire miner recalled: 'It were the best twelve months of me life. I hadn't seen a complete summer since I were fifteen. I right enjoyed it. I walked miles.'[53] Many men left the industry at the end of the strike. Some of them were militants driven out by management harassment, or working miners who were bullied by former strikers; some, though, seem simply not to have wanted to go back to the coalface.

Doubt about whether or not mining was a desirable job was illustrated by the family of Iris Preston. Her two sons were miners and she campaigned vigorously during the strike to defend their jobs. Both her sons went on strike, but one of them, Tarrance, refused to undertake picket duty. After the strike, Tarrance asked his mine manager if he could be paid redundancy money. When the manager said no, because the pit was not going to be closed, Tarrance resigned. He said that he could not bear working with 'scabs'. His mother, though, recognized that Tarrance had been unenthusiastic about his job even before the strike and that, after it, he was simply frightened by the prospect of underground work. However, she, the mother, preferred not to think about the reasons for this fear because her other son was still working underground.[54]

There was also something oddly double-edged about the way in which the British public responded to the miners' strike. Every opinion poll showed that the public was dissatisfied with the power exercised by trade unions and that this dissatisfaction had helped to bring the Conservatives to power in 1979. The Conservatives had always been open about their desire to curb union power, and their more specific plans to deal with the NUM had been widely discussed since the late 1970s. Beating the miners was not a radical Thatcherite policy that broke with mainstream Conservatism. Conservatives disagreed about timing and tactics but almost all of them agreed about the need to defeat the NUM, and the defeat was eventually achieved under the leadership of the most important cabinet 'wet'. Indeed support for government on this issue, and on unions generally, went much wider than the Conservative Party. Members of the Social Democrat Party, allegedly the defender of the 'post-war consensus', were often particularly enthusiastic about containing trade union power. In the summer of 1984 David Owen, a leader of the SDP and a man who had in 1972 put up striking miners in his London house, urged Thatcher not to back down to the NUM.

Why then, as Thatcher's ministers sometimes asked themselves,[55] did the Conservative Party not get more credit for the outcome of the coal strike? Its poll ratings were poor in the spring of 1985 and it suffered heavy losses in local government elections soon afterwards. The strike left a nasty taste. This was partly because of the winner. It would have been hard to find a more unattractive face of international capitalism than Ian MacGregor. The nasty taste was also associated with the nature of the losers in the strike. Trade unionists and strikers were often portrayed in contemptuous terms. Descriptions of workers at the British Leyland plant at Longbridge in Birmingham or of printers in Fleet Street made much of their laziness, 'Spanish practices', and (in the case of printers) high pay. The miners were different. No one thought that they were lazy or dishonest. Coal mines were harsh and dangerous places: thirty miners were killed at work in the year before the strike. A number of politicians knew all too well what it was like to work in a mine: Neil Kinnock and Roy Jenkins were both the sons of miners. Keith Joseph had spent a week working in a mine near Rotherham during a university vacation in the 1930s; with his characteristic honesty, he admitted that he would not have cared to spend a second week there.

The very hopelessness of the strike increased the regard in which miners were held. They were not striking for higher pay or shorter hours. Towards the end of the strike, it was not clear that they were fighting for any material benefit at all. Dennis Skinner, a left-wing Labour MP and ex-miner, said that the strike was: 'The

most honourable strike this century [because it] was not about
money but about people fighting for their jobs, communities and
the futures of their children.'[56] Many Conservatives who did not
want the miners to win were, nevertheless, fascinated by their
courage. The historian Raphael Samuel, writing shortly before the
miners accepted defeat, advanced an interesting theory as to why
this was so. Samuel was sympathetic to the strikers, but he also
recognized that they were in a curious way conservative, and even
that they incarnated some of the 'Victorian values' that were
sometimes associated with Margaret Thatcher. The miners
represented solidarity and tradition. The very efficiency with which
the government dealt with the strike – the careful preparation, the
deployment of well-equipped policemen, the centralization of
power – all seemed 'unEnglish'. One miner complained that the
roadblocks which he had to get through were 'Soviet style'; a miner
of Polish origin likened the government's action to that which was
taken against the Solidarity trade union in Gdansk.[57]

People who regarded themselves as 'traditional Tories' and as
defenders of an 'organic' and settled society were particularly prone
to self-deception when they recalled the strike. In truth, such
people had often been particularly exercised by trade union power
and were keen to see the miners beaten, but they began to feel
uncomfortable about their victory after the event. In 2005 the
journalist Peregrine Worsthorne wrote: 'the physical methods . . .
adopted by the Thatcher revolution to put down the Scargill
miners were . . . alien, owing more to France's brutal revolutionary
tradition of treating all protests as incipient insurrections – a
tradition loyally upheld by the CRS [riot police] to this day – than
to Britain's preference for beer and sandwiches in Downing Street'.[58]
No one reading this passage would guess that Worsthorne had
poured abuse on the miners during the strike itself, or that he had
said in private that the chairman of the NCB deserved to be fêted
'as Wellington after Waterloo'.[59]

The truth, perhaps, was that the British people wanted the miners to be beaten, but they did not want to be associated with the means by which this victory was achieved. In a strange way, Thatcher's very success in the miners' strike laid the way for her eventual failure. Concern about the power of the trade unions had been one of the most important reasons for Thatcher's electoral popularity. When the most terrifying of the British trade unions had been broken, the usefulness of her style of politics had ended. Expressing admiration or concern for the miners became a discreet way in which Conservatives could distance themselves from the government. Harold Macmillan, the man who had recognized, back in 1972, that the miners would one day have to be beaten, delivered his maiden speech in the House of Lords in November 1984: 'It breaks my heart to see what is happening to our country – this terrible strike with the best men in the world, who beat the Kaiser and who beat Hitler too, who never gave in. Pointless, endless. We cannot afford that.' In January 1985 an obscure upper-class Tory MP made a speech in which, whilst deploring the miners' aims, he stressed that the strikers had something to 'teach us about solidarity'.[60] The MP was Anthony Meyer, who was five years later to become the first person to challenge Thatcher for the leadership of the Conservative Party.

Chapter 8

SERIOUS MONEY, 1983-8

Sexy greedy *is* the late 80s.
　　　　　　　Caryl Churchill, *Serious Money* (1987)

The 1983 election ought to have been Margaret Thatcher's great moment of triumph. She had been the emblematic figure of the Conservative Party during the election, and that election produced a sharp increase in the party's majority, from 43 to 144. The Labour Party was even more inward-looking after the election than it had been before. The party's new leaders, Neil Kinnock and Roy Hattersley, were good at dealing with internal dissent in their own party but famously ineffective in their attacks on the government. Senior Tories regarded them with a contempt that they had never shown to Foot or Healey, and senior Labour politicians doubted whether Kinnock could ever win a general election.

Thatcher was now strong enough to insist that her own supporters dominate the cabinet. Not all of her appointments worked. She abandoned plans to make Cecil Parkinson foreign secretary when she discovered that his mistress was pregnant; he was forced to resign from the government altogether a few months later when the scandal broke. As for Leon Brittan, he just looked wrong for the part of home secretary and had to be moved in 1985. Two more durable appointments were Nicholas Ridley and Norman Tebbit. Ridley, who came into the cabinet in 1983, was the younger son of a viscount. His father had insisted that he study engineering at university in order to be able to make his own living. However, Ridley was, in some ways, a rather unworldly man who had wanted to be an architect (he was the grandson of Edwin Lutyens), and who spent his spare time painting watercolours. Thatcher said that he 'could have been a figure from Wilde or Coward'.[1] Ridley, a chain smoker who did nothing to disguise his upper-class drawl, made no concessions to populism; in March 1990 he said: 'Every time I hear people squeal, I know that we are right.' Norman Tebbit was a very different kind of man. He had been in the cabinet since 1981 but he now became more prominent and in 1985 was made chairman of the party. He was a grammar-school boy from Edmonton who had become a pilot during his national service – fighting his way out of a burning Meteor jet at an age when some of his future cabinet colleagues were still at university. He was a more careful politician than Ridley (John Mortimer described him as 'an illusionist without illusions') and one who never caused offence unintentionally. What united Ridley and Tebbit was contempt for the pre-1974 political order and fierce personal loyalty to Margaret Thatcher.

The most momentous of Thatcher's ministerial promotions after the 1983 election was that of Nigel Lawson. He became chancellor, a position that he held until his resignation in 1989. No cabinet minister, other than the prime minister, stayed in a single post for longer than Lawson, and in many ways Lawson was second only to Thatcher in the influence that he exercised over British politics during the period. Elected to the House of Commons for the first time in 1974, and not appointed to the cabinet until 1981, he had risen fast. Other men who enjoyed such meteoric careers – Brittan or John Moore – were marked by the perception that they were Thatcher's creatures. Lawson, by contrast, was known as one of the few ministers who regularly stood up to the prime minister. He was the only senior minister who had never been talked about as a possible leader of the party

– his disdain for certain kinds of public relations and his impatience with those whom he regarded as his intellectual inferiors made it inconceivable that he would ever build an independent following. Curiously, these qualities were strengths rather than weaknesses. Thatcher never regarded him as a possible rival, but she could also never dismiss him as a political runner-up. Though he sometimes reflected on the charms of being foreign secretary, Lawson himself had effectively achieved the highest of his ambitions when he entered Number 11 Downing Street. This gave him an aura of success and self-confidence, as well as the knowledge that a return to the back benches would not mean cutting off his career before its peak.

For Tebbit and Ridley, Thatcherism was intertwined with personal loyalty to the prime minister. Lawson was different. He was, more than any other member of the cabinet, prone to reflections on political philosophy and he was keen to put the government's actions into the broad sweep of history. Ross McKibbin suggested that Lawson was not a Thatcherite at all.[2] The truth was more complicated. Lawson emphatically was a Thatcherite, as Thatcher recognized.[3] But, for him, loyalty to Thatcherism meant loyalty to a set of ideas (ideas that he regarded himself as particularly qualified to expound) rather than loyalty to a person. For Lawson, Thatcherism was not 'whatever Margaret Thatcher herself at any time did or said'.[4]

In spite of her new parliamentary majority and Thatcherite hegemony in the cabinet, Thatcher recalled the aftermath of the 1983 election in curiously melancholy terms. Early Thatcherism had often seemed ascetic. There was a sense that economic virtues – thrift, independence, responsibility – were to be encouraged as much because they were virtues as because they were economic. After 1983 the economic benefits of Thatcherism seemed more dramatic and more widely experienced. Privatization, the sale of council houses, rising property prices and deregulation in the City of London sometimes seemed to offer people the very thing that the first Thatcher government had defined as being impossible – money for nothing.

The new economic mood of Thatcher's second term was felt first in the City of London. In the early 1980s jobbers (who bought and sold stock and made their profits from the differences between the prices of these two operations) were required to be separate from brokers (who acquired stock on behalf of their clients and charged a fixed commission). Gilts were sold, on behalf of the government, by a single broker and then sold on by a small group of other recognized dealers. Only individuals, rather than corporations, were allowed to be members of the Stock Exchange and, in practice, this excluded foreigners. Until 1973 women were not allowed to be members of the Stock Exchange. In 1971 Graham Greenwell, a partner in a broking firm that employed a number of people who would become advisers to Margaret Thatcher, objected to 'modernization' of the City in these terms: 'In essence, both the Stock Exchange and the Baltic [Exchange] are private men's clubs and not business institutions . . . The Stock Exchange is not an institution which exists to perform a public service.'[5]

The City was dominated by small institutions that had been established for a long time. Nepotism and back-scratching flourished. Lord Carrington remembered how his Eton housemaster had advised him that stockbroking (along with farming and the army) was a suitable profession 'for a really stupid boy'.[6] S.G. Warburg, a merchant bank founded by a German-Jewish émigré in 1946, was the only firm that stood outside the culture of the City. It pioneered Eurobonds and also, in the battle for control of British Aluminium in 1958–9, suggested that shareholders might have the right to sell their shares to the highest bidder regardless of the wishes of the company's management. S.G. Warburg, however, was the exception that proved the rule. Respectable bankers regarded it as pushy and vulgar.

The Stock Exchange was, in fact, facing the prospect of prosecution by the Office of Fair Trading for restrictive practices

when the Conservatives came to power in 1979. Ministers in the
first Thatcher government were not inclined to stop this prosecution.
Many of them believed that British financial institutions gave
insufficient support for industry. This belief often featured in the
theories of industrial decline that influenced the Conservative
Party so much in the late 1970s (see below), and it had been
strengthened by the way in which banks had apparently sought
profits in property rather than industrial investment during the
'Barber boom' of 1972–3. Thatcher had no particular affection
for the City – she said that her father had seen the Stock Exchange
as a form of gambling.[7] Disdain for the City was especially marked
amongst those ministers who had actually worked in it. This was
true of John Nott, secretary of state for trade from 1979 to 1981,
who had chosen to begin his business career with S.G. Warburg
in 1959 precisely because of Warburg's reputation for being an
outsider in the City club.[8] It was also true of Cecil Parkinson,[9]
who headed the Department of Trade and Industry during the
few months between the 1983 election and his public disgrace.
However, Parkinson decided on a change of tactic. In July 1983
he called off the OFT in return for a promise that the Stock
Exchange would reform itself.

The reforms were to be implemented on a single day (the 'Big
Bang') on 27 October 1986. Brokers and jobbers were no longer
to be separate, fixed commission was to be abolished, corporate
membership of the Stock Exchange was to be permitted and the
trade in gilts was to be opened to anyone who could obtain a
licence. The Big Bang did not seem likely to bring unqualified
benefits for those who worked in the City. Just before the deregulation
of the City, one of the biggest of the UK merchant banks, Morgan
Grenfell, had a stock market capitalization of £664 million; this
compared to £5 billion for the American Citicorp and almost £20
billion for the largest Japanese investment bank.[10] Many thought
that British institutions would be elbowed aside in a more aggressive
market, and that a brief flurry of investment, as new opportunities

opened up, would be followed by redundancies and bankruptcies. As one American banker put it: 'Sure as dammit, 50 per cent of the Eurobond and gilt traders are going to be driving taxis in five years' time, and the best business to be in will be a second-hand Porsche dealership.'[11]

As it turned out, few traders ever drove taxis. The prospect of reform meant that banks and brokers became bigger. Firms merged in order to create companies that would be able to work in several different areas. Foreign banks bought their way into the City. All of this brought new prosperity. Brokers and jobbers were bought out at generous premiums. Barclay's Bank bought the broker De Zoete and Bevan and the jobber Wedd Durlacher Mordaunt in 1986. It was said to have paid close to £150 million for the two; three years earlier the estimated capitalization of *all* brokers on the London exchange put together had been between £150 and £200 million.[12] The desire to acquire expertise pushed up salaries. The average income of directors in Morgan Grenfell had been £40,000 in 1979; by 1986 it was £225,000. At the stock broker Cazenove, profits during the same period (to be divided amongst a pool of partners that had barely increased at all) multiplied by seven.[13]

The City of London was also transformed by a new attitude to mergers and acquisitions. In 1985 Burton brought Debenhams for £579 million – the largest takeover in stock market history; by the end of 1989 there had been twenty acquisitions for more than £500 million. Hanson Trust, which bought the Imperial Group for £2,564 million in 1986 and Consolidated Gold Fields for £3,275 million in 1989, specialized in such operations. Particularly important to the City after the Big Bang in the late 1980s were 'hostile takeovers', that is to say takeovers, such as the one of British Aluminium that had so shocked City opinion in 1958–9, that were opposed by the existing management of the target companies. The mid-1980s saw a wave of such takeovers. Newspapers ran vituperative advertisements in which the managers of firms that were locked in battle abused each other in an attempt to win shareholders over to their side. Share prices were pushed higher and corporate finance departments became ever more aggressive in their pursuit of victory. The language of the takeover began to penetrate the whole world view of prominent Conservatives. Norman Tebbit suggested that the Church of England was like a poorly managed company that would benefit from the attentions of Charles Hanson.

One takeover bid which, though relatively small in business terms, had particular political significance was the attempt by the American company Sikorsky to take over Westland helicopters in 1985–6. The Sikorsky bid was supported by the Westland management but, against Thatcher's wishes, Michael Heseltine, the defence secretary, conjured up an alternative bid by a consortium of European companies. Westland divided the cabinet, caused the resignation of two ministers and almost brought Thatcher herself down (see chapter 11). It also revealed how interwoven the worlds of Conservative politics and corporate finance had become. Hanson Trust and News International, both companies whose owners were close to Thatcher, rode to the support of the Sikorsky bid; GEC, an established British industrial company, was the key component in the European consortium. This was not, however, a simple matter of political positions 'expressing' economic interests. In purely economic terms, the Westland company was not very important (until the artificial pressure of a contested takeover pushed its share price up, the company was valued at around £30 million) and many of the companies that became involved in its affairs did not really have any business interest in helicopters. The truth seems to have been that business and political interests were entangled in complicated ways, and that politics drove business as much as the other way round. Two figures in the takeover battle (John Nott, at Lazard, which advised Westland, and James Prior at GEC) had been ministers in Thatcher's early cabinets. Gordon Reece, who advised Westland, was an important figure in Thatcher's inner court. Indeed, the most significant lesson of Westland was that the state influenced the economy even after a supposedly free-market revolution. Westland was, after all, a defence company that would always do most of its business with governments – the only debate was whether the governments in question should be European or American. Furthermore, all the companies involved understood the importance of political patronage. The chief executive of GEC had worried, even before the Westland affair, that his takeover of Plessey might be blocked,[14] whilst the government's decision not to refer Hanson Trust's takeover of Imperial to the Monopolies and Mergers Commission was widely seen as a reward for Hanson's intervention during the Westland affair.

The wealth associated with the new City came to obsess cultural commentators. In March 1986 Nicholas Coleridge, himself the son of the chairman of the Lloyd's of London insurance exchange, identified the 'New Club of Rich Young Men':

> It is difficult to estimate the number of young investment bankers, stockbrokers and commodity brokers earning £100,000 a year. Perhaps there are only a couple of thousand, but they are so mobile and noisy that they give the impression of being far more numerous. Most are aged between 26 and 35, and two years ago they were being paid £25,000, in some cases even less, until the opening of the City markets precipitated an epidemic of headhunting and concomitant salaries.[15]

Caryl Churchill's play *Serious Money*, which was first performed at the Royal Court Theatre in March 1987, was set amongst the traders of the London International Financial Futures Exchange. It was intended as an attack on Thatcher's Britain. However, the cast (mainly earning the minimum Equity wage of £130 per week) developed a horrified fascination with traders who earned £40–£50,000 per year by the time they were twenty-three. Traders themselves seemed to relish the image of them that Churchill portrayed: on two occasions banks booked every seat in the theatre for works outings.[16] The whole style of the City – flickering screens, arcane jargon and implausibly large sums of money – seemed glamorous. Some writers felt that the City was supremely 'postmodern'; though Cecil Parkinson, the principal architect of the Big Bang, claimed, rather improbably, to have been a disciple of F. R. Leavis.[17]

Merchant banks gave money to the Conservative Party, and an increasing number of men who had begun their careers in banks or as brokers became advisers to ministers and, eventually, ministers themselves. John Richardson, a corporate financier at Cazenove, was an early admirer of Margaret Thatcher, and his subsequent recruitment by N.M. Rothschild may have owed something to the bank's celebrated talent for maintaining political contacts. Some saw a strand of Thatcherism as an instrument of London finance: 'City interests received political and ideological expression through Sir Keith Joseph's conversion to monetarism and anti-statism and through the role of leading City commentators and financial journalists as the organic intellectuals of a new economic strategy.'[18]

In spite of these links, there were always tensions between the Thatcher government and the City. The fact that a successful banker could expect to be paid several times the salary of a cabinet minister did nothing to smooth relations. Thatcher was said to disapprove of the cavalier attitude to the law that some banks took – the exclusion of Morgan Grenfell from almost all privatization business was believed to be a punishment for the improper actions of some of its executives during the battle to take over Distillers in 1986.

The success of the City also raised questions about the whole nature of Thatcherism. The members of Thatcher's first government had been haunted by the idea of Britain's relative economic decline. Geoffrey Howe's first budget speech compared the statistics relating to British productivity with those of France and West Germany. Three interpretations of British decline had a particular influence on the Thatcherites. The first of these was the report on the state of British engineering prepared by a committee under the chairmanship of Sir Monty Finniston. The report had been commissioned by the Labour government in 1977, but it was finished in 1979 and, in large measure, implemented under Thatcher. Finniston's committee blamed Britain's poor economic performance partly on the low prestige of British engineers and partly on the poor quality of British technical education, particularly relative to that in France and Germany.

The second interpretation was contained in the dispatch that Sir Nicholas Henderson, about to retire as ambassador to Paris, composed in March 1979 on 'British Decline: its causes and consequences'. Henderson too made much of the need to improve the status of engineers. More generally he talked about the need for technological modernization, for fewer strikes and less shop-floor resistance to management. He also argued that Britain was too rooted in a comfortable pastoral vision of itself and too resistant to industrial values. He bemoaned the propensity of intelligent young people to go into the civil service or the City rather than into industry. The dispatch was leaked, as Henderson almost certainly intended that it should be, and published in the *Economist*. It provided Thatcher's supporters with useful ammunition against the Labour government during the election campaign.[19] Thatcher referred to the dispatch with approval soon after she took office,[20] and, indeed, cited it again in one of the last speeches that she made as prime minister.[21] She brought Henderson back from retirement to become British ambassador in Washington.

And thirdly, Martin Wiener, an American historian, published *English Culture and the Decline of the Industrial Spirit, 1850–1980*, in 1981.[22] Some of the arguments of this book ran parallel to those of Henderson – one of Thatcher's advisers wrongly believed that Henderson had 'quoted Wiener' in his dispatch[23] – and also to the arguments that were advanced, a few years later, by the English historian Correlli Barnett.[24] Wiener argued that British industrial decline was rooted in aristocratic values and a celebration of rural

Arcadia that had been passed to the middle classes via British public schools and ancient universities. Wiener contrasted the British middle classes unfavourably with those of other nations, especially Germany and America, and argued that they had become excessively inclined to seek their fortunes in the 'gentlemanly capitalism' of merchant banking rather than in manufacture. Shirley Robin Letwin (a Tory intellectual who was herself hostile to the assault on gentlemanly values and liberal education) lamented that her friend Sir Keith Joseph had made the 'Barnett/Wiener thesis' into a 'Thatcherite theme song'.[25]

There was something odd about the enthusiasm with which some Conservatives embraced the various theses about Britain's 'anti-industrial culture' in the early 1980s. They had *étatiste* implications. Their proponents often thought that redemption might come through nationalized industry – Finniston had run British Steel. Henderson was fascinated by the *grands corps* of elite civil servants who exercised such power over the French economy. The very notion of 'relative decline' suggested that the state ought to determine the 'right' economic performance for a country. Enoch Powell, a true free-marketeer, regarded economic decline as a meaningless concept. He also expounded the Arcadian vision of Englishness that men like Wiener regarded as responsible for industrial decline; Wiener's book is shot through with disapproval of Powell. The oddest feature of Wiener and Henderson, when seen through the prism of the later Thatcher government, is that both men seemed closer to Heathite technocracy than to Thatcherite free enterprise.[26] Heath had, indeed, been staying at the Paris embassy in the month before Henderson sent his dispatch, and it seems likely that he had some influence over the views that Henderson expressed.[27]

Far from suggesting that the state was causing problems for society, proponents of the 'anti-industrial culture thesis' suggested that society itself had problems that might be cured by state intervention. John Hoskyns, an admirer of Henderson's dispatch, wanted 'ten years of vulgarly pro-business and pro-industry policies'.[28] He supported special grants for engineering students and, in January 1981, he wanted the government to bail the computer company ICL out of its financial difficulties, partly on the grounds that it was in a 'growth' industry.

The deregulation of the City had important implications for theories of national decline. First, and most simply, it was less obvious that Britain had declined. Reversal of fortunes was especially obvious amongst the upper-middle classes. In 1979 Nicholas Henderson had envied the privileges of the French *grands corps*; by the mid-1980s, members of the French elite drooled at the thought of the money earned by 'les golden boys' in the City. In 1985 Jacques Attali – the man who best epitomized the French educational and administrative elite – published an admiring biography of the London banker Siegmund Warburg.[29]

The new direction of the British economy went with new thinking about Europe. John Redwood and Peter Lilley, important figures on the anti-European wing of the Conservative Party, had made their fortunes in the City.[30] Conservative enthusiasm for European integration during the late 1970s and early 1980s had gone, in part, with a belief that British capitalism had lessons to learn from France and West Germany. This belief was less influential as the City of London became more successful. Increasingly, it seemed that Europe might learn lessons from Britain; in certain respects, particularly with regard to privatization, it did. Judged as financial centres, Paris and Frankfurt looked provincial, and the important competitors for London were now New York and Tokyo.

The success of the City also had implications for the kind of economy that might be possible in Britain. Talk about decline in the 1970s and early 1980s had often gone with a belief that Britain's fortunes were tied to the success of manufacturing. British merchant banks were blamed for being too interested in short-term returns and too prone to invest abroad. The City was seen as a feature of Britain's archaic economy. In the mid-1980s all this began to change. Conservative talk about the possibility of an economy based on service rather than industry, which had looked like rather desperate special pleading in the early 1980s, suddenly began to seem plausible.

Notions about decline had also gone with a wider sense about the whole of British society. Theorists of decline had made much of the survival of 'pre-industrial' values in Britain – values that they associated with the ruralism of the upper classes and with the outdated ethos of the public schools. An odd feature of such theories was that the very people who propounded them so often seemed to epitomize the qualities that they denounced. This was true, to an almost absurd extent, of Sir Nicholas Henderson. Henderson had spent his formative years in the Vanbrugh gardens that surround Stowe School. His life in France revolved around hunting parties and tastings of vintage claret. Even his perception of national decline was rooted in a Foreign Office view of the world: one that saw prosperity as primarily useful because it supported the exercise of national power or prestige.[31] He had an almost *ancien régime* sense of status – after dining with the rector of the Sorbonne, he fussed about whether Oxford dons were still being waited on by flunkeys in white gloves. He epitomized the archaic aspects of the British diplomatic service: he had run a ruthless campaign of press leaks to undermine the team sent by a cabinet think tank in the mid-1970s to enquire into why, for example, the British embassy in Paris needed eleven official cars when the French embassy in London made do with one.[32]

Ministers in the first Thatcher government were also notable for their lack of contact with the industrial virtues that they extolled. The only minister who had much direct experience of industrial technology was the prime minister and, perhaps because of this, she was always rather hostile to attempts to make the British education system more 'practical'.[33] Indeed, so removed from the world of industry were most ministers that discussion of 'anti-industrial culture' often became a means by which they attacked each other. Wiener's book almost provided the occasion for a libel action between two former cabinet colleagues. On Christmas Day 1984 Rupert Edwards gave his father, Nicholas Edwards, the secretary of state for Wales, a copy of Wiener's book. Inspired by his reading, Nicholas Edwards made a speech in which he denounced British companies for their lack of entrepreneurship. He cited GEC, then noted for its refusal to plough its large cash reserves back into the business, as an example. Jim Prior, chairman of GEC and, until recently, a cabinet minister, complained and threatened to sue. Edwards apologized.[34] Rupert Edwards, whose present caused such trouble, had been schooled in the gritty realities of industrial life at Radley and Trinity College Cambridge. After graduation he (like the sons of many of Thatcher's ministers) went to work in the City.

The striking feature of the new prosperity that came from the City was that it strengthened, and was strengthened by, the very culture that the 'declinists' had denounced. There was much talk about the role of 'barrow boys' and cockney dealers. Grimes, the dealer in *Serious Money*, has 'one CSE in metalwork'. In reality, however, it was members of the established upper-middle class who were the big winners from the prosperity of the City. Kate Mortimer was a more typical figure than Grimes. She became the first ever female director of a UK merchant bank in 1984. In social terms, however, she was hardly a parvenu. Her father had been bishop of Exeter and she had built up a network of powerful friends (including a future Tory minister) whilst working in the Central Policy Review Staff during the premiership of Edward Heath. Most bankers had been educated in the very institutions that Wiener and Barnett blamed for Britain's 'anti-entrepreneurial' culture. Oliver Letwin was a banker and adviser to Margaret Thatcher, as well as being the son of Shirley Letwin, who had expressed such hostility to the 'Wiener/Barnett thesis'. Oliver Letwin illustrated the full range of his 'liberal education' by publishing *Ethics, Emotion and the Unity of the Self* in 1987, the year before he published *Privatizing the World*. The young men who left Oxford and Cambridge and went into the City in the mid-1980s had sometimes acquired a fascination with wealth by watching the television series based on that supreme celebration of aristocratic values, *Brideshead Revisited*, in 1981. Many of these people poured their new money back into old commodities: country houses, well-stocked wine cellars and expensive public-school educations for their own children.

The new confidence of the aristocracy and upper-middle class in the 1980s was summed up in the phrase 'Sloane Ranger'. Sloane Rangers were young women from good families who were characterized by their gentility, conservatism and interest in country pursuits. Peter York and Ann Barr, the journalists who popularized the term, described how the 'Magic Money . . . brass without muck' of the City funded this new group. The epitome of the Sloane Ranger was Lady Diana Spencer, who married the Prince of Wales halfway through the first Thatcher government. The curious relationship between the old world of the hunt ball and the new world of the post-Big Bang City was illustrated by the widely reported rumour that, in the late 1980s, the Princess of Wales was having an affair with a man who worked in the corporate finance department of the bank that had once stood for everything that was most vulgar in the financial world: S.G. Warburg.

Most British people had probably never heard of S.G. Warburg. For them, the economic effects of the 1980s were felt as a result of less spectacular changes. One of these was privatization. The Conservatives had never liked nationalized industries, but had not on the whole tried to translate this dislike into action. Before 1970 they made only one attempt to reverse a nationalization (that of the steel industry). Thatcher said, shortly before her election to parliament in 1959: 'The government could not de-nationalise things as easily as they had been nationalised.'[35]

A group of Conservatives dreamt of more radical denationalization. Nicholas Ridley had produced an internal party report on the matter in the late 1960s.[36] The Heath government had sold off a few insignificant companies – the Thomas Cook travel agency and a network of pubs in the North East – that had come into the possession of the state, more or less by accident, at various times. However, more significantly, it had nationalized Rolls-Royce when the company seemed on the verge of bankruptcy – a move that was defended by Margaret Thatcher.

Ridley had chaired a second internal party committee to investigate 'problems in the nationalized industries' that began work in 1976 and reported in 1977. Denationalization had many advantages for the Conservatives. It would cut state spending (since most nationalized industries enjoyed large subsidies), and the sale of state assets might even bring money to the government. Denationalization would also weaken the unions, which were strong in nationalized industries, and might create a more flexible free-market economy. It would even change the formal structure of British industrial leadership – since the heads of nationalized industries were represented in the Confederation of British Industry.

In spite of all this, the Conservatives were hesitant in their approach to nationalized industries. Keith Joseph summed up matters with his usual mixture of radicalism and uncertainty:

Presumably we do not think that denationalization is practicable. Who would buy under Labour threats? Can we go half-way – BP? We must study. Anyway, I assume – but I may be wrong – that we are agreed to manage them [nationalized industries] at arm's length, phasing out subsidies, and seeking to cut overmanning as hard as we can. I am very conscious of a reservoir of disenchanted experience among our colleagues, and hope that suggestions will be made for fruitful thought and study.[37]

Ridley's report of 1977 on the nationalized industries became notorious for the way in which one of its annexes seemed to anticipate a confrontation between a future government and the miners (see chapter 7). However, the proposals in the main part of the report, and the discussions that preceded it, were modest. Even in internal party discussions, Tories did not suggest that all nationalized industries suffered from the same kinds of problem or were amenable to the same kinds of reform. Nationalized industries considered to control 'natural monopolies' were on the whole regarded as unsuitable for sale. Ten years before the first British Gas shares were traded on the Stock Exchange, a radical group of Conservatives in a private party document concluded that 'the denationalization of the gas industry would be neither practicable nor beneficial'.[38] The denationalization of the British National Oil Corporation (achieved just two years after the Conservatives came to power) was regarded as a 'long-term ideal'.[39]

The idea that it would be possible to sell large numbers of state-owned enterprises was seen as almost quixotic. Managers of nationalized companies were reluctant to discuss the idea – partly because they feared the confusion that would be caused if they moved in and out of the private sector.[40] When Norman Fowler, shadow minister for transport, presented some modest proposals about privatization to his colleagues, he was worried that they might be seen as too radical – he later concluded that they got through only because the shadow cabinet was not terribly interested in transport.[41] In 1976 the CBI insisted that they wanted the existing balance of private and public sector companies left as it was.[42] For much of the 1970s, Conservatives, including Thatcher and Joseph, seemed more concerned to defend the existing 'mixed economy' against further nationalization than to sell off companies that belonged to the state.[43] Enoch Powell presented denationalization as one of the means by which he would reduce taxation in the alternative budget that he presented on the fringes of the Conservative Party conference in 1968, but this was after his front-bench career had ended and Powell later recognized that his proposals had been 'political satire'. The most enthusiastic proponent of denationalization before 1979 was not an MP or a businessman but Michael Ivens, a poet whose distaste for state power had, in his youth, taken him close to anarchism and who, in the 1970s, ran the free-market pressure group Aims of Industry.[44]

The 1979 manifesto barely mentioned denationalization. The truth was that 'privatization' (a word that began to be widely used in 1981 and which Thatcher always disliked) was easier to talk about than to implement. It was not terribly clear who, in law, owned a nationalized corporation and ownership had to be transferred to special companies before it could be sold to anyone.[45] It was hard to value companies that had no existing share on the stock market, no profits and, in some cases, nothing that anyone in the private sector would have recognized as a set of accounts. The Tory discussion papers of the 1970s had recognized that any value that might be ascribed to nationalized industries, for the purposes of forcing them to make a certain return on capital, was pretty much 'arbitrary'. Should such companies simply be given away to the public or to their employees? This possibility was discussed – though, in truth, some parts of nationalized industries had such liabilities that they might be worth less than nothing. Should shares be offered by tender – that is to say, should buyers be invited to bid for them? Should shares be offered at a price that had been fixed after consultation with bankers and, if so, how was the government to ensure that the bankers, who had an interest in undervaluing shares that they also underwrote, did not take advantage of the ambiguity surrounding valuation?

The government embarked on early privatizations with trepidation. When Cable and Wireless was sold to the public in 1981, the value of the shares offered (around £240 million) was the largest that had ever been sold in a company that had no previous stock market valuation. There was no way of telling how the market would react to such an offer. Some privatizations seemed to confirm the government's worst fears. Amersham International was a spin-off from the nationalized nuclear industry – its assets were largely composed of patents on unproven technologies. The government offered its shares at a fixed price that was, as it turned out, much below what the market was willing to pay. The lucky buyers made quick profits. A year later, the sale of Britoil produced the opposite kind of problem. This time the sale was conducted by tender. However, when the bids were in, a few casual remarks by a Saudi Arabian minister knocked 20 per cent off the price of oil. No one wanted Britoil shares and the underwriters were left with heavy losses.

Companies could be privatized only if they had the right kind of managers. Getting such people was easier said than done. Occasionally, a successful industrialist could be tempted into running a nationalized industry that seemed on the verge of privatization – this was how Sir John King was brought to British Airways. However, before privatization had begun, it was hard to persuade anyone to endure the travails of public sector management in the hope that they might still be there on the day of stock market flotation. Matters were not made easier by Margaret Thatcher who insisted that managers of nationalized industries were performing a 'public service' and should not therefore expect to be paid the kind of money that they might attract in private companies.[46] Some strong-willed chairmen were more concerned to hold their industrial empires together than to increase market choice or profitability. Denis Rooke bullied the government into selling the gas industry as a unified whole; Walter Marshall resigned as chairman of the Central Electricity Generating Board rather than preside over the break-up of his beloved conglomeration.

Most of all, though Conservatives were rarely very open about this, privatization raised questions about party politics. In general terms, it was obviously in Conservative interests that large numbers of people should own shares of any sort and, more particularly, that they should own shares in companies that might be renationalized if Labour were to regain power. However, the very threat of a Labour government also made privatization difficult. Until the summer of 1982 it seemed likely that the Tories would lose the next election, and highly possible that the Labour Party would form the next government. Labour was committed to renationalizing privatized companies in a manner that would deprive shareholders of all profits; Tony Benn talked of nationalization without any compensation at all. This made it hard to sell shares in state-owned companies; every privatization prospectus was required to spell out Labour Party policy.

After the Conservative election victory of 1983, things changed. The chance that a Labour government might reverse privatization policy now seemed remote. Privatization was pursued with new ambition and energy. Until 1983 annual receipts from privatization never exceeded half a billion pounds. After 1983 they were never less than one billion pounds, and they peaked in 1988–9 at £7.1 billion. The change was seen in the privatization of British Telecom in 1984. Previous privatizations had involved relatively small companies, ones that had often been nationalized recently and ones that did not do business directly with the general public. British Telecom was a national company that did business with almost every householder in Britain. It was also the holder of what had seemed to be a natural monopoly. Its privatization was facilitated partly by technological change, which seemed to undermine its monopoly and also to offer new possibilities for profitability as a private company. BT shares were sold at a fixed price and with special provisions to ensure that ownership of the shares should be as widely distributed as possible. The share sale was publicized with a vast mailshot and telephone answering service – at one point, over 36,000 enquiries per day were being fielded.[47]

The sale was, in terms of the government's ambitions, a success. British Telecom was followed by other big sell-offs – British Gas in 1986, British Airways and the British Airports Authority in 1987, the electricity generating companies in 1990. By the time

Thatcher left Downing Street, forty companies, employing a total of 600,000 people, had been sold off. Privatization was also a notable success for the City of London: banks were engaged to advise all the relevant parties in each privatization and to underwrite the shares that were issued. The grander banks tended to be sniffy about the comparatively small fees that were offered for underwriting privatizations,[48] and very indignant on the rare occasions when some unexpected movement in the share price forced them to do something in return for those fees.[49] However, privatization work in the UK reinforced the general sense that London-based banks were the frontier warriors of corporate finance, and provided them with the route to more lucrative work overseas as other countries began to sell-off state assets. N.M. Rothschild established a special department (employing Oliver Letwin and John Redwood) to 'sell' privatization abroad.

In some ways, the focus on the very visible transformation that was brought about by the sale of shares obscured the wider problems that Conservatives had identified with state control of industry. Privatization, in itself, did not necessarily bring greater efficiency or more competition. The airline industry illustrated the contradictions in the Thatcherite approach. In the 1970s Freddie Laker's Skytrain had offered cheap transatlantic fares in competition with British Airways. Thatcherites, such as John Nott and Cecil Parkinson, had seen Laker as a kindred spirit.[50] Thatcher herself praised him and supported his legal actions against the British government to ensure his right to operate. However, during the 1980s Laker brought an anti-trust suit against British Airways in the American courts – a case that made privatization difficult and eventually forced the government to delay it. Then Thatcher became the enemy of Laker. She appealed directly to the US president in a bid to quash the anti-trust suit and protect British Airways.[51] There were other ways in which British Airways seemed to benefit from government's willingness to smother competition. A sharp-eyed merchant banker noticed that the privately owned airline

British Caledonian seemed to find it difficult to get routes or landing rights when their state-owned rival was being prepared for privatization.[52]

Privatized companies were not always models of the free market. Several of them preserved monopolistic positions. Their prices were often subject to control and the government sometimes retained a 'golden share', which allowed it to veto certain operations, particularly the sale of 'strategic' companies to foreign buyers. So far as could be told, productivity in most companies increased more dramatically in the period preceding privatization than in that immediately after it.[53] A supporter of privatization would no doubt have argued that increases in productivity were brought about by the prospect of privatization; an opponent would argue that state-owned companies were being fattened for sale through sleights of the accountant's hand that disadvantaged taxpayers or customers.

The proportion of the British public that held shares increased from 7 per cent to 29 per cent during the 1980s. However, this change was not as dramatic as it sounded. The proportion of shares held by individuals rather than institutions in 1990 was still lower than it had been in 1950. Furthermore, shares in privatized companies did not really change people's attitude to shareholding in general, or to the management of companies. Most people bought shares in privatized companies because the shares were easy to buy, and because they were known to command an instant premium. Few buyers went on to buy other shares or followed the fortunes of the companies that they 'owned' with any great attention. Indeed, Edward du Cann, the chairman of the 1922 Committee and an intermittent nuisance to the Thatcher government, had probably done more through his promotion of unit trusts during the 1960s to promote share ownership than Nigel Lawson or Cecil Parkinson.

Did privatization have a wider impact on British society? In 1986 government ministers began to talk about 'popular capitalism'

(Thatcher had vetoed Lawson's original formulation of 'people's capitalism' because it sounded too 'East European'). Popular capitalism was never, in fact, that popular. This was partly because, for the reasons described above, the distribution of shares was not as spectacular as it looked. It was also because take-up was not spread across all social classes or even all regions. The typical customer who enquired about buying shares in British Telecom was 'male, middle-class and over 45'.[54]

The government did gain from privatization. In the simplest terms, it made money from selling state assets. The culture of industry changed. Privatized industry, especially when privatization was accompanied by the break-up of companies, created a less benign climate for the exercise of union power. The government found it easier to distance itself from pay negotiations once companies had been sold off. A whole section of the establishment, with which Thatcherites had had such fraught relations, was swept away when management of nationalized industries ceased to exist. There were political gains too. Nationalization/privatization is an area in which political parties find it hard to change the status quo. Just as the Conservative Party had hesitated to put denationalization forward as a policy during the 1970s, or even during the first Thatcher government, so the Labour Party realized after 1983 that renationalization would be a complicated and messy operation – one that would alienate some voters, cost a lot of money and make merchant bankers (probably the same ones who had gained from privatization) even richer. Gradually, Labour's threats about renationalization were abandoned. In 1989 Enoch Powell remarked that 'the transfer of ownership and control of industries and services to a wide public gave the Conservative government precisely the sense of irreversibility that is daunting to political opponents'.[55]

Privatization brought relatively small profits to individual buyers, and benefits tended to be enjoyed by people who were already wealthy. The sale of one sort of state asset, however, was different.

This was housing. In 1979 about a third of all housing in Britain was owned by local councils – making the British state the largest landlord in western Europe. Many council houses had been built quickly during slum clearance campaigns in the 1960s. Rapid building had all sorts of unfortunate consequences. When Tottenham's Broadwater Farm estate, which was to be the scene of a violent riot in 1985, was built, the council architect realized, after the building contracts had been signed, that important features such as drainage had been omitted. About 2000 large estates – each of which contained between 500 and 2000 properties – were regarded as particularly difficult places in which to live. These estates tended to be composed of flats in high-rise buildings that had been built in line with the modernist fashions of the 1960s. Raised walkways and underground car parks – ideas that looked good on the drawing board – encouraged crime and vandalism. Difficult estates soon got into a vicious circle because only people with no choice would agree to live there and/or because councils deliberately allocated them to 'problem' families.[56]

The Conservative Party was particularly keen to sell council houses. Partly this was a matter of crude politics. They knew that council tenants were likely to vote Labour and that home owners were more likely to vote Tory. Proponents of the free-market also pointed to the 'rigidities' in the labour market that were created by council houses – because tenants were reluctant to abandon their safe and subsidized housing and move to areas where work might be more available. This argument was used with increasing frequency during the 1980s as unemployment rose in the north of Britain. Patrick Minford, a Thatcherite economic cheerleader with a taste for boldly implausible claims of statistical exactitude, argued that the rigidities of the housing market pushed the rate of unemployment 2 per cent above its natural level.[57]

Some Tory strategists considered simply giving council houses away to their tenants. This idea was abandoned, partly because it would have outraged middle-class home owners who were still paying mortgages. Instead, in 1980 the government introduced the 'right to buy' council houses. The right was granted to all tenants who had occupied a property for three years or more (this was lowered to two years in 1984). Prices were fixed at a fraction of the market rate that diminished according to the length of time that the property had been occupied – eventually some tenants were able to buy their houses for just 30 per cent of the market value. The implementation of the scheme was one of many things that brought the government into conflict with Labour-controlled councils. Legislation forced councils to allow sales and also prevented them spending their share of receipts from sales, at a time when the government was keen to cut all public spending.

Over a million council houses were sold in the 1980s. Subsidy of housing was the one area of government spending that dropped sharply during the 1980s. The receipts from council house sales amounted to £17,580 million in the ten years after 1979 and, until 1984, sale of council houses raised more money than the rest of the privatization programme put together.[58] The government also made political capital out of the policy. Those who bought their houses at reduced prices were understandably grateful.[59] More importantly, perhaps, home ownership was popular with the population as a whole, and the sale of council houses forced Labour councils into a position where they looked as though they were against home ownership in general.

The wider social and political effects for which some had hoped from the sale of council houses were harder to discern. About a sixth of all council properties were bought by their tenants. This did not, however, transform a feckless underclass into a breed of sturdy householders. On the whole, houses rather than flats attracted buyers, and many sales took place in relatively desirable locations in southern England. Buyers were mainly middle-aged, married couples from the skilled working class. Council policies for the allocation of housing had tended to favour people who were defined as 'respectable' when distributing the most desirable properties for rent, and the sale of council houses gave an added advantage to this already privileged section of the working class.

Council house sales on problem estates in areas of high unemployment were low – they amounted to between 1 and 5 per cent of properties.[60] Council estates looked more like social ghettos than ever before. The least desirable estates were the ones in which people were least likely to buy. Tenants in such places did not have the money to buy, even when granted substantial discounts, or to pay the high service charges and rates that went with difficult estates. A building society survey of council tenants in 1983 found that many of them did want to own their own homes, but that only about a fifth of them wanted to buy the properties in which they currently lived.[61]

The economic benefits that some had hoped to see from the sale of council houses were elusive. Sales would hardly contribute to labour mobility if the only people who bought were those who already had jobs in relatively prosperous areas. Furthermore, property ownership created its own 'rigidities', which were particularly marked for former council houses because tenants were prevented from realizing the full profit from their acquisition if they sold within a short period of buying. Indeed the most mobile population in Britain was composed of tenants on difficult council estates – where turnover sometimes reached 40 per cent per year.

Most Tories argued that the sale of council houses was justified on grounds that transcended economic or political calculations. They believed that the ownership of property made people into better citizens with a 'stake in society'. Thatcher was a particularly strong exponent of the virtues of home ownership[62] – though she and Denis had not bought their first house until the late 1950s.

There was, however, a tension in Conservative attitudes to home ownership during the 1970s and 1980s. Housing was an area in which the free market conspicuously did not function. Council housing was subsidized by the state; private landlords were prevented from charging a market rent for their property by legal controls; owner occupiers benefited from subsidy in the form of tax relief on their mortgages. The Thatcher government increased the operation of the free market for rental accommodations – by cutting subsidies to council houses and by relaxing rent controls. It did not, however, intend to expose home owners to the unrestricted free market. Thatcher herself had once been the front-bench advocate of the Conservative Party's extraordinary proposal, during the general election campaign of October 1974, that the government should prevent repayments on all mortgages from rising above a certain level.

Thatcher never felt comfortable with the notion of direct government subsidy to mortgage payers. She was, however, an enthusiastic proponent of subsidizing home ownership via the tax relief that was granted on mortgage repayments. Lawson disagreed with her. His belief in property-ownership was less fervent than hers – he had sold his London house on moving into Number 11 Downing Street in 1983. He wanted to make the revenue system simpler and more efficient. He was also keener on a genuine free market in accommodation that would mean the revival of privately owned housing for rent.

Lawson and Thatcher reached an unwieldy compromise by which the amount on which tax relief could be granted was increased – though not as fast as the price of houses increased during the late 1980s. The total tax relief granted to mortgage holders increased from £1,639 million to £5,500 million between 1979 and 1989; subsidy to local authority housing dropped from £1,258 million to £520 million during the same period.[63] House price inflation – driven by a general sense of middle-class prosperity as well as by tax advantages – became a defining feature of the late 1980s. Attempts to revive the privately owned rental sector produced few results, largely because its economic logic was overridden by a British (or at least English) obsession with home ownership. Inflation of house prices was particularly marked in London and parts of the south east. There were times when the average London house 'earned' more than its owner.

The housing market was also transformed by the blurring of the division between building societies and banks (many of the former were 'demutualized' and then reborn as banks), and by the removal of the formal or informal restrictions that had previously existed on the granting of personal credit. In the ten years to November 1988 non-housing loans given by UK banks increased from £4 billion to £28 billion; during the same period, housing loans increased from £6 billion to £63 billion.[64] Borrowing on this scale sat oddly with a government that talked about the need to live within one's means.

During the booming 1980s the City was always haunted by the fear of a bust. There were many who could still remember the disastrous year of 1974 when shares had plunged. There was also, perhaps, a strain of apocalyptic puritanism in English middle-class culture. The very articles that gave currency to the notions of new prosperity in the City almost invariably finished with some allusion to the prospect of future crisis. A character in Caryl Churchill's *Serious Money* muses on how 'it' will all end: 'Will it be Aids, nuclear war or a crash?'

As it turned out, the end (or at least a kind of end) came with a storm. On Friday 16 October 1987 an extraordinarily high wind, said to be the most severe since 1703, hit southern England. Ancient trees were uprooted, roads were blocked, the plate glass on the new buildings that housed London banks shattered and the whole City was brought to a halt by power cuts. The following Monday world stock markets crashed – a crash that seems to have been exacerbated by automated computer trading systems that sold stock in an attempt to prevent loss. The value of shares quoted in

London fell by more than a quarter in a single day – the most dramatic fall in history. Briefly it seemed that the whole transformation of the City during the previous few years might just have been a dream.

Things were not as bad as they had looked on 19 October 1987. Equity prices mainly recovered within a year. In the long run total employment in the City did not drop. The crash did, however, have an important effect on government policy. Nigel Lawson cut interest rates, partly to boost confidence in the UK and partly because he wanted to avoid the pound rising against the currencies of other countries that were cutting rates. The government was, in fact, faced with an odd situation since sterling was rising against other currencies at a time when Britain's balance of payments deficit was also rising. The political divisions over currency and interest rates were now very different from the ones that had existed in the early 1980s (see chapter 5). Thatcher, who had once been so concerned to lower interest rates, was now worried about the possibility of inflation and willing to see sterling reach its 'natural' level. Lawson wanted to keep sterling and interest rates low. The argument was to help bring Thatcher down (see chapter 11).

At the time, Lawson's budget of March 1988 seemed to be a triumph. It looked as though he had headed off the dangers of recession that had loomed just six months earlier. In addition to this, his budget had two striking features. First, he announced that he would be repaying public sector debt (the last chancellor to do this had been Roy Jenkins in 1968), and he added that 'henceforth a zero PSBR will be the norm'. Secondly, Lawson cut income tax. The basic rate was reduced from 27 pence in the pound to 25 and the top rate was reduced from 60 pence to 40. The second of these cuts was relatively unimportant in terms of government revenue, but significant in terms of public perception; for the first time since the Second World War, rich people in Britain could expect to keep most of the money that they earned. Someone earning the average male income in 1988 (£245 per week) would, after Lawson's budget, pay a slightly higher proportion of their income in taxes, rates and national insurance contributions than someone in the same situation would have done ten years previously. Someone earning five times the average male income would be paying about 15 per cent less of their income in tax.[65]

In the long term, Lawson's budget came to be seen in a less favourable light. In some respects it seemed like a negative version of Geoffrey Howe's budget of 1981. Whereas Howe's budget earned retrospective admiration for having dared to increase taxes during a recession, Lawson earned retrospective condemnation for having cut taxes at a time when the economy was 'overheating'. Lawson himself claimed that his budget was misunderstood – that people failed to appreciate how well public spending had been contained or how small tax cuts were as a proportion of GDP. Even he, however, recognized that the tone of the budget contributed to a sense of expansiveness in the economy.

Perhaps, in fact, the single most important measure in the budget was one that appeared at first comparatively trivial. Mortgage tax relief was to be limited to covering £30,000 per property rather than £30,000 per borrower. The main effect of this was to prevent unmarried couples (who were taxed separately) from obtaining tax relief on £60,000 of mortgage. Implementation of the decision, however, was deferred for four months (apparently for administrative reasons). The effect of this deferral was to further heat the property market as people hurried to complete purchase during the last few months when they would be entitled to double tax relief.

The aftermath of the 1988 budget was curious. Everyone had expected that the crash would primarily affect shares; as it turned out, it affected the one thing that the British middle classes had come to regard as safe: houses. From October 1988, for the first time since the 1940s, UK property prices dropped. They continued to do so until the early 1990s. This was, so far as most people were concerned, the most visible sign of a wider economic downturn. It was a downturn that was to strain the relations between Lawson and Thatcher, with important political consequences for them both.

Chapter 9

DIVIDED KINGDOM?

If we are to act in the name of patriotism, as our party has traditionally been respected for doing, we must define the patria.

Keith Joseph, 1975[1]

Mr President, before I begin, there is just one thing I would like to make clear. The rose I am wearing is the rose of England.

Margaret Thatcher to Conservative
Party conference, 1986[2]

For most of the period since the partition of Ireland in 1920, the United Kingdom had been an uncontentious administrative formality that aroused few strong feelings. In the decade after 1968, though, questions of devolution inside the British Isles became increasingly pressing. This was most obvious in Northern Ireland, where the violence of the Provisional IRA, and their loyalist opponents, came to overshadow all other political developments in the 1970s. Events on the mainland were less dramatic. Nationalist parties gained some purchase in both Scotland and Wales during the 1970s. The Labour government responded to this by putting forward plans for a limited 'devolution' of powers to local parliaments. Thatcher's shadow cabinet was trapped by a commitment to Scottish devolution given by Edward Heath in

1968. For this reason, the Conservative Party claimed to support devolution, but opposed the particular form that was proposed. In practice, devolution divided both parties. Alick Buchanan-Smith, the Tory spokesman on Scotland, resigned in protest at the party's failure to support devolution more vigorously, as did his deputy, Malcolm Rifkind. Meanwhile George Gardiner, who had been an important figure in Thatcher's leadership campaign, organized opposition to devolution. In the end, referenda in Wales and Scotland in March 1979 did not produce the majority that had been required under the legislation for such measures to be introduced. In the 1970s two governments fell partly because of nationalist movements inside the United Kingdom. Heath might have been able to cobble together a parliamentary majority in 1974 if he had still been able to depend, as previous Tory leaders had, on Ulster Unionist support (see chapter 1). Callaghan was finally forced into calling an election in 1979 partly because the Scottish Nationalists, angry at his failure to deliver devolution, withdrew their support, and partly because a member of the Social Democratic Party, a representative of Catholic nationalists in Northern Ireland, angry at the government's failure to reform the Ulster electoral system, abstained in the key vote.

When Margaret Thatcher came to power in 1979, the constitutional questions of the 1970s seemed to have been settled, or at least to have reached the kind of stasis that is produced when no one believes that any further settlement is practicable in the near future. Scotland and Wales were not to have devolved government. Northern Ireland was to remain in a peculiar constitutional limbo – it was ruled from London, though its parliamentary representation at Westminster was smaller than an equivalent population on the mainland would have enjoyed and though the legislation underwriting its position had to be renewed every year. Furthermore, because of anti-terrorist laws, its inhabitants did not enjoy all the rights that they would have done on the mainland. In terms of party politics, a stasis had also been achieved. Until 1974 the Official Ulster Unionists had taken the Conservative Party whip. This was no longer the case when Thatcher became the leader of the party, though the Conservatives, like all the major mainland parties, refrained from contesting elections in Ulster.*

The Conservative Party did field candidates in Scotland and Wales, but its electoral success in these areas was more limited than that which it enjoyed in England. In part, this was due to a long-term decline that predated Thatcher. Wales was an area of heavy industry (coal and steel) and nonconformist religious traditions. Even the presence of Lloyd George's son on the Conservative benches after 1945 did not make the Welsh susceptible to the charms of Toryism. The Conservative electoral performance in Wales was not, in fact, disastrous during the Thatcher years – they gained seats in the 1983 election, though their gains were more limited than those they made in Britain as a whole, and for several years they managed to find a secretary of state for Wales, Nicholas Edwards, who sat for a constituency in Pembrokeshire and who could make semi-plausible claims to be Welsh. However, Conservative support in Wales dropped quite sharply in the late 1980s and the Tories began to look like a foreign army of occupation – the head of the Welsh Development Agency had formerly been chairman of the Monaco branch of Conservatives Abroad.[3] There was an increasingly strong sense of cultural divide between Wales and the Thatcher government. Every single Labour leader that Thatcher faced between the resignation of Harold Wilson in 1976 and her own resignation in 1990 (i.e. Callaghan, Foot and Kinnock) sat for a Welsh constituency.

The proportion of people in Wales who defined themselves as 'Welsh', rather than 'British', had dropped to a low point of 57 per cent after the failure of devolution in 1979. Two years into

---

* The Conservative Party did authorize the formation of four associations in Northern Ireland in 1989.

the Thatcher government, this proportion had risen to 69 per cent.[4] Thatcherites seemed sometimes to take it for granted that Wales would epitomize everything that made them uneasy. Sir Keith Joseph once told an audience in Cardiff that the Welsh language had no word for 'entrepreneur'; he was disconcerted when a member of the audience asked him what the English word might be.

The problems of Scotland were more painful for the Conservatives. There had once been a strong Scottish Conservative Party and important figures in the party – Willie Whitelaw and Alec Douglas-Home – thought of themselves as Scottish. Thatcher had been greeted rapturously during a brief visit to Scotland shortly after she became leader of the party and she seems to have assumed that the country of Adam Smith would be 'naturally' Thatcherite – indeed, that the Scots 'invented Thatcherism'.[5] This assumption, perhaps cultivated by the small group of free-market radicals at St Andrews University, was wrong. The Conservative Party lost votes in Scotland throughout the 1980s, as Labour, the Nationalists and the Liberal/SDP Alliance gained them. In March 1982 Roy Jenkins, who had been born in Wales and who sounded like a caricature of an upper-middle-class Englishman, won the Glasgow Hillhead constituency from the Tories in a by-election. By 1983, there were only eleven Conservative MPs from Scotland.

Almost every statistic showed that Thatcherism made less progress in Scotland and Wales than in England – or, more precisely, than in the south of England. Ministers with responsibility for Wales boasted of a 'Welsh economic miracle' during the late 1980s, sometimes implying that this miracle was the result of rather unThatcherite policies that they had pursued in the principality. It is true that unemployment dropped sharply in Wales during the second half of the decade, that foreign companies were persuaded to bring inward investment, and that industries associated with the provision of services or high technology rose as the old industries of steel and mining declined. This was not, however, a miracle that would have survived much scrutiny by a statistician: the Welsh economic recovery of the late 1980s looked dramatic precisely because Welsh industry had taken such a bad hammering during the recession of the early 1980s. Furthermore, an increase in employment did not bring a dramatic increase in household income. Many of the new jobs were comparatively unskilled and lowly paid. Often men who had held down well-paid jobs in heavy industry were replaced by women who held more precarious positions on assembly lines. Even the best jobs were less lucrative than those being created in London and the South East. Employment in banking and financial services increased from 50,000 to 75,000, but these were mostly clerical jobs in 'back offices'.[6]

The Scots were particularly resistant to attempts to strengthen the private sector. The proportion of people employed by the public sector was higher in Scotland than in England, as was that of people who belonged to trade unions. Scots were less likely to own shares than English people and, in particular, were less likely to buy shares in the companies that were privatized during the mid-1980s. Scots were more likely to live in council houses and, again, were less likely to buy such houses under the Conservative legislation of the 1980s.

The imposition of Thatcherite economic policies outside England was made more difficult by the fact that the ministers for Wales, Scotland and Northern Ireland often saw it as being their job to maintain public subsidies for the areas under their aegis. Debates on the steel industry, for example, did not simply pit Treasury ministers against those with more interventionist instincts; they also pitted the secretary of state for Scotland, who was determined to defend the steel works at Ravenscraig, against his counterpart for Wales, who tried, with less success, to defend the works at Port Talbot. The tendency of regional ministries to become centres of opposition to certain Thatcherite policies was exacerbated by Thatcher's own use of these offices as a political Siberia to which her most determined cabinet opponents could be exiled: Peter Walker was allowed to run a semi-autonomous economic policy in Wales from 1987 to 1990, as an alternative to keeping him in an economically sensitive ministry with influence over England.

All the problems presented by Wales and Scotland during the 1980s were dwarfed by those of Northern Ireland. In 1920 Ulster had been granted home rule. A parliament met at Stormont. The majority of the province's population were Protestant and electoral manipulation ensured that Protestants monopolized political power. Quite important parts of the British post-war settlement simply never applied to Ulster. The welfare state was more limited, and, not surprisingly, worked in ways that tended to advantage Protestants over Catholics. The education system was divided, to a much greater extent than on any part of the mainland, along religious lines. Birching for young offenders, the abolition of which on the mainland had so offended Margaret Thatcher, remained in force in Northern Ireland until the 1980s.

During the first two decades after the Second World War, conservatively minded English people sometimes regarded Ulster as a tranquil land, one which was refreshingly free of the 'troubles' caused by left-wing activism, trade union power and immigration on the mainland. Brian Faulkner, the Ulster prime minister, remarked in 1963: 'I doubt whether there is any other country which has shown such universal political stability as Ulster.'[7] By 1968 all this had changed. The Civil Rights movement began the long period of violence that the Northern Irish came to refer to as 'the Troubles'.

More than 850 people were killed by terrorists in Northern Ireland during the 1980s. Violence was particularly acute early in the decade. In 1980 and 1981 Republican prisoners went on hunger strike in an attempt to regain the special status as political prisoners that they had enjoyed until 1976. The government made no concessions and ten hunger strikers eventually starved themselves to death; each death provoked riots. Bobby Sands, the most

prominent of the strikers and the one who died first, was elected
to parliament during the last months of his life.

In spite of all this, Northern Ireland in the 1980s never produced
the sense of general crisis of the British state that it had produced
during the early 1970s. Politicians on the mainland were less
fearful that disorder in Ulster might become associated with
disorder on the mainland. The rate of killing was lower than it
had been for most of the 1970s and this reflected a new strategy
by the IRA, which now recognized that it was in for a long war.
The government too dug in for a struggle with no immediate
end in sight. The legal and constitutional initiatives of the 1970s
were replaced by policies of 'Ulsterization', which meant, so far
as possible, replacing the British army with the Royal Ulster
Constabulary, and 'criminalization', which meant prosecuting
terrorists for particular offences rather than interning whole
categories of people.

There was no particularly Thatcherite view on Northern Ireland.
The Conservative Party had fought the 1979 election with a vague
proposal to introduce 'regional councils' in Ulster. This proposal
seems to have been designed to assuage Unionist desire for home
rule without re-establishing the Stormont parliament. Two people
who were close to Thatcher – Airey Neave and Ian Gow – had a
strong interest in Northern Ireland; both were assassinated by Irish
republicans. But these men were political fixers rather than policy
makers. In any case, Neave was dead by the time that Thatcher
formed her first government and Gow resigned from the government
in protest at its Ulster policy. There were Conservative MPs who
cared about the union of Britain and Ulster but these were isolated
figures – such as Ivor Stanbrook[8] or Sir John Biggs-Davison – who
often took a range of slightly eccentric positions that prevented
them from forming a coherent group. The behaviour of Ulster
Unionists themselves seemed increasingly at odds with the economic
dynamism of Britain in the 1980s – Ferdinand Mount, once head
of Margaret Thatcher's policy unit, wrote in 1986: 'the Unionists

appear so irredeemably *foreign*, far more alien, say, than Mr Lenny
Henry or Mr Clive Lloyd.'[9] Mount's remarks would have offended
Unionists even more if they had realized that he had authorized
the section on Ulster in the draft Conservative manifesto for 1983.[10]
After the Anglo-Irish agreement of 1985, of which more below,
Unionists finally broke their last formal links with the British
Conservative Party. They also sought to organize their forces on
the British mainland, with little success. The affairs of Ulster barely
impinged on the electorate of the mainland. James Black contested
the 1986 Fulham by-election on a 'Democratic Rights for Northern
Ireland' ticket. He got 98 votes – placing him just behind John
Creighton's Connoisseur Wine Party (127 votes) and Screaming
Lord Sutch's Monster Raving Loony Party (134 votes).

Thatcher's own attitude (or perhaps, more precisely, her lack of
a clear attitude) to Ulster can be highlighted, as is often the case,
by comparing her position with that of Enoch Powell. Powell, to
Thatcher's surprise,[11] supported 'integration' – that is to say he
wanted Northern Ireland to be ruled by the Westminster parliament
under the same terms as the rest of the United Kingdom. He also
opposed any measure that seemed to dilute the sovereignty of the
British government or to suggest that the Irish Republic might
have any voice in Ulster affairs. Powell's focus on what he saw as
vital matters of sovereignty went with near indifference to the day-
to-day question of terrorism.

Thatcher, on the other hand, was obsessed with terrorism. Some
of her closest associates were killed or injured by republican terrorists
and she herself came close to being killed when IRA volunteers
planted a bomb next to her hotel room during the Conservative
Party conference at Brighton in 1984. The passage in her memoirs
that deals with Northern Ireland is in large measure a recital of
killings and bomb attacks. Often Thatcher seemed to see Northern
Ireland as one front in a world-wide battle between democracy
and terrorism[12] rather than as a specific place that raised particular
constitutional issues for the British government.

In terms of policy, Thatcher claimed to be a unionist rather than an integrationist. In theory, she wanted to restore devolved government; in practice, she never made any move that brought such restoration closer. Throughout her government, Northern Ireland continued to exist in constitutional limbo with its status, as well as the anti-terrorist legislation that had most effect on people from Northern Ireland, being renewed every year. Far from seeking clarity about the status of Northern Ireland, Thatcher often seemed intent on generating the greatest possible degree of ambiguity. This was particularly obvious in talks with the Republic of Ireland about the status of Ulster, talks that ultimately produced the Anglo-Irish agreement of 1985. The Anglo-Irish agreement was designed to give the Republic some say in the affairs of Ulster. The defining quality of the agreement was lack of definition. It gave the government of the Republic of Ireland a consultative role in the affairs of Ulster, without specifying what that might mean. Even the negotiation of the agreement generated peculiar doubts – at one point Margaret Thatcher insisted that discussions of this matter should circumvent ordinary political and diplomatic channels entirely, and that they should be conducted orally by the cabinet secretary, thus leaving no written record. This vagueness provoked the violent hostility of Unionists, who often convinced themselves that the anodyne phrases of the agreement must carry some secret meaning that would be apparent to the Vatican or the CIA.

Thatcher's relations with the secretaries of state for Northern Ireland revealed much about the oddity of her own position over Ulster. Many of them were driven to distraction by her unwillingness to grasp the detailed problems of the province. She repeatedly suggested some border adjustment that would put all Catholics into the Republic and bring all Protestants into the six counties; she had repeatedly to be reminded that most Northern Irish Catholics lived nowhere near the border.[13] She was much given to historical analogies; she once compared Ulster Catholics to Germans in the Sudetenland, hardly a point calculated to reassure either side. It says much about Thatcher's general attitude that her favourite Northern Ireland secretary was not Douglas Hurd or Jim Prior (both subtle men) but Tom King. Thatcher recognized that King had no great grasp of detail but felt that his 'manly good sense' was what Ulster needed.[14]

If Thatcherite economics failed in Scotland and Wales, they were not even attempted in Ulster. In 1977 Geoffrey Howe wrote a despairing report in which he commented on the extent to which Ulster Unionism had become effectively allied with the Labour government on the mainland: 'Ulster shows so many signs of becoming (like the North East) a "natural" for state-subsidized Socialism.'[15] In practice nothing was done to assuage Howe's fears after the Conservative election victory of 1979. One British journalist wrote of the 'Independent Keynesian Republic of Northern Ireland, where monetarism remains unknown'.[16] Jim Prior, secretary of state for Northern Ireland from 1981 to 1983, had been, along with Peter Walker, one of the most determined defenders of pre-Thatcherite economic policy to remain in the government. Most of the Conservatives who filled the various posts at the Northern Irish Office were smooth, often rather patrician, men who seemed equally distant from both the culture of Ulster Unionism and that of those who were directing economic policy in London. Rhodes Boyson, who was responsible for industry in Northern Ireland when Douglas Hurd was secretary of state, was probably the only one of them who would have described himself as a Thatcherite, and even he conducted an interventionist policy when he got to Belfast.

Economic intervention in Ulster was mainly rooted in pragmatism rather than ideology. Unemployment in the province was higher than on the mainland and it was twice as high among Catholics as among Protestants. Economic failure and terrorist violence fed each other and the government recognized that subsidizing jobs might have political benefits even if it did economic damage. It was estimated that 90 per cent of all industrial jobs in the province were supported by some kind of government subsidy.[17]

The state was more visible in Northern Ireland than it was on the mainland – not least because of the agencies associated with security. About 40 per cent of all jobs in the province were in the public sector.[18] Such jobs could be sustained only by moving money across the Irish Sea. Subsidies from the mainland to Ulster rose from £100 million in 1972 to £1.6 billion in 1988–9 (£1.9 billion if money from the European Community and money spent on the army were taken into account). One curious result of all this was that average household income in Northern Ireland, racked by unemployment and state dependency, overtook that in Wales, which had 'adjusted' so well to the new realities of free-market economics.

Huge areas of Thatcherite politics meant nothing in Northern Ireland. Crushing the power of local authorities was unnecessary because direct rule had already stripped those authorities of much of their power, partly to prevent them from favouring Protestants. Council housing in Northern Ireland was under the control of a central Housing Executive. On a less formal level, paramilitary groups took a keen interest in the housing of 'their people', and it is unlikely that the sale of council houses on, say, the Garvaghy Road would have been brisk even if the government had tried to implement such a policy. The level of government subsidy to housing in Northern Ireland dropped by only 27 per cent, during a period when it fell by 79 per cent on the mainland.[19]

If direct rule weakened local authorities, it strengthened another agency that was sometimes seen as being inimical to Thatcherism: the civil service. Decisions that might have been taken by elected politicians anywhere else were taken by administrators in Northern Ireland. 'Apoliticism', which Thatcher's ministers often regarded with suspicion on the mainland, seemed eminently desirable in Ulster. The whole sprawling Ulster state produced complexities that only specialists could hope to understand, and this increased the power of both the Northern Irish civil service, which retained a strong sense of its own identity, and of civil servants in London – indeed 'rule from Whitehall' describes Ulster's position better than 'rule from Westminster'.

Education policy was different because Ulster had never abolished its grammar schools, and the Conservatives exerted no pressure for it to do so. There was no poll tax in Northern Ireland. Trade union legislation was applied in the province more slowly than on the mainland. The delay was justified on the grounds that industrial relations posed less severe problems in Ulster than they did on the mainland. In view of the role that the Ulster Workers' Council had played in opposing government policy in 1974, with a strike that was much more blatantly political than anything attempted by the NUM, this was a bizarre argument – though the simple fact that there were no coal mines in Ulster may have played a role in government thinking. The truth was that trade unions in Northern Ireland were so intertwined with sectarian divisions that even Norman Tebbit preferred not to open this particular *panier de crabes*.

What of Thatcherism's relation with the wider world, and particularly with that substantial part of it that had once been ruled by Britain? In 1978 a group of Tory MPs had said: 'The Nation has been damaged . . . by the denigration of its "colonialist" history. Let's stop apologizing for our history.'[20] There was, in fact, little evidence that Thatcher had ever started 'apologizing for our history'. She carried little imperial baggage. For her, the Empire was an admirable chapter in the British story but a chapter that was now finished. She repeatedly insisted that she was proud of the Empire and she sometimes did so in extraordinary contexts (inhabitants of the Congo must have been disconcerted to hear the European civilizing mission lauded in a speech that she gave in Belgium). However, Thatcher never expressed regret about the loss of Empire either and seems to have had remarkably little sense that Britain might in any way be overshadowed by its imperial past. One of her admirers wrote:

> For the fifty years before Thatcherism, the Conservative Party struggled with Britain's imperial heritage, never quite shaking off a belief in or at least a nostalgia for empire. Thatcherism, in its post-imperial modernity, has suffered no such hang-ups. It has concentrated instead on the revival of Britain as an independent island power.[21]

Thatcherites sometimes regarded the attachment to particular pieces of land as mere sentimentality. Nicholas Ridley put matters bluntly when, discussing the Falklands with Argentine diplomats in 1981, he said that the only former British possession that he cared about was Bordeaux – 'because of the wine'.[22]

Some saw the Falklands War as associated with a bid to restore an imperial quality to Britain's role in the world. The truth is that the Falklands War did not mark any turning point in Britain's world role. It was justified on the very unimperialist principle of 'self-determination'. Military success may have seeped into British self-perceptions but the Falklands themselves hardly did so at all: there was no sense that the islands constituted some exciting new frontier. Most of all, the Falklands War did not change British strategy towards any of its other dependencies. There was, in particular, no attempt to change the timetable for handing over Hong Kong, a more economically and strategically important residue of Empire, to China.

The area of the world in which the legacies of the British Empire still mattered most was southern Africa. Here two governments – in South Africa and Rhodesia – had broken away from the British Empire in order to resist the imposition of black majority rule. Britain had, eventually, imposed economic sanctions on both countries. A large group of Tory MPs, and a noisy group in the Conservative Party outside parliament, were, however, against sanctions. Thatcher's own views were open to more than one interpretation. She expressed doubts about sanctions. She said that they were hypocritical, because they were not applied to regimes that repressed their people on the basis of something other than race, and cruel, because they caused unemployment and suffering amongst the black population. In 1978, after the government of Rhodesia had made some concessions to the majority population, party whips ordered Conservative MPs to abstain in the vote on renewing sanctions, but 114 Tories voted against renewal. Many of these rebels – George Gardiner, Stephen Hastings, Julian Amery and Patrick Wall – regarded themselves as being personally loyal to Margaret Thatcher and sometimes believed that she took an indulgent view of their rebellion.[23] Stephen Hastings was knighted in 1983; Julian Amery was given to understand that he might be made foreign secretary. All this might mean that Thatcher was privately in favour of white minority rule, or at least that she regarded it as the least bad of the available options, but that she was obliged to support sanctions for reasons of political advantage. It might equally well mean that Thatcher simply found discreet gestures of consideration towards some right-wing MPs to be a good way to keep the support of a useful group in the party.

One clear fact is that Thatcher rarely gave a member of the pro-South Africa and Rhodesia lobby any office that might have given them influence over government policy. This was particularly striking in the case of Julian Amery. He was the son of a senior minister, Leo Amery, and the son-in-law of a former prime minister, Harold Macmillan. He had been a junior minister in the early 1960s, but he never held any office at all, let alone that of foreign secretary, under Thatcher. Furthermore, though support for white minority rule often went with personal loyalty to Thatcher, it was not much associated with Thatcherites – that is to say those people who were most involved in implementing the broad range of government policies, particularly those that related to economics. Thatcher's first chancellor, Geoffrey Howe, was the strongest opponent of white rule in South Africa on the Conservative front bench. He had made an unauthorized visit to Soweto during the 1970s[24] and, when he became foreign secretary, he sent British soldiers to protect Botswana against South African raids.

In practical terms, the affairs of southern Africa impinged most sharply on the Thatcher government during its first year in office. Rhodesia's rulers had come to recognize that white rule could not survive. They hoped to manage a relatively gentle transition away from this regime with a constitution that protected some white privileges and with a government that would be formed by Bishop Abel Muzorewa, who was seen as the least threatening representative of black rule. The British government convoked a conference of interested parties at Lancaster Gate in London in 1979, and Lord Soames was sent out as the last governor of Rhodesia to preside over elections, which were won by Robert Mugabe's radical Patriotic Front. Thatcher claims, rather improbably, that she did not appreciate the significance of the Lancaster Gate settlement because she did not realize that Mugabe's party was likely to win. More generally, historians have tended to assume that the real architect of Lancaster Gate was Lord Carrington, the foreign secretary, and that Margaret Thatcher, inexperienced in foreign affairs and still unsure of herself in cabinet, was manoeuvred into an agreement that went against her own instincts.

The coming of black majority rule in Rhodesia was significant for another reason. For much of the twentieth century some British people had seen the Empire/Commonwealth as a place in which 'British values' might thrive even if they were snuffed out in the British Isles themselves. After 1945 the sense that parts of the Commonwealth might provide a refuge from socialism and economic decline at home grew stronger. H. V. Morton, who had written evocatively about *'l'Angleterre profonde'* in the 1930s, made his home in South Africa. Noël Coward and Ian Fleming

spent much of their time in the West Indies, and it was to
Fleming's Jamaican house that Anthony Eden went when he
was licking his wounds after Suez. Nevil Shute fantasized about
Australia as a land of new opportunity for dynamic Europeans,
in which the voting system would be changed to reflect the rights
of education, property and service. Race also played an important
part in these fantasies. As immigrants from Africa and Jamaica
arrived in England, certain kinds of English people were attracted
to places where blacks knew their place (as seemed to be the
case in the West Indies until the 1970s) or where black people
were shown their place (as in southern Africa or, until the 1960s,
in Australia).

Some of Thatcher's ministers had been tempted by emigration.[25]
In 1976 Thatcher talked of 'those who leave this country in
increasing numbers for other lands'.[26] In the 1970s Thatcher told
a friend that she and her husband would stay if socialism came
to power again, but that they would ensure that their children
were settled in Canada.[27] The idea of Britain overseas, however,
seemed less and less reassuring. Thatcher had remarked as early
as 1961 that 'Many of us do not feel quite the same allegiance
to Archbishop Makarios or Doctor Nkrumah or to people like
Jomo Kenyatta as we do towards Mr Menzies of Australia.'[28] By
1980 even Australia – more republican and less 'white' than it
had been in the 1960s – was not an entirely comfortable place
for an English conservative.

Rhodesia was the last place in which the notion of an overseas
refuge could still seem plausible. Its white population had come
mainly from England and had mostly done so quite recently. The
capital city had the air of an English provincial town and bore
the name of a Tory prime minister. The prime minister – Ian
Smith – was a former Spitfire pilot who argued that Winston
Churchill would have felt more at home in Rhodesia than in present-
day England. Giving up Rhodesia meant giving up the notion that
there was anywhere for English conservatives to run. It was, though

Thatcher probably did not appreciate it, as symbolically important as the moment when the Romans burnt their boats on the coast of Kent. After this, a certain section of the English middle class had no choice but to stand and fight in their own country.

All this brings us back to Britain and, especially, to England. Thatcherism was an English phenomenon. It never commanded an electoral majority in any of the other constituent parts of the United Kingdom. Its most cherished policies worked better in England – especially southern England – than they did in Scotland, Wales and Ulster. The Thatcher government was pretty much indifferent to Britain's former imperial possessions overseas and never seems to have been infected with any nostalgia for the 'greater Britain' of Empire.

The policies of the Thatcher government provoked various forms of nationalist reaction in Wales, Scotland and Northern Ireland. Thatcherites were, however, remarkably unconcerned with the nationalistic implications of their own acts. The Falklands War, to choose an obvious example, was seen as having important implications for the United Kingdom by Unionists in Northern Ireland, which was why they supported it so vigorously, as well as by nationalists in Wales – Plaid Cymru was the only party represented in parliament to oppose the war (partly because there were so many Welsh-speakers in Patagonia). The government, however, seems not to have thought about such matters at all. Even the decision that the Scots and Welsh Guards should be sent to the South Atlantic seems to have been taken on grounds of military expediency, without regard for any messages about Scottish or Welsh national feelings.

Thatcher often talked of patriotism and of Britain, but this was a curiously undefined concept in her mind. She seems, in private at least, to have allowed for the possibility that both Ulster and Scotland might split away from England. The American alliance was the centre of her thinking. She saw America both as the pivot of a Cold War coalition against Communism and as the leading

country in an axis of English-speaking peoples. Even her apparently
'English' enthusiasms – Kipling, Churchill and the English language
– were very transatlantic ones. The American and/or anti-Soviet
alliance often cut across any particularly British loyalties. Thatcher
barely protested in 1983 when the Americans, in the name of anti-
Communism, invaded the island of Grenada, which was a member
of the Commonwealth and which recognized Elizabeth II as head
of state. The Tory writer T. E. Utley complained that Thatcher
cared more about the anti-Soviet guerrillas of Afghanistan than
about the Unionists in Ulster.[29]

Religion underlay a great deal of nationalism in Wales, Scotland
and, especially, Ulster. It is revealing that the Thatcher government's
periodic spats with the Church were concerned entirely with matters
of social and economic policy. No mainstream Tory ever took
much interest in what might have been *English* about the Church
of England. Questions of liturgy, language and the nature of
authority over the established Church were all discussed during
the 1980s – especially when it seemed that the Church was seeking
to circumvent parliamentary control over the prayer book.[30] But
these were matters that concerned only a handful of eccentric
parliamentarians and there was no particularly Tory approach to
them.

Most strikingly, the Thatcher government said little about English
nationalism. Some significant Conservatives – such as Stanley
Baldwin and Enoch Powell – had talked a great deal about
Englishness. Both Baldwin and Powell had delivered important
speeches to the Royal Society of St George. Thatcher was to
become a vice president of the society in 1999, but there is not
much evidence that she took any interest in England's patron saint
when she was in power – indeed, the only time she mentioned St
George was on 1 April 1987, when she drew attention to the fact
that he was also the patron saint of Georgia.[31]

Race played a peculiar role in Thatcherism. The perception
that the Conservatives were 'tough' on immigration certainly played

a role in their electoral success, especially in 1979. However, Thatcher's enemies were wrong to say that her party was simply 'racist' or unable to conceive of an English identity that was not white. In some ways the problem for Thatcherism was that Thatcherites could not agree on any conception of English identity at all. There were men, such as Howe and Nott, who stood on the Left of their party, and indeed to the Left of James Callaghan, on race and immigration. However, even those Thatcherites who were most 'right-wing' on this issue, did not really live, or want to live, in a racially 'pure' society. The back-bench MP George Gardiner was opposed to immigration and supported the Apartheid regime in South Africa, but he was also close to leaders of the British Sikh community, whom he saw as incarnating the robust moral and martial qualities that Thatcherites admired. Thatcher was Philo-Semitic – she occasionally talked as though the Chief Rabbi was the head of the established Church – and some of her most important allies were Jews. This too meant that Conservatives approached issues of race with mixed feelings. In 1975 Keith Joseph had told the shadow cabinet: 'Mass immigration was imposed against the wishes and forebodings of the overwhelming majority of the people. The concept of the nation has been progressively diminished towards becoming a mere residence qualification.'[32] However, Joseph does not seem to have felt comfortable with a political appeal based on race, and he urged his colleagues not to make immigration an electoral issue. Both Joseph and Lawson, who had also talked about immigration in internal party documents,[33] were disconcerted when it emerged in 1983 that the Conservative Party had attracted a former member of the National Front as a parliamentary candidate.[34]

Nationalism in the United Kingdom was associated with the political death throes of Margaret Thatcher. There was a Welsh element in the opposition to Thatcherism inside the Conservative Party. Sir Anthony Meyer, the first person to challenge Thatcher for the leadership of the party, sat for a Welsh constituency (though he was also an upper-class English Europhile of German-Jewish descent who had served in the Scots Guards), and Michael Heseltine believed that every single one of the three ministers at the Welsh Office voted against Thatcher in the leadership challenge that he made to her in the following year.[35]

Scotland also played a part in the general crisis that seemed to beset Thatcher during the last two years of her government. The poll tax was introduced in Scotland a year before it was introduced in England and Wales (see chapter 11). Though there was less violent disorder during protests against the tax than in England, resistance to paying was in fact more determined in Scotland.[36] Thatcher attempted to impose a more ideologically committed leader of the Conservative Party north of the border. She also used an address to the General Assembly of the Church of Scotland on 21 May 1988 as an opportunity to lecture the Scots on the virtues of her economic policy. Neither of these moves was terribly successful. In October 1990 Thatcher was obliged to accept that Michael Forsyth, the man whom she had imposed as chairman of the Scottish Conservative Party in the previous year, did not command enough support. She replaced him with the more 'traditional' Lord Russell Sanderson.[37] All the evidence showed that the attempt to Thatcherize Scotland failed. When Thatcher attended the Scottish Cup final between Celtic and Dundee at Hampden Park in 1988, the fans waved specially issued red cards to 'send her off'.

The irony of this was that Thatcher was beginning to talk, apropos of European integration, about the inherent instability of federal states at the very moment that some of the British nations seemed most hostile to her government. In the aftermath of Thatcher's Bruges speech, some of her supporters began to use the phrase 'nation state' as a rough translation of de Gaulle's '*patrie*'. This was a dangerous phrase to use – since a defining quality of de Gaulle's 'Europe des Patries' was that it should exclude the British Isles. Furthermore, there is not much evidence that

British Conservatives actually understood what might be particularly national about the kind of state that they desired. When Alan Clark was challenged on the subject by the economist Samuel Brittan, he could only say: 'If you don't *know* what the Nation State is, you're decadent.'[38]

Chapter 10

EUROPE

The Lady is going to make a speech at Bruges on the occasion of some Euro-anniversary or other. The Eurocreeps have written for her a really loathsome text, *wallowing* in rejection of our own national identity . . . They even managed to delete a ritual obeisance to Churchill, his ideals, all that and substituted the name of *Schuman*. Really!

Alan Clark, September 1988[1]

The Bruges speech of September 1988 did not turn out as the 'Eurocreeps' had intended. Instead of making the 'positive' statement on Europe that the foreign secretary had hoped for when he first suggested that she make the speech, Thatcher delivered her most celebrated attack on the European Community. Towards the end of her time in office, and perhaps more importantly after it, some admirers of Margaret Thatcher talked as though opposition to European integration was the defining element of her philosophy. The Bruges speech was treated as a kind of political testament – the Bruges Group, established by an Oxford undergraduate in early 1989, became one of the most important guardians of the Thatcher shrine. Thatcher's downfall was rooted partly in argument over Europe, and she became increasingly bitter in her denunciations of pro-European Tories, even urging members of her own party to vote against a three-line whip on the Maastricht Treaty of 1993.

Foreign secretaries who served under Thatcher had trouble in explaining the evolution of her views. Douglas Hurd thought that she moved 'slowly from the vague enthusiasm for the EEC which she had shown during the referendum campaign of 1975 to the almost total hostility to Europe which she has shown in recent years'.[2] Geoffrey Howe wrote:

> I was driven finally to conclude that for Margaret the Bruges speech represented, subconsciously at least, her escape from the collective responsibility of her days in the Heath Cabinet – when European policy had arrived, as it were, with the rations . . . Margaret had waited almost fifteen years to display her own distaste for the European policies which she had accepted as a member of that same government.[3]

Her civil service advisers were equally confused. Charles Powell, her private secretary for foreign affairs from the end of 1983, said that Thatcher had come into power with little experience of foreign affairs but:

> She had certain strong instincts, and one of them was the importance of a very close attachment to the United States of America. The second was a very strong sense of anti-communism, that communism was evil and had to be confronted. Also, one has to say, a strong support for British membership of the European Community. She had led the Conservative 'Yes' Campaign in the referendum in the early 1970s and therefore came with a basis of belief that Britain had a role in Europe and had to play that role.[4]

Percy Cradock was the prime minister's foreign policy adviser and had an office just yards away from Powell's in Number 10 Downing Street, but he recalled her attitude to Europe in very different terms: '[it] ranged from suspicion to undisguised hostility. She did not like the Europeans; she did not speak their languages; she had little time for their traditions . . . Continental penchant for grand generalizations offended her lawyer's mind.'[5]

Thatcher's downfall owed much to the way in which her attitude to Europe irritated Howe and Nigel Lawson (see chapter 11). Europe split her party. In the autumn of 1980 George Gardiner, a Thatcher loyalist who had stressed Thatcher's 'Europeanism' in the admiring biography that he had written of her, was elected as chairman of the Parliamentary Committee on European Affairs, defeating Hugh Dykes. In his memoirs, Gardiner suggested that this marked the beginning of a civil war in the party between 'federalists' who wanted European union to be political and those, like himself, who merely hoped for a common market.[6] By 1998 Europe had taken both Dykes and Gardiner out of the Conservative Party altogether – the former joined the pro-European Liberal Democrats; the latter joined the Referendum Party, which campaigned for a plebiscite on Britain's continued membership of the European Union. However, divisions such as these became apparent only slowly. In the early 1980s Dykes was still sufficiently sure of the Tory Party's pro-Europeanism to resist an invitation to join the Social Democratic Party.[7] Gardiner would still have described himself as pro-European. Alistair McAlpine, the Tory treasurer, would eventually join Gardiner in the Referendum Party but until the mid-1980s most people would still have assumed that his position was defined by his role in organizing the 'Yes' vote in the 1975 referendum on continued British membership of the European Community.

Thatcher never opposed Britain's membership of the European Community/Union. One of her earliest statements on the matter, in 1961, sounded remarkably like the kind of thing that pro-European Conservatives were to say thirty years later when they attacked the Bruges speech: 'Sovereignty and independence are not ends in themselves. It is no good being independent in isolation if it involves running down our economy and watching other nations outstrip us in both trade and influence.'[8] For most of her time as leader of the Conservative Party, Thatcher emphasized her *pro-European* feelings as something that divided her from Labour. She appointed and promoted pro-European ministers throughout her time in office. Hurd, for example, joined the cabinet in 1984, and Kenneth Clarke did so in 1987.

Europe reveals the difficulty of looking for some consistent spirit of 'real Thatcherism' that underlay the twists and turns of political expediency. The truth was that the position of both Thatcher and of other Thatcherites changed, but also that these changes were linked to the way in which the whole political spectrum, in terms of world alliances as well as British parties, changed.

Edward Heath was the politician who engineered Britain's entry into the Common Market. However, Thatcher's challenge to Heath was not seen to involve hostility to his European policy. On this issue, Thatcher had always supported Conservative policy, which since the early 1960s had been to secure British entry into the Common Market. After she had become leader of the party, Thatcher paid tribute to Heath who had 'brilliantly led the nation into Europe in 1973'.[9]

In 1975 Harold Wilson called a referendum to decide on whether Britain should remain in the Common Market, a move which owed much to his need to manage divisions in his own party. Thatcher opposed the very idea of a referendum as being outside British constitutional tradition. Both parties left their members free to campaign as they wished in the referendum. In practice, however, opposition to British membership came mainly from the Left of the Labour Party and from groups such as the Ulster Unionists. Thatcher stressed that Conservative MPs were overwhelmingly in favour of Britain remaining in the EEC, and that both the shadow cabinet and all the members of the last Conservative cabinet were united on this issue.

Some observers pointed out that Thatcher said relatively little about European integration during her campaign for the leadership of her party, and that she allowed Heath to make the running in the 'Yes' campaign in the 1975 referendum. No one, however, regarded these facts as particularly significant. Most assumed that Thatcher was just seeking to avoid alienating one or other wing of the Conservative Party – it was, perhaps, a sign of her success that people disagreed about which wing she belonged to.

Whatever Thatcher's personal feelings may have been, the Conservative Party was seen as pro-European, until at least halfway through her premiership. Simple electoral advantage played a part in this. The Labour Party was divided over Europe during the 1970s, and in 1980 the party conference passed a motion calling for British withdrawal – a motion that was eventually finessed into an expression of support for withdrawal within the lifetime of the next Parliament. The two men whose influence in the Labour Party rose most during the early 1980s (Tony Benn and Michael Foot) were almost caricatures of 'Britishness' – Benn had even complained about the new European passports that had begun to be issued in the 1970s. Labour Party strategists, who thought that their party's position on this issue would lose them votes, were slightly surprised that the Conservatives did not make more of the issue in the 1983 election.

The Conservative Party itself was touched by the process of European integration. The European parliament, previously made up of representatives delegated from national parliaments, was to be chosen by direct elections from the late 1970s onwards. Douglas Hurd recalled that Thatcher 'never challenged the principle of direct election, but she found it uncongenial'.[10] The prospect of direct elections meant that European parties had an interest in forming alliances across national frontiers. This presented the Conservatives with interesting problems. The most important non-Socialist parties in Europe – especially in Belgium, Holland, West Germany and Italy – were Christian Democrats. Christian Democracy implied an opposition to Marxism, a defence of private property and a belief in the family. However, Christian Democrat parties were not 'conservative' – they were mostly new parties and keen to play down any associations with embarrassing political ancestors from before the Second World War. They were also emphatically not 'liberal', which in continental terms meant that they were not supporters of an unrestricted free market. Christian Democrats also worked in political systems that contained more than two parties, and they sometimes governed in coalition with Socialists.

Douglas Hurd was put in charge of negotiations with European parties. The most important of his interlocutors was the German CDU. This was a successful party in a successful country and the very nature of West Germany, founded and defended by the Western allies, forced its leaders to think in international terms. The CDU was at the centre of an alliance of Christian Democrat groups (the European People's Party) that eventually contested elections to the European parliament in 1979, but it was also interested in a wider alliance of Centre-Right groups (which would include parties that were not Christian Democratic and countries that were not part of the EEC). Hurd himself became a moving force behind this latter group, which was eventually christened the European Democratic Union (EDU).[11] Debate about the value of 'Christian democracy' rumbled on amongst the more thoughtful Tories for many years:[12] Hurd was to describe himself as a 'Christian democrat' when he stood for the leadership of the Conservative Party in 1990. Conservatives seem to have regarded the EDU as a success. Thatcher met Helmut Kohl, the leader of the CDU, for the first time in 1976. Hurd's diary entry on this meeting indicated some of the reasons why there might in the long run be tension between Kohl and Thatcher. The former, Hurd wrote, had 'very much Ted's philosophy of human nature'.[13] However, at the time and for many years to come, Thatcher seems to have admired Kohl. Indeed, in the 1980s she was to describe Kohl, along with herself and Reagan, as the 'Trinity' of Cold War leaders.[14] In an address to the EDU in April 1978, Thatcher managed to make the British Conservative Party sound remarkably like a continental Christian

Democratic party – she even emphasized the role that trade unionists played in the party.[15] The centrist language that the Conservatives often spoke during the late 1970s owed a great deal to the need to maintain good relations with continental parties. Thatcher drew explicit links between the association of European political parties and the association of European states (and implied that she thought that both processes were good):

> It is nearly two years since I spoke at the Congress of the C.D.U. in Hanover. This was one of the first major European commitments which I undertook after becoming Leader of the Conservative Party, and it made a deep impression on me. I came home from Germany confirmed in my belief that the main inspiration behind the European ideal was political rather than economic – and convinced that the Parties of the Centre and Right in Europe had so much in common and so much at risk that they must learn to work together more effectively.[16]

Conservative enthusiasm for links with continental Europe went with enthusiasm for capitalism. The party's leaders were painfully aware that productivity was higher in France and Germany than in Britain and that, in some ways, capitalism was more secure in these countries. Enoch Powell said that the British bourgeoisie was 'bolting for Europe' because it had lost faith in its ability to defend capitalism with its own resources in its own country. Thatcher referred to the German president, Helmut Schmidt, as 'that rare person, a Socialist who believes in the market economy';[17] she even claimed in 1976 that some Communist parties of continental western Europe were less 'extreme' than the Labour Party.[18] Even more importantly, support for Europe went with opposition to Communism. Thatcher became leader of the Conservative Party at a time when the Soviet threat seemed to be increasing. Soviet protégés took power in Vietnam and Angola. Discussions amongst Conservative leaders involved much agonizing about the weakness of the West, and about the alleged links between foreign threat and internal subversion. Under these circumstances, the European Community was important partly because it underwrote an alliance of west European states that were grouped under the American aegis. Even during her anti-European old age, Thatcher continued to stress that Jean Monnet had been a vigorous supporter of the Atlantic alliance.[19] Thatcher was very conscious that West Germany was the front line of the Cold War in Europe. Her speech to the conference of the German CDU on 25 May 1976 was largely devoted to calling for both military and intellectual defence against Communism.[20] In her article of 1978 for a Hamburg newspaper, Thatcher talked of the alliance between Conservative and Christian Democrat parties in western Europe as rooted in the need to contain 'Marxism'.[21] Sometimes, indeed, she described the whole EEC in these terms. After a meeting with Thatcher in 1979, Roy Jenkins noted that she was 'thinking always a little too much of the EEC and NATO as two bodies that ought to be amalgamated'.[22]

The Cold War got colder in the late 1970s and early 1980s. The Soviet Union invaded Afghanistan on Christmas Day 1979, and in 1981 the Communist government of Poland declared martial law in a bid to contain the Solidarity trade union. The Thatcher government's response to these events was to strengthen its links with the 'Western alliance', and 'Western allies' were, in large measure, European ones.

America was the richest and most powerful of the NATO countries, but Thatcher did not initially regard the United States with unqualified admiration. American society in the 1970s did not provide a model that many English Conservatives – often worried by crime, racial tension and social disintegration in their own country – were keen to imitate. As her party's education spokesman, Thatcher had suggested that American schools epitomized all the dangers of comprehensive education.[23] Thatcher disliked the policies of détente that had been pursued by Henry Kissinger in the early 1970s, and she did not have good relations with Jimmy Carter, the American president from 1976 until 1980. Relations were, of course, better once Ronald Reagan entered the White House, but they were not without tension. West Europeans and Americans clashed when the Americans wanted to impose economic sanctions on the Soviet Union and in particular to prevent the construction of a pipeline to transport Soviet gas to western Europe. Over sanctions, Thatcher was strongly in the west European camp. Debates on American missile deployment also brought out a specifically European dimension to Thatcher's strategic thinking. She was against Reagan's Strategic Defence Initiative and against plans to reduce the number of long-range nuclear weapons, because she felt that such policies might leave Europe without American support. American short-range cruise missiles did lead the Thatcher government to take a pro-American stance (to an extent that was unpopular with the British electorate), but these policies also brought Thatcher closer to other west European governments. The missiles were, after all, being deployed very largely in Germany. Furthermore, it was the Socialist, but anti-Communist, François Mitterrand (president of a country that was in the EEC but not in NATO) who pronounced the most robust defence of cruise missiles – when he told his own compatriots in 1983 that 'The missiles are in the East and the pacifists are in the West.'

Why, then, did Thatcher's attitude to European integration change during the 1980s? Money had something to do with it. The Thatcher government made much of the fact that British contributions to the community budget were disproportionately large, especially in view of the fact that Britain was now poorer than France or Germany. During her first few years in office, Thatcher devoted much of her energy to negotiating a rebate on British contributions; her determination on this point disconcerted even some of her more abrasive ministers. It is indicative of the extent to which the EEC was seen in terms of anti-Communism that some of her own backbenchers, men usually seen as being on the Left of the party, implied that Thatcher was wrong to 'divide' the Western allies at a time when the Soviet peril was so high.[24]

More generally the very satisfaction that Thatcher came to feel about her own achievements in Britain made her less admiring of continental Europe. Before 1979 British Conservatives had pointed to Germany as a country where unions accepted capitalism more easily than their English counterparts. This seemed less attractive after, say, 1985, when British unions themselves had been so clearly humbled. Furthermore, Thatcher came to see the European Community itself as a means by which statism or corporatism might be imposed on member countries. The most striking passage in the Bruges speech was this: 'We have not successfully rolled back the frontiers of the state in Britain, only to see them reimposed at a European level, with a European super state exercising a new dominance from Brussels.'

Finally, changes in the Communist world affected Thatcher's attitude to Europe. In late 1984 her aides hunted around for a Soviet leader from the younger generation with whom the prime minister might talk. They vaguely thought that Viktor Grishin, the Moscow party secretary, or Grigory Romanov, from Leningrad, might fit the bill. As it turned out, the first person to respond to their invitations was Mikhail Gorbachev, recently appointed to the Politburo with special responsibility for agriculture. The meeting between Gorbachev and Thatcher was a success and Thatcher concluded it with the statement that she and Gorbachev could 'do business together'. Just a few months later, Gorbachev was general secretary of the Soviet Communist Party.

Reform in the Soviet Union had implications for Thatcher's attitude to the rest of Europe. West European unity had mattered to her largely because it promised to help contain the Soviet Union; if the Soviet Union ceased to be a threat, European unity mattered less. Changes in the Communist world also opened up the possibility of a new kind of Europe. Even before the advent of Gorbachev, Thatcher and her ministers had made discreet overtures to the Communist-ruled nations of central Europe. Hungary, the most liberal state in the Warsaw Pact, was the first target for the British government's attempts at seduction. Janos Kadar, the general secretary of the Hungarian Communist Party, was invited to Britain and Thatcher visited Hungary. Later Poland, which Thatcher visited in 1988, became the most important focus of Britain's attention. The shift was significant, perhaps more so than Thatcher's advisers realized at the time. In Hungary, 'reform' meant primarily a move towards free-market economics and was conducted under the aegis of the Communist government. In Poland, 'reform' meant the Solidarity trade union. It was less economic (the union defended the Gdansk shipyards at a time when heavy industry was being shut down in Britain), more nationalistic and less likely to be contained within a system dominated by the Soviet Union.

Whatever the broad reasons for Thatcher's change of emphasis over Europe, the change was not quick or clear-cut. Many of her closest associates seem to have been genuinely perplexed by her behaviour during the second half of the 1980s. In late 1985 Thatcher attended the Luxembourg conference which led to the signing of the Single European Act, by which European governments ceded some of their powers to the Commission. She claimed, in retrospect, that 'The Single European Act, contrary to my intentions and my understanding of formal undertakings given at the time, had provided new scope for the European Commission and the European Court to press forward in the direction of centralization.'[25] Howe, Thatcher's foreign secretary, and Charles Powell, her private secretary for foreign affairs, men who recalled matters from very different perspectives, both insisted that Thatcher had a clear sense of what she wanted out of the Luxembourg discussions, though Powell did believe that the Commission subsequently took advantage of agreements that they had secured, and that 'we should have been more alert to the Commission's duplicity in some of these matters'.[26]

Thatcher seems to have gone along with the Single European Act because it removed so many barriers to free trade in Europe. Much of the work to prepare for this had, in fact, been done by Arthur Cockfield, who had been one of Thatcher's ministers from 1979 until he was dispatched to Brussels as a European commissioner in 1984. Howe defined this as 'Thatcherism on a European scale', and argued that the concessions that Britain made to secure this agreement were calculated and moderate.[27]

Even on the national currency, Thatcher's position had not always been inflexible. Ever since the 1970s a number of European currencies had been linked to the Exchange Rate Mechanism, which prevented currencies from moving against each other by more than a certain margin. In 1978 Thatcher had mocked the Labour government for its refusal to take sterling into the ERM, and pledged that the Conservatives would do so, when the time was right. In practice, the matter was not much discussed during the early years of the thatcher government – though Lawson, as financial secretary to the treasury, raised the possibility of joining the ERM in June 1981,[28] and Thatcher apparently asked him, when the pound had seemed about to fall to parity with the dollar in January 1985, why sterling was not already in the ERM and thus 'protected from all this'.[29]

During the second Thatcher government, support for the ERM amongst Thatcher's ministers became more vocal. At a key meeting in November 1985, John Biffen was the only minister who spoke against the proposal, but Thatcher vetoed it outright. Attitudes to sterling were to haunt her for the next five years. Lawson believed that, even if Germany was no longer a micro-economic model for Britain to emulate, she could still be a macro-economic one, and that tying sterling to the Deutschmark might create 'international monetarism'. To this end, he ensured that the value of sterling shadowed that of the Deutschmark during the late 1980s. The policy was never announced in any official way and Thatcher claimed that she found out about it only when

journalists from the *Financial Times* showed her a graph that
illustrated the movements of the two currencies. Lawson's policy
with regard to the Deutschmark broke down in the spring of
1988 under financial pressure from the markets and political
pressure from the prime minister. However, Lawson and Howe
finally faced Thatcher down on the eve of the Madrid summit
in 1989. Apparently with threats of resignation, they forced her
to concede that sterling should now move towards entering the
Exchange Rate Mechanism.

Though monetary union became important to Thatcher, it was
not an issue on which there was a clear-cut division between
Thatcherites and their opponents in cabinet. Norman Tebbit,
usually seen as Thatcherite and anti-European, had to everyone's
surprise supported joining the ERM in November 1985. Howe
and Lawson – both Thatcherite opponents of Thatcher on
monetary issues – did not agree about the most desirable outcome.
Howe was in favour of creating a single currency eventually;
Lawson merely wanted to achieve greater stability in the exchange
rate.

In any case, arguments over Europe became intertwined with
other disputes – often of a rather petty nature. Cockburn was
dismissed, partly because Thatcher saw his support for European
tax harmonization as a sign that he had 'gone native' in Brussels.
Jacques Delors, the president of the European Commission, became
a particular target for Thatcher's ire. Delors was a Socialist and a
trade unionist – though one whose links to the Catholic Church
probably made him the closest thing that Fifth Republic France
had to a Christian Democrat. Thatcher had a high opinion of
Delors's ability, which may be why she was annoyed by his public
statements and especially by two of his speeches in 1988. In one,
he claimed that 80 per cent of legislation affecting member states
would soon be enacted by the European parliament; in another,
delivered to the British Trade Union Congress, he urged unions
to undertake collective bargaining at European level.

All of this fed into Thatcher's Bruges speech of September 1988. Howe had originally urged her to make the speech because he hoped that it would give her the opportunity to lay out a slightly more pro-European position – though, as drafts of the speech were passed from the Foreign Office to Downing Street and back, it became clear that Howe was going to be disappointed. Alan Clark wrote: 'by their [the Foreign Office's] interference and provocation they have turned a relatively minor ceremonial chore into what could now well be a milestone in redefining our position towards the Community.'[30]

The Bruges speech took up many characteristic Thatcher themes. It insisted Europe was older than the European Community. It also drew attention to a Europe that extended beyond the members of the Community and, indeed, into the Communist world: 'We shall always look on Warsaw, Prague and Budapest as great European cities.' It insisted on the importance of national cultures. It urged that the Community should be based on a minimum of regulation – 'we in Britain would fight attempts to introduce collectivism and corporatism at the European level – although what people would wish to do in their own countries is a matter for them'. A large part of the speech was devoted to insistence on the continuing importance of NATO and nuclear weapons.

Like many of Thatcher's most notorious pronouncements, the speech was notable for its tone rather than for containing any concrete proposals for a change in policy. Nothing in it implied that the EEC should not exist or that Britain should not be a member of it. One diplomat noted that, with a slightly different spin and in a slightly different context, parts of the speech might have been interpreted as 'pro-European'. There was no marked change in British policy after Bruges and there seemed to be an uncomfortable tension between what everyone now took to be Thatcher's private beliefs and her government's actions. Geoffrey Howe likened his time as foreign secretary during this period to the experience of a vicar's wife whose husband has said that he does not believe in God.

If Thatcher was not pro-European, what was she? Her speech was applauded by Enoch Powell and John Biffen; Howe suggested that Thatcher had revealed some true 'Powellite' identity. However, Powell and Biffen had both voted against British accession to the EEC; they were both clear that defence of the 'Nation' should be put above the defence of free-market economics. Powell associated opposition to the EEC with fierce anti-Americanism. Biffen associated opposition to Franco-German domination with a call for a Europe that would be wider, looser and somehow less worthy – when the EEC first began to expand beyond its original core, he had implied that he rather welcomed the fact that the 'European club' was becoming less like the Athenaeum and more like the Playboy.[31] Thatcher did not really go along with either of these visions.

The Bruges speech contained a revealing line: 'Utopia never comes, because we know that we should not like it if it did.' In some ways, the greatest problem for Thatcher was precisely that Europe did seem to totter on the brink of a kind of Utopia in 1989 and 1990. Thatcher's whole vision of the world had been formed during the Cold War. Her own success owed much to the sense that she had been particularly resolute in standing up to the Soviet Union. The Cold War had also meant that Britain was able to use its military power to increase its leverage in Europe; during a sterling crisis in late 1986, Thatcher had threatened to withdraw the Rhine Army if the Bundesbank did not buy pounds.[32] The end of the Cold War, however, raised awkward questions about what the victors might really want. This was particularly noticeable with regard to the issue that absorbed much of Thatcher's attention in early 1990 – the reunification of Germany. Ostensibly, reunification had been the aim of the Western allies for many years. But, as late as October 1987, even those Foreign Office discussions that were specifically initiated to plan for reunification did so on the assumption that it would not happen for many years. An official remarked that Thatcher had always been in favour of German reunification 'as long as it was not a realistic prospect'.[33] With the fall of Communist rule in the German Democratic Republic, reunification suddenly seemed all too possible. America and, after some hesitation, France supported it. Thatcher was unhappy, though there was, as it happened, little that she could do to stop Germany from reunifying, or to prevent the unified state from being admitted to the EEC and NATO. She made much of German refusal to guarantee its frontiers with Poland. Nicholas Ridley had to resign from her cabinet after giving a tactless interview in which he said that handing the European Union over to a unified Germany under Kohl would be like handing it over 'to Hitler'.

In two respects, Thatcher's position was contradictory, or at least ambiguous. First, she had always insisted that European unity should not come at the expense of relations with the United States (it was a point that she had made emphatically at Bruges), and yet her own relations with America took a turn for the worse in 1988, as Ronald Reagan left the White House and was replaced by George Bush. She was particularly discomfited by the fact that Bush turned out to be a supporter of German reunification. Secondly, Thatcher was keen to help Gorbachev in the Soviet Union and argued that German reunification might weaken his position. British diplomats complained that their own country was 'more pro-Russian than the Russians'.[34] However, she was also worried about the prospect that western Europe might prove too weak in the face of some future incarnation of the Soviet Union, and consequently she was hostile to any suggestion that Germany might be disarmed or distanced from NATO. Personal relations played a role in Thatcher's attitude. Her growing dislike for Kohl was one aspect, but so too was her respect for Mitterrand and Gorbachev. One British diplomat maliciously recalled: 'Mrs Thatcher, as she noted interestingly in her memoirs, was hoping for a sort of alliance between her and

Gorbachev and Mitterrand in order somehow or other to stop something or other.'[35]

Was there such a thing as Thatcherite, rather than Thatcher's, policy on Europe? Some of her admirers (Tebbit and Ridley) thought there was, and rooted this in an Anglo-Saxon concern for intellectual clarity and legal principle. There were some wonderfully confused references to racial characteristics – Lord Young thought that Helmut Kohl had a typically Latin outlook. Thatcher's enemies also came to believe that anti-Europeanism was hardwired into Thatcherism. Stuart Hall and Martin Jacques wrote:

> Since the whole project has been hinged, ideologically, around the narrowest, most racist, exclusive and backward-looking definition of English national identity, and focused on the ancient symbols of empire and nation, hearth and family, kin and culture, the idea that Thatcherism could lead the nation to embrace a European identity and future always lacked conviction.[36]

It was wrong to say that there had been a consistent Thatcherite line on Europe and silly to say that Thatcher's attitude to Europe was rooted in racism (there were, in any case, plenty of racists in the European parliament), but Hall and Jacques were on to something when they suggested that Europe exposed the 'contradictions' of Thatcherism. There had always been a certain conflict between the populist element of Thatcherism, often concerned with non-economic issues, and the governmentalist element, which had often meant the willingness to take unpopular economic measures. Thatcher had contained this conflict by implying that on certain issues she was a populist opponent of her own front bench. This approach worked with regard to short-term issues (such as interest rates in the early 1980s or the pace of trade union reform); it worked with issues that were seen as unimportant (such as whether or not to continue sanctions against South Africa); and it worked on issues that were not matters of party policy (such as the death penalty). The tactic could not, however, work on Europe. Thatcher could hardly disassociate herself from the Single European Act, which she had signed; she could hardly claim that the question of sterling's relation to other European currencies was a peripheral matter and, if she had stayed in power for long enough, she could not have avoided facing the simple question of whether or not she wanted Britain to stay in the European Union.

In the short term, Thatcher's European policy distanced her from the two men who had been most influential in her governments during the 1980s – Howe and Lawson – and brought her closer to people who played more minor roles in British politics – Alan Clark believed that he was helping her to compose 'Bruges II' in early 1990, though he also recognized that he might be helping her to 'dig her own grave'.[37] During her early years in power, Thatcher had devoted much of her energy to domestic policy and left much diplomacy to the Foreign Office. She had also focused in all her policies on what was concrete and attainable rather than on grand abstractions. During her last years in power, Thatcher changed. Her distrust of the Foreign Office, which dated back at least to the Falklands War, was now more openly expressed. She thought more about world affairs and less about domestic ones. Her last six months in office were framed by two grand international summits (in Houston and Paris). She also began to look to the long sweep of history. She cited Paul Kennedy's book on the Great Powers to an interviewer from the *Wall Street Journal*,[38] and she convoked a group of historians to Chequers to discuss the possible consequences of German unification in March 1990. The minutes of this meeting, quickly leaked to the press, listed 'abiding' German characteristics in alphabetical order: 'angst, aggressiveness, assertiveness, bullying, egotism, inferiority complex, sentimentality'.[39]

Thatcher opened the Chequers meeting with historians by saying that 'Europe had come to the end of the post-war period.' However, whilst others interpreted this end as meaning that they should move forward and concentrate on things that had happened since the fall of the Berlin Wall, Thatcher seemed to feel that the pre-1945 past was now pushing its way out of the history books and back into contemporary politics. Welcoming Vaclav Havel to Britain, as the president of an independent Czechoslovakia, she expressed her shame at the Munich agreement. More than any major politician, she wanted Britain to make some formal statement about the Nazi murder of the European Jews.

Thatcher's reinvention of herself as an actor in world history, rather than in British politics, came at an inopportune time. She liked to claim that she had 'prophesied' the fall of Communism and the end of the Cold War. The truth was, however, that the Cold War had helped Britain to conceal – perhaps mainly from itself – its long-term decline in power. Thatcher's own prestige had owed much to the perception that she was particularly resolute in standing up to the Soviet Union and particularly loyal to the United States. As Communism fell, these qualities mattered less. Britain now had to face the fact that it was, as it had been for decades, a middle-ranking European power.

Chapter 11

THE FALL

One is, after all, finite.

Margaret Thatcher, 24 October 1989[1]

Thatcherism's ending has to be explained too. Otherwise it might seem as if it was a gigantic experiment, which ultimately failed – like some vast science fiction concept which missed out one vital consideration and was never heard of again.

Nicholas Ridley, 1991[2]

I wish that cow would resign.

Intercepted telephone call from Richard Needham (minister at the Northern Ireland Office), 11 November 1990[3]

Margaret Thatcher never lost an election. Under her, the Conservative Party won parliamentary majorities in 1979, 1983 and 1987. On the last of these occasions, the Conservative Party obtained a majority of 101 seats – a smaller margin of victory than in the 1983 election but still bigger than the one the Conservative Party had enjoyed in 1979. Winning another large majority without the patriotic surge of 1983 and after the sharp dip in Tory fortunes that followed the Westland affair in 1986 (see below) was impressive. In retrospect the victory of 1987 carried intimations of trouble. Apparent Tory invincibility, and the more general sense of upper-middle-class prosperity, made even the government's supporters feel uneasy. Peregrine Worsthorne, editor of the *Sunday Telegraph*, complained of 'bourgeois triumphalism'. Furthermore, the Conservatives had been elected on an unusually detailed manifesto (very different from those of 1979 and 1983). The old hands in the party who remembered their manifesto of 1970 (or, for that matter, those who had bothered to read the Labour manifesto of 1983) thought that such specific commitments were unwise. Thatcher herself believed that the manifesto was the best ever produced by the Conservative Party – though the fact that the party had been so explicit about its intentions does not seem to have done it much good when the electorate began to turn against its policies.

Thatcher also won all the internal elections that she fought in her party. On the three occasions when she stood for the leadership of the Conservative Party (in 1975, 1989 and 1990) she obtained more votes than any other candidate – though on the last of these occasions her support fell short of the absolute majority that would have prevented a second round of the contest, and, as Thatcher eventually recognized, this left her too weak to continue as leader. The nature of her political demise encouraged some to hint darkly that she had been the victim of a conspiracy by ambitious rivals. Thatcher herself became convinced that her colleagues had behaved badly. This belief soured her relations with her successor, and overshadowed the Conservative Party for a decade. Actually, there is not much evidence of a conspiracy; the various actors in Thatcher's downfall do not seem to have worked together. It *is* true that many Conservatives wanted Thatcher to resign as leader, and that at least one of them believed that he would be the right person to replace her. However, few Conservatives wanted her to leave in the circumstances in which she did. Some came to regret that she had resigned – not because they thought that she could realistically have resurrected her leadership of the party, but rather because they came to believe that the party would have been better off if she had been allowed to go down to defeat in a general election.

Thatcher's biggest problem was not her enemies but her friends. She was increasingly isolated from ordinary life. She was, especially after the Brighton bomb of 1984, surrounded by bodyguards. It was probably twenty years since she had last had a conversation with anyone who did not know who she was. A group of advisers provided her with much of her information. The two most important members of her entourage were Bernard Ingham, her press secretary, and Charles Powell, who had become her private secretary for foreign affairs in 1983, though he sometimes preferred to be known as her foreign policy adviser. Ingham and Powell were different kinds of men. The former had spent his early years in Hebden Bridge, Yorkshire and worked his way up through jobs on local newspapers to a staff post on the *Guardian*. He had been a member of the Labour Party and, before working for Thatcher, his most significant post had been with Tony Benn.[4] Powell was a diplomat and married to a glamorous Italian socialite. What he and Ingham had in common was their peculiarly close relation to the prime minister. Both men were nominally civil servants but had, in practice, escaped from the usual routine of the civil service – one colleague from the Foreign Office said that Powell was as much a 'courtier' as a clerk.[5] Nigel Lawson wrote that Powell considered that his job was not to challenge Thatcher's prejudices but to 'refine the language in which they were expressed'.[6] Powell and Ingham resisted attempts to move them on (an increasingly desperate Foreign Office had tried to tempt Powell out of Downing Street with the offer of various embassies). Both men probably knew that their official career would pretty much end with Thatcher's departure, and both knew that the prestige and contacts they had acquired would serve them well in the outside world.

Advisers sometimes crossed swords with ministers. Powell seems to have encouraged Thatcher to redraft the Bruges speech in terms that were bound to annoy the foreign secretary (see chapter 10). Ingham had provoked a run on the pound in 1985, when he had told journalists that the government was not attached to any particular value of sterling, thus arousing the ire of Nigel Lawson.[7] Tim Bell, an advertising executive who remained close to Thatcher personally even when he left the agency Saatchi and Saatchi that held the Tory account, quarrelled with Norman Tebbit, the chairman of the Conservative Party, during the 1987 election campaign.

The adviser at the centre of Thatcher's most spectacular row with her senior ministers was the economist Alan Walters. Unlike Powell or Ingham, Walters was not a civil servant and not a fixture in Downing Street. He had advised Thatcher informally in opposition and worked in Downing Street for a time in the early 1980s before taking up an academic post in America. In 1989 he returned when Thatcher was in a state of undeclared war with her chancellor over the exchange rate. Walters was from a humble background and had made his reputation with work on a quite specialized area – the economics of transport. All this aroused much scorn from the Keynesians of Trinity and King's, and a little condescension from some of the grander monetarists. Lawson resented the fact that the prime minister was taking advice on the economy from someone other than himself. In October 1989 Walters indicated that he did not believe in the Exchange Rate Mechanism, which Lawson and Howe had just persuaded Thatcher to agree to join. Lawson demanded that Thatcher dismiss her adviser. When she refused, Lawson resigned – though Walters also resigned immediately afterwards.

What of the cabinet itself? By late 1990 no one talked of 'wets' and 'dries'. Thatcher's most bitter opponents in Cabinet – Pym, Prior, Gilmour and Soames – had gone, but so had her most fiercely loyal supporters – Tebbit and Ridley. There was a technocratic flavour to Thatcher's last government. In the acknowledgements to *Britain Can Work* – his anti-Thatcherite tract of 1983 – Gilmour had thanked three Tory MPs. By 1989 all three of them were in the government,* and one was in the cabinet. This did not mean that they had changed their views or that Thatcher had changed hers; it simply showed that senior Conservatives had in large measure given up discussing what their policies ought to be and now dedicated their energies to seeing how policies might be implemented and sold to the public.

Increasingly ministers were chosen because of their perceived competence rather than because of their ideological sympathy. For much of the later 1980s, Thatcher's favourite minister was David Young. Young had trained as a solicitor and then made a fortune in business. He was closer to being one of Thatcher's advisers than he was to being an ordinary minister – he had been parachuted into the House of Lords without having held a seat in the Commons. He entered the cabinet in 1984 and became secretary of state for trade and industry in 1987. Thatcher said of him: 'Others bring me problems; David brings me solutions.' In practice the 'solution' that Young preached most fervently was 'enterprise', which on close examination turned out to mean producing a lot of expensive advertisements to show how companies would flourish if they were given a certain indefinable 'whosh' that would be imparted by reading glossy brochures from the DTI, itself briefly renamed the Department of Enterprise. Young resigned to pursue his own business interests in July 1989. His place as Thatcher's favourite purveyor of 'solutions' was taken by Kenneth Baker. Baker had entered the cabinet in 1985 and become chairman of the Conservative Party in July 1989. 'Technology' had for a time been his own magic cure for the nation's ills, and, in the early 1980s, whilst the battles over monetarism raged in cabinet, Baker had invented a job for himself as minister for technology and spent much of his time getting photographed with clumsy-looking pre-Amstrad computers.

* Richard Needham, Chris Patten and John Patten.

By the time Thatcher resigned, Douglas Hurd was the longest-serving member of her cabinet. The son and grandson of Tory MPs, Hurd had been educated at Eton and Trinity College Cambridge, joined the Foreign Office and then worked for Edward Heath before entering parliament in 1974. He was associated with those who wanted to modernize the Conservative Party (such as his friend Chris Patten) whilst also thinking of himself as rooted in the traditional values of Anglicanism (he was one of the few senior Tories who cared about the Church) and rural England. On a personal level he did not much like the new men who began to rise up the Conservative Party under Thatcher: 'stiff-collared accountants from Stratford on Avon'.[8] Hurd's position, however, might better be characterized as 'post-Thatcherite' than 'anti-Thatcherite'. He entered parliament shortly before Thatcher took over the party and he joined the cabinet only after Thatcher and her allies had won the economic debates of the early 1980s. He had sympathized with the 'wets' and advised Ian Gilmour to resign rather than wait to be sacked. Hurd himself, however, never seems to have contemplated resignation. He worked within the Thatcherite order, sometimes achieving concessions by stealth rather than confrontation. The fact that he never held a position in an economic ministry kept him out of the firing line, and he seems to have found it useful to cultivate the impression that he knew nothing of economics – though his business career since leaving politics suggests that he was not as innocent as he liked to pretend.

Thatcher's last appointments were all men who could at best be seen as efficient implementers of her policy rather than passionate believers in her vision. Tony Newton, who took over Social Security in July 1989, or Chris Patten, who became secretary of state for the environment in the same month, were known to be on the Left of the party. Thatcher's last appointment of all – William Waldegrave – was also seen as being on the Left, though he managed to maintain good relations with both Enoch Powell and Edward Heath. He was an old Etonian fellow of All Souls from an aristocratic family, who had once been engaged to Lord Rothschild's daughter. It looked as though the ghost of Ian Gilmour had come back to haunt the cabinet table – though Thatcher described Waldegrave as 'a sort of Norman St John-Stevas without jokes'.[9]

Thatcher's own view of her ministerial colleagues was an odd one. She could be a bully. Paddy Ashdown recorded her behaviour at the ceremony of remembrance in November 1988 in his diary: 'Maggie fussed around, bullied us into two lines ... then she proceeded to go down the lined-up Cabinet like a sergeant major, inspecting new recruits, straightening the Foreign Secretary's tie, flicking specks of dust off the Chancellor's coat etc.'[10]

Thatcher was not always able or willing to reward loyalty. She had made, and then disposed of, a succession of protégés. Cecil Parkinson had once been her favourite, but she had not been able to keep him in her government after it was revealed, in 1983, that he had broken a promise to marry his pregnant mistress. Parkinson came back to the cabinet in 1987, but he was now badly weakened. A man who might once have been chancellor or foreign secretary had to content himself with being secretary of state for energy and then transport. Furthermore, Parkinson's behaviour – his undignified return to his wife rather than his original affair – had made him look ridiculous, even in the eyes of his admirers. Parkinson knew that he had nothing going for him except Thatcher's affection. He did not try to stay in the cabinet after her resignation.

Tebbit too had been weakened by personal misfortune. He had been injured in the IRA attack at Brighton in 1984, which had left his wife crippled. After this, he had less energy for politics and, having returned to the front-rank as chairman of the party, he stepped down in 1987. Tebbit remained loyal to Thatcher – though some Tories had the uncomfortable sense that she, always dubious about any minister with an independent power base, was not completely loyal to him. Tebbit refused Thatcher's invitation to rejoin her cabinet, as education secretary, in early November 1990.

Other men rose and fell with disconcerting speed. Leon Brittan had owed his rise largely to Thatcher's favour. He had entered the cabinet, as chief secretary to the treasury in 1981, just seven years after being elected to parliament. Two years later, he was home secretary. He had seemed almost slavish in his willingness to do the bidding of his mistress – solemnly repeating her absurd view that people who refused to denounce terrorism in Ulster should be 'denied the oxygen of publicity' and calling for the restoration of the death penalty, when many believed that he was privately against it. However, Thatcher demoted Brittan as soon as he seemed to fail at the Home Office, and then sacrificed him during the Westland crisis of early 1986. John Moore was the next minister to rise on the strength of Thatcher's patronage, and was talked of as a possible successor. He too entered the Commons in 1974, joined the cabinet as minister for transport in 1986 and became minister for health and social security in the following year. However, the health part of his portfolio was taken away from him after just over a year, and a year after that he was out of the cabinet for good.

Ministers were moved around like pawns on a chess board. John Major, Thatcher's last protégé and the one who had the dubious good fortune of holding the parcel when the music stopped, rose from almost nowhere to occupy two of the most important offices of state (foreign secretary and then chancellor of the exchequer) in the space of less than six months. Thatcher did not like being reminded of her own political mortality and, for this reason, being her anointed dauphin was always an uncomfortable position. She constantly implied that the only potential heirs were 'not ready yet'. In her memoirs, she claimed that she had become convinced that her successor must be drawn from a generation younger than her own, but her definition of 'young' in this context was arbitrary – the 'younger generation' included Hurd (born in 1930) but not Heseltine (born in 1933).[11]

Two politicians had partly alleviated the impact of Thatcher's isolation. William Whitelaw was useful to her because he possessed the qualities that she lacked. He was popular and well connected in the party and particularly close to those sections of it – aristocrats, Heathites and people with liberal views on law and order – who sometimes felt estranged from Thatcher. He was suspicious of ideology and good at listening to people. On the other hand, he was also a man with a strong sense of duty to the leader, as he had shown in 1974, and, at least after the Falklands War, he never seems to have considered supporting any move to dislodge Thatcher. He was the only major politician who could argue with Thatcher without making her doubt his loyalty, and he saw it as his job to head off dangerous initiatives and to maintain amicable working relations between ministers. Whitelaw, however, was ill and old. He went into the House of Lords in 1983, and withdrew from the cabinet in 1988.

Much was also made of Ian Gow. Gow, born in 1937, sometimes seemed to be a caricature of a particular kind of Tory MP. When he first stood for parliament in 1966, *The Times* wrote that he wore his 'public school manner as prominently as his rosette'.[12] He had, like Whitelaw and many of Thatcher's associates, been educated at Winchester. He had performed his national service in the cavalry, and then worked as a solicitor at Joynson-Hicks (a firm founded by a Conservative Home Secretary who had himself been something of a caricature). Gow was Thatcher's parliamentary private secretary from 1979 to 1983 and served as a link between her and the Conservative back benches – planting questions, massaging egos and keeping an eye on potential opposition. As a Powellite free marketeer, he was sympathetic to the government's aims and he was fiercely loyal to Thatcher personally. Gow, however, ceased to be Thatcher's parliamentary private secretary in 1983 and took office as a junior minister, first for housing and construction and then at the Treasury. He resigned from the government in 1985, in protest at the Anglo-Irish agreement. On 30 July 1990 he was killed by an IRA bomb that had been planted under his car.

Some thought that Gow's political antennae would have saved

Thatcher from some of the faux pas that she made during her last two years in office, and, particularly, that he might have healed the rift between her and Geoffrey Howe – Gow was a friend of Howe and had managed his leadership bid in 1975. However, it is hard to see how Gow could have remained as Thatcher's parliamentary private secretary for ever, and his access to the prime minister had always depended on holding this post. Personal friendship might have healed the Thatcher/Howe rift but it is equally possible that Gow's own Eurosceptic opinions would have made things worse, or that his loyalty would simply have made Thatcher more impervious to criticism. It is not, in any case, clear what Gow would have wanted to do. In May 1990 Alan Clark and Gow talked in the smoking room of the House of Commons. After the conversation, Clark wrote in his diary: 'What could we do to succour the Lady? Do we even want to?'[13] In one sense at least, Gow's assassination certainly damaged Thatcher: it brought a by-election at Eastbourne in October 1990, which the Tories lost.

All of this tied in with wider problems that afflicted the Conservatives during their last few years in power. The first of these, discussed in a previous chapter, was Europe. Within a few years, the role of Europe in British electoral politics was turned on its head. It went from being an issue that gave the, mainly pro-European, Conservatives an advantage over a divided Labour Party to being an issue that divided the Conservatives themselves. Disputes over Europe underlay the resignations of Nigel Lawson in 1989 and Geoffrey Howe in 1990. These resignations were bad blows. Both men made carefully judged resignation speeches in the House of Commons that were designed to damage Thatcher. Howe's speech contained the line 'It is now time for others to consider their own response to the tragic conflict of loyalties with which I myself have wrestled perhaps for too long.' It was hard to interpret this as anything other than a call for Thatcher's removal from office.

The changing role of Europe in British politics was in part linked to the fact that the European Community of 1989 was different from that of 1979. However, it was not inevitable that these changes would have the particular impact that they did on the Conservative Party nor that they should prove so damaging to Thatcher's position. After all, Thatcher had gone along with the Single European Act and the possibility of British entry into the European Exchange Rate Mechanism. What annoyed her pro-European colleagues was the tone of her remarks, especially those she made off-the-cuff, rather than the specific policies she advocated.

The second problem that afflicted the Tories was public service reform, particularly of the National Health Service. The cost of health care was increasing (because of ever more expensive treatments and an ageing population) and the difficulty of managing health care costs would have faced any government in the late 1980s. However, health was a difficult issue for a right-wing Conservative government, for the same reasons that defence had been a difficult issue for a left-wing Labour Party. The electorate was likely to suspect that any move to control costs reflected a lack of commitment to fund the service at all. The appointment of Kenneth Clarke as secretary of state for health in July 1988 did not make things any easier. Thatcher recognized that Clarke was not on her wing of the party but argued that he was 'an energetic and persuasive bruiser, very useful in a brawl or an election'.[14] She might have added that Clarke's breezy bad manners made him an awkward man to have on your side if you were trying to explain the need for complicated reform of a popular public service. In 1988 ambulance crews struck for higher pay. It was probably the first major strike to attract wide public support since 1972; Clarke's tone, and particularly his description of the strikers as 'glorified taxi drivers', grated.

The third problem for the government in the late 1980s was local government finance. Money for local government had been raised by charging home owners and businessmen 'rates' in proportion to the value of the property that they owned. Thatcher, and some of her supporters, had always disliked the rates, believing them to be unfair because only part of the population paid (especially unfair because ratepayers were likely to be drawn from 'our people'). Thatcher was deeply rooted in the politics of municipal resentment – her own father had represented a ratepayers' alliance in Grantham.

Resentment of the rates was nothing new in the Conservative Party. There was much talk of 'little old ladies' living on their own who paid the same rates as large families living next door to them – this talk was particularly common in Tory constituency associations, which tended to contain a lot of old ladies.[15] Various alternatives to the rates had been discussed, but nothing had come of them. Thatcher had talked of abolition during the general election of October 1974, but, when she got into power, she was in no hurry to act in this matter. When Michael Heseltine said in 1979 that the revaluation of rateable properties would generate discontent, Thatcher briskly responded that the way to avoid this was not to revalue.[16]

Pressure to do something about the rates came partly from Tories in Scotland, where legislation made it impossible to defer the revaluation of property beyond the mid-1980s. Reform of the rates also became part of a more general struggle between the government and Labour-controlled local councils. The government disliked the profligacy of councils, especially when that profligacy involved support for left-wing causes. The conflict had all sorts of fall-out. The metropolitan counties and the Greater London Council, the latter led by Ken Livingstone, were abolished in 1986. The government also began to 'cap' rates in a bid to contain local government spending and this brought it into conflict with some councils that simply refused to set rates.

Some wanted to abolish the rates and replace them with a flat-rate direct local tax that would be paid by all adults. New arrangements were bound to be expensive and bureaucratic. There was, in fact, something ominously Heathite about the whole discussion of local government finance. Indeed, the key advice was given by a group of civil servants, ministers and advisers – notably, William Waldegrave, Anthony Mayer and Victor Rothschild – who had first worked together in Heath's think tank. It was never entirely clear that the various advisers entirely believed in their own proposals. Some of them seem simply to have relished the challenge of grappling with a complex problem but not to have considered the political consequences of their proposal.[17]

Thatcher was initially sceptical about reform, but, in 1985, she finally agreed to the proposal for a new tax (soon to be known as the 'community charge' and to be christened by its enemies as the 'poll tax'). From then on, Thatcher embraced the new scheme with enthusiasm. Some of her younger and less obviously ideological ministers seem to have promoted it because they thought that doing so would demonstrate their loyalty to the prime minister. Opposition often came from the battle-hardened veterans of the first Thatcher government. Lawson hated the poll tax. It brought new people into the tax system when he was trying to take them out, it introduced new complexities when he was trying to simplify, and it seemed likely that the whole thing would end up costing central government money (first to pay for establishing the new scheme and then to provide subsidies that would alleviate its effects). Biffen, a man whose dislike of complicated novelties was even greater than Lawson's, found it hard to disguise his disdain as he 'defended' the proposal in the House of Commons.[18]

The poll tax illustrated the curious disintegration of the Thatcher government. Her early cabinets had been characterized by simplicity and clarity of thought. They focused on the essentials and they did not get into fights that could not be won. They avoided complicated legislation that would be difficult to enforce – Norman Tebbit had once remarked that the key aim of his trade union legislation was to *prevent* any trade unionist from having an excuse to get himself locked up. After 1985, and even more after 1987, ministers got buried in a complicated and messy legislative programme. A new law appeared to be the response to any problem. When a madman opened fire in Hungerford, the government introduced new restrictions on the possession of firearms – a measure calculated to annoy millions of rural Tories. When it emerged that a couple of old men who might once have been concentration camp guards were living in Scotland, the government introduced a war crimes bill – a retroactive measure that was bound to disturb Conservative lawyers. Thatcher's hyperactivity became a source of derision – one journalist claimed that he carried a card saying: 'In the event of an accident, I do not wish to be visited by the Prime Minister.'

Legislating for the poll tax was a long and wearing process. There was a bill for Scotland, introduced at the end of 1986, and one for England and Wales, introduced at the end of 1987. Many Tory MPs had doubts. Michael Heseltine, who had walked out of the cabinet on another issue minutes before it was due to endorse the poll tax in January 1986, was one of those who voted against its implementation in England. Whips twisted arms, called in favours and, in doing so, stoked up a mood of ill-will and confusion. Tory peers had to be dragged away from their estates to vote the measure through the House of Lords. In the end, the tax was introduced in Scotland in April 1989; it came to England and Wales a year later.

The poll tax had particularly awkward consequences for the Tories. Opponents of the tax rioted. Magistrates sent people to prison for refusal to pay – though the law surrounding such punishments was complicated and many sentences were overturned on appeal. The demonstrations and riots were not in themselves important. They involved a relatively small group of people and one that was not, in any case, likely to vote Tory, or to vote at all. Labour leaders feared that violent protests might in fact damage the Left. More importantly, the tax provoked discontent amongst middle-class people; Chris Patten described it as a 'heat-seeking missile aimed at voters in marginal constituencies'.[19] It annoyed the kind of self-righteous people who are liable to write letters to the authorities – often, one suspects, the same 'little old ladies' who had previously complained about the rates. Tory MPs found themselves buried under a deluge of correspondence, much of which required specific and detailed answers. The Tory chief whip had to deal with one of Thatcher's most loyal backbenchers, who was worried about the impact of the tax in Surrey, and had to explain to another irate MP why the tax in Spelthorne was more than twice as high as it was in neighbouring Slough.[20]

No amount of muttering in the tea room of the House of Commons would have had any effect on Thatcher's position if no one had been willing to stand against her. Technically, leaders of the Conservative Party were required to submit themselves for re-election every year; in practice, no other candidate had put themselves forward during Thatcher's first fourteen years in the post. In the autumn of 1989 this changed. Sir Anthony Meyer announced that he would challenge Margaret Thatcher. Meyer was a little-known MP from Wales who gave the impression of being a character escaped from *A Dance to the Music of Time*, an impression strengthened by his heroic lack of contrition when the press revealed that he had conducted a twenty-five-year affair with the jazz singer Simone Washington. His background and style evoked the world of patrician superiority that so exasperated some Thatcherites. He was formed by Eton (his father turned down a scholarship to prevent him from being corrupted by contact with clever boys), Oxford, the Guards (he was badly wounded in 1944) and the Foreign Office. Meyer came to play up to his upper-class image. He described his visit to Cecil Parkinson, when the latter was chairman of the Conservative Party and was trying to persuade Meyer to stand down as a parliamentary candidate, thus:

> I have to say that I felt as if I had strayed into the servants' hall of a not very well run stately home, rather than the nerve centre

of a great political party at a critical stage in its battle for supremacy.
I also reflected on how very differently Lord Thorneycroft, the
previous Party Chairman, would have handled the interview with
me. I am sure he would have had me round to lunch at Whites,
oysters and champagne, a lot of talk about how he was sure I
would understand the needs of the Party at a time like this, a vague
suggestion that there would be all sorts of ways in which I could
render great service to the state in some other place, and would
have come away from the lunch, quite possibly having agreed to
stand down, or, if not, feeling that I was behaving like a cad.[21]

Meyer saw himself as being on the liberal end of the Conservative
Party. He had, however, supported the economic policies of the
government during the early 1980s, and he expressed misgivings
about government economic policy (or at least about its social
consequences) only after other issues had alienated him from the
bulk of the Conservative Party. The turning point of his career
was the Falklands War. He was one of the few MPs to speak out
against the war. He despised the jingoism of the House of Commons
– though he seems to have been more concerned about the fate
of Lord Carrington than that of Welsh Guardsmen or Argentine
conscripts.

After the Falklands, Meyer was increasingly recognized as an
awkward MP by Tory whips, who would probably not have been
sorry to see him lose his seat in parliament. European unity had
always been the political cause closest to Meyer's heart and, as
Thatcher's tone became increasingly anti-European, he became
increasingly anti-Thatcher. Meyer's criticisms of the prime minister
were couched in a code of transparently insincere loyalty that
anyone in Westminster could have cracked. He invited her to pay
homage to the memory of Jean Monnet, or to celebrate the measures
that Peter Walker, the last supporter of government economic
intervention left in the cabinet, was taking to revive the Welsh
economy.[22]

In himself, Meyer posed no threat to Thatcher. He was not a serious candidate for high office, he had no following in the parliamentary party and he was unknown to the general public. During the Westland crisis, the Thatcher loyalist George Gardiner had sarcastically offered to sign the nomination papers if Meyer ran against the prime minister. In the very different context of the autumn of 1989, however, Meyer was more dangerous. His very obscurity meant that the choice between him and Thatcher was all the more stark. This was not an election that pitted two rival candidates or rival programmes against each other. The thirty-three MPs[23] who voted for Meyer were, in effect, saying 'anyone but Thatcher'.

The real, though undeclared, rival to Margaret Thatcher was Michael Heseltine. Heseltine, a flamboyant and famously ambitious man, had made a fortune in publishing and property before establishing a reputation as an effective minister and barnstorming performer at Conservative Party conferences. Thatcher had remarked privately in the early 1970s that Heseltine had 'everything that it takes to succeed in politics except brains'.[24] It was widely said that he had, as an undergraduate at Oxford, sketched a career plan on a restaurant menu. The plan involved becoming a millionaire in the 1960s and a cabinet minister in the 1970s before becoming prime minister in the 1990s.[25]

Heseltine, who had been secretary of state for defence since January 1983, resigned from the cabinet on 9 January 1986 over the fate of the Westland helicopter company. Westland was in financial trouble, and its management were keen to sell a stake to the American Sikorsky company. Heseltine suddenly took an interest in this comparatively small operation. He wanted Westland to join a consortium of European manufacturers and he tried to persuade a group of European 'National Armaments Directors' (i.e. officials responsible for buying weapons) that non-European manufacturers should be excluded from future European purchases. This produced a bitter argument between him and Thatcher, which also came to involve Leon Brittan, who, as secretary of state for trade and industry, was responsible for authorizing the takeover.

What was the dispute about? Heseltine favoured European integration. He also sometimes seemed to be interested in a policy of industrial intervention (the cabinet position that he most coveted, after that of prime minister, was trade and industry). However, this was not really a dispute that divided the cabinet on such lines – Norman Tebbit, one of the anti-European and anti-interventionist ministers, was initially sympathetic to Heseltine's proposal. Nor was it really, as Heseltine liked to claim, a dispute about the collective responsibility of the cabinet – collective responsibility imposes obligations on ministers but does not give them rights, and in any case almost all cabinet ministers seem to have concluded that Heseltine's 'European option' was just not realistic. The points on which Heseltine was subsequently able to embarrass Thatcher, and which almost brought her downfall, involved nice questions of constitutional procedure. A civil servant leaked a letter from the solicitor general to Heseltine, and thus breeched the convention that the advice of law officers to ministers should remain secret, and Leon Brittan denied having received a letter from the chairman of British Aerospace, thus opening him to the charge of having misled the House of Commons. Brittan was forced to resign and for a brief period Thatcher feared that she would have to do the same.

Westland was not significant because it raised important issues, but rather because it showed how the Thatcher government was increasingly vulnerable to the damage caused by comparatively trivial matters. Thatcher and her allies would have won the debate in cabinet easily if they had been more patient. They could probably have damaged Heseltine if they had allowed him to pursue his 'European option'. Instead Westland showed the prime minister's impatience, her tendency to use civil servants and advisers against ministers whom she regarded as disloyal (there was much dark muttering about the role of Bernard Ingham during the Westland affair) and her inability to help ministers, such as Brittan, who had been loyal.

Heseltine did not call for Thatcher's resignation after Westland (the only Tory MP to do so was Anthony Meyer), and he ostentatiously voted in the government lobbies during the vote of confidence that was moved by the opposition in the aftermath of the affair. For the next four years, Heseltine was to insist that he 'could not foresee the circumstances' under which he might challenge Margaret Thatcher for the leadership of the party.

Being a very rich man (he even took his ministerial driver with him when he resigned), Heseltine could afford to conduct a long private campaign to maintain his reputation in the Conservative Party. He addressed endless constituency associations (108 of them during the 1987 election campaign) and wrote a couple of worthy books. Michael Mates and Keith Hampson became unofficial parliamentary private secretaries and fixers for Heseltine in the House of Commons.

But Heseltine was in an awkward position. His links with those who had remained in the cabinet were weak. He was not a clubbable man and was actively disliked by some powerful ministers. Whitelaw, probably the man who most resented Heseltine's habit of wearing a Brigade tie on the strength of a few months' national service with the Welsh Guards, was an enemy. After his own resignation, Geoffrey Howe rebuffed an approach from Heseltine. Heseltine's resignation looked bad – probably even worse to those who believed Heseltine's own story that it was carried out in a moment of spontaneous exasperation than to those who assumed that it was a calculated challenge to the prime minister. Heseltine was also acutely aware that the Tory rank and file valued loyalty and would not forgive him for an open challenge to the leader. A Tory whip commented on his 'delicate balancing act between rebellion and oblivion'.[26] Heseltine summed up his dilemma with the phrase: 'He who wields the dagger never wears the crown.'

Michael Heseltine did not publicly support Meyer's candidacy and abstained in the vote on the leadership in 1989 – though one of his associates did talk to Meyer, apparently without Heseltine's authorization. Heseltine's enemies argued that he was seeking to damage Thatcher, in the hope that she would resign, whilst not being willing to take her on directly. An article in *The Times*, which Heseltine believed to have been inspired by Ingham, said that he should 'either put up or shut up'. Heseltine felt that such accusations were damaging him. Like Meyer before him, he also seems to have been annoyed by the belief that his enemies had agitated in his own constituency. Quite large parts of his account of the events leading to his decision to stand involve the machinations of obscure people in Henley-on-Thames rather than politicians in Westminster. Finally, on the day after Howe's resignation speech of 13 November, Heseltine announced: 'I am persuaded that I would now have a better prospect than Mrs Thatcher of leading the Conservatives to a fourth electoral victory and preventing the ultimate calamity of a Labour government.'

Thatcher responded badly to the challenge. Her campaign, which had been so well organized in 1975, was inept in 1990. George Younger was nominally the leader of Thatcher's campaign but was distracted by his business commitments. Norman Tebbit became recognized as the real leader – though he was hardly the man to draw together a broad coalition and though, like other senior Tories, he seems by this stage to have been more interested in stopping Heseltine than preserving Thatcher.[27] Peter Morrison was Thatcher's parliamentary private secretary. A wealthy man from an established political family (his father and brother had both supported Heath against Thatcher in 1975), he was not well equipped for the kind of street-fighting that his mistress needed in 1990. He seems to have pursued his canvassing of MPs with remarkably little vigour. He told Thatcher that 'if you have not won then an awful lot of Conservative MPs are lying' – a remark that will live on in the annals of political naïvety.[28]

Some blamed Thatcher for going to attend a meeting of leaders of industrial powers in Paris at a crucial moment when Heseltine was campaigning vigorously. This probably misunderstands Thatcher's nature. She had won the leadership when fighting as an outsider against an aloof and unpopular leader, but she was not the kind of person who could have won MPs over with displays of intimacy and bonhomie in 1990.

In any case, the notion that getting the extra few votes to give her an absolute majority in the first round of the leadership election would have saved Margaret Thatcher is far-fetched. She would have been wounded by the leadership election under any circumstances and would almost certainly have found it impossible to restore her fortunes afterwards. Indeed, Heseltine's campaign manager – Michael Mates – was later to reproach himself for having missed a trick by not having his candidate withdraw after the first round. If Heseltine had done this, he would have looked gracious, and he would have denied other candidates the chance to compete in the second round. However, he would not in reality have saved Margaret Thatcher. She would have limped on for a few months before being finished off when the next crisis made the Conservative Party nervous.

In truth, Margaret Thatcher's authority was ebbing away in 1990 for reasons that were only partially linked to the electoral arithmetic behind a formal leadership bid. A parliamentary party with a large majority is, almost by definition, nervous, because it contains many MPs who represent relatively marginal seats. In addition to this, the social changes of the 1980s created problems. The cost of bourgeois life had increased (school fees were an object of special concern to many Tory MPs), but the means that MPs had to pay for such a life diminished. Relatively few of them now had private incomes; the new professionalism and urgency of business life made it harder to combine a career in parliament with one in the City or at the Bar. Most Conservatives lived on their salary, their parliamentary allowances and (in many cases) on business activities that involved peddling political influence. Some of the new-style Tories would have found it hard to make a living outside Westminster. Such men were frightened at the thought that the next election must occur no later than 1992, and that public opinion polls were turning against them.

Lack of faith in Thatcher acquired a circular quality. Once Tory MPs began to feel that Thatcher would not last, then their thoughts increasingly turned to the question of who would be her successor. The prime minister's powers of patronage disappeared when no one believed that she would be able to exercise them in the long term.[29] This ebbing of support was illustrated by Alan Clark. Thatcher recalls a slightly farcical meeting with him after the first round of the leadership contest, in which he told her that she should fight on – not because she could win but because 'it was better to go out in a blaze of glorious defeat than to go gentle into that good night.' She does not seem to have taken Clark very seriously; she likened the meeting to the porter's scene in Macbeth, but she was glad 'to have someone unambiguously on my side even in defeat'.[30]

In reality, there was nothing 'unambiguous' about Clark's support for Thatcher. As early as April 1990 he had doubted whether she ought to stay on. The month before her fall, he had encouraged Douglas Hurd to put himself forward as Thatcher's replacement.[31] Clark was almost obsessively concerned with prime ministerial powers of patronage. When Carla Powell, a significant figure in Thatcher's personal court, asked for his help in reversing the dismissal of Bruce Anderson, a journalist on the *Daily Telegraph*, Clark said: 'we were all in limbo. No one, not even Mrs T herself could today cut any ice at all with anyone.'[32] Clark worried about the impact that a new prime minister would have on his career – on whether he would get into the cabinet, whether he would get on to the Privy Council, whether he would get a knighthood.

Clark got none of the things he desired – a more realistic man might have understood that he had actually been lucky to achieve office as a junior minister. In such circumstances, it is hardly surprising that cabinet ministers, who really did have something to lose, were reluctant to stand at the salute on the sinking battleship of HMS Thatcher. The only unqualified support for the prime minister came from those political kamikazes – Ridley and Powell – whose political careers were already destroyed.

Thatcher saw the leadership contest as a matter of 'loyalty', but loyalty could mean more than one thing. Some who respected Thatcher personally had reached the point when they genuinely believed that her own reputation would suffer if she stayed in office. Many put loyalty to the party, and particularly to its election prospects, above loyalty to its leader. Rank-and-file Tory members had much influence on the MPs who represented them, and opinions amongst this group were more complicated than the orchestrated displays of enthusiasm at the annual conference made them appear. Most members of the Conservative Party were old; they understood that the party had existed before Thatcher and hoped that it would exist after her. It is significant that members of the Conservative Party seem to have been especially loyal to John Major in the early 1990s, at the very moment when Thatcher was beginning to regard him as a 'traitor'.[33] Conservatives were reluctant to express their concerns in public – for reasons that may have been linked to feelings about good form as much as calculation of personal interest. George Walden conducted an interesting experiment. He asked his constituency officers in Buckinghamshire for a show of hands over whether Thatcher should stay. Most said that she should. He then approached those who had voted in favour of Thatcher and asked them their private opinions: three quarters said that she should go.[34]

After the first round of the leadership contest (in which Thatcher got 204 votes and Heseltine got 152), Thatcher consulted her cabinet colleagues. Almost all of them said, with various nuances, that they would support her if she maintained her candidature, but that they thought it unlikely that she could win. She was later to rage at the betrayal involved in the polite formula. Hurd,

Waldegrave and Baker were amongst the very few ministers who left a favourable impression. It does not seem to have occurred to Thatcher that all three of these men had been intimates of Edward Heath, and consequently had some experience in handling a defeated leader who felt bitter at 'betrayal'.

The defeat for Thatcher was not a defeat for the policies that had been espoused by the early Thatcher governments. Even Anthony Meyer, who had been a critic of the Thatcher government since 1982, stressed that he was favourable to much of its economic and social legacy. Heseltine had served in the Thatcher governments for seven years and never implied that he regretted much that he had done in that position. The two people whose resignations did most to bring Thatcher down – Lawson and Howe – were both Thatcherites *de la première heure*. Will Hopper, a former member of the European parliament, who had supported the chancellor over the 1981 budget, urged Howe to make a leadership bid in 1990, precisely in order to make it clear that opposition to Thatcher was not a 'wet European thing', but that it went with a restoration of the austere virtues of the first Thatcher government.[35] No one suggested that overthrowing Thatcher should go with reversing her government's policy on trade unions, the sale of council houses, the promotion of the free market or privatization: John Wakeham was distracted from his duties in the Thatcher leadership campaign team partly by his efforts to privatize the electricity companies.

Thatcher's opponents sometimes disliked the poll tax – though this was hardly, except in Thatcher's own mind, a matter of great principle. Europe was a more substantial issue (the only matter of policy that was mentioned at all in Heseltine's declaration of his intention to stand for the leadership of the party). However, this too was hardly a matter on which policy differences brought Thatcher down. Her opponents were themselves divided on matters such as the desirability of a single currency. Only opposition to Thatcher united them, and this opposition was aroused more by her tone than by any concrete proposal that she made.

In a curious way, Thatcher's fall might be interpreted as a sign that Thatcherism had succeeded. She was a natural leader at a time of conflict. Her image was burnished at the height of the Cold War. She had challenged the leader of her own party at a time when no one else dared to do so and fought for four years against a Labour government. She had persisted with unpopular policies in the early 1980s, led her country in a war and denounced the 'enemies within'. Her success had changed the very circumstances that had once made her supporters regard her as uniquely useful. By the time she resigned, Soviet troops were pulling out of Eastern Europe, the National Union of Mineworkers was broken and over a million council houses had been sold. The problem for this unconsensual politician was that she had created a new consensus.

CONCLUSIONS

Is it serious or is it just the usual wank?
William Shelton, junior education minister, to
Ferdinand Mount, head of Number 10 Policy Unit[1]

William Shelton was, by any definition, a Thatcherite. He was a monetarist who had despaired during the last years of the Heath government. He was one of just two MPs whose support Margaret Thatcher knew she could rely on when she first declared her candidacy for the leadership of the Conservative Party in 1975.[2] The fact that such a man could also see that many individual policies of the Thatcher government were silly, contradictory or unoriginal does not mean that he did not also recognize that there was some overall thrust behind the Thatcher government which made it, in his eyes, worthwhile. In short, Shelton recognized that the frequently drawn contrast between the Thatcher government as an ideologically driven revolution and the Thatcher government as just another piece of Tory 'statecraft' is misleading. There were always elements of both, and the fact that Thatcherism was often mythologized, by its most unworldly supporters as well as by its bitterest enemies, does not mean that it was a myth.

What did Thatcherites themselves mean by Thatcherism? Nigel Lawson gave a speech on Thatcherism to Swiss bankers in 1981, which in his memoirs he recalled thus:

Thatcherism is, I believe, a useful term, and certainly was at the time. No other modern Prime Minister has given his or her name to a particular constellation of policies and values. However, it needs to be used with care . . . The right definition involves a mixture of free markets, financial discipline, firm control over public expenditure, tax cuts, nationalism, 'Victorian values' (of the Samuel Smiles self-help variety), privatization and a dash of populism.[3]

Lawson's definition of Thatcherism is revealing. He mentions privatization, which hardly featured in the 1979 manifesto and was not much practised until after the 1983 election, and 'Victorian values' – a phrase that was coined by a television interviewer and only really used by Thatcherites themselves for a few months in 1983. His 1992 definition, on the other hand, makes no mention of monetarism, though this would have been seen as a crucial aspect of Thatcherism until at least 1982 and Lawson's lecture of 1981 had in fact been mainly about control of the money supply. As for populism, no one would deny that it was an element of Thatcherism – though a paper that Lawson had helped draft in 1978 came close to suggesting that populism and the practice of free-market economics might prove mutually exclusive.[4] Neither in 1981 nor in 1992 did Lawson mention the issue that many came to define as central to Thatcherism, and that eventually produced the rift between Lawson himself and Thatcher: Europe.

One might argue that there were really several different Thatcherite projects and that they overlapped only to a limited extent. Before the 1979 election, Thatcherism meant, in large measure, certain attitudes to crime, race and disorder. It was known that powerful Conservatives were monetarists, but it was not clear how far the party leader had embraced this doctrine or how far it would be applied in government. After the 1979 election, the focus on a particular kind of economic policy became so intense that many commentators talked as though monetarism was a synonym for Thatcherism. After the 1983 election, monetarism was discussed less. Privatization played an increasing role in the government's image, as did the booming stock market. After 1988, and even more after 1990, Thatcherism was increasingly interpreted as meaning opposition to Britain's further integration into Europe – though, in fact, some prominent people associated with early Thatcherism supported such integration.

Does all this mean that, as some came to argue, there was no continuity or coherence in Thatcherism? There is a peculiar risk that a political phenomenon will be dismissed because of its success. If Margaret Thatcher had been forced to resign in 1981, then historians would find it easier to agree on what her government stood for. The very fact that the government remained in power for so long meant that it was bound to encounter new problems, to adjust to circumstances and to seem 'inconsistent'.

Underneath the tactical adjustments, however, it is possible to discern certain general themes in the Thatcher government. It sought to promote the free market, to reduce public spending (or at least to reduce its rate of increase) and to place the control of inflation above that of unemployment. Economics was at the core of Thatcherism – this explains why Thatcher always placed her allies in economic ministries while being less concerned with who occupied, for example, the Home Office; it also explains how a man like Geoffrey Howe, who disagreed with Thatcher on many areas of social and foreign policy, could still think of himself as a Thatcherite. It would, however, be wrong to assume that Thatcherism was just about economics or that economics could be entirely separated from other elements of the project. A concern for 'order' or 'discipline' was discernible in almost everything the Thatcher governments did and to some extent this concern transcended the division between economic and non-economic policies. Dealing with strikes and trade unions, to take an obvious example, can be seen as both an attempt to re-establish order (something that should be placed alongside Thatcherite concern with crime), and as an attempt to make the economy more productive. It is true that there was nothing particularly new or distinctive about many broad aims of

Thatcherite economic policies. T. E. Utley argued in 1986: 'Her two major achievements – the control of inflation and the reduction of the trade unions to size – were simply the climax of a series of unsuccessful attempts by Labour and Tory governments alike to cope with what were increasingly seen as the two most important evils from which the country was suffering.'[5] There were, however, two distinct novelties. First, the techniques by which the Thatcher government tackled both inflation and labour relations – particularly its refusal to use formal pay controls – were different from those used by governments in the 1970s. Secondly, and crucially, there is a difference between governments that *try* to do things and governments that *do* things, especially when they do things over a long period of time, as in the case of the Thatcher government.

THATCHERITE MORALITY

During the 1970s both Thatcher's supporters and her opponents understood that the political battle was not likely to be won or lost entirely, or even mainly, through debates on economics.[6] Discussions of electoral strategy in the shadow cabinet made much of immigration, crime and patriotism. Thatcher's opponents sometimes argued that Thatcherism needed to be understood as part of a larger movement that took in Enoch Powell's attitudes to race and the views of Mary Whitehouse on sexual morality.[7]

> The rejection of progressive 'Keynesian' conservatism was therefore also accompanied by . . . marked hardening of the party's attitudes on questions of immigration, law and order and the family. From a feminist perspective the Thatcherite project was very successful in exploiting gender and race issues to win popular support for its wider programme.[8]

Sexual morality intersected with the discussion of other political issues in all sorts of peculiar ways during the 1980s. The feminists who campaigned against nuclear weapons at the Greenham Common airbase were pitched against Lady Olga Maitland's Families for Defence. Supporters of striking miners made much of the transformation of women's status that was alleged to have taken place in pit villages during the strike; whilst the Union of Democratic Miners (which represented men who had refused to strike) supported a Parents' Rights Group in its bid to sue Haringay Council for supporting homosexual causes.[9] William Rees-Mogg suggested in 1983 that there was a link between Keynes's disregard for the 'natural' rules of economics and the homo-erotic atmosphere of Forsterian Cambridge.[10]

There was never, however, as clear a link between politics and morality in Britain as there was in America during the 1980s. Religion was a more pervasive and explicit influence on politics in America. The American 'moral majority' was united by commitment to particular policies – in favour of the death penalty and against abortion. There was no such coherence in Britain. There was not always a link between particular positions on race, crime and sexual morality. Enoch Powell was the most prominent opponent of non-white immigration, but he was also one of the most articulate opponents of the death penalty. On sexual matters, Powell was 'liberal' over homosexuality and 'illiberal' over abortion. Victoria Gillick, who campaigned to prevent girls under sixteen from being given contraceptive advice without their parents' consent, had taken a Powellite line on immigration during the early 1970s. She seemed to change her position during the 1980s though, partly because some black and Muslim groups sympathized with her view of sexual morality.[11] Conservatives were particularly numerous amongst those who voted in favour of restoring the death penalty or restricting abortion, but these were never matters on which political parties imposed whips, and the running was primarily made by backbench MPs – often people, such as Jill Knight, Cyril

Townsend, Bernard Braine or Geoffrey Dickens, who were not taken very seriously by their senior colleagues. Voting on all these issues cut across party lines.

Conservatives, and even Thatcherites, were never united around a single line. Thatcher refused to admit that she was a 'feminist', but many MPs in her party – ranging from Teresa Gorman on the libertarian Right to Emma Nicholson on the liberal Left – would have described themselves in that way. Christine Chapman – the journalist who once told Thatcher, 'We still believe in Thatcherism but I wonder if you still do'[12] – had no time for moral authoritarianism. Thatcher's two most important chancellors sought to reform the tax system in ways that would give equality to married women, and at least one of them thought of this in feminist terms.

The Conservative leadership's association with 'moral' issues was strongest during the period when Thatcher was leader of the opposition. Some prominent Tories seem to have seen such issues largely as a matter of electoral advantage, and the attempt to present Thatcherism in terms of some overall moral code resurfaced briefly before the 1983 election. Thatcherites as policy makers were very different from Thatcherites as electoral campaigners. On some issues – notably immigration – the Conservatives did not really differ much (in terms of policy rather than tone) from Labour, whilst on other issues they took no party line. Dealing with Gillick's campaign against the provision of contraceptive advice to girls under sixteen, the Conservative government managed to give the impression that it supported the general moral thrust of the campaign whilst appealing against legal judgments that went in Gillick's favour.[13]

Hostility to homosexuality was often seen as an important part of the Thatcher government's morality – especially when a clause seeking to prevent councils from 'promoting' homosexuality was inserted into the local government bill of 1988.[14] In fact, though, the fuss over this single clause, which was vague to the point of meaninglessness and which was never tested in court, helped to conceal the fact that the Thatcher government had in many ways been remarkably liberal. It had responded to the AIDS crisis with medical advice rather than moral homilies[15] and it had, in accordance with European law, legalized homosexuality in Northern Ireland.[16]

The gulf between words and action was particularly notable with reference to the two issues with which Thatcher had been strongly associated during her early career: comprehensive education and the death penalty. In practice, the Conservative government did almost nothing to reverse the move towards comprehensive schools that had occurred during the 1960s and 1970s. As for capital punishment, this undoubtedly played an important part in Thatcher's public image. In her memoirs she implies that the failure of more Conservative MPs to vote in favour of restoration in 1983 was an omen of disappointments and betrayals to come. However, the Conservative leadership was never united on this issue – many Thatcherite ministers were opposed to restoration – and, as Thatcher must have known, putting the matter to a free vote was tantamount to accepting that it would be defeated (a number of Tory MPs voted in favour of hanging only because they knew that the motion that they 'supported' had no chance of winning). Thatcher's own position seems to have been more complicated than she admitted, perhaps even to herself. Jim Prior, who was sitting next to her on the government benches when the result of the 1983 vote in the Commons was announced, believed that she was privately relieved and that she would not have welcomed the practical difficulties that would have sprung from being forced to put her own principles into action.[17]

For all this, race, crime and family were important to the image of Thatcherism and part of the electorate clearly saw the Thatcher government as having a consistent and coherent position on such matters, even if it did not do so. Here, as was often the case, attacks on Thatcherism helped to define it in the public mind. There was a strange tacit complicity between parts of the Left and parts of the Right on certain kinds of disputes that revolved around 'values'. It suited the Left to be shocked by Thatcherites and it suited the Thatcherites to shock. Both sides could avoid asking awkward questions about their own positions. The Left could avoid asking how the election of Britain's first woman prime minister could be construed as an assertion of 'patriarchy' or whether Yorkshire miners were the natural allies of feminists. The Right could avoid stating precisely which bits of the 'permissive society' it would seek to destroy. Both sides reduced their dispute into a vague and ahistorical juxtaposition of two periods. 'Progressive' values were associated with 'the radical movements and political polarizations of the 1960s, for which "1968" must stand as a convenient, though inadequate, notation'.[18]

Just as the 'Sixties' came to be the expression of everything that Thatcherites were supposed to dislike, so the Victorian age was used to sum up everything that they were supposed to like. The history of the phrase 'Victorian values' is itself revealing. It was coined not by Thatcher but by the television interviewer Brian Walden. Walden had been a Labour MP and was sometimes seen as Thatcher's most hostile journalistic interlocutor[19] (he once asked her whether she was 'off her trolley').[20] But he had seriously contemplated defecting to the Conservative Party during the late 1970s and seems to have been close to Thatcher in private during the 1980s.[21] 'Victorian values' illustrated the curious way in which references to Thatcherism's morality could be double edged – descriptions perceived as attacks by the Left could be seen as benign by Thatcherism's own supporters. Thatcherites adopted the phrase 'Victorian values' with enthusiasm but this enthusiasm was fairly brief, mainly confined to the period immediately before the 1983 election. The Left's interest in the phrase was more durable (books on the subject were still pouring off the presses when Thatcher resigned) and almost certainly played into her hands by helping to give her government a certain moral brand – Michael

Foot's introduction to Labour's catastrophically unsuccessful 1983 manifesto pledged to 'end the long Victorian night'.*

Some discerned a 'contradiction' between Thatcherism's economic policies and its attitudes to other matters. They believed that there was something incongruous about the fact that a government that seemed so committed to freedom in economic affairs was authoritarian and moralistic in other spheres. They saw a conflict between an expensive defence policy and the desire to cut public spending or protect capitalism. Thatcherites themselves sometimes recognized that their policy was double-sided and that, for example, the Falklands War involved a conflict between desire to reassert British greatness and desire to cut public spending.

More commonly, however, Thatcherites argued that their attitudes to economics, foreign policy and morality fitted together. There were three elements to this. First, Thatcherites were not in fact defenders of an utterly unrestricted free market. All of them recognized the need for social services that were provided by the state. All of them also recognized that the state needed to regulate economic activity in certain respects – indeed their criticism of British politics in the 1970s revolved around the fact that the state had become too 'big' (in that it interfered in too many things) but also that it had become too 'weak' (in that it was unable to enforce its will in those things that really mattered).

Secondly, Thatcherite policies, including economic policies, were not just about economics. Keith Joseph wrote in 1975:

> It is characteristic of the past two decades that almost exclusive obsession with economics by governments, and competitive claims to usher in utopia, have coincided with economic failure. A healthy economy is possible only in a healthy body politic – with self reliance, thrift, respect for laws and confidence in a system of rewards and sanctions.[22]

* Foot was quoting the Welsh poet Idris Davies.

Thatcher's opponents often presented the battle against her as a battle between the market and morality. Thatcherites, however, thought that the market was moral. The free market encouraged individual virtue. It produced people who were robust, independent and willing to take responsibility for the consequences of their own actions. Shirley Robin Letwin, who both commented on and influenced Thatcherism, wrote that 'The Thatcherite conception of the individual is the most important and at the same time the least understood element of Thatcherism.'[23] For Letwin, this aspect of Thatcherism revolved around promoting the 'vigorous virtues'. She argued, for example, that privatization might have raised more money, and done more to promote industrial efficiency, if it had involved the sale of state assets to existing companies rather than attempts to spread share-ownership as widely as possible. She added:

> [T]he privatization programme has indeed been 'ideologically driven', in the sense that it had aims other than that of merely increasing economic rationality. The privatization programme has been specifically designed not merely to resuscitate economic vitality, but also to promote the vigorous virtues in individuals, to strengthen the family, and to bring the paradigm shift to bear on industrial policy.[24]

Thirdly, economic success was seen as a prerequisite for national greatness. The sense of crisis that afflicted the British establishment in the 1970s, and which helped to give birth to Thatcherism, was always a crisis about *relative* decline rather than about the extent to which people enjoyed the fruits of prosperity within their own frontiers – indeed some 'declinists' seemed to think that the British people needed to live *less* comfortable lives. The Thatcher government was always interested in British prestige and influence. Ministers were reluctant to cut defence spending and, when Britain was at war in 1982, the government disregarded financial considerations entirely. Margaret Thatcher admired Switzerland, but she never thought that a nation exercising no influence beyond its frontiers could be a model for Britain.

THE ECONOMY

As she left Downing Street for the last time, Margaret Thatcher said 'we are very happy that we leave the United Kingdom in a very, very much better state than when we came here eleven and a half years ago'. How far, in economic terms, was this true? Generally speaking, judgements on the Thatcher government's economic record have been marked by grudging and reluctant concessions on the part of Thatcher's critics. Andrew Gamble wrote: 'There was an improvement in the 1980s, but no miracle.'[25] At first glance, this is not very extravagant praise, but the mere suggestion that Thatcherism should be discussed in terms of 'improvement' shows how far debate has shifted since the 1980s – a time when Gamble's commentaries were published in an official organ of the British Communist Party[26] and when one of Britain's best-known economists talked of imminent 'apocalypse'.[27]

British productivity improved during the 1980s. Those who are less favourable to the government's record point out that the improvement was smaller than that enjoyed by some other countries during the 1980s and than that which Britain itself had enjoyed during the 1960s.[28] These are unfair comparisons. Britain always faced the problems of apparent relative decline that came from having been the first industrial nation. In terms of international comparison, two points are worth noting. First, by the mid-1980s, some foreign observers had come to regard some aspects of the British economy as a model to be imitated, which would certainly not have been the case in the mid-1970s. Secondly, those who were least favourable about British economic growth tended to move the goal posts – they compared Britain with France in 1978, Japan in 1987 and increasingly with a variety of entities – the Rhone–

Alps corridor, for example – that had been dreamt up in research seminars.

Britain was not the most 'successful' economy in the world at any point during the 1980s (or, for that matter, at any point since 1851). There were, however, important, and unexpected, successes in the 1980s. At the time many worried about the nature of these successes. The diplomat Nicholas Henderson wrote in 1987, consciously making himself a spokesman for establishment opinion, that the recession of the early 1980s had done irredeemable damage to much of British manufacturing industry. He thought it unlikely that an economy based on services would be able to fill the gap that was left by this.[29]

Sir Nicholas was right about the collapse of manufacturing industry. This is also an area in which it is fair to look at the Thatcher government's record, because Thatcherites did assume that 'reversing decline' meant improving the state of British manufacturing – indeed Henderson's own lament on this subject in 1979 influenced Thatcher and some of her associates. Members of the Thatcher government did not want or expect the recession of the early 1980s to be as severe as it was. The emphasis on 'services' in Thatcherite economic discourse emerged largely as a rhetorical expedient to justify the unintended consequences of government economic policy.

Having said this, the consequences of Thatcherite economic policy did not turn out to be as bad as many, including some of Thatcher's supporters, feared they might be. An economy based on services did produce prosperity for parts of Britain – especially because of the, largely unplanned, way in which reforms in the City of London intersected with the growth of international finance. Nicholas Henderson himself did rather well out of this new economy – in retirement he became a consultant for Hambros merchant bank and a director of Sotheby's auction house. As for the losers of the early 1980s – those who worked in manufacturing industry – it is not, in retrospect, clear what might have been done to help them. Manufacturing industry declined in most of the more prosperous Western countries during the 1980s and 1990s. Britain had particular long-term problems of low investment, poor industrial relations and weak technical training that would have meant that industry performed badly even in the best of circumstances. The most brutally simple verdict on the Thatcher government's relations with industry in the early 1980s was that it merely turned off the life-support system for a patient that was already dead.

A defender of the Thatcher government's economics might also point out that these need to be seen as a whole. The shock of its policies – particularly during the recession of the early 1980s or the miners' strike of 1984 to 1985 – was meant to be therapeutic. Thatcherites probably did not then understand the full scope of the policies they were going to implement, but they did know that things were going to have to change dramatically and that the country needed to be prepared for a new kind of economy. They might argue with some justice that the 'successful' policy of privatization would not have been possible without the humiliation of the trade unions, seen most clearly with the miners' strike, and that the defeat of the miners would not have been possible if the high unemployment of the early 1980s had not left much of the rest of the working class too subdued to help the miners.

There was also a sense in which the whole debate about economics and society changed during the 1980s. Enoch Powell once said: 'The life of nations no less than that of men is lived largely in the imagination.'* The remark was sometimes quoted disapprovingly as an example of Britain's flight from the hard realities of the economic world. Curiously, commentators from parts of the Left, which had once made much of material conditions, became more sympathetic to interpretations that stressed subjective experience during the late 1970s and 1980s, and this influenced

* The remark was originally made in a speech at Trinity College Dublin in 1946.

their views of Thatcherism. In 1989 Charles Leadbeater (whose own curious status on the frontiers of financial journalism, business consultancy and policy advice reflected the social transformations wrought by Thatcherism) pointed out that 'progress' had once been measured largely at national level and largely in quantifiable terms relating to material goods and accepted by both Right and Left. In the previous decade, all this had changed:

> A simple balance sheet of progress and regress is not enough because the accounting conventions to draw up the balance sheet are changing. They are changing with the shift to new times and post-Fordism. But Thatcherism is ensuring that they are shifted to the Right as they are brought up to date.[30]

Thatcher's own advisers, especially from the world of advertising, were increasingly influenced by the knowledge that there was not a precise relationship between people's economic situation and their own perception of their social class and/or political interests. It is significant that the most important resource for British sociologists in the 1960s and 1970s was *British Social Trends*. In 1984 this annual publication was supplemented by another – entitled *British Social Attitudes*.

WHIG OR TORY?

It was often alleged that Thatcher had broken with a true Tory tradition that saw social obligations as more important than market relations. The charge was levelled from both the Left and the Right. Ian Gilmour talked of a 'traditional' Toryism that was defined by interest in fairness and, in particular, in reducing unemployment. On the other side of the spectrum, journalists – such as T. E. Utley and Peregrine Worsthorne – talked of a Conservatism that was defined in terms of hierarchy and deference:

both men were close to the historian Maurice Cowling who had written in 1978 that the free market interested Conservatives only in so far as it was a means 'to maintain existing inequalities or restore lost ones'. A few of Thatcher's supporters occasionally showed interest in the notion that she was not really a Tory. John Nott wrote in 1982: 'I am a nineteenth-century Liberal. So is the Prime Minister. That is what this government is all about.'[31] There clearly were people around Thatcher who felt some affinity with Liberalism (or at least with the Liberal Party of an earlier age). Geoffrey Howe had voted Liberal in 1945 and Nott had technically been elected to parliament as one of the last representatives of the National Liberals, who did not finally and formally merge into the Conservative Party until 1974.

It would, however, be wrong to make too much of this. It is not possible to draw a clear line between Liberalism and Toryism – after all, Gladstone was once a Tory and Winston Churchill was a Liberal for a time. Late twentieth-century Conservatism drew from a variety of traditions (an important group of Thatcher's advisers had once been active on the Left), but it confronted problems that would have been inconceivable in the nineteenth century. There was an element of point-scoring in the use of historical analogies – and it is significant that both Thatcherites and 'wets' were prone to label their enemies in the party as 'Whigs'.

In any event, the case that Thatcher was 'not really a Tory' was never made very convincingly. Nott himself changed his mind on Thatcher's Liberalism. He came to argue that she was never really sympathetic to the logic of free trade and that 'it is a complete misreading of her beliefs to depict her as a nineteenth-century Liberal'.[32] Characteristically, Nott did not mention the fact he himself had put this particular myth into circulation. Besides, there were other Thatcherites who emphatically saw themselves as not being Liberal. In particular, Nigel Lawson – one of the most vigorous defenders of free-market economics in the government – insisted that his political ancestor was Disraeli not Gladstone, though he also pointed out that Disraeli and Gladstone had actually shared important economic assumptions.[33] Finally, it is worth pointing out that Thatcherites made most of 'Liberalism' at a time when they seemed threatened by an alliance of the Liberal and Social Democrat parties – it seems likely that a large part of their enthusiasm was rooted in the well-established Tory tradition of electoral calculation.

The self-appointed spokesmen of 'true Toryism' did not put a very consistent case. In many respects, Gilmour was to the Left of his friend Roy Jenkins and recognized in retrospect that his references to Burke served mainly as 'covering fire'[34] for suggestions that owed much to Keynes. As for Worsthorne and Utley, they represented a dissident faction within Thatcherism, rather than a Tory opposition to it. When the chips were down, as they often were in the late 1970s and early 1980s, both men described themselves as 'Thatcherites'.[35] Besides, there was a degree of affectation in those Tories who pretended that they cared about fox hunting and the prayer book more than they cared about crushing the unions and controlling inflation. In February 1979, Utley talked of 'the scrannel piping of some of the agitated economists who surround Mrs Thatcher',[36] but this did not prevent him from writing speeches for the leader of the opposition.

Denunciations of Thatcher for departing from 'Toryism' often implied that the market in which she placed such faith was a thing of 'Gradgrindesque' impersonality – hence the glee with which her detractors fastened on her remarks about there being 'no such thing as Society'. These denunciations missed the point. For some Conservatives, the market itself could be an organic and natural thing. Strains of such thinking can be found in Keith Joseph and Nigel Lawson – both men who combined a defence of the free market with an insistence that they were 'Tories'.[37] Thatcher expressed such ideas to the conference of the Scottish Conservative Party in 1990:

We realise, with Edmund Burke, that 'to be attached to the sub-
division, to love the little platoon we belong to in society, is the first
principle (the germ as it were) of public affection. It is the first link
in the series by which we proceed towards a love to our country
and to mankind'. What the class warriors of the Left refuse to
grasp, however, is that markets are living, bustling, spontaneously
generated communities. And it's not surprising that the first great
champion of markets, Adam Smith, was the friend of Edmund
Burke.[38]

THATCHER'S PERSONAL ROLE

How much did Margaret Thatcher personally confer coherence
on the Conservative Party during the time she led it? Her closest
associates were sometimes rather dismissive of her. Alfred Sherman
wrote: 'In the eight years that we worked closely together I have
never heard her express an original idea or even ask an insightful
question. She left no memorable sayings, apart from one quoted
against her out of context.'[39]

Thatcher drew heavily on the opinions of advisers. Her speeches
were mainly composed by other people. Some of the key phrases
of the Thatcherite revolution were in the first instance coined by
its enemies – what single phrase did more to define Thatcher than
'Iron Lady', first used in the pages of the Red Army newspaper?
It is certainly true that Thatcher's exposition of Thatcherism was
less systematic than that of some of her advisers and ministers.
She did not value intellectual coherence as an end in itself, and
she made few general statements of principle. Her very importance
sprang from these facts. For all her apparent dogmatism, she was,
at least at crucial moments in her career, a pragmatist who avoided
fights that could not be won and who recognized the importance
of tactical flexibility.

Those who worked with Thatcher also recognized that – though
she often seemed to lack a theory of politics – she did have certain

beliefs or instincts that pervaded much of what she did. She rarely coined phrases, but when presented with choices she often had a strong sense of which words might capture her views. As has been suggested, she preferred 'community' to 'society' and 'popular capitalism' to 'people's capitalism'. She disliked 'privatization', 'supply side' and 'detente' – though no one ever came up with satisfactory alternatives to these words. One aide summed up Thatcher's speech-writing manner thus:

> A speech-writing discussion with Margaret Thatcher was like a session on the psychiatrist's couch, though I was unsure who was the patient and who the psychiatrist. One would usually sit with others, in her study at No. 10, pen poised over notepad, hanging on her every word. Phrases, themes, single words would be scribbled down as one tried to identify – from the stream of consciousness, often inchoate, that poured from her brow furrowed and with that penetrating gaze turned inward – some thread from which to form sentences and paragraphs. One could sense the specks of gold in the ore, but it was agonizingly difficult to capture them as she darted quickly from subject to subject and from theme to theme.[40]

Margaret Thatcher's image was always an important part of the reason for her government's success – not because she was popular, but because she had a particular appeal for a part of the electorate that would not otherwise have voted Conservative. Here Thatcher's apparent lack of systematic and clear thinking often turned out to be an advantage, in that she conveyed the impression that she disliked many aspects of elite liberal thinking, but she did so without being explicit about how she would do things differently and without making many binding promises.

AGAINST CONSENSUS?

Thatcher hated the word 'consensus'.[41] Many of her enemies assumed that this hatred focused on a particular kind of consensus – that which had grown up around Keynesian economics and the welfare state in post-war Britain. Some of her colleagues also came, at least after 1990, to relish the image of themselves as enemies of the political orthodoxies that had allegedly pervaded both parties during the 1950s and 1960s. There are three reasons, however, why we should hesitate before labelling Thatcher as the destroyer of the post-war consensus. First, the Thatcher government's attack on government spending, especially welfare spending, was less dramatic than its enemies alleged. Government spending in many areas rose during the 1980s. Secondly, the Thatcher government never really denounced the whole post-war period. Thatcher herself was polite about the ministers of the Labour governments who held office immediately after the war. None of Thatcher's ministers ever suggested that it might, for example, be desirable to dismantle the National Health Service. For all their occasional talk about Victorian values or periodic attempts to rehabilitate the 1930s, it was, in fact, pretty clear that the golden age for Thatcherites was the 1950s.[42] This was the very period during which the Conservatives had embraced the post-war consensus. Thatcher recalled the 1950s thus:

> I am always astonished when people refer to that period as a time of repression, dullness or conformity – the Age of Anxiety etc. The 1950s were, in a thousand different ways, the reawakening of normal happy life after the trials of wartime and the petty indignities of post-war austerity.[43]

There was a sense in which Thatcherites attacked the 'progressive consensus'; that is to say, the way in which establishment opinion evolved during the 1960s and early 1970s. In an important shadow cabinet discussion of 1975, Angus Maude dated the moment at which the 'consensus' had moved to the Left very precisely: 1962.[44] Thatcher thought 'things started to go wrong in the late Sixties'.[45] Thatcherites did not challenge the existence of the welfare state but they did complain about the growing proportion of the national wealth that it consumed. They resented specific aspects of 'progressive' opinion – notably that relating to comprehensive schools. However, even if the 'progressive' rather than the 'post-war' consensus is considered, attacks on it had more effect in terms of Thatcherite rhetoric than policy – the Thatcherites did not in fact reverse many of the policies that had been enacted in the late 1960s.

Secondly, the post-war consensus was not just about Keynesianism and the welfare state. It also encompassed a view of Britain's role in the world. The two parties agreed that loss of the Empire should not mean the loss of Britain's great power status. They both sought to maintain this through membership of NATO, through a particularly intimate alliance with the United States and through Britain's possession of an independent nuclear bomb. Both parties also accepted, though neither was very successful at doing anything about it, that they needed to reverse Britain's economic decline relative to other countries, particularly in western Europe, that became visible during the 1960s. By the mid-1970s most major politicians agreed that British membership of the European Economic Community was a crucial part of reversing this decline.

In the contexts of great power status and attitudes to economic decline, the Thatcher government did not merely accept the post-war consensus; it was a strong defender of it. Thatcher's relatively conventional views on this matter in the 1960s and 1970s are thrown into focus by comparison with someone who really did challenge the consensus: Enoch Powell. Later the most revealing comparison was with the political Left: in 1983 it was Thatcher's Conservative Party that defended the pre-1979 consensus – revolving around the American alliance, nuclear weapons and the EEC. It was Michael Foot's Labour Party that attacked it.

There was, however, one sense in which Thatcher did attack consensus. This did not involve the specific policies of the post-war period; rather it was a question of style. Thatcher's attacks on consensus did not on the whole involve reference to post-war Britain at all. Sometimes she just attacked the very notion of consensus: 'a soft wishy washy word'.[46] Often her insistence on the superiority of 'conviction' to 'consensus' swept across the centuries to take in Greek philosophers, old testament prophets and reformation theologians.[47] She represented a view of politics that saw vigorously expressed disagreement as inherently desirable.

In early 1979 Norman Tebbit explained what he saw as being special about Margaret Thatcher in revealing terms:

> She's not a Conservative like, say, Stanley Baldwin or some of those leaders who were essentially compromisers and stayers in office and trimmers to keep the ship of state just going that way. She sees that we need a much more radical change of direction than that, and that's what made her attractive to people like myself.[48]

The reference to Baldwin is significant. He could hardly be accused or representing the post-war consensus — some suggested that such a consensus had been built in conscious opposition to everything that Baldwin stood for.[49] What Thatcherites disliked about Baldwin was his manner rather than his policies. He was a tough-minded politician in terms of what he *did* (it was, after all, as a result of Baldwin's economic policies that Norman Tebbit's father had been obliged to 'get on his bike and look for work'), but he was emollient and conciliatory in terms of what he *said*. Baldwin had an odd afterlife during the 1980s. Though he had been the most electorally successful Tory prime minister of the twentieth century, Thatcher could barely bring herself to say his name — indeed, she referred to Jack Baldwin, the professor of organic chemistry at Oxford, almost as often as she referred to Stanley Baldwin the politician.[50] Baldwin also became a significant figure for those Conservative politicians who wanted to distance themselves from Thatcher's style without condemning her policies. Julian Critchley, delighted to find something that would annoy both Michael Foot and Margaret Thatcher, campaigned during the early 1980s to erect a statue of Baldwin in the House of Commons.[51] William Whitelaw gave the Baldwin Memorial Lecture in 1980,[52] Edward Heath insisted that Baldwin represented the true Conservative Party,[53] and Thatcher's successor, John Major, announced that Stanley Baldwin was his political hero.

Thatcher's combative style accounted for much of her early success but it also explained the increasing distance between her and her ministers: many of them worried that their leader saw conflict as an aim in itself. After a shadow cabinet discussion of trade union reform, Hailsham wrote in his diary: 'Margaret wants to fight. But about what?'[54] Radical Thatcherites allowed for the possibility that they would have some hard fights to impose their vision on Britain, but, like Howe, they saw no gain to be had from unnecessary disagreement and, like Lawson, they anticipated a moment when a consensus might be built, or resurrected, around their own ideas.[55] John Biffen illustrates the changes in the Conservative Party most strikingly. Biffen was willing to take unpopular positions when he thought it necessary – Thatcher regarded his open support for Powell as an act of political suicide in the early 1970s. However, Biffen's apparently extreme stance was designed for a specific and limited purpose. He told John Hoskyns that 'wild men on the Right' would help move the centre of the Conservative Party.[56] By the mid-1980s Biffen believed that redefinition of the party's centre had gone far enough and began to talk about 'balanced tickets' and consolidation. Men such as Biffen were increasingly worried by what they saw as Thatcher's 'Maoist' enthusiasm for new battles even after the old ones had been won.

A THATCHERITE PEOPLE?

Thatcher won three general elections with comfortable majorities, but opinion polls showed that Thatcher personally was not always popular with the electorate. They also showed that two thirds of British people in the late 1980s regarded the phrase 'Thatcher's Britain' as evoking something unpleasant.[57] Polls consistently showed that British people were suspicious of free-market values and sympathetic to notions of communal solidarity – particularly as expressed in the welfare state.

All this evidence needs to be used with care. Opinion poll results depended on the questions people were asked. Voters often seemed to distinguish between what was 'good' and what was 'good for me'. Polls about 'values' often implied the existence of a scale with 'collectivism' or 'government action' at one end and 'individualism' at the other, but such a scale did not really capture the complexity of the choices in British politics during the 1980s.[58] Respondents tended to dislike unrestrained free-market economics and anything that they perceived as a threat to the welfare state. On the other hand, they were positive about, say, trade union reform. Indeed, in this area, the Thatcher government was marked by caution rather than radicalism. Norman Tebbit said that he aimed in his trade union legislation to 'stay one step behind public opinion'. An important part of the electorate was also quite closely aligned with Thatcherism, or at least with what was perceived as being Thatcher's personal position, on issues such as race and crime. One might in any case argue that people's statements about economic 'values' reflected a sense of the worthy opinions they were expected to express but that the votes they cast in general elections were a more realistic reflection of the ways in which they calculated their own interest. Thatcher's ministers seem to have been cynically aware that the electorate was 'unThatcherite' in every respect except its repeated willingness to re-elect governments led by Margaret Thatcher.[59]

Another interpretation would stress the peculiarity of the British electoral system. Margaret Thatcher's Conservative Party obtained more votes than any other party in every election that it contested, but it never got a majority of British people's votes. In fact, the Conservative share of the vote declined between 1979 and 1983 – though the Conservative representation in parliament increased between these two dates. Part of the reason lay in the foundation of the Social Democratic Party (SDP) in 1981. Initially, it seemed likely that the SDP would eat into the Conservative electorate. However, Conservative fortunes revived, particularly after the Falklands War, and this transformed the electoral position of the three main parties. The Conservatives, gaining more votes than any other party, won a disproportionate share of seats in the 1983 election. The SDP and their Liberal allies, gaining fewer votes than the other parties, won a disproportionately small number of seats in parliament.

Some commentators argued that this reflected the fact that Thatcherism had not succeeded in electoral terms, but rather that its opponents had failed. They pointed to the division of the 'anti-Thatcher vote'. They also, at least in 1983, often talked about the 'unelectability' of the Labour Party: committed, particularly on defence, to policies that were unpopular with the electorate and led by a man, Michael Foot, who was seen as an improbable prime minister.[60] Often debate about the electoral success of Thatcherism was tied in with debates about the post-war consensus. Those who urged the unification of the anti-Thatcher vote assumed that post-war consensus was a kind of default option to which a large part of the electorate would revert as soon as squabbles on the Left were resolved. This analysis understates the extent to which Thatcher was actually a defender of the post-war settlement, especially in the 1983 election, and to which the Labour Party was its enemy. It also underestimates the extent to which individual voters regarded their votes as having a significance that went beyond the simple instrumental question of whether or not they managed to eject a government they disliked. It overestimates the extent to which there was some natural centre ground on which the Labour Party and the SDP, or at least their voters, might have been able to come together. In fact, it is wrong to see a clear division between a broad mass of leftist and centrist positions and an extreme right-wing Thatcherite position. Many issues cut across the party divisions in ways that aligned parts of the political centre with Thatcherism. Nuclear weapons was not an issue that divided a broad Left from the Conservative Party – on the contrary this was an issue that placed the Conservatives, along with the SDP and part of the Labour Right, on one side, with the Labour Left and part of the Liberal Party on the other. On industrial relations, the Labour Party – especially its 'moderate', centrist wing – was closely attached to the trade unions. The SDP leadership, on the other hand, had broken away from the Labour Party partly in protest at the institutionalization of trade union power. SDP MPs were divided on the trade union laws that the Thatcher government introduced in 1982 – five of them voted against and seventeen voted in favour. Most rank-and-file members of the SDP were hostile to trade unions.

On economic management, there was, again, no clear-cut division. Those who talked of a broad anti-Thatcher coalition sometimes wanted to revive a 'Keynesian' consensus. The truth was, though, that the Labour Party official policy (at least during the early 1980s) was not very Keynesian. Its emphasis was on direct state control rather than broad macro-economic management. As for the SDP, its members seem to have wanted to see higher levels of state spending (perhaps because some of them worked for the public sector) but the position of its leaders vis-à-vis economic Thatcherism was not one of unqualified hostility.

Most of all, emphasis on Thatcherism's electoral failure assumes that Thatcherism ought to have been different from any other political movement and that it ought to have converted a majority of the population to its point of view. There is no evidence that

Conservative electoral strategists thought in these terms – they were happy with a working parliamentary majority and not overly exercised by the question of how it was obtained.

The 'success' of Thatcherism did not necessarily mean electoral success. Thatcher certainly wanted to win elections and stay in Downing Street. Some of her supporters, however, were very aware of the difference between being 'in office' and being 'in power' and were sure that they preferred the latter to the former. As a young radical in the Centre for Policy Studies during the early 1980s, John Redwood recalled that a great deal of his work was predicated on the assumption that the Conservatives were in fact likely to lose the next election, and for this reason 'In our policy discussions we would always include the question of whether the change we were proposing could be made irreversible.'[61] The area in which Redwood and his colleagues were most successful in establishing 'irreversibility' was, eventually, privatization. Privatization stood in an odd relation to electoral success. The Conservatives needed to be reasonably secure in office before they could get significant numbers to buy shares in privatized industries and, at least as long as Labour threatened to renationalize, privatization may have contributed to Conservative success. But privatized companies were never popular; rather, like nationalized companies in the 1960s and 1970s, they were simply accepted as part of the economic landscape. The Conservatives had not so much won the argument as persuaded the British people that there was no argument to be had.

How far, though, did the Thatcher government mobilize some wider change in values? Thatcher was pessimistic. Referring to the period after the 1983 election, she wrote:

> there was still too much socialism in Britain. The fortunes of socialism do not depend on those of the Labour Party: in fact, in the long run it would be truer to say that Labour's fortunes depend on those of socialism. And socialism was still built into the institutions and

mentality of Britain. We had sold thousands of council homes; but 29% of the housing stock remained in the public sector. We had increased parents' rights in the education system; but the ethos in the classrooms and teachers' training colleges remained stubbornly Left wing. We had grappled with the problem of bringing more efficiency into local government; but the Left's redoubts in the great cities still went virtually unchallenged. We had cut back trade union power; but still almost 50 per cent of the workforce in employment was unionized.[62]

Perhaps looking for ways in which the British public might have embraced Thatcherism with enthusiasm is deceptive. Marxists who were interested in how Thatcherism might achieve ideological hegemony in Britain often talked about the way in which it might change perceptions of 'common sense'. This is a significant phrase because it was one that Thatcherites, especially Margaret Thatcher herself, frequently used.[63] Common sense did not necessarily imply a belief that Thatcherite policies were good, but rather that they were inevitable or 'natural'. The success of Thatcherism in these terms was to be measured not just in the way that its supporters expressed their enthusiasm, but also in the ways that its opponents (or victims) expressed their acquiescence. Unemployed people who recognized that unemployment was 'no one's fault' were, in one sense, Thatcherite, even if they did not belong to that section of the unemployed (24 per cent in 1983) who voted Conservative.[64]

Some argued that submission was not the same as acceptance. They stressed the ways in which 'dull compulsion of economic relations' forced people to do things without implying that they had undergone any sort of ideological or cultural conversion. However, even 'the dull compulsion of economic relations' is a cultural construct. The fact, for example, that increasing numbers of workers sought to protect their jobs by accepting increasing levels of workplace flexibility rather than by going on strike is a sign that they had to some extent accepted the government's definition of 'economic realism'. Indeed the ways in which Thatcherism redefined 'economic realism' can be seen amongst those Tories who did not think of themselves as Thatcherites. In 1978 a secret report warned Thatcher of the 'harsh reality' that 'Strong unions and advanced technology operated by their members . . . mean that no government these days can "win".'[65] Fourteen years later, Ian Gilmour, who had been a member of the committee that drew up the secret report, argued that the decline in working-class power was the 'harsh reality' and that 'the succession of British acts of parliament registered rather than caused the decline of the trade unions'.[66]

The complexity of what it might mean to 'accept' or 'submit' to Thatcherism is illustrated by the single group of people whose opinions were most intensively studied during the 1980s: miners during the strike of 1984–5. At first glance, the division amongst miners might seem a simple one between those who struck and those who crossed picket lines. The former were the warrior class of the British Left in the mid-1980s; the latter were 'scabs' despised by the Left for their selfishness. The first problem with this division is it does not work for all miners. Only a minority of them worked throughout the strike and only a minority held out until the National Union of Mineworkers called for a return to work in March 1985. Between these two extremes lay a large group of men who struck (and who were sometimes militant supporters of the strike) but who returned to work before March 1985. Strikers themselves sometimes distinguished, after the event, between 'super scabs', who had worked from the beginning, and 'hunger scabs', who had returned to the pits halfway through the strike. This is a division that seems to overlap with that between people who accepted Thatcherism and those who merely submitted to the 'dull compulsion of economic relations'.

It should be stressed, however, that even the 'super scabs' of the Nottingham coalfield were not enthusiastic supporters of the Thatcher government. As far as can be told, few of them voted

Conservative. Furthermore, in one respect the stated aims of those who broke the strike were rather similar to those of men who struck: both wanted to preserve their own jobs in a nationalized industry. Working miners remained members of a trade union. It is true that some broke away to join the Union of Democratic Miners, but even then a large proportion of the members of the UDM would have liked to reunite with the NUM. Whatever their enemies may have said, working miners thought of their interests in very collective terms – indeed most working miners, just like most strikers, seem to have been driven by a desire to fit in with their neighbours and workmates. There were also ways in which the more general values of the 1980s cut across the division between strikers and strike-breakers in the coalfields. Both sides were very affected by that most Thatcherite institution: home ownership. Men who worked often did so because they needed to pay mortgages; equally strikers often believed that owning their houses had given them a particular attachment to their pit villages and sometimes argued that the closure of pits would bring a fall in house prices.[67]

LEGACY

What was left of Thatcherism after Margaret Thatcher had gone? Thatcher was by this stage an emphatic believer in a Thatcherism that would go on after her political demise. Her desire to secure the election of John Major as her successor was partly linked to the desire to secure the survival of Thatcherism – though it also had a good deal to do with personal bitterness, and her feelings about the succession were not shared by all Thatcherites. To many people's surprise, the Conservative Party did win the 1992 general election, but it was not a successful party for most of the fifteen years after Thatcher's resignation. Between 1997 and 2005, it ran through four different leaders and lost three general elections.

Some commentators had always worried, or hoped, that Thatcher would induce intolerable divisions in her own party. As early as 1983, one of her admirers wrote: 'History's verdict on Mrs Thatcher could yet be that she saved the nation, and dished her party. It might be a verdict that all three deserved.'[68] In 2005 John Sergeant expressed a common argument when he wrote that 'Maggie's fatal legacy' had been to destroy the Conservative Party. Sergeant attributed this destruction to divisions over Europe and to the bitterness caused by the circumstances of Thatcher's departure.[69]

The notion that the Conservative Party has been 'destroyed' looks less convincing in 2009 than it did in 2005. Besides, viewing Thatcher as the 'destroyer of the Conservative Party' risks, as is often the case with interpretations of Thatcherism, painting an excessively benign picture of what came before 1979. For one thing, such a view assumes that there was a secure patrician 'old' party that was displaced by Thatcherism during the 1970s. Actually, the party had already changed frequently, which was partly why it was so electorally successful. Besides, Thatcher did not simply sweep away an old Tory style of patrician paternalism and social liberalism. Even 'traditional' Conservatives had often concluded that 'old' solutions, particularly with regard to labour relations, were not working during the 1970s. Furthermore, Thatcherism did not just mean free-market economics. The ultimate Tory grandee – Alec Douglas-Home – was closer to Margaret Thatcher on issues of race or foreign policy than he was to Edward Heath. Major General Sir Brian Wyldbore-Smith DSO was very much an old-style Tory. He was a Master of Hounds for the Belvoir Hunt who regretted the passing of national service, disliked professional politicians and thought immigration and urbanization would destroy English values. He was, however, also a moderately important Thatcherite – director of the Conservative Board of Finance from 1970 until 1992 and a trustee of the Thatcher Foundation.[70]

There is in any case no reason why political parties should survive and, judged in an international context, it is odd that British politics should still be so influenced by a party that was founded in the early nineteenth century and that exists, in theory at least, to defend the monarchy, the Union and the established Church. Between 1974 (the moment when Heath called for a government of national unity) and 1982 (the moment when electoral support for the Social Democrat Party began to decline), there was a period when many thought that the British party system might be restructured in ways that would mean the end of the Conservative Party. Thatcher was one of the very few Tory politicians who believed that the battle against socialism could be carried out exclusively through her own party and, in this sense, she was the saviour of her party rather than its destroyer.

Alongside the view of Thatcher as the destroyer of her party has often gone the view that Thatcherism was the intellectual ancestor of New Labour. In March 1986 the journalist Woodrow Wyatt met John Smith – Labour's shadow chancellor who was to become leader of the party six years later. Apparently, Smith agreed with Wyatt that the Labour Party owed a 'big debt' to Thatcher for having 'tamed the unions' and made reform of the Labour Party possible. Wyatt subsequently told Thatcher about this meeting and suggested that she had 'shifted the centre about two hundred miles to the Right', to which Thatcher replied: 'Yes but not far enough.'[71] The changes in the Labour Party that happened after 1990, of course, dwarfed those that had happened during the 1980s. In 1984 Andrew Gamble wrote:

The real question to ask about Thatcherism . . . is how far it is creating [a] . . . broader consensus for its policies and objectives . . . the Labour Party must be brought to accept it or the Labour Party must never govern again. In the first case this would mean the Labour Party abandoning Clause IV; accepting the priority given to the control of inflation; renouncing protectionism . . . to shield any sector of the British economy from the need to be competitive; and accepting a much smaller state sector, with lower taxation, selective rather than universal welfare provision, as well as permanent weakening of trade union organizations . . . No one really expects Labour to head down this road.[72]

By 1997 Labour had in fact adopted many of the policies that Gamble regarded as being inconceivable in 1984. Indeed, there was an odd personal flirtation between Margaret Thatcher and Labour prime ministers: Tony Blair attended her eightieth birthday party and Gordon Brown invited the woman whom he had once derided as an 'Anglo Poujadist' to tea at Number 10 Downing Street.

Does this mean that the Labour Party had become Thatcherite? Clearly Labour accepted that elements of what the Thatcher government had done were now irreversible. There was no attempt to renationalize companies that had been privatized. The trade union laws of the 1980s were not repealed. However, there was such a wide shift in all political attitudes between the mid-1970s and the mid-1990s that it is sometimes hard to construct a meaningful spectrum on which politicians can be compared. There is no doubt that John Smith was a more right-wing Labour leader than Michael Foot, but saying whether Tony Blair was more right-wing than James Callaghan is a trickier proposition – partly because the Labour Party turned through such a collection of sharp political hairpin bends in the 1980s and partly because some of the issues that confronted politicians in the late 1990s were just different from those that had confronted politicians in the late 1970s.

It should also be stressed that changes in the Labour Party should not just be seen as a reaction to Thatcherism. They were also in part responses to international changes that affected left-wing parties throughout western Europe regardless of what kind of opponents they faced. Capitalism seeped into the most unexpected corners of political life. A monument to Antonio Gramsci (whose writings exercised such an influence over English Marxist understanding of Thatcherism) is now located in the entrance hall to the business school of the accountancy firm Ernst and Young, which bought the building that had formerly housed the headquarters of the Italian Communist Party.

Changes in the Labour Party lead us to the broader sorts of change in the whole pattern of politics. What would the Thatcherite position on the break-up of Yugoslavia be? Thatcher was vigorously pro-Bosnian, but some of her advisers took exactly the opposite point of view. What might a Thatcherite position on climate change be – especially in an era when support for coal-fired power stations is seen as a 'right-wing' policy? What about international events since September 2001? Thatcher always laid a heavy emphasis on international law (including the legal restraint that might prevent states from pursuing terrorists outside their own frontiers). Thatcherites are divided on whether British involvement in the invasion of Iraq in 2003 was a good thing and, indeed, disagree with each other on what Lady Thatcher's own position on this matter might be.[73] In 1983 Conservatives denounced Labour proposals to nationalize banks; now (early 2009) both Labour and Conservative politicians seem to recognize that the acquisition of a controlling interest in British banks by the state is a necessary and, they devoutly hope, temporary evil.

The truth is that Thatcherism was not composed of political constants that can be traced back to the nineteenth century or transported forward into the twenty-first. It was rooted in particular problems posed by the expansion of Soviet power after the Vietnam War, the development of 'progressive opinion' after 1968 and the British elite's obsession with notions of economic decline during the 1970s. Thatcherism also exploited certain opportunities opened up by North Sea Oil, the growth of international finance, the election of Ronald Reagan as president of the United States and the spread of reform in Communist Europe. Thatcherism belonged to a particular time, and it is probably significant that Thatcher seems to have become most interested in the idea of Thatcherism as a timeless phenomenon at precisely the moment when she was herself losing touch with political reality.

SOME THOUGHTS ON SOURCES

The way to study Conservatives is to meet Conservatives;
and here Leftist writers are at a loss. They resemble early
Victorian anthropologists, whose willingness to pronounce
on the nature of man bore no relation to their readiness
to commune with natives by sleeping in straw huts.
Naturally self-imprisoned in their intellectual ghetto,
Leftists concentrate on the printed text, which, in Tory
terms, means the ephemeral, the tangential and the
epiphenomenal.

John Vincent[1]

Professor Vincent is unfair to 'Leftists' – to judge from the
interview pages of *Marxism Today* in the late 1980s, of which
more below, one might think that Beatrix Campbell and her
colleagues spent practically all their time talking to Tories.
Furthermore, some Thatcherites took ideas seriously: the 'printed
text' was less 'ephemeral' to, say, Nigel Lawson than it would have
been to Alec Douglas-Home.

The peculiar circumstances of the 1980s also did something to
subvert another distinction that is dear to historians: that between
primary and secondary sources. Many books and articles about
Thatcherism deserve to be treated as primary sources – either
because they draw directly on the experience of the authors or
because they were themselves intended to be political statements.

Equally, many of Thatcher's allies were aware of their own historical importance. Their memoirs are rarely just based on memory. Ministers and advisers knew quite a lot about the academic debate that swirled around the events in which they had taken part – sometimes ministerial memoirs were in fact ghost-written, edited or otherwise influenced by professional historians. Mark Garnett, to take the most obvious example, is a historian who has produced his own accounts, and also a kind of academic midwife who has helped Tory politicians deliver their accounts. He wrote biographies of Keith Joseph and William Whitelaw – the latter book being an official biography that seems, with the complicity of its subject, to have revealed things that had been skated over in Whitelaw's own memoirs.[2] However, Garnett also edited Alfred Sherman's bilious attack on the Thatcher government from the Right and encouraged Sir Ian Gilmour to produce his display of urbane sulkiness from the Left of the Conservative Party.[3] In writing their autobiographies, ministers drew on accounts by other people of the governments in which they had served.[4] They also looked to historians to place their own actions in some longer-term context. The work of Andrew Roberts was so important in moulding the retrospective view that Thatcherites had of what they had done* that intelligent observers often assume that Roberts came to prominence in the 1980s[5] – actually, he must have been at school in 1980 and did not publish his first book until 1991.

Because journalistic accounts were so important to the image of the Thatcher government, including the image that its members often had of themselves, it is worth pausing to think about the backgrounds of the British political journalists – Peter Hennessy, Peter Jenkins, Simon Jenkins, Peter Riddell and Hugo Young – who wrote most about Thatcher. All belonged to that fraction of the British establishment that encompasses academia, parts of Fleet Street (especially pre-Murdoch *The Times* and the *Economist*)

---

* Roberts's work is cited by John Hoskyns and John Nott.

and the administrative civil service. The title of Hugo Young's biography of Margaret Thatcher – *One of Us* – is an implicit joke because Young, and most of his readers, did not really think that Thatcher was 'their kind of person'. Looking back, however, I wonder whether the joke was not on 'us' rather than her. Thatcher, after all, was explicit about what she stood for. People who wrote about her often did so through the prism of unspoken assumptions that sprang from their own background. Young writes that Thatcher 'possessed no trace of the effortless superiority of the Balliol men, Macmillan and Heath, who went before her'.[6] Readers of these lines might not be surprised to hear that Young himself was a Balliol man.

The grander journalists drew from their extensive connections with the great and the good. Sometimes it seems to me that they end up being sucked into the spider's web of their well-placed sources. For example, Simon Jenkins insists that Britain would have been unable to fight the Falklands War if it had taken place after the defence cuts envisaged by John Nott had been implemented.[7] No doubt this is what senior figures in the Admiralty told their journalistic contacts, but it is almost impossible to predict the outcome of a hypothetical war fought with hypothetical resources. Anyone who reads Jenkins's confident pronouncements on this subject might do well to recall that he is the man who said that the battle for Baghdad in 2003 would be as savage as that for Stalingrad in 1943.[8]

In a similar vein, consider one of the most striking passages in Hugo Young's biography of Margaret Thatcher. Young describes Thatcher's propensity to interfere in every aspect of policy and illustrates this with an account of how she threatened to take personal control of the hunt for the Yorkshire ripper (a serial killer of women) in 1980: 'so vexed was the prime minister that she summoned the Home Secretary and announced her intention of going to Leeds that weekend to take personal charge of the investigation'.[9] This story seems to refer to a meeting between

Thatcher and the home secretary (in the presence of various civil servants) on 25 October 1980.[10] An account of it is now in the public domain. It reveals that Thatcher said that violence against women was a serious matter, suggested that the local police had not been very effective and asked whether it might be useful to hand over the enquiry to Scotland Yard. The official transcript of the meeting gives no hint of a threat to take personal charge of the case. All of Thatcher's comments sound sensible and her intervention may have had an effect because the team investigating the case was changed shortly after it and the murderer was caught. It is easy to imagine how this story might have passed from a succession of civil servants to a succession of journalists (probably over a succession of lunches at the Garrick) and become progressively more colourful in the telling – 'Have you heard what happened to Willie? Now the bloody woman thinks she's Sherlock Holmes.'

There were of course some influential journalists who were, at least to start with, self-consciously outside the establishment. Particularly important in the 1980s was the journal *Marxism Today*. Founded in 1957, it was the official organ of the Communist Party of Great Britain (CPGB). Nigel Lawson described it as 'recherché' and 'briefly influential' – the mere fact that a senior Conservative minister could be bothered to be rude about it is probably a sign of its importance. The journal had an odd symbiotic relation with Thatcherism. Martin Jacques became editor in 1977 and began to rethink the politics of the Left. The fact that the British Communist Party entertained no real fantasies about ever holding power gave some of its intellectuals an Olympian open-mindedness. During the 1980s *Marxism Today*'s circulation grew from 4,000 to 15,000 (its readership was larger than the membership of the CPGB), and it became a glossy magazine that stood uncomfortably on the doorstep of consumerism – it carried advertisements for Nicaraguan rum and Zimbabwean wines. Leading Tories (Biffen, Heath, Heseltine) were interviewed in its pages and, on at least one occasion, Thatcher quoted from it.[11] It ran important articles by Hall, Jessop, Gamble and others, some of which formed the basis of later books.

Marxism Today was, however, neither a party-line Communist journal nor the exponent of a systematic theoretical viewpoint. Marxists often denounced work that appeared in *Marxism Today*, and, indeed, it seemed as though the most bitter arguments about Thatcherism took place between different kinds of Marxist. Roger Scruton – surveying matters from the other side of the spectrum, or perhaps just the other side of Birkbeck senior common room – parodied an Open University sociology course that pitted Dave Spart, who believed that 'the capitalist class as a class controls the means of production', against Chris Toad, who believed that 'the bourgeoisie as a class controls the power structures from which workers as a class are excluded'.[12]

For some contributors to *Marxism Today*, the urgency of their day-to-day analysis of Thatcherism seems to have gone with a declining interest in Marxist theory. It would certainly be hard to tell from his articles in the journal whether or not Andrew Gamble considered himself to be a Marxist.[13] Arthur Seldon, one of *Marxism Today*'s many Thatcherite admirers, argued that the second word in its title was more important that the first.[14] Between 1975 and 1990 a certain kind of left-wing affiliation sometimes seemed more like a fashion statement than a political or intellectual manifesto – this was a period when a group of art school students named their pop band Scritti Politti, in homage to the work of Antonio Gramsci. The jibe by Peter Jenkins that Thatcherism was 'more a style than an ideology' might equally well have been directed at many British Marxists and, indeed, the article in which the very unMarxist Jenkins made this point was published in *Marxism Today*.[15]

As time went on, the analysis of some left-wing writers began to bear an odd resemblance to that of some writers who were looking at matters from a more obviously establishment perspective.[16] This was particularly notable with regard to the sentimentalization of the period between 1945 and 1979. At first, writers from the Left tended to be highly critical of post-war social democracy, and often saw Thatcherism as associated with changes that had begun a long time before Thatcher's arrival on the stage of British politics. However, the Falklands War and the Conservative victory in the 1983 election seem to have brought a change. Anthony Barnett's *Iron Britannia* (published in 1982 and written at the beginning of the Falklands campaign) was probably the last left-wing analysis to emphasize the things that Thatcherism and post-war social democracy had in common rather than the things that separated them. After this, left-wingers were increasingly prone to see themselves as part of a broad anti-Thatcher alliance, and to celebrate the pre-1979 period. Eric Hobsbawm was the most important contributor to this new mood. He was a regular writer for *Marxism Today* and a card-carrying member of the Communist Party, but he saw political salvation in a political alliance of the Labour and Social Democratic parties, and he seems to have had more respect for Healey than for Benn, Foot or Kinnock. His notion of a 'golden age' throughout the Western world from 1945 to 1975, a notion that influenced many historians of Europe, seems in effect to have meant 'anything before Thatcher'.

Questions about sources are particularly pressing now because the thirtieth anniversary of Thatcher's election, when this book is to be published, is also the time when the cabinet papers relating to the Thatcher government will begin to be opened to historians. Is it folly to write without having full access to the sources that will soon be available? My own feeling is that the archives to be opened over the next decade will be useful to historians in all sorts of ways. I dare say that some of my own assumptions will be proved wrong, that some questions will be answered, and some new questions (quite a large number I suspect) will be raised.

I am, however, sceptical about the idea that there is some pot of gold at the end of the archival rainbow.[17] Consider, for example, the Westland crisis, which almost brought Thatcher down in 1986.

Many participants in this believe that there is a document somewhere that will vindicate them, or reveal what really happened. Leon Brittan told a friend that the truth of the matter would come out 'after thirty years' (i.e. when the cabinet papers were opened). Michael Heseltine became obsessed with finding out what 'really happened'. He nagged the Italian industrialist Gianni Agnelli, who had been involved in a takeover bid for Westland, to tell him – Agnelli wisely said that he could not remember.[18] Heseltine even printed his own email address in his memoirs in case a reader could shed light on the matter.[19] One journalist believed that Colette Bowe, a civil servant at the centre of the case, had her own account locked away in a safe.[20]

All this reveals the slight absurdity of an interest in 'secret' documents. What document is likely to reveal something that none of the principal participants in the affair knew or understood themselves? Over half of the ministers who sat in cabinet on the day that Heseltine walked out have now published their memoirs. But these accounts do not agree about the most simple details of the affair – whether Heseltine intended to resign when he first arrived for the meeting and whether Thatcher was already prepared for him to do so. Nicholas Ridley opens his account by saying: 'I have a clear memory of the first Cabinet in 1986 after the Christmas recess, on 16 January.'[21] The meeting actually took place on 9 January. Geoffrey Howe describes his own contribution to cabinet discussion and then adds, with a characteristic mixture of asperity and self-deprecation, that no one else seems to recall his intervention.[22] In any case, Westland hardly revolved around hidden documents; the whole scandal was rooted in the fact that so many documents had been improperly leaked to the press. There were no fewer than three official enquiries into Westland, which means that the events surrounding a small Somerset firm in late 1985 and early 1986 have been investigated in more depth than almost any other episode in recent British history. It is very hard to imagine that cabinet papers will tell us anything that we do not already know. Perhaps the fury of the main protagonists in the affair sprang from the fact that they themselves were uncertain of what had really happened.

The Westland affair does draw our attention to sources that are available, even before the opening of cabinet papers. Firstly Thatcher's ministers were notoriously indiscreet. Furthermore, a group of journalists built up particularly good personal relations with important figures in the Conservative Party during the fifteen years when Margaret Thatcher led it. By the time he came to write his account of Thatcher's fall, Alan Watkins reckoned that he was on first-name terms with over a hundred Tory MPs and that it was quicker to list those people who had refused to talk to him than to acknowledge those who had done so.[23] Sometimes leaks were used, especially by the prime minister's own entourage, as a means of conducting political battles. Sometimes indiscretion seems to have been built into the psychology of the government in ways that divided even men who agreed with each other about policy. Cecil Parkinson, not the most discreet of men, believed that John Wakeham, leader of the House of Commons, had briefed journalists about cabinet business even as he walked back from Downing Street.[24]

All this makes it easier to study Thatcherism but leaks have to be used with care. Indeed my general sense is that the release of archives will not produce startling 'revelations' but rather tend to put information that has already been revealed into a context that will make it appear a bit less startling. One of the important leaks from Thatcher's shadow cabinet concerned the Ridley report, which apparently anticipated a confrontation between a future Tory government and the National Union of Mineworkers. The report was published in the *Economist* in 1978 under the headline 'CIVIL WAR OR APPOMATTOX'. Six years later, when the government did take on the miners, many left-wingers assumed that it was acting on the Ridley plan and well-thumbed photocopies of the *Economist* article circulated on picket lines. However, the shadow cabinet papers, which are now available, remind us that Ridley's view on the miners formed just one small part of a long report on other matters, and that Ridley was a relatively junior figure. His report probably illustrated the way in which senior Conservatives were thinking but it did not necessarily *influence* that thinking much. Ministers in 1984 were not following the Ridley plan – it is not clear, in fact, that anyone in Central Office even knew where Ridley's report had been filed.[25]

The second source for the study of the Thatcher government lies in the memoirs published by those who participated in politics during the period. Almost twenty of the people who held office in Thatcher's cabinets have now published some kind of autobiography – as have many other Tory politicians and other well-connected figures in British public life. Once again, the very acrimony that the Thatcher government generated means that these memoirs can be revealing. The bland tones of self-satisfaction and mutual congratulation that characterize an earlier generation of Tory autobiography are usually absent. Enoch Powell famously likened reading Harold Macmillan's memoirs to 'chewing on cardboard'. Anyone who reads the memoirs of, say, Alistair McAlpine or John Nott will sometimes feel as though they are choking on broken glass.

A willingness to say frank things does not, of course, mean that authors are being frank about everything, especially their own motives. In his diaries, Alan Clark, a junior minister in the late 1980s, describes amongst other things his intermittent desire to stand on the window ledge outside his seventh-floor office in the Department of Trade and Industry and urinate on the passers-by in Victoria Street beneath him.[26] On the other hand, the entry in this diary for 29 October 1990 does not mention the fact that on that day Clark went to urge a senior minister to put himself forward as Thatcher's replacement as leader of the Conservative Party.[27]

The very differences between the accounts provided by various participants in the Thatcher government can themselves be revealing. Kenneth Baker suggests that Nicholas Ridley considered the Falklands War to be 'mad', something that the reader would not learn from Ridley's own memoirs.[28] On the other hand, a reader of Baker's memoirs would not discover that Baker had, according to his friend Max Hastings, said in the late 1970s that a future Conservative government should avoid conflict with the miners.[29] Geoffrey Howe draws attention to the support that Tebbit apparently gave in 1985 to British entry into the Exchange Rate Mechanism,[30] a support that Tebbit does not mention in his own memoirs.[31] Several of Thatcher's advisers allege that it was Thatcher, acting on the advice of Alan Walters, who forced Geoffrey Howe into his radical budget of 1981. In his own memoirs, Howe comments on the commentaries thus: 'Most of the participants have been keen to take credit . . . So there has been no lack of over-simplification . . . Most of the subsequently alleged battle-lines were by no means apparent (to me at least) at the time.'[32] Howe, himself, however, is not always above 'over-simplification'. He cites the speeches that he delivered in August and September 1978 as examples of the way in which Conservative policy on trade unions was developing.[33] He makes no mention of the draft speech on trade unions that he sent to Thatcher in January 1978 and on which she wrote: 'Geoffrey this is not your subject. The press will crucify you for this.'[34]

The ways in which an autobiography can reveal and conceal are illustrated by the works of Douglas Hurd – works that are interesting precisely because Hurd writes in a more serene and less obviously partisan tone than many of his colleagues. Hurd has written three books about his own political involvement. First, he kept a diary throughout his career. This diary has never been published – though Hurd quotes it in other works and also read out long chunks of it to his biographer.[35] Hurd writes interestingly about the diary, suggesting that entries made at the end of an exhausting or annoying day may be less 'true' than recollections recorded at a greater distance.

Secondly, he published an *End to Promises* in 1979, an account of the government of Edward Heath, whom Hurd had served as an adviser. Hurd sought to defend aspects of Heath's record, but his book was also addressed to the people who had taken power in the Conservative Party after Heath's fall. Hurd recognized that the age that had produced Heath and Macmillan might now seem as remote as the age of Baldwin had seemed to those who had risen to prominence after the Second World War.[36] Hurd was frank about the government's faults, and the diary entry that he quotes from February 1972 – 'The Government now wandering vainly over the battlefield looking for someone to surrender to – and being massacred all the time'[37] is probably the single sentence that is most often cited in accounts of Heath's failure.

Thirdly, Hurd published his memoirs in 2004. Most of his cabinet colleagues had already published their memoirs and, though he is rarely explicit about it, this gives Hurd the last word on some matters. Quotations from the diary were less inhibited in 2004 than in 1979. He quotes his entry for 23 November 1975: 'Listen to a talk by a typical Thatcherite – dark suited, articulate, 55, accountant, full of sourness.'[38] It is revealing that Hurd seems privately to have regarded 'Thatcherite' as a term of abuse – all the more interesting when we remember that he served in Thatcher's cabinets for longer than Nott or Parkinson, and that he was still serving in one of them after both Howe and Lawson had resigned.

In his memoirs Hurd discusses his personal life to a greater extent than most of his colleagues and sometimes he does so in ways that raise interesting questions – one notes, for instance, how many prominent Conservatives got divorced, or lived through some other personal crisis, in the mid-1970s, and one wonders how this might have been related as cause and/or effect to their wider sense of crisis about British politics during the period. Finally, Hurd's memoirs are often most interesting for what they leave out. For example, though his political career involved foreign affairs, security and Ulster, he says nothing at all about an episode that was associated with all three of these – the shooting by British soldiers of three members of the IRA on Gibraltar in 1987.

I should end by emphasizing that any study of Thatcherism published now or at any point in the near future will have a provisional quality. In addition to the opening of papers under the thirty-year rule, documents that are currently exempt from Freedom of Information legislation, such as letters from working miners during the miners' strike of 1984–5, will one day be available to historians.* Many of Thatcher's ministers have not published their memoirs, and some of them will presumably do so. Charles Moore, who, as editor of the *Spectator* from 1984 to 1990, was a participant in Conservative politics during the 1980s, is writing the official biography of Margaret Thatcher.

I have sought to stress throughout this book that the Thatcher government should be seen as an episode in history rather than an aspect of present-day politics. All the same, views of the 1980s will clearly be influenced by things that have happened more recently. I am writing these words in October 2008. In the last few weeks Britain has seen a financial crash, a burst of state intervention in the economy and an apparent revival in the fortunes of the Labour Party. I must admit to worrying that aspects of my book may seem quaintly out of date by the time I see the proofs.

---

* I made requests under the Freedom of Information Act to see the following collections of documents in the National Archives: Coal 31/362, Coal 31/441 and Coal 26/510. My requests were turned down.

NOTES

Place of publication is London, unless otherwise specified. Date of publication refers to the edition cited in this book.

Abbreviations used:

TFW – Margaret Thatcher Foundation website
NA – National Archives

INTRODUCTION

1 Ian Deary, Simon Wessely and Michael Farrell, 'Dementia and Mrs Thatcher', *British Medical Journal*, 291, 21–28 December 1985.
2 *The Times*, 8 December 2005.
3 Andrew Gamble, *The Free Economy and the Strong State* (1994, first published 1988); Stuart Hall and Martin Jacques (eds.), *The Politics of Thatcherism* (1983); Bob Jessop et al., *Thatcherism. A Tale of Two Nations* (Cambridge, 1988); Peter Jenkins, *Mrs Thatcher's Revolution. The End of the Socialist Era* (1987); Dennis Kavanagh, *Thatcherism and British Politics. The End of Consensus?* (Oxford, 1990, first published 1986); Peter Riddell, *The Thatcher Decade. How Britain Changed during the 1980s* (Oxford, 1989); Robert Skidelsky (ed.), *Thatcherism* (1988); Hugo Young, *One of Us. A Biography of Margaret Thatcher* (1990).
4 Stuart Hall, 'The Great Moving Right Show', *Marxism Today*, January 1979.
5 Raphael Samuel, Barbara Bloomfield and Guy Boanas (eds.), *The Enemy Within. Pit Villages and the Miners' Strike of 1984–5* (1986), p. 20.
6 TFW, Thatcher interview with David Frost for TV-AM, 7 June 1985 (105826).
7 John Campbell, *Margaret Thatcher*, Vol. 1, *The Grocer's Daughter* (2000) and Vol. 2, *The Iron Lady* (2003).

8   Andrew Gamble, 'The Reading of a Decade', *Marxism Today*, May 1989: 'The term was first used by Stuart Hall in *Marxism Today* . . . [whose] seminal article "The Great Moving Right Show" appeared in January 1979.'

9   Nigel Lawson used Thatcherism, as he believed, for the first time in 1981, but then wrote: 'I later discovered that it had been used by the recherché and now defunct journal *Marxism Today* before we had even taken office in 1979', Nigel Lawson, *The View from No. 11. Memoirs of a Tory Radical* (1993), p. 64.

10 T. E. Utley, *Spectator*, 9 August 1986, reprinted in Philip Marsden-Smedley (ed.), *Britain in the Eighties. The Spectator's View of the Thatcher Decade* (1989), pp. 146–50.

11 Bob Jessop, Kevin Bonnett, Simon Bromley and Tom Ling, 'Authoritarian Populism, Two Nations and Thatcherism', *New Left Review*, 1, 147, September–October 1984.

12 TFW, Thatcher speech to Conservative Central Council, 15 March 1975 (102655): 'Do we become extremist Right-Wingers? Because that is what our opponents will say, that's what they've been saying. To stand up for liberty is now called Thatcherism. (Laughter.)' Thatcherism was also quite widely used in the press during the late 1970s. See for example, *The Times*, Business Diary, 2 September 1977.

13 John Hoskyns, *Just in Time. Inside the Thatcher Revolution* (2000), p. 118. The phrase was coined by Norman Strauss.

14 Peter Clarke, *A Question of Leadership. From Gladstone to Thatcher* (1991); E. H. H. Green, *Thatcher* (2006).

15 David Cannadine, 'How I Inspired Thatcher'. A Point of View from BBC website, 9 December 2005. Cannadine wrote an article on that very unThatcherite hero Harry Flashman in *New Society* and later heard that his friend Matthew Parris had drawn the article to Thatcher's attention.

16 Campbell, *The Grocer's Daughter*, p. 60.

17 'Playing with the Casino's Money', John Mortimer interview with Tebbit, *Spectator*, 24 May 1986, reprinted in Marsden-Smedley (ed.), *Britain in the Eighties*. pp. 139–46.

18 E. H. H. Green, *Ideologies of Conservatism* (Oxford, 2001), p. 221.

19 The only Thatcher minister to refer to Law in his memoirs is John Nott, but these memoirs were published some time after Nott's

resignation and Nott quite often draws the general historical background of his memoirs from the works of historians rather than personal memory. John Nott, *Here Today, Gone Tomorrow, Recollections of an Errant Politician* (2003), p. 134.

20   Simon Jenkins, *Thatcher and Sons. A Revolution in Three Acts* (2006).

CHAPTER 1. THATCHER BEFORE THATCHERISM

1   Alfred Sherman, *Paradoxes of Power. Reflections on the Thatcher Interlude,* edited by Mark Garnett (Exeter, 2005), p. 20.

2   TFW, Margaret Thatcher, enclosing account of her early career to Donald Kaberry MP, 16 March 1956 (109939).

3   Margaret Thatcher, *The Path to Power* (1996), p. xiii.

4   TFW, Memorandum of conversation between Margaret Thatcher and official of US embassy at Connaught Hotel, 22 May 1973, enclosed with letter from Annenberg to State Department, 25 June 1973 (110554).

5   George Gardiner, *Margaret Thatcher. From Childhood to Leadership* (1975).

6   On the circumstances of his biography's composition and his own life, see George Gardiner, *A Bastard's Tale* (1999).

7   Paul Halloran and Mark Hollingsworth, *Thatcher's Fortunes. The Life and Times of Mark Thatcher* (2005).

8   Leo Abse, *Margaret Daughter of Beatrice. A Politician's Psycho Biography of Margaret Thatcher* (1989).

9   John Campbell, *Margaret Thatcher,* Vol. 1, *The Grocer's Daughter* (2000), p. 33.

10   Ibid., pp. 8–15.

11   For an account by one of her less privileged fellow pupils, who seems not to have fond memories of Margaret Roberts, see Joan Bridgman, 'At School with Margaret Thatcher', *Contemporary Review*, 9 January 2004.

12   Julian Critchley, *A Bag of Boiled Sweets* (1995), p. 49.

13   TFW, Thatcher speech to Conservative Party conference, 13 October 1989 (107789): 'I went to Oxford, but I've never let it hold me back.'

14   *The Fourth Protocol* was published in 1984. It concerns an attempt by elements in the Soviet Union to bring Thatcher's downfall and engineer the election of a left-wing Labour government in 1987. Forsyth dabbled

in Conservative politics. See Frederick Forsyth, *Britain and Europe. The End of Democracy? Tenth Ian Gow Memorial Lecture* (2001).

15 Percy Cradock, *In Pursuit of British Interests. Reflections on Foreign Policy under Margaret Thatcher and John Major* (1997), p. 20.

16 On Thatcher's meeting with Bloom, see George Walden, *Lucky George. Memoirs of an Anti-Politician* (1999), p. 273.

17 Anthony Powell, *Journals, 1982–1986* (1995), p. 40, entry for 26 October 1982.

18 TFW, Thatcher speech on the opening of Buckingham University, 6 February 1976 (102954).

19 TFW, Speech by Harry Giles, 24 February 1950 (100873).

20 Angus Calder, *The Myth of the Blitz* (1991).

21 TFW, Thatcher speech to rally in Cardiff, 16 April 1979 (104011): 'Is this the nation that stood alone in 1940 against the collapse of European Civilization?'

22 TFW, Thatcher speeches: 21 May 1985 (106055), 1 November 1989 (107812) and 29 August 1990 (108179).

23 TFW, Thatcher speech to Conservative Party conference, 13 October 1989 (107789): 'Let us never forget Poland's role in our own finest hour.'

24 George Urban, *Diplomacy and Disillusion at the Court of Margaret Thatcher. An Insider's View* (1996), p. 34: 'I provided some Churchillian words and metaphors for Margaret Thatcher, not because I believed her to be quite of Churchillian stature – though my respect for her was immense – but rather because I thought that she was the most persuasive and eye-catching representative of the new Western determination to stop the Soviet Union.'

25 TFW, Nigel Lawson, 'The New Conservatism', speech to Bow Group, 4 August 1980 (109505): 'This, for a whole generation, was Britain's finest hour: it was also a time when the State was seen to arrogate to itself, in a cause whose rightness was not open to question, all the apparatus of central planning and direction of labour. In fact what is sensible in war, when there is a unique unity of national purpose and when a simple test can be applied to all economic activities (namely whether or not they further the success of the war effort), is wholly inappropriate in time of peace, when what is needed is a system that brings harmoniously together a diversity of individual purposes of which the State need not even be aware. Nevertheless, the apparent

beneficence, rationality and justice of central planning cast a spell that long outlived the wartime world to which it belonged.'

26 Peter Tatchell, the unsuccessful Labour candidate in the Bermondsey by-election of 1983, expressed his admiration for Wintringham in his pamphlet, *Democratic Defence. A Non-Nuclear Alternative* (1985).

27 TFW, Thatcher speech to Scottish Conservative Party conference, 10 May 1985 (106046): 'One of the world's ugliest tyrannies had to be defeated so that we could live in peace and human dignity. It was a war of the common man – our own, Russian, French and American. We all fought, rich and poor, men at the front, women in the factories, fought together in a common cause which transcended all our differences ... Many were at constant risk – in London streets; at Anzio, at Coventry, at Murmansk.'

28 Richard Hillary, *The Last Enemy* (1942).

29 Barbara Cartland, *Ronald Cartland* (1942).

30 John Peyton, *Without Benefit of Laundry* (1997), p. 1.

31 Peter Rawlinson, *A Price Too High. An Autobiography* (1989), p. 17.

32 TFW, Waldron Smithers to J. P. L. Thomas, 5 February 1949. This document is quoted in the editorial comments attached to the memo from Cook to Thomas, 1 February 1949 (109917).

33 Roy Jenkins, *A Life at the Centre* (1994), p. 554.

34 James Prior, *A Balance of Power* (1986), p. 17.

35 Carol Thatcher, *Below the Parapet. The Biography of Denis Thatcher* (1996).

36 Woodrow Wyatt, *The Journals of Woodrow Wyatt*, Vol. 1, *1985–1988*, edited by Sarah Curtis (2000), entry for 19 January 1986, p. 62.

37 Petronella Wyatt, *Father, Dear Father. Life with Woodrow Wyatt* (1999), p. 158.

38 Thatcher's candidacy seems to have been supported by Central Office but resisted by constituency associations. John Ramsden, *The Winds of Change. Macmillan to Heath, 1957–1975* (1996), p. 117.

39 TFW, Harris to Kaberry, 15 July 1958 (109944).

40 Dennis Walters, *Not Always with the Pack* (1989), p. 104.

41 Rawlinson, *A Price Too High*, p. 246.

42 TFW, Thatcher to Kaberry, 18 August 1958 (109946).

43 TFW, 'What My Daughter Must Learn in the Next Nine Years', Thatcher article for *Daily Express*, 4 March 1960 (100948).

44 Campbell, *The Grocer's Daughter*, p. 95.

45 TFW, Thatcher interview for the *Hornsey Journal*, 21 April 1978 (103662). Thatcher denied being a feminist – though the interviewer tried to insist that the mere fact of being leader of the Conservative Party made her a feminist, if not a militant one.

46 The quickest way to find all her statements on feminism is to do a keyword search on the Thatcher Foundation website with the word 'strident'. See, for example, TFW, Thatcher press conference in Glasgow, 26 April 1979 (104045).

47 TFW, Thatcher interview for Thames TV, 13 December 1982 (105071).

48 TFW, Thatcher general election address, 3 February 1950 (100858).

49 Denis Healey, *The Time of My Life* (1990), p. 487.

50 Most literature on the subject in recent years has, in fact, been devoted to showing that consensus was a 'myth'. See Dennis Kavanagh, *Thatcherism and British Politics. The End of Consensus?* (Oxford, 1988); Ben Pimlott, 'The Myth of Consensus' in Lesley Smith (ed.), *The Making of Britain. Echoes of Greatness* (1988); Harriet Jones and Michael Kandiah (eds.), *The Myth of Consensus* (1996); Scott Kelly, *The Myth of Mr Butskell. The Politics of British Economic Policy, 1950–1955* (Aldershot, 2002).

51 Norman Tebbit, *Unfinished Business* (1991), pp. 17–19.

52 Nicholas Ridley, *My Style of Government. The Thatcher Years* (1991), p. 3.

53 Thatcher, *The Path to Power*, p. 116.

54 Campbell, *The Grocer's Daughter*, p. 151.

55 TFW, Interview for Scottish Television, 21 February 1975 (102632). Thatcher said, 'He [Macmillan] was a marvellous politician and it was fascinating to work with him and watch him. He was working towards the things which I believe in.'

56 Gardiner, *Margaret Thatcher*, pp. 67 and 68: 'Even now, Macmillan is the Tory leader for whom Margaret seems to have the greatest admiration.'

57 TFW, Thatcher interview for the Finnish newspaper *Suomen Kuvalehti*, 7 November 1984 (105512). Interviewed by Alastair Burnet for *TV Eye*, 24 January 1985 (105949), Thatcher drew attention again to the fact that Macmillan had been in power at a time when public spending consumed about 33.3 per cent of national income – though now, at a time when Macmillan's attacks on her were becoming more open, her own tone was more petulant. On 22 February 1983, Hugo Young, interviewing Thatcher for the *Sunday Times* (105088), asked: 'Were the

Macmillan years an aberration?' Thatcher replied: 'I don't think I have changed the direction of Conservatism ... don't forget that in the Macmillan years the proportion of public expenditure was lower than it is now.'

58 TFW, Thatcher interviewed by Brian Walden, *Weekend World*, 1 February 1981 (104472).

59 TFW, Thatcher interviewed by Hugo Young, *Sunday Times*, 22 February 1983 (105088): 'The Employment 1944 White Paper is excellent but it's on my side.' Later in the same interview, she said: 'I really am the true Keynesian, when you take him as a whole.' Favourable references to Keynes from Thatcher were relatively rare – though they were quite common in the speeches of her mentor Sir Keith Joseph.

60 TFW, Thatcher speech to the Institute of Socio-Economic Studies in New York, 'Let Our Children Grow Tall', 15 September 1975 (102769).

61 Richard Cockett, *Thinking the Unthinkable. Think Tanks and the Economic Counter-Revolution, 1931–1983* (1995).

62 John Nott, *Here Today, Gone Tomorrow. Recollections of an Errant Politician* (2003), p. 137.

63 Geoffrey Howe, *Conflict of Loyalty* (1994), pp. 30–31.

64 TFW, Thatcher speech to Conservative Political Centre, 'What's Wrong with Politics?, 11 October 1968 (101632).

65 *The Times*, 5 November 1969.

66 Oliver Franks, *Britain and the Tide of World Affairs. The BBC Reith Lectures, 1954* (1955).

67 Thatcher, *The Path to Power*, p. 91.

68 TFW, *Sun*, 10 April 1970 (101809).

69 John Pardoe cited in Campbell, *The Grocer's Daughter*, p. 155.

70 TFW, Thatcher speech in Friern Barnet, 3 April 1959 (101016).

71 *Financial Times*, 23 October 1969.

72 Thatcher interview for *The Times*, 5 November 1969.

73 TFW, Thatcher speech at Haberdasher's Aske School, 17 September 1971 (102138).

74 On Heath's life, see his autobiography – *The Course of My Life* (1998) – and John Campbell, *Edward Heath. A Biography* (1993). On the Heath government, see Martin Holmes, *The Failure of the Heath Government* (1997) and Stuart Ball and Anthony Seldon (eds.), *The Heath Government, 1970–1974. A Reappraisal* (1996). For the sense of crisis in the early

1970s, it is worth reading Victor Rothschild, *Meditations on a Broomstick* (1977).

75 John Ramsden, *The Making of Conservative Party Policy. The Conservative Research Department since 1929* (1980).

76 TFW, transcript of meeting at Selsdon Park Hotel, morning session, 31 January 1970 (109512).

77 TFW, 'Advance hints on Walden's thinking', with covering letter signed Bruce Anderson, 14 September 1977 (archive/2008/gl.pdf).

78 Howe, *Conflict of Loyalty*, p. 76.

79 Jeremy Smith, 'Relations between the Conservative Party and the Ulster Unionist Party during the Twentieth Century', *English Historical Review*, CXXI, 490 (2006), pp. 70–103. See also Jeremy Smith, 'Walking a Real Tight-Rope of Difficulties: Sir Edward Heath and the Search for Stability in Northern Ireland, June 1970–March 1971', *Twentieth Century British History*, 18, 2 (2007), pp. 219–53.

80 TFW, 'Events leading to the resignation of Mr Heath's administration, 4 March 1974' (thorpe.pdf): Telegram from Mr Harry West, 2 March; Mr Pym's advice on Mr West's Telegram; reply to Mr West's Telegram; note of the meeting with Thorpe on 2 March. See also John Ramsden, *The Winds of Change. Macmillan to Heath, 1957–1975* (1996), p. 387.

81 NA, PREM 15/985, Strike Report 5/6 February (day 28/9) 1972.

82 NA, PREM 15/986, Note to or from Prime Minister signed E, 23 February 1972.

83 Douglas Hurd, *An End to Promises* (1979), p. 81.

84 For an account of Heath's fall, see TFW, 'Events leading to the resignation of Mr Heath's Administration on 4 March 1974' by Robert Armstrong, 16 March 1974 (110605). This document is different from the one listed above with the same title.

85 Nott, *Here Today, Gone Tomorrow*, p. 146.

86 Arthur Scargill, interviewed in *Marxism Today*, April 1981.

87 Gerald Nabarro, *Exploits of a Politician* (1973), p. 101.

CHAPTER 2. THATCHERISM BEFORE THATCHER? ENOCH POWELL

1 Cited in Douglas Schoen, *Enoch Powell and the Powellites* (1977), p. 261.

2 Simon Heffer, *Like the Roman. The Life of Enoch Powell* (1998), p. 958.

3 TFW, House of Commons, Prime Minister's Question Time, 4 June 1981 (104660).

4 *The Times* diary, 10 September 1974.

5 *Observer*, quoted in Richard Shepherd, *Enoch Powell* (1996), p. 217.

6 Schoen, *Powell and the Powellites*, p. 11: 'The deepest instinct of the Englishman – how the word 'instinct' keeps forcing itself in again and again – is for continuity.' The Tory MP Stephen Hastings wrote of Powell's 'massive castles of logic steadily constructed rampart upon unassailable rampart, yet sometimes founded on some simple, instinctive, romantic conviction'. Stephen Hastings, *The Drums of Memory* (1994), p. 240.

7 'No answers blowing in the wind' first published in the *Spectator*, 9 October 1976, reprinted in Rex Collings (ed.), *Reflections of a Statesman. The Writings and Speeches of Enoch Powell* (1991), pp. 341–5.

8 'A battalion in which fifty per cent deserve the VC is a battalion that destroys itself . . . Still, you have to have somebody within the ranks who says, "I'll charge that machine gun!"' Powell quoted in John Ranelagh, *Thatcher's People* (1991), p. 184.

9 Shepherd, *Enoch Powell*, p. 231.

10 Quoted in ibid., p. 246.

11 Douglas Hurd, *An End to Promises* (1979), p. 23.

12 Geoffrey Howe quotes Powell's speech approving of the abolition of exchange controls in *Conflict of Loyalty* (1994), p. 143. Note too one of the rare occasions when Thatcher herself said: 'I entirely accept the right honourable gentleman's rebuke', House of Commons, Prime Minister's Question Time, 13 May 1980 (104363). Powell had rebuked her for suggesting that the civil service made policy.

13 Douglas Hurd, *Memoirs* (2003), p. 308.

14 Collings (ed.), *Reflections of a Statesman*, p. 137. Powell replied that he was not sure that what Thatcher meant by Powellism was the same as what he himself meant by the term.

15 Cecil Parkinson, *Right at the Centre* (1992), p. 124.

16 John Nott, *Here Today, Gone Tomorrow. Recollections of an Errant Politician* (2003), pp. 135–8.

17 Powell used the phrase in a speech in Birmingham on 13 June 1970.

18 Powell has excited an extraordinary amount of attention from biographers; Simon Heffer has written the definitive work. T. E. Utley, *Enoch Powell. The Man and His Thinking* (1968) is also very important – Utley was sceptical about some aspects of the Powell myth, perhaps because he himself had done a good deal to invent it.

19 TFW, Thatcher speech to Finchley League of Jewish Women, 18 November 1968, reported in the *Finchley Press*, 22 November 1968 (101636).

20 TFW, Memorandum of conversation between Margaret Thatcher and official of US embassy at Connaught Hotel, 22 May 1973, enclosed with letter from Annenberg to State Department, 25 June 1973 (110554).

21 John Ramsden, *The Winds of Change. Macmillan to Heath, 1957–1975* (1996), p. 279.

22 Thatcher's remarks about Powell in her own constituency were always made in terms of studied inscrutability. Asked about Powell's views on immigration in November 1968, she said: 'I think that you should always be willing to take your views to the final test; and I hope that Enoch will put his views before the parliamentary forum.' TFW, Thatcher speech to Finchley League of Jewish Women, 18 November 1968 (101636).

23 Shepherd, *Enoch Powell*, p. 292.

24 TFW, Thatcher speech to Young Conservative conference, 12 February 1978 (103487).

25 Christopher Bland, reviewing T. E. Utley's biography of Powell in a liberal Tory journal, argued that Powell's views on race were the least interesting and attractive part of his political platform, *Crossbow*, January–March 1969.

26 Howe, *Conflict of Loyalty*, pp. 476 and 480.

27 Quoted in Heffer, *Like the Roman*, p. 748.

28 Cited by Ronald Butt in 'The Importance of Being Enoch', *Crossbow*, April–June 1966.

29 Cited in Shepherd, *Enoch Powell*, p. 388.

30 Ibid., p. 427.

31 Heffer, *Like the Roman*, p. 97.

32 Collings (ed.), *Reflections of a Statesman*, p. 577.

33 Schoen, *Powell and the Powellites*, p. 11. Powell made these remarks in 1964.

34 John Wood (ed.), *Enoch Powell. Freedom and Reality* (1969), p. 241.

35 Shepherd, *Enoch Powell*, p. 248.

36 Ridley was speaking on *Panorama*; quoted in Collings (ed.) *Reflections of a Statesman*, p. 12.

37 Quoted in Shepherd, *Enoch Powell*, p. 267.

38 TFW, Thatcher interviewed by David Frost for TV-AM, 30 December 1988 (107022).

39 Simon Heffer, *Like the Roman*, p. 934.

CHAPTER 3. BECOMING LEADER

1 Quoted in Patrick Cosgrove, *Margaret Thatcher. A Tory and Her Party* (1978), p. 11.

2 TFW, Annenberg to State Department, 25 June 1973 (110554).

3 David Butler and Dennis Kavanagh, *The British General Election of October 1974* (1975), pp. 237 and 264. According to Hailsham, Thatcher, Macmillan (fils) and Joseph had been the only members of the shadow cabinet to oppose an approach to the Liberals in March 1974, TFW, Hailsham diary, entry for 1 March 1974 (111117).

4 TFW, Joseph speech, 'Inflation is Caused by Governments', Preston, 5 September 1974 (110607).

5 Morrison Halcrow, *Keith Joseph. A Single Mind* (1989), p. 9.

6 Cited in John Ranelagh, *Thatcher's People* (1991), p. 137.

7 Bruce Anderson, *The Times*, 31 August 2006.

8 Alfred Sherman, *Paradoxes of Power. Reflections on the Thatcher Interlude*, edited by Mark Garnett (Exeter, 2005), p. 97.

9 Ferdinand Mount cited in Halcrow, *Keith Joseph*, p. 90.

10 Sherman, *Paradoxes of Power*, p. 55.

11 Denis Healey, *The Time of My Life* (1990), p. 488.

12 TFW, Hailsham diary, 9 March 1977 (111176). Hailsham seems to have been reporting remarks made by Jo Grimond and Lord Plowden.

13 Ibid., entry for 29 March 1977 (111182), after meeting Carrington.

14 Ibid., entry for 6 October 1977 (111187), after meeting Carrington and Whitelaw.

15 The precise purpose of the speech is unclear. Joseph's biographer believes that it was designed to form part of a bid for the leadership of the Conservative Party, Halcrow, *Keith Joseph*, p. 81.

16 Sherman, *Paradoxes of Power*, p. 56.

17 Halcrow, *Keith Joseph*, pp. 86–7.

18 Margaret Thatcher, *The Path to Power* (1996), p. 266.

19 Cited in Halcrow, *Keith Joseph*, p. 76.

20 Edward du Cann, *Two Lives. The Political and Business Careers of Edward du Cann* (Upton upon Severn, 1995).

21 Nigel Fisher, *The Tory Leaders. Their Struggle for Power* (1977), p. 146. For Fisher's activities earlier in the year, see TFW, 'Events leading to the resignation of Mr Heath's administration, 4 March 1974' (thorpe.pdf): 'Message from Mr Nigel Fisher', 3 March 1974. Fisher, a friend of Jeremy Thorpe's, said that he believed the Liberals would find supporting the government easier if it had a different leader.

22 Baker says that Kitson was the manager. Kenneth Baker, *The Turbulent Years. My Life in Politics* (1993), p. 44. John Ramsden says that Baker and Kitson jointly managed the campaign. John Ramsden, *The Winds of Change. Macmillan to Heath, 1957–1975* (1996), p. 447.

23 For an analysis of the votes in the 1975 leadership election (conducted with access to private documents and anonymous interviews), see Philip Cowley and Matthew Bailey, 'Peasants' Uprising or Religious War? Re-Examining the 1975 Conservative Leadership Contest', *British Journal of Political Science*, 30, 4 (2000), pp. 599–629.

CHAPTER 4. OPPOSITION, 1975–9

1 TFW, Hailsham diary, 29 March 1977 (111182).

2 TFW, Kissinger briefing for Ford, 8 January 1975 (110510).

3 Edmund Dell, *A Hard Pounding. Politics and Economics Crisis, 1974–1976* (Oxford, 1991), p. vii.

4 TFW, Angus Maude and others, 'Themes', 16 February 1978 (109853).

5 TFW, Thatcher speech to Institute of Socio-Economic Studies, 'Let Our Children Grow Tall', 15 September 1975 (102769).

6 See Peter Jay, 'How is Your Gloom Resistance?', *The Times*, 8 July 1974 and 'Pursuit of Group Self-Interest Seen as Main Threat to Liberal Democracy', *The Times*, 4 September 1974.

7 Auberon Waugh, 'Of Human Bondage', *New Statesman*, 13 September 1976. Reprinted in Auberon Waugh, *In the Lion's Den* (1978), pp. 71–4.

8 TFW, shadow cabinet, 11 April 1975 (109958). Tim Raison said: 'We should support Mr Healey if he produces a sensible budget.'

9 *Sun*, 15 October 1972.

10 Alistair McAlpine, *Once a Jolly Bagman* (1998), p. 211.

11 James Prior, *A Balance of Power* (1986), p. 112.

12 Kenneth Morgan, *Callaghan. A Life* (Oxford, 1997).

13 This remark was apparently quoted by Tim Bell to Larry Lamb; see Mark Hollingsworth, *The Ultimate Spin Doctor. The Life and Fast Times of Tim Bell* (1997), p. 71.

14 TFW, Steering Committee, 13 May 1975 (109965).

15 John Nott, *Here Today, Gone Tomorrow. Recollections of an Errant Politician* (2003), p. 174 and McAlpine, *Once a Jolly Bagman*, p. 205.

16 *The Times*, 30 May 1978, 'Loyalty and Leadership'.

17 In her memoirs, Thatcher suggests that Patten's main use was to turn the CRD into a 'secretariat for the Shadow Cabinet'; a secretariat was particularly necessary because the shadow ministers were so often divided amongst themselves. Margaret Thatcher, *The Path to Power* (1995), p. 293. In fact, Thatcher eventually took away Patten's functions as secretary to the shadow cabinet though she stressed that this was in no way a demotion. See Thatcher letter to *The Times*, 31 May 1978.

18 John Hoskyns, *Just in Time. Inside the Thatcher Revolution* (2000), p. 16.

19 Ibid., p. 28.

20 Thatcher, *The Path to Power*, p. 399.

21 Stephen Hastings, the right-wing Tory MP who was also involved in some of these committees, described Crozier's account as 'rather colourful'. Stephen Hastings, *The Drums of Memory* (1994), p. 236.

22 Brian Crozier, *Free Agent. The Unseen War, 1941–1991* (1993), pp. 128–48.

23 TFW, Patten, 'Implementing our Strategy', 21 December 1977 (109847).

24 TFW, Joseph, 'Notes Towards the Definition of Policy', 4 April 1975 (110098).

25 TFW, Shadow cabinet, 11 April 1975 (109958).

26 TFW, Hailsham's note on shadow cabinet meeting, 11 April 1975 (111134).

27 TFW, Shadow cabinet, 11 April 1975 (109958). Raison argued: 'that the fulcrum of the political see-saw lay not between the Labour and Conservative Parties but half way across the Labour Party'.

28 Ibid.

29 David Stirling expressed his support for a written constitution. TFW, Hailsham diary, entry for 8 November 1974 (111124).

30 TFW, Joseph to Thatcher, 22 July 1975 (111219), on meeting with Val Duncan, of RTZ, Marcus Sieff and Hector Laing. Joseph alluded to 'a brief reference to the old subject of electoral reform' – though he suggested that Duncan was more realistic about the limited benefits of such reform than some of the industrialists whom he represented.

31 TFW, Maudling, 'Incomes Policy', 24 May 1976 (110140). Adam Ridley sent the paper to Thatcher with a note saying that he had tried, and failed, to persuade Maudling to amend his paper to allow that 'monetary policy and the level of demand did have some influence on the rate of inflation'.

32 TFW, Joseph lecture, 'Monetarism is not Enough', 5 April 1976 (110796).

33 TFW, Howe, 'The Economic Prospect and the Party's Political Position', 16 December 1975 (110128).

34 TFW, Kissinger briefing for Ford, 16 September 1975 (110527).

35 TFW, Thatcher interviewed by Peter Jay on *Weekend World*, 9 May 1976 (102836). Thatcher said: 'There are times when for temporary purposes you have to have an incomes policy.' Pressed on whether the Labour government's current pay policy was necessary, Thatcher replied: 'I certainly thought that the initial impact was temporarily needed.'

36 TFW, Maudling, 'Incomes Policy', 24 May 1976 (110140).

37 TFW, Lawson to Thatcher, 'Thoughts on "Implementing Our Strategy"', 15 January 1978 (110321).

38 Geoffrey Howe, *Conflict of Loyalty* (1994), p. 100.

39 Ibid., p. 63.

40 TFW, Howe, 'The Economic Education of the Public. Proposals for Concerted Action and Fighting Inflation', 16 May 1977 (109761).

41 TFW, Thatcher annotation on letter from Howe, 26 May 1977 (109784).

42 TFW, Thatcher annotation on Howe proposed speech on trade unions, 11 January 1978 (109796).

43 Thatcher, *The Path to Power*, p. 423. For the discussion of the Stepping Stones report, see TFW, Meeting of leader's steering committee, 30 January 1978 (109832).

44 Norman Fowler, *Ministers Decide. A Personal Memoir of the Thatcher Years* (1991), p. 93.

45 Nott, *Here Today, Gone Tomorrow*, p. 172.

46 'Tory Leader Denies Split in Party Over Closed Shop', *The Times*, 14 September 1988.

47 Thatcher, *The Path to Power*, p. 451.

48 Konrad Zweig wrote a pamphlet, prefaced by Howe, on the social market economy for the Centre for Policy Studies. He also published *The Origins of the German Social Market Economy. Leading Ideas and Their Intellectual Roots* with the Adam Smith Institute in 1980.

49 TFW, Howe, 'The Economic Education of the Public. Proposals for Concerted Action and Fighting Inflation', 16 May 1977 (109761).

50 TFW, Maudling, 'Incomes Policy', 24 May 1976 (110140).

51 Peter Hennessy, 'Mrs Thatcher Warned in Secret Report of Defeat in Confrontation with Unions', *The Times*, 18 April 1978. For a more detailed, and less defeatist, account of this committee, see TFW, Authority of Government Policy Group, Final Report, 22 June 1977 (111394).

52 TFW, 'Themes' by Angus Maude and others, 16 February 1978 (109853).

53 TFW, Hailsham diary, entry for 20 January 1976 (111153).

54 It is worth noting Callaghan's own remarks on the eve of the 1979 election: 'You know there are times, perhaps once every thirty years, when there is a sea-change in politics. It does not matter what you say or what you do. There is a shift in what the public wants and what it approves of. I suspect there is now such a sea-change – and it is for Mrs Thatcher.' See Bernard Donoughue, *Prime Minister. The Conduct of Policy under Harold Wilson and James Callaghan* (1987), p. 191. The remarks are widely quoted in memoirs of the period – see, for example, David Owen, *Time to Declare* (1991), p. 413.

55 David Butler and Dennis Kavanagh, *The British General Election of 1979* (1980), p. 337.

56 TFW, Joseph, 'Our Tone of Voice and our Tasks', 7 December 1976 (110178).

57 TFW, *Weekend World*, 18 September 1977 (103191).

58 Howe, *Conflict of Loyalty*, p. 104.

59 The Tories proposed a register of Commonwealth citizens whose family links might give them the right to settle in Britain. Their home affairs spokesman privately regarded the proposal as unworkable and, after the election, it was dropped. Howe, *Conflict of Loyalty*, p. 104.

60 Hoskyns, *Just in Time*, p. 94.

CHAPTER 5. PRIMITIVE POLITICS, 1979–83

1 Nigel Lawson, *The View from No 11. Memoirs of a Tory Radical* (1993), p. 46.

2 Robert Armstrong and Clive Priestley in 'The Civil Service Reforms of the 1980. The Demise of the Civil Service Department and the Resignation of Sir Ian Bancroft as Head of the Civil Service, November 1981', seminar held 17 November 2006, Centre for Contemporary British History, 2007, p. 67.

3 John Newsinger, *Dangerous Men. SAS and Popular Culture* (1997).

4 TFW, Hailsham diary, entry for 8 November 1974 (111124).

5 John Harvey-Jones, *Getting it Together. Memoirs of a Troubleshooter* (1991), p. 361.

6 Nicholas Henderson, *Mandarin* (1994), p. 406, entry for 4 July 1981. Henderson added, however: 'I am not sure that it's Maggie's fault or that it will not come right in the end.'

7 TFW, Richard Allen, memo for the president, 31 July 1981 (110522).

8 Quoted in Henderson, *Mandarin*, p. 363, entry for 3 October 1980.

9 Denis Healey, *The Time of My Life* (1990), p. 433.

10 Geoffrey Howe, *Conflict of Loyalty* (1994), p. 144. Howe did not believe that his party should have committed itself to sustain such increases in defence spending.

11 Edmund Dell, *A Hard Pounding. Politics and Economics Crisis, 1974–1976* (Oxford, 1991), p. 70.

12 Howe, *Conflict of Loyalty*, p. 204. Lawson, *The View from No. 11*, p. 93.

13 Tim Renton went home as the measure taxing banks was put to

parliament, hoping that the opposition would not force a vote and expose his absence. As it was, there was a vote and the whips gave Renton a choice between inventing some duplicitous excuse for his absence or resigning. He resigned. He was quickly offered office again, but was reluctant to forgo his lucrative City employment (perhaps becoming known as a defender of banks had not done his extra-parliamentary career any harm). Tim Renton, *Chief Whip* (2005), p. 12.

14 Milton Friedman comment on Patrick Minford, 'Inflation, Unemployment and the Pound' in Subroto Roy and John Clarke (eds.), *Margaret Thatcher's Revolution. How it Happened and What it Meant* (2005), pp. 50–66, p. 66: 'I am a great admirer of Margaret Thatcher, but I have no great expertise on recent British experience.'

15 American ambassador in London to secretary of state, 15 September 1983 (109408): 'Thatcher and Howe are skeptical of Administration arguments that inflationary expectations – rather than deficits – are the major influence on interest rates.'

16 On Tory resentment at the programmes by Galbraith, and the suggestion that the BBC restore 'proper balance' by broadcasting Friedman or Hayek, see TFW, Howe to Joseph, 22 March 1976, 'Economics and the BBC' (110039).

17 Biffen, interviewed by Beatrix Campbell in *Marxism Today*, 6 December 1989.

18 John Hoskyns, *Just in Time. Inside the Thatcher Revolution* (2000), p. 135.

19 Ibid., p. 127.

20 Quoted in David Richards, *The Civil Service under the Conservatives, 1979–1997* (1997), p. 191.

21 Peter Hall, *Governing the Economy. The Politics of State Intervention in Britain and France* (1986), p. 97.

22 Enoch Powell, 'The Conservative Party', in Dennis Kavanagh and Anthony Seldon (eds.), *The Thatcher Effect. A Decade of Change* (1989), pp. 80–88, p. 81.

23 Lawson, *The View from No. 11*, p. 45.

24 Howe, *Conflict of Loyalty*, p. 109.

25 Ibid., p. 162.

26 TFW, Lawson, 'The New Conservatism', speech to the Bow Group, 4 August 1980 (109505).

27 The financial secretary to the treasury ended the practice, begun by the Labour government in 1975, whereby the government imposed limits on the amount that building societies were allowed to lend in each quarter. However, he discreetly refrained from breaking up the cartel that existed amongst building societies, because it suited him that some interest rates at least should not fluctuate. Lawson, *The View from No. 11*, pp. 86–7.

28 Lawson, The *View from No. 11*, pp. 78–80.

29 TFW, 'Fentiman Road Economic Seminar', 18 May 1975 (109968): 'It [a floating exchange rate] poses the threat of higher interest rates, with the consequent difficulty of "dealing with" the mortgage situation . . . Probably the most important political and practical constraint on monetary policy, particularly in the context of a floating rate, is the housing mortgage market. A stabilization scheme that would have the effect of insulating this is an essential concept to have on hand . . . The question arises whether this two-tier interest rate structure needs to be extended in other directions.'

30 Gordon Pepper, *Inside Thatcher's Monetarist Revolution* (1998); Gordon Pepper and Michael Oliver, *Monetarism under Thatcher. Lessons for the Future* (2001); Patrick Minford, *The Supply Side Revolution in Britain* (1991).

31 Ferdinand Mount claims that 'Alan Walters was the driving force behind the 1981 budget', Ferdinand Mount, *Cold Cream. My Early Life and Other Mistakes* (2008), p. 283.

32 Ian Gilmour, *Dancing with Dogma. Britain under Thatcherism* (1992), p. 26.

33 Patrick Minford, 'Inflation, Unemployment and the Pound', in Roy and Clarke (eds), *Margaret Thatcher's Revolution*, pp. 50–66.

34 Philip Booth (ed.), *Were 364 Economists All Wrong?* (2006). This pamphlet can be downloaded from the website of the Institute of Economic Affairs.

35 *Guardian*, 16 March 1982, cited in Howe, *Conflict of Loyalty*, p. 209.

36 Mount, *Cold Cream*, p. 283.

37 *The Times*, 9 March 1984, letter from Hahn and Solow.

38 Peter Bazalgette in *Philips and Drew Market Review*, cited in David Kynaston, *The City of London, IV, A Club No More, 1945–2000* (2001), p. 587.

39 TFW, Nigel Lawson, 'Thoughts on the Coming Battle', 15 October 1973 (110312).

40 James Prior, *A Balance of Power* (1986), p. 129.

41 Margaret Thatcher, *The Downing Street Years* (1995), p. 151.

42 George Gardiner, *A Bastard's Tale* (1999), p. 141. The rebels wanted to remove legal immunity from unions involved in all secondary action (not just strikes), to require unions to hold ballots before strikes and to require ballots on all existing closed shops.

43 Peter Dorey, 'One Step at a Time: the Conservative Government's Approach to the Reform of Industrial Relations since 1979', *Political Quarterly*, 64, 1 (1993), pp. 24–36. And Simon Auerbach, 'Mrs Thatcher's Labour Laws: Slouching Towards Utopia?' in ibid., pp. 37–48.

44 Peter Ingram, David Metcalf and Jonathan Wadsworth, 'Strike Incidence in British Manufacturing in the 1980s', *Industrial and Labor Relations Review*, 46, 4 (July 1993), pp. 704–17.

45 Roy Jenkins, *European Diary, 1977–81* (1998), p. 479, entry for 14 July 1979.

46 Hoskyns, *Just in Time*, p. 147.

47 Michael Edwardes, *Back from the Brink* (1983), p. 89.

48 TFW, Thatcher interview for *Weekend World*, 18 September 1977 (103191): 'I've never seen anyone take Clive Jenkins to the cleaners as Hugh Scanlon does.'

49 Donald MacDougall, *Don and Mandarin. Memoirs of an Economist* (1987), p. 231.

50 Brian Wyldbore-Smith, *March Past* (2001), p. 135.

51 On the decline in donations to the Tory party, see the report by the Labour Research Department of 1977 – mentioned in *The Times* Business Diary, 2 September 1977. On 29 March, Hailsham reported Carrington's view that 'they [the big industrialists] much resented the hectoring way she lectured them'. TFW, Hailsham diary, 29 March 1977 (111182).

52 Hoskyns, *Just in Time*, p. 345.

53 Lawson, *The View from No. 11*, p. 58. MacDougall denies that the CBI leaders 'caved in' during their subsequent meeting with Thatcher.

54 Ivor Crewe and Anthony King, *SDP. The Birth, Life and Death of the Social Democratic Party* (Oxford, 1995), p. 113.

55 David Butler and Dennis Kavanagh (eds.), *The British General Election of October 1974* (1975), p. 237.

56 TFW, Meeting of shadow ministers and economists, 8 July 1975 (109986).

57 TFW, Joseph speech at Preston, 'Inflation is Caused by Governments',
    5 September 1974 (110607): 'But you will ask, how do I square this
    with the monthly unemployment statistics which receive banner
    headlines and strike gloom into politicians' hearts – 500,000 – 600,000
    – 800,000 – fears of one million unemployed?'

58 MacDougall, *Don and Mandarin*, p. 211. MacDougall himself prepared
    a report in November 1979 which suggested that, by 1983, inflation
    would stand at 5 per cent, output would barely regain its 1979 level
    and unemployment would reach 2 million. He thought that the Tories
    would find it hard to win an election with such statistics – as it turned
    out, they won with inflation and output at roughly the levels MacDougall
    had guessed, and unemployment at 3 million.

59 Kenneth Morgan, *Michael Foot. A Life* (2007).

60 Eric Heffer, *Never a Yes Man. The Life and Politics of an Adopted Liverpudlian*
    (1991), p. 176. Heffer identifies the key figures behind Foot's candidacy
    as being himself, Clive Jenkins, Ian Mikardo, Moss Evans, Bill Keyes,
    Alec Smith and Arthur Scargill.

61 TFW, CBTV programme, 13 December 1982 (105071): Child: 'What's
    the three things you admire in Michael Foot?' PM: 'Oh my goodness
    me. Can I give you just one? He's a very effective journalist.'

62 David Butler and Dennis Kavanagh (eds.), *The British General Election
    of 1983* (1984), pp. 60–63.

63 Cecil Parkinson, *Right at the Centre* (1992), p. 229. McAlpine himself
    gives a slightly different figure. Alistair McAlpine, *Once a Jolly Bagman*
    (1998), p. 254.

64 David Owen, *Time to Declare* (1991), p. 495.

65 William Rodgers, *Fourth Amongst Equals* (2000), p. 201.

66 John Golding, *Hammer of the Left. Defeating Tony Benn, Eric Heffer
    and Militant in the Battle for the Labour Party*, edited by Paul Farrelly
    (2003).

67 Ken Spencer, Andy Taylor, Barbara Smith, John Mawson, Norman
    Flynn and Richard Batley, *Crisis in the Industrial Heartland. A Study of
    the West Midlands* (Oxford, 1986), p. 42.

68 David Lazar, *Markets and Ideology in the City of London* (1990), p. 42.

69 Gallup Poll, 21–26 May 1987, cited in David Butler and Dennis
    Kavanagh (eds.), *The British General Election of 1987* (1988), p. 248.

70 *British Social Attitudes Survey* (1984), pp. 48–9.

71 Paul Bagguley, *From Protest to Acquiescence? Political Movements of the Unemployed* (1991), p. 202.

72 In December 1982, only 38 per cent of unemployed people blamed the government for their plight. Martin Holmes, *Thatcherism. Scope and Limits, 1983–1987* (1989), p. 92. Paul Bagguley did stress that the attitudes of the unemployed varied according to how questions were phrased and how much contact they had with wider political movements. Bagguley, *From Protest to Acquiescence?*

CHAPTER 6. UNEXPECTED VICTORY: THE FALKLANDS

1   TFW, James Rentschler, 'Falklands Diary', 1 April–25 June 1982, entry for 1 April.

2   Julian Critchley, *A Bag of Boiled Sweets* (1995), p. 181.

3   Lawrence Freedman, *The Official History of the Falklands Campaign*, Vol. 1, *The Origins of the Falklands War* (2005), pp. 114–27.

4   Sir Michael Armitage, in 'The Falklands War', seminar held 5 June 2002, http:/www.icbh.ac.uk/witness/Falklands/, p. 22.

5   Cecil Parkinson, *Right at the Centre* (1992), p. 165.

6   TFW, Telegram from American embassy, Buenos Aires, for Assistant Secretary of State Enders, 3 March 1982 (109418): 'He [Galtieri] reportedly wants to find a formula that will permit him to continue in a dual capacity [i.e. as head of the army and head of state]. This is likely to emerge as the key political question in the months ahead.'

7   The precise reasons for the Argentine decision to invade the Falklands at the moment when they did are still a matter of debate. Lawrence Freedman and Virginia Gamba-Stonehouse suggest that the British reaction to the Argentine landing in South Georgia forced the Argentinians to act before the British could send forces to the Falklands. Lawrence Freedman and Virginia Gamba-Stonehouse, *Signals of War* (1990), pp. 65–83.

8   Douglas Hurd, *Memoirs* (2003), pp. 88 and 280.

9   Henry Leach, in 'The Falklands War', seminar held 5 June 2002, http://www.icbh.ac.uk/witness/Falklands/, p. 29.

10 Sir Michael Quinlan denied that the money for Trident had come

from the navy budget, 'The Nott Review', seminar held 20 June 2001, http://www.icbh.ac.uk/witness/nott/, p. 36.

11 John Nott, *Here Today, Gone Tomorrow. Recollections of an Errant Politician* (2003), p. 240.

12 Keith Speed, *Sea Change. The Battle for the Falklands and the Future of Britain's Navy* (1982), p. 109.

13 Kim Sabido (ITN correspondent), cited in Robert Harris, *Gotcha. The Media, the Government and the Falklands Crisis* (1983), p. 26.

14 Ewen Southby-Tailyour. *Reasons in Writing. A Commando's View of the Falklands War* (2003). It illustrates the relative unimportance of the islands to British planners that Southby-Tailyour had been posted to the Falklands, in 1978, as an unofficial punishment after an argument with a superior.

15 Rentschler, 'Falklands Diary', p. 3.

16 Jacques Attali, *Verbatim. I. Première Partie, 1981–1983* (1993), pp. 298–9.

17 Nott, *Here Today, Gone Tomorrow*, p. 305.

18 See, for example, Anthony Barnett, *Iron Britannia*, special issue of the *New Left Review* (1982): 'If the "profusion" of unexploded Argentine bombs had gone off, the story might have had another ending.'

19 Sandy Woodward with Patrick Robinson, *One Hundred Days. The Memoirs of the Falklands Battle Group Commander* (1997), p. 99.

20 Roger Jackling referred to a letter from John Nott's office to the prime minister which said: 'from four to six escorts and an aircraft carrier – they were likely losses.' 'The Falklands War', seminar held 5 June 2002. http://www.icbh.ac.uk/witness/Falklands/, p. 45. Leach said that he was never told of this and that he never asked directly about possible losses but that he would have expected them to amount to 'six destroyers/frigates, I would have been perfectly prepared to tolerate at least double that number'. He added that the landing might have been cancelled if both aircraft carriers had gone before it, but that they would have pressed on if the carriers had been destroyed after it. Leach to ibid., p. 46. Woodward said, in ibid., that he had understood that the loss of one carrier would mean that the landing would have been called off.

21 Roger Curtis, in 'The Falklands War', seminar held 5 June 2002, http://www.icbh.ac.uk/witness/Falklands/, p. 45, said that he had

taken the figure 'from the top of his head' to impress the seriousness of the affair on the war cabinet. Roughly 3000 men took part in the first landings at San Carlos Bay. So perhaps Leach's 'worst-case scenario' simply anticipated that all of these would be lost.

22　Cecil Parkinson, in 'The Falklands War', seminar held 5 June 2002, http://www.icbh.ac.uk/witness/Falklands/, p. 44.

23　Quintin Hailsham, *A Sparrow's Flight. Memoirs* (1991), p. 408: 'The one thing I had always been taught in the army was that an opposed landing from the sea was a peculiarly hazardous undertaking, required air superiority, and should be undertaken only with a secure and fairly short line of communications.'

24　Julian Thompson, *No Picnic. 3 Commando Brigade in the South Atlantic, 1982* (1992), p. 31.

25　Nott, *Here Today, Gone Tomorrow*, p. 247.

26　Guy Bransby, *Her Majesty's Interrogator* (1996), p. 48. It should be added that the Falklands War involved an unspoken alliance with Pinochet's regime in Chile. Bransby's wife was the daughter of a Chilean officer.

27　Kevin Foster, *Fighting Fictions. War, Narrative and National Identity* (1998), p. 28.

28　Alan Clark, *Diaries, 1972–1982. Into Politics* (2001), p. 366, entry for 29 October 1982.

29　Ibid., p. 370, letter to Michael Jopling, 4 November 1982.

30　Hugh McManners, *Falklands Commando* (1987), p. 24.

31　Ted Rowlands, cited in Freedman, *The Falklands War*, p. 75.

32　Jock Bruce-Gardyne, *Ministers and Mandarins. Inside the Whitehall Village* (1986), p. 166.

33　Kenneth Baker, *The Turbulent Years. My Life in Politics* (1993), p. 69: 'I also remember Nick Ridley telling me . . . that . . . "She is mad and will have to go."' Ridley himself mentions no such conversation in his memoirs.

34　Geoffrey Howe, *Conflict of Loyalty* (1994), p. 453. In *Cold Cream. My Early Life and Other Mistakes* (2008), Ferdinand Mount, an opponent of the Falklands War who was appointed as an adviser to Thatcher immediately after it, gives a more colourful account of Walters's proposals and suggests that they were, in fact, put to Thatcher at the time.

35　Ian Lang, *Blue Remembered Years* (2002), p. 58.

36 Geoff Eley, 'Finding the People's War: Film, British Collective Memory, and World War II', *American Historical Review*, 106, 3 (2001): 'Thatcherite reinscription of Churchillian "greatness" in the little-Englander animus against "Europe" licensed by the Falklands-Malvinas War.' Eley also writes: 'By 1983, Thatcherism was evoking the other Churchill of late imperial militarism and racialized cultural superiority, exchanging ideals of social justice for patriotism pure and simple.'

37 Cecil Parkinson, in 'The Falklands War', seminar held 5 June 2002, http://www.icbh.ac.uk.witness/Falklands/, p. 70.

38 David Butler and Dennis Kavanagh (eds.), *The British General Election of 1983* (1984), p. 256. Only 28 per cent of their sample of Conservative candidates referred directly to the Falklands.

39 Harris, *Gotcha*, p. 89.

40 Eric Hobsbawm, 'Falklands Fallout', in Stuart Hall and Martin Jacques (eds), *The Politics of Thatcherism* (1983), pp. 257–70.

CHAPTER 7. VICTORY FORETOLD: THE MINERS

1 Andrew Richards, *Miners on Strike. Class, Solidarity and Division in Britain* (1996), p. 125.

2 Brian Towers, 'Running the Gauntlet: British Trade Unions under Thatcher, 1979–1987', *Industrial and Labor Relations Review*, 42, 2 (1989), pp. 163–88.

3 Norman Tebbit, *Upwardly Mobile* (1989), p. 302.

4 TFW, Thatcher interview for *Weekend World*, 18 September 1977 (103191). Walden anticipated a first successful strike over pay and then a second strike over pit closures that would challenge the authority of the government.

5 TFW, Report of the Nationalized Industries Policy Group, 30 June 1977 (110795).

6 See, for example, Penny Green, *The Enemy Without. Policing and Class Consciousness in the Miners' Strike* (1990), p. 29. Alex Callinicos and Mike Simons, *The Great Strike. The Miners' Strike of 1984–5 and its Lessons* (1985), p. 36: 'Thatcher's six years in office have followed with eerie precision the pattern laid out in the Ridley Report'. John Saville, 'An Open Conspiracy: Conservative Politics and the Miners'

Strike, 1984–5', *Socialist Register* (July–August 1985), pp. 295–329: 'The Ridley plan began to be inserted into the statute book within a year of the Thatcher government taking office.'

7 Martin Adeney and John Lloyd, *The Miners' Strike, 1984–5. Loss Without Limit* (1986), p. 73. Tim Eggar was apparently unable to find a copy of the report when drafting the 1983 manifesto. The report had anticipated confrontation between six and eighteen months after a Conservative election victory. Anyone reading it in 1982 might well have concluded that the report had already been implemented in the government's handling of strikes in steel and the civil service or, for that matter, in the government's 'surrender' to the miners in February 1981. According to *The Times*, the annex to the report was not circulated to members of the shadow cabinet, Michael Hatfield, 'Tory Views on Unions Embarrass Leaders', *The Times*, 27 May 1978.

8 TFW, Report of the Nationalized Industries Policy Group, 30 June 1977 (110795).

9 John Hoskyns, *Just in Time. Inside the Thatcher Revolution* (2000), p. 73. On 13 November 1978, an opposition working group had asked: 'What is a Tory government's response to an "unbeatable strike" (miners' or power-workers')?' Prior apparently told Hoskyns in 1977 that he believed a government would have no option but to surrender to the miners. Ibid., p. 39.

10 Ian MacGregor with Rodney Tyler, *The Enemies Within. The Story of the Miners' Strike, 1984–5* (1986), p. 145.

11 Hoskyns, *Just in Time*, p. 143.

12 Alan Clark, *Diaries. Into Politics, 1972–1982* (2001), entry for 25 January 1974, p. 40.

13 Joe Gormley, *Battered Cherub* (1982), p. 186.

14 Roy Ottey, *Strike. An Insider's Story* (1985), p. 41. Ottey resigned from the NUM executive in October 1984 in protest at Scargill's refusal to hold a strike ballot.

15 Eric Heffer, *Never a Yes Man. The Life and Politics of an Adopted Liverpudlian* (1991), p. 180. After reading an article in the *Financial Times*, Scargill rebuked Heffer for having refused to support Tony Benn in the election for deputy leader of the Labour Party.

16 'The New Unionism', *New Left Review*, July–August 1975, pp. 3–33. Scargill interviewed by 'RB' and 'HW'.

17 Peter Walker, *Staying Power. An Autobiography* (1991), p. 167.

18 'The New Unionism', *New Left Review*.

19 Sir John Herbecq, 'The Civil Service Reforms of the 1980s: the 1981 Civil Service Strike', seminar held 17 November 2006, Centre for Contemporary British History, http://icbh.a.uk/downloads/ civilservicereforms, p. 40: 'It was absolutely clear [after the civil service strike of 1981] that there would be a succession of strikes by the more familiar suspects, those who really would cause the government trouble. In July 1979, Christopher Foster . . . and I were having private meetings with one or two other outsiders and Michael Portillo (who was special adviser to David Howell at the Department of Energy) about a miners' strike. It actually took until the scare of the spring of 1981 to get the government to grapple with preparing for a miners' strike, which conservatively we reckoned would take two years.'

20 Gormley, *Battered Cherub*, p. 173.

21 Nigel Lawson, *The View from No. 11. Memoirs of a Tory Radical* (1993), pp. 145–51.

22 Margaret Thatcher, *The Downing Street Years* (1995), p. 341.

23 Lawson, *The View from No. 11*, p. 154.

24 Thatcher expressed her dislike of both Ezra and Villiers, of British Steel, in private conversations as early as July 1979, see Roy Jenkins, *European Diary, 1977–1981* (1989), p. 480, entry for 14 July 1979.

25 Roy Mason, *Paying the Price* (1999), pp. 73–6 and 236; Lawson, *The View from No. 11*, p. 156. Mason knew that his name had been discussed as chairman of the NCB and believed that Thatcher had vetoed his appointment.

26 Giles Shaw, *In the Long Run* (2001), p. 128.

27 MacGregor, *The Enemies Within*, pp. 168, 171 and 209.

28 Bob Haslam, *An Industrial Cocktail* (2003), p. 113.

29 MacGregor, *The Enemies Within*, p. 146. Mick McGahey of the NUM met Jimmy Cowan of the NCB at Christmas. In spite of their differences, the two men were friends and McGahey advised Cowan to get out of the industry because there would soon be a strike.

30 Ibid., p. 166.

31 Andrew Taylor, *The NUM and British Politics*, Vol. 2, *1969–1995* (Aldershot, 1995), p. 229. There were nine regional ballots of which

only one, in Northumberland, favoured the strike – though the result in Derbyshire was very close.

32 Adeney and Lloyd, *The Miners' Strike*, p. 262.

33 In May 1984 Eric Hammond, the right-wing leader of the electricians' union, wrote a private letter to an NUM official offering to shut the power stations if only the NUM executive won a ballot of its members on the strike. Eric Hammond, *Maverick. The Life of a Union Rebel* (1992), p. 47. The letter was apparently sent to Peter Heathfield of the NUM on 24 May 1984. Hammond must have known by this stage that there was no chance that the NUM executive would hold a ballot.

34 MacGregor insists that he himself decided to abandon the NCB's legal action and that he also discouraged other heads of nationalized industries from suing. MacGregor, *The Enemies Within*, p. 218.

35 Walker, *Staying Power*, p. 173.

36 Haslam, *An Industrial Cocktail*, p. 105.

37 Adeney and Lloyd, *The Miners' Strike*, p. 93.

38 Bill Sirs, *Hard Labour* (1985), pp. 122–4.

39 Mike Ironside and Roger Seifert, *Facing up to Thatcherism. The History of NALGO, 1979–1993* (Oxford, 2000), pp. 171–2.

40 Adeney and Lloyd, *The Miners' Strike*, p. 152.

41 Walker, *Staying Power*, p. 175. Walker claims that he dissuaded the cabinet from sacking MacGregor on the grounds that this would appear to give Scargill a victory. Walker seems to have approached Robert Haslam, then at British Steel, in 1985 and suggested that he be appointed to the NCB in a move to force MacGregor out. Haslam did become deputy chairman of the NCB and did eventually replace MacGregor as chairman. Haslam, *Industrial Cocktail*, p. 113.

42 TFW, Peter Walker to Ian MacGregor, 12 February 1985 (strikend.pdf); the letter is taken from MacGregor's files – the originals of which can be found at Kew, National Archives Coal 31/438.

43 National Archives, Coal 26/500. Tables on number of strikers. The NCB believed that 43 per cent of miners were not on strike on 1 February 1985 and that 52 per cent of them were not on strike on 1 March.

44 Woodrow Wyatt also seems to have helped the National Working Miner's Committee, though the precise nature of the help was often

rather symbolic. After the strike, most leaders of working miners seem to have felt rather marginalized. Wyatt helped one of them, Tony Morris, to obtain a sufficiently good redundancy deal from the NCB to buy himself a bar in Marbella. Woodrow Wyatt, *The Journals of Woodrow Wyatt*, Vol. 1, *1985–1988*, edited by Sarah Curtis (1998), pp. 224 and 336, entries for 14 November 1986 and 30 April 1987.

45 Peter Gibbon and David Steyne (eds.), *Thurcroft. A Village and the Miners' Strike. An Oral History* (1986), p. 152.

46 Tony Parker, *Redhill. A Mining Community* (1986), p. 41. Interview with Harry Hartley: 'most of them were only 9 out of 10 mentally ... They didn't know what day it was ... What was worse they didn't know what would happen to them.'

47 Roger Seifert and John Urwin, *Struggle Without End. The 1984/85 Miners' Strike in North Staffordshire* (Newcastle, Staffs, 1987), p. 6.

48 *The Times*, 5 March 1985.

49 Herbecq, 'The Civil Service Reforms of the 1980s', p. 40.

50 Hammond, *Maverick*, p. 56. Basnett and Laird both criticized the NUM after the strike was over.

51 Tony Benn, *The Benn Diaries, 1940–1990*, edited by Ruth Winstone (1996), p. 564, entries for 5 May and 15 May 1984.

52 Gibbon and Steyne (eds.), *Thurcroft*, p. 148.

53 Quoted in David Waddington, Maggie Wykes and Chas Critcher, *Split at the Seams. Community, Continuity and Change after the 1984–5 Coal Dispute* (Milton Keynes, 1991), p. 97.

54 Raphael Samuel, Barbara Bloomfield and Guy Boanas (eds.) *The Enemy Within. Pit Villages and the Miners' Strike* (1986), interview with Iris Preston, pp. 240–50.

55 Tebbit, *Upwardly Mobile*, p. 302.

56 Introduction to Seifert and Urwin, *Struggle Without End*.

57 Samuel et al., *The Enemy Within*, interview with Steve Ciebow, pp. 199–202.

58 Peregrine Worsthorne, Preface, in Subroto Roy and John Clarke, *Margaret Thatcher's Revolution. How it Happened and What it Meant* (2005), pp. vii–xvi.

59 Cited in Wyatt, *The Journals*, entry for 29 September 1986, p. 198.

60 Samuel et al., *The Enemy Within*, p. xi, Meyer does not mention this speech in his own autobiography.

CHAPTER 8. SERIOUS MONEY, 1983–8

1   Margaret Thatcher, Tribute to Nicholas Ridley, *Sunday Times*, 7 March 1993.

2   Ross McKibbin, *London Review of Books*, 23 November 1989. 'Although Mrs Thatcher and Mr Lawson are closely associated in the public mind their aspirations are very different. Mrs Thatcher, for her part, is not really interested in the economy at all. She has little idea how it works, no notion of its complicated and delicate relationships and only the most elementary conception of how it might work better . . . Mr Lawson is not in her sense a Thatcherite, not one of us. A form of economic neo liberalism is central to his politics – not, as with her, secondary. He differs also from Mrs Thatcher in other important respects: he is a bon viveur, is not, I would think, an admirer of Mrs Whitehouse and has openly declared his dislike of the inquisitorial and moralizing state which seems to mean so much to the prime minister. Mr Lawson has been called "the brains of Thatcherism" in the press: but that he and Mrs Thatcher adhere to apparently similar economics is partly accidental and partly just a matter of convenience.'

3   Margaret Thatcher, *The Downing Street Years* (1995), p. 308: 'if it comes to drawing up a list of Conservative – even Thatcherite – revolutionaries I would never deny Nigel a leading place on it'.

4   Nigel Lawson, *The View from No. 11. Memoirs of a Tory Radical* (1993), p. 64.

5   Graham Greenwell, letter to *The Times*, 25 June 1971. The letter, which also contained reference to 'the Guards', banging of drums in 'primitive countries' and doctrinaire dons, 'possibly of the female sex', aroused embarrassed dissent from younger brokers, including Greenwell's own son.

6   Peter Carrington, *Reflect on Things Past. The Memoirs of Lord Carrington* (1988), p. 20.

7   John Campbell, *Margaret Thatcher,* Vol. 1, *The Grocer's Daughter* (2000), p. 30.

8   John Nott, *Here Today, Gone Tomorrow. Recollections of an Errant Politician* (2003), p. 95.

9   Cecil Parkinson, *Right at the Centre* (1992), p. 87: 'Insider trading could not have been made illegal in the Fifties, it was almost a way of life.

The best stockbrokers were the best connected. Through their connections they found out what was going on, and passed on to their clients as "tips" the information gained quite often over that famous institution, the two-hour city lunch.'

10 *Economist*, 'The City Revolution. Big Bang and After' (1986), p. 3.

11 Karl Van Horn, Head of Asset Management at Amex, quoted in ibid., p. 16.

12 Dominic Hobson, *The Pride of Lucifer. The Unauthorized Biography of Morgan Grenfell* (1991), pp. 211 and 200.

13 David Kynaston, *Cazenove & Co. A History* (1991), pp. 301–32.

14 Woodrow Wyatt, *The Journals of Woodrow Wyatt*. Vol. 1, *1985–1988*, edited by Sarah Curtis (1998), p. 27, entry for 8 December 1985.

15 *Spectator*, 15 March 1986, reprinted in Philip Marsden-Smedley (ed.), *Britain in the Eighties. The Spectator's View of the Thatcher Decade* (1989).

16 Elaine Aston, *Caryl Churchill* (2001), p. 74.

17 Parkinson, *Right at the Centre*, p. 67.

18 Bob Jessop, Kevin Bonnett, Simon Bromley and Tom Ling, 'Authoritarian Populism, Two Nations and Thatcherism', *New Left Review*, 1, 147 (September–October 1984).

19 Nicholas Henderson, *Mandarin*. (1994), p. 269, entry for 24 May 1979. For a sceptical response to Henderson, see R. W. Johnson, 'Dear Peter . . .' in *The Politics of Recession* (1985), pp. 13–17, first published in *New Society*, 21 June 1979.

20 TFW, Thatcher off-the-record press briefing after meeting French president, 5 June 1979 (104089): 'I must say that I found it a very, very interesting despatch. If I might say so, some of the things which [Lord Carrington] Peter and I have been saying with my [*sic*] less panache and much less style were said in that.'

21 TFW, Thatcher to House of Commons, 22 November 1990 (108256): 'I remind the House that, under socialism, this country had come to such a pass that one of our most able and distinguished ambassadors felt compelled to write . . . a famous dispatch, a copy of which found its way into *The Economist*.'

22 For an idea of the impact made by this book, see James Raven, 'British History and the Enterprise Culture', *Past and Present*, 123 (1989), pp. 178–204.

23 John Ranelagh, *Thatcher's People* (1991), p. 186. Henderson did cite

Wiener in his book *Channels and Tunnels* (1987), in which he revisited the debate that he had aroused in 1979.

24   On Barnett's influence, see Lawson, *The View from No. 11*, p. 607.

25   Shirley Robin Letwin, *The Anatomy of Thatcherism* (1992), p. 251.

26   Curiously, Wiener suggested, in retrospect, that his book was written as a hostile response to Heath: 'He had absorbed this whole anti-urban and anti-enterprise culture.' Interview with Martin Wiener in Richard English and Michael Kenny (eds.), *Rethinking British Decline* (2000), pp. 25–36, p. 34. I think that Wiener is rewriting his own history here. In 1981, he had seen Heath as a proponent of modernization – though not necessarily a successful one. See Martin Wiener, *English Culture and the Decline of the Industrial Spirit, 1850–1980* (Cambridge, 1981), p. 164.

27   Henderson, *Mandarin*, p. 250, entry for 25 February 1979.

28   John Hoskyns, *Just in Time. Inside the Thatcher Revolution* (2000), p. 110.

29   Jacques Attali, *Un homme d'influence, Sir Siegmund Warburg, 1902–1982.* (1985).

30   John Redwood, *Singing the Blues. The Once and Future Conservatives* (2004), p. 35. Redwood claimed that, at least in the 1970s, his opinions were considered unorthodox by his fellow bankers.

31   For the extent to which Henderson's views were shared by other senior diplomats, see Percy Cradock, *In Pursuit of British Interests. Reflections on Foreign Policy under Margaret Thatcher and John Major* (1997), p. 28.

32   Tessa Blackstone and William Plowden, *Inside the Think Tank* (1988), p. 162.

33   Thatcher expressed reservations about business studies. TFW, Thatcher speech to First Engineering Assembly, 3 September 1985 (106120).

34   Nicholas Crickhowell, *Westminster, Wales and Water* (Cardiff, 1999), p. 69.

35   TFW, Thatcher speech in Friern Barnet, 3 April 1959 (101016).

36   Nicholas Ridley, *My Style of Government. The Thatcher Years* (1991), p. 4.

37   TFW, 'Notes Towards the Definition of Policy', 4 April 1975 (110098).

38   TFW, Nationalized Industries Policy Group, 12 January 1977 (110844).

39   Ibid.

40   Norman Fowler, *Ministers Decide. A Personal Memoir of the Thatcher Years* (1991), p. 97. See also Joseph to Heseltine, 10 September 1976 (111237), reporting a conversation with industrialist Arnold Hall 'who

believes that we would be wrong to commit ourselves to total denationalisation of the aircraft industry – since that would only renew uncertainties'.

41 Fowler, *Ministers Decide*, p. 99.

42 Donald MacDougall, *Don and Mandarin. Memoirs of an Economist* (1987), p. 231.

43 TFW, Joseph to Thatcher, 19 July 1976 (111232). Joseph had met the banker Minos Zombanakis who believed that Healey was looking for an excuse for *'nationalization à la française'*. See also, Thatcher speech to Institute of Directors, 6 June 1975 (102702); Thatcher article for CBI review, 3 November 1975 (102794).

44 Michael Ivens wrote the introduction to Ian Gow, *A Practical Approach to Denationalization* (1977). Ivens seemed more radical than Gow and lamented that 'many Conservatives seem to have accepted that the extending frontiers of nationalization cannot be flung back'.

45 Leo Pliatzky, *The Treasury under Mrs Thatcher* (1989), p. 106.

46 Bob Haslam, *An Industrial Cocktail* (2003), p. 112.

47 Karin Newman, *The Selling of British Telecom* (1986), p. 77.

48 Lazard consistently refused to underwrite privatizations. See Nott, *Here Today, Gone Tomorrow*, p. 336.

49 TFW, Letter from a variety of American bankers (apparently led by Goldman Sachs) to Sir Peter Middleton (permanent secretary to the treasury), 28 October 1987, about the losses that they had endured from underwriting BP shares. This letter is attached to the letter from Howard Baker to Goldman Sachs, 8 December 1987 (110640).

50 Nott, *Here Today, Gone Tomorrow*, p. 171; Parkinson, *Right at the Centre*, p. 137.

51 On Thatcher's attempt to quash the case involving British Airways and the by now defunct, Laker Airways, see TFW, Memorandum for the president from William P. Clark, attached to letter from Reagan to Thatcher, 6 April 1983 (109328).

52 David Lazar, *Markets and Ideology in the City of London* (1990), p. 33.

53 Leslie Hannah, 'Mrs Thatcher, Capital Basher', in Dennis Kavanagh and Anthony Seldon (eds.), *The Thatcher Effect. A Decade of Change* (Oxford, 1989), pp. 38–48. Stephen Martin and David Parker, *The Impact of Privatizations. Ownership and Corporate Performance in the UK* (1997).

54 Newman, *The Selling of British Telecom*, p. 77.

55 Enoch Powell, 'The Conservative Party', in Kavanagh and Seldon (eds.), *The Thatcher Effect*, pp. 80–88.

56 Anne Power and Rebecca Tunstall, *Swimming Against the Tide. Polarization or Progress on 20 Unpopular Council Estates, 1980–1995* (1996), p. 15.

57 Patrick Minford, Paul Ashton and Michael Peel, 'The Effects of Housing Distortions on Unemployment', *Oxford Economics Papers*, 40, 2 (1988), pp. 322–45.

58 Alan Murie, 'Housing and the Environment', in Kavanagh and Seldon (eds.), *The Thatcher Effect*, pp. 213–25.

59 Alistair McAlpine, *Once a Jolly Bagman* (1998), p. 255.

60 Power and Tunstall, *Swimming Against the Tide*, p. 32.

61 Anne Power, *Property before People* (1987), p. 114.

62 TFW, Thatcher article for *Daily Telegraph*, 'The Owner-Occupier's Party', 1 July 1974 (102377).

63 Murie, 'Housing and the Environment', in Kavanagh and Seldon (eds.), *The Thatcher Effect*, pp. 213–25.

64 Margaret Reid, 'Mrs Thatcher and the City', in ibid., pp. 48–63.

65 Pliatzky, *The Treasury under Mrs Thatcher*, p. 148.

CHAPTER 9. DIVIDED KINGDOM?

1 TFW, Joseph, 'Notes Towards the Definition of Policy', 4 April 1975 (110098).

2 TFW, 10 October 1986 (106498).

3 Dylan Griffith, *Thatcherism and Territorial Politics. A Welsh Case Study* (1996), p. 63.

4 Ibid., p. 25.

5 TFW, Thatcher speech to Scottish Conservative Party conference, 13 May 1988 (107240).

6 Griffith, *Thatcherism and Territorial Politics*, p. 77.

7 Cited in Marc Mulholland, *Northern Ireland at the Crossroads. Ulster Unionism in the O'Neill Years, 1960–1969* (2000), p. ix.

8 Ivor Stanbrook, *A Year in Politics* (1988). No pagination, but see entry for 16 January 1986, for an attempt to found a 'nation-wide' organization of unionists. On 30 January Stanbrook complained that

Thatcher herself had started to talk of union 'as long as the majority in Northern Ireland want it'.

9 Ferdinand Mount, 'Hypernats and Country Lovers', *The Spectator*, 18 February 1989, reprinted in Philip Marsden-Smedley (ed.), *Britain in the Eighties. The Spectator's View of the Thatcher Decade* (1989), pp. 158–68.

10 Ferdinand Mount, *Cold Cream. My Early Life and Other Mistakes* (2008), p. 334.

11 On Thatcher's surprise at hearing of Powell's position see TFW, Mrs Thatcher's call on the prime minister, 10 September, report dated 11 September 1975 (110717).

12 TFW, Thatcher speech to the American Bar Association meeting, 15 July 1985 (106096). Thatcher's phrase about denying terrorists the 'oxygen of publicity', which was subsequently used as a justification for the ban on broadcasting the voices of some Northern Irish politicians, was first used in a speech to American lawyers with no suggestion that this remark was particularly linked to Ulster.

13 Douglas Hurd, *Memoirs* (2003), p. 302.

14 Margaret Thatcher, *The Downing Street Years* (1995), pp. 420–1.

15 TFW, Report of Howe's visit to Ulster, 3 and 4 July 1977 (109789).

16 Ian Aitkin cited in Frank Gaffikin and Mike Morrissey, *Northern Ireland. The Thatcher Years* (1990), p. 35.

17 Ibid., p. 76.

18 Ibid., p. 28

19 Ibid., p. 47.

20 TFW, Angus Maude and others, 'Themes', 16 February 1978 (109853).

21 Shirley Robin Letwin, *The Anatomy of Thatcherism* (1992), p. 37.

22 Lawrence Freedman, *The Official History of the Falklands Campaign*, Vol. 1, *The Origins of the Falklands War* (2005), p. 107.

23 George Gardiner, *A Bastard's Tale* (1999), p. 127.

24 Geoffrey Howe, *Conflict of Loyalty* (1994), p. 476.

25 Cecil Parkinson, *Right at the Centre* (1992), p. 83. Angus Maude had, in fact, lived in Australia for a time during the 1960s.

26 TFW, Thatcher speech to Conservative Party conference, 8 October 1976 (103105)

27 John Campbell, *Margaret Thatcher*, Vol. 1, *The Grocer's Daughter* (2000), p. 362.

28 TFW, Thatcher speech to Finchley Conservatives, 14 August 1961 (101105).

29 T. E. Utley, 'A Monstrous Invention', *Spectator*, 20 October 1987.

30 See David Martin, 'The Stripping of the Words: Conflict over the Eucharist in the Episcopal Church', *Modern Theology*, 15, 2 (1999), pp. 247–61. See also Bernard Palmer, *High and Mitred. A Study of Prime Ministers as Bishop-Makers* (1992). Charles Moore, A. N. Wilson and Gavin Stamp. *The Church in Crisis* (1986).

31 TFW, Thatcher speech at official dinner in Georgia, 1 April 1987 (106784).

32 TFW, Joseph, 'Notes Towards the Definition of Policy', 4 April 1975 (110098).

33 TFW, Lawson, 'Thoughts on "Implementing our Strategy"', 15 January 1978 (110321): 'we must not shirk the immigration issue'.

34 David Butler and Dennis Kavanagh, *The British General Election of 1983* (1984), p. 99.

35 Michael Heseltine, *Life in the Jungle* (2000), p. 365.

36 Rodney Barker, 'Legitimacy in the United Kingdom: Scotland and the Poll Tax', *British Journal of Political Science*, 22, 4 (1992), pp. 521–33.

37 Ian Holliday, 'Scottish Limits to Thatcherism', *Political Quarterly*, 63, 4 (2005), pp. 448–59. Holliday argues that Forsyth continued to exercise some influence, via Downing Street, even after he ceased to be chairman of the party.

38 Alan Clark, *Diaries* (1993), p. 301, entry for 8 June 1990.

CHAPTER 10. EUROPE

1 Alan Clark, *Diaries* (1993), p. 225, entry for 13 September 1988.

2 Douglas Hurd, *Memoirs* (2003), p. 244.

3 Geoffrey Howe, *Conflict of Loyalty* (1994), p. 538.

4 TFW, Charles Powell interviewed by Chris Collins, 12 September 2007 (111049).

5 Percy Cradock, *In Pursuit of British Interests. Reflections on Foreign Policy under Margaret Thatcher and John Major* (1997), p. 125.

6 George Gardiner, *A Bastard's Tale* (1999), p. 136.

7 Ivor Crewe and Anthony King, *SDP. The Birth, Life and Death of the Social Democratic Party* (Oxford, 1995), p. 114.

8 TFW, Thatcher speech to Finchley Conservatives, 14 August 1961 (101105).

9 TFW, Thatcher speech to Conservative Party conference, 10 October 1975 (102777).

10 Hurd, *Memoirs*, p. 243.

11 TFW, Hurd and Baroness Elles, 'The European Democratic Union', circulated paper for shadow cabinet, 12 April 1978 (110134) and Hurd, 'Alliance of Centre/Right Parties in Europe', 22 March 1976 (110314).

12 See David Willets, 'Conservatism and Christian Democracy', speech to Viennese Institute for Human Sciences, 9 December 2003.

13 Hurd, *Memoirs*, p. 246.

14 Ian Lang, *Blue Remembered Years* (2002), p. 57.

15 TFW, Thatcher speech to founding conference of EDU in Salzburg, 24 April 1978 (103663).

16 TFW, Thatcher article for *Hamburger Adenblatt*, 13 May 1978 (103683).

17 TFW, Thatcher speech to Engineering Employers' Federation, 21 February 1978 (103622): 'A few years ago when Helmut Schmidt – that rare person, a Socialist who believes in the market economy – visited this country, he was compared by *The Times* to "the headmaster of a famous public school, come to give out prizes at a struggling comprehensive".'

18 TFW, Thatcher speech to Conservative Party conference, 8 October 1976 (103105).

19 TFW, Thatcher speech to Aspen Institute, 4 August 1995 (108346).

20 TFW, Thatcher speech to CDU, 25 May 1976 (103034).

21 TFW, Thatcher article for *Hamburger Adenblatt*, 13 May 1978 (103683).

22 Roy Jenkins, *European Diary, 1977–1981* (1989), p. 450, entry for 21 May 1979.

23 TFW, Thatcher speech to National Association of Head Teachers conference, 25 May 1970 (101752): 'America has spent a good deal more on education than on defence; she has had virtually a total comprehensive education system . . . But she still has colossal problems.' See also Thatcher speech to Westminster Catholic Parents Association, 1 May 1970 (101742): 'In the USA they have had all children going

to the same school for a long time, yet it doesn't seem to me that they have created either the kind of society that would suit us, nor have they got rid of their social problem, nor have they got supreme educational standards.'

24 *The Times*, 1 May 1980, letter from Sir Anthony Meyer: 'Is it acceptable that the attention of Europe and America should be concentrated during the next few weeks on side issues when the Soviet threat is so huge and so imminent?' See also the letter in the same issue from Hugh Dykes.

25 Margaret Thatcher, *The Path to Power* (1995), p. 473.

26 TFW, Charles Powell interviewed by Chris Collins, 12 September 2007 (111049).

27 Howe, *Conflict of Loyalty*, p. 456.

28 Philip Stephens, *Politics and the Pound. The Tories, the Economy and Europe* (1997), p. 16.

29 Ibid., p. 29.

30 Clark, *Diaries*, p. 227, entry for 16 September.

31 John Biffen, 'The Europe of Tomorrow', in ibid., *Political Office or Political Power. Six Speeches on National and International Affairs*, foreword by Margaret Thatcher (1977), pp. 19–25.

32 Stephens, *Politics and the Pound*, p. 65.

33 Colin Munro, 'Anglo-German Relations and German Reunification', seminar held 18 October 2000, Institute of Contemporary British History, http://www.icbh.ac.uk/icbh/witness/germanreun//, p. 37.

34 Hurd, *Memoirs*, p. 383.

35 Sir Roderic Braithwaite, 'Anglo-German Relations and German Reunification', seminar held 18 October 2000, Institute of Contemporary British History, http://www.icbh.ac.uk/icbh/witness/germanreun//, p. 28.

36 Stuart Hall and Martin Jacques, 'March without a Vision', *Marxism Today*, December 1990.

37 Clark, *Diaries*, p. 281, entry for 20 February 1990.

38 TFW, Interview with Robert Keatley, *Wall Street Journal*, 24 January 1990 (107876).

39 TFW, Charles Powell's minutes of meeting held at Chequers on 24 March 1990 (111047).

CHAPTER 11. THE FALL

1 TFW, Thatcher interview for TV-AM, 24 November 1989 (107829).

2 Nicholas Ridley, *My Style of Government. The Thatcher Years* (1991), p. 2.

3 Richard Needham, *Battling for Peace. Northern Ireland's Longest Serving British Minister* (Belfast, 1998), pp. 209–22.

4 Robert Harris, *Good and Faithful Servant. The Unauthorized Biography of Bernard Ingham* (1990).

5 Percy Cradock, *In Pursuit of British Interests. Reflections on Foreign Policy under Margaret Thatcher and John Major* (1997), p. 15.

6 Nigel Lawson, *The View from No. 11. Memoirs of a Tory Radical* (1993), p. 680.

7 Ibid., p. 485.

8 Douglas Hurd, *Memoirs* (2003), p. 234, quoting diary entry for 23 November 1975.

9 Margaret Thatcher, *The Downing Street Years* (1995), p. 835.

10 Paddy Ashdown, *The Ashdown Diaries*, Vol. 1, *1988–1997* (2002), p. 18, entry for 11 November 1988.

11 Thatcher, *The Downing Street Years*, p. 755.

12 *The Times*, 19 March 1966.

13 Alan Clark, *Diaries* (1993), p. 296, entry for 1 May 1990.

14 Margaret Thatcher, *The Downing Street Years*, p. 835.

15 David Butler, Andrew Adonis and Tony Travers, *Failure in British Government. The Politics of the Poll Tax* (Oxford, 1993), p. 52.

16 Ibid., p. 61.

17 Ibid., p. 48.

18 Ibid., p. 103.

19 Quoted in John Sergeant, *Maggie. Her Fatal Legacy* (2005), p. 91.

20 Tim Renton, *Chief Whip* (2005), p. 37.

21 Anthony Meyer, *Stand Up and Be Counted* (1990), p. 101.

22 TFW, Prime Minister's Question Time, 10 November 1988 (107378) and 16 June 1988 (107263).

23 Robin Oakley, 'Victory with Just a Dent', *The Times*, 6 December 1989. For an assessment of the political situation after Meyer's challenge see TFW, Post-Mortem Notes, prepared by George Younger and a number of Thatcher's supporters in parliament, 6 December 1989 (111437). The notes concluded that the result was less good than the

figures made it appear, Tristan Garel-Jones said: 'We are talking about the beginning of the end of the Thatcher era.' Everyone seemed to agree that Thatcher's advisers were a serious problem: 'Charles must go . . . Bernard is the one they all really hate.'

24 TFW, Memorandum of conversation between Margaret Thatcher and official of US embassy at Connaught Hotel, 22 May 1973, enclosed with letter from Annenberg to State Department, 25 June 1973 (110554).

25 Julian Critchley, *Heseltine. The Unauthorised Biography* (1987).

26 Renton, *Chief Whip*, p. 13.

27 Kenneth Baker, *The Turbulent Years. My Life in Politics* (1993), p. 387.

28 Perhaps Morrison was not really so naïve. Bernard Ingham reports that Morrison had built a 'lie factor' of 15 per cent into his calculations; Bernard Ingham, *Kill the Messenger* (1991), p. 393.

29 On 15 November 1990 John Major told Edwina Currie: 'Don't be too close to her, or you could go down with her too.' Edwina Currie, *Diaries, 1987–1992* (2002), p. 209.

30 Thatcher, *The Downing Street Years*, p. 853.

31 Hurd, *Memoirs*, p. 398.

32 Clark, *Diaries*, p. 357, entry for 20 November 1990.

33 Paul Whiteley, Patrick Seyd and Jeremy Richardson, *True Blues. The Politics of Conservative Party Membership* (1994), p. 61. Asked to rank Tory leaders, at a time when Major was particularly unpopular with the electorate as a whole, party members gave him an average rating of 80; this compared to 78 for Thatcher, 70 for Hurd, 64 for Heseltine and 41 for Heath.

34 George Walden, *Lucky George. Memoirs of an Anti-Politician* (1999), p. 302.

35 Geoffrey Howe, *Conflict of Loyalty* (1994), p. 610.

CONCLUSIONS

1 Ferdinand Mount, *Cold Cream. My Early Life and Other Mistakes* (2008), p. 313.

2 Nigel Fisher, *The Tory Leaders. Their Struggle for Power* (1977), p. 163.

3 Nigel Lawson, *The View from No. 11. Memoirs of a Tory Radical* (1993), p. 64.

4 TFW, Angus Maude and others, 'Themes', 16 February 1978 (109853).

5 'A Monstrous Invention', *Spectator*, 9 August 1986. Note that eighteen months after having proclaimed the non-existence of Thatcherism Utley was writing: 'I deplore the end of Thatcherism'; see 'Why I Shrink from 1988', *The Times*, 28 December 1987.

6 Stuart Hall, 'The Great Moving Right Show', *Marxism Today*, January 1979: 'Neither Keynesianism nor Monetarism win votes in the electoral market place.'

7 Whitehouse was a particular target of mockery for left-wing intellectuals. In *Policing the Crisis* (1978), Hall wrote that Whitehouse's Festival of Light gave the Right 'considerable popular depth of penetration in the aroused middle classes'. See Martin Durham, *Moral Crusades, Family and Morality in the Thatcher Years* (New York, 1991), p. 162.

8 Andrew Gamble, *The Free Economy and the Strong State* (1994, first published 1988), p. 198.

9 Anna Marie Smith, *New Right Discourse on Race and Sexuality: Britain, 1968–1990* (Cambridge, 1994), p. 194.

10 William Rees-Mogg, 'Confessions of a Justified Monetarist', *The Times*, 10 November 1983.

11 Durham, *Moral Crusades*, p. 39.

12 TFW, Chapman interviewing Thatcher for Channel 4's *Diverse Reports*, 16 July 1985 (106097).

13 Beatrix Campbell, 'A Taste of Edwina Currie', *Marxism Today*, 20 March 1987. Campbell suggested that Thatcher supported Gillick and Whitehouse – though she seemed to recognize that Currie was not part of this moral consensus. In her book, *Iron Ladies. Why Do Women Vote Tory?* (1987), Campbell suggested that Kenneth Clarke, the secretary of state for health, opposed Gillick whilst Thatcher supported her.

14 Adam Lent and Merle Storr, introduction, no pagination, 'Section 28 and the Revival of Lesbian, Gay and Queer Politics in Britain', seminar held 24 November 1999, icbh.ac.uk/downloads/section28.pdf., p. 11.

15 Norman Fowler, *Ministers Decide. A Personal Memoir of the Thatcher Years* (1991), p. 252.

16 Note that Matthew Parris used the legalization of homosexuality in Northern Ireland in 1982 as the occasion to try to announce his own homosexuality to the House of Commons. It is indicative of the

atmosphere of the times that it suited both sides to ignore his declaration. Matthew Parris, *Chance Witness. An Outsider's Life in Politics* (2002), p. 261.

17   James Prior, *A Balance of Power* (1986), p. 225: 'On the one hand, her strong personal prejudice meant that she wanted to win, but on the other, her reason told her that she would be very happy to lose.' See also Douglas Hurd, *Memoirs* (2003), p. 341: 'She was reasonably content with a situation in which she could record her own views, . . . without any chance of their prevailing.'

18   Hall, 'The Great Moving Right Show', *Marxism Today*, January 1979.

19   Gertrude Himmelfarb – a rare example of an academic historian who was sympathetic to both Margaret Thatcher and to Victorian values – thought that Walden had used the phrase 'Victorian values' 'rather derisively'. Gertrude Himmelfarb, *The Demoralization of Society. From Victorian Virtues to Modern Values* (1995), p. 3.

20   TFW, 28 October 1989, 'The Walden Interview' (107808).

21   TFW, Hailsham diary, entry for 1 October 1976 (11159). Ronald Millar, *A View from the Wings. West End, West Coast, Westminster* (1993), p. 293.

22   TFW, 'Notes Towards the Definition of Policy', 4 April 1975 (110098).

23   Shirley Robin Letwin, *The Anatomy of Thatcherism* (1992), p. 32.

24   Ibid., p. 101.

25   Andrew Gamble, 'Theories and Explanations of National Decline', in Richard English and Michael Kenny (eds.), *Rethinking British Decline* (2000), pp. 1–22, p. 19.

26   In fairness, one should say that *Marxism Today* had by the end of Thatcher's premiership begun to express a remarkably nuanced view of government economic achievements; see John Wells, 'Miracles and Myths', *Marxism Today*, May 1989.

27   Margaret Jones, *Thatcher's Kingdom. A View of Britain in the Eighties* (1984), p. 15. Wynne Godley apparently objected to an article that Jones had written on the grounds that it was not pessimistic enough. He predicted 'apocalypse'.

28   Christopher Johnson, *The Economy under Mrs Thatcher, 1979–1990* (1991).

29   Nicholas Henderson, *Channels and Tunnels. Reflections on Britain and Abroad* (1987), pp. 109–140. Henderson lists about fifty people whose opinions he had canvassed about the British economy.

30   Charles Leadbeater, 'Back to the Future', *Marxism Today*, May 1989.

31 Cited in E. H. H. Green, *Thatcher* (2006), p. 31.

32 John Nott, *Here Today, Gone Tomorrow. Recollections of an Errant Politician* (2003), p. 183.

33 TFW, Lawson, 'The New Conservatism', speech to the Bow Group, 4 August 1980 (109505): 'Those Conservatives who none the less feel ill at ease with the new Conservatism are inclined to suggest that it smacks far too much of classical liberalism. The charge is a strange one. Nineteenth-century politics was about wholly different issues. There was, behind the rhetoric, a fundamental consensus on economic policy. Disraeli may have used the Corn Laws and protection to secure the leadership of the Conservative Party, but in practice he was operating in precisely the same world of non-intervention in industry, adherence to the gold standard (and thus to stable money) and free trade as was Gladstone. They had their differences outside the field of economic policy, but what matters to us today is what they had in common – which is scarcely surprising given that Gladstone himself was a Conservative Cabinet Minister before becoming the embodiment of Liberalism. Of all forms of heresy-hunting, this variety seems particularly futile.'

34 Ian Gilmour, *Dancing with Dogma. Britain under Thatcherism* (1992), p. 25.

35 Peregrine Worsthorne, Preface in Subroto Roy and John Clarke (eds.), *Margaret Thatcher's Revolution. How it Happened and What it Meant* (2005), pp. vii–xvi, p. vii: 'This excellent book has reminded me why, from the beginning of "the Thatcherite era" to the bitter end, I was an ardent fan, devoted both to the person and the creed.' Characteristically, Worsthorne follows this with several pages denouncing much of what Thatcher did.

36 *Daily Telegraph*, 11 February 1979.

37 TFW, 'Notes Towards the Definition of Policy', 4 April 1975 (110098): 'Our vision is embodied in social market policies, which recognise economic life as something organic but largely autonomous.'

38 Thatcher speech to Scottish Conservative Party conference, 12 May 1990 (108087).

39 Alfred Sherman, *Paradoxes of Power. Reflections on the Thatcher Interlude*, edited by Mark Garnett (Exeter, 2005), p. 26.

40 Ian Lang, *Blue Remembered Years* (2002), p. 82.

41 TFW, Thatcher article, 'Consensus or Choice' *Daily Telegraph*, 19 February

1969 (101650): 'In politics, certain words suddenly become fashionable. Sometimes they are just words. Sometimes they reveal a whole attitude of mind and influence the development of thought. Then they can be dangerous and set us on a false trail. Consensus is one of these.'

42 TFW, 'The Right Approach', Conservative Policy Statement, 4 October 76 (109439): 'In the 1950s, for example, there was a substantial and soundly based increase in prosperity.' There were more guarded references to the 1950s in Keith Joseph, TFW 'Monetarism is not Enough', 5 April 1976 (110796), in which he talked of 'the mid 1950s, the silver age of Churchill's post-war administration' and in Geoffrey Howe's budget speech of 26 March 1980 (109498): 'Even in the 1950s and early 1960s our economy was lagging behind those of our competitors. But it was a period of low inflation and rising growth rates. Seen in retrospect, that period was something of a golden age.'

43 Margaret Thatcher, *The Path to Power* (1995), p. 77.

44 TFW, Hailsham diary, 11 April 1975 (111134).

45 TFW, Thatcher interviewed by Hugo Young for the *Sunday Times*, 22 February 1983 (105088).

46 *The Times*, 3 May 1983.

47 TFW, Speech to Conservative rally in Cardiff, 16 April 1979 (104011) and Sir Robert Menzies Lecture, Monash University, 6 October 1981 (104712).

48 TFW, Norman Tebbit, interviewed on *Weekend World*, 7 January 1979 (103807). Note also Nicholas Ridley's sarcastic suggestion of 1978 that the Labour Party might sponsor a statue of Baldwin because Callaghan was his natural successor. 'Why a Tory Wants a Statue of Baldwin', *The Times*, 21 February 1978.

49 Philip Williamson, 'Baldwin's Reputation. Politics and History, 1937–1967, *Historical Journal*, 47, 1 (2004), pp. 127–68.

50 For example, Thatcher referred to Stanley Baldwin in the speech that she made on the opening of Buckingham University – when she cited his view of 'intellectuals', TFW, 6 February 1976 (102954). She cited him again in a speech to the Cambridge Union, 12 March 1976 (102981). She referred to Jack Baldwin twice – in a speech at the Oxford Centre for Molecular Sciences on 4 August 1989 (107748) and in a speech to the Parliamentary and Scientific Committee on 6 December 1989 (107839).

51 *The Times*, 27 February 1982, Julian Critchley, 'Why Baldwin Deserves His Place in the House'.

52 Mark Garnett and Ian Aitken, *Splendid. Splendid! The Authorized Biography of Willie Whitelaw* (2002), p. 263.

53 No Prime Minister', interview between Hugo Young and Edward Heath, *Marxism Today*, 16 November 1988.

54 TFW, Hailsham diary, entry for 2 February 1976 (111154).

55 TFW, Lawson, 'The New Conservatism', Lecture to the Bow Group, 4 August 1980 (109505): 'The old consensus is in the process of being re-established.'

56 John Hoskyns, *Just in Time. Inside the Thatcher Revolution* (2000), p. 39.

57 Ivor Crewe, 'Values: the Crusade that Failed', in Dennis Kavanagh and Anthony Seldon (eds.), *The Thatcher Effect. A Decade of Change* (Oxford, 1989), pp. 239–50.

58 Noel Malcolm, 'Margaret Thatcher, Housewife Superstar', *Spectator*, 25 February 1989, reprinted in Philip Marsden-Smedley (ed.), *Britain in the Eighties. The Spectator's View of the Thatcher Decade* (1989), pp. 168–73: 'such a scale cannot measure the effects of a populism which favours both individualism in private life and a crude but powerful cult of government action'.

59 Lawson, *The View From No. 11*, p. 696.

60 Paul Hirst, *After Thatcher* (1989), p. 11: '"Thatcherism" is a myth that tries to justify Conservative victory by ascribing it to fundamental social and attitudinal changes, rather than to the defeat of any credible political force.'

61 John Redwood, *Singing the Blues. The Once and Future Conservatives* (2004), p. 63.

62 Margaret Thatcher, *The Downing Street Years* (1995), p. 306.

63 TFW, Thatcher speech at Conservative rally (European Election), 11 June 1984 (105703): 'It's interesting to see how catching these policies of sound finance have become – whether they're called honest money, or monetarism or just plain commonsense, or Thatcherism'. Press conference for American correspondents in London, 10 January 1986 (106300): 'many of them [European countries] have come closer to Thatcherism than they had ever intended. That is not because it is Thatcherism; it is because it is common sense!'

64 Bob Jessop, Kevin Bonnet, Simon Bromley and Tom Ling, *Thatcherism. A Tale of Two Nations* (Cambridge, 1988), p. 74.

65 Peter Hennessy, 'Mrs Thatcher Warned in Secret Report of Defeat in Confrontation with Unions', *The Times*, 18 April 1978.

66 Ian Gilmour, *Dancing with Dogma. Britain under Thatcherism* (1992), p. 82.

67 Peter Gibbon and David Steyne (eds.), *Thurcroft. A Village and the Miners' Strike. An Oral History* (1986), p. 46.

68 Jock Bruce Gardyne, *Mrs Thatcher's First Administration. The Prophets Confounded* (1984), p. 82.

69 John Sergeant, *Maggie. Her Fatal Legacy* (2005).

70 Brian Wyldbore-Smith, *March Past* (2001).

71 Woodrow Wyatt, *The Journals of Woodrow Wyatt. 1, 1985–1988*, edited by Sarah Curtis (1998), entries for 17 and 20 March 1986.

72 Andrew Gamble, 'The Lady's Not For Turning: Thatcherism Mark III', *Marxism Today*, June 1984.

73 See Douglas Hurd's review of Ferdinand Mount's *Cold Cream* in the *Spectator*, 9 April 2008.

SOME THOUGHTS ON SOURCES

1 Quoted in Campbell Storey, 'The Poverty of Tory Historiography' in The School of Historical Studies Postgraduate Forum, e-Journal, Edition Three, 2004.

2 Mark Garnett and Andrew Denham. *Keith Joseph. A Life* (2001); Mark Garnett and Ian Aitken, *Splendid, Splendid! The Authorized Biography of Willie Whitelaw* (2002); William Whitelaw, *The Whitelaw Memoirs* (1989).

3 Ian Gilmour, *Dancing with Dogma. Britain under Thatcherism* (1992), preface and acknowledgements: 'Mark Garnett, who suggested I write this book, has given very freely of his own ideas and has been a tireless critic of mine.'

4 See, for example, Norman Fowler, *Ministers Decide. A Personal Memoir of the Thatcher Years* (1991), p. 148, which draws on Hugo Young's biography.

5 Alan Bennett, 'The History Boy', *London Review of Books*, 3 June 2004.

6 Hugo Young, *One of Us. A Biography of Margaret Thatcher* (1990), p. 137.

7 Simon Jenkins, *Thatcher and Sons. A Revolution in Three Acts* (2006), p. 74: 'The war was won because the Argentinians invaded before her "weak" defence policy had been implemented.'

8 'Baghdad Will Be Near Impossible to Conquer', *The Times*, 28 March 2003.

9 Young, *One of Us*, p. 237.

10 TFW, Account of this meeting in letter from Clive Whitmore to John Halliday of the Home Office, 25 November 1980 (110839). Other documents relating to the Ripper case can be found on the Home Office website.

11 TFW, Thatcher speech to Conservative rally in Edinburgh, 2 June 1987 (106861).

12 'Chatshows with a Touch of Class,' *The Times*, 31 July 1984.

13 This was particularly striking when events, such as the Westland crisis, invited an analysis based on some theory about how capitalism worked, see Andrew Gamble, 'Tarzan Takes the High Ground', *Marxism Today*, February 1986. Gamble seems to have slipped discreetly away from Marxist language in his academic work. An intriguing note in the second edition of his book on Thatcherism informs us that the term 'economic strategy' has been substituted for 'accumulation strategy'. Andrew Gamble, *The Free Economy and the Strong State* (1994 edition), endnote p. 257.

14 Steve Lohr, 'A Magazine Reflects a Shift in the British Left', *New York Times*, 25 April 1988.

15 Peter Jenkins, 'Thatcher's Statism', *Marxism Today*, July 1985.

16 Note how often *Marxism Today* published articles by non-Marxist authors such as Hugo Young or, as has already been mentioned, Peter Jenkins.

17 As an adviser to Margaret Thatcher, Ferdinand Mount sat in on a number of cabinet meetings. He suggests that minutes were often drafted in a manner that was designed to smooth over differences and that in any case the cabinet secretary could not always keep up with the pace of conversation. Ferdinand Mount, *Cold Cream. My Early Life and Other Mistakes* (2008), pp. 310 and 311.

18 Michael Heseltine, *Life in the Jungle* (2000), p. 302.

19 Ibid., p. 326. MRDH@haynet.com.

20 Alan Watkins, 'The Force is with Cook and He Will Prevail', *Independent*, 5 July 1998.

21 Nicholas Ridley, *My Style of Government. The Thatcher Years* (1991), p. 48.

22 Geoffrey Howe, *Conflict of Loyalty* (1994), p. 467.

23 Alan Watkins, *A Conservative Coup* (1991), p. 3. Watkins said that only three Tories had refused to speak to him and that these were Cranley Onslow, chair of the 1922 Committee, Sir Peter Morrison, Thatcher's parliamentary private secretary, and Tim Renton, the chief whip. Renton did subsequently publish his own account.

24 Alan Clark, *Diaries* (1993), p. 56, entry for 14 December 1983.

25 Martin Adeney and John Lloyd, *The Miners' Strike, 1984–5. Loss Without Limit* (1986), p. 73. According to these authors, Tim Eggar was unable to find a copy of the report when drafting the 1983 manifesto.

26 Clark, *Diaries*, p. 15, entry for 23 June 1983.

27 Douglas Hurd, *Memoirs* (2003), p. 398. Hurd attributes Clark's silence on this point to a desire to make himself seem loyal to Thatcher. Actually Clark is pretty open about the fact that he thought Thatcher would have to go. My guess is that he did not want to reveal that he had supported Hurd for the leadership of the party at a time when John Major was prime minister.

28 Kenneth Baker, *The Turbulent Years. My Life in Politics* (1993), p. 69.

29 Max Hastings, *Going to the Wars* (2001), p. 271.

30 Howe, *Conflict of Loyalty*, p. 449.

31 Norman Tebbit, *Upwardly Mobile* (1990) and *Unfinished Business* (1991).

32 Howe, *Conflict of Loyalty*, p. 200.

33 Ibid., p. 106.

34 Undated but referring to a speech that Thatcher had given on 9 January 1978.

35 Mark Stuart, *Douglas Hurd. Public Servant* (1998).

36 Douglas Hurd, *An End to Promises* (1979), p. 91.

37 Ibid., p. 103.

38 Hurd, *Memoirs*, p. 234.

BIBLIOGRAPHY

L isted below are all books and journal articles referred to in this book. Articles in newspapers or individual documents taken from the Thatcher Foundation website are not listed. Readers seeking these should consult the Notes.

BOOKS

Abse, Leo, *Margaret, Daughter of Beatrice. A Politician's Psycho Biography of Margaret Thatcher* (1989)

Adeney, Martin and Lloyd, John, *The Miners' Strike, 1984–5. Loss Without Limit* (1986)

Ashdown, Paddy, *The Ashdown Diaries*, Vol. 1, *1988–1997* (2002)

Aston, Elaine, *Caryl Churchill* (2001)

Attali, Jacques, *Verbatim. I. Première Partie, 1981–1983* (1993)

—, *Un homme d'influence, Sir Siegmund Warburg, 1902–1982.* (1985)

Bagguley, Paul, *From Protest to Acquiescence? Political Movements of the Unemployed* (1991)

Baker, Kenneth, *The Turbulent Years. My Life in Politics* (1993)

Ball, Stuart, and Seldon, Anthony (eds.), *The Heath Government, 1970–1974. A Reappraisal* (1996)

Barnett, Anthony, *Iron Britannia* (1982)

Benn, Tony, *The Benn Diaries, 1940–1990*, edited by Ruth Winstone (1996)

Biffen, John, *Political Office or Political Power. Six Speeches on National and International Affairs* (1977)

Blackstone, Tessa, and Plowden, William, *Inside the Think Tank* (1988)

Booth, Philip (ed.), *Were 364 Economists All Wrong?* (2006)

Bransby, Guy, *Her Majesty's Interrogator* (1996)

Bruce-Gardyne, Jock, *Ministers and Mandarins. Inside the Whitehall Village* (1986)

—, *Mrs Thatcher's First Administration. The Prophets Confounded* (1984)

Butler, David, and Kavanagh, Dennis (eds.), *The British General Election of October 1974* (1975)

—, *The British General Election of 1979* (1980)

—, *The British General Election of 1983* (1984)

—, *The British General Election of 1987* (1988)

Butler, David, Adonis, Andrew, and Travers, Tony, *Failure in British Government. The Politics of the Poll Tax* (Oxford, 1993)

Calder, Angus, *The Myth of the Blitz* (1991)

Callinicos, Alex, and Simons, Mike, *The Great Strike. The Miners' Strike of 1984–5 and its Lessons* (1985)

Campbell, Beatrix, *Iron Ladies. Why Do Women Vote Tory?* (1987)

Campbell, John, *Margaret Thatcher.*, Vol. 1, *The Grocer's Daughter* (2000)

—, *Margaret Thatcher*, Vol. 2, *The Iron Lady* (2003)

—, *Edward Heath. A Biography* (1993)

Carrington, Peter, *Reflect on Things Past. The Memoirs of Lord Carrington* (1988)

Cartland, Barbara, *Ronald Cartland* (1942)

Clark, Alan, *Diaries, 1972–1982. Into Politics* (2001)

—, *Diaries* (1993)

Clarke, Peter, *A Question of Leadership. From Gladstone to Thatcher* (1991)

Cockett, Richard, *Thinking the Unthinkable. Think Tanks and the Economic Counter-Revolution, 1931–1983* (1995)

Collings, Rex (ed.), *Reflections of a Statesman. The Writings and Speeches of Enoch Powell* (1991)

Cosgrove, Patrick, *Margaret Thatcher. A Tory and Her Party* (1978)

Cradock, Percy, *In Pursuit of British Interests. Reflections on Foreign Policy under Margaret Thatcher and John Major* (1997)

Crewe, Ivor, and King, Anthony, *SDP. The Birth, Life and Death of the Social Democratic Party* (Oxford, 1995)

Crickhowell, Nicholas, *Westminster, Wales and Water* (Cardiff, 1999)

Critchley, Julian, *A Bag of Boiled Sweets* (1995)

—, *Heseltine. The Unauthorised Biography* (1987)

Crozier, Brian, *Free Agent. The Unseen War, 1941–1991* (1993)

Currie, Edwina, *Diaries, 1987–1992* (2002)

Dell, Edmund, *A Hard Pounding. Politics and Economies Crisis, 1974–1976* (Oxford, 1991)

Donoughue, Bernard, *Prime Minister. The Conduct of Policy under Harold Wilson and James Callaghan* (1987)

du Cann, Edward, *Two Lives. The Political and Business Careers of Edward du Cann* (Upton upon Severn, 1995)

Durham, Martin, *Moral Crusades. Family and Morality in the Thatcher Years* (New York, 1991)

Edwardes, Michael, *Back from the Brink* (1983).

English, Richard, and Kenny, Michael (eds.), *Rethinking British Decline* (2000)

Fisher, Nigel, *The Tory Leaders. Their Struggle for Power* (1977)

Forsyth, Frederick, *Britain and Europe. The End of Democracy? Tenth Ian Gow* Memorial Lecture (2001)

—, *The Fourth Protocol* (1984)

Foster, Kevin, *Fighting Fictions. War, Narrative and National Identity* (1998)

Fowler, Norman, *Ministers Decide. A Personal Memoir of the Thatcher Years* (1991)

Franks, Oliver, *Britain and the Tide of World Affairs. The BBC Reith Lectures, 1954* (1955)

Freedman, Lawrence, *The Official History of the Falklands Campaign*, Vol. 1, *The Origins of the Falklands War* (2005)

Freedman, Lawrence, and Gamba-Stonehouse, Virginia, *Signals of War* (1990)

Gaffikin, Frank, and Morrissey, Mike, *Northern Ireland. The Thatcher Years* (1990)

Gamble, Andrew, *The Free Economy and the Strong State* (1994, first published 1988)

Gardiner, George, *A Bastard's Tale* (1999)

—, *Margaret Thatcher. From Childhood to Leadership* (1975)

Garnett, Mark, and Aitken, Ian, *Splendid, Splendid! The Authorized Biography of Willie Whitelaw* (2002)

Garnett, Mark, and Denham, Andrew, *Keith Joseph. A Life* (2001)

Gibbon, Peter, and Steyne, David (eds.), *Thurcroft. A Village and the Miners' Strike. An Oral History* (1986)

Gilmour, Ian, *Dancing with Dogma. Britain under Thatcherism* (1992)

—, *Britain Can Work* (1983)

Golding, John, *Hammer of the Left. Defeating Tony Benn, Eric Heffer and Militant in the Battle for the Labour Party*, edited by Paul Farrelly (2003)

Gormley, Joe, *Battered Cherub* (1982)

Gow, Ian, *A Practical Approach to Denationalization* (1977)

Green, E. H. H., *Thatcher* (2006)

—, *Ideologies of Conservatism* (Oxford, 2001)

Green, Penny, *The Enemy Without. Policing and Class Consciousness in the Miners' Strike* (1990)

Griffith, Dylan, *Thatcherism and Territorial Politics. A Welsh Case Study* (1996)

Hailsham, Quintin, *A Sparrow's Flight. Memoirs* (1991)

Halcrow, Morrison, *Keith Joseph. A Single Mind* (1989)

Hall, Peter, *Governing the Economy. The Politics of State Intervention in Britain and France* (1986)

Hall, Stuart (ed.), *Policing the Crisis* (1978)

Hall, Stuart, and Jacques, Martin (eds), *The Politics of Thatcherism* (1983)

Halloran, Paul, and Hollingsworth, Mark, *Thatcher's Fortunes. The Life and Times of Mark Thatcher* (2005)

Hammond, Eric, *Maverick. The Life of a Union Rebel* (1992)

Harris, Robert, *Good and Faithful Servant. The Unauthorized Biography of Bernard Ingham* (1990)

—, *Gotcha. The Media, the Government and the Falklands Crisis* (1983)

Harvey-Jones, John, *Getting it Together. Memoirs of a Troubleshooter* (1991)

Haslam, Bob, *An Industrial Cocktail* (2003)

Hastings, Max, *Going to the Wars* (2001)

Hastings, Stephen, *The Drums of Memory* (1994)

Healey, Denis, *The Time of My Life* (1990)

Heath, Edward, *The Course of My Life* (1998)

Heffer, Eric, *Never a Yes Man. The Life and Politics of an Adopted Liverpudlian* (1991)

Heffer, Simon, *Like the Roman. The Life of Enoch Powell* (1998)

Henderson, Nicholas, *Mandarin* (1994)

—, *Channels and Tunnels. Reflections on Britain and Abroad* (1987)

Heseltine, Michael, *Life in the Jungle* (2000)

Hillary, Richard, *The Last Enemy* (1942)

Himmelfarb, Gertrude, *The Demoralization of Society. From Victorian Virtues to Modern Values* (1995)

Hirst, Paul, *After Thatcher* (1989)

Hobson, Dominic, *The Pride of Lucifer. The Unauthorized Biography of Morgan Grenfell* (1991)

Hollingsworth, Mark, *The Ultimate Spin Doctor. The Life and Fast Times of Tim Bell* (1997)

Holmes, Martin, *The Failure of the Heath Government* (1997)

—, *Thatcherism. Scope and Limits, 1983–1987* (1989)

Hoskyns, John, *Just in Time. Inside the Thatcher Revolution* (2000)

Howe, Geoffrey, *Conflict of Loyalty* (1994)

Hurd, Douglas, *Memoirs* (2003)

—, *An End to Promises* (1979)

Ingham, Bernard, *Kill the Messenger* (1991)

Ironside, Mike, and Seifert, Roger, *Facing Up to Thatcherism. The History of NALGO, 1979–1993* (Oxford, 2000)

Jenkins, Peter, *Mrs Thatcher's Revolution. The End of the Socialist Era* (1987)

Jenkins, Roy, *A Life at the Centre* (1994)

—, *European Diary, 1977–1981* (1989)

Jenkins, Simon, *Thatcher and Sons. A Revolution in Three Acts* (2006)

Jessop, Bob, Bonnet, Kevin, Bromley, Simon, and Ling, Tom, *Thatcherism. A Tale of Two Nations* (Cambridge, 1988)

Johnson, Christopher, *The Economy under Mrs Thatcher, 1979–1990* (1991)

Johnson, R. W., *The Politics of Recession* (1985)

Jones, Harriet, and Kandiah, Michael (eds.), *The Myth of Consensus* (1996)

Jones, Margaret, *Thatcher's Kingdom. A View of Britain in the Eighties* (1984)

Kavanagh, Dennis, *Thatcherism and British Politics. The End of Consensus?* (Oxford, 1990, first published 1986)

Kavanagh, Dennis, and Seldon, Anthony (eds.), *The Thatcher Effect. A Decade of Change* (Oxford, 1989)

Kynaston, David, *The City of London. IV. A Club No More, 1945–2000* (2001)

—, *Cazenove & Co. A History* (1991)

Kelly, Scott, *The Myth of Mr Butskell. The Politics of British Economic Policy, 1950–1955* (Aldershot, 2002)

Lang, Ian, *Blue Remembered Years* (2002)

Lawson, Nigel, *The View from No. 11. Memoirs of a Tory Radical* (1993)

Lazard, David, *Markets and Ideology in the City of London* (1990)

Letwin, Shirley Robin, *The Anatomy of Thatcherism* (1992)

MacDougall, Donald, *Don and Mandarin. Memoirs of an Economist* (1987)

MacGregor, Ian, with Rodney Tyler, *The Enemies Within. The Story of the Miners' Strike, 1984–5* (1986)

Marsden-Smedley, Philip (ed.), *Britain in the Eighties. The Spectator's View of the Thatcher Decade* (1989)

Martin, Stephen, and Parker, David, *The Impact of Privatizations. Ownership and Corporate Performance in the UK* (1997)

Mason, Roy, *Paying the Price* (1999)

McAlpine, Alistair, *Once a Jolly Bagman* (1998)

McManners, Hugh, *Falklands Commando* (1987)

Meyer, Anthony, *Stand Up and Be Counted* (1990)

Millar, Ronald, *A View from the Wings. West End, West Coast, Westminster* (1993)

Minford, Patrick, *The Supply Side Revolution in Britain* (1991)

Moore, Charles, Wilson, A. N., and Stamp, Gavin, *The Church in Crisis* (1986)

Morgan, Kenneth, *Michael Foot. A Life* (2007)

—, *Callaghan. A Life* (Oxford, 1997)

Mount, Ferdinand, *Cold Cream. My Early Life and Other Mistakes* (2008)

Mulholland, Marc, *Northern Ireland at the Crossroads. Ulster Unionism in the O'Neill Years, 1960–1969* (2000)

Nabarro, Gerald, *Exploits of a Politician* (1973)

Needham, Richard, *Battling for Peace. Northern Ireland's Longest Serving British Minister* (Belfast, 1998)

Newman, Karin, *The Selling of British Telecom* (1986)

Newsinger, John, *Dangerous Men. SAS and Popular Culture* (1997)

Nott, John, *Here Today, Gone Tomorrow. Recollections of an Errant Politician* (2003)

Ottey, Roy, *Strike. An Insider's Story* (1985)

Owen, David, *Time to Declare* (1991)

Palmer, Bernard, *High and Mitred. A Study of Prime Ministers as Bishop-Makers* (1992)

Parker, Tony, *Redhill. A Mining Community* (1986)

Parkinson, Cecil, *Right at the Centre* (1992)

Parris, Matthew, *Chance Witness. An Outsider's Life in Politics* (2002)

Pepper, Gordon, *Inside Thatcher's Monetarist Revolution* (1998)

Pepper, Gordon, and Oliver, Michael, *Monetarism under Thatcher. Lessons for the Future* (2001)

Peyton, John, *Without Benefit of Laundry* (1997)

Pliatzky, Leo, *The Treasury under Mrs Thatcher* (1989)

Powell, Anthony, *Journals, 1982–1986* (1995)

Power, Anne, *Property before People* (1987)

Power, Anne, and Tunstall, Rebecca, *Swimming Against the Tide. Polarization or Progress on 20 Unpopular Council Estates, 1980–1995* (1996)

Prior, James, *A Balance of Power* (1986)

Ramsden, John, *The Winds of Change. Macmillan to Heath, 1957–1975* (1996)

—, *The Making of Conservative Party Policy. The History of the Conservative Research Department since 1929* (1980)

Ranelagh, John, *Thatcher's People* (1991)

Rawlinson, Peter, *A Price Too High. An Autobiography* (1989)

Redwood, John, *Singing the Blues. The Once and Future Conservatives* (2004)

Renton, Tim, *Chief Whip* (2005)

Richards, Andrew, *Miners on Strike. Class, Solidarity and Division in Britain* (1996)

Richards, David, *The Civil Service under the Conservatives, 1979–1997* (1997)

Riddell, Peter, *The Thatcher Decade. How Britain Changed during the 1980s* (Oxford, 1989)

Ridley, Nicholas, *My Style of Government. The Thatcher Years* (1991)

Rogers, William, *Fourth Amongst Equals* (2000)

Rothschild, Victor, *Meditations on a Broomstick* (1977)

Roy, Subroto, and Clarke, John (eds.), *Margaret Thatcher's Revolution. How it Happened and What it Meant* (2005)

Samuel, Raphael, Bloomfield, Barbara, and Boanas, Guy (eds.), *The Enemy Within. Pit Villages and the Miners' Strike of 1984–5* (1986)

Schoen, Douglas, *Enoch Powell and the Powellites* (1977)

Seifert, Roger, and Urwin, John, *Struggle Without End. The 1984/85 Miners' Strike in North Staffordshire* (Newcastle, Staffs, 1987)

Sergeant, John, *Maggie. Her Fatal Legacy* (2005)

Shaw, Giles, *In the Long Run* (2001)

Shepherd, Richard, *Enoch Powell* (1996)

Sherman, Alfred, *Paradoxes of Power. Reflections on the Thatcher Interlude*, edited by Mark Garnett (Exeter, 2005)

Sirs, Bill, *Hard Labour* (1985)

Skidelsky, Robert (ed.), *Thatcherism* (1988)

Smith, Anna Marie, *New Right Discourse on Race and Sexuality: Britain, 1968–1990* (Cambridge, 1994)

Southby-Tailyour, Ewen, *Reasons in Writing. A Commando's View of the Falklands War* (2003)

Speed, Keith, *Sea Change. The Battle for the Falklands and the Future of Britain's Navy* (1982)

Spencer, Ken, Taylor, Andy, Smith, Barbara, Mawson, John, Flynn, Norman, and Batley, Richard, *Crisis in the Industrial Heartland. A Study of the West Midlands* (Oxford, 1986)

Stanbrook, Ivor, *A Year in Politics* (1988)

Stephens, Philip, *Politics and the Pound. The Tories, the Economy and Europe* (1997)

Stuart, Mark, *Douglas Hurd. Public Servant* (1998)

Tatchell, Peter, *Democratic Defence. A Non-Nuclear Alternative* (1985)

Taylor, Andrew, *The NUM and British Politics*, Vol. 2, *1969–1995* (Aldershot, 1995)

Tebbit, Norman, *Unfinished Business* (1991)

—, *Upwardly Mobile* (1989)

Thatcher, Carol, *Below the Parapet. The Biography of Denis Thatcher* (1996)

Thatcher, Margaret, *The Path to Power* (1995)

—, *The Downing Street Years* (1995)

Thompson, Julian, *No Picnic. 3 Commando Brigade in the South Atlantic, 1982* (1992)

Urban, George, *Diplomacy and Disillusion at the Court of Margaret Thatcher. An Insider's View* (1996)

Utley, T. E., *A Tory Seer. The Selected Journalism of T. E. Utley* (1989)

—, *Enoch Powell. The Man and His Thinking* (1968)

Waddington, David, Wykes, Maggie, and Critcher, Chas, *Split at the Seams. Community, Continuity and Change after the 1984–5 Coal Dispute* (Milton Keynes, 1991)

Walden, George, *Lucky George. Memoirs of an Anti-Politician* (1999)

Walker, Peter, *Staying Power. An Autobiography* (1991)

Walters, Dennis, *Not Always with the Pack* (1989)

Watkins, Alan, *A Conservative Coup* (1991)

Waugh, Auberon, *In the Lion's Den* (1978)

Whitelaw, William, *The Whitelaw Memoirs* (1989)

Whiteley, Paul, Seyd, Patrick, and Richardson, Jeremy, *True Blues. The Politics of Conservative Party Membership* (1994)

Wiener, Martin, *English Culture and the Decline of the Industrial Spirit, 1850–1980* (Cambridge, 1981)

Wood, John (ed.), *Enoch Powell. Freedom and Reality* (1969)

Woodward, Sandy with Robinson, Patrick, *One Hundred Days. The Memoirs of the Falklands Battle Group Commander* (1997)

Wyatt, Petronella, *Father, Dear Father. Life with Woodrow Wyatt* (1999)

Wyatt, Woodrow, *The Journals of Woodrow Wyatt*, Vol. 1, *1985–1988*, edited by Sarah Curtis (2000)

Wyldbore-Smith, Brian, *March Past* (2001)

Young, David, *The Enterprise Years. A Businessman in the Cabinet* (1990)

Young, Hugo, *One of Us. A Biography of Margaret Thatcher* (1990)

Zweig, Konrad, *The Origins of the German Social Market Economy. Leading Ideas and Their Intellectual Roots* (1980)

ARTICLES

Auerbach, Simon, 'Mrs Thatcher's Labour Laws: Slouching Towards Utopia?', *Political Quarterly*, 64, 1 (1993), pp. 37–48

Barker, Rodney, 'Legitimacy in the United Kingdom: Scotland and the Poll Tax', *British Journal of Political Science*, 22, 4 (1992), pp. 521–33

Biffen, John, interviewed by Beatrix Campbell in *Marxism Today*, December 1989

Bland, Christopher, review of T. E. Utley's biography of Enoch Powell, *Crossbow*, January–March 1969

Bridgman, Joan, 'At School with Margaret Thatcher', *Contemporary Review*, 9 January 2004

Butt, Ronald, 'The Importance of Being Enoch', *Crossbow*, April–June 1966

Cowley, Philip, and Bailey, Matthew, 'Peasants' Uprising or Religious

War? Re-Examining the 1975 Conservative Leadership Contest', *British Journal of Political Science*, 30, 4 (2000), pp. 599–629

Crewe, Ivor, 'Values the Crusade that Failed', in Dennis Kavanagh and Anthony Seldon (ed.), *The Thatcher Effect. A Decade of Change* (Oxford, 1989), pp. 239–50

Currie, Edwina, interviewed by Beatrix Campbell, *Marxism Today*, March 1987

Deary, Ian, Wessely, Simon, and Farrell, Michael, 'Dementia and Mrs Thatcher', *British Medical Journal*, 291, 21–28 December 1985

Dorey, Peter, 'One Step at a Time: The Conservative Government's Approach to the Reform of Industrial Relations since 1979', *Political Quarterly*, 64, 1 (1993), pp. 24–36

Eley, Geoff, 'Finding the People's War: Film, British Collective Memory, and World War II', *American Historical Review*, 106, 3 (2001), pp. 818–38

Gamble, Andrew, 'The Reading of a Decade', *Marxism Today*, May 1989

—, 'Tarzan Takes the High Ground', *Marxism Today*, February 1986

—, 'The Lady's Not for Turning: Thatcherism Mark III', *Marxism Today*, June 1984

Hall, Stuart, and Jacques, Martin, 'March without a Vision', *Marxism Today*, December 1990

Hall, Stuart, 'The Great Moving Right Show', *Marxism Today*, January 1979

Hannah, Leslie, 'Mrs Thatcher, Capital Basher', in Dennis Kavanagh and Anthony Seldon (eds.), *The Thatcher Effect. A Decade of Change* (Oxford, 1989), pp. 38–48

Heath, Edward, interviewed by Hugo Young, *Marxism Today*, November 1988

Hobsbawm, Eric, 'Falklands Fallout', in Hall, Stuart, and Jacques, Martin (eds.), *The Politics of Thatcherism* (1983), pp. 257–70

Holliday, Ian, 'Scottish Limits to Thatcherism', *Political Quarterly*, 63, 4 (2005), pp. 448–59

Ingram, Peter, Metcalfe, David, and Wadsworth, Jonathan, 'Strike Incidence in British Manufacturing in the 1980s', *Industrial and Labor Relations Review*, 46, 4 (1993), pp. 704–717

Jenkins, Peter, 'Thatcher's Statism', *Marxism Today*, July 1985

Jessop, Bob, Bonnet, Kevin, Bromley, Simon, and Ling, Tom, 'Authoritarian Populism, Two Nations and Thatcherism', *New Left Review*, (September–October, 1984)

Leadbeater, Charles, 'Back to the Future', *Marxism Today*, May 1989

Martin, David, 'The Stripping of the Words: Conflict over the Eucharist in the Episcopal Church', *Modern Theology*, 15, 2 (1999), pp. 247–61

Minford, Patrick, Ashton, Paul, and Peel, Michael, 'The Effects of Housing Distortions on Unemployment', *Oxford Economics Papers*, 40, 2 (1988), pp. 322–45

Murie, Alan, 'Housing and the Environment', in Dennis Kavanagh and Anthony Seldon (eds.), *The Thatcher Effect. A Decade of Change* (Oxford, 1989), pp. 213–25

Pimlott, Ben, 'The Myth of Consensus', in Lesley Smith (ed.), *The Making of Britain. Echoes of Greatness* (1988)

Powell, Enoch, 'The Conservative Party', in Dennis Kavanagh and Anthony Seldon (eds.), *The Thatcher Effect. A Decade of Change* (Oxford, 1989), pp. 80–88

Raven, James, 'British History and the Enterprise Culture', *Past and Present*, 123 (1989), pp. 178–204

Saville, John, 'An Open Conspiracy: Conservative Politics and the Miners' Strike, 1984–5', *Socialist Register*, July–August 1985, pp. 295–329

Scargill, Arthur, interview, *Marxism Today*, April 1981

—, interview, *New Left Review*, July–August 1975

Smith, Jeremy, 'Walking a Real Tight-Rope of Difficulties: Sir Edward Heath and the Search for Stability in Northern Ireland, June 1970–March 1971', *Twentieth Century British History*, 18, 2 (2007), pp. 219–53

—, 'Relations between the Conservative Party and the Ulster Unionist Party during the Twentieth Century', *English Historical Review*, CXXI, 490 (2006), pp. 70–103

Towers, Brian, 'Running the Gauntlet: British Trade Unions under Thatcher, 1979–1987', *Industrial and Labor Relations Review*, 42, 2 (1989), pp. 163–88

Wells, John, 'Miracles and Myths', *Marxism Today*, May 1989

Willets, David, 'Conservatism and Christian Democracy', speech to Viennese Institute for Human Sciences, 9 December 2003

Williamson, Philip, 'Baldwin's Reputation: Politics and History, 1937–1967', *Historical Journal*, 47, 1 (2004), 127–68.

WEBSITES

Margaret Thatcher Foundation
www.margaretthatcher.org
The Margaret Thatcher Foundation has provided a unique historical resource by putting almost all of Margaret Thatcher's public statements online. This is a very important reserve of material – much larger than anything that exists for figures even as major as Churchill and de Gaulle. It is possible to carry out keyword searches of all Thatcher's statements which can yield interesting results. In view of the frequency with which her enemies invoked the links between the Conservative Party and Mary Whitehouse's Festival of Light, for example, it is significant that Thatcher used the words 'Festival of Light' only twice – both times she was referring to the Hindu festival of Diwali.

In addition to this, a number of speeches and writing by other people can be found on the Thatcher Foundation website. Particularly important are long speeches or lectures by Keith Joseph and Nigel Lawson.

Finally, the Thatcher Foundation website gives access to a number of archival sources, which is constantly expanding as new material is released. The most significant of these are documents from the National Archives relating to the Heath government; documents from the Conservative Party archives relating to Thatcher's early career; documents from the Conservative Party archives relating to the discussions of the shadow cabinet between 1975 and 1979; documents (released under the Freedom of Information Act) from the National Coal Board relating to the miners' strike of 1984–5; and documents from a variety of archives in the United States relating to aspects of British politics (not just Anglo-American relations).

Samuel Brittan

www.samuelbrittan.co.uk

The financial journalist Samuel Brittan has his own website. Its autobiographical component in particular will be interesting for anyone who wishes to understand the social and cultural context in which economic discussion took place.

Centre for Policy Studies

www.cps.org.uk

The website of the Centre for Policy Studies contains the full text of important pamphlets by people such as John Biffen.

Institute of Economic Affairs

www.iea.org.uk

The website of the Institute of Economic Affairs contains much interesting material – notably the text of the pamphlet (edited by Philip Booth) *Were 364 Economists All Wrong?* (2006), about the 1981 budget.

Marxism Today

www.amielandmelburn.org.uk/collections/mt/
index_frame.htm

The complete run of *Marxism Today* from 1978 to 1991 can be consulted online.

The Institute of Contemporary British History
www.icbh.ac.uk
The Institute of Contemporary British History has organized a succession of witness seminars that touch on the Thatcher years. These can all be consulted on the ICBH's website. Particularly important are those on German reunification; the Civil Service Reforms of the 1980s; the Nott Defence Review; the Falklands War; and the opposition to Clause 28.

NATIONAL ARCHIVES KEW, LONDON

PREM 15/985
PREM 15/986
Coal 26/500

INDEX

(the initials MT in subentries denote Margaret Thatcher)

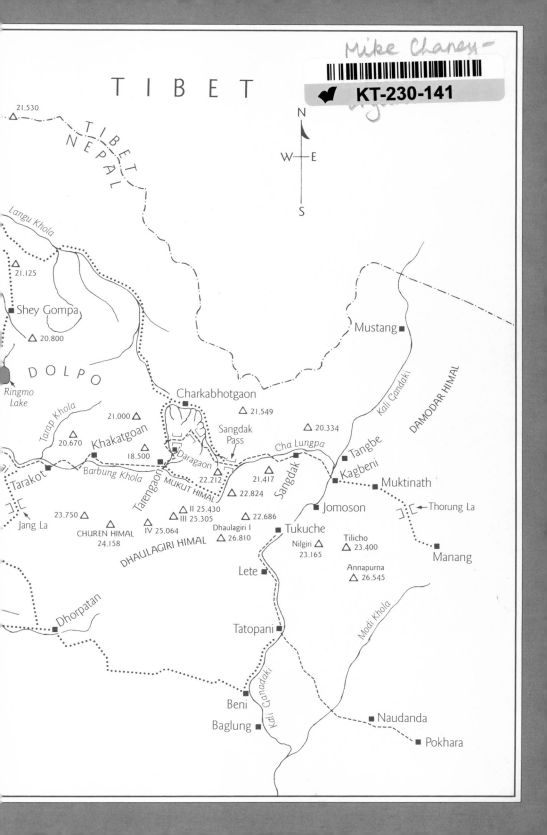

T I B E T

△ 21,530

T I B E T
N E P A L

Langu Khola

△ 21,125

■ Shey Gompa

△ 20,800

D O L P O

Ringmo Lake

Tarap Khola

21,000 △

△ 20,670

■ Khakatgoan

△ 18,500

Charkabhotgaon

△ 21,549

Sangdak Pass

△ 20,334

Cha Lungpa

Mustang ■

Kali Gandaki

DAMODAR HIMAL

■ Daragaon

Barbung Khola

22,212 △

21,417 △

Sangdak

△ 22,824

Tangbe ■

Kagbeni ■

Muktinath ■

■ Tarakot

Tarengaon

MUKUT HIMAL

△ II 25,430
△ III 25,305

△ 22,686

Jomoson ■

Thorung La

23,750 △

△
CHUREN HIMAL
24,158

IV 25,064

Dhaulagiri I
△ 26,810

Tukuche ■

Nilgiri △
23,165

Tilicho
△ 23,400

Manang ■

Jang La

DHAULAGIRI HIMAL

Lete ■

Annapurna
△ 26,545

■ Dhorpatan

Tatopani ■

Modi Khola

Kali Gandaki

Beni ■

Baglung ■

■ Naudanda

Pokhara ■

HIMALAYAN
ODYSSEY

HIMALAYAN ODYSSEY

ODYSSEY

The Perilous Trek
to Western Nepal

by

PARKER ANTIN

with

PHYLLIS WACHOB WEISS

DONALD I. FINE, INC.
NEW YORK

Library of Congress Cataloging-in-Publication Data
Antin, Parker.
Himalayan odyssey : the perilous trek to western Nepal / by Parker Antin, and Phyllis Wachob Weiss.
p. cm.
Includes index.
ISBN 1-55611-197-5
1. Nepal—Description and travel. 2. Hiking—Nepal. I. Weiss, Phyllis Wachob. II. Title.
DS493.53.A55 1990
915.496—dc20 90-55333
CIP

Manufactured in the United States of America

10 9 8 7 6 5 4 3 2 1

Designed by Irving Perkins Associates

For Nora

ACKNOWLEDGMENTS

This is a true story, presented with minor changes of some names and places—minor in that they camouflage the truth only when necessary to protect those with whom I shared these experiences.

I wish to express my sincerest thanks to Phyllis Wachob Weiss for persuading me to begin this project. Her boundless enthusiasm buoyed us through many difficult months of writing. Don Weiss gave up both the serenity of his home and the companionship of his wife to the singular task of writing this book. For those sacrifices, and for providing helpful advice concerning the choice of photographs, I thank him. I am also indebted to Jerry Athearn for arranging the initial meeting between Phyllis and me.

The many insecurities and doubts that accompany the writing of a first book were eased by the early interest and encouragement of our editor, David Gibbons. My parents, Tony and Jean, were equally supportive, and patient. For only in reading this book did they finally learn the "whole story." My father, a writer by trade, tirelessly edited our many manuscript drafts and added much, but not himself, to the book.

Of those who helped put this book in its final form, I am grateful to Mushkeel Baba, who lent his extensive knowledge of the Himalayas and their peoples to a critical reading of the final manuscript, and to Niranjin Koirala, who patiently corrected the grammar and spelling of my "tourist Nepali," with little more than an occasional smirk and raised brow.

My debt to Prem Tshering Lama, Akaal Bahadur, Jeet Bahadur and Pema Tshering Sherpa is best expressed in the text that follows. Their enthusiasm and spirit of adventure kept us constantly veering toward the less trodden routes. I also wish to thank the many fellow travellers who influenced my thoughts, among them Randy Smith, Mark Castagnoli, Andre DeCary, Charlie and Debbie Weinberger and Peace Corps volunteers Sean Gaffney and Robert R. Bell, Jr.

Finally, I wish to express my deepest gratitude to J.B. Gross; friend, Sensei, and world class wanderer.

PROLOGUE

BALANGRA PASS, DOLPO, WESTERN NEPAL
Monday, March 26, 1984, 4:00 P.M.

IN the high mountain forest, the late afternoon sun cast a golden light onto the green of hemlock trees. As I climbed towards 12,000 feet, the air cooled. In the stillness of the afternoon I heard no sounds except an occasional shrill whistle from the yak herders on the slopes somewhere below me. Prem, my *sirdar*, had moved ahead of me, the porters had fallen behind. The trail contoured along the hillside curving into four deeply forested side canyons before again emerging onto an open ridge.

I saw her sitting on a grassy knoll beside the trail. A young Tibetan woman, startling in her beauty. No more than eighteen, she held a suckling infant at her breast. Her long jet-black hair fanned out around her, enveloping the child in dark gossamer. With half closed eyes, a smile of enchanting radiance lit her rosy-cheeked face as she turned it towards the warmth of the sun's last rays. I stood mesmerized. Despite poverty, hunger, disease, ignorance, this woman-child who held life itself in her arms personified the quietly persistent will to live of these mountain people, especially their elemental ability to experience each moment just as it came to them. The guileless smile on her exotic Asian face captivated me—and, for a moment, I saw my Clara as we said goodbye in Kathmandu.

The encounter lasted less than a minute, but it lingered with me as I strolled on in the forest. The amber hue of the setting sun dappled light onto the forest floor. Huge masses of moss hung from the oak trees forming a canopy over my head. I sat on a lichen-covered rock that beckoned me.

I held my breath and heard . . . nothing. At that time of afternoon, the wind had died, leaving the forest at peace. The earth was silenced. I sat for several minutes, motionless, barely breathing, challenging the magnificence of nature around me to blink, to break the spell.

My eye caught a movement on the trail ahead. An animal had bounded onto it and was coming towards me. Perhaps four feet from nose to tail, marten-like but huskier, with chestnut-red fur and a raccoon face; a red panda, one of the rarest of Himalayan animals. He leapt gracefully in undulating strides until barely thirty yards away. Then he picked up my scent and stopped, looking directly at me through the camouflaging foliage. Rearing up slightly, he inspected me for several seconds with an odd, dancelike swaying motion, and then was gone, off the trail and out of sight.

I sat for several more minutes and felt a deep sense of melancholy overtake me. My eyes moistened and filled, and, surprised, I brushed tears from my cheeks.

I'm not sure why the tears came. This was not what I expected when I came to Nepal. The pull of the Himalayas for many is a religious quest, a search for enlightenment, personal fulfillment, a guru, the Way. Having scoffed at all that, I now began to understand, to feel the essence of life as I never had before. By coming halfway around the world, by removing myself in multiple cultural and physical layers from my upper-middle-class existence in America, I was beginning to learn a lesson in what it meant truly to *live* on this earth. The lovely young Tibetan mother, the red panda, the moss-laden trees, the magnificent mountains; the spirits of all of them were inextricably tied together, and so was I. This connection between man and the earth on which he lives was a link missing from my experience of life. The tears made me suspect that Asia, in all its unfathomable complexity, was profoundly altering my life; something was happening to me on this journey to western Nepal.

CHA LUNGPA GORGE, DOLPO, WESTERN NEPAL
Wednesday, April 11, 1984, 3:00 P.M.

My foot touched but did not hold on the sloping sand-covered rock, and I slipped off into the void.

Instinctively, I spun around as I fell, arresting my fall by bearhugging the rock I had slipped from. My chest and chin slammed into the boulder, knocking the wind out of me and driving my teeth into the side of my tongue. I sucked for breath that wouldn't come. My feet flailed in empty space. I started to slip.

Frantically grabbing for a more secure hold, my hands met only grit, sliding across the uneven rocks. Sand trickled onto my face. Then torn fingers clutched something firm and I stopped slipping. My feet dangled, and I swung them around blindly, wildly searching for purchase on anything.

Nothing below me. Realizing the futility of searching for nonexistent footholds, I put everything I had into pulling myself up. Forearms shaking, I hauled myself up until the side of my face pressed against the crumbling wall. With a contortionist's maneuver I dragged one foot onto the rock. With shallow, painful gulps of air, I pulled and pushed myself to my feet.

Prem and the porters watched in utter silence, their mouths agape. Auri Bahadur, who was closest to me, finally spoke, *"Bistaari, Sahib"* ('Go slowly, sir').

I stood on the rock embedded in the compacted dirt conglomerate until my breath returned and my forearms uncramped. Looking down was inconceivable, I didn't want to know what I had missed this time. A fall to my death. Or worse, a fall that would have left me bone-broken deep in the gorge, wishing I had died quickly.

Hacking pink globs of blood and spit into the air, I tentatively explored the damage to my tongue, which felt numb. Along with the blood came bits of a front tooth. After a few minutes I gathered enough control to make my way, ever so cautiously, back the remaining ten feet to where the others waited.

SAN FRANCISCO, CALIFORNIA

February, 1990

I returned from Asia five years ago, but it has taken most of the intervening years to truly come back. In 1983, when this story begins, I was twenty-seven, fresh out of graduate school and eager to see the world. One could say with some truth, given the pattern of my life till then, that I was looking for a rite of passage. In my youthful ignorance and arrogance, I challenged the greatest mountain range on earth— the Himalayas. With my friend J.B. Gross, I formed the "Everest K2 Trans–Himalayan Expedition." Our avowed purpose: to traverse the entire Himalayan range, from Sikkim to Pakistan.

I did not set out to prove my manhood or to risk my life. I had nothing in mind to conquer, I meant simply to trek, walk up and down the mountains, see exotic cultures. But by March 1984, six months into the trip, the expedition had been reduced to one sahib (myself), a *sirdar* (guide) and two Nepalese porters. I was in Dolpo, the most remote, most inaccessible part of western Nepal. I didn't have the proper permits, enough money or enough food; and information about what lay ahead was nonexistent. I had good reason to fear the Tibetan nomads, the villagers, the police and military, not to mention the mountains themselves.

I found myself extended to my physical limits; lost, starving, facing death itself in the stark haunting mountains. I had plunged myself into a world totally dissimilar to what I had known. A world with life stripped of its pretenses, where man coexists with and does not attempt to compete with nature. Dolpo, in the winter of 1984, also brought a new consciousness of the mental, emotional and, most unexpectedly, the *spiritual* center of myself. An awareness that alternately made me exalt and despair, laugh and sob, understand and wonder. A spiritual core that I had never allowed anyone to see or sense, even myself.

Although I returned from Nepal physically unscathed, the spiritual odyssey continues.

CHAPTER
ONE

KATHMANDU lay wrapped in a dark gray cloak except for soft lights on Swayambhunath, the Monkey Temple. I could see them quite clearly from my window on the fourth floor of the hotel. Voices came from the big room at the head of the stairs and hearing them, I downed my cup of coffee and went to join J.B. and the others.

Although Prem and our porters, Akaal Bahadur and Jeet Bahadur, had walked three miles from Prem's place clear across town, they had arrived only twenty minutes after J.B. and I had wakened at 4:00 A.M. The night before, Prem had carefully directed the packing of our equipment into the funnel-shaped bamboo *doko*s (baskets) the porters would carry. Now, in the early morning hours, they whispered to each other as they shouldered their loads and stepped quickly down the stairs.

Clara, accompanied by her friend Sera, had come to say goodbye. In May, I would see Clara again in Darjeeling, but that seemed a long uncertain time away as we moved into the darkened stairwell. She pressed a round pendant into my hand, a good-luck charm.

"Good luck, I will miss you." Her soft voice and averted eyes said more. Our bodies moved closer and she grabbed my shoulder. "Parker, please, you must come to see me in Darjeeling."

1

Incapable of expressing what I felt, I only nodded my reply. Awkwardly we kissed in the predawn twilight.

I ran down the concrete staircase to the open courtyard below. I carried one porter load in a *doko* on a tumpline around my forehead, not something I would recommend to anyone who, like myself, had never done it before. At the far side of the courtyard I paused and looked back to the fourth-floor balcony where Clara stood. I waved. She raised her hand slowly, then turned and was gone. With an ache I knew that I would think of her often in the days ahead.

The cool, forty-five-degree February morning was damp and overcast, the sky a pearl gray. We piled into the back of a minitruck, and creaked through the awakening streets. Sweepers with long brooms made piles of yesterday's trash and set them on fire, leaving smoking mounds every few yards along the streets. Porters carrying produce-filled baskets hurried through the narrow alleys, stopping at their favorite shrines with offerings before delivering their loads to the early morning bazaar and setting out vegetables for sale. We met the bus near the post office, and after securing our gear on the roof we left, more or less on time, at 5:30 A.M. Eight hours later, we arrived in Pokhara, Nepal's second largest city, and our first stop on a much longer road trip towards Nepal's western border with India.

The next morning, Prem and I walked for an hour from the Himalayan Hotel near the airport to the Tibetan camp. With the passing years and the continued Chinese occupation of Tibet, the refugee camp had become a permanent village of stone and mud houses. Here we hoped to hire an extra porter who also was knowledgeable about the routes through the Karnali, Mugu and Dolpo regions of Nepal's far west. Neither Prem nor our Kathmandu porters had traveled further west than the Kali Gandaki River Valley of central Nepal. For two weeks before leaving the Kathmandu Valley, we had searched vainly for such a porter around the great stupa of Bodnath, a winter gathering place for Tibetans from the far reaches of the Himalaya. We had found no one, but hoped for better luck in Pokhara.

Prem stopped and spoke with some young Tibetan women. We were in luck, for extreme cold had driven many people out of the Himalaya and south along the Kali Gandaki. Porters from Dolpo would arrive soon, possibly tomorrow.

We continued our search through the scattered village houses. A man dressed in a black *chuba*, the voluminous Tibetan topcoat, stepped forward and offered to guide us. He hesitated, however, when told of our intention to bus to the western border with India and then travel back towards Kathmandu along the crest of the Himalaya. He outlined another plan: walk north out of Pokhara up the Kali Gandaki to Jomoson, then west into Dolpo. Both Prem and I had already rejected this option, as the 18,000—foot passes into Dolpo would be buried under snow this time of year. Also, since the final 1975 shootout with the anti-Chinese Khampa rebels in Dolpo, this area was closely guarded. We became suspicious, as our would-be guide must have known that we would never make it past the police and military checkposts. He would just make a few easy rupees before we were turned around. Our suspicions grew when bystanders whispered to us that he stole from the trekkers he guided. Disappointed, we returned to the Himalayan Hotel, still without an extra porter.

I suspected that Prem was secretly relieved. He didn't like or trust these Tibetans, considering them a shiftless, dirty lot. As in our crossing of eastern Nepal last fall, he was our *sirdar*, and would continue to be no matter who we took on here. Even though I might choose who we hired, he would have to establish his authority and a porter who ranked also as a guide had him a little worried.

I, too, felt relieved. The Everest K2 Trans—Himalayan Expedition, never a well-financed one, could certainly use the money saved in salary and bus fare. Now, rather than return to the Tibetan camp, we decided to wait until we got to the west to hire any porters.

We spent our last day in Pokhara writing letters, repacking and doing last-minute shopping in preparation for our three-day bus ride two hundred and fifty miles to the west of Nepal.

I first met James Bernard ("J.B.") Gross at the Philadelphia Judo Dojo. In 1978 I had moved to Philadelphia to begin graduate school in biology at the University of Pennsylvania. Although I had begun studying judo at the age of ten, I dropped it when I started college. Now, in the summer of 1981, I had been invited to the Olympic Training Center in Colorado Springs. But I hadn't been on the mat in several years.

Panicking, I looked in the phone book and called the only listing,

the Philadelphia Judo Dojo on North Broad Street. A recorded message gave the hours of the classes.

At six o'clock the following Wednesday, in the war zone of North
Philadelphia, I opened the battered yellow metal door with *JUDO*
stenciled on it and climbed four flights of grimy wooden stairs. A
worn, white canvas-covered mat, twenty-five by forty feet, covered
most of the big room. The dojo was empty. I walked around the mat
and looked into the office. I found J.B. sitting behind the desk.

I introduced myself and explained why I needed to get into shape
quickly. He nodded, "Locker room's in the back."

My first impression was *big*. An understandable assessment of a
man with a neck as wide as his head, standing six foot two and
weighing anywhere from 225 to 280 pounds, eight inches taller than
I and nearly twice my weight. In his early thirties, he had short light-
brown hair and wore a military-issue green T-shirt. I soon learned
that J.B. had recently returned from five years studying judo in Japan
and had just taken over as the sensei (teacher) of the dojo.

We got to know each other over the requisite beers after practice
and I learned that his early years differed markedly from mine. He had
grown up along the south Jersey shore. Although quiet and unfailingly well-mannered, he had always been bigger than his classmates and never quite fit in. His father's stories of the South Pacific
during World War II planted the seed of wanderlust. At sixteen, J.B.
graduated from high school and immediately shipped out with the
Merchant Marine. He returned two years later to attend Annapolis.
But at the last minute, he broke his mother's heart by enlisting in the
Marines instead. He wanted to fight in Vietnam, and four years of
officer training was too long to wait.

War wounds put him in the hospital for twenty-two months and
the doctors said he would never walk again without canes. He proved
them wrong, not only walking but returning to judo and even playing
professional football.

Almost from the beginning he talked longingly of getting back on
the road. I didn't take him seriously until late one night in a bar.

"Parker, I'm tired of the kind of people we get at the dojo. And I'm
bored to tears with Philadelphia. I want to get out of here."

"I never understood why you left Japan," I countered.

J.B. sighed, "The culture's hard on foreigners. For a year it's not so
bad, but then you realize that you're forever a second-class citizen. But
I've been to a lot of other places in Asia that I'd like to get back to." He

turned to me. "You'll be through with grad school in a year. You're the only one around here that I'd consider going with. Parker, let's *do* something."

In a deep corner of my mind a similar notion had been banging around, as yet it was nebulous, nothing more than a faint feeling of discontent. My life until then had been school, vacation, college, vacation and graduate school. I was supposed to be set for life, on the track to a career, family, mortgage and the proverbial white picket fence. But something seemed missing. Life couldn't possibly be so simple, so pat, so superficial. I didn't know, and the more I thought about it, the more elusive the answer became. So perhaps in search of something, perhaps for the sheer thrill of the thought, I was willing to follow J.B. to Asia.

I received my Ph.D. in Biology in July, 1982. That same week we started planning—a 4,000-mile walk across China, from Harbin in the northeast to Kashgar in the far west. J.B. was a dreamer, and he dreamt big thoughts. And he yearned to follow in the footsteps of the characters in his oft-read books. Men who had traipsed the barren plateaus and steppes of Asia. Heinrich Harrer and Peter Aufschnaiter. Wilfred Thesiger. And who was I to suggest that we start with something just a bit shorter?

For several months our preparations continued at full speed until one day we received a phone call from our contact at Mountain Travel. China, having just opened its doors to foreigners, was also embracing the capitalist philosophy. Our "permit fee," the China expert informed us, had been set at something in excess of $100,000, payable in cash directly to the Chinese government.

So we pulled out a map of Asia and looked again. If not China, then how about something further south—perhaps a traverse of the Himalayas? At first glance our qualifications seemed impeccable. J.B. had spent a month trekking in Nepal a few years earlier, and I had once climbed New Hampshire's Mount Washington—all 6,288 feet of it. Who needed more experience than that?

Thus the Everest K2 Trans–Himalayan Expedition was born.

We both set to work researching and organizing. Despite its humble origins, our expedition soon took on the trappings of a serious undertaking. Johnson Camping Incorporated gave us Eureka tents. Because It's There, an expedition equipment outfitter in Seattle, gave us sleeping bags. Nike supplied shoes.

That spring and summer I had papers to finish for my postdoctoral work. Pressure mounted from my friends, my colleagues and my professors, who frowned and shook their heads. "You'll ruin your career, you know, dropping out like this." The trip organization took time and long nights stretched me thin. I extricated myself from a sound relationship with Susan, my girlfriend of two years. I found it difficult trying to tell her that it had nothing to do with her. Not that I was afraid of commitment (*Just keep telling yourself that, Parker*), but I wasn't "husband" material just then.

In April, I injured my back in a judo accident. It hurt. For three weeks, I lay in the University of Pennsylvania hospital, not two hundred yards from the lab in which I had been working. Sadly, I watched solid muscles turn to flab from inactivity. Exactly six weeks before I left I had disc surgery, but was up and walking the same day. I told my body there simply was no time for a leisurely recovery.

Three days before leaving, I moved back to my parents' house in Darien, Connecticut, sick with the flu. Three days in which I tried to ignore the largely unspoken concerns of my parents. My mother quietly seemed to accept my going with more grace than my dad, somehow sensing better than I the need for this "adventure." My father, always the one to worry, shook his head. How could his only son, armed solely with some Boy Scout merit badges and not a single day of serious mountain climbing, plunge himself into the vast maw of Asia, to trek across the most daunting mountain range in the world? I suspected he felt it was all "damned foolish," that I would fall off a cliff or be gored by a rhinoceros and never come home.

Before I had time to think I stood at the Air India desk at JFK. Four hundred Indians, 1,600 oversized suitcases, the bewildering screech of a dozen languages and the exotic smells of curry. And me. My father stood transfixed and mumbled, "Oh my God." There wasn't time to say proper goodbyes, I was gone so quickly.

To pluck myself from the entanglements of my family, my job and my expected course in life, and to fly off to Asia so suddenly was hard—the second hardest thing I have ever done.

Since the Himalayan Hotel in Pokhara stood a mile out of town, we made arrangements for the bus to Butwal to pick us up. At 5:30 A.M. we piled our supplies along the side of the road and waited. Just before 7:00 A.M., a particularly aged and dirty TATA bus wheezed to a halt across the road, already overloaded with passengers and cargo. Akaal Bahadur and Jeet Bahadur immediately climbed onto the roof and, deftly untying and rearranging cargo, secured our loads in the safest center spot.

We squeezed inside the bus to find our reserved seats occupied. We argued, we righteously waved tickets, Prem threatened the driver. But we lost. Four of us, one of whom was J.B., squeezed into a space meant for three small Nepalese.

Murphy's Law worked without a hitch all day, a very long day. At a tea stop in a dingy village of squalid hovels we ate *daal bhaat* (lentils and rice) from filthy metal plates. For two hours, we waited as six boys pried one of the bald tires from its rim, found and then patched the leak and, after a break for tea and a smoke, rebolted it to the bus. An agonizing procedure to watch because we had witnessed the same protracted exercise on each and every bus trip of the last six months. We piled back onto the bus . . . and sat for another thirty minutes. Exasperated, J.B. leaned out of the window to berate the lazy driver, but stopped in midsentence.

"No, no," he muttered. "Parker, take a look, you're not going to believe this one."

I stuck my head out the window just in time to see a young Nepalese boy empty the contents of a large beer bottle into the bus's gas tank. Then he turned and ran to a fifty-five-gallon drum twenty yards away, where he refilled the bottle.

Refueling, one beer bottle at a time.

Cramped and desperate for some fresh air, J.B. and I pushed our way outside and climbed a ladder at the back of the bus to the roof rack. Just then the bus lurched forward, and quickly we found comfortable spots amidst luggage and large bales of wool. Except for inhaling an occasional bug, we found the roof a refreshing place to ride in good weather. A rumor had made the rounds (J.B. claimed that if it weren't for the unending stream of rumors, Nepal would have dried up and blown away a long time ago), that on this same road a low wire had neatly sliced off half of a roof-riding foreigner's head. We saw picture-postcard images of the Himalayas to the north, but no wires.

Twelve and a half hours after leaving Pokhara, the bus ground to a halt in the town of Butwal. Like all *terai* towns, its single main street was lined with poured concrete buildings, the kind that seemed to be taking over the Third World. We had passed through this border town only the month before while playing the visa extension game. Now, with twelve hours to kill until our next bus heading further west to Nepalganj, we found a filthy, windowless room in a filthy hotel on the second floor of one of the concrete boxes. I threw my pack on the jaundice-colored mattress with suspicious stains in suspicious places, and eyed the hovering mosquitos warily. Having lived above 3,000 feet continuously for the past several months, I had stopped taking antimalarial drugs.

To speed the hours, we sent Prem to the bazaar for a bottle of Kukri rum, which we drank out of greasy water glasses with Coke, real Coke. At least we weren't across the border in India and forced to drink our rum with Campa Cola, a sickly sweet brown liquid whose color is its only relation to The Real Thing.

I lit a mosquito coil and J.B. pulled out a worn deck of cards. We played hand after hand of our ongoing gin rummy game. After midnight, we pulled tattered mosquito nets down around us and tucked them in. We fell asleep, but not for long.

I guess just about every American kid has heard, "Sleep tight, don't let the bedbugs bite." But no one I knew in grade school had ever seen one, let alone been bitten by one. And a good thing. As hardened Third World travelers, we thought we could handle a few bedbug bites. We were wrong. These unsavory mattresses crawled with the evil little beasties. Scratching and cursing, we tore the mosquito nets down and wrapped ourselves in them. Unfortunately, tattered mosquito nets don't stop bedbugs. We slept intermittently between the scratching.

At four-in-the-middle-of-the-night, a bus horn blasted us awake and kept on blasting. A cup of sweet, milky tea and a couple of *rotis* (unleavened flatbread) did for breakfast, then we stumbled into the dark to find our bus. The "navigator" on our overbooked bus told us the road between Butwal and Nepalganj was closed for repairs and had been for weeks. The bus driver/owner, however, had sold every seat twice over, so he was willing to have a go. Chaos reigned as we hoisted our loads to the roof and then found our seats. We felt lucky to get seats, but then cursed our luck when the driver popped a tape into his tape deck, and the incessant wailing of Hindi songs began to emanate from a cheap plastic speaker right above our heads. We cringed at the screeching female voice, but our fellow passengers seemed to love it.

Our companions were a hodgepodge of locals, rich and poor. Three ex-Gurkha soldiers, a group of wild looking Nepalese of an undetermined tribe, women weighed down with silver ankle and wrist bracelets, coin necklaces and nose rings. Some men wore the dress of typical hill tribesmen; baggy white jodhpurs, *topees* (hats) of multicolored cloth and large *kukris* (Nepalese knives) in wooden scabbards stuck into dark waist sashes.

Four wild-eyed Tibetans in greasy black chubas pushed down the aisle and took up residence on the floor just behind us. The "navigator" came back and told them in Nepali that they couldn't block the door with their piles of belongings. The Tibetans merely fingered their silver-handled knives, stared through the boy and smiled wild, demented smiles. The navigator backed away, the Tibetans and their bundles stayed put for the entire trip.

With a blast of horns that would have brought down the walls of Jericho, the bus lumbered out of Butwal and immediately came to the first obstacle, a two-hundred-yard-wide river. The water rose to the axles as the bus churned over the rocky river bottom. Just upriver we saw the disintegrating concrete pilings of an unfinished bridge. On the far bank, a gravel road ascended into the green Siwalik hills. As dawn broke misty gray we saw that the road sliced a bloody gash into the steep mountainsides of red clay. Workers stopped and stared as we drove past. Where an entire hillside had washed away, we dropped back down to a dry riverbed and followed its course over the rocks and sand in the narrow canyon. With the monotonous sway of the bus, my eyelids closed. I woke a short time later to the sound of retching, and opened my eyes just in time to see the five-year-old in the seat in front of me heave a stream of chunky yellow vomit onto my left boot.

It began to rain. Soft mist rapidly turned into a downpour as we came out of the canyon and back onto the road. Soon the bus bogged down in a depression of soft clay turned to mud. The navigator told us that we might like to push, so we stumbled out into the pouring rain. Leaning into my piece of bumper, I found myself next to two of the still-grinning Tibetans.

"*Tapaaiko gaarma kahaa ho?*" ('Where is your house?') I asked, impressed with my imagined command of Nepali and eager to know where they came from. They merely grinned.

"*Ek, dui, tin*" ('One, two, three'). We pushed. Suddenly the bus lurched and swerved like a drunken hippo, sending a Gurkha and two jodhpured Nepalese sprawling face down in the muddy quagmire. Laughs froze in our throats as the wildly spinning wheels sprayed the rest of us with flying globs of muck. The bus regained the firm road bed and slowly picked up speed. Realizing that the driver had no intention of stopping, we chased after the bus and re-boarded on the run. As we continued through the gray afternoon, I dozed off.

A rock crashed into the side of the bus just below my window. I bolted awake. "What the hell . . . ?"

"Do not worry, Parker Sahib. It is just the road workers. They are attacking us," Prem answered nonchalantly.

Struggling to clear my head, I peered out. Through the rain-streaked window I saw groups of workers alongside the road ahead. They hurled rocks and mud and sticks as we sped by them at thirty miles an hour. Irate that we might destroy their half-finished repairs, they had erected barricades along the road.

A quarter-mile beyond one such barrier, we came to a halt. Prem and I went forward to investigate the commotion and witnessed a mutiny on the bus. Several passengers argued with the driver, urging him to keep moving. He refused, fearing for his bus and/or his limbs. A round Newari in Western clothes dislodged the driver from his seat, and the other mutineers shoved him towards the rear. Taking the wheel, the Newari quickly accelerated back onto the road amidst a barrage of mud and cow dung. With a blaring of horns we crushed two dogs in our path, then flew down the embankment of a washout and jolted to a stop at the bottom. With a grinding of gears and the smell of burning clutch, our driver rocked the bus back and forth before we broke free and climbed the far side.

Both darkness and rain fell and we reached Nepalganj at 9:00 P.M. Yet another dirty transportation *terai* town. At this hour all of the shops were shuttered, so we dined on a bit of our yak cheese and warm vodka.

Once again, our wake-up call came at 4:00 A.M. with the blasting of horns. We gathered our gear as Prem searched for our bus heading west towards Dhangarhi. Ten minutes later Prem returned—with bad news. "The roads ahead, they are washed away. We cannot go farther west."

This news necessitated a major change in plans. Short of crossing the border into India, which would invalidate our visas, our only choice was to head for Surkhet, eliminating at least a hundred miles of trekking in the far west. Prem had already spotted the bus. We loaded our gear and climbed aboard for another eight-hour bus ride.

As we crested the final tortuous switchback, the bus belched billowing clouds of acrid gray smoke. From the top of the ridge, a broad flat valley lay before us. Surkhet was spread out at the far end, its whitewashed buildings shining like a beacon in the slanting afternoon sunlight. I stuck my head, then half my body, out of a window for a breath of fresh air. I squinted into the sun as the wind flattened my hair against my head. Imagining the warm wind washing away the sweat and dust that had accumulated during the last three days, I smiled to myself as we barreled the final few miles towards Surkhet. I eagerly looked forward to escaping this cramped, noisy bus and to getting back onto the trail.

The road was paved, barely, and lined with local villagers traveling towards the "city." The driver, perhaps emboldened by the sight of our destination, leaned incessantly on his horn as we maintained a continuous weaving course at forty miles per hour through the increasingly thick throngs of people.

Bright multicolored banners arched across the road every fifty yards for mile after mile, all the way into Surkhet. In gold letters they welcomed His Majesty King Birendra Bir Bikram Shah Dev, scheduled to arrive in Surkhet that afternoon! The people had decorated every roadway in the region on the remote chance that His Majesty might pass their way. For these isolated villagers, he is truly a god, a reincarnation of Vishnu.

Because our trekking permits did not include Surkhet, we nervously eyed the troops and police lining the road. We had hoped to keep a low profile, but lost that hope as soon as we stepped off the bus. We couldn't help attracting attention. Men in Nepal over six feet tall are a rare sight and revered in a way, as if they harbored unusual powers. J.B., as the biggest man most Nepalese had ever seen, was an attraction wherever we went. Our porters called him "Buddha." Naively we thought we could just slip into Surkhet and trek out on our merry way.

The bus had stopped in the midst of a large flock of bleating goats, seemingly abandoned in the central square. A crowd of onlookers instantly gathered to stare at Buddha while Akaal Bahadur and Jeet

Bahadur straddled our baggage to prevent theft. A small band of pleading porters competed with the goats and onlookers for our attention, hoping to earn a rupee or two carrying our loads. Prem quickly took control and from the midst of the boisterous, beseeching crowd selected two of the sturdiest porters. J.B. and I hoisted the remaining loads and our entourage set off, trailing a stream of children and luckless porters to a small house a half-mile beyond the town center.

The house, a classic Nepali dwelling, was beautiful in its simplicity. Burnt orange covered the first five feet of mud walls, the rest was whitewashed. The floors were packed dirt, and rough beams supported the high-angle thatched roof. We were settled into a small room on the second floor, surprisingly cool despite the heat outside. Leaning back against my pack, I looked out the window. A yellow moon rose above the surrounding hills.

CHAPTER
TWO

As the first order of business, after a pot of *chang* and a plate of *daal bhaat*, we had to obtain information about the route between Surkhet and Jumla. We laid our purple ammonia-dye map out on the floor. It was entitled "Latest Trekking Map Jomoson to Jumla and Surkhet, showing whole of the Dhaulagiri Himal and Kanjiroba Himal."

With his finger, Prem traced our route north, then east to Jumla. We had heard rumors of food shortages to the north, which meant we would have to carry enough to be self-sufficient to Jumla.

J.B. studied the map, then questioned Prem. "What do you think, Prem? How long will it take us to reach Jumla?"

"Carrying all our food, ten or twelve days, I think. Walking long days and with good weather. And we will need two, maybe three more porters to carry the food."

J.B. thought for a moment. "That means eight people. Lots of rice. Fifty kilos ought to do it."

"Sixty at least, maybe more," replied Prem.

I leaned over the map and traced our route north further, beyond Jumla to the Tibetan border then east through 250 miles of the remotest region in the Himalayas, Dolpo. Thirty days, maybe more,

13

with no chance of resupply. If we needed three more porters just to carry to Jumla, how did we expect to carry our food for thirty days? Speed would be critical. Our lives might depend on how fast we could move, and on not getting lost. The magnitude of our intended journey began to hit home.

Prem's voice brought me back to Surkhet. "We will have no problem getting porters, many were asking at the bus. We can find them in the bazaar."

But preparations could wait for another day. In thanksgiving for surviving the three-day bus ride, we bought two bottles of apple *rakshi*, the homemade distilled liquor found everywhere in Nepal, and a large jug of *chang*, the local beer made from whatever grain was available. Our guest house hostess cut her last strips of *suggotti*, dried buffalo jerky, from above the hearth, and soon the pungent smell of the meat frying with onions and garlic filled the room. We had designated tomorrow as a rest day to hire more porters and buy provisions, so we ate well and drank better before stumbling off one by one into the darkness and sleep.

I woke just before nine to the excited racket of Surkhet, already several hours into its busy day. The king's visit had swollen the town's populace by several thousand, and it seemed they had all chosen to execute their vociferous business beneath my window. J.B. and I had a quick snack of *chapattis* (unleavened bread) and tea, a light meal in deference to our pounding heads, and sent Prem and the porters to the bazaar.

Two hours later, they returned with three new dokos and three Thakuri porters. Two of them had carried our loads from the bus the day before, the other was an acquaintance from their home village near Jumla. Soon we found ourselves back in the bazaar to buy provisions, and also socks and the favored Chinese sneakers for the newly hired porters. If we expected our porters to make it through the deep snow we might have to cross in the mountains during the next two weeks, they needed something more than the usual bare feet or rubber flip-flops.

For an hour we peered into every stall in the market before Prem chose an especially small and decrepit one. Then began the lengthy bargaining process for our rice supply of sixty-five kilos. Prem, Akaal Bahadur and Jeet Bahadur fingered one lot after another, engaged in animated discussion about the relative merits of each. Because they came from a culture that survived on rice, this was serious business. J.B. and I were never once consulted, for it had been determined months and hundreds of miles before that we possessed unsophisticated rice palates, and thus were next to useless for making such important decisions.

As three pairs of watchful eyes confirmed that the correct amounts were weighed out, I peered into the dim interior from just outside. Above the shopkeeper's head hung a curved two-foot-long *kukri*, more sword than knife. The merchant's small child squatted and deposited a stream of yellow diarrheal feces on the flat stones of the street not eight inches from my foot.

After twenty minutes, Prem nodded his satisfaction that the correct quantity of rice was now safely stowed in our burlap bags. He paid the shopkeeper with crisp blue fifty-rupee notes. With a few deft jabs, using homespun thread and a large sewing needle, Akaal Bahadur and Jeet Bahadur sewed the bags shut.

At the local bank we converted several thousand rupees into five-, ten- and twenty-rupee notes. In the remoter regions of Nepal, bills of over twenty rupees (about U.S. $1) were seldom seen and sometimes impossible to change. In exchange for our large bills, the teller handed us several stapled bundles.

"Parker, we'd better check them all. You know how hard it is to get people to take torn bills around here," J.B. said, handing me a 500–rupee bundle of twenties.

I pried a brass staple out of the first packet. "Isn't it ironic that *nobody* wants old or torn money, but the banks start out by punching holes in every single note, even the new ones?"

The teller stood behind the counter and blinked at us as we carefully examined the stacks of bills. The bank's lone guard, brandishing his ancient twelve-gauge shotgun, sauntered over to peer over our shoulders.

"Here's one right in the middle of the stack. Sneaky bastards." J.B. held up a five-rupee note, nearly torn through a crease down the center, oily from hundreds of dirty hands and many shades darker than the rest.

I laughed. "What do you expect? The bank gets stuck with them like everybody else. They may as well fob them off on some other unsuspecting fools."

A half hour later, the teller smiled sheepishly and wobbled his head from side to side as we confronted him with more than two hundred rupees' worth of useless paper.

"I want *new* bills, *brand new* bills," J.B. demanded, towering over the teller.

We got them.

Returning to the guesthouse, we spent the next several hours packing and repacking loads, carefully hoisting each one innumerable times to judge its weight. Our three new porters would demand loads of equal weight. Besides the rice we bought in the bazaar, we had two large buffalo salamis, a large wheel of yak cheese, cooking oil, Tibetan rock salt, tea, chilies, curry powder, garlic and two #10 cans, one each of coffee and hot chocolate. We planned to buy more rice in Jumla.

Surveying the gear spread out around the room, I realized that we had considerably less now than when J.B. and I arrived last summer. It would be a leaner expedition, this journey to western Nepal.

J.B. had arrived in Delhi on August 1, 1983. When I landed at 1:00 A.M. on August 31, he met me at the Delhi airport. Me and 390 pounds of extra gear. At the door of the plane, a wall of treacly monsoon humidity embraced me. Sweat gathered along my spine, trickled down and pooled in the small of my back; my underwear chafed.

First, I needed to shepherd my large pile of expedition gear through the inevitable tangle of customs paperwork. We had worked six months with the embassy in Washington and the consulate in New York accumulating the appropriate forms to avoid paying customs duty. Now, as I negotiated with the customs officials, all the carefully prearranged paperwork was "totally unacceptable." Two hours later, I capitulated and slipped the agent the requested *baksheesh* (bribe), a crisp fifty-dollar bill. Then I joined the battling throngs at the money exchange window before emerging into a monumental downpour. Standing under the crowded eaves, I counted my wad of multicolored bills. I was twenty-six rupees short. Cheated at the government exchange window. *Welcome to India, Parker.*

An Indian business associate of my father's, Vivian D'Souza, met us at the airport with his car. The aged but well-maintained Ambassador was a blessing, a lifeboat that sailed through the monsoon puddles while the taxis refused to travel the flooded roads into the city from the airport. We crammed our hillock of gear into the car with only breathing space to spare.

"You are staying in one of the hotels near the airport?" Vivian asked as he negotiated the throngs at the curb. Perhaps he was thinking of the Sheraton or the Hilton.

J.B. gave me a sideways smile and replied, "No, we're staying at the Hotel Chanakya. In Paharganj."

Vivian slowed, then brought the car to a squeaking stop at the side of the road. He turned and looked directly at J.B. "Surely you are joking?" he asked hopefully with a nervous giggle.

"No, really, Paharganj."

"Our expedition is just a bit tight on cash," I chimed in, sensing Vivian's shock and knowing the kinds of places J.B. might find appealing.

After a long pause, Vivian replied. "It is no problem, really. I will take you wherever you wish to go."

That first ride through the dark streets was a fantastic nightmare, a hallucinatory journey into the abyss.

"This being your first exposure to Asia, I thought it only proper that you should dive right in, body and soul," J.B. announced as the car wound slowly through the narrow darkened streets. "Nonstop, JFK to the slums of Delhi."

"Looks like straight to the ninth circle of Hell," I muttered.

J.B., who had spent years in Asia, kept up a running commentary on the significance of the monstrous ghostly white cows with huge humps and curving horns that materialized from the gloomy sidestreets. Dark forms covered the wet sidewalks, huddled onto thin bamboo mats. "Some of those people are probably beggars. They say they mutilate their own children so they'll have ugly scars and twisted legs and get more money."

"This is true, this is true," Vivian nodded. "Such a sad and evil thing in India."

Long after three o'clock we gingerly stepped over sleeping bodies to get into the hotel door. Later we referred to it as Fort Chanakya, in one of the oldest, dirtiest parts of Old Delhi.

A week's living and eating in Paharganj left me with an acute case of Delhi belly, and the heat kept us confined to our room under a slowly revolving ceiling fan. J.B. had time to fill me in on the planning he had been doing for the expedition.

"Last month, August, while I was waiting for you to get here, I went out to Rajasthan. I was staying at the Evergreen Guest House in Jaipur. A real traveler's hangout. People used to say they named it after the swimming pool, a real grungy green. Evergreen." He laughed.

"One day I was in the dining room and I saw this little brown man in the corner, sweating his nuts off. I thought he looked like a Sherpa. So I went up and introduced myself. His name is Pema Tshering Sherpa and he owns a shop in Kathmandu. He got himself into a brawl and had to lay low for a while, so he was hiding out in Jaipur. Nobody's going to look for a Sherpa in the desert in August."

"So he's going to help us?" I asked.

"He's our outfitter. He's a former high-altitude porter and climber. Knows everybody. He owns the International Mountaineering and Equipment House in Kathmandu and was really excited about us trying to traverse the Himalayas."

The journey from Delhi to Kathmandu was one of those Asian epics; an overnight train, a bus, another train, a horse-drawn two-wheeled *tonga*, spending the night (all three hours of it) in a shabby hotel on the border, another nine-hour bus ride with goats, people and plenty of noise. After uncounted switchbacks, at five in the afternoon we crested one last ridge and there before us lay the Kathmandu Valley. The Himalayas, glaciers gleaming yellow in the late afternoon sun, loomed over the lush green valley. I had looked forward for so many years to being in that fabled city, the mythical Kathmandu, exotic starting point for reaching into the Himalayas, the emperor of mountain ranges. In my naivete, I thought then that I had reached Nirvana.

Now Pema took over, organizing the first part of our expedition, actually two treks: the first from the eastern border west to Kathmandu, and the second from the western border east to Kathmandu. For the first part, we would bus to the eastern border of Nepal and then trek back to Kathmandu, stopping at Everest Base Camp to "touch go." We would leave about October 1 and be back in time for Christmas in Kathmandu. For the second part, on January 1, we would bus to the western border and trek back in an easterly direction to Kathmandu. Because of impassable snow in the region just north of Dhaulagiri in January, we would start our journey in the lower areas of the far west. That way we would reach the higher passes in late spring when the deepest snows had melted. Both of the Nepal portions of our expedition would be coordinated by Pema from his shop in Thamel.

The list of equipment and food supplies lengthened rapidly, and we soon realized that our expenses were rising far above our original expectations. We had not counted on buying *all* of the equipment for the trek. We also had to buy a sleeping bag, parka, boots and climbing gear for our *sirdar*. All this would be his to use on the trek and then to keep or sell afterwards. Our porters needed gloves, hats, sunglasses, socks, shoes, pants and specially made pullovers. We weren't going to eat *daal bhaat* every day, so the list of foodstuffs grew and grew. Pema sold us the leftovers from a British military Everest expedition; two boxes of high-altitude rations, which supplemented our local supplies.

After mornings of gathering supplies from shops hidden in narrow alleyways around Asan Tole, in the heart of Old Kathmandu, we had our afternoons free. Prem Tshering Lama, our *sirdar*, J.B. and I often had tea together in the garden of the Kathmandu Guest House where J.B. and I were staying. In leisurely, informal conversations, we learned about the man who was to be our guide and companion for the next eight months. He grew up in Darjeeling, India, and in Ilam in eastern Nepal. He weighed 110 pounds and stood a dignified five foot four under a full head of unusual curly black hair. Eyes so dark they seemed black offset a walnut-tan complexion. A well-educated man, Prem was intelligent, articulate and spoke excellent English as well as Nepali, Tamang and a little Tibetan. And he needed all these skills because a *sirdar* on a trek has a complicated and demanding job; combination travel guide, chief of staff, interpreter and liaison with the local population.

Quiet, with an impassive face, Prem didn't confide much in anyone. In fact, like me, he was perhaps a bit too introspective. He worked in the mountains by choice. With his education and intelligence he could have found more lucrative employment, but he felt strongly the lure of the mountains. Months later I found that my earliest intuitions had been correct: the Himalayas were a Siren tempting him to deeds beyond those expected of him. As they did me.

On October 5, we left Kathmandu with nine porters, Prem as *sirdar*, a cook and two sahibs—thirteen in all. We took a bus to Ilam on the eastern border with India and started trekking west from there. The lush, corrugated hill country of the east, an area few foreigners ever reached, introduced me to life on trek.

After the two weeks fattening up in Kathmandu, I felt relieved to be out on the trail. I had spent so much of the previous year in a frenzy of preparation, work and emotional turmoil that I looked forward to immersing myself in physical activity. It was also a time to rebuild my body and clear my brain. Four weeks in a hospital bed prior to my back surgery had turned my legs to jello.

Walking alone for hours, I let my mind wander down unexpected paths, allowing myself to explore ideas for which I seemed to have no time back home. The beauty of nature and the daily physical exertion seemed to encourage creative thought, and my perspective seemed far clearer and healthier.

The two-month trek in eastern Nepal, while not filled with death-defying excitement, nevertheless was more than just interesting. We crossed four hundred and fifty miles of rugged eastern Nepal hill country. By luck we happened upon the Mani Rimdu festival at Thyangboche Monastery in November. We did our duty to Everest Base Camp, our theoretical starting point, and thought about our destination at K2 Base Camp in Pakistan, fifteen hundred miles to the west.

But the most important benefit from the traverse of eastern Nepal was confidence gained in the art of Himalayan trekking. I went in green and came out seasoned, both physically and mentally. I learned the lay of the land, what to expect out of a day's journey. I learned rudimentary Nepali, enough to talk to the porters and communicate my needs, ask directions and receive information. Our routine was laid down as a team, Prem's duties as *sirdar*, the porters' duties along the trail and in camp.

Then, a half day north of Lukla on our way out, we temporarily lost J.B. His service in Vietnam, plus years of football and judo, had left him with legs both literally and figuratively shot. He had walked across eastern Nepal without a misstep. Now, in a moment of careless levity, while racing one of our porters into camp, he stepped on a loose stone and sprained his ankle badly. He limped into Lukla, and that ended his trekking for the time being.

As we said goodbye at the Lukla airport from which he would fly back to Kathmandu, I realized for the first time that I had, indeed, become seasoned. Last August, J.B. had brought me to Asia; I was a neophyte, he had lived for more than eight years in various parts of the Orient. He showed me many things: how to hold my place in a line of two hundred clamoring Indians, the finer points of bartering, and the judicial, lubricating use of *baksheesh*. He told me to watch closely as my letters were franked in the post office, lest my stamps be stolen and my letters remanded to the "never send" pile. He showed me his favorite haunts in Kathmandu, the westernized restaurants, the local gin joints, places like the Momo Cave. As I watched him hobble to the plane, I thought, *See you later, you lucky bastard. In less than an hour, it will be beer, pizza, steak, apple pie . . . and women.*

I stayed behind with Prem and the porters and we walked, or more accurately, we ran eighty miles and 60,000 vertical feet out of the Khumbu region. Hospitably waylaid in the village of Mugli, home of five of our porters, we feasted on chicken and chang. It would have been impolite to refuse anything. How could we spend time in one man's house and not another's? How could we drink only one bottle of *chang* and not three? In a bloated, drunken stupor, Prem and I were held captive for three days as I grew increasingly frustrated in my yearning to return to the delights of the city of Kathmandu.

Finally we got underway, but missed the early bus out of Karantichop because Akaal Bahadur had to pay one last conjugal visit to his wife. The later bus unloaded at Ratna Park well past midnight. Because I had only one rupee left, we jogged through the dark streets towards Thamel. The narrow, dirty alleyways in the old parts of the city were quiet as we headed to the Kathmandu Guest House where I had a rendezvous with J.B.

Thuli, the desk boy, peered sleepily at me from beneath his blankets.

"I'm looking for J.B. Gross. Where is he?"

"Sorry, Sahib. No J.B. here," Thuli murmured.

"I know he's here. Let me see the ledger!"

As Thuli blundered through stacks of paper to find the ledger, I continued fuming and mumbling about life on the Indian subcontinent. "Two and a half months on the trail. The only thing that's kept me sane the last week was the thought of getting here, of having a bed, a hot shower, a beer."

Fortunately, Thuli had worked at the KGH for several years and was well acquainted with foreigners gone berserk. I flipped through the pages—no J.B.

"Sorry, Sahib. But no rooms here."

"What?"

Thuli was also a swift thinker and had a ready answer. "But next door there are rooms."

As I walked up the stairs to my assigned room, coincidentally directly over Pema's trekking shop on the main drag of the district of Thamel, I heard the barred front door close behind me and a lock scrape. I was hungry, filthy, exhausted and had an overwhelming craving for one of those gassy Golden Eagle beers.

When we had left Kathmandu in early October, Thamel had been a sleepy area. Shops were shuttered by eight, and there was no night life. But now I heard raucous music coming from across the street, a song I hadn't heard before. Prying open my window, I peered through the iron bars and listened.

"*Do you come from the land down under?*" What in the hell was that? (I later learned that this was a new album from the Australian band Men at Work.) Crazed people on the second floor of the shabby white building across the way stomped and yelled and screamed this song like some newfound national anthem.

This cannot be happening, I thought. A mirage with a sound track, the final hallucination before total mental cave-in. Locked in my hotel, and not forty feet away I could hear and see the action I craved—and I couldn't get to it.

In desperation I swallowed ten milligrams of Valium, lay down on the bed fully clothed and turned out the light. Finally, at 4:00 A.M., the music ended.

At 7:00 A.M. I roused myself to look for J.B. Christmas season in Kathmandu filled the hotels, including the KGH, so J.B. had booked a room in another hotel just two doors down. Now, with the company of friends we had made the previous September, the hotel's fourth floor became ours. Although it was mid-December, the weather in the valley was pleasantly warm during the day and we had a large sunny balcony. That first afternoon I found a comfortable chair in the sun and lined up four ice-cold, twenty-two-ounce Golden Eagles. Rags (Californian Randy Smith), the quintessential party man with a serious spiritual bent lurking somewhere just below the surface, punched on the boom box. With the first strains of Roxy Music's "Avalon" drifting off towards Swayambhunath, I poised on the brink of the most outrageous partying of my life.

My goal in preparation for our journey through western Nepal was

The author in training for trek to western Nepal; Kathmandu, December, 1983.

to pack on as much weight as possible. So I ate four or five meals a day, plus generous slabs of cake and pie. After a few days, I ate alone. No one could bear to watch!

Crazy times reigned in Kathmandu. A series of seemingly unrelated political events had combined with the inherent corruptibility of Third World bureaucracies to turn this Himalayan backwater into a wide open country. For a few brief months, the green light blinked on for smugglers of all descriptions. Electronics, gold, heroin, money— with the apparent complicity of the government—flowed into and out of the country. U.S. dollars by the millions, bought on the black market from tourists, went to Hong Kong, then were converted into gold and smuggled back into Nepal or India for a tidy profit. Heroin from the Golden Triangle of Burma, Laos and Thailand came over-land across the Tibetan Plateau and down into Nepal. From there it was smuggled out to corners of the drug-craving West, including the U.S. Lots of money, lots of risk. In all my naivete, months passed before I realized that many of my good friends survived by muling contraband through Tribhuvan International Airport.

For those so inclined, drugs were everywhere. The pharmacies conveniently supplied Valium, Quaaludes and little white Dexedrines at five or ten rupees for twenty-five tabs. Hashish was ubiquitous. The Pheasant Lodge next door sported a thirty-foot marijuana tree in its central courtyard. Although not as flagrantly advertised, heroin was available and addicts swarmed into Kathmandu. Though they played it close to the vest, they apparently played it very seriously. I woke one morning to the news that John, a regular at our fourth-floor parties, had O.D.'ed on heroin and almost died the night before.

"You mean John, the quiet accountant from Oklahoma?" Only then did it dawn on me how many of my acquaintances had intimate knowledge of the stuff.

Kathmandu was an odd sort of place, at the end of the line, not really on the way to or from anywhere. Within the sanctuary of this idyllic valley one could wear any mask, play any role. Thus it attracted an eccentric amalgam of would-bes and has-beens, outcasts, castoffs, con artists, mercenaries and dope smugglers, in addition to the stan-dard trekkers, climbers and pajama-wearing nirvana seekers. Within the cheap hotels in Thamel, they all swam in the same social soup.

The wild party I had heard my first night back had been at a new bar, the Up and Down, which I took to calling the Bar at the End of the Universe. In addition, the Marine Bar, open only on Friday nights, K.C.'s Bambooze Bar and Restaurant and the Copper Floor, a particularly sleazy establishment, were favorite hangouts for foreigners, and we frequented them all. These places were not in any way Nepal, but rather an intrusion of the worst degenerate customs of the western world, endured and condoned because of the insatiable lust for the tourist dollar. The mixing of East and West in the bars, with the ignorance of accepted norms of social behavior on one side and intolerance on the other, occasionally precipitated serious altercations.

Barroom brawls were commonplace. One night just before Christmas, it turned bloodier than even the bloody norm. The Up and Down's proprietor, a slight, bearded man who owned an immaculate two-tone 1956 "Chevrolette," had hired a crew of bouncers to maintain order and to turn away most of the Nepalese who tried to get in. By a system indecipherable to me, the bouncers knew exactly which of the locals were permitted. This screening was for the safety of all, as the majority of fights could be traced to friction between well-meaning but wasted Nepalese and unenlightened foreigners.

One of the bouncers was Sita Ram, a twenty-year-old just five foot four but solidly built. With a short stubble covering his recently shaven head, he looked like a misdirected remnant of Genghis Khan's Mongol hordes, fearsome-looking but unfailingly polite. I liked him and we had started to meet several times a week in the afternoon. I taught him English; he helped me with my Nepali.

On this particular night Sita Ram had tangled with a Manangi, refusing to let him into the bar. The Manangis came from the small isolated village of Manang, high in the Himalayas behind Annapurna. Tagged with the reputation as an unfriendly, aggressive people, they were now, rumor had it, deeply involved in the heroin trade. Rolling in money but new to the sophisticated social whirl of Kathmandu, they had no idea how to conduct themselves. The Manangi that Sita Ram turned away had recently indulged in the latest fad, a Kawasaki motorcycle. When refused admission to the Up and Down, he cracked Sita Ram on the head with his visored helmet, splitting open a long, deep cut in the bouncer's scalp.

Arriving moments later, I found Sita Ram covered with blood. The owner, whom I knew quite well, asked if I would help. I ran upstairs and grabbed a guy we called "Life," a Swedish doctor, bizarrely attired in a bow tie, white ruffled shirt and black dinner jacket. Throwing Sita Ram in the back of the owner's Chevrolette, we screamed through the streets, our patient bloodying the floor like a drain gutter in a slaughterhouse. We stopped at Life's house, gathered up sutures and sped on to Bir Hospital.

The emergency room was a scene from a Hieronymus Bosch painting. In the open dingy green room with a dirty floor, cots and gurneys held people in silent agonies. We asked the hospital staff for needles and they pointed to an old stainless steel tray of translucent bluish liquid. Some needles rattled at the bottom, thrown there when someone had finished with the previous job. We laid Sita Ram on his stomach on a table and, with no anesthetic, started sewing him up with Life's sutures. We wouldn't let anyone else touch him, although it was doubtful that they would have known what to do anyway. Life and I took turns sewing up his head; it was hard work forcing the needle through the skin on his scalp. There weren't any clamps and we pulled the needle through with our hands. The atmosphere seethed with infectious bacteria, and when I asked for antiseptic, I was handed a can of white powder which we sprinkled liberally on Sita Ram's head.

Throughout the whole ordeal Sita Ram never made a sound. Alternately, depending on who was stitching, one of us held his hand, and with every stitch he would nearly crush the hand holding his. After forty-odd stitches, I stepped back to admire our handiwork. Sita Ram looked pretty good, in a Frankenstein monster sort of way, and he thanked us for sewing him up. We took him back to the Up and Down and he returned to his station by the door.

To show his thanks, the owner led me upstairs, cleared a stool and told the bartender to start pouring—on the house. Three quick shots of Johnnie Walker Red brought me to an appropriate frame of mind to enjoy the rest of the evening. I ordered a beer chaser and turned to peruse the crowd.

The Aussie kayakers who had led the fracas the night I arrived were already stoked, pounding beers and making time with some fine-looking Norwegian women, new arrivals in town. On the dance floor a growing crowd of sweating bodies moved to the throbbing beat of Bob Marley. Just as the scotch began to kick in, I spotted Rags, J.B. and the rest of the group just across the room. Which reminded me that Rags, he of the golden tongue, had arranged a date for me that night. I signaled the bartender and he slid me a final peg, this time of Kukri rum. Not the most appealing stuff, but I downed it anyway. Grabbing my beer, I waded through the mass of people. Rags met me in the middle of the dance floor with two nurses from New Zealand on holiday. One of them slid her arm around me and I began to see that the evening, for all of the earlier blood and gore, was shaping up nicely. A pipe appeared out of the crowd. I took a long drag and passed it on. The music switched to Men at Work, the Aussies hit the dance floor and the energy level popped up a couple more notches. The music pounded, the crowd was in a frenzy. I was flying. And it was only a quarter to nine.

Several hours and many beers later I turned at the sound of another argument. A drunk Manangi, reeling around the floor, bumped into a girl dancing with an SAS soldier (British Special Forces in Nepal to train the crack Nepalese troops). The SAS man whacked the Manangi just once, and that did it. Confederates from both sides jumped in. Prudently we backed into a corner and watched. Bottles smashed through the mirrored shelves behind the bar; barstools, fists and bodies flew everywhere. And in minutes the brawl grew from the Nepalese fighting the British to an authentic riot in the streets outside between rival Nepalese factions. A law in Nepal says that in self-defense, you can shoot an attacker below the waist. One of the Nepalese turned to me.

"Parker, you're a foreigner, you can get out of here. There's a Winchester rifle in my car. Please go and bring it back for me."

I declined as politely as I could. Unfortunately his lackey got it for him. Someone called the police, but it seemed like hours before they arrived. Meanwhile, we kept drinking beer. We had friends in all factions. And, despite our condition, we still had enough sense to stay away from flying fists and bottles. When the police arrived, they cleared everybody from the street in front of the bar, and we moved the party to the fourth floor of our hotel. Just another night in Kathmandu.

The three Thakuri porters we had hired arrived at our guesthouse in Surkhet promptly at six on the morning of February 14. They were three of the filthiest human beings on earth. Their tattered homespun clothes had accumulated sweat and oils from continuous wear and

were encrusted with the dirt of daily living. In contrast, Akaal
Bahadur and Jeet Bahadur stood out markedly because of their clean-
liness.

Golden rays of sunshine filtered through the sparkling morning
mist as we followed a rutted dirt track to the edge of town. At six-
thirty, dawn had just arrived, fresh, sweet, the start of a new journey.
All of our porters, especially Akaal Bahadur and Jeet Bahadur, carried
excessively heavy loads. Lingering behind to take some photos, I
watched our small band spread out two hundred yards ahead of me,
mist swirling at our feet, green hills surrounding us.

Our crossing of eastern Nepal had been in many ways just a re-
hearsal for the journey confronting us now. We had planned a venture
into the unknown, a trip to legendary places. In hushed whispers in
the back of Pema's Kathmandu shop, we had thrashed through several difficult decisions about our passage through western Nepal.
While the trails in the east had been mapped and traveled by our

Our three Thakuri porters.

companions, this journey to the west would lead us into unfamiliar territory. Where would we find food, porters? Would the trails be passable? We had concluded that our only hope of making it in, around, through and, if necessary, over the Himalayas and back to Kathmandu was to go as fast and as light as possible.

Pema had insisted we leave ropes, climbing gear and crampons behind. We argued with him and won only on the issue of ice axes. I wondered, as I watched our porters carrying our meager supplies down the trail in front of me, what this might mean in the weeks ahead. Would we have need of our ropes, our crampons? What use would we make of our ice axes? Food weighed us down now, but would we be able to resupply?

Once the sun had burned away the mist, the day turned clear and hot. The porters' loads slowed our steady ascent, but to my surprise I found my climb really no chore at all. Five months ago, during our first days trekking in eastern Nepal, I had been so out of shape that just about any small hill had filled me with consternation. Glad to be

Leaving Surkhet at dawn on February 14, 1984, heading north towards the Himalaya of western Nepal.

back on the trail, putting one foot in front of the other, I found myself deep in thought, pondering innumerable ideas, ending the mental stagnation that had become habit in Kathmandu. The hedonism of Kathmandu had been necessary after two and a half months on the trail, but I was ready once again for some physical work as well as some cerebral activity, which for me go hand in hand.

The second day out of Surkhet, we ascended the first major ridge and dropped back down to camp for the night. The porters still moved slowly, though we knew their loads would lighten as we continued to eat our food supplies. We were also slowed by snow and ice along the trail. As we headed north, we would move further into spring, but we also would go higher into the Himalayas.

I could feel the history of the trail we followed, one of the oldest trading routes in Nepal. Before the Chinese takeover of Tibet, the Tibetans and Nepalese traded actively. Each year, the Tibetans collected rock salt from lake beds in central Tibet and made the long journey down through Mugu and Jumla. They traded with the Nepalese for grain and other food supplies. This trading relationship, which over hundreds of years linked individual families of Tibetans and Nepalese, was drastically curtailed by the Communist Chinese. The trade had not stopped altogether—the Chinese had not been willing or able to police the high border passes—but it had diminished greatly.

Hindus of various castes and tribal groups inhabited the region we passed through now. The Nepalese easily identified one another as belonging to a certain group by dress, language and facial features. Further north, in the high mountains, the people were Buddhists, mostly of Tibetan stock. The Tibetans had moved gradually south into Nepal over the last two hundred years. In some areas where the valleys were easy to reach, lowland people moved north and adopted Tibetan Buddhism, even though they were ethnically Nepalese. This trail was used by all of these people, Tibetans and Nepalese, Hindus and Buddhists.

That night, the full moon rose white and brilliant. With us far from any artificial light, it shone brighter than I had ever seen. I took my heavy, bound journal, the one embossed on the front with *Everest K2 Himalayan Expedition* and my name in gold letters, and recorded the day's events by the glowing light.

* * *

I recalled now that I had spoken to Clara for the first time by the light of the full moon. I first saw her in late December. One sunny afternoon as I lazed on the fourth floor balcony, I saw two women come up the stairwell.

The first held my glance. Only slightly shorter than I, she had shoulder-length, raven black hair and shining black eyes. Her attire seemed inappropriate for her Nepalese features, a plaid pleated skirt, white knee socks and red wool sweater. She faced me briefly, then started up the open stairs to the roof with her friend.

I called out to them, "Hello."

She turned to me and smiled, deep dimples in her cheeks, warmth in her wide-set eyes. "Hello," she answered. Then they continued up.

I watched her disappear behind the low wall along the roof's edge. Something in that first look drew me towards her.

One evening a few days later, I stood on the balcony as the huge yellow orb of the moon rose out of the Himalayas far to the northeast around Everest. Just at that moment, Clara and her friend Sera came up the stairs.

"Come and look at this." I pointed to the moon. "Isn't it beautiful?"

Clara came and stood next to me, leaning out to see the moon. I could feel her body's warmth near me. I looked at her thick black hair caught in a clip at the nape of her neck and watched the expressions flit across her clear, fresh face, the color of warm honey.

Though it had only been two months before, now I couldn't remember the rest of the conversation. Small talk baffles me and this conversation had been trite, inane, not overly coherent, words spoken only to make contact.

The thoughts of Clara broke my concentration. And so reluctantly I left the moon and my journal and crawled into my sleeping bag.

CHAPTER
THREE

THE moon played funny tricks on me that night. I dreamt I was a professional baseball player. That image segued into watching the rock group The Who play in the basement of K.C.'s Bambooze Bar and Restaurant, which has no basement. I gave no thought to the Jungian significance of descending into basements, but I did have to get up three times in the night to heed the call of nature. Each time the moon stared benevolently down on me, a cold, white, silent blessing on our journey.

Soon after breaking camp, J.B. and I moved out ahead of the porters along the broad, gently descending trail. The sun cleared a ridgeline, and with its first warming rays I stopped to strip off my gray bunting jacket and wool hat. Even this early in the day, J.B. wore only his green military-issue T-shirt, already sweatstained from his broad shoulders to the small of his back. Stopping to wait while I packed my gear, he wiped his brow with a small blue towel tied to one pack strap. A habit he picked up in the jungles of Vietnam, he had told me, when he was with the Marine Corps, First Force Reconnaissance. Secret, sensitive missions, with a life expectancy measured in weeks. J.B. had endured for months and was wounded twice, the second time nearly costing him his life.

32

An hour later, we stopped at a trickling stream and washed the sweat from our faces before resting in the shade of a teahouse. A barefoot girl in a tattered red smock offered us soothing glasses of cool *dahi* (yogurt). J.B. sat on a flat rock along the trail's edge. I found a low wicker stool on the porch of the hut.

From around a bend in the trail, a uniformed man and a woman on horseback approached us. Two policemen, burdened with weighty loads, followed hurriedly on foot. This was the first time I had seen anyone on a horse, which, along with the silvery bars atop the epaulets on the man's shoulders, denoted a high-ranking officer. I watched as he reined in a few feet from J.B.

He eyed J.B. intently for a few seconds before asking, in perfect English, "Where are you going?"

"To Jumla," J.B. replied offhandedly.

"And what is your purpose?"

"Trekking and to see the views."

Concentrating on the foreigner in front of him, the officer hadn't spotted me yet, obscured as I was by the low eaves of the porch. Certain that this police officer would detain us if he learned we traveled without the appropriate permits, I formulated a plan. If he asked to see J.B.'s trekking permit, I would walk through the door into the teahouse, and then out through the kitchen in the back. I knew J.B. would say nothing.

For fifteen seconds, the man stared down at J.B., then with a flick of his gleaming black riding boots, he nudged his horse back onto the trail. His wife followed and the junior officers trotted along behind them. For me, it had been an unsettling meeting; J.B., though, just shrugged it off.

At ten-thirty, we stopped at a group of bamboo and thatch huts built on stilts for our first meal of the day. While trekking we had formed the habit of eating as the Nepalese do, twice a day. We ate first in the late morning, after we had walked for two to four hours. In the evening, we ate our second meal, after the day's work.

Prem, both *sirdar* and cook, built a small fire to begin cooking as I unfolded my map of western Nepal. "Prem," I asked, "how many police checkposts do you think lie between here and Jumla?" Shopkeepers in Surkhet had said none, but J.B. and I hesitated to believe them.

Prem turned to our newly hired Thakuri porters and spoke quickly. "They say three, perhaps four."

Four too many, I thought. J.B.'s encounter with the policeman, the hard stare and ominous tone of voice, had shaken me. I had not expected to be concerned about the police until we began trekking north of Jumla, into the Mugu region. Because we had no idea how we would cross western Nepal, when we applied for our permits in Kathmandu we had the only route available—through Beni, Baglung, Dhorpatan and Jarjakot—written on them. However, this route passed through hill country and our intent was to traverse further north, through the Himalayas themselves. Now we were trekking 250 miles west of where we were supposed to be and traveling without proper paperwork on this trail from Surkhet to Jumla.

After our meal, Prem spoke. "If we come to a checkpost, I think it will be best for you to split from us. You and J.B. stay together, the porters and I will go separately, one at a time."

I thought about Prem's words, trying to decipher his meaning. After five months together, I had become attuned to the nuance of his speech. "I think it best for you" meant Prem was certain of the course to take, but unwilling to explain further. Perhaps, in the Asian way, he would lose face, or he had learned something he thought it better we not know. Language and cultural barriers created many complexities. The phrase was one Prem used rarely, and I didn't ask for an explanation.

I recalled a conversation we had in Surkhet, in which Prem had suggested that the police might deal harshly with him and the porters for leading foreigners into restricted areas. Plainly he was afraid of getting caught with us, and I couldn't blame him for not wanting to find himself staring at the four walls of a Nepalese jail. *But what about us? What would J.B. and I do about not having the proper permits?* Before I could ask, J.B. came up with a plan.

"Parker, remember the police in Pokhara telling us about the banditry problems due to the Tibetan refugees in the area around Dhorpatan? We can just say that to avoid all that mess, we decided to hop on a bus and start from Surkhet. Maybe throw in a little of the 'lost and confused foreigners' routine."

"The best plan is to avoid the police checkposts altogether," I answered. "Prem, can we find out from the Thakuris where those checkposts are?"

"I will ask them, Parker Sahib, but I am not sure we should believe what they say. They do not lie to us, but they are very simple men. Sometimes they make up things just to please us."

The Thakuri porters still huddled on their haunches around the embers of their fire, cooking more of their flatbread rotis to be squirreled away for future meals. Prem squatted and talked casually with them.

He returned to our fire. "It is certain that one checkpost can be found in Dailekh, two or three days ahead. A big one, they say, with a military garrison. After that, they cannot tell me. They say the checkposts sometimes move from village to village."

"Then let's find a way around Dailekh," I replied. "I certainly don't want to walk right into the middle of an entire garrison."

With a belly full of rice, I reclined on my pack and watched J.B. leave. Thirty yards down the trail, three barefooted girls tumbled from a hut, intent on a secret game among themselves. The urchins were about six years old. They surrounded J.B. almost before he spotted them.

"*Namaste! Namaste!* What time? What time? Give me your pen!" one screeched at him, practicing her English and hoping for that most precious commodity, a pen to take to school.

I smiled at their innocent, unfettered gaiety. Not taught to be afraid of strangers, as yet untouched by the harsh existence that awaited them, they played happily, thinking of nothing but their current game.

J.B. stopped, leaned on his walking stick and namasted them back, speaking a few words of Nepali. Startled, their chattering stopped, and their large eyes stared from dirty faces at this impossibly huge human being. J.B. resumed his pace and left them huddled together, three little girls on a dusty trail, wondering who this light-haired giant could be. A ghost? A yeti? A mythical personage from out of the past?

I noticed that J.B. favored his left ankle, the one he had injured in the Khumbu and then reinjured in a pothole in Kathmandu. Fearing he would hold us back, he left before the rest of us in the morning, and again now, after our lunch stop. But our porters, laden with a two-week food supply, dictated our pace, and I thought it unnecessary for him to go ahead. Lingering with the slowest porter would have been kinder on his mending ankle. But I said nothing, deciding that he could take care of himself. Only later did I realize that J.B.'s absence at crucial decision-making times would become a problem.

I left last, after lazing in the midday sun. Soon, though, I caught and passed Prem and the porters. I pushed myself recklessly downward, straining to regain the timing necessary to rapidly negotiate the steep rocky trails. Six weeks of inactivity had softened my body, and now leaden thighs and burning feet screamed their protest. In preparation for this crossing of western Nepal, I had purchased a used green Tibetan pack. With my slight build, dark hair and brown eyes, I hoped to pass unnoticed as a foreigner. Now the pack, with its primitive suspension system, bounced awkwardly and scraped at my back.

As I sat resting on an exposed promontory, I saw J.B. 1,500 feet below approaching the village of Dungibara, fifty or more houses situated on a flat green expanse at the confluence of two rivers. Fearing he might go right through the village and run into a check-post, I cut my rest short and hurried after him.

A hundred yards before the village, I found J.B. resting atop a boulder set in a rice paddy. He, too, had worried about the village and pulled off to wait.

Fifteen minutes later, several policemen materialized above us. They stared for half a minute, then slowly continued into the village. One, a black turbaned adolescent in oversized olive trousers, stopped several times to watch us before disappearing between the houses. J.B. pulled out his binoculars and scanned the village, hoping to spot them emerging from the other side. No one appeared.

Three-quarters of an hour later, Prem showed up with the porters, the Thakuris sheepishly admitting they had forgotten about the *chaulki* (checkpost) in the village center. A path led off to the left, skirting the village. Prem proposed we take this path, camping where the stream spilled into the Katia Khola river a quarter of a mile beyond the settlement.

We started along this trail, but just abreast of the village a police-man appeared on a rooftop, waving and yelling in our direction. He left no doubt that he wanted us to go into the village and visit his checkpost. Prem muttered a few obscenities and we conferred hurriedly to get our stories straight.

As we made our way along the narrow paths, balanced atop paddy dikes, Prem called back over his shoulder. "Do not be concerned, they can do nothing to us."

"Nothing but throw our butts in jail," I muttered to no one in particular, feeling none of Prem's confidence.

We entered the courtyard of the *chaulki* smiling, hands pressed together. *Namaskar!* Eight officers in military green, wearing felt berets and with black wooden batons cradled in folded arms, stared sternly at us from the porch. In the middle of the slate courtyard, a short mustached man sat at a small table, scribbling in a notebook. The pungent smell of high-quality tobacco from his black pipe filled the air. He motioned me towards a small stool near the table. J.B. sat on the porch. Prem conversed with two officers, answering their questions. I understood just enough to hear him say he had met us on the trail only this morning.

"Passports," snapped an assistant.

J.B. handed me his and I handed both to the officer. He took them but, continuing his mad scribbling, handed them on to an assistant. The younger officer opened a large ledger and began to transcribe information. Our many entry and exit stamps perplexed him and he flipped back and forth, pulling out the extra accordion pages we both had in our passports. I helped him find the information for each column in his log: Name, Passport Number, Date of Visa, Purpose of Journey, Trekking Permit Number.

Damn, I thought, sweat trickling down between my shoulder blades. *They've got us now!*

But he didn't notice our trekking permits and continued his aimless flipping. I saw a glimmer of hope. Maybe he had never seen a trekking permit. Quickly I diverted him to the visa numbers, and he dutifully recorded them in the Trekking Permit column.

After all the paperwork was complete, the mustached man looked up from his writing and spoke softly in heavily accented English. "Where are you going?"

"To Jumla," I answered.

"And what is the purpose of your journey?"

"To view the scenery."

"Where will you go after Jumla?"

"Back to Kathmandu through Dhorpatan," I replied evenly.

His face softened. "I grew up in Kathmandu. I have spent time in Hong Kong. Now I have been here in Dungibara since three years. So boring here. I wish I could go with you! Okay, you can go after signing the book." He pointed to the ledger. We signed it, hoisted our packs and bid them farewell. We had made it through the first checkpost!

We set camp just beyond a large wooden bridge spanning the Katia Khola. After a wash in the river and a meal of *daal bhaat*, we were joined by Prem in our tent.

Our relief at bluffing our way through the checkpost was promptly shattered by Prem's first words. "The police have sent a runner to Dailekh, three days to the north. They will ask to see your trekking permits when you get there."

"How do you know?" I asked.

"At the checkpost they did not know what to do with you. First they thought they would keep you there while they sent word to Dailekh. I told them to wait and let the police in Dailekh find you, you would walk there anyway. But they talked and then the head officer ordered one man to leave for Dailekh to warn them of you. So now I think we must go through Dailekh."

That night I lay awake for a long time, staring at the tent walls. Late-night doubts took over, and for the first time I thought of what lay ahead, what might happen to us if we were taken by the police. Traveling quasi-legally through these areas was one thing; playing hide-and-seek with a military police force was another. We could avoid Dailekh, try to bypass the checkpost, try to outrun the police. But with our heavy loads we would lose for sure. The other option, to go brazenly to the checkpost, present ourselves with bravado and confidence, also worried me. What if they didn't buy our story? What if they threw us in jail?

At dawn three days later, gunmetal gray storm clouds scudded low across the sky, threatening rain below, still more snow above. A morning's climb brought us to within a half mile of Dailekh, its whitewashed buildings straddling the ridgeline.

We opted for the role of innocent, disoriented trekkers. The same passport game we played in Dungibara would be our strategy. And if the situation turned against us, we could always try spreading *baksheesh* around.

The wind rose as we approached the first clusters of houses on the outskirts of town. Dust devils swirled and the first large drops of rain spattered on the cobbled streets. Hurriedly, we jogged with bodies bent against the rising winds. We passed an ancient stone fortress, the remnant of an earlier era fifty or more generations past, when Nepal lay fragmented into small kingdoms, each struggling to defend itself against the others and against periodic waves of marauding invaders. Now the weathered stonework lay abandoned and covered in vine, a relic slowly returning to the soil.

In the central square, the police post appeared on our right. Two uniformed men watched us. We walked to the far side of the square and stopped next to a huge banyan tree. Just then, with a flash and a thundering boom, the skies let loose a torrential downpour. Searching for shelter, we retreated two hundred yards through nearly horizontal sheets of rain to a small lodge.

Within fifteen minutes the storm had passed. Prem told the porters to go ahead, one by one. J.B. and I followed five minutes behind; Prem brought up the rear.

As we walked, J.B. suggested a different plan. "Look, they know we're here, and they haven't paid us much attention so far. Maybe we can just walk by."

As we entered the square, we could see that the porters had passed through unchecked. I glanced across to the checkpost forty yards away. Policemen inside talked with one another, but no one emerged.

I was still calculating our chances of being chased down and thrown into some grimy jail cell when J.B. queried again, more insistently. "C'mon, Park, what do you think? Should we give it a try?"

"No balls, no glory," I replied with a shrug. "Let's go for it. Just keep looking straight ahead."

With that, we casually strolled side by side past the checkpost to the far end of the square, between two houses and out of sight. We looked back. No one followed. Prem caught up with us a few minutes later near the edge of town; he had not been stopped either. Our prospects looked good. We found the porters waiting just beyond the last buildings.

"Why don't we camp near here?" suggested J.B. "That'll give the police a chance to check on us if they really want to."

Although we had decided not to try to outrun the authorities, nonetheless I felt that we should at least keep moving, if not actually running. But instead of voicing my opinion, I merely shrugged. There wasn't a suitable camping place, anyway.

So with a decision made by default, we all kept moving and left J.B. standing alone. We climbed to an exposed ridge, then stopped for a rest. J.B. caught up with us and once again suggested we camp, this time in the lee of a large wall surrounding a water works. Despite the wall, the site was exposed, and the winds still whipped around close to thirty miles an hour. Once again I said nothing, but looked at Prem. I sensed he didn't like J.B.'s choice of a site either, although he was reluctant to contradict the sahib who paid his wages.

Prem hesitated, kicked a few stones around, then looked up and down the trail. He beckoned to Akaal Bahadur and whispered a few words in his ear. Akaal Bahadur dropped his load and went on ahead—to check for a better campsite, I assumed. He returned in a few minutes and conferred with Prem. The porters then hoisted their loads and went down the trail. The decision had obviously been made to go on a little further.

J.B.'s mood turned dark. "Hell, if we go on a little further, we might as well walk the whole damn afternoon!" He grabbed his pack with an angry jerk, and stormed off.

Prem and I caught up with him an hour later as he sat on a stone wall in the small village of Khursanbari. Prem poked his nose into one of the houses and, wishing to give J.B. a wide berth, suggested to me that we camp in a nearby field for the night. As we cleared a space for the tents, a middle-aged man in jodhpurs and topee talked to Prem, urging him not to camp outside in the fields.

Prem translated his grisly tales of recent robberies and murders, the last incident occurring only the night before.

"A man who lives just there," Prem pointed to a thatched-roof house not two hundred yards away, "asked a Gurkha soldier to stay in his house for the night. After going to bed, the Ghurka had a bad feeling. So he got up from his bed and went out of the house. Then, a little while later, the man's son came home from drinking and slept in the same bed. Later, the man, his father, went into the room to cut and kill the Gurkha, but killed his own son instead. He says this happened just last night. Parker Sahib, I think we should do as this man says, stay inside tonight."

I agreed. Throughout our conversation J.B. sat on the wall thirty yards away. When I told him of our change of plans, he exploded.

"Who's making the decisions around here anyway? Prem's job is to take orders, not give them."

I struggled to maintain an outward calm, but my quavering voice betrayed me. "I didn't like the campsite you chose this afternoon, either. It was too close to town, it was exposed."

"Then why didn't you say so? You could have said something earlier instead of making it look like our *sirdar* was calling all the shots."

Anger simmered on both sides, and we went to bed with the issue unresolved.

* * *

We had had this sort of argument before. While J.B. and I were good friends, we were not perfectly matched to take this trip together. We came from different backgrounds and had differing views on decision-making.

More than once, J.B. complained that I was not forceful enough in expressing my opinions. In a sense he was right, but I had my reasons. For the last five years, I had spent my time first in graduate school, then in a high-powered biomedical research lab. Day after day, long hours, stress, conflict. The last six months had emptied me completely. Back surgery, relationships left hanging, unfinished scientific manuscripts, leaving my job, reducing my worldly possessions to a backpack and a duffel, family fears of never returning home—all had sapped my mental energies. I embraced the idea of finding myself on the trail with nothing more to do for the next year but walk. I sought peace, not conflict.

I had imagined that one could take a motley group of six to thirteen people of two nationalities and put them on the trail for two months without trouble. I was wrong. There had been conflict. And J.B. disagreed with me on how to handle it. His approach, born of the Marine Corps, was one of active leadership, of being on top of and involved with each decision, a firm hand on everything. Although I had exercised my share of leadership in the past and could adopt this style when necessary, I found a laissez-faire approach more effective with Prem and the porters.

Prem, as *sirdar*, had charge of the details of everyday life: cooking, setting and breaking camp, keeping the porters moving, purchasing food. Because of the language barrier and his authority over the porters, I found it best to let him do his work. Only if I disagreed with or questioned a decision, would I intervene.

I was never quite sure whose style was more effective, J.B.'s or mine. But clearly our attitudes differed and this difference caused friction and then outright arguments during months on the trail.

Two days later, we pushed above 9,000 feet, and here, on a broad trail through intermittent rhododendron and conifer forest, we found snow. Towards late afternoon, Prem went ahead in his daily task of selecting our campsite for the evening and I walked on alone.

The trail became steeper as it followed the ridge crest, and having lent my ice axe to Jeet Bahadur, I negotiated the slippery descents cautiously, sidestepping on precarious footholds. On one stretch I found myself reduced to backing down on all fours. I topped a knoll and my altimeter recorded 9,200 feet, our highest altitude thus far. Another slippery descent brought me to a broad saddle that dropped off on either side into steep, tortuous ravines. Far below and to the west, clouds clung to a broad valley floor. Nearer, a succession of deeply forested side canyons dominated the landscape.

I stopped briefly and fished out my Nikon to take some photographs. As I removed my pack, I heard a brief muffled yell from somewhere back up the trail. I listened but heard nothing more, and wondered if I might have imagined the sound. I took a number of photos, then hoisted my pack and continued on down the trail.

Prem waited for me at a squalid farmhouse a short ways ahead. A small boy, incongruously dressed in a red wool jacket and matching red and white striped hat, played with a decaying corn cob. His sister, barefoot and wearing a homespun smock, leaned against the doorway clutching an empty metal bowl. From between her legs a wizened mongrel growled and showed his teeth.

A half hour later, J.B. hobbled into view on the trail above us. Prem and I hurried to help him the last few yards. We sat him down on a low wall.

"I fell on one of those steep places. Think I whacked it a good one this time." J.B. grimaced as he spoke.

"I heard you yell. Here, let me get your boot off." Gingerly I pried the heavy boot from his foot, then cut through two layers of socks. The ankle seemed okay, but his Achilles tendon was pulled bowstring tight with pain centered on two spots. "You might have partially torn your Achilles, J.B. Not the best news."

"Jesus, it's starting to really hurt. Where are those Demerols?"

I gave him two fifty-milligram tablets, then wrapped his foot and ankle in a compression bandage. By the time the Demerol had taken effect, we had the tents set up. Carefully, four of us helped him into our tent.

Just at dusk, it began to snow, and Prem brought mugs of tea into our tent.

"What do you think we should do, J.B.?"

"We don't have a whole lot of options, do we?"

"No, I don't guess we do." I lit a candle and handed Prem my map. Unfolding it, we traced our route to Jumla. "How long do you think it will take us, Prem?"

He marked out distances and thought. "I cannot tell, Parker Sahib. Maybe five days if we all are in good health. Now, I think seven or eight if J.B. Sahib can walk."

"That puts us equal distance to Surkhet or Jumla. But Marbu Lekh is between us and Jumla. With this weather moving in, getting over that mountain could be quite a chore." I paused, then suggested the obvious. "It would be easier to retrace our way back to Surkhet. From there you can bus to Nepalganj, then fly back to Kathmandu."

J.B., who had been lying flat, now struggled unsteadily onto one elbow. With his fur hat pulled down over his head, and with his sun-grayed beard, he looked and smelled every bit like a burly eighteenth-century trapper. "There is no way I am going to make the rest of you backtrack to Surkhet. That would waste two weeks and jeopardize this entire segment of the expedition. I don't care if I have to crawl, we're going to Jumla. Supposedly planes fly in there several times a week carrying rice. I can hitch a ride on one of the rice charters."

"It is a long way, J.B. Sahib. We must cross Marbu Lekh the next two days with deep snow, then go 7,000 feet down to the Tila Khola." Prem pointed out the route to J.B. "Then three more days along the river to Jumla."

J.B. remained unswayed. "You said yourself that it's about the same distance, north or south. We're going to Jumla. Period. No back talk from either of you."

Prem and I remained silent. We had nothing to say. I felt grateful to J.B. for his willingness to continue north instead of returning south. Backtracking always depressed me, and I wasn't sure I would have the drive, once reaching Surkhet, to turn around and cover the same ground a third time.

Finally Prem set forth the plan. "If you cannot walk in the morning, J.B. Sahib, we *must* go south. We will need many porters, maybe thirty or more, to help carry you. And we will find no one on Marbu Lekh."

"Then I will walk tomorrow," replied J.B. with finality as he fell back onto his sleeping bag. I prayed he was right.

So J.B. would head back to Kathmandu. He would have up to four months to heal before we started through the Himalaya of northern India. But where did that leave me now?

Alone.

We had meant this section between Surkhet and Jumla in western Nepal as a warmup, to hone our bodies and our team for the far more treacherous crossing of the regions to the north and east of Jumla. Through Mugu and Dolpo, one of the most remote inhabited regions on the planet. Surprisingly, I was more excited than frightened. I had never thought of doing it alone.

Snow and high winds rocked our tent during the night. For more than an hour during the darkest period I lay awake, unable to sleep as the curved tent poles bent towards the ground. Worried that our tent might fail, I lay in my sleeping bag fully clothed.

When Akaal Bahadur brought us "bed tea" to start the day, my thoughts immediately turned to J.B. Could he walk? The drugs had left him groggy, and it was after eight o'clock when he finally unzipped the tent door and tested his leg. I helped him upright, then handed him his walking stick. Cautiously, he placed some weight on his left foot and took a tentative step, then another. He could walk. We would head north towards Jumla.

The snowstorm had turned to rain in the night and cleared the trail ahead. J.B. moved steadily with surprisingly little pain until we hit snow once more just before noon. We stopped for a quick meal, then continued. Because few braved this route in the middle of winter, we laboriously cut our own trail through two feet of wet snow. At one-thirty, on a narrow ledge engulfed in clouds, J.B. pulled up.

"This is about as far as I can go today, Park. It's tightening up fast."

I called ahead to Prem and suggested we find a place to camp. He disappeared into the windblown whiteness as I dropped off the ridgeline to search for a suitable flat spot. Twenty minutes later, I found Prem waiting.

"No place to camp above," he said. "The trail goes up and down steeply."

"The slopes below seem to drop off for quite a way. I couldn't find a flat place either," I replied.

J.B. interjected. "I can go on a bit. Let's keep moving up, so we'll have less to climb in the morning."

The trail became steeper and the snow deeper. I remembered my gaiters, the one extra item I had allowed myself, and stopped to put

Ascending Marbu Lekh, the weather deteriorates.

them on. Removing my pack, I rummaged deeply into it, extracting the brand new, bright green gaiters. Just then, I looked up and saw one of our Thakuri porters laden under his thirty-kilo load. Clad in thin pants and torn coat, summer socks and shoes woven from old string, he sank with each step almost to his waist. Only the day before, I had learned that even before leaving Surkhet the porters had given the Chinese sneakers we had bought for them to their families. As I watched our porter struggle through the snow, my hands tightened around the gaiters. Ashamed, I hastily shoved them deep into my pack and quickly moved on through the snow.

Prem and I alternated in the lead, laboriously kicking steps in the steeper sections for the others to follow. Although J.B. said nothing, he leaned heavily on his walking stick and grunted with each step. His pace slowed and I worried that we might be forced to bivouac out in the open. At one near vertical descent, I turned to J.B. and asked him to give me his pack.

"No. I can carry it."

"Dammit, J.B., now is not the time to let your ego get the best of you. It's not just you I'm worried about. If you tear that Achilles tendon right through, it's going to mean trouble for all of us. Now give me your pack!"

Reluctantly, he passed it to me. I put it on backwards so it rested on my chest.

At 10,580 feet, as the trail switchbacked up a steep exposed slope, J.B. slowed and then stopped. He could go no further. His Achilles tendon was tight, and an ominous knot appeared midway between heel and calf.

Prem and I searched through blowing snow and cloud for a small patch of level ground. We found a spot just where the switchbacking trail turned itself. Using cooking pots as shovels, Akaal Bahadur and I cleared away the snow and fashioned a ledge from a mixture of rock, ice and dirt—an area just large enough for the two tents. The swirling gusts raked the unprotected site.

With a final, gargantuan effort, J.B. hobbled the last two hundred feet and we quickly settled him inside a tent.

Earlier in the day I had noticed three local men trailing us. Afraid to cross the lekh (mountain) alone, they had attached themselves to us, and now they huddled without any form of shelter just outside our tents. Fearing for their survival, Prem and I used our blue cooking tarp to construct a lean-to, and then stacked the porters' loads to close off the open side. After we finished, our friends crawled in and silently hunkered down for a long, cold night.

Just before dusk, the wind slackened. Hoping to take some photos, I scrambled a short way above our encampment. The clouds rose vertically around me and intermittent breaks gave spectacular views of forested ridgelines stretching south towards the plains of India. Closer, I glimpsed sunlit fields 8,000 feet below, just as the clouds settled in once again. The winds came up stronger than before, driving horizontal sheets of freezing rain and snow across the sky. I retreated to the relative warmth and dryness of our tent, exhausted after a long, hard day.

At daybreak, my thermometer showed just four degrees Fahrenheit. I unzipped the tent door and peeked out. Despite the bitter cold, the skies were clear and half a foot of fresh snow blanketed the surrounding mountains. Pulling on my boots, I clambered outside just as our hangers-on emerged stiffly from their makeshift shelter, like bears arising from a winter's hibernation.

In the brittle morning air, Prem prepared large mugs of sticky sweet tea for everyone. The porters sat on their haunches around the small fire, slurping loudly and warming their hands on the steaming metal mugs.

Hoping to take advantage of the good weather we broke camp hastily, without eating. In foregoing food, we committed ourselves to reaching the pass and descending to treeline on the north side of Marbu Lekh before stopping for our first meal. I wondered if J.B. could make it up and over the top in one push. He seemed more agile than the day before, but we had more than 1,500 feet of steep snowy trail above us. Before setting off, I distributed sunglasses to the porters. Snowblindness was one malady we could prevent.

We followed the faint impression of the switchbacking track beneath two feet of snow. Soon the trail narrowed and then climbed for several hundred feet up a near-vertical face before opening out into a series of large open bowls. Spectacular alpine scenery unfolded before us; rocky, snow-laden peaks, vast cirques of unmarked snow, bright sun and azure sky.

Suddenly J.B. stopped. "Parker, listen."

Standing still, I heard it, the *wupp-wupp* of a helicopter. With a mixture of amazement, amusement and horror, we saw a white helicopter, only half a mile away, clear a notch in the ridge to the north.

"Good God, it's the king," J.B. exclaimed.

I, too, recognized the helicopter from the times I had seen it parked in its special hangar at Tribhuvan International Airport. An experienced pilot, the king often took to the air to visit the remoter regions of his kingdom, much to the consternation of his security forces. Close behind, two green military helicopters also cleared the ridge, and the three flew in a triangular formation, passing us at eye level just a quarter of a mile away.

I pointed to the white helicopter and exclaimed to our porters, "*Sri Paanch, Sri Paanch!*" The king's nickname meant "five sirs," in reference to the five honorifics that preceded his name. Our Surkhet porters stood wide-eyed at the sight of their god-king, he of the same Thakuri caste, in a great white flying machine. As the choppers receded, the porters pressed their palms together and, bowing slightly, raised them to their foreheads in salute.

The top of the pass now seemed just a few hundred feet above us. Another delicate traverse across unstable snow and another series of steep switchbacks. At the top, a summit cairn, its windward side and lone prayer pole caked with several inches of windblown snow, stood in stark defiance of the harsh elements. By my altimeter, we stood at 12,300 feet, with surrounding peaks rising another thousand feet above us. To the south our entire route was laid out behind us, to the first ridge just north of Surkhet, and beyond to the Gangetic plain of India sixty miles away. To the north stood the broad snow-capped ridge of Chuli Lekh.

Relieved to have reached the top before eleven o'clock, and that the skies had remained clear, we turned our thoughts now to getting down below treeline before the regular afternoon winds began. As I set out behind the rest, I saw that the north slope opened onto a broad gentle valley. Our toil seemed largely behind us, for now we began the 7,000–foot descent to the Tila Khola, followed by an easy thirty miles along its banks to Jumla.

Just fifty yards below the cairn, I saw how premature my relief had been. For on this gentler north-facing slope, the trail disappeared beneath chest-deep snow, a slick veneer of breakable crust glistening under a midday sun. I watched our laden porters break through up to their waists with each step, one foot buried, the other jammed up against their buttocks. Then a slow roll to one side and a struggle to right their loads. Only to repeat the process with the next step. "Postholing," I found, proved as exhausting as it looked. For J.B.

with his injury and the porters with their loads, it proved a colossal effort.

Half a mile from the pass we hit the treeline and rested on the exposed trunk of a fallen fir. Looking to the north and east, I glimpsed for the first time the Himalaya of western Nepal. An unbroken wall of snowbound peaks stretched across the horizon. Forty miles away, beyond Jumla at the far end of the Tila Valley, stood the Sisne, Patrasi and Kanjiroba Himal. Further east, hardly more than a mirage on the horizon, shimmered the 25,000-foot peaks of the westernmost portion of the Dhaulagiri range.

This, then, was the challenge, this jumble of mountains that lay between us and Kathmandu. Somewhere amongst those jagged spires of rock, snow and ice, over high mountain passes, through steep canyons, across churning rivers of glacial waters, we hoped to find a passage. But first, we had to deliver J.B. safely to Jumla.

We continued down in deep, soft snow through conifer and rhododendron forest until 1:00 P.M. Exhausted, we hacked out a campsite in the drifted snow. From a standing dead pine we collected mounds of firewood for a large fire and a hot meal.

With great relief I unrolled my sleeping bag and fell back onto it. We had crossed Marbu Lekh without a major mishap. J.B. had found the downs much easier on his ankle than the ups, although he confided that he thought the day's efforts had further damaged his ankle. The pain had worsened as soon as he stopped. He took another one hundred milligrams of Demerol and was asleep by 7:00 P.M.

The crossing of Marbu Lekh had invigorated me. Having seen our destination, the big peaks of western Nepal, I yearned to be there quickly. But I thought about J.B.'s injury and the porters' struggle through the deep snow, and kept my yearnings to myself.

The next day we continued under sunny skies, but deep crusted snow slowed us to a crawl. With clear weather, Chetri and Thakuri men in twos and threes passed us on their way up to Marbu Lekh. Soon after we stopped for our first meal, I spotted three such porters, each carrying a heavy basket, approach from below. It seemed late in the day to try for the top. Still 3,000 feet below the pass, they would have another 2,500 feet down on the south slope before finding shelter. At 1:30 P.M. the winds had already picked up, and clouds formed over the peaks. As the men passed, stepping in each other's footsteps in the snow, I saw they walked on nothing more than the thick callouses of their bare feet.

Late in the afternoon, the highest village on the north side of Marbu Lekh appeared below us; its natural beauty captivated me. Thatch-roofed houses sat in picturesque disarray, backdropped by the snowy Chuli Lekh. The first shoots of spring turned the terraced fields a tender green, patchworked with the brilliant yellow of flowering mustard. As we approached, the sounds of village life rose up to greet us: roosters and dogs, the high-pitched chatter of children at play.

The pastoral beauty of Dillikot, however, like many villages in Nepal, was best appreciated from afar. For upon entering, the idyllic vision disintegrated. The villagers, children and adults alike, were filthy with soot-blackened skin, covered with tattered and unwashed clothes. A thick stench from rotting garbage and human excrement greeted me. I swatted ineffectually at clouds of flies.

As we threaded our way through narrow passageways between houses, the villagers' stern, unfriendly faces glared at us. Suddenly and without warning, a black mongrel leapt silently from a darkened doorway. Reflexively, I sidestepped the blur of black fur and flashing teeth that hurled itself at me and swung the flat blade of my ice axe, catching the animal a glancing blow to the back of his head. He hesitated, momentarily stunned, then with a terrifying growl, turned to renew his attack. Prem, twenty yards ahead, grabbed a broken length of fence post and rushed to my aid, crashing the stave down on the dog's back. Yelping, the beast fell to the ground, and in an adrenaline-induced rage I closed in, intent on making this day his last. Just as I swung my ice axe, he slid under a fence, and the sharp blade embedded itself in the fence post inches from his rear leg. Taken aback at my intention to maim this animal, I pulled the blade from the wood and turned to see two young women and a grizzled old man standing, expressionless, in the doorway from which the dog had leapt. With Prem at my rear, we continued cautiously and found J.B. at a campsite just beyond the village.

The next day, we followed a silty stream downwards towards the Tila Khola. Preoccupied with calculations of money and food supplies, I hardly noticed when I entered a hamlet of thatch-roofed huts. A small girl stood by the trail, and as I passed, she fell in step beside me, grasping my hand in both of her grubby ones.

"Hello, Japanese. Whoayou? Whoayou?" She giggled and skipped along at my side for a few steps, giving my hand a gentle tug, as if beckoning me to follow. Then she wheeled and darted on chubby little legs back towards her home.

Unprepared for this gesture of communion with her world, a spontaneous touch from this Asian child's sphere, I stopped. I experienced a momentary tightness in my throat, then a deep smile came from within. My world of finances, food, petty concerns of the trek, had made me forget for a time the joys of life, the laughter, the pleasure of another's company. She had come from nowhere to change my day, this child of the Himalayas.

I turned back; the tiny face disappeared in the shadow of the door. I called, "*Namaste!*" ('I greet the god within you.')

She reappeared, still half hidden in the darkness and placed her hands together gravely in front of her oval face. "*Namaste!*" Such a tiny voice.

Early the next morning, we crossed the Tila Khola on a cantilevered wooden bridge. Formed of tremendous rough-hewn planks pegged together like some child's oversized toy, the posts on either end stood adorned with grotesque carvings; incongruously, one was capped by the wooden likeness of an airplane. On the south-facing slope of this deep gorge at only 5,800 feet, the sun had baked the earth brown. We stopped in the shade of granite boulders to study our map. Jumla, we estimated, lay only two long days ahead. For the first time, I felt confident J.B. would make it under his own power.

We hoped to cover ten miles or more on this hot afternoon, but after waiting impatiently at a rest stop, Prem confided angrily that the Surkhet porters deliberately lagged behind. The Tila trail was virtually flat, and since we'd eaten most of our food, the loads were now half their original weight. Suspecting trouble, Prem had instructed Akaal Bahadur and Jeet Bahadur to stay close to the Thakuris. We would pass close to their village tomorrow, and Prem worried they might slip off with our supplies. At the least, by going slowly they could squeeze an extra day's wages from us.

Finally they arrived, Akaal Bahadur and Jeet Bahadur at the rear as if herding them along. The Thakuris fiddled sheepishly with their loads as Prem chastised them, announcing that we would make Jumla tomorrow, no matter what. With our slow going that day, I privately doubted that we could cover the distance.

Ornately carved posts on a cantilevered wooden bridge spanning the Tila Khola, one capped by the wooden likeness of an airplane.

At six-thirty the next morning, J.B. packed his gear and headed out. "I'm making Jumla today, come hell or high water."

I didn't understand his reasoning, and after our misunderstandings at Dailekh, I resolved to voice my concerns. "J.B., I don't think that's a smart move. It would be a lot better on your ankle if you took it easy."

"No, Parker, I know I can make it. I'll see you there."

"But the porters are carrying your gear and all of the food. And you probably won't get there until well after dark. If the rest of us don't make it, you'll be stuck. Where will you sleep?"

"The sooner I get to Jumla, the sooner I get to Kathmandu and have this foot looked at."

"The faster you go, the more likely you are to do more damage." I was exasperated at his obstinacy. "Besides, you can't leave for Kathmandu until the porters reach Jumla. We're not going to haul your gear hundreds of miles through the mountains."

"I'll see you in Jumla. I'm leaving." With that, J.B. started off down the trail.

Prem and I left an hour later with the porters, but given Prem's desire not to lose J.B., he and I walked without a break for three hours. Where the marble black waters of the southward-flowing Sinja Khola blended into the Tila, we came upon the village of Nangma. Here we found J.B. resting at a teahouse. Prem and I ordered a meal of *daal bhaat*, but as the shopkeeper hefted his *kukri* to go find the wood to build the fire to cook our rice, we realized the delay this would cause us. J.B. said little and, impatient, ate just a small snack and left.

We lounged amidst dusty midday heat and meddlesome flies, in the shade of a tremendous ancient pine. An hour and a half drifted by, and still no food. The porters, as slow as our cook, also languished some- where behind. Frustrated at trying to appease J.B. and keep the porters moving, Prem suddenly rose to his feet and jammed his ice axe defiantly into the soft earth.

"This is not good! We should not get so apart! I do not understand, why is J.B. Sahib far ahead, when the porters are still behind? I am the *sirdar*. It is my job to organize food, the camp, to make certain you and J.B. Sahib are safe. How can I do this when we are everywhere at one time? First rule, Parker Sahib: stay together!" As he talked, Prem, more angry than I had ever seen him, pulled his ice axe from the earth and swung it around wildly.

Finally our rice arrived, the pinkish long-grained Kashmiri variety brought ages ago to this region near Jumla, and a tasty yellow *daal*. We finished quickly and greedily licked our fingers clean.

After our meal, Prem and I continued eastward along the Tila Khola, not waiting for the porters. We trusted Akaal Bahadur and Jeet Bahadur to keep an eye on our gear. As we neared Jumla, the gorge opened into a valley. Under a disorienting white sun, we traced a broad flat trail as it paralleled the riverbed. We walked steadily for several hours, scanning ahead in hopes of spotting J.B.

At the village of Raku we stopped at a decrepit teahouse to escape the sun. This rough village, though typical, looked even more primi- tive and dirtier than any other we had seen in western Nepal. Dark- skinned Thakuris watched us intently as Prem ordered two glasses of tea, ladled from a large open kettle, a pale liquid in oily metal cups. Ash and fragments of sticks floated on the surface. Prem caught my eye, and, of a single mind, we surreptitiously emptied our glasses onto the thirsty earth. From the bottom of my glass fell a crumpled black beetle.

The trail wound past crude two-story dwellings; the bottom levels housed livestock, the upper ones, unwashed humanity. Locals stared silently from the flat roofs as we passed. From somewhere behind us, a stone was launched, then another. They landed and rolled just a few feet in front of us. Enraged, I whirled to confront the throwers. Two dozen faces glared at me.

"Do not stop, Parker Sahib. We should get away."

I stared for a moment longer, recording indelibly the scene of these uncharacteristically inhospitable people. Turning, I jogged a few steps to Prem's side and we strode quickly past the last buildings.

Two school-age boys fell in a few feet behind us, laughing and taunting us with rapid staccato bursts of Nepali.

"They think we are both foreigners and cannot understand their language," Prem whispered.

We endured the slurs for several minutes, then Prem had heard enough. With a speed that surprised even me, he whirled and confronted them with his ice axe. The boys backpedaled, wide-eyed and silent, out of his range. Prem raged at them for thirty seconds before we continued on our way.

Several minutes later, in a subdued voice, Prem commented on the incident. "They were poking fun at us because we were strangers. Calling us stupid and worse. Calling us stupid! They who live as animals, so backward and lazy, and still we are the stupid ones. Never have I seen such people in Nepal, Parker Sahib."

Except for the villagers at Dillikot, neither had I.

Towards late afternoon, a soft golden haze settled across the sky, but the heat and stultifying humidity remained. A dull ache crept up my legs, and my feet burned from the long day's walk. Drawn to the gently tumbling waters, I veered and sat at the river's edge. I removed my boots and socks, then plunged my feet to mid-calf in the icy waters. Prem stopped and we soaked our feet together.

"I do not understand, Parker Sahib, why we must go to Jumla today. It is a very old village, and surely it will be there tomorrow and the next day."

"Prem, I have no idea why J.B. insists on reaching there today. Even if he goes on, I am sure he won't make it much before midnight."

Passersby kept us informed that the *tulo maanchhe* ('big man') walked thirty minutes ahead of us. Although we increased our pace, we could not catch him.

Two hours later, as a purple-gray dusk settled on the valley, we rounded a bend along the river and spotted J.B. on the trail a half mile ahead. Head down, supported by his stave, he plodded purposefully along. Helpless to stop him, we merely watched in frustration and anger as his form slowly faded into the growing darkness.

Why didn't he stop? He knew as well as we that the next village was still two hours ahead, Jumla easily another hour beyond that.

"To hell with it. We'll spend the night at the teahouse just ahead. Let J.B. fend for himself," I muttered.

"Yes," Prem said wearily. "I can do only so much. Let him find his own way."

We ate a spartan meal of *daal bhaat* and *alu* (potatoes), then were shown to a room upstairs. A lone wooden bed hugged one wall, and Prem insisted I take it. The proprietor gave us each a single blanket. Prem found a spot on the earthen floor and lay down. In this chimneyless house, the oily pine fire below soon filled our room with acrid, sooty smoke. Around three o'clock, I fell into a fitful sleep.

At dawn, Prem shook me awake. A thin layer of soot covered everything and had darkened our faces and hands by several shades. Our heads pounded from inhaling the smoke. After a quick cup of tea, we set out towards Jumla. Both Prem and I felt terrible, with headaches and grumbling bowels. Our progress was interrupted by frequent dashes into the bushes.

Within three hours, the river valley opened into a broad plain of gently terraced fields. Twenty miles in the distance, the valley abruptly ended in a wall of towering glaciered peaks, the Himalaya of western Nepal. Several miles ahead on the left bank of the river, mustard-and-white flags on four towering poles rose above the main temple of Jumla. For an hour, we trudged towards them. Spitefully they seemed to recede before us. I had run out of drinking water and with incessant diarrhea, I became weak and disoriented.

As we approached the first building a mile before Jumla, we found J.B. waiting on a small wall. Depleted of all energy, I felt dehydrated, my feet hurt, my guts hurt and I hadn't eaten since the night before. I exploded with the frustrations of the last two days.

"What was the goddamned rush for?"

J.B. sighed. "I wanted to get the walk over with."

"But what about the rest of us? The porters aren't even here yet!"

"I thought they would get here even if they had to walk all night. Prem told them we were going to Jumla yesterday. I got here last night about nine, and I didn't think they would be too far behind. Where were you?"

"Don't ask!"

"Well, I was attacked by one of those Tibetan mastiffs at the edge of town. I just managed to hold him off with my walking stick. Where were you?"

"Fighting off smartass boys in Raku."

"Yeah, I had a run-in with those little bastards myself. They bounced a rock off my shoulder, but I managed to knock one off his feet with my stick. So where did you spend the night?"

"In a cold, smoky teahouse about ten miles back. We saw you ahead of us just at dusk, but couldn't catch up. Why didn't you stop when it got dark?"

"Because I want to get back to Kathmandu to get this foot looked at. The sooner the better."

I was exasperated. "If you could walk thirty miles in a day, it must not be bothering you so much that an extra day would make any difference. Yesterday probably did more damage than taking three days to cover the same distance."

Speechless and drained, I wondered whether I might be seeing this in the wrong light. J.B. and I had never experienced such conflict before. What had gone wrong here?

Then I realized that tomorrow or the next day J.B. would be on a plane back to Kathmandu and that would resolve the whole issue. Enough said.

I shouldered my pack and stomped the last few hundred yards to Jumla.

CHAPTER
FOUR

Tuesday, February 28, 1984

A FADED metal sign hung from the second-floor balcony of the weathered wooden building: "Sherpa Hotel." *How had a Sherpa ended up in Jumla, hundreds of mountainous miles from his native Khumbu?* Whatever the answer, the sign brought back memories of the good food and sincere friendliness we had enjoyed in the Sherpa inns of eastern Nepal.

I waited in the shadow to catch my breath. Feeling anger and frustration from my encounter with J.B., I had half run the last third of a mile, leaving him and Prem far behind.

Now I took a hard look at some buildings clustered behind a barbed-wire enclosure about a hundred yards ahead.

Just then, J.B. arrived and nodded towards the buildings, "That's the police garrison. I passed it late last night. This morning when I came back to wait for you, they seemed pretty interested but didn't stop me."

"Damn. I was hoping we could get around to the other side of town without running into the police. We're already getting the once over from those two in bush hats."

By the route on our trekking permits, we should have entered

Jumla from the east instead of the west, the direction from which we now walked. Our permits had not been stamped since leaving Kathmandu, and I had hoped that by skirting around the checkpost and approaching from the opposite direction, we might avoid additional permit hassles.

"We should stay here," Prem said. "Let them come and find us."

The "Sherpa's" name was Pema, although he called himself a Tamang, the same caste as Prem, Akaal Bahadur and Jeet Bahadur. A gregarious and diverse group of people who inhabit the hill country north and east of Kathmandu, Tamangs, like Sherpas, are of Tibetan descent—some say descendants of the Tibetan cavalry of centuries past.

Pema's lodge, although spartan, was typical of Sherpa inns in the Everest region. The hotel business in Jumla, however, was far from booming. We registered as his first guests in more than a month, then followed him to the second floor and along the balcony. Removing two oversized padlocks from the door, Pema led us into a darkened, musty room. Half a dozen wooden beds, strewn with colorful Tibetan carpets, cluttered the room. Silk-framed *thangkas* (religious paintings) lined the walls, and a Buddhist altar filled the far end. Three large golden statues, butter lamps, prayer books, cymbals and drums, and at the center, a small postcard likeness of the Dalai Lama draped in white prayer scarves. Pema said we could have the whole room to ourselves. Before leaving, he lit the row of butter lamps lining the altar.

Within minutes, a boy appeared at our door, a runner sent by the police to request our presence at their compound. Immediately!

J.B., Prem and I entered the compound and were shown to three wooden chairs in the middle, just opposite a small school desk. We sat in our own sweaty stench under the hot noonday sun for almost a half hour before a stocky man in crisply pressed military greens approached from a nearby building.

He stopped next to the desk and spoke in excellent English. "Good morning. I am Narayan Shrestha, the head officer here in Jumla."

An assistant held the chair as he sat down. He asked Prem several questions before turning to J.B. and me. "Passports, please, and your letters for trekking."

He leafed through both sets of documents, flipping back and forth, checking them against each other. Finally figuring out that we had permits to trek from Dhorpatan, but not from Surkhet, he directed a frowning question in Nepali at Prem. Although a fool might have guessed the topic, for our benefit Prem answered Narayan in English. "In Pokhara, they heard of much banditry just near to Dhorpatan. The police in Pokhara said they should change the route and go from Surkhet. And not to worry about the permits."

Narayan screwed up his face and looked incredulously at Prem. Sensing his skepticism, Prem quickly added. "Of course, I know just what they have told me. They hired me only in Surkhet as their cook."

Narayan shot back another question in Nepali. Prem again answered in English. "The police along the way saw us but just waved at us. They did nothing."

Narayan shook his head in obvious disgust at the ineptitude of the village police, then, thankfully, moved on to the subject of our travel plans after leaving Jumla. He launched into a rambling ten-minute monologue that left us glancing quizzically at one another.

"Please, you must understand my professional duties here in this city of Jumla. I am the chief officer here, but not anywhere else. I do not have any control outside of this place. If someone were to stop you, the police in another village, what can I do? Even if you have the proper paperwork, this has nothing to do with me." He leaned forward and eyed us intently. "I can do nothing to help you." I sensed hidden meaning in his tone, but did not understand what he was trying to tell us.

After a weighty pause, he continued. "Now, your permit says that you wish to visit RaRa Lake. This is four days to the north. You must understand that you cannot go further into the restricted areas of Mugu or Dolpo. I can have no control over what happens if you do."

He asked us if we had a map, and I pulled out our slowly disintegrating ammonia-dye trekking map.

"The best way back to Pokhara," the officer said, tracing the route with a pen, "is to cross these passes and follow this river here, to the Bheri River, then south to Jarjakot and east to Dhorpatan. It is faster to go over the Jang La, but to do this you would need to go to Dolpo, and this is forbidden. The best way for you is through Jarjakot." He stood, signaling the end of our interrogation.

"Before you leave Jumla, you must come to me again to tell me the date of your departure. *Namaste*."

An assistant showed us to the gate.

"I got it," I announced as I returned late that evening to our second-story room in the Sherpa Hotel. I waved the plane ticket in the air.

J.B., lying on a bed, smiled broadly. "Good going, Park. How'd you do it?"

"Not easy," I replied, slumping onto a bed, still wearing the same clothes I had arrived in that morning. "It took a while to find the RNAC office, and they were hopelessly overbooked for tomorrow. I've been arguing for hours. Finally I told the clerk that I would pay tourist rate, which came to 1,575 rupees—the Nepalese pay 375 rupees. Plus 100 rupees 'surcharge.' A seat just suddenly materialized."

"Money talks."

To our immense relief, the Thakuri porters had appeared late that afternoon, shadowed closely by Akaal Bahadur and Jeet Bahadur. After dropping their loads, the Thakuris disappeared into the Jumla bazaar. Akaal Bahadur and Jeet Bahadur crashed on the extra beds in our room.

Now my conversation with J.B. turned to the possible routes through Mugu and Dolpo, and how J.B. might organize a search party if we didn't show up in Kathmandu. We didn't speak about our conflicts of the last three days, and I felt a subtle shift of attitude. A rapprochement of sorts had occurred as soon as I had arrived with the ticket. Although both still simmering, we seemed tacitly to agree to leave our misunderstandings behind us along a thirty-mile stretch of the Tila Khola.

Twenty feet off the ground a Pilatus Porter, the single-engine work-horse aircraft of the Himalayas, gunned its engines and still barely cleared the barbed-wire fence before setting down on the bumpy pasture that served as a runway. Although the plane brought precious rice supplies from the terai town of Nepalganj, its arrival was always uncertain. But that day the flight arrived on time at 8:00 A.M. and a crowd mobbed the airport's tiny open-air building. Beyond the fifteen or so ticketed passengers, a group of clamoring Tibetans had descended upon a waifish Nepalese in white jodhpurs who held the day's manifest aloft. I assumed they were attempting to cajole or bribe their way on board, the same tactic I had used.

After an hour of milling around, the jodhpured Nepalese led his entourage towards the runway gate, where a vague semblance of a queue formed. J.B., as the only foreigner on board, was permitted to board last. The rest of the passengers, Mugulis from the region just to the north, seemed intent on thwarting the tight weight restrictions necessary on the short-takeoff-and-landing runway. One at a time, they were allowed onto the runway where an attendant asked each one to raise his arms. From deep within their oversized black *chubas*, a veritable cascade of hidden treasures—bowls, knives, jewelry, half-eaten pieces of meat and assorted bric-a-brac—tumbled onto the ground, to the great amusement of the onlookers.

Finally, after sorting out the Mugulis and their seat assignments, J.B. was called to board.

"Best of luck, Parker, see you in Kathmandu," J.B. said with a firm handshake. A quick wave at the plane's doorway and he was gone.

I had mixed emotions about seeing J.B. leave. I knew things would go easier without him. A residue of anger remained and I actually felt relieved to see him go, but also guilt at feeling that way. I also felt sorry for him. He had endured so many physical injuries, bouncing back again and again, only to be injured one more time.

The engines revved to full throttle, then the plane shot forward down the runway, lifting off only thirty yards shy of the fence. As I watched the tiny plane rise into the sky and disappear into the snowy peaks to the east, I felt a twinge of loneliness and apprehension. I would go on alone, with Prem, Akaal Bahadur and Jeet Bahadur.

A cheerful female voice with an American accent caught me off guard. "Hello. You look like you could use a shower."

I spun around, but she continued before I could reply. "I have the only hot shower in western Nepal. Would you like to use it?"

Too tired and not in the mood to brave the Tila Khola's icy waters the day before, I smelled worse than a week-old pair of gym socks. By the time I could manage a reply, the tall woman in her fifties had already loaded the packages she had received on the plane into a backpack, and had begun walking towards town.

"I guess I *could* use a shower," I called after her. "Thanks for the offer. Where do you live?"

"Over by the RNAC office. I saw you leaving there yesterday. Just ask around for the Youngkins' place."

An hour later, I reveled in my first hot shower since leaving Kathmandu. Afterwards, Anita invited me in for homemade muffins and coffee, and, as I was leaving, asked me to dinner that evening with some United Mission workers.

Anita proved an old hand at adapting recipes to the supplies at hand. Dinner was excellent, and dessert an indescribable treat, angel-food cake topped with real whipped buffalo cream. Anita and Frank Youngkin had worked for twenty-seven years as missionaries in Asia—twenty-three in Thailand, the last four here in Jumla. In Nepal, where proselytizing was strictly forbidden and swiftly punished, they built schools, taught and worked on forestry and agricultural projects. After dinner, we talked of their experiences living in Jumla, and their efforts on behalf of the Nepalese. And we talked of religion.

Throughout my life I had sustained a uniformly negative view of Christianity. At Sunday school, my earliest memories were of well-meaning teachers presenting fantastical stories, which seemed as plausible to me as Santa Claus or the tooth fairy. I was too young to perceive them as allegories. And the elders of our tribe offered no help, presenting these stories as truth "because the Bible tells us so." Their insistence on belief in the Bible without question turned me away from religion. If religion meant embracing the kind of dogma peddled by the Sunday morning Presbyterians, then I called myself an atheist. Unfortunately, in my homogeneous environment, alternative approaches to religion did not exist.

The Youngkins, however, had infused reality into their brand of Christianity. I thoroughly enjoyed my evening with these people, who worked selflessly to better the lives of others.

Later that night, back at the Sherpa Hotel, Prem and I discussed the next day's tasks; hiring porters and resupplying for the long push ahead.

As we talked, Prem and I drank fiery apple *rakshi*. Soon, Prem emptied his glass and turned in. I sat up for a time, finishing the last of the bottle in the soft light of two butter lamps. Their yellow glow bathed the altar in an eerie flickering light that left mysterious shadows. The Buddha's eyes watched me.

Did they just blink? I thought so. Under their benevolent gaze, my thoughts turned to what lay ahead. An unknown route through remote and forbidding Dolpo. Could I handle it? Would these mountains defeat me, or would I conquer them? Just before leaving for Asia

I had finished Rick Ridgeway's book, *The Last Step*, about the first American ascent of K2. One phrase in particular, Barry Bishop's statement about the first American ascent of Everest, stuck with me: "There are no conquerors—only survivors." Alone in the far outback of western Nepal, I sensed that at best there would be only survivors. In the past, my anxieties and fears had been about such things as passing a test, winning a judo match, finishing graduate school. Contrived goals. If I failed, life would go on. What I faced now was far more visceral—survival itself.

Then, late at night, three sheets to the wind, staring into the eyes of that blinking Buddha, I ran head-on into the question, *What was I doing here?*

I was doing what I had always done. That is, doing instead of talking about it. My parents approached life with a "can do" attitude and made sure that I acquired this same air of confidence. Fearing that I, small for my age, would become withdrawn or feel insecure, my father involved me in the martial arts and joined in the learning experience. A neighborhood football team was organized and, recognizing that I was being left out, my father quietly suggested I be given the ball to run with. Being fast and agile, I soon became a star running back. Without his guidance, I might have languished on the sidelines, in sport and in life.

As I grew older, through intense physical training in both scholastic sports and judo, I glimpsed what the martial artist has always known: that spiritual development is attained through physical discipline. That true insight is acquired by doing rather than by thinking. That clarity and vision come spontaneously, often at wholly unexpected times and from oblique angles. That when we are totally extended, stretched to the limits of both body and mind, the barriers to understanding seem sometimes to drop and we glimpse some truth, if only for a moment. Thus it is that humans strive upwards, to be the first, the best, to perform the task in the purist way, risking their lives to stand for a moment or two on a mountaintop. Willing to die for the reason of being.

And thus I found myself, on February 29, 1984, about to set off into the unknown. As I finished the gritty residue in my glass, I had an uncanny feeling, as if I had always known I would find myself here, on this day and at this time. J.B. had been the early driving force behind our expedition that had brought me to Asia. Now he was gone. It frightened me a little, but I never entertained any doubts about my continuing. It was as if I couldn't *not* go.

Pulling myself up, I stumbled to the altar. A smile creased the corners of my mouth as I gazed a final time into the eyes of the golden Buddha. *Would we make it, Siddhartha?* No answer, just the silent serenity of that all-knowing expression. I leaned down and extinguished the butter lamps.

The next morning, we set off for Jumla's bazaar. One of the largest towns in western Nepal north of the *terai*, Jumla was nonetheless smaller and more primitive than I had expected. Although it was the starting point for most of the trekking in western Nepal, there were virtually no tourist facilities there. A government official had told us that only fifty trekkers had registered with the police during the past year. The Sherpa Hotel, the only trekker's lodge in town, rarely housed guests, and the town lacked electricity and any semblance of sanitation facilities.

The bazaar lay at one end of a two-hundred-yard cobbled "main street." A mixture of rough Nepalese hill people and Tibetans loitered in front of the squat flat-roofed buildings lining the street. As Akaal Bahadur and Jeet Bahadur set off through the throng, searching for trustworthy porters, Prem and I bargained for food supplies. We quickly learned how scarce and expensive foodstuffs were in this region. After scrounging through stall after stall, we gathered only minimal supplies. Thirty kilos of rice at thirteen rupees per kilo; twenty-two mannas of sugar, which came to eleven kilos, at twenty-four rupees per kilo; packets of instant noodles, soap, kerosene and the small red screaming-hot chilies without which Prem and the porters could not eat their meals.

Foolishly, perhaps, I thought also of adding to my disguise in hopes of passing myself off as a Tibetan. In Kathmandu, I had discarded my western pack in favor of the external-framed, faded green canvas variety popular with Tibetan traders. Pema had found a tailor to make me a billowing black Tibetan *chuba*. Now I spotted a tall Tibetan wearing a Chinese army-green hat with fake-fur flaps. This hat, available only in Tibet, would place the owner as Tibetan. I approached the man and, through hand signals, bartered on fingers for several minutes. We settled on 120 rupees and a packet of Yak cigarettes, not available in Jumla but which the Tibetan had seen sticking out of Prem's pocket. The cigarettes I cared little about, although Prem parted with them grudgingly.

After paying the 120 rupees, however, I realized I had forgotten to collect J.B.'s extra money from him before he left. I had spent valuable cash on his plane ticket and we had yet to pay off the Surkhet porters. Now, by my calculations, it seemed that my money might not last us to Kathmandu. I sighed. Nothing I could do about it now.

On the way back to the hotel, I stopped at the police garrison. Narayan greeted me cordially. "Ah, yes, Mr. Parker, the American. Are you leaving us?"

"Yes, we're heading north to RaRa Lake tomorrow."

"Very good. When you come back to Jumla, please check in once again. I will look for you in two weeks. Goodbye."

After washing the caked black dirt from my new fur hat, I sat down to write J.B. a letter. I outlined our prospective route. We would go north several days and then east to the village of Dalphu, then continue east along what we came to call the "high route." This would take us across the northern reaches of Dolpo, near and parallel to the Tibetan border. Once into Dolpo, our route would depend on trail conditions—or even finding trails—and food supplies. One option took us south past Shey Monastery, then east to the Kali Gandaki, over the Thorung La to Manang and back to Kathmandu by early May. Perhaps four hundred miles in all. J.B. had agreed that if we didn't show up in Kathmandu by late May, he would organize a search party.

By early afternoon, Prem returned to the hotel with good news. He had found two porters who knew the region well, and he had brought one back with him, a wiry, bronze-skinned man with high-cheekboned Tibetan features. He greeted me with a smile, and I was astonished at how remarkably like a Native American he looked. Smiling, he proudly showed us a photo of himself and Bob Adams, a former Peace Corps volunteer in Jumla whom J.B. and I had met by chance on the trail in eastern Nepal. In broken English, he told us of a French photographer from Kathmandu, a man whom he had guided several times through Dolpo and who planned to return in two months' time to make another foray. This information cross-checked with what Bob Adams had told us.

This Tibetan guide, however, was pessimistic about our proposed route. The trail north and east beyond Dalphu lay under deep snows—up to eight feet, he said, with many dangerous glacier crossings. To attempt to go along the high route through Dolpo to the Kali Gandaki was certain death. He spoke rapidly in Nepali, and I caught only fragments of the conversation. Anxious to know for myself, I pointed to our route and asked him, "*Baato jaanasakchha?*" ('Trail is possible to go?')

"*Sakdaaina! Sakdaaina!*" ('Not possible!') came the emphatic reply.

I didn't know how to gauge such comments. Although this man apparently had extensive experience traveling through Dolpo, I knew of no areas north of the Dhaulagiris where we might encounter "many glacier crossings." What little snow fell generally evaporated quickly in the arid, high-altitude desert. I had read that the peoples of the Himalayas were poorly adapted culturally to their high, cold environment, and remained remarkably fearful of the elements. Perhaps they also feared disturbing the local deities, and used the threat of snow and glaciers as an excuse.

The Tibetan, however, remained adamant in his assessment. After conferring, Prem and I both remained skeptical, but decided to go to Dalphu and reassess the situation there.

Later, a little after eight, the Tibetan returned with our other newly hired porter. We shut the door to our room and talked in hushed tones. Our topic: the police and military presence in the region. The porters told us of a large garrison in Gum Gadhi and another in Mugu. But the police did not venture far from these villages because the Tibetan people in the area didn't like or trust the authorities. Stories abounded of Tibetan *drokpa*s (nomads) setting upon police traveling between villages. So, they assured us, as long as we could skirt the villages of Gum Gadhi and Mugu, we should encounter no problems. But while I felt hesitant to believe their assessment of the trails in Dolpo, I was reluctant to believe we would pass through that area so easily.

They repeated stories—actually rumors which circulated in the bazaar—that shed some light on the police chief's odd monologue. One involved a French couple who had hired two Dolpo men to guide them back to Kathmandu. Deep in the mountains, the Tibetans murdered the French couple, burying them in a shallow grave. With cameras, money and traveler's checks, the Tibetans headed towards Kathmandu. The police in Jomoson were alerted, and apprehended the murderers as they attempted to sneak through town at night. They confessed to the police chief in Jomoson, but convinced him to take a bribe in exchange for their release. The Tibetans then continued on to Kathmandu, where they tried to cash the traveler's checks. That undid them and, upon their arrest, they told the entire story to the authorities, who subsequently arrested the Jomoson police chief. He was sent to prison in Jumla, under the watchful eye of his good friend, Narayan Shrestha, Jumla's chief of police.

Now the rambling oratory of two days earlier began to make sense. Narayan was telling us that, should we run into any trouble, he could no longer be bribed into helping us because the authorities were watching him.

Our new porters told us another story that troubled me more than the first. Prem translated as they spoke.

"Just last year, a French trekker on his way to RaRa Lake, with proper permits, was taken in by the police in Gum Gadhi. Even with the permit, they put him in jail. It was months before his friends found out. They came to Gum Gadhi and had to pay big *baksheesh*, many rupees, before they let him out. These police, they are so far away, they can do as they want, like a king."

Permits or not, I decided to avoid all police. I had heard yet another story about trouble in Dolpo from Bob Bell, a Peace Corps volunteer stationed in far western Nepal. He got the story directly from the chief of police in Silgarhi, who conducted the investigation. According to this story, another Peace Corps volunteer, proficient in Nepali and well-traveled in other parts of Nepal, went alone into Dolpo. Two months later, he was reported missing, and the U.S. embassy applied pressure on the Nepalese government to investigate the case. The police chief of Silgarhi himself went into Dolpo and came upon a local woman wearing one western-style sneaker. Asked where she got the shoe, she replied that she got it from her sister, who had the other one, and whose husband had removed the pair from the body of an American. The husband confessed to dropping a rock on the American's head while he slept, because he wanted his shoes. The body was found in a superficial grave, fully clothed, the pack still on his back. Inside the pack they found an expensive camera and camping gear, untouched.

All of these stories naturally disturbed me and made me resolve firmly to stay close to our group and to avoid all villages containing police or military posts.

* * *

By eight the following morning, four bulging *doko*s leaned against the balcony railing outside our room. Prem had carefully directed their packing, for the new porters had given hints they might balk at carrying heavy loads. The loads of Akaal Bahadur and Jeet Bahadur weighed close to thirty kilos. I hefted the other two loads a few inches off the floor and estimated their weight at twenty-five and twenty kilos, respectively.

The new porters arrived, and as they mounted the stairs their cheerful smiles turned to somber frowns at the sight of the *doko*s. The posturing began.

"Parker Sahib," Prem reported. "They say the loads are too heavy."

"Ridiculous," I answered. "They are less than our porters' loads and much lighter than the ones the Thakuri porters carried from Surkhet. Even I am carrying twenty kilos."

"I know, Parker Sahib. I have told them, but they think because they know the way that they can get us to make their loads smaller."

The conversation escalated to a heated argument. A Tibetan woman stepped forward, offering to carry for us. One of the porters—her husband, we later learned—backhanded her across the face. At this, Prem took a step towards the man and the argument rapidly degenerated into a shoving match. The two men advanced on Prem. Akaal Bahadur, Jeet Bahadur, Pema and I stepped in to turn the numbers in our favor. We backed them down the steps but they didn't leave, sullenly conferring twenty yards away. From a small crowd that had gathered to watch the altercation, a stocky man in his late thirties came forward and quietly offered to work for us. The two disgruntled porters angrily threatened him with a beating and chased him away.

Prem, whose normally reserved manner hid a hot temper, exploded. With the rest of us behind him, he advanced on the two troublemakers, warning them to leave or he would find the police. Waiting only for the would-be porters to melt into the crowd, Prem, Akaal Bahadur and Jeet Bahadur set off for the bazaar. They returned within a half hour with two new porters.

One was Puraba, the man who had offered to carry for us during the altercation. With only a hint of a smile, he introduced his companion as eighteen-year-old Shera Punzo. The chubby-faced boy looked no more than fifteen. Both lived in a village near Dalphu, our immediate destination. To avoid another unpleasant encounter, we arranged to meet our new hirees at the northern edge of town. Within the hour, we were off.

Porter problems came as nothing new to us. In eastern Nepal, we had up to nine Tamang porters with us. Tamangs are a gregarious caste, quick to laughter but also explosive if provoked. One memorable fight broke out after forty days on the trail.

We had just entered the Khumbu region from the east, and had eaten enough of our supplies to no longer need one porter. Prem had asked Akaal Bahadur to split the porter's remaining equipment among the rest of the loads. Akaal Bahadur did this, including a few kilos for our deaf cook boy, Buddhiman. An argument immediately broke out as Buddhiman objected to carrying anything not belonging to the "kitchen." A shoving match ensued, and Buddhiman, about five foot five inches and unusually muscular, quickly gained the upper hand against Akaal Bahadur. Shiro, Akaal Bahadur's brother and also one of our porters, picked up a rock and advanced on Buddhiman. J.B. and I had watched all of this unfold from the sidelines, but now we intervened. I jumped Shiro and quickly pinned him to the ground. Meanwhile, behind me, Buddhiman had grabbed Akaal Bahadur by the hair and thrown him to the ground. Grabbing a nearby ice axe, Buddhiman made a wild swing, adze end first, towards Akaal Bahadur's head. Fortunately, at the last second, Akaal Bahadur twisted his head to the side. The ice axe stuck in the ground inches from his face. Buddhiman had raised the ice axe overhead for a second blow when J.B. rushed to Akaal Bahadur's rescue. Arresting Buddhiman's swing, J.B. applied an armlock and almost broke Buddhiman's arm before the boy cried out and dropped the weapon.

That ended the actual fight, but tensions remained high and minor altercations occurred during the next few days. Finally, we threatened to dock their wages or even fire any porters caught fighting again. I never found out, and Prem would not tell me, what had started the incident. But I could never believe that just a few extra items loaded in a *doko* had precipitated such a nasty feud.

In planning for our trip to western Nepal, we consulted with Prem and selected two of the porters to go with us. Endless stamina, trustworthiness and spirit of adventure were the attributes we sought. Every one of our eastern Nepal porters wanted to go. For them, it meant a long period of employment with almost no opportunity to squander their earnings. The experience might also lead to other portering jobs, or even the chance to become a *sirdar*. Ultimately, we chose the two who showed the most promise of becoming *sirdars* themselves someday.

Akaal Bahadur was taller than most Nepalese, almost five foot eight, and a bit huskier, although still weighing less than 140 pounds. Because of his robust, outgoing personality, matched by his square-jawed good looks, women often hovered around him. He had a ready laugh and a wild sense of humor, but could become quite volatile at times. Jeet Bahadur was not only unrelated to Akaal Bahadur, but in many ways he was his total opposite. At five foot three and not much over 110 pounds, he was neither as strong nor as outgoing. He had thick, almost bushy, black hair, and was more Tibetan than Nepalese in feature. He spoke little, and I could remember stretches of two or three days when I did not hear him utter a single word. But what Jeet Bahadur lacked in physical size and strength, he possessed in character; I would trust him with my life. And he could carry, on what often seemed sheer will power, any load, all day long, albeit sometimes at a slow pace.

Both Akaal Bahadur and Jeet Bahadur, who together knew no more than two hundred words of English, expressed eagerness to learn more. And their desire to speak English complemented my desire to learn Nepali. So we taught each other. They both spoke Nepali, the umbrella language for the country, and Tamang, a Tibetan dialect, often confusing me by combining both within the same sentence and creating a pidgin language.

Their sense of humor surfaced when they took advantage of my eagerness to learn by teaching me nonsense phrases, telling me they were everyday expressions. They told me *musalai kaideo* meant "very good." When my repeated attempts to use this phrase backfired, leading to shocked expressions (and barely concealed guffaws from the porters), I began to suspect some subterfuge. Several months later, one of my Peace Corps friends told me it meant, "The mouse ate it." *The sneaky bastards.* Thereafter I began to use the expression in more appropriate situations, and to plot my revenge.

We followed a stream due north out of Jumla, ascending gradually towards the 12,000-foot Danphya La pass. A half hour out of town, we came to a stone-walled compound containing several large, beautifully constructed slate-roofed stone buildings, the finest buildings I had seen in Nepal outside of the Kathmandu Valley. On the spacious grounds, twenty boys happily played volleyball. Prem translated the sign on the front gate, and I realized this was the school only recently completed by the United Mission workers. The Youngkins had told me the school was completely self-sufficient, and as we climbed past the main cluster of buildings I saw greenhouses and cultivated fields.

At midafternoon, we crossed an open pasture known as Charya Chaur. Just beyond, in a stand of pine with magnificent views of snow-covered peaks to the south, we set camp for the night.

An hour after first light, on our fourth day out of Jumla we topped the final pass separating us from the gorge of the mighty Mugu Karnali River. Forty miles to the north, a spine of snowy peaks marked the Tibetan border. Gum Gadhi and its police garrison lay far below on this south side of the Mugu Karnali watershed.

The trail descended through dense stands of Himalayan fir and pine. First imperceptibly, then precipitously, the track steepened as we wound down into the gorge of the north-flowing Lumsa Khola, a tributary of the Mugu Karnali.

Although having passed this way many times, Puraba remained unsure of the exact location of Gum Gadhi. He stopped two girls as they passed us. They pointed to a ridgeline rising above the dark depths of the Mugu Karnali. Gum Gadhi lay there, they said, two and a half hours away. Not wishing to go closer until late in the day, we stopped in an open field for our first meal.

Since leaving Jumla, Prem and I had talked often about how we would approach the checkpost at Gum Gadhi. Questions laced our plans with uncertainty. Did the checkpost lie within the village? How vigilantly did the police watch the main trail that skirted several hundred feet below the village? Could we make our way along this trail in the dark? Would our new porters balk at moving at night?

The stories we heard in Jumla had convinced me of one thing: to avoid the police at all costs. With or without proper paperwork, they could stop us and very well might detain us. To avoid being seen, we decided to time ourselves so as to pass rapidly just at dusk below Gum Gadhi, where the Lumsa spilled into the Mugu Karnali. Then, following the Mugu Karnali east, we would walk for an hour or two in the dark before setting camp. Hoping to disguise myself,

I took out my Chinese cap and borrowed back my Tibetan *chuba* from Puraba, to whom I had lent—or more likely given—it two days earlier.

In a barren rice paddy hidden from the trail, we languished in the warm sun, waiting. Then, as the amber sunlight rose off the west-facing slopes, we set off, following the Lumsa Khola steeply down towards its confluence with the Mugu Karnali. Small hamlets clung to the trail.

Although I wore my Chinese cap pulled down over my head, to my dismay it did little to disguise me. From a hundred yards and more, locals spotted me and stared. *What part of my appearance, what movement labeled me a foreigner?* I wondered. I wore drab gray pants, a tan shirt, my Chinese cap, and carried a weathered Tibetan pack, and still something shouted my presence off the canyon walls. I became alarmed.

"Prem, what is it about me that makes me stick out? I wear clothes the same as yours. My pack is old and dirty. What is it?"

Prem stepped back and perused me from head to toe. Then, with a condescending smirk, he replied "It is everything, Parker Sahib, from the inside you are a foreigner. You cannot hide it from them."

Great, I have some kind of foreign aura! I pulled my black Tibetan *chuba* from my pack and began to put it on. Prem intervened.

"Parker Sahib, it is no use. This coat will not help."

"C'mon, Prem. The only thing left showing is a bit of my chin. I know I have a beard and nobody else does, but I can hide that." I hunkered down into the oversized robe.

Prem merely shook his head and continued.

At the next cluster of houses I hung close to Akaal Bahadur, using his large *doko* as a shield. Prem and Puraba had walked by without being noticed. But as we approached, a group of men raising the centerbeam of a new house stopped their chatter and watched us pass. Two young boys stepped out into the trail to stare at me. Guise or no, they could tell. Feeling like an overaged adolescent out on Halloween, I hurried out of their sight and took off the *chuba*. I caught up with Puraba and held it out to him. "*Linos*" ('Take it'), I said, embarrassed.

Soon the trail split. The upper strand led directly into Gum Gadhi. We followed the lower trail that continued along the Lumsa Khola. At dusk we found ourselves still an hour or more from the Mugu

Karnali. We had miscalculated, or the young girls had not told us the truth. In any case, we wouldn't get off this steep trail until well after dark. We pushed on.

Negotiating the rock-strewn trail in the murky twilight became difficult for the porters. We stopped and Prem asked them. "*Ke garne?*" ('What to do?') "Should we go on? Can you make it?"

All agreed that we should keep moving—except Shera Punzo.

"It's too dark," he sniveled.

"You are a small child, a baby," Akaal Bahadur shot back.

Since leaving Jumla we had come to find that Shera Punzo often acted even younger than his true age of fifteen. At first his requests to carry less, or to rest more often, had been amusing. Quickly, however, we lost our patience, and no one more so than Akaal Bahadur.

Shera Punzo cowered behind Puraba. "I cannot see. I will fall."

"We will be here, no one will fall." Prem said.

"What are you afraid of? It's dark every night!" Akaal Bahadur spat out the words in Nepali.

But nothing could sway Shera Punzo. Resigned to spending the night along the trail just below Gum Gadhi, we groped in the dark for a resting place. Behind a nearby stone wall, we cleared a small space of stinging nettles. Using long sticks as tongs, Akaal Bahadur and Jeet Bahadur collected the bristled leaves in our large pot. A half hour in boiling water would turn them into an unsightly but surprisingly edible green slurry called *sisnu*.

Fearing that our tents would be conspicuous, we used our kitchen tarp and ice axes to fashion a shelter close against the wall. With little available fuel, we ate half-cooked rice and *sisnu*, then settled in for several hours' sleep. I set the alarm on my watch for 3:00 A.M. Prem and I had quietly decided that no matter what, we would move out well before first light, dragging Shera Punzo if necessary.

Peering over the wall, we could see the lanterned windows of buildings along the ridge directly above us. Puraba identified them as the garrison barracks. This was *not* my idea of a good campsite. Worried that our cooking fire had been spotted, I slept only intermittently through the night.

By 3:15 A.M. we were on the trail. Surprisingly, Shera Punzo had put up no protest, although with the moon having set, the night was now pitch black. In Jumla we had bought two more Chinese flashlights, bringing our total to three. But to conserve our meager supply of batteries, we now used only one. This slowed us to a crawling pace along the precipitous rocky trail. A few feet to our right, the slope dropped away into the night—how far, we couldn't tell.

Suddenly, from behind, I heard Puraba's muffled yell and the scraping of body and basket. I rushed back to find him lying on a large rock, his *doko* half-crushed beneath him. Through skill or good fortune, he had twisted as he fell, avoiding serious damage. I bent to help him, but with injured pride he waved me off.

Prem, in the lead with the flashlight, had stopped at Puraba's outcry. To avoid more falls, we continued on as a human chain, each of us holding the load of the person ahead for guidance. Although slow, this method provided both stability for negotiating the trail and security for Shera Punzo, who by now was keeping up a constant litany about the blackness, his load, the rocky trail, his desire to stop and wait until daylight. We placed him second in line behind Prem, both to keep him moving and to make sure he didn't disappear into the night with our equipment.

After an hour, the trail flattened out along the Lumsa Khola. Here on flat ground, other travelers had spent the night. Even at this early hour, people stirred. Ahead, the light of a fire lit the trail. I waited in the cover of darkness while Prem went ahead to check. He returned smiling. No police. Just travelers cooking an early-morning meal. Nevertheless, as we passed I hid behind Akaal Bahadur, his large *doko* providing a shield from inquisitive eyes.

Ahead, the persistent roar of the river grew louder. We crossed a small wooden bridge spanning the Lumsa Khola, and turned a corner. Below us rushed the dark waters of the Mugu Karnali, one of the few rivers to pierce the Himalayas completely. From its source somewhere to the north and east along the Tibetan Plateau, it runs as the Mugu Khola south where it merges with the Langu Khola, then turns due west to form the Mugu Karnali. From Gum Gadhi, the waters run another forty miles west before merging with the Humla Karnali and Kubori Kholas to create the Karnali River.

For two hours we headed east, contouring again along the sheer walls of the steep river canyon. Gradually, the eastern sky lightened. At dawn we stopped for tea and a quick meal.

I dropped behind some rocks, which partially hid me from the trail, feeling greatly relieved at having passed Gum Gadhi so easily. Maybe my worries were unfounded; perhaps we would have no trouble with police or permits. We had seen no one since reaching the Mugu Karnali. It seemed almost too easy.

Soon, however, Tibetans in groups of threes and fours began passing on the trail. As dawn turned to day, their numbers increased. And once again, with little more than my Chinese cap visible above the rocks, the *bideshi* (foreign) aura stopped them cold. Everyone paused to stare. I scrunched down lower, completely out of view, and waited for five minutes. Then I cautiously stuck up just an eyeball's worth of head, and, incredulously counted twelve of them watching me. At my appearance, they commented and smiled, as if engaged in some spectator sport.

I had hoped to travel through this region quietly, causing only the merest ripple, slipping through the bureaucratic cracks, leaving nary a trace. *How was I supposed to do that when so many people knew I was here?* I could almost hear them saying, "Over there. Behind those rocks. Don't you see him slinking down, trying to make us think he is a local by hiding under that stupid hat? Doesn't he know we can smell him from half a mile away?"

I gave up and, like a kid found in a game of hide-and-seek, joined the others around the fire at trail's edge. With another checkpost in the village of Mugu several days ahead, there were bound to be officials as well as these Tibetans using this trail. Once again, the demons of doubt crept into my thoughts.

I might as well give myself up right now. Because probably sooner than later, the soldiers will come along and drag my ass off to some dingy jail cell. How many months will I languish, like that poor Frenchman, until someone realizes that I'm not coming back? What exorbitant price will they demand for my release?

I turned to Prem. "I thought there wasn't supposed to be any traffic along this trail. Who are all these people?"

He sensed my rising agitation and responded in a reassuring tone. "Only the local people, nothing to worry about, Parker Sahib."

"But they've seen me! All two hundred and fifty of them!"

"This is no problem, Parker Sahib. Come, let us go." Prem smiled over his shoulder as he headed off.

"No problem, Parker Sahib," I mimicked. "Whose ass is on the line here, Prem?" Muttering obscenities, I hurried along behind him. "Prem, if the shit hits the fan, I want you right here with me. You are going to do all of the explaining."

"No problem, Parker Sahib."

The trail gently undulated as it followed the river course. Falling in with the local traffic, we matched their quick pace for almost two hours without a pause. The trail remained crowded, but gradually I realized that almost everyone moved in our direction, away from Gum Gadhi. I was certainly the object of their curiosity, but in a friendly, nonaggressive way. They nodded and smiled, I smiled back.

Towards midday, we came upon a medieval village straddling the trail. Lumsa consisted of a series of dilapidated, flat-roofed, two-story structures, many of which leaned at dangerous angles. In the small, dusty central square, I stopped to change a roll of film. Several silvery black water buffalo tethered to stakes eyed me skittishly. Dung, decomposing animal carcasses and piles of unidentifiable organic debris created a nauseating stench in the midday sun. A glassy-eyed villager dressed in blackened homespun stared at me with benign curiosity from a doorway. Clouds of flies and the stench urged me onward.

Just beyond Lumsa, the trail dropped two hundred feet to the riverbed. Here the gorge opened, and we set out across fields to the river's edge. Tired from having started our day so early, we took an extended lunch break, snoozing under makeshift shelters that protected us from the searing sun.

Later, sitting by a small bridge spanning a side stream, I saw that the trail was now deserted. Only then did I understand Prem's cavalier attitude that morning, for the traffic we had encountered was just the normal early-morning traffic heading from Gum Gadhi towards Mugu and the Tibetan frontier. These ruddy-faced Tibetans were little threat to us. Given their dislike of authority, they had no reason to turn us in, and it might be just like them to protect us. Certainly we were never in any danger, and Prem knew this. I forgave him. After all, he had said, "No problem, Parker Sahib."

At four we rose and walked several slow miles through afternoon heat into the early evening. We set camp along the river, and I turned in early after another meal of rice and *sisnu*.

At one-thirty I awoke, cursing myself for not having brought a piss bottle with me as I had in eastern Nepal. Finally, I struggled out of my warm sleeping bag, unzipped the tent door and stepped a few feet into the cool night. The skies remained clear; directly overhead, the Milky Way streaked the sky. A crescent moon rose over the ridges to the south. How many times had I watched that moon wax and wane in these last months? I had never imagined that I would become so attuned to its cycles. But then, I had never before lived outdoors for months at a time, away from the obscuring glow of artificial light. Here the moon took on new meaning, new importance for me. At its fullest, I could write in my journal by its light. In its absence, we stumbled and fell along the trail. By the rising full moon of December, I had met Clara.

Every afternoon I waited. Clara and her friend Sera would come up to the fourth floor, then climb the stairs to the rooftop to smoke cigarettes and talk. A low wall, three feet high, hid them from the prying eyes of the other Nepalese who worked in the hotel. Sometimes I followed them up to the roof and there Clara and I talked. From the beginning she made it obvious she wished to keep our meetings and conversations a secret.

I learned that although she was Nepalese, she came from Darjeeling and was raised as a Catholic, hence her Christian name. Accustomed to wearing skirts and blouses at her convent school, she and the other Darjeeling girls who lived in Kathmandu continued to wear western clothes. She spoke clear, precise English and appeared sophisticated and westernized.

Perhaps that's what led me to ask her out. Looking back now, it seemed such a naive thing to do. Because we had little privacy to talk, we fell into the practice of communicating by passing notes.

One afternoon as we sat hidden by the wall, I surreptitiously passed her a note.

Dear Clara,

I would be most pleased if you could accompany me for dinner this evening.

Parker

She read the note and then smiled at me in such a beautiful way I thought she might say yes. With hindsight, I could see that she probably smiled because she felt it was a sweet thing for me to suggest—but such a naive boy! She thought for a moment after reading the note, then scribbled a reply.

Dear Parker,

    I would more than anything like to go to dinner with you, but I cannot. Please, you must understand, there are many things you do not know and my life does not always go the way I would like, so full of complications. But I thank you anyway.

Clara

    I crawled back into my sleeping bag and pulled the drawstring close around my head. "I will miss you," she had said. I missed her.

CHAPTER FIVE

Mugu Karnali Gorge
Wednesday, March 7, 1984

At dawn, we quietly disassembled the tents and packed them away before other travelers appeared along the trail. I wanted to attract as little attention as possible. We walked steadily until ten-thirty, when the sun began to beat down on us. Once again, we rested and cooled ourselves with a five-hour midday break.

Grass fires dotted the steep slopes on the opposite side of the river. Set intentionally, they burned the dry grasses but left the huge pine trees unharmed.

Later we passed through an area burned some weeks previously, and I guessed at the reason for it. Fresh green shoots pushed through the tufts of burned grass, perfect fodder for the many cows, yaks, goats and sheep that grazed on the slopes. The only detrimental effect was that the flames destroyed the small saplings, preventing new forest growth. Only the large trees escaped unharmed.

The "only" detrimental effect—destroying the young trees—might, as in other parts of Nepal, ultimately prove catastrophic. Here the population pressure wasn't as great as in eastern Nepal, where entire forests had been axed to supply firewood and make way for fields. In addition, the intensive pressures of trekking in Sagarmatha

National Park in the Everest region has led to massive deforestation with subsequent problems of landslides and loss of fertile topsoil. Here, in remote western Nepal, we alone would not threaten the supply of wood, but what if others followed us? The native population's needs, even in these remote valleys, could easily lead to environmental degradation. Was I, one lone Westerner, starting an outsider problem here too? Trekking in this part of Nepal was years away, but very likely it would come; bringing in some tourist money, true, but environmentally possibly doing more harm than good. Would the countries from which the trekkers came, mine included, help with foreign aid, family planning, medical delivery systems? Too many questions, no answers.

After our lunch break, we walked quickly, following the increasingly spectacular Mugu Karnali Gorge. As we moved upstream, the gorge narrowed, the slopes steepened. The view offered an occasional glimpse of the himal in the distance.

Towards midafternoon I came to a high stone bench built at just the right height for resting a load if one backed onto it. No need to take off your load or set it on the ground, less energy expended. Five Tibetans, three men and two women, whom I had followed for the past hour, stopped too. Since passing Gum Gadhi I had relaxed and for the first time looked closely at our fellow travelers.

Virtually everyone carried something. The loads ranged from twelve-foot lengths of iron pipe to month-old pieces of meat wedged into the bottom of homespun bags. They dripped blood and fat and each trailed a cloud of flies. Even though we were at 7,000 feet, it was hot at midday and we could smell these loads from many yards away.

These Tibetans had deep olive complexions, high cheekbones, and eyes with a deeper fold than that found on the lowland Nepalese. The three men wore gray wool *chubas*, the traditional oversized Tibetan topcoat, and homespun wool trousers. Two sported dark-colored hats. Each man had earrings of a different design.

The first had a gold hoop, three inches across, pierced through his right ear and soldered closed. The second man had rings in both ears, five-inch-long pieces of hide on which hung a piece of turquoise flanked by two strips of smooth orange-pink coral. He had wrapped both around his ears, the stones facing forward, but as I watched, one came loose and flopped down to his shoulder. Laughing, he deftly twisted it back into place. The oldest man's earlobes were distended

Puraba, our porter, showing his heavy silver hoop earring, set with an oval piece of turquoise in a flared section that faced forward.

by the weight of heavy silver hoops set with oval pieces of turquoise in a flared section that faced forward. Around his neck hung a heavy necklace alternating turquoise with coral beads.

Turning to look at the women, I immediately sensed their strength and self-confidence. Unlike some Nepalese women, they looked directly into my eyes. The younger of the two had cheeks so rosy that if it were not for the dirt, I would have sworn she wore makeup. The other woman did wear a strange type of cosmetic, oblong patches of dark green henna spread on her chin, forehead and cheeks. Sleeveless black dresses with multicolored aprons of dark red, charcoal gray and light tan topped the most incongruous aspect of their outfits, blue and green Chinese sneakers. They draped a piece of wool, the same color pattern as their aprons, over their heads. I had become used to seeing nose jewelry on Nepalese women, but the Tibetan women had none. Six-inch hoops of silver dangled from their ears. Both wore magnificent necklaces of alternating coral and turquoise; the roughly polished hunks of turquoise varied from pea-size to apricot-size.

I tried to take photographs, especially of the women, but they turned shy, giggling and covering their mouths when they caught me pointing the camera their way. Always struggling to take candid shots, I felt awkward and intrusive. But I knew I would regret it later if I didn't at least try for a photographic record of these people.

These Tibetan Bhuddists had their spiritual home in Lhasa. Soon after the Chinese takeover of Tibet in 1959, however, the Dalai Lama had fled to India, taking with him the spiritual center of Tibetan Buddhism. The result now is a religion and cultural heritage in disarray, fragmented by both political boundaries and Chinese oppression. Confronted already with tourists in Nepal and with the impending influx of tourists into Tibet, I wondered how long the nomadic culture of these Tibetans would survive in the face of the encroachment of western influences.

Late in the afternoon, another grimy Tibetan came running after us, shouting loudly. Even as he approached, the pungent smell of his unwashed body enveloped us. *Oh no, another government official!* For several minutes, Prem and I tried to ignore him, until we realized he was only trying to tell us his house lay just ahead. He invited us in for *chang*. The ninety-degree afternoon made the idea of a cool sit-down appealing. So we crossed a cantilevered wooden bridge and walked to his house, a one-story stone-and-mud building. He led us into a large gloomy room with a crude fireplace, yak skins on the floor and drying meat strips hanging from the beams. Smiling, with two prominent gold teeth, his wife served us thick, cool *chang*. Only after a couple of glasses did we realize why the man had been so anxious to have us come to his house. He charged forty rupees per pitcher!

Noticing a pile of potatoes, we bargained with the Tibetan for two paathis' worth, about ten pounds. We paid him for the *chang* and potatoes, then walked back outside into the blinding sunlight.

A man dressed in a green sweater and pants crossed the bridge with a purposeful stride and marched up the path in our direction. I spotted him first and recognized him immediately as police. Tall and spindly, with his army sweater a size too small, he carried a small baton. The slanting sun disoriented me momentarily, and I felt a cold sweat on my forehead. Dizzy, flushed from the *chang*, I felt oddly detached from the scene. Certain that he would confront me, I tried frantically to formulate a plan of escape, a lie, a strategy. But before my addled brain could engage gears, he passed not more than a foot away, ignoring me completely, and walked into the house.

Seizing the opportunity, I jumped to my feet. With my head still swirling I jammed my Chinese cap down tightly. Prem and I jogged across the bridge and collected our porters. We walked for another hour before setting our camp near the village of Dhungedhara at just over 8,000 feet.

That evening I still felt lightheaded and nauseated, although I couldn't determine why. I lay awake in my sleeping bag for a long time. Serious doubts began to erode my confidence. Before leaving Kathmandu for the west, I had mentally prepared myself for the possibility of physical adversity. Steep passes, snow and ice, long, hard up-and-down climbs, storms, concerns about food. But I hadn't seriously considered engaging in a game of dodge-'em with the police and military. Perhaps naively, I had assumed that our paperwork from Kathmandu would get us by. A little fudging here and there, a bribe or two . . . I had learned the tricks of getting by in Asia—I thought. Now I knew I had grossly underestimated the true remoteness of western Nepal. I drifted off to sleep about one o'clock, but woke up at three-thirty with a fever, exploding bowels and paralyzing cramps.

Poisoned. By the *chang*, by the gnawing doubts, by my own anxieties. I reached for the Lomotil and the local opium-laced cough syrup. They eased my pain, but I was up four more times, squatting in the cool, still night. I hadn't been weaned in this part of the world where legs become accustomed to this position and by the last time I could no longer squat. With leaden legs and heavy eyes, I watched the eastern sky turn gray and then pink with the coming dawn.

Mercifully, we slept late. At eight, Akaal Bahadur brought me bed tea. Having become dehydrated during the night, I accepted it gratefully, downing the steaming sweet liquid in a few gulps. I dragged myself up and into the already hot sun, my legs trembled under me, my eyelids heavy from the drugs and lack of sleep. Prem and Puraba had also become sick during the night and I offered them Lomotil, which they accepted with thanks.

We weren't as quick off the mark that morning, but moving proved easier than remaining still. Not long after we left camp we passed through a large *chorten* built over the trail. The *chorten* (*stupa* in Sanskrit) is the quintessential symbol of Buddhism. The square base faces the four cardinal directions and represents the earth element. Above the base a circular mound is surmounted by a spire, representing the fire element. On the most elaborate *chortens*, a crescent, representing the air element, and a ball of flame, representing the ethereal element, sit atop the spire. Funerary monuments of important *lamas*, or monks, *chortens* vary greatly in size and style. But they can be found on the outskirts of villages and their appearance alerted us to human habitation. I looked up from the inside of this particularly elaborate *chorten* to see the entire twelve-foot-high ceiling and half the walls painted with intricate religious artwork, exquisitely detailed, colorful scenes and figures.

Two miles on, we came to the convergence of two rivers, the Mugu Khola and the Langu Khola, also known as the Dolpo Chu, from Dolpo. They merged at this point to become the Mugu Karnali. Each khola had cut a gorge several thousand feet deep, and we could see a trail following each, precarious silver threads winding high along the near-vertical walls. A half day's walk to the north, the trail following the Mugu Khola passed through the village of Mugu, then crossed the frontier into Tibet. This, the main trading route between Tibet and western Nepal and India, had accounted for virtually all of the traffic we had seen since leaving Gum Gadhi.

The other route, following the Langu Khola due east towards Dolpo, marked our destination. We estimated our immediate target, the village of Dalphu, to be less than two days' walk.

We stopped just where the kholas merged for our first meal, Prem, Puraba and I eating only plain rice. Puraba, who never complained, and Shera Punzo, who complained all the time, both indicated that we were in for a long uphill climb from here to Dalphu. It *was* steep. For two hours we ascended steadily until we reached a ridge 2,000 feet above the Langu Khola. From there we looked down three hundred feet to the village of Kimri. Although the terrain we had followed along the Mugu Karnali Gorge was rugged, several thousand feet deep, what faced us now was even steeper, deeper and rockier.

Across the river, the village of Tika perched above a 2,000-foot buttress which dropped sheer to the river below. Nestled in its aerie, the village lay beneath slopes that rose in rocky crags and spires for several thousand feet before disappearing from view. It was a formidable location for a village and I wondered what sort of people could inhabit such a place. Did its inaccessibility affect them in some strange ways? Or did it perhaps make them feel safe from the marauding bands of invaders so prevalent in the past?

We continued ascending to Kartik and camped next to a *gompa* (monastery) just above the village.

We left early the next morning to begin the most difficult day of trail-hiking I had yet experienced. Although Dalphu was only five miles from Kartik, the undulating, rocky, near-vertical terrain turned this distance into eleven miles of tortuous, treacherous travel. Cumulatively, we ascended and descended 10,000 feet before reaching Dalphu, although it was only 1,000 feet higher than Kartik.

The trail was a feat of engineering that did credit to the villagers who maintained it. In places, stone retaining walls one hundred feet high buttressed the two-foot-wide path along near-vertical cliffs. In high winds and during the monsoon season, the landslides along the trail made it impassable and Dalphu remained isolated for months at a time. I found it remarkable that trails existed at all in some of these remote areas of Nepal. But without a trail there could be no village, and these tenuous tracks served as lifelines to the outside world.

Late in the morning we came to an active slide and I wondered how we could possibly continue. The slide, a forty-yard highway of rock and earth pulled by gravity towards the riverbed below, started 2,000 feet above us and continued 2,500 feet down to the *khola* below. Looking up, we could see specks that with terrifying speed grew into near boulders as they hurtled down and then crashed past. I looked into the faces of Prem and the others and they looked wordlessly back at me, Prem impassive, Puraba fingering his prayer beads, Shera Punzo ready to turn back. We all knew what we had to do, and feared it.

"Okay," I said to Prem. "One at a time and run like hell. I'll go first." I moved to the head of the party under a protective overhang.

Prem stepped back several yards to get a view of the slide above. "Parker Sahib, I will tell you when to go."

I crouched against the wall as several rocks bounced by, trailing growing amounts of debris with them. During a lull, I heard Prem's signal and darted out. Moving as quickly as I could through the loose dirt, scrabbling, balancing on moving earth, I surprised myself by reaching the other side without incident.

Gasping from the effort, I turned to watch a large rock smash and obliterate my footprints just twenty feet behind me.

Akaal Bahadur came next, then Jeet Bahadur, Puraba, Shera Punzó and finally Prem. Miraculously, within half an hour we all stood safely on the far side.

The trails did not simply contour the terrain on one level. The steep slopes formed by streams originating in snowfields thousands of feet above made this impossible. Thus, we would descend 1,500 feet into a side canyon only to climb 2,000 feet out on the far side, gaining only 500 feet in altitude and only a third or half a mile in distance, but actually walking two miles. All with the knowledge that the precious 500 feet of altitude would soon be lost in our descent into the next side canyon.

The final climb to Dalphu was the highest and steepest, and we took it slowly. As we labored, I was surprised by the chatter of female voices behind me. Turning, I saw an adolescent girl and her grand-mother rapidly gaining on us. Local inhabitants routinely used these trails and took the perilous slide crossings in stride.

We stopped to rest and as they came abreast of us, I saw large silver-hooped earrings stretching the old woman's earlobes to eight inches. Around her neck were strung large, rounded hunks of amber and coral. And at the bottom of the necklace hung an intricately decorated silver amulet box, roughly three-by-four-by-one-and-a-half inches. I tried to take her photograph, but she protested, shaking her head vigorously. This didn't surprise me, for I had received a similar re-sponse from older people in other parts of Nepal. *But maybe the young girl*. For a moment she seemed willing to pose, then laughed and turned away before I could focus.

Shortly after a rest stop, we came to an unusually level, muddy place on the trail. Casually I glanced down at Prem's bootprint in the soft mud. Then I did a double take. There, only an inch from the boot mark, I saw a paw print three inches across. It had to be the track of a snow leopard. Comparing the relative freshness of the two sets of prints—that of the cat and Prem's boot—I speculated that the snow leopard had passed within the hour. Excitedly I searched the slope above me, but saw nothing except a pair of brilliant blue snowcocks.

Chortens split the trail and we dutifully kept them to our right as we approached the upper reaches of the village of Dalphu.

We crested the last ridge and looked out on the terraced fields of Dalphu, barren and dusty after five months without rain. Boys and girls tending goats in the fields stopped and stared as we walked past. A line of *chortens* split the trail, and in deference to Buddhist tradition we dutifully kept them to our right as we approached the upper reaches of the village proper.

Puraba led us to the uppermost building. The rest of the village lay below us, a primitive apartment complex of two-story dwellings, eight or ten in a row. Several tiers of these buildings comprised the village.

From above, the clean, light-tan rooftops stretched for several hundred feet down the slope, prayer flags on long poles above each house fluttering in the breeze. On the rooftops, children played, lambs brayed, women spun wool and men conversed in small groups surrounded by grain spread to dry in the sun. Once they spotted us, more villagers gathered on the roofs to talk and stare openly at us. They seemed friendly and genuinely curious.

From the rooftop, Puraba led us down a ladder into the main room of the house. The only light in the semidark interior came from a small

The village of Dalphu is a primitive apartment complex of two-story dwellings, eight to ten in a row.

partially covered roof hole, which served also as a crude chimney. A middle-aged woman placed her hands together in greeting and then motioned for us to sit. Acrid smoke from the open fire stung my eyes, and I quickly moved to my designated place on the coarse wooden floor next to the hearth.

Chang appeared in silver-lined wooden bowls. It was pale yellow and almost clear, in contrast to the milky white of most *chang*s, with a slight carbonation and an aftertaste very similar to the mass-produced American beers. Made of barley, it was the closest thing to an ice-cold Michelob that I had tasted since leaving home.

The mayor's son played on
the rooftops of Dalphu.

The author with the children of Dalphu.

By the time I finished the customary third bowl, my eyes had adjusted to the dim light. The room measured approximately fifteen feet square, with a fireplace abutting the wall opposite the doorway, next to which stood a small Buddhist altar. On the altar I saw a photograph of the Dalai Lama, small brass cups containing oil and water burning with a primitive wick, assorted hand-held prayer wheels and Tibetan scriptures. Crude wooden chests, decorated with regularly spaced splotches of whitewash, lined another wall. In the far corner, a ring of flour surrounded a hand-powered grinding wheel, and a sack of unground barley rested nearby.

An incredible clutter of bric-a-brac, both old and new, lay randomly strewn about. Huge copper urns containing water or perhaps barley fermenting for *chang*, yak skins piled in a heap, a small box of worn plastic shoes and galoshes for children, mats for bedding, plastic jerry cans, assorted bowls and plates made of brass or silver, shredded pieces of old blankets, torn and discarded clothing, foam sleeping pads. All were covered with a layer of soot, the result of burning pinewood so laden with oils that a large splinter could be lit and used as a candle.

"Parker Sahib," Prem leaned towards me. "This man is the *pradhan panch*, the—how do you say—mayor of Dalphu. He knows all the foreigners who come here."

"Have other foreigners been here recently?"

"Yes. Now there are three or four who are studying the snow leopard. They have a camp not far from here, four hours' walk. They work for the National Geographic."

Perhaps that's where the *pradhan panch* had gotten his shoes. I eyed his pair of Nike Gore-Tex Approach shoes identical to the pair I was wearing.

"Two weeks ago," Prem said, "one man received a snow-leopard bite. The snow leopard was sleeping. Put asleep by the man."

"Tranquilized."

"Yes. He was afraid the snow leopard would give him rabies. So he went to Jumla quickly so that he could go to Kathmandu."

"That was the guy we just missed in Jumla, Rodney Jackson. The Youngkins told me about him. Well maybe we can visit their camp. Four hours, you say?"

"Only four hours' walk, Parker Sahib."

"Well, not tonight. I've emptied too many bowls of *chang*. Time for bed."

We staggered up the log ladder to the roof where our tents had been pitched. Trail-weary and *chang*-filled, we had no trouble falling asleep.

Next morning, we faced a big decision. Where were we going next? Our plan had been to follow the Langu Khola east into Dolpo along what we called the high route, past the village of Phapagaon fifteen days' travel to the east. From there, we hoped to go either south towards Shey Gompa and eventually southeast over several unknown high passes towards the Barbung Khola, or to continue eastward on the high route along the Tibetan frontier towards Charkabhotgaon, another fifteen to twenty days beyond Phapagaon. Either way, it would be a long, tough and treacherous journey.

Thus far, for all the difficulties and risks, we had really encountered only the normal problems of serious trekking. But we had been warned repeatedly by the locals that the routes we now planned were impossible this time of year, that it would be suicide to head into Dolpo by this route. On the other hand, I didn't believe much of what they said, knowing the locals' inordinate and irrational fear of the weather and terrain. In fact, we learned that some of the people near Jumla had become afraid of *us* because we had braved the Marbu Lekh in a storm. Actually, if it hadn't been for J.B.'s ankle, we could have done it even more easily and faster, because under normal circumstances it was a straightforward crossing.

To get a clearer view of the land ahead, Prem and I walked east about a mile and a half beyond Dalphu. On an outcropping perched 1,500 feet above the Langu Khola, we stopped and sat silently side by side, staring at the formidable terrain.

As I contemplated this twisted jumble of mountains, the sheer walls of snow and rock along our intended path, I realized that nothing in my past years of trekking and climbing had prepared me for the scene of geological devastation that lay before us. The fears, the doubts, the worst-scenario nightmares—they were no longer abstractions in some hazy future time. They were here.

Neither of us wanted to admit his fears to the other, so Prem and I sat for a long time, saying nothing. Because we could carry only limited supplies of food, we both knew that once we got a certain distance away from Dalphu, we would reach a point of no return. From that point we would either make it through or die somewhere amidst the mountains of Dolpo. It wasn't just a matter of food. It was still winter, and we could run into bitter weather. Storms, blizzards could trap us for days while we consumed precious food supplies. Or we could lose our way, fall off the trail, be overcome by snow too deep to traverse. Injuries and illness could plague us, and there would be no helicopter rescues in these areas. Ahead we might face slow starvation, agonizing injury or, merciful by comparison, a quick fall to our deaths.

My head reeled as I tried to think through all the possibilities. What to do? Take the chance and go on into the unknown or turn around and retrace our steps?

Finally, Prem spoke. Though soft, his voice cut firmly through the atmosphere of doubt. "Parker Sahib, I think we should do it. Jeet Bahadur, Akaal Bahadur, you and me. We have come a very long way. Too far to simply go back. We must try."

"Do you know the risks? The food we will have to carry, the mountains we will have to cross, the trails?"

Prem closed his eyes and nodded slowly, thoughtfully. Then he waited as I pondered the decision I would have to make, because in the end it was *my* decision. Actually, I had already decided for myself, but hesitated to make such a weighty decision for the others. I turned to Prem. "We will depend on Akaal Bahadur and Jeet Bahadur to help us get through. It's not just you and me. We have to talk to them. See if they understand the risks. We must get their okay, too."

He nodded again.

Back in Dalphu, we ate boiled potatoes, carefully peeled and dipped in fiery *achar* (chili sauce) and crushed Tibetan rock salt. After our meal, Prem, Akaal Bahadur, Jeet Bahadur and I walked a short way up the slope behind Dalphu, out of earshot of the villagers.

Prem explained to Akaal Bahadur and Jeet Bahadur what we had discussed earlier. I understood roughly half the interchange, but I heard the excitement in their voices. The two porters' eyes sparkled and they smiled animatedly. The thrill of adventure had captured them.

"Parker Sahib, they say they will go. They are strong, they can carry our food, they can carry very heavy loads. They will go anywhere you go," Prem said. The porters' enthusiasm was contagious and I smiled at their eagerness.

Then in my best broken Nepali I spoke to all three of them, mustering the most serious tone I could. "Now things will be different. This is not like the other treks. This isn't like being with J.B.

Sahib and me in eastern Nepal. This isn't like going from Surkhet to Jumla. We, the four of us, are together. We are equals. No sahib, no *sirdar*, no porters. Do you understand?"

They all nodded gravely.

"If you want to go back now, you must choose. I will not stop you, this is your choice."

Again they nodded, matching the solemn expression on my face. I knew they would come with me for they trusted me. And I trusted them with my life. But I also knew that the cultural differences would not disappear. I could see in their eyes that although I said we were equals, and they agreed, it was not and never could be so. I would always be sahib to them; nothing I could say or do would change this.

We returned to our tents to work out the logistics. We figured we needed to carry food for twenty-five days minimum, and potatoes were the only food available. When we computed one and a half pounds of food per person per day, times four people, it came to 150 pounds extra weight. This meant three extra porters to carry our food. But since they ate too, we would need still another porter just to carry potatoes for the three porters. Four more porters, with one possibly returning to Dalphu when we had eaten one load of food. The others would have to come all the way to Kathmandu with us, which meant paying their transportation costs home.

I checked our money supply, which was dangerously low, since J.B.'s plane ticket had taken a large bite out of our treasury. After counting carefully, I determined that we could afford to offer forty rupees per day for each porter.

We approached the *pradhan panch* with our request to hire porters. He scowled and shook his head grimly. It would be difficult for him to help us just now.

Prem raised his eyebrow and smiled sideways at me. Then turned back to the *pradhan panch* with a serious expression. A finder's fee could be arranged if he was successful in helping us. That lit up the mayor's face, and he immediately left to visit the other households in the village.

An hour and a half later, he returned and spoke to Prem.

"He says it is impossible, Parker Sahib. No one will go with us. Not even if we pay them eighty rupees per day. They say it is impossible to go our way."

"Maybe we can find porters in Wangri. Puraba and Shera Punzo live there. Maybe they can help us. Besides, we still haven't asked Puraba if he wants to go with us. I'd like him to. Not Shera Punzo, though. He's too young and weak."

"Tomorrow we should go to Wangri," Prem said.

I agreed, as the village was only on the other side of the gorge and should take us just a few hours to reach.

"Parker Sahib, the *pradhan panch* wants to sell us more *chang*."

I couldn't resist, and eventually bought six bottles of the delicious golden beer, which we shared with Akaal Bahadur and Jeet Bahadur.

CHAPTER SIX

Monday, March 12, 1984

S N O W fell during the night but with little accumulation. By morning the storm had blown through, leaving the temperature in the twenties.

Before leaving for Wangri, Prem approached me. "Parker Sahib," he said with a sigh. "Shera Punzo wants to leave the kerosene and stove here at the *pradhan panch*'s house so he doesn't have to carry it. He says we can come back for it later. I think this is a good idea."

I agreed, then looked around at the small pile of gear to be left behind. "What's this?" I picked up several packets of noodles. "Why are we leaving these behind? They don't weigh anything."

"Shera Punzo!" Prem called to the boy sharply.

"Lazy kid," I muttered.

Akaal Bahadur turned and sneered at Shera Punzo, making another snide remark in Nepali on the inadequacies of our youngest porter. Shera Punzo's almost constant complaining and shirking had come to a head.

"First it was funny," I said. "All that whining about needing more food and more clothes. Now it's just damn tiresome."

"And he complains about how much money he makes!" Prem said.

"He is making forty rupees per day. This is more than he has made ever in his life."

"We're only paying Akaal Bahadur and Jeet Bahadur twenty-five rupees per day." (These being standard Kathmandu wages.) "We've got to get rid of Shera Punzo soon."

"Yes, Parker Sahib. At Wangri we can find other porters, much better ones."

"Certainly ones that eat less. Have you seen how much rice he eats?"

Prem laughed. It had been a recurring joke, the enormous amounts Shera Punzo could consume at one sitting. I carried more weight, but he ate more food. "No problem, Parker Sahib. Soon he will go."

The trip to Wangri, less than two miles across the canyon, took us four grueling hours. First we dropped to the Langu Khola, then puffed up the steep face on the far side.

Crumbling *chortens* guarded the trail as we neared the village. Three small girls, dressed in rags, appeared out of the underbrush a hundred feet above to watch us. Puraba shouted and waved as a small boy ran down to greet him. Puraba hadn't seen his children since leaving for Jumla last November.

The village came into view above us, a maze of interconnected multilevel dwellings, denser than in Dalphu but in every other way similar, cluttered with log ladders, prayer flags on long wooden poles and the necessities and debris of daily life. Puraba led us into the village and up to the roof of his house, situated in the middle of a dozen connected dwellings that formed a row fifty yards long.

Within ten minutes, we had attracted a crowd of more than forty children and adults. I sensed their excitement. Few foreigners made it this far, and Prem, Akaal Bahadur and Jeet Bahadur were just as foreign here as I. I squatted down to the level of the children and started kidding with them, making faces and teasing. Soon the children were laughing and the adults smiling.

"*Ausadhi?*" ('Medicine?') someone asked.

"*Ausadhi chhainna*" ('I don't have any medicine'), I answered, denying yet another request for the coveted western commodity.

"Where are you from?"

"Kathmandu," Prem answered. A few nodded their heads, but just as many looked puzzled. "They don't know where Kathmandu is, Parker Sahib. What would happen if we tried to tell them you were from America?"

Puraba's Children.

Looking out over the rooftops of the village of Wangri towards Dalphu.

A child of Wangri.

"Kathmandu is far enough away."

"Yes, to them I am a foreigner, too. They think it is strange that I wear western clothes. They do not know where Darjeeling is. It is as far away as America."

"Japanese, Japanese," someone identified us.

This wasn't the first time I had been called Japanese. Caucasians automatically were called Japanese by many in the Himalayas. This seemed odd, because of all the foreigners who traveled the Himalayas, the Japanese, being Asian, looked most like the indigenous people.

"Parker Sahib," Prem called me away from the crowd of children. "Come this way."

We climbed down the ubiquitous log ladder, steps hewn in a single log split in two, and into Puraba's dark and smoky home. Once again, we were served golden barley *chang*. Each time we drained our silver-lined bowls, Puraba attentively refilled them. We drank several large bottles' worth to avoid offending Puraba or his grandmother, who ran his household for him. The old woman was in her eighties and had severe conjunctivitis. She, too, asked for medicine, but again I couldn't provide it. The smoky atmosphere in the house did nothing to ease her condition. Although in almost constant pain, she was cheerful and cordial to us.

After three hours of drinking *chang*, we stumbled up the log ladder to the roof, had a quick dinner and turned in.

We planned to rest the next day in Wangri. We would spend time learning more about the possible routes ahead, finding porters, washing and, if possible, resting a little. Another clear, cold morning dawned. I huddled in my sleeping bag until eight-thirty when the sun climbed above the towering 8,000-foot rock face a half mile away, across the side canyon on which Wangri perched at 11,000 feet.

At ten o'clock, Prem, Akaal Bahadur and I went further up the side canyon to scout a possible route over the Khapre La to the south in the event we couldn't find porters to carry for us east into Dolpo. We stopped by the stream that flowed down into the village, built a fire and left Akaal Bahadur to wash clothes. Prem and I continued up the canyon past several *chortens*.

Crossing the jumbled remains of two avalanches, we ascended through a birch and pine forest. A route marked on our maps continued up this trail and over the 17,000-foot Khapre La. After two miles, we stopped and looked towards the snow-covered peaks.

"Well, Prem. What do you think? Is it possible?"

"Yes, Parker Sahib. I think it is possible. Maybe it will be good for seeing all the mountains."

I glanced at Prem by my side and smiled affectionately. Without question Prem could have earned a better living doing something else, but he enjoyed this life: trekking, guiding, being in the open air, in the mountains. I could empathize with that.

We bent over the map. "Look, if we go this way," I traced the dotted line with my finger, "we'll be able to see the Sisne, the Kanjiroba, the Patrasi and the Jagdula Himals. It should be beautiful."

"From here we cannot see this pass, but I think it will be possible," Prem said. "Even though there is snow, we can do it."

I turned and looked once again at the steep, snow-blanketed slope above. "If we can't go east, let's give it a try."

Excitedly, we hurried back down the trail. Halfway back to the village, I saw them. Stopping abruptly, I motioned Prem to do the same. In front of us on the trail was a set of fresh snow leopard tracks, made in the sun-softened mud since we had passed this spot on our way up the canyon.

The mysterious and shy snow leopard (*Panthera unica*) inhabits only these remotest mountain areas of the Himalayas. They prey primarily on the bharal (blue sheep) although with the destruction of habitat and human depletion of their natural prey they have more recently turned to domestic animals for food. This threat to livestock has led to extensive hunting by local villagers, and a precipitous drop in their numbers. Because their spotted coats give them superb camouflage and their reclusive habits keep them out of sight, it was unlikely we would actually see one of these big cats. Counted among the endangered species, even a glimpse of one of these rare and beautiful animals would have made my day.

Hardly daring to breathe, we followed the tracks downhill for twenty-five yards until they veered off into the brush along the trail. Intently, hopefully, we scanned the sparse forest and open meadows above us. We stood there, eyes searching for several minutes, but nothing broke the stillness of the cobalt blue sky and midday sun. Far above us, a pair of lammergeiers spiraled upwards in ever higher circles.

Disappointed, we returned to the stream where Akaal Bahadur waited. We washed ourselves—thoroughly—for the first time in the ten days since leaving Jumla.

Back in Wangri, I spent the afternoon relaxing in the sun on the roof and writing in my journal. Puraba's grandmother came up a log ladder, sat and smiled toothlessly at me. Not far away, a woman wove cloth from homespun wool yarn. Attached to one end of her ten-foot-long loom was a dowel to which was tied fifty pieces of yarn. The woman sat at the other end in a harness, keeping an even tension on the loom. She passed a large ball of yarn between the two layers of stretched yarn and went through a complex series of maneuvers I couldn't follow. Her expert fingers moved quickly and deftly. Fascinated, I watched her repeat this procedure over and over as a piece of cloth slowly emerged.

She seemed to be the only one busy, however. A few men sat about. Some children played. Otherwise, nothing seemed to be happening.

What an idle lifestyle, I thought to myself. These people grew their barley, made *chang*, cooked their simple food. The women made cloth, but so few household chores occupied them. Without schools, the children played on the rooftops or in the terraced fields. They were filthy, their hands, ankles and necks blackened and encrusted with dirt. I knew that if they washed, their skin would be light brown.

Laughing to myself, I looked at my own hands; they had accumulated a layer of grime just since that morning's wash.

Life was hard in Wangri, and what seemed laziness to me was perhaps to them a rest from difficult travel between villages or spurts of intense work in the fields. During the last several days I was also beginning to feel the dulling effects of several weeks of spartan diet. I could only imagine what effects a lifetime of malnutrition could have on one's mental and physical capabilities. And malnutrition was just one of the factors that trapped them in a vicious cycle of poverty and poor health. *You must judge them by their own standards, Parker.*

Late in the afternoon we had more *chang*, then dinner. After dinner, a man in his late forties joined the group around our campfire on the dirt roof of Puraba's house. He asked a few questions, then launched into a tirade. I caught a few words, but couldn't understand much else. When he paused for a moment, Prem translated for me.

"He is angry, Parker Sahib, about the foreigners. He says that some foreigners are here without the proper papers. Even those who have permits, he doesn't like. The foreigners who study the snow leopards, he says they should not be here."

"Why does he say that? What are his reasons? What are they doing here that he doesn't like?"

Ever loyal, Akaal Bahadur and Jeet Bahadur stood and began arguing with the man. Forceful gestures showed their anger and intense passions.

"He does not say why, Parker Sahib. He only says that the foreigners are stupid and ignorant."

The argument went on for almost an hour. Prem was unable to elicit any concrete answers from him. Finally the angry man stood up, shouted a few sentences, turned on his heel and faded into the night. I looked inquiringly at Prem.

"He says that he is going to Gum Gadhi tomorrow to talk to officials about a new bridge. He gave you a threat. He said he would teach you a lesson."

Puraba tried to ease the situation, telling Prem that the man, a former village official, was just blustering, trying to show off, to prove he still held some authority. But he also gave Prem more ominous news, which Prem related to me.

"Shera Punzo has been boasting. He told all the village people that we passed Gum Gadhi at night. And he has told them that we wish to travel to Dolpo."

"That useless little jerk," I said. "We told Puraba and Shera Punzo to keep quiet about that."

"He is too young, that boy," Prem said. "He wants to tell everyone how much money he makes, and how he cheated the police at Gum Gadhi."

Uncharacteristically, the anger rose inside of me and my hands clenched, yearning for Shera Punzo's throat. "Come to my tent, everybody."

Prem, Akaal Bahadur, Jeet Bahadur and I piled inside my tent. Prem was furious and I heard muttered curses under his breath.

"I think, Parker Sahib, that it is not possible to get porters here to go east into Dolpo. I think they are afraid of the mountains and also of demons."

"You're right, Prem. I don't think we can get anyone to go with us over Khapre La either."

"But if we can go over Khapre La, it will save many days," Prem countered.

"Without extra porters, we can't do it. We'll just have to go back through Gum Gadhi to Jumla."

"We don't like to do this, Parker Sahib. To go back."

"I don't like it either, but we can't afford to take any chances that the man was bluffing. We'll just have to head back towards Gum Gadhi as fast as we can to get there before he does. And we'll have to pass it again at night."

We went to bed unhappy, discouraged, angry. I couldn't get comfortable and didn't feel like sleep.

"Damn," I said, suddenly sitting upright. "And we'll have to go back to Dalphu to get our kerosene and stove. Shera Punzo left them there so he wouldn't have to carry them."

Our hopes of doing the high route, of going deep into the wilds of Dolpo, had been dashed. We now found ourselves at a dead end, unable for lack of porters to go east into Dolpo or south over Khapre La. My anger burned hot. I hadn't realized until now how much I wanted to take this high route through Dolpo. It was the most difficult, the furthest out, the purest line through the Himalayas. Ultimately, style was important to me.

Now I couldn't do that. And at least in part because some juvenile wanted to boast to anyone who would listen. All the frustrations of the trip—being unable to bus further west than Surkhet, J.B.'s injury, the porter problems, being alone, the need to avoid local authorities, periodic illness—built one atop the other, eroded my strength and will. Nothing, it seemed, happened as intended. The Himalayas continually forced us to alter our plans, to play it by ear, to take one thing at a time, one day at a time. Perhaps this was the lesson.

But now I didn't feel philosophical. Lying awake, the demons of frustration and doubt tormented me, taunted me, hunted for my weak spots. They would not leave me.

The entire village turned out for our departure the next morning, including Puraba's grandmother. Her bent figure appeared on the furthest roof in the village, standing with hands pressed together, tongue sticking out in the traditional Tibetan greeting. As we descended to the Langu Khola, I turned back several times, and each time I saw her standing there, watching us through half-seeing eyes.

We reached Dalphu at one o'clock and headed to the mayor's house to drink more of his golden *chang*. He greeted us from his rooftop and spoke excitedly. Prem translated.

"Yesterday two people from the snow leopard camp came here to drink *chang*."

"The *pradhan panch*'s *chang* is the best in the region, obviously."

"But they drank too much and when they wanted to go home, they were too drunk. They fell many times. So they returned and last night they slept here. But they left this morning."

"That's a shame. I'm disappointed to have missed them. And now we're not even going to have time to visit their camp. I'm sure they could have used the company. I know I could."

Before leaving the next morning, we sold our ten liters of kerosene to the mayor. We were getting desperate for money, and we could do without the weight. Prem convinced me that firewood would be readily available along the route ahead. I neglected to press him too hard on this point, but I wondered how he could be so confident about it. Besides, we weren't sure where we were going after retracing our steps back towards Jumla.

The backtracking had struck a sour chord in all of us. Kathmandu was over thirty days away, a depressingly long time to contemplate. All that work, day by day, trekking through canyons, over passes. Wangri had been a dead end for us; from here on out our journey seemed as though it would be anticlimactic.

Our first hurdle in getting to Kartik was retracing our steps up and down 10,000 feet and crossing the same slide areas we had crossed before. The day's intense sun reflected from the exposed rock, burning our faces as we struggled through contour after contour into the side canyons.

*Puraba's grandmother pressed her hands together and stuck out her tongue in
the traditional Tibetan greeting.*

Then we came to the slide area we had traversed days earlier. We glanced uphill apprehensively. Akaal Bahadur, having looked up and seen nothing coming, launched himself across the danger zone. Then, as though it had been waiting, a football-size rock hurtled down right at his head. His bulky load proved both hindrance and salvation. It kept him from dodging, but pulling his head in like a turtle, he swiftly turned his load toward the hillside. The rock seemed almost vengeful as it bounced off the basket and smashed into Akaal Bahadur's arm, tearing through his shirt and wounding him. He barely hesitated as he scurried swiftly to safety. After the rest of us crossed, we stopped long enough for me to bandage Akaal Bahadur's shoulder. And then we moved on.

We reached Kartik at dusk, tired and thirsty. Once again we pitched our tents on the roof of a house. I was grateful for the absence of tourists. In Khumbu and other places visited by many trekkers, householders charge for camping. They also sell firewood, sometimes asking sixty or eighty rupees for enough to cook a meal. Here we were given wood, and only sometimes would people ask for a rupee or two.

Trekking groups in eastern Nepal must by law use kerosene or other cooking fuel, not wood, to help prevent deforestation. Unfortunately, there was no such rule for the porters that accompany treks, and there are sometimes twice or three times as many porters as trekkers, plus camp staff. The porters use wood to cook their meals, so the deforestation continues, even in supposedly protected areas.

In our desire to travel quickly, we covered the distance to Gum Gadhi in two days, one and a half days faster than our outward journey. When we camped just short of Gum Gadhi, the porters thought it time for a celebration because Shera Punzo and Puraba would be leaving us soon. Shera Punzo saw the celebration as a farewell in his honor, but the rest of us would be celebrating for a different reason.

In a small village nearby, Prem bargained for three chickens, alive and squawking, and five bottles of *chang* for our feast. When it came time to slaughter the birds, Jeet Bahadur asked Puraba to do the honors.

Puraba recoiled in horror. As a devout Buddhist, he couldn't possibly kill anything. Akaal Bahadur turned to Shera Punzo. He, too, backed off, shaking his head. Disgusted with what he considered Buddhist squeamishness, Jeet Bahadur grabbed a knife in one hand

and a chicken in the other. Pinning the squawking animal to a rock, he sawed through its neck, blood squirting everywhere, the chicken flapping in desperation.

"*Om mani padme humji, om mani padme humji,*" Puraba chanted as loudly as he could over the horrendous noises made by the dying chickens. Over and over, until all three chickens were slaughtered, Puraba kept up his monologue of prayer.

The thought of killing may have been abhorrent to Puraba and Shera Punzo, but when it came time to eat the birds, they were first in line. They apparently reasoned that although killing animals was disgusting, as long as someone else did it there was no sense in letting good meat go to waste.

I drank too much *chang* and sneaked off to bed at nine, leaving the party still going strong. I planned to be up with Prem in six hours to make a nighttime passage through Gum Gadhi. The others would follow at daylight. I tried not to dwell on Shera Punzo's loose tongue, which forced us to go at night yet once again. I wasn't willing to risk the chance that the man from Wangri hadn't tipped off the police.

Prem and I moved out quickly in the chilled darkness, just after 3:00 A.M. We walked rapidly along the flat trail as it paralleled the Mugu Karnali River and made the five miles to Gum Gadhi in an hour. The cold, hard light of the full moon was our guide. Once again I was amazed at the brilliance of the moon so far away from city lights. Our eyes adjusted easily and we could see every rock, every undulation in the trail.

Below Gum Gadhi we left the Mugu Karnali and followed the tributary Lumsa Khola. At the confluence, Prem led the way across on a small wooden bridge. Just as I stepped onto the bridge, my foot broke through the boards, trapping my leg at midcalf.

As I tried to free my leg, my knee twisted and pain shot up my leg. "Prem," I called. I saw his receding figure move on across the bridge. "Prem," I yelled again. But the roar of the river drowned my calls and Prem kept going, the dark shadows swallowing him up.

Taking a deep breath, I tried to work my leg out, but intense pain stopped me. The wood pressured my calf and shin; my knee throbbed. I grabbed for the post at the end of the bridge. Using it as leverage, and gritting my teeth, I twisted and pulled and finally yanked my leg out of the hole.

With my leg free, I let go of the end post. That's when I saw that my hand had been resting on a crude carving of a female holding her labia open with her hands. A *dhauliya* figure found everywhere in this region, she protected the villages from evil of all kinds. These figures had survived from ancient animistic religious beliefs. Under different circumstances, I might have thought it either funny or grotesque, but now I just slumped against the post and tried to catch my breath.

Realizing that I wasn't behind him, Prem returned to look for me. He was relieved that I hadn't slipped off the trail or into the river, and he helped me clean up my scrapes. My knee throbbed. I tested it and then gingerly stood. At least I could still walk.

The moon set over the ridges to the west just at dawn. Soon the sun rose to greet and warm us. A steep and tiring ascent brought us to our prearranged stopping place. By eight-thirty we had covered twelve miles. We stopped and spent the day in the open loft of a trailside teahouse. We munched on our high-altitude rations and slept.

We camped near the teahouse that night and discussed a change in plans. Instead of heading directly back to Jumla, we decided to head further east towards Dunai in the Dolpo district. This would avoid the police checkpost in Jumla and also save a few days' travel time.

The next morning it was time to pay off Shera Punzo. Customarily we would have paid him his salary plus a tip—*baksheesh*—but considering his laziness and the trouble he had caused us, Shera Punzo would not get a rupee more than agreed upon in Jumla weeks ago. We called Puraba and Shera Punzo into our tent.

I had Prem translate my sentiments to Shera Punzo. "You are lazy. You have gossiped when you were told not to, you have carried less than anyone else, including me. You have asked for more food and clothing. We will pay you what we have agreed upon, 640 rupees, less your advances and no more. You will get no *baksheesh* because you don't deserve it. Do you understand?"

Shera Punzo looked nonplussed. He turned and whined to Prem. "Parker Sahib," Prem said incredulously. "This boy says he wants some money for *chang*!"

I clenched my fist and shook it in Shera Punzo's face. "Get out of here now. Get out of this campsite and don't look back."

He needed no translation and left immediately.

Puraba, looking alarmed at this outburst, was calmed by Prem. We made it clear to Puraba that we were dissatisfied only with Shera Punzo and not with him. He had been a good porter and a faithful friend and this was appreciated. Although we asked him to go with us to Kathmandu, he declined, saying he would leave us in a few days.

By nine o'clock we were on our way again. The next three days would take us through an area without villages, and we were running low on food. By midafternoon we reached the last village in which we could possibly buy supplies, Mandu.

From a distance, it was a beautiful village surrounded by lush green fields and trees in full bloom, their pink and white blossoms scattering in the wind. But when we entered the village what seemed idyllic from a distance proved squalid at close range. We smelled no perfume of delicate blossoms, but rather the stench of dirt and feces that lay everywhere amidst thousands of buzzing flies. We turned into a central courtyard, dusty and full of debris.

A woman, a huge goiter swelling her neck, pounded millet into dust amidst the filth. The children stared at us. Their clothes, if they wore any at all, were rags.

The bloated bellies of the children, their thin reddish hair and scabrous scalps were signs of malnutrition. Two small girls sat side by side on a pile of pine needles. I set down my pack and took out my camera, thinking they would make a nice composition. The girl on the left raised one arm to rub her eye, but she had no hand. I lowered my camera and stared at the end of her arm—a a dirt-blackened stump. Leprosy had left no vestige of a hand. Now her limb was useless except as a wand to wave at the numerous flies that gathered around her. Averting my eyes from the child, I looked at the girl on the right. She sat with dulled eyes, oblivious to her surroundings, perhaps mentally retarded or just malnourished. It was no longer a nice composition, but rather a grim record as I took their picture, two children of Mandu sitting side by side on the bed of pine needles.

Prem had been trying for fifteen minutes to buy some food. "Parker Sahib, they say they have no food. I think this is true."

"Keep trying, Prem. We need something else for the next three days, even if it's only some millet, anything."

Finally he found someone who would sell us a few potatoes and enough millet dust for two or three days. He also came to me with another request.

"Parker Sahib, could we buy some *ganja* (marijuana) for the porters? This woman has some. It costs only two rupees."

I followed Prem and the woman into the ground floor of a dwelling

Distended bellies, thin reddish hair falling out in clumps—the signs of malnutrition in the children of Mandu.

Leprosy had left no vestiges of a hand on this child of Mandu.

which smelled worse than the courtyard outside. The woman bent down and scraped a pile of debris up off the floor and filled a small plastic bag with a horrible mixture of sticks, chicken shit and mari-juana leftovers. I thought that if it kept the porters happy, then I was happy. There was about a half ounce of the vile-looking stuff and I wondered how long it would last.

Leaving Mandu, we followed a newly constructed trail up Riyan Lekh, ascending through a lush pine and hemlock forest. We made camp above 10,000 feet in a small open area sheltered by towering pines several hundred years old. The loam underfoot cushioned each step, muffling the sounds of setting camp. The Nepalese called this the "jungle," and it had an ominous connotation to them. Danger and bandits, lions and tigers and bears.

Two children of Mandu on a bed of pine needles.

Their fears had a degree of validity. Bandits and plunderers, particularly the Tibetan nomads, did roam these forests. But we faced far less chance of a confrontation now than in the past. And the same for attacks by leopards and bears. Few such large mammals remained in the Himalayas. But at dusk the forest came alive. Animals reclaimed the land through which we trespassed. Flying squirrels floated from tree to tree above us in an eerie, silent aerial display. Just beyond the light of our campfire, we felt the presence of unseen eyes, heard the hooting of owls and the barking of the deer.

The forest and its animals lifted my depression somewhat, but I couldn't entirely shake the melancholy with which Mandu had filled me. Amidst those lush fields and groves of fruit trees, roaring streams and lofty pines, such disease and famine. The United Mission workers in Jumla had told me the problem was not lack of water or arable land, but education. Now I knew they were right, for I had seen it that day. The people of Mandu knew nothing of basic hygiene or effective farming practices. And the lack of education made it almost impossible to effect meaningful change.

The missionaries had told me the story of a Peace Corps volunteer who had brought vegetables into the area a few years ago. He had taught the people how to grow them, and also how to prepare seeds for the following year. Just before the harvest, however, his father became ill and he returned to the U.S. When he returned to Nepal a month later, the people had harvested and eaten all the vegetables, saving nothing for seed. When he asked them why, they replied that it was too much trouble. They had lived without vegetables for many years, and could do so again. Such attitudes would take many years to change. Could one Peace Corps volunteer really expect to do much in a year or two?

I thought of my home town, Darien, Connecticut, an enclave surrounded by a neat white picket fence. Republican ladies having teas, good little boys and girls going to school, people opening their pretty shops in town or riding off to the city every day to well-paying jobs. We knew no poverty in our world, no prejudice against our neighbors—against whom in our homogeneous society could we show prejudice? We all led healthy lives, got our teeth straightened and enjoyed every opportunity to realize our full potential. I thought of the contrast between my older sister, Betsy, born mentally retarded, and the children of Mandu. Unlike them, Betsy had attended school and had a small army of trained professionals working with her, guiding her and helping her to become a productive member of society. She had received the best medical care available and now, in adulthood, is, I believe, happy. Those children of Mandu who perhaps shared her disability would not be so lucky. Without food and proper medical care, it seemed unlikely that they would even live to adulthood. Now they simply sat and stared blankly at a bleak future.

I fell asleep that night, troubled by what I had seen. But my last thoughts were of more immediate problems: we had only a two-day supply of food left. We had to continue to make good time to reach the place called Chaurgaon to resupply, or . . .

CHAPTER
SEVEN

THE GREAT FOREST, RIYAN LEKH
Monday, March 19, 1984

THE unmistakable aroma of marijuana woke me in the morning. *That's it. We won't get anywhere for the next two weeks, not till all that stuff is gone.*

Akaal Bahadur and Jeet Bahadur giggled, happy as schoolboys with a forbidden treat. Out on the trail, however, they were high-spirited and nothing more. When we came to difficult sections, I feared they would stumble. But quietly and deliberately, they took their time and carefully negotiated even the most intricate passages.

Our gradually ascending path lay through still more pine-canopied forest. Groves of ten-foot-high bamboo grew beneath the canopy. Then, just after lunch, the trail petered out at the crest of Riyan Lekh. Prem and I sat down with the map.

"Look," I pointed at the map. "If we head southeast this way, we should intersect with this trail."

"Yes, Parker Sahib, if this map is right."

"We'll have to trust it." I looked out ahead at the proposed route. "We'll just have to bushwhack, that's all."

Ridges separated a series of verdant, forested bowls. But snow, ice and mud covered the north sides of each ridge, making conditions

even more difficult for the porters with their bulky loads. And slowing our progress even more, the porters stopped for frequent smokes, rolling their marijuana cigarettes with oily birchbark instead of paper.

Near evening, we came to a small khola. While trying to cross it on a log, I fell in. *No harm done, just a little wet.* But as I shook out my pack, pulling things out to dry, I found a roll of film I had finished but had neglected to put back into its watertight plastic canister. Ruined. Wet through. I checked the others. All dry, except one with its snap top lid slightly ajar. As I pulled the top off, water trickled out. Another roll lost. It was always effort enough to prod myself. *Parker, take out your camera, take that picture.* Now I had lost two rolls of film. I sighed, and wondered what images I would never see again.

We had a one-day supply of food left.

Next morning, fifteen minutes after breaking camp, we crossed a faint path that ultimately ran into the trail on the map leading to the village of Chaurgaon. We lunched beside the Sinja Khola, the same river we had camped beside many miles downstream the day after leaving Jumla seventeen days before. We followed the gently undulating trail through the jungle for several hours, until, at three-thirty, we broke out into a high meadow. A long, broad valley stretched for twenty miles below us and off to the southeast. Chaurgaon, our destination, lay at the near side of the valley, about four miles away, and to the east rose the 22,000-foot peaks of the Patrasi Himal. Snow-covered Hinchuli Patan, 19,750 feet, loomed to the south.

The trail descended gently for two miles through lush conifer forest. At a split in the trail, we stopped. One path, directly in front of us, headed towards Chaurgaon. I started down the trail but fifty yards on turned at Puraba's shout from behind. He signaled that we should follow the path leading off to the right, towards Jumla.

"We can't go that way," I shouted back at the others. "We don't want to go towards Jumla. We want to go to Chaurgaon." They didn't move, so I backtracked to the fork.

"Parker Sahib," Prem said apologetically. "We told Puraba that we would go to the village of Chaubesi, near the village where he has another house. It is not the same place as Chaurgaon."

It was a long, two-hour walk along a stream called the Chaubesi Khola. We arrived at the village at three-thirty, tired and hungry.

That evening, while drinking *rakshi* with some of the locals, I learned that Chaubesi was also known as Luma or Lum, which I located on our map. Once again I cursed the map makers of Kathmandu and wondered if we might be better off with no map. Distances and names were often inaccurate, trails and villages appeared in the wrong places, contour lines bore little resemblance to reality.

The next day was a rest day in Chaubesi/Lum. Early in the morning, Akaal Bahadur and Jeet Bahadur set off to Jumla to restock our rice, sugar and spice supplies. Replacement batteries for our Chinese flashlights completed the shopping list. The men were also to look for another porter.

Puraba left us that morning heading for Larpa, a village an hour's walk away. There he had another house where his wife waited for him. We paid Puraba 690 rupees and said our thanks.

"*Tapaai asa maanchhe*" ('You are a good man'), I told him in Nepali.

He grinned his appreciation, then swiftly moved out on the trail. I watched him go. *A gentle hardworking man.* I would miss him.

At eight that evening, Akaal Bahadur and Jeet Bahadur returned from Jumla. They had found the necessary food supplies, but no additional porter. For their extra effort, I bought them a bottle of *rakshi* and we made sure they had a hearty meal. They had earned it.

Early the next morning, Prem and Akaal Bahadur set out through the village in search of a porter. They returned at eleven o'clock empty-handed.

"Parker Sahib," Prem said. "No one wants to go with us because they are afraid to walk back to their village alone. But we have told everyone. We will wait for a time and see."

A few minutes later, a man in his late twenties dressed in black jodhpurs, dusty suitcoat and black *topee* arrived at our camp. He was willing to travel with us the entire way to Pokhara if we could guarantee his safe return.

"Tell him, Prem, that we will fly him to Jumla."

"Yes. He will go if he can fly in an airplane," Prem announced happily. "He has never been in an airplane."

And so we hired Auri Bahadur Raut, a Chetri.

Within the hour we were once again on the trail, following the open river valley to the southeast. A few miles from Chaubesi/Lum, we crossed the trail that came from Wangri over Khapre La.

"Look, Prem," I pointed up the trail towards Khapre La. "There's the trail. Just think of how many days it would have taken us from

Wangri if we had come this way. Three, maybe four. But it took us ten."

"If we had been able to hire porters in Wangri . . ."

"All that way. All for the lack of two decent porters. Don't remind me. I'll get mad all over again."

The next day, the thirty-ninth since leaving Surkhet, we camped near the village of Chautri where Prem convinced a villager to sell us a chicken. As soon as the squawking bird arrived in camp, the butchering took place. Akaal Bahadur and Jeet Bahadur cleaned the chicken thoroughly and divided the pieces into three different dishes.

The first course included the heart, lungs, liver, kidneys, brain and intestines. Fiery red chilies made a mouth-burning but tasty stew. For the second course we had the legs fried. The final course consisted of all the rest of the chicken, hacked with a *kukri* into small pieces, bones and all, and made into a curry. We wasted nothing.

I bit into the stringy chicken as deep as I could get my teeth. Then I sucked every bit of meat off the bones. Amused, I thought of all the meat I had left on bones over the years, good food that went wasted into garbage cans.

The next day we continued heading southeast, then turned south to struggle up the steep but short Mauri Lekh. The north-facing slope presented a quagmire of snow and mud melting in the afternoon sun. I gave my ice axe to Jeet Bahadur and hacked a functional walking stick from the underbrush for myself.

We sat and rested near a *chorten* that guarded the crest of the ridge. Prayer flags snapped briskly in the rising afternoon winds. "*Om mani padme hum*" ('Hail to the jewel in the lotus') hurtled endlessly, a perpetual muffled prayer that hastened before the breeze across Dolpo, Mugu and on into Tibet. The glaciered peaks of the Kanjiroba Himal played a power game of hide-and-seek with the rapidly building storm clouds. A few heavy drops of rain and hail spattered on the surrounding rocks, and the distant reports of thunder spurred us to retreat several hundred feet down to the treeline.

The mighty Bheri Khola, 9,000 feet deep, lay two ridges away, although the river's course was visible for many miles. Following the descending trail until almost dusk, we arrived at the village of Chaurikot, where we set camp for the night.

Early in the morning, we followed a wide trail hugging the steep river valley. Two thousand feet below, the seething waters swept by.

The morning was still and clear, and by nine we felt the full heat of the sun. Beside a tumbling stream at the edge of the trail, we stopped for a meal. Before eating, I slid off my pack and dug out a bar of soap. I stripped to the waist, hanging my shirt over a bush to dry the sweat. Then, luxuriating in the cold, clean water, I washed my head and scrubbed my upper body for the first time in five days.

By noon, the winds had risen and the daily build-up of thick, bilious cumulus clouds over the Himal to the north and east had begun. Above us eagles and falcons soared with the thermals to thousands of feet over our heads, then in single mad downwind dashes covered what might take us a day or more to do on foot. Before we finished, a half dozen Tibetans with their monstrous full-blooded yaks stopped to share our stream. As we set out again, swirling dust devils played around our feet.

Far below, another trail wended its way along the river's edge. Destination: Jarjakot, six days to the southwest. I stopped, contemplating this fragile path. Auri Bahadur had traveled this way many times, and he had told us about the flat, easy trail along the river's edge. From Jarjakot, the route led due east through Dhorpatan, then Beni and Baglung.

"That's it, Prem," I said. "The last chance to go the easy way."

"O Parker Sahib, it would be too hot."

"Yes, and too boring. If we had been able to go to the north, through Phapagaon . . ."

"So which way do we go?"

"This way." I waved with a broad, vague gesture towards the east.

Prem gave me one of his crooked smiles and nodded with understanding. Though we had not discussed it, we both knew we would go on through Dolpo with little food, no guide and our all-but-useless map.

Prem and I quickened the pace, hoping to outrace the coming storm. The trail descended gently through the open fields of the Buddhist village of Rimi and on towards Kaigaon and Hurikot on the edge of the Bheri Khola. Luckily, the rains held off until we reached the valley floor and the shelter of a crudely constructed building beside the trail. I quickly ducked under the porch and was leaning against an upright post when Prem arrived just a minute later. He looked up and translated the sign above our heads: "Kaigaon Secondary School, Dolpo District." My surprise at finding a school here was overshadowed by the realization that we had slipped into the most restricted area of Nepal; we had entered Dolpo.

Heavy rain splashed against the earth as the porters arrived some twenty minutes after us, completely drenched. We dashed over a wooden bridge and found shelter for the night in the empty front room of a small abandoned house. In a rough hearth dug into the dirt floor, we built a fire, brewed tea and were enjoying the warmth when Akaal Bahadur rose, pulled a tent from his *doko* and left the smoky room.

"Akaal Bahadur, where are you going?" I asked as he disappeared in the rain.

"He is putting up the tent, Parker Sahib," Prem answered for him.

"But it's pouring out there!"

"It is too smoky in here. He will put the tent up for you and for me to sleep in."

Exasperated, I went to the door and looked out. Through the obscuring downpour I saw Akaal Bahadur struggling alone with the tent. He could put it up by himself, he had done it many times before. But I had to stop myself from going out into the rain to help him. I knew I wasn't wanted, my offer of help would be refused. So I just watched as Akaal Bahadur erected the tent, then dug a small trench around the edges to deflect the runoff.

"Prem, I've said this before. We can't be sahib and porter, we can't be master and servant. Not here."

"But Akaal Bahadur wants to do this, it is his job."

"Where I come from, we all share. I don't always have to have bed tea, or the best place around the fire, or the best portions of food."

Prem looked at me. His eyes—gentle, silent, pleading—tried to tell me that here things were different.

"Look how wet he is," I started to protest again.

Prem reached over and touched my arm. "You must forgive us, Parker Sahib, for it is our way."

Defeated, I slumped down on the small carpet we had placed next to the fire. His reply had been so simple and so complete. It was their way. How could I pretend to alter anything so fundamental?

Five minutes later Akaal Bahadur returned, dripping wet. I started to get up, to offer him my warm place by the fire. But the weight of centuries, of their way, pushed me back to my appointed place. He smiled at me. Despite the mud clinging to his feet, the rain-slick hair plastered to his face, his worn clothes soaked completely through, nothing could detract from the man's dignity. He had completed his task; I had not shamed him by interfering. Joining us by the fire, he stretched out his hands to warm them.

Within an hour we were set upon by a dozen villagers, all wanting to know in that Asian way where we had come from and where we intended to go.

"*License chhaa*?" ('Do you have a permit?')

"*Ho, license chhaa*" ('Yes, we have a permit'), we answered again and again.

We offered *chang* to every visitor and the villagers soon became our friends. They repeatedly informed us that we needed special permission to be here or to continue further into Dolpo. We were consistently evasive in our replies, but equally insistent that we had trekking permits. We must have finally convinced them that all the necessary documents were in order, for the awkward questions stopped.

Late in the afternoon, the steady rains changed to snow and hail, and three inches blanketed the ground by sundown. Several pitchers of thick *chang* took the edge off our discomfort.

After a meal of rice and potatoes, we sat around the fire in the small, smoky room and rehashed the events of the last two days. Prem commented on the wild appearance of the group of Tibetans from Lhasa, the ones who had shared our lunch spot earlier in the day.

Through the *chang* haze, pictures began to flash through my mind, an eerie late-night slide show. I saw myself barechested, washing by the stream. Then a slow zoom focused on my necklace lying on a rock where I had put it after taking it off to wash. That picture now made me grab at my chest. My necklace! Aghast, I realized that I had left it at the edge of the stream. Hung on the chain was a silver good-luck scarab from Susan and, much worse if lost, a military-style dog tag with my name, nationality, social security number and blood type.

"Prem. I left my necklace by the stream. I have to go back to get it. I don't know how I could have been so stupid to leave it there. I'll get up early so we won't lose any time."

Prem turned to Akaal Bahadur and said a few words.

"Akaal Bahadur will go with you, Parker Sahib," Prem said.

"We will go at three o'clock," I said to Akaal Bahadur as I made my way outside to my tent.

Snow still fell gently as I ducked inside. Setting my watch, I fell asleep instantly.

My wristwatch alarm resonated from underneath my makeshift pillow through to my head, giving me a painful reminder of last night's *chang*. Unzipping the tent a few inches I peered at the star-filled sky. The storm had passed, leaving in the still night four inches of frozen snow. I dressed quickly, stuffed my pockets with the few remaining snacks from our British high-altitude rations and went to awaken Akaal Bahadur.

Within minutes we were off in the predawn darkness, silent except for our steady breathing and the crunching of snow underfoot. Without packs we moved rapidly and soon I fell behind Akaal Bahadur. Breathing in labored gasps, I strained to maintain his pace as he skipped effortlessly up the trail. We had been on trek for forty days and I believed I was in excellent condition. But a lifetime of porter's labor had given Akaal Bahadur fitness far surpassing mine. If he chose, he could have left me floundering within three hundred yards.

He danced, I struggled up the gently ascending trail for three miles before stopping for a break. As I gulped down draughts of air, he lit a cigarette as if to taunt me further. As soon as he had it glowing, he set off once again at the same blistering pace.

The eastern sky lightened and the stars disappeared one by one. We passed through two small villages, eerily silent at that early hour. But then, as though given a signal, roosters at farmhouses scattered along the mountainside greeted the new day in crowing unison.

We covered the seven miles to our previous lunch spot in an hour and a half, and my hopes were high that the foul weather had dissuaded anyone from lingering along the stream's edge. Once there, I went immediately to the rock where I had carefully placed the necklace. Nothing. It was gone. We cut leafy branches and swept away the accumulated snow from the ground. Nothing.

Angry, tired and embarrassed at having dragged Akaal Bahadur all this way for nothing, I brushed the snow off a small rock and sat at the stream's edge. Swollen now from the rains of the day before, the stream carried bits of decaying leaves, twigs and shards of schist, sweeping them towards the Bheri River far below. Could my necklace be traveling on this same course? Could it be tumbling, rolling, catapulting down to the Bheri and beyond, to the mighty, sacred Ganges?

More likely, it had found a new home around a Tibetan's neck. The

Khampa traders we had encountered here the day before were heading to Lhasa. That it might find a home in this forbidden city was of some solace, for it might see places I could only hope to visit one day.

We snacked on fig cookies and the last few pieces of chocolate from the rations kit before beginning our return to Kaigaon. The sun was now upon us, turning the snow under our feet to mud as we dashed along. It took less than an hour for our return journey. Prem had our first meal ready for us, and we ate quickly. Akaal Bahadur and I were on the trail with the others by ten-thirty, having already walked fourteen miles.

Our route ascended to a ridgeline just south of Kaigaon. Sloppy with mud, the track switchbacked up through broad open fields interspersed with cool shaded stands of hemlock and birch. Our presence startled into flight a huge flock of sparrowlike birds. They flew as one, changing directions in midflight several times before settling among the moss-laden oaks. As we stopped to rest from the midday sun, I roused them back into flight with a well-hurled rock and watched them wheel, spin and turn as one again and again. I looked for the leader, the headman of the tribe that dictated the erratic but unified movement of this large flock of birds. Within a few minutes, though, I realized that I searched in vain, for with each change of direction the lead bird became the last and the last became the newly followed leader.

Another half hour of walking brought us to a hogback. Across a deeply forested valley, the snow-covered peaks blocked our view to the south. A fresh breeze soothed us and dried our sweat into salty streaks on our faces. As we rested on the ridgecrest, a local Chetri villager stopped to talk.

"He gives us a warning, Parker Sahib," said Prem. "He says that the land ahead has Khampas. These men are from Tibet, from the east. They are nomads, they follow their sheep and goats and yaks."

"Like the Tibetans we saw yesterday?"

"The same. He says we should be careful, not to trust them because they will steal from us. He says we should be careful in the night, that we should not camp next to them."

"Sounds like a good idea to me," I said and started to leave.

Prem remained engaged in a heated discussion with the Chetri. I could catch little except Prem's repeated firm, "No!"

Then I caught the gist of the conversation. 'Shoes, socks, boots, sugar or cigarettes' were his demands. I laughed. For what? Just for telling us to watch out for thieving Tibetans?

Coincidentally, just then three Tibetans, one astride a beautiful white Tibetan horse, approached us from up the trail. They smiled broadly, their perfectly white, even teeth offset by one gold tooth each. When they stopped abreast of us, the sickly sweet, pungent smell of those who never wash came with them. They spoke to us in broken Nepali.

"Where are you going?"

"Where are *you* going?" Prem turned the question.

After a few desultory comments their attention settled on our porters' *dokos*, chock-full of interesting and enticing new objects. While Akaal Bahadur, Jeet Bahadur and Auri Bahadur sat under the nearby trees, puffing *beedies*, cheap cigarettes, and unaware of what was happening, Tibetan hands greedily delved into our baskets. Exclaiming with wide-eyed wonder about utensils, knives, sugar, plastic storage bottles and rice, they fingered every object. "How much for this, and for this?" they asked, holding each object aloft.

Inexplicably, just then Prem hoisted his pack and began heading up the trail, leaving me to deal with the rapidly deteriorating situation.

"Not for sale!" I shouted in Nepali, stepping forward and showing them my ice axe gripped in my hand. "Akaal Bahadur, Jeet Bahadur. *Jaau!*" ('Let's go!') I used my best angry-sahib voice in a desperate attempt to get their attention.

Looking up from their smokes, the porters now realized the danger and jumped to their feet. Snatching items from out of the grasping hands of the Tibetans, they repacked and secured their loads.

"How much for this?" came the last bargaining demand from one of the nomads.

"Thirty-five rupees, last price," I said forcefully as I reached for the empty leaky kerosene container in his hands.

"Thirty-two rupees."

"No, thirty-five rupees." I pulled the container away from him.

This last demand was answered by the Tibetans with hard, leering smiles.

"*Jaau, jaau,*" I urged the porters. "Pick up your loads and let's go."

I took up the rear with my ice axe still held determinedly and in obvious view. Before a bend in the trail, I turned to see the Tibetans still staring after us as we followed the trail out of their sight.

In the high mountain forest, the late afternoon sun cast a golden light onto the green of hemlock trees. As I climbed up towards 12,000 feet, the air cooled. The trail contoured along the hill-side, slipping into four heavily wooded side canyons before again emerging.

Beside a rushing stream in the deepest recess of one of these side canyons, I stopped to catch my breath. I sat on the trunk of a huge, downed hemlock, resting the weight of my pack on the stub of a broken branch. The stream emerged from a dense forest and above me I could see its source, a vast, treeless alpine meadow that formed the northern ridge of the valley. To the southeast, this ridge met the 15,000-foot, snow-covered peaks across the valley. A deep notch marked the Balangra Pass, a natural gateway to Tibrikot, Dunai and the forbidden interior of Dolpo.

Stampeding hooves jolted my attention from the view. Whirling, I saw two enormous yaks rushing down the stream bed—right at me! In a panic, I jumped from my seat and leapt aside just before the yaks thundered by, their huge shaggy bulks passing directly over the spot where I had been seated. I think now that if I had stayed put, they would have veered off to another course. But at that moment my heart pounded with adrenaline. I wondered what had frightened them as they hit the trail below me.

"*Namaste.*"

Startled, I swung around. I looked into the gold-toothed smile of a man about my age, but many inches taller and broader. He wore a patched and dirty Tibetan *chuba*, and a long Tibetan knife with a silver handle and sheath hung from his hip next to a small silver-and-leather purse. His oily black hair, braided with red yarn and wound around his head, framed his high-cheekboned face.

He laughed at my discomfort at being surprised, but then his throaty laughter subsided into a chilling smile. In broken Nepali he asked where I came from. And then, without waiting for a reply, "*Kahaa jane ho?*" ('Where are you going?')

Another question followed, frightening in its transparency, "Are you alone?"

It was asked hopefully. Alone, I was vulnerable. I thought about the Chetri's warning and the stories of other foreigners who had been murdered for their money, their cameras, their boots.

"No," I answered in Nepali. "I have a guide ahead and many porters behind me."

He looked both directions along the trail and, seeing no one, smiled at me again. I'm not sure he believed me.

He pointed to his mouth. *"Ausadhi?"* ('Medicine?')

"Ausadhi chaainna" ('No medicine').

He moved past me and strode slowly up the steep trail. With his hands clasped behind his back and shoulders hunched, he walked in the splay-footed duck walk so characteristic of the Tibetan nomads. He motioned me to follow, indicating that he had friends further up the trail.

Wonderful, more of them. Pretending that my twenty-kilo pack was too heavy, I slackened my pace, hoping my newfound companion would go on ahead.

Looking up, I spotted Prem several hundred yards ahead and above me in an open pasture. I swung my arms wildly, frantically indicating he should wait for me. I continued slowly, but my guide stopped every few yards to let me catch up. Another Tibetan emerged from the bushes beside the trail. He was equally as tall and wide, although much older and stooped. He fell in directly behind me and so close that I could smell his fetid breath and unwashed body.

I stopped several times and wheezed in an exaggerated manner, indicating with my hand to the Tibetan that he should go on ahead and not wait for me. He spoke in broken Nepali, saying that he was in no hurry, he would wait for me. I sat on a rotten log and with slow deliberation hacked at it with my ice axe.

Prem was waiting for me on a grassy knoll. He smiled as I dropped down beside him, heaving a sigh of relief. Behind me came the two Tibetans with three yaks and a calf in tow. They were camped a few hundred yards ahead amidst an ancient moss-covered scree field, and they urged us to join them for the night.

Prem declined politely, saying that we were headed for the pass and hoped to cross before sundown—an obvious lie since it was now almost 5:00 P.M. and a good two hours to the pass. And our porters were still another half hour behind us. Nevertheless, we walked quickly past the Tibetans' camp and on up the trail. Prem walked on even faster as he began his daily search for firewood, water, a place to camp for the night. I let him go.

It was here, as I walked on alone, that I met a young Tibetan mother and her child. I stopped in a silent grove of ancient trees and watched a red panda bounding along the trail.

The sight of the lovely and innocent mother nursing her gift of new life, of the rare red panda surrounded by the moss-laden trees—all juxtaposed with the massive and eternal mountains, dramatized the fleeting, transient nature of life. My environment had never before moved me to such thoughts, such powerfully felt emotion. As I sat there, tears slid down my cheeks.

Two tremendous lammergeiers cruised the steep slope, the wind rustling their feathers as they passed less than sixty feet over my head. Wingtip to wingtip, the bearded vultures flew in unison, one a perfect shadow of the other as they searched hopefully along the slope. They thermaled upward, ascending rapidly in a tight spiral. I followed their moves, watching intently for several minutes until they were 2,000 feet above the ridgeline. I blinked twice, and the two specks were lost in the blue afternoon sky.

As the giant birds disappeared, I heard the familiar Tamang folk songs I had enjoyed so many times before in eastern Nepal in October and November. Then I saw the porters appear from out of a side valley half a mile away. Akaal Bahadur and Jeet Bahadur, prodigious vocalists, sometimes sang for hours on end as they carried their loads up and down the valleys of Nepal. Now I heard Auri Bahadur chime in on a song.

The wind increased, and as the sun dropped behind a snow-covered *lekh*, the temperature dropped towards freezing. Hurrying up the trail, I found Prem at a splendid campsite a mile below the head of the pass. Beneath an ancient oak tree bedecked with hanging moss, a small fire already burned. When the porters arrived, they quickly dropped their loads, pitched the tents and scurried to gather firewood.

After a meal of rice and *tarkaari* (curried vegetables), I slipped into my sleeping bag. It had been a long day full of inspiring contrasts. By the light of the fire coming through the open tent flaps, I inspected the map and the next few days' route. Tibrikot, Dunai, Tarakot. Police. Military. The next week promised to be interesting. And long.

Our spirits were high, however. Tomorrow we would cross the Balangra Pass and head further into Dolpo. The challenge excited us all. The sheer sport of it had Akaal Bahadur in his highest spirits of our journey to the west. His boisterous attitude infected all of us, and smiles circled the campfire that night. *Let's just do it well, fellows, because I for one have no desire to see the interior of a Nepalese jail.*

Sinking into the warmth of my sleeping bag, I thought again of the

Tibetan mother and her child. She seemed so at peace with herself, her surroundings. She didn't fight the natural forces of her world, she lived with them. After all these months trekking, I was beginning to see some of the rewards of this way of life. I had noticed time and again that my Nepalese companions looked at so many things differently. Time was not measured in minutes and quarters of hours that someone paid for. They did not see themselves as masters of their fate, controlling their lives, directing its course towards carefully planned goals. Theirs was life without the hurry, the status-seeking, the sheer cussedness of western existence. I began to think about the possibility of not going back, ever. Of staying here, of being part of this world where people seemed so much more content with themselves.

CHAPTER
EIGHT

BALANGRA PASS
Tuesday, March 27, 1984

W E crested the Balangra Pass at 12,700 feet before 9:00 A.M. Without stopping, I tossed a few stones on the summit cairn and began the long descent along the tributary gorge of the Balansuro Khola towards the deep canyon of the Thuli Bheri River, still ten miles to the southeast. Somewhere near their confluence lay the village of Tibrikot and a police checkpost. A day's walk further east along the Thuli Bheri, the village of Dunai, with both police and military garrisons, stood in our way. My trekking permit did not mention Dunai, and once again, I wanted to avoid contact with anyone in an official capacity and bypass the checkposts.

Not since our passage of Gum Gadhi at night had I felt so tense about my high visibility as a foreigner.

As we passed before the entrance to a government yak farm and agricultural project, I shielded myself with Akaal Bahadur's load. Soon after, we stopped to rest and eat, and I secluded myself behind a stone wall.

Again I looked at my creased and dirty trekking map. It showed the trail continuing along the northeast side of the Balansuro gorge to the Thuli Bheri, where it passed through Tibrikot. Perhaps by crossing over to the other side of the gorge and following along the south side of the Balansuro until it reached the Thuli Bheri we could bypass Tibrikot. My map showed no trail on the south side, only a village called Huma. But where there was a village, there had to be a trail.

For two hours we kept to the north side of the gorge. Gradually it opened into a valley, the treeless slopes having long ago lost their forests to the human demand for fuel, fodder and tillable fields. Several miles ahead we saw three villages, which on our map were called Pahad, Para and Liku.

Reaching a breezy promontory with a view of the entire valley and the brooding canyon of the Thuli Bheri in the distance, we again stopped to rest.

"Prem, we need to know exactly where Tibrikot lies and which trail we can take to avoid it. What do you think about crossing to the other side of the river? My map says that there is a village. Maybe we can reach the Thuli Bheri from there and miss Tibrikot."

"Perhaps this is so. But we should find out from the local people."

Prem turned to the porters and instructed them to scatter and see what they could find out about the routes and checkposts. Akaal Bahadur soon returned with a grizzled man and his simpleminded son. Standing on the promontory, the man pointed to the tiny white speck of a building barely discernible in the middle of Liku village, several miles ahead.

"Parker Sahib, this man says that white house is a police checkpost. We cannot see Tibrikot, it is beyond Liku where the rivers meet." Prem asked the man a few more questions.

Jeet Bahadur and Auri Bahadur returned, having asked three or four people and receiving as many different answers. From these stories we wove together the common threads of information we thought most likely to be true. Yes, they said, we could reach the Thuli Bheri and bypass Tibrikot by following a trail on the south slope of the valley.

Filled with the false confidence that this information provided, we descended and crossed the Balansuro, at this point a lively stream with many water-powered mill houses. By late afternoon we had reached the village of Huma. We stopped to buy a few potatoes and to ask our way.

Prem reported to me. "Parker Sahib, I am sorry. These people say we cannot go this way to the Thuli Bheri. Ahead there are steep cliffs."

Looking southeast from below the Balangra Pass towards the Thuli Bheri River and the village of Tribikot. The north side of the Dhaulagiri Himalaya rises in the distance.

"Then why were we told otherwise just two hours ago? So where does the trail go?"

"The trail goes down to the river, to the Balansuro, then it goes up on the other side. To Tibrikot."

"So the terrain is funneling us right towards Tibrikot. There doesn't seem to be any way out."

Reluctantly we followed the contouring trail out of Huma as we descended once again towards the Balansuro. An hour later we stopped for our second meal. I conferred again with Prem.

"Look, if we bushwhack down the slope here," I pointed down eight hundred feet to the Balansuro, "we can follow the river to the Thuli Bheri. That way we should pass below Tibrikot, which the villagers told us sits several hundred feet above the river."

Prem thought for a minute. "But Parker Sahib, there is no moon, it will be very dark and we have almost no batteries. And the locals say there is no trail following the river."

"Prem, you know there are always trails along rivers. People go there to get water, to wash clothes, and to shit. And I'm sure we can find some way to get down there."

We waited until the last lingering twilight, just after eight o'clock. What looked from above to be an easy way turned into a steep, loose scree slope. Prem was right; without the moon, movement was treacherous. For more than two hours we slipped, slid and blundered our way down until we reached the riverbed. As I had figured, a faint trail followed the river bank. We moved steadily for an hour through the blackness as the roar of the Thuli Bheri grew steadily louder.

Just before the confluence, we came to another bridge embellished with erotic sculptures, and crossed the Balansuro for the last time. We rounded a corner and the roar of the roiling Thuli Bheri overwhelmed us. The water charged over immense boulders and plunged through piles of debris, the din so loud we had to shout into each other's ears just to be heard.

Stopping to rest, we sat directly in the trail, our backs supported by the cliffs behind us. Our feet dangled over the edge just above the sheer one-hundred-foot drop to the river. No one attempted to speak above the roar of the river, that tremendous display of power, the demonstration of the immense forces of nature all around us. The red glow of the porters' *beedies* brightened and dimmed as they inhaled.

As we rose to continue, Prem came close to me and yelled in my ear. "Parker Sahib, we are very lucky that we passed Tibrikot so easily. Now we should be safe until we reach Dunai."

"I'm sure that getting through Dunai will be easy too," I shouted back. "Let's go, but still no flashlights, we're too close to Tibrikot."

We had become adept at this night travel, even in the blackest times, as now without moon or flashlights. After months together on the trail, we had also come to know one another's movements well. Little needed to be said, as we knew almost instinctively what the others were thinking and what to do. Auri Bahadur, our newest porter, seemed to fit in easily. He was quiet but with an inner toughness that meshed with the others. I was sure he hadn't the faintest clue what he was getting himself into when he signed on with us. But he appeared unflappable and readily went along with our nighttime sojourns.

From our resting spot, the trail switchbacked steeply up the face of the river gorge. Loose rocks and gravel churned up by yak caravans made for a slow, dusty ascent. The roar of the river slowly diminished. After several hundred feet, a ghostly apparition loomed out of the night, a newly erected *chorten* that split the trail.

We stopped beside it to rest while Prem went ahead to check the trail, which appeared to level off. He returned before the porters had extinguished their *beedies* and silently signaled us to move on.

In a low, tense voice, he whispered to all of us. "Keep together, very close. Very, very quiet."

Not until we had passed the second house along the trail did I realize the cause of his concern. For it was then that the dogs began to bark. First, off in the distance, then closer as they moved towards us from several directions. We moved quickly, close together in single file, with Prem in the lead, then me, Jeet Bahadur, Auri Bahadur and Akaal Bahadur bringing up the rear.

More houses and crude structures lined the trail. A village. But which one could be so close to Tibrikot?

Ahead, the trail split; one path maintained a flat course, the other headed further up the hillside. Prem veered and took the upper trail. For a hundred feet we climbed, but soon realized that this path led only to a large Hindu temple. Communicating with hand signals, we rapidly reversed direction and went back to the fork.

The level trail that we had avoided the first time led directly into the

Prem

Jeet Bahadur

Akaal Bahadur

Pema

J.B. Gross, immediately after his injury
on Marbu Lekh.

The captivating village of Dillikot on the north side of Marbu Lekh.

Ascending Marbu Lekh, looking south over rugged hill country towards the plains of India.

The great stupa of Bodnath, Kathmandu Valley, by night.

Reaching the pass on Marbu Lekh at 12,300 feet.

Village below Dillikot, near the Tila River.

The author with children of Dalphu.

A girl from the village of Dalphu.

Prem and the porters along the Barbung Khola east of Tarakot.

Lama Dorje and his children in the village of Tarengaon. Dressed in tattered homespun, they pose in front of their house. A carved stone mask is embedded in the wall.

Eroded terrain looking east of the Barbung Khola beyond Tarengaon.

A remarkable gompa at Daragaon, built directly into the crumpled sedimentary layers.

Ascending above Daragaon, at 17,000 feet, looking west at the mountains of Dolpo.

Does the river flow north or south? Frozen river encountered after descending from the first pass east of Daragaon.

Descending off the second pass east of Daragaon. Frozen rivers, snow-capped mountains, crumbling cliffs of burnt umber and gray.

Three boys in the village of Sangdak.

Descending through the Cha Lungpa Gorge, Akaal Bahadur helps Jeet Bahadur along a crumbling face of rock and dirt.

Leaving Sangdak, looking back at the ocher-colored buildings, with the Sangdak Pass beyond.

We reached the Kali Gandaki watershed and looked south towards the Annapurnas. Tilicho and Nilgiri form a sheer 10,000 ft. wall of rock and hanging glaciers.

center of the village. Prem waved for absolute silence. The dogs that we had shaken off when taking the upper trail now caught our scent again and began barking with renewed vigor. Ice axes at the ready, we moved deeper into the center of the village with a pack of a dozen dogs surrounding us.

Some were knee-high mongrels. The larger ones, huge beasts of mastiff stock, gave us more hesitation as their deep, gruff growls echoed among the moving shadows of the night. Hearing the mounting frenzy behind me, I turned, thinking to help Akaal Bahadur fend them off.

With little warning, a black mastiff attacked. Wielding his ice axe with wicked accuracy, Akaal Bahadur sidestepped and slammed its flat blade down against the dog's skull, inches before the animal could sink his teeth into Akaal Bahadur's leg.

The dog yelped, then fell to the ground, stunned. Slowly it slunk back into the night. Instead of putting the pack on guard, Akaal Bahadur's defense seemed to incite the others, and they moved in closer, increasing their barks to a furious cacophony. Quickly I stepped to Akaal Bahadur's side and we both walked backwards, protecting ourselves with readied ice axes. As we moved through the village their number slowly diminished until we were left confronting only two malnourished mongrels.

At an airy whistle from Prem, Akaal Bahadur and I turned and followed the others, trotting slowly towards the far side of the village. Ahead, a thirty-foot-long enclosed archway spanned the trail. Long benches lined either wall, a table partially blocked the far end.

Following the trail that passed directly beneath the structure, I paused briefly halfway through, thinking this must be some kind of *gompa* or covered *chorten*. A shallow drainage ditch crossed the trail and in the dark I stumbled momentarily. Akaal Bahadur heard my staggering step and turned to me. Grabbing my arm, he whispered urgently, "*Chitto, Sahib!*" ('Hurry, sir!')

We ran. As quickly as our loads permitted we raced down the trail for a hundred yards. Then slowing, Akaal Bahadur turned to me, a broad grin splitting his face.

"*Chaulki, Sahib, chaulki*" ('A checkpost, sir'), he said excitedly, pointing back to the covered structure.

I looked back at the faint outlines of the police checkpost. With a shiver, I realized that we had literally passed through the very thing we had desperately sought to avoid, the checkpost in the village of Tibrikot.

We continued to run as best we could and caught up with Prem and the other porters several hundred yards down the trail. They had hidden among some boulders.

I found Prem leaning back against a rock. Sweat streaked his face. He shook his head gently back and forth. "Parker Sahib, we were very lucky. The police must have been sleeping. But the dogs made so much noise. Maybe the police will get up and come after us." He peered nervously back along the trail.

"You're right. We should walk all night. Put as much distance between us and Tibrikot as we can. Let's go. And no lights, it's still too risky."

We hoisted our loads and continued along the trail, contouring high above the Thuli Bheri River.

Stunned by our mistake of entering directly into the village when we thought we had passed it, disturbed by the attack of the village dogs and shaken by the encounter with the police checkpost, I walked quickly despite the dark. My one thought was to get away, leave this place behind as soon as possible.

For long stretches the trail clung precariously to the vertical face, hundreds of feet above the rumbling torrent that we could hear in the darkness below. Because we had no lights, the going was tricky. To traverse the stretches more quickly and safely, we kept close together, each placing an outstretched hand on the load of the person ahead. In this manner, we moved like a snake winding its way along the trail.

We walked all night, stopping only twice for short breaks. In the warm and humid night sweat soaked my clothes, stung my eyes. Only during our brief stops did I begin to dry out. I was tired and hungry, but still I felt a growing exhilaration at having passed the checkpost and now traveling at night further into Dolpo.

With Tibrikot behind us, I also sensed the porters' excitement. Akaal Bahadur laughed a satisfied throaty chortle as he retold the story of urging Sahib to hurry up and get out of the police *chaulki*. Their mood recalled the childhood thrills of going to horror movies or sneaking around haunted houses on Halloween. It was a game to them.

The trail gradually descended to the riverbed, and just before dawn we crossed a bridge spanning the Thuli Bheri. Soon we began to see others on the trail—Tibetan porters carrying heavy loads, travelers on horseback.

"Prem, it's time to stop," I said. "Too many people."

"Yes, Parker Sahib. We must find a safe place to eat and sleep. But where?" We looked up at the near-vertical canyon walls.

"We'll just have to keep looking for a flat place somewhere off the trail."

For two miles we continued on the narrow trail. From around a bend, two figures on horseback appeared several hundred yards up the trail and heading our way. I spotted the telltale khaki green of their uniforms.

"Parker Sahib," Prem intoned warningly.

"I see them." Quickly we ducked behind some boulders at the trail's edge.

As we crouched behind our screen, waiting for the men to pass, I leaned towards Prem. "Now. We have to get off this trail *now.*"

He nodded, then cocked his head, straining to catch a sound over the roar of the river.

I heard it too, the unmistakable sound of an airplane. I knew an airport existed at Dunai, but within this narrow, precipitous canyon it seemed inconceivable that an airplane could find a place to fly.

Within a minute, from the direction of Dunai, a single-engine Pilatus Porter came into view. It flew three hundred feet above the river, following the contours of the deep canyon. It passed almost overhead and then, still constrained by the canyon walls, disappeared out of sight around a bend in the river.

The khaki-clad horsemen passed. I scanned the cliffs above and from our hiding spot could just make out a small ledge three hundred feet above the trail. A breathless scramble up the steep, loose scree brought us to a flat spot covered with large thorny bushes. We cleared out the small brush as best we could, then laid out our gear in the open spaces underneath the larger bushes. I fell back on my bedroll, exhausted after twenty-four hours without sleep.

A quick meal of rice and potatoes satisfied our immediate hunger pangs, and by eleven o'clock we were all spread out among the bushes, resting or sleeping. Finally out of sight of the trail, I relaxed and tried to sleep, but large, noisy flies buzzed around my face and arms. "Too tired to sleep"—the phrase seemed apropos.

Late in the afternoon, we ate another large meal, then waited until eight. Prem and I figured it should take a couple of hours to reach Dunai, but it made no sense to expose ourselves to the late afternoon traffic. Because of the narrow canyon, there was no place else to hide. Not until after dark did we abandon our hiding spot and descend to the trail.

By ten-thirty we reached what we assumed was the outskirts of Dunai. Prem motioned us off the trail and we hid in some bushes.

For two hours we crouched waiting, listening . . . Silence. At twelve-thirty Prem rose and we followed suit, bunched closely together. Without a word we headed off into the night. Prem and I had discussed earlier in the day a way to bypass Dunai altogether. If we could find a path leading towards the river, we might find a bridge and cross to the opposite side.

We walked for fifteen minutes until we reached the outskirts of the town.

Suddenly the path veered away from the river and crossed a large flat area. For ten minutes we continued, but then stopped.

Prem spoke with Akaal Bahadur, then turned to me. "Parker Sahib, this trail is too big. We should look for a small trail near the river and away from the *chaulki*."

Just then Akaal Bahadur turned on his flashlight and shone it across the flat expanse of ground between us and the river. Panning the light across the open space, he paused to illuminate a two-story building. Seconds later he doused the light, swearing colorfully in Nepali.

The flat space was the airport and the building was the flight tower! There was a collective intake of breath at the realization that we were so close to this official installation, and we quickly moved on.

A dog's incessant barking emerged and echoed from a farmhouse behind us as we followed the trail ever closer to the center of Dunai. I was beginning to hate dogs. The trail, which until now had been loose gravel and dirt, suddenly became a raised slate path five feet wide. Buildings appeared ahead, and with them came the dogs.

In ones and twos, then in larger groups, they appeared. They barked, setting each other off. Two stalked us from behind, grizzled mongrels in the shadowy darkness.

"Parker Sahib," Prem whispered, breaking the self-imposed silence. "What to do?"

I approached him, our heads together as we talked softly, trying not to rouse the ire of the fiends circling our feet. "You go ahead," I said.

"Akaal Bahadur and I will follow. Then Jeet Bahadur and Auri Bahadur. You can talk to the police or anyone who stops you. I can hide behind Akaal Bahadur's *doko*."

"Okay, Parker Sahib. If someone stops me, I will talk very loudly so you will know to hide. We must go quickly."

Akaal Bahadur and I waited until Prem was out of sight, then stepped out into the trail. Soon the raised trail became lined on either side with barbed wire fencing. Behind it we saw the outlines of several long, low buildings. A hundred yards further on we came to two opposing archways that led to the buildings. Signs, large and freshly painted in red and white, identified the compounds as police and military barracks. The trail had funneled us into the largest police and military garrisons in the region.

I walked behind Akaal Bahadur, peering right and left, alert for lights or any signs of movement. The barracks remained dark.

We left the garrison behind and entered the village proper. Small, shuttered houses and shops lined the street, and apparently each harbored a dog. Akaal Bahadur walked ahead, ice axe ready. A small pack followed us, lunging periodically. I kept them at bay to the rear, but my ice axe seemed merely to infuriate rather than drive them off.

"Sahib," whispered Akaal Bahadur over his shoulder. "*Chaulki*."

Looking around Akaal Bahadur's *doko*, I saw a small building ahead. A light flashed and the figure of a man emerged.

I immediately stepped off the trail and hid behind a boulder. Akaal Bahadur held his ground on the trail, fending off the growling, snarling dogs that surrounded him. The man, using a flashlight to guide his way, crossed the trail and disappeared down an embankment on the far side.

For two minutes I waited in the shadows. Then, feeling safer, I emerged and rejoined Akaal Bahadur on the trail. Just as we reached the *chaulki*, however, the man reappeared and aimed the beam of his flashlight directly at us.

With the quickness of hyperalert senses, I shielded myself on the far side of Akaal Bahadur's *doko*. Grabbing the flaps of my Chinese hat with both hands, I pulled it low over my brow. Without hesitation, we walked past him and into the cover of darkness.

"*Chitto, chitto*," I urged Akaal Bahadur. We broke into a half trot and soon left the dogs and most of the village behind us.

A hundred yards beyond the *chaulki* we found Prem waiting near a small shed. We stopped, breathing heavily, sweatsoaked in the warm night.

"Prem, did you see anyone?"

"No, Parker Sahib, no one."

"Well, we did. And he saw us." I told him what had happened. Just as I finished, Jeet Bahadur and Auri Bahadur appeared and the five of us moved out onto the trail. We jogged silently, intent on putting as much distance as we could between us and Dunai.

I looked back. Two flashes of light bobbed along the trail. Someone was coming after us.

Akaal Bahadur took my arm roughly and pushed me ahead of him. "*Chitto*, Sahib, *chitto*," he urged, his voice tight.

I ran. After a hundred yards I glanced behind me, but saw only the swaying bulk of Akaal Bahadur's *doko*. My breath came more easily. We continued, but again fear caused me to look back.

They came, two yellow bouncing lights still behind us.

With a burst of speed I ran to catch Prem.

I saw Prem's swiftly moving figure ahead but hesitated to call out his name. I lunged and grabbed his arm.

"Prem," I said. "They are coming!"

Prem stopped and turned to face me. We had only seconds to make a decision. We had no time to even ask the question, "What should we do?"

"Run," he said.

"I'll find someplace to hide and wait for you."

"We will talk with them," he assured me. "Go!"

I dashed ahead, looking for a hiding place. The trail, which once again followed the river, was bounded to the left by a sheer fifty-foot drop to the river, to the right by raised fields. A small lean-to came into view and I scrambled behind it. One last glance told me I was just in time as the two lights reached Prem, now waiting with the porters.

From my vantage point I listened carefully and heard the low murmur of conversation. Struggling to keep my breath even and soft, I monitored the encounter between the authorities and my Nepalese staff. What were they saying?

After three minutes I saw the two lights heading back towards Dunai. Waiting another cautious minute, I reemerged and walked silently back towards Prem and the porters.

I found them sitting by a house, not talking, their silence ominous. At the sound of my footsteps, Prem turned.

Jumping up he grabbed me by the shoulders and pushed me down the trail. "They are coming!"

Looking behind me I saw lights approaching. Not more than thirty seconds, I judged, and they would be on me. This time I saw four dim beams weaving in the darkness. By the pale yellow light I saw that each man carried a long object in his other hand. They had rifles.

Run.

That primitive reaction prompted by adrenaline gave me strength.

Run. And I ran into the cover of darkness. My eyes were accustomed to the absence of light, I could feel the trail under my feet, hear the roar of the river to my left and sense the closeness of the crude retaining wall to my right.

Run. My mind focused on the flight, to put distance between me and those rifles, and to look for a place to hide.

I ran for several agonizing minutes. My pack jolted and swung wildly with every step. My eyes searched the blackness for an escape.

Finally I glimpsed a tiny break in the retaining wall. With a heave, I pulled myself over it and fell silently into a muddy field. Lying flat on my stomach and pressing myself into the freshly plowed earth, I struggled to catch my breath.

My heart pounded. *Be quiet. Be calm. Deep regular breaths.* I willed myself silent.

As soon as the sounds of my gasping breath died away, I peered over the wall. I saw no one coming, but the darkness could have hidden a person. And the river below bellowed its presence, masking any silent footfall. I took off my light-colored jacket but put my Chinese hat back on. Removing my pack I rummaged for my water bottle and downed half the quart of water I carried.

I took stock of my situation. I had no food, little water, no flashlight and spoke poor Nepali. I did have 3,000 rupees in cash. If Prem and the others were taken by the police, I would be alone, a foreigner in forbidden Dolpo.

Going alone further east into Dolpo, I knew, would be foolhardy and possibly suicidal. Even if I survived the elements I might be murdered just for the boots I wore. But I was on the wrong side of Dunai to get back to Jumla. What should I do?

The only reasonable course was to wait. Wait until sunrise at least. If Prem and the porters did not show up by then, I would try to make my way past Dunai and return to Jumla. Passing Dunai, especially during the day, would be difficult. Most likely I would be caught and thrown in jail.

I found a place just off the trail to sit and waited. Visibility was less than thirty feet and the noise from the river muffled any footsteps. Although I wanted enough warning to hide if someone approached, I didn't want Prem and the porters to pass me by. If they went ahead, I would be on my own. I looked at my watch. One-fifteen.

The sounds of the river engulfed me. It was alive with the crunch and boom of rocks as the waters powerfully pushed and ground the boulders downstream. Nature creating another feature on the land-scape, carrying the land before it like a giant bulldozer.

I was covered with sweat. I resisted drinking all of my water, even though my mouth was dry. Where were Prem and the porters?

At 2:10 A.M., silhouettes moved out of the darkness towards me. I leapt back over the retaining wall and lay flat. Seconds later they passed, and I made out the tops of our porters' loads. Were they alone? It was too dark for me to see, but I couldn't take the chance of letting them pass me by. I had to stop them. I crawled to the edge of the wall and leaned out over the trail.

"Prem."

"Come, we are going," came his cryptic reply.

Still concerned that they were not alone, I waited until they had passed me, then hopped back onto the trail and followed fifty yards behind.

Twice, the last person in line stopped to wait for me, but each time I, too, stopped until the group moved on. It was impossible to count how many they were, and I was afraid one or two policemen accompanied them.

After an hour I closed in and grabbed Jeet Bahadur from behind, pulling him off the trail. "Everything okay?"

"No problem, Sahib."

A half hour later we stopped to rest and I heard their story.

"There were four men, police. They had guns," Prem said.

"Yes, I saw them," I said. "I ran, but they didn't follow me, did they?"

"No, they did not see you. They talked to us there by the small house. I told them we worked for a sahib who took an airplane from Jumla just two days ago. That we walked all day and all night to go back to Pokhara. I said we tried to save our sahib money by going very fast. They didn't believe me."

"No wonder. What porter goes fast to save a foreigner money?"

Prem chuckled and continued. "So they made us untie our loads. And they counted the bowls and spoons to see how many people in our party. We have all given them the wrong names. I was Bira Bahadur Rai." He laughed again.

"So what happened?"

"Nothing. What can they do? We are Nepalese, we do not need any permits. No problem, Parker Sahib. They let us go. They didn't want to, but they let us go."

We walked along the Thuli Bheri until three-thirty, then pulled off the trail. Not bothering with tents, we threw our bedrolls out underneath a large conifer tree and fell asleep.

CHAPTER
NINE

A HAND pressed firmly down on my head and woke me from a deep slumber.

"Do not move," Prem whispered.

Pulling my head inside my sleeping bag, I heard the jingle of harness bells, then the sound of hooves approaching.

"*Namaste,*" Prem called out.

"*Namaste. Kahaa jaane ho?*" ('Where are you going?') A man's voice, warm, unthreatening. I relaxed. Prem spoke to him for several minutes, then the sound of bells and hooves receded.

"It is okay now, Parker Sahib."

Rising up on one elbow, I saw three *lama*s astride sturdy Tibetan ponies twenty yards down the trail. Their flowing red robes and brightly colored saddlebags shone resplendently in the midmorning sun.

"Parker Sahib," Prem said. "The *lama*s have said that the crops were very bad this year, and that there is little food in the villages ahead."

"What about Tarakot?"

"We have two days of food left, we can easily get to Tarakot. But the *lama*s said that even there it may be difficult to find more."

142

After a cup of tea and some cold potatoes, we got quickly under-way, walking along the increasingly spectacular gorge of the Thuli Bheri River. Hazy morning sunlight silvered the sheer rock walls, which rose on both sides of us for thousands of feet before disappear-ing from view. In such rugged terrain the only conceivable place for a trail was here, just beside the river.

By late morning, the sunlight had descended the walls of the gorge to the riverbed. The temperature soared. The sun soon baked our brains and sent us in search of cover. We stopped for a meal, then hid in the cool alcoves of some boulders that we shared with menacing black spiders. In the sultry afternoon heat I dozed and caught up on my journal. With the pace of events during the last few days, I hadn't had much chance to record what had happened.

I wrote about the day before the Balangra Pass, meeting the Tibetans, seeing the young mother with her child, the panda, and my emotional response to that inspiring day. Now, lazing in the heat, having been cheated out of a good many nights' sleep, I wondered what in the hell I was doing here. Where were the mountains I'd come to see? I was avoiding not only the police, but the local people, most of whom wished me no harm. This wasn't what I'd come to do. I consoled myself with the thought that in just one more day we would be past all these checkposts and into the high mountains just north of Dhaulagiri. Then we could relax, enjoy ourselves, take it easy . . .

Also our nocturnal schedule of late had left me sluggish and not thinking clearly. Perhaps our diet of rice and potatoes, which did not provide me with enough calories and nutrients, had dulled my mind. There seemed little chance, however, that our diet would improve as we traveled further into Dolpo. Only a small portion of the wheel of yak cheese remained, and our buffalo salami also was almost finished. Both had by now petrified so that they required extended cooking just to make them edible. In the mornings, we had taken to breaking off a small chunk of the yak cheese which we sucked throughout the morning as it slowly softened. Both our cheese and salami would soon be gone, and with them our only source of protein.

This was not to suggest that my diet lacked taste. During the past few weeks, my fare had changed in a manner that more than counter-balanced its increasing monotony. Before Jumla, J.B. and I had eaten the same food as the porters, with one exception—chilies, or in Nepali *korsani*. Prem and the porters seemed addicted to them. When

Prem prepared the food, he would serve J.B. and me and then add the chilies to their portion. Time and again, I had watched Prem eat half a dozen large chilies with a meal. Then, with swollen lips and tearing eyes, he would lament. "O Parker Sahib, I eat too many *korsani*. I must stop." But at the next meal, the story would be the same; he could not lay off the chilies. Prem and the porters lost their appetite and had little desire to eat without them. For them, running out of *korsani* and running out of rice were equally grim prospects.

Just before Tibrikot, we had passed a man carrying an entire basket of bright-red dried chilies. Our progress halted for almost an hour while Prem and Jeet Bahadur bargained for a large sack. Though that was only days ago, those chilies were already half gone. Since Jumla and J.B.'s departure, the Nepalese had me far outnumbered. They figured that Parker Sahib would eat whatever they cooked. And they cooked with chilies. I remembered their smiles as they served me those first few meals, then waited for my reaction. My lips tingled, my tongue burned, my face flushed, but I said nothing. The food got hotter by increments until finally it was wholly to their liking, the equivalent of five or six dried *korsani* per serving, ground up so they could not be removed. Now I feared I, too, was addicted, which seemed to have been their intent all along. Sneaky bastards.

Because of the heat and traffic on the trail, including police, we waited until eight-thirty when the western sky held only the faintest trace of gray light. We left our hiding spot and followed the trail, which recrossed the river several times before climbing hundreds of feet up the canyon walls.

We walked until twelve-thirty, when dogs barking in the distance gave us a hint in the dark night that the village of Laban was close by. We had planned to stop near it for the night and the next day obtain information about the route ahead. Our sketchy information indicated that the last police checkpost along this route through Dolpo lay somewhere ahead of us in the village of Tarakot. Tarakot, capital of the former kingdom of Tichu Rong, was known also by the locals as *Dzong* (Fort), for it once held the fort that controlled this medieval kingdom.

In the dark we stumbled about, searching for a flat area large enough for all of us to sleep. We looked through dense thickets of thorny scrub, to no avail. Then, hacking our way through heavy brush, we climbed a steep run-off gully and found a near-level area. We cleared a spot right in the middle, then squeezed five of us in a space big enough for only three. After several minutes of flailing arms and legs, we found the only mutually agreeable position, stacked front to back like a set of spoons. Exhausted, I slept soundly.

Just after dawn two Magar men and a girl spotted us from above. In the Nepalese manner, they came to snoop, to find out who we were and where we were going. Prem shook me awake and warned me of their approach. I pulled my sleeping bag over my head, then listened as best I could to the conversation.

First they asked why we were sleeping here when their farmhouse was only two hundred yards above us. Answer: We couldn't have seen it in the dark. Where were we going? Answer: None of your business.

Prem, of course, didn't give these answers but said just enough to keep them talking as he listened to everything they could tell us about the route. These farmers hung on to chit-chat for an agonizing sixty minutes as my bladder nearly burst. Smothered in my sleeping bag, even I couldn't stand the rank odor of my unwashed body. *As bad as a Tibetan.*

As soon as they left, we took up our loads and got under way. Once more we headed down to the river and crossed it on a cantilevered bridge, the large posts on either side of which were decorated with erotic carvings. Many of the Magars who live in this area called Tichu Rong speak Tibetan and practice a form of Tibetan Buddhism, although they are ethnically related to people who live further south in the lower valleys of Nepal. They migrated north, adopting Tibetan ways, but hold themselves aloof from the ethnic Tibetans found in other parts of Dolpo.

At a rest stop, Prem and I discussed our strategy for the next few days.

"These Magars have said that the Jang La going south from Tarakot is not passable because of snow," he said.

"We didn't want to go that way anyway," I answered.

"They said that we can go this way." He pointed along the Thuli Bheri. "We can follow the river all the way to Mustang."

"But our map doesn't show any route that way."

Prem looked at me quizzically. "Maybe the map is wrong."

"You're right. It's been wrong before. I have this feeling that some

Kathmandu bureaucrat who once came this way twenty years ago sat there in his office, probably half-crocked, and said, 'Oh, I remember the trail went this way.' And so that's what he put on the map. I'm pretty sure of one thing though, we're going to have to cross a mountain barrier somewhere up ahead."

I took the map and spread it out. The printing had begun to fade in the sunlight and flecks of curried vegetables stained it. I traced the thick line of the Barbung Khola as it wound around the Dhaulagiri Massif, then followed a route east over the mountains to the Kali Gandaki River. "Look," I pointed. "Once down to the Kali Gandaki we can go over the Thorung La to Manang and then on towards Kathmandu. But that's weeks away ... what did the farmers say about the checkpost at Tarakot?"

"They said there was no checkpost," Prem answered.

"How can they say that? They must know that's not true!" I fumed in frustration. Why was it so hard to get accurate information? Why did people lie to us? The mountains and rivers threw physical barriers in our path, but the helpless feeling at the lack of information created a mental frustration that weighed at least as heavily upon us.

Just before noon we stopped just below the village of Tarakot. Sitting three hundred feet above the river plain, we saw the roofs of a few buildings standing out against the deep blue sky. White prayer flags on long poles rippled in the breeze.

As we started to prepare a meal, a Tibetan approached us from the east. Prem hailed him and offered a cup of tea, hoping to learn of the route ahead. After a short exchange, Prem hurried to my side.

"Parker Sahib, this man says there is a checkpost just above us." Prem pointed to one of the buildings. "We can see it. He says the police look for people from the roof with binoculars."

I looked up and, sure enough, on the roof I saw the silhouette of a person. Sliding down behind some rocks, I reached for my binoculars and carefully focused on the building.

A man watched the trail.

I pulled back. Despite the heat, I jammed my Chinese hat down on my head as far as I could. Lifting the binoculars again, I took another peek. The man watched but seemed to pay no particular attention to us.

"Parker Sahib," Prem said. "Let me look."

Prem scanned the village and the trail ahead.

"What do you think, Prem?" Sweat trickled down my face.

"They do not see us."

"So we should be thankful for small favors," I mumbled. "Let's put some miles between us and this place."

"But first we need food, and Tarakot is perhaps the only place between here and the Kali Gandaki."

"Let's get out of this spot, away to a more secluded place. Then we can send the porters into the village to buy food."

"Yes, Parker Sahib. But let us go one by one. Maybe the police will look for a group."

"Auri Bahadur," I called softly. "*Chuba dinos*" ('Give me your coat'). I mimed putting on his Tibetan coat.

Auri Bahadur looked puzzled for a moment, then, with a grin, nodded. I wanted to borrow his Tibetan *chuba* as a disguise. He untied his *doko* and extracted it.

Now with my Chinese hat, green canvas pack and the black Tibetan *chuba*, I attempted to pass as a local, hoping my foreign aura didn't extend as far as the checkpost.

Prem went first. I waited until he was out of sight, then followed. The three porters brought up the rear. For nearly a third of a mile the trail crossed a flat expanse directly below the village and within sight of the checkpost.

I walked rapidly with my head down, silently cursing our bad luck, or our stupidity, at not passing this checkpost at night as we had the others. I remembered the remarks of the police chief in Jumla and Prem's assessment of these remote outposts of the Nepalese government. Although the medieval fortress no longer stood on the hillside, the modern equivalent of the 'king of Tichu Rong' probably lurked in the buildings above.

I found Prem a mile down the trail. He had stopped at a small stream amidst some boulders far enough off the trail to hide us for the day. Once the porters arrived, we set camp and cooked a meal.

Then Prem and I sat down with Akaal Bahadur and Auri Bahadur. They were to go into town to buy food, matches, batteries for our Chinese flashlights and to obtain information. To keep from attracting undue attention, they left thirty minutes apart.

Early in the afternoon I drifted out of camp to a place near the stream. As soon as I was out of sight of Prem and Jeet Bahadur, I slipped out of my pants and began to wash away the grime and filth from weeks of wear. This work normally was done by the porters, but I figured that Jeet Bahadur could use the rest. I could wash my own clothes this once.

I wet them in the icy stream and then rubbed in the soap. Just as I began to pound them on a flat rock, Jeet Bahadur silently appeared.

"Sahib," he said, squatting on his haunches beside me.

"Yes," I answered cautiously, perhaps feeling a little guilty for being found out. A sahib washing his own clothes.

He told me that Prem wanted to see me, he had something important to talk about. I looked at Jeet Bahadur and he steadily returned the gaze. Silently, I left my task and went to look for Prem. It was a lie and I knew it, for Prem had nothing important to say that couldn't wait. But I couldn't do anything about it. I had already offended Jeet Bahadur by trying to wash my own clothes; to insist on continuing would have been an insult.

Some tasks I was permitted to do. Akaal Bahadur and I usually set the tents, which was easier with two people anyway. Maybe because they were western tents, the porters made an exception. Also, I usually got away with collecting firewood. I frequently arrived at our camping spot before the porters and hurriedly collected enough wood to last the evening, sparing the porters that one task. It was a small enough contribution.

But I know that I frequently offended them by undervaluing the status given me by birth, by taking on tasks not meant for me. In trying to change our daily routine, I tried to change history, to negate thousands of years of the caste system, plus hundreds of years of British occupation in the Indian subcontinent.

Their social structure was so different from mine; would I ever understand the cultural gaps, let alone bridge them? And should I even attempt to do so? The only answer that came to me now was that I should give up gracefully, to allow Jeet Bahadur to finish his task unobserved, not embarrassed by the bumbling sahib, who didn't always know his place. This was the best I could do. Complaining to Prem would do no good. He had lectured me before. *Parker*, I told myself, *don't impose your values on them. Leave it.*

Akaal Bahadur and Auri Bahadur had been gone for several hours. Worried, Prem had just asked Jeet Bahadur to go find them when they appeared out of the surrounding boulders. They had been delayed by their inability to find food and matches. I had fallen into a river just past Mandu, ruining several packets of matches and seriously depleting our supplies. I had also lost my plastic lighter, something that upset Prem a great deal more than me. One of the cheap, sealed-plastic disposables made in Hong Kong and Bangkok, it had been refilled in Kathmandu by someone who drilled a hole in the bottom. Stories of these unstable lighters exploding in users' faces, or even in someone's pocket, made me nervous about having one and I was relieved to have lost it. Matches, even the warped, undependable Nepalese ones, were preferable to me. But in Tarakot those had been in short supply as well, and Akaal Bahadur and Auri Bahadur paid eight rupees per packet. They bought fifteen kilos of rice, a sack of potatoes and, of course, *korsani*, the addictive chilies. Twenty packets of *beedies* were my bonus to Prem and the porters. They found no batteries.

Canvasing the bazaar for information, they had received conflicting reports about the route ahead. Locals confirmed that the Jang La to the south was buried in deep snow. They heard several different stories, however, about the route east along the Thuli Bheri. Some said the trails were impassable; others said we could reach Jomoson in only a few days' time. It was exasperating.

"Prem. What is the truth?"

"I do not know, Parker Sahib."

We looked at each other. Once again our constant obstacle—lack of information.

"How long will our rice last?"

Prem checked our supplies. "We bought fifteen kilos today, plus a little left from before. If we eat two kilos every meal, we have eight meals of rice."

I laughed: almost a pound of *uncooked* rice per person. Much more when cooked. It never failed to astonish me how much rice a small Nepalese could eat. I had never heard a porter say he was full, although Prem occasionally refused more food. *My* problem was an inability to consume such vast quantities of rice and potatoes, which meant I was slowly wasting away, starving for lack of a large enough stomach. I hitched my belt two notches tighter these days, an indication of how much weight I had lost. Jeet Bahadur had also grown perceptibly thinner, and I urged him to eat more rice, hoping I didn't look as gaunt as he.

"What else do we have?" I asked.

"Some potatoes. And *korsani*!" Prem laughed.

* * *

The next day the porters began singing again and that lifted my spirits. I hadn't realized how much I missed their songs. In eastern Nepal they had sung almost nonstop as they carried their loads along the trail. In western Nepal the singing had stopped suddenly above Jumla. I realized that the tension over the authorities had been weighing on all of us. Now with the checkpost at Tarakot behind us, we all felt lighter, unburdened.

By now I knew many of Akaal Bahadur and Jeet Bahadur's favorite songs by heart and I sang along with them—quietly, so they wouldn't hear. Like the Tamang people, their songs were boisterous and full of life. I didn't know what the Tamang words meant, but the melodies seemed somehow appropriate to these mountains. With each song, my mood lightened.

The air, free of dust and moisture, allowed spectacularly clear views down the canyon and above to the mountains. The cloudless blue sky, the glaciered peaks, the deep thrust of the canyon—all seemed closer. Late in the morning we passed a tributary that rushed out of a chasm from the north, its water tumbling into the Thuli Bheri. The Tarap Khola drained a large valley of the same name in the interior of Dolpo to the east of Shey Gompa and Crystal Mountain. Once past this confluence, the river we followed changed its name to the Barbung Khola. And it was this Barbung Khola to which we now seemed tied. Possibly we would make a pilgrimage to its source on our way to cross the mountain barrier between Dolpo and the Kali Gandaki watershed.

In the afternoon, while walking alone, I rounded a large boulder in the trail. Deep in thought, I didn't see the group of people sitting there until I ran into them. I had to place my hands on the shoulders of two of them to avoid tripping. Embarrassed, I mumbled an almost incoherent "*Namaste*."

Then, I looked at the group of six Tibetans around a small fire just at the trailside—six of the scariest people I had ever seen. I put my hands together with a bow and took two steps to keep moving along the trail.

"*Namaste*," came the thickly accented reply from one who stepped into the trail directly in front of me.

I looked up and up. He was easily six foot three, and another two inches were added by the thick black hair wound around his head. His girth, accentuated by his oversized sheepskin *chuba*, was the greatest I had seen in a Tibetan. His right arm hung out, leaving his shoulder and torso bare. Around his waist a leather belt held a satchel and a long, silver-handled sword. The ubiquitous multicolored, yak-soled Tibetan boots adorned his feet.

I smelled his foul breath and unwashed body. He smiled and I saw that half of his teeth were gone and one of the few remaining was capped in gold. Instinctively, I took a step backwards.

I almost fell over the large aluminum box that two of the others now opened. Jammed inside were cigarettes, tobacco, chilies, chocolate, coral, yak rope and other bric-a-brac I couldn't identify.

In halting Nepali, the tall Tibetan asked, "You want to buy something?"

"No. I have very little money."

With a chilling, twisted leer, he asked another question. "Where is your house?"

"America."

"Ahhhhhh," came a chorus from around the fire.

"Where are you going?"

"Jomoson." It was the best I could think of quickly, as I felt the hairs on the back of my neck stand up. Two more rose to their feet.

"How much for your boots?" Three frightening Tibetans now surrounded me, asking a question I had answered at least three dozen times before in my travels. They stared at my feet, assessing the potential value of my footgear.

"Not for sale. They are the only pair I have."

I continued smiling all this while, as the Tibetans smiled back. Despite my outward calm, my heart pounded and jumbled chaos raced through my mind. They were Khampas—nomads, drifters, ex-CIA allies against the Chinese. Feared for centuries in Tibet for their lawless ways, they had drifted into Nepal, seeking a livelihood. They had continued in their old professions as bandits, businessmen and mercenaries. I remembered the stories about the murdered French couple and Peace Corps volunteer.

"Who are your friends?" came the next question. I knew what these bizarre words meant. They wanted to know if I was alone, just as had the Khampas I'd encountered before the Balangra Pass.

"Many porters coming behind and a guide," I answered, hoping fervently that one of the aforementioned would suddenly appear around the boulder. Unfortunately I was feeling strong that day and had marched out ahead of the others. I guessed that Prem and the porters were twenty minutes back. *At least I have my ice axe. Get out of here. Move.*

"*Namaste*," I said, walking around the towering Tibetan, who still stood resolutely in front of me, and hurrying on down the hill.

I continued at a bruising pace for half a mile. Then I became worried about Prem and the porters, how they might fare with the Tibetans. I climbed fifty feet up and off the trail to a spot where I could see but not easily be seen and waited.

How confident I had been getting! How presumptuous to think that just because we had passed the police checkposts all of our problems were over! So many had warned us of precipitous trails and high mountain passes covered in snow. But it was not the wilderness I had feared that day. It was the wildness of men whose cultural values differed so much from my own.

Fifteen minutes later Prem appeared along with Akaal Bahadur. I slipped back onto the trail.

"Prem, did you meet the Khampas?"

"Yes, Parker Sahib."

"*Na ramro maanchheho*" ('Not good men'). Akaal Bahadur shook his head.

Prem seemed as shaken as I, and related their conversation. "First they wanted us to buy things from them. Then they wanted to buy our pots and containers. They wanted to look in Akaal Bahadur's *doko*. Then, Parker Sahib, they wanted us to camp with them."

"*Na ramro maanchheho*," Akaal Bahadur commented again.

"Camp with them!" Prem was indignant. "But I told them we would go on until dark."

"Which way are they going?" I asked.

"I do not know," Prem answered.

"Real smart of us, forget to ask them the same questions they asked us. Everybody in Nepal asks 'Where are you going?' except us! Let's keep a sharp eye to our rear."

Jeet Bahadur and Auri Bahadur arrived ten minutes later. Closer together, we walked steadily for two hours, hoping to put distance between us and the fearsome Tibetans.

We set camp well off the trail and immediately next to the river, which was smaller now and not so foreboding since becoming the

Barbung Khola above its confluence with the Tarap Khola. As soon as we set camp, we sent Auri Bahadur back along the trail to keep an eye out for our "friends."

We cooked and ate our second rice meal of the day, and this favorite food lifted the porters' spirits considerably. I thought that Prem had done this intentionally to lighten their mood. As we sat around our small fire, the earth shuddered for a second, then suddenly jolted. Startled, we looked at each other. An earthquake. I had never felt one before, but it was an unmistakable tremor. "Earthquake," I said.

The porters laughed and told me the Nepali word for it. We heard the sharp reports of falling rock above, but far away and no danger to us. Over quickly and no harm done.

As I crawled into my tent, I mulled over the words of the Magar farmers of Tarakot. Five days to Jomoson, they had said. Seeing how little we had covered so far, I found this assessment preposterous. Now I was no longer so confident.

CHAPTER TEN

BARBUNG KHOLA GORGE

Sunday, April 1, 1984

THE gorge narrowed. Beyond the dirt, rocks and glacial debris we saw a wooden bridge spanning the Barbung Khola. But the trail traversed for sixty feet along a vertical rock wall a hundred feet in the air. A trail had been created along the sheer face with long poles bracing two tree trunks that spanned the gap, a rough scaffold. The trunks were one and a half feet wide, and below them was nothing but air.

We approached this section cautiously. No one spoke. Prem and I went first, facing forward with our slender packs, but the porters with their bulky loads had to face the wall as they inched along, six inches at a step. We crossed safely, one at a time, but I fervently hoped we would meet no more trails like this one. It slowed us down—worse, it scared the hell out of us all.

Beyond the bridge we tramped down through loose rock and dirt to the riverbed, a torrent tumbling through huge boulders. In the warm sun I stripped to the waist and washed my head and upper body in the icy water.

Beyond this narrow gorge the valley opened up into a broad flood plain, the river meandering haphazardly through it. We kept to the north side of the river, threading through scattered stands of towering conifers and ancient deodar cedar.

The trail passed through a tremendous walk-through *chorten* in partial ruin. Although the near entrance was blocked with rubble, the opposite side remained open. Cautiously I crawled through scattered debris to get inside. Shafts of sunlight shone through the shattered roof and illuminated the interior. High above the collapsed entrance, four painted figures sat serenely streaked by the rare rainwaters that entered freely through the ruptured roof.

The whole structure stood twenty-five feet high, and the guts of it

A tremendous chorten in partial ruin, the paintings streaked by the rainwaters that entered freely through the ruptured roof.

had spilled out so I could see the tons of various sized rock that had been used to construct it. Large wooden crossbeams and joists formed a framework for a carefully constructed outer dry wall of rock. Although spiritually it meant little to me, I was unsettled to see the *chorten* in ruin. Perhaps an earthquake had done the damage. If so, it had yet to be mended, and in the meantime the harsh climate was tearing it apart. I could not help but feel that I was observing a culture and religion in decline.

Late afternoon sun illuminated the squat stone houses of the village of Khakotgaon, a medieval fortress that clung to the base of the cliffs along the north wall of the gorge. Curious villagers came out on the roofs to stare down at us, foreigners from far away. Prem asked to buy food and we purchased four eggs, ten kilos of potatoes and three kilos of *tsampa* (roasted barley flour).

A young man stepped in front of me with a broad smile. His western dress and facial features identified him as another outsider.

"Good to see you. I need English," he said slowly and with a heavy Nepali accent.

Taking this to mean that he wanted to speak English with me, I attempted a conversation. Unfortunately, we didn't seem to speak the same variety of that language and we lapsed into Nepali. I learned that he was a schoolteacher from the *terai* sent here to establish a school. He had served fourteen months of his "sentence," with ten months to go before he could leave.

He leaned close to me. "Very lonely. Not good people," he whispered.

Beyond the village, a series of *chorten*s spaced two hundred yards apart stretched out across the barren plain. Further ahead on the south side of the river, a side canyon rose 13,000 feet in one continuous upsurge to the northern ramparts of the 24,000-foot Churen Himal. So vast was the vertical rise that the scene looked surreal, like a painting. In the flame-colored late afternoon light it seemed the most beautiful mountain I had ever seen. We stopped by a small *chorten* to rest.

As we sat, a man and a lame boy approached and rested thirty feet from us. After a minute, the man spoke to Prem in passable Nepali, although he looked and dressed like a Tibetan—more aristocratic version, though, than the Tibetan Khampas we had met the day before. His black hair was interwoven with red wool and wound around his head. He wore a monk's robe.

Beyond the village of Khakatgoan, a series of chortens stretched across the barren plain.

Still nervous after our encounter with the Khampas the day before, Prem talked only briefly with him. The sun dipped below the mountains to the southwest and the temperature plunged. Saying a hurried goodbye to the man and his boy, we moved on to find a place to camp a mile from Khakotgaon.

On the south side of the Barbung Khola, a canyon wall rises 13,000 feet to the northern ramparts of the 24,000-foot Churen Himal.

We stopped by a chorten to rest; from left to right: Jeet Bahadur, Akaal Bahadur, the author, Auri Bahadur Raudt.

As we set camp, I asked Prem about the man.

"He says his name is Lama Dorje, Parker Sahib. He lives in the village of Tarengaon, one or two days' walk. He wanted to camp with us."

"I don't like that idea, Prem. Not after yesterday."

"But Parker Sahib, they are only two, we are five. Maybe they think of the Khampas too."

"Maybe. What did you find out in Khakotgaon about the route?"

"They told me about a trail over the Mukut Himal. It is shorter, but very high and may have deep snow. One man said '*Mukut baato mateeeeeee*'—Mukut trail is high. His voice was very high like the trail."

"I think it must be close to twenty thousand feet. I don't like the idea of taking the porters that high this time of year."

"In Tarakot they told us that the Mukut baato was not possible."

"Tarakot seems pretty far away now. I'm not sure they knew what they were talking about."

The next day we passed behind the Dhaulagiri Massif and entered a barren desert terrain almost totally devoid of vegetation. In the cool morning we followed the Barbung Khola. The trail alternated between hugging the river and climbing the steep slopes on either side. A few times it traversed slide areas several hundred feet above the river—active slides that cascaded rock and dirt in intermittent barrages across the trail and down to the cold waters of the river.

At one fifty-yard-wide slide, I stopped to take a picture of one of the porters as he crossed carefully but quickly. Then I changed film. The camera jammed. Cursing, I fiddled with it for several minutes, spooling in a new roll. By the time I had finished, I was alone; the others had gone ahead.

Remembering that we had promised to keep together, I wanted to catch up and hurriedly stepped out onto the edge of the slide. As lightly and as quickly as I could, I tiptoed through the loose rock, creating mini-slides with every step. Stopping would have meant sliding with the debris. Halfway across, a large rock, five feet in diameter and partially embedded in the slope, gave me the idea to pause briefly. I stepped onto the rock. It moved. I lost my balance and fell backwards. From beneath my feet, the boulder disappeared down the slope. I swung my ice axe over my head and with a gratifying *clunk* I felt it dig into the earth. An instinctive movement, it had checked my fall, but I realized the axe might not hold, that the whole mountainside could follow the large rock down to the river bed.

My body hung over the void left by the boulder. For sickening seconds I swung, suspended from above by my ice axe stuck into conglomerate that threatened to rip apart at any moment. Over my shoulder I saw debris raining down on either side of me, picking up speed as it slipped down the slope. A growing cloud of dust rose from the avalanche of earth around me. Breathing shallowly, I tested my ice axe. It still held, nothing over my head moved. The ground immediately surrounding me seemed stable. I dropped into the small depression created two feet below me by the missing boulder. *Quick, before it starts moving.* With three jerks, I worked my ice axe free, then looked across the remaining twenty-five yards to the trail. I saw sandy soil that wasn't moving. With no time to waste working out a strategy, thinking of what to do, I just went with fast, light steps, straining to reach the trail. Behind me the mountainside continued to move, gathering speed, noise and dust.

Stable ground under my feet! I stopped. My lungs sucked for air. *Calm down.* I looked back. The leading edge of the landslide had just reached the canyon floor. I had not noticed the noise in my attempt to reach the trail again. But now it filled the air, a roaring freight train accompanied by a thick and rising cloud of fine dust.

Impervious to sound while on the slope, I now felt weak, especially my knees. I sat down and threw myself backwards as the blood rushed from my head. For several minutes I lay lightheaded and out of breath.

Finally my breath returned more or less to normal and I sat up, propping myself against a rock on the uphill slope. Still feeling weak, I looked once more at the hillside. Only thin tendrils of sand now spilled over the small rocks towards the river below. Leaning forward, I could just see the terminus of the slide area at the river's edge. Dust obscured the tons of rock and dirt that had just fallen.

Dark clouds scudded across the sky, adding to the forbidding view of the barren and lifeless mountain terrain of inner Dolpo to the north. After our confrontation with the Tibetans we should have hung together, but now I was alone. It was too easy for the last person in line to fall behind without being noticed. What would have happened if I had fallen into the landslide? I could have been entombed forever in this vast desert and no one would have known what happened. My epitaph would have been a simple "Lost in the Himalayas of western Nepal."

I did not want to be alone now. Cinching the shoulder straps on my pack, I headed out rapidly along the trail, jogging as best I could. A half mile ahead I saw the last porter round a promontory and then disappear from view. Determined not to stop until I had caught up with them, I picked up my pace. A half hour later I found them resting beside a small bridge spanning a narrow section of the frigid waters of the Barbung Khola. I approached and sat on a wall without saying anything, breathing heavily. Glad only to be in their presence again, I had no words.

For the first time on this trip, I felt totally vulnerable. Even with the fear of the police, the military and the Khampas, I was always quickly able to revive feelings of confidence, assuredness, strength. I knew I would make it through western Nepal alive. But I felt deeply shaken by this brush with death.

It had been so close! If my ice axe had not held, if I hadn't found the bit of solid footing, I would have been hurled down to the river, a fragile human body crushed in the midst of tons of dirt and rock, buried in a crude tomb. I shuddered as I envisioned the helpless plunge, the pain, the fine dust covering my face, cutting off light and air and then suffocating me. But strangely, sitting there under the dark gray sky, I came to feel something else—something new to me. I realized how attuned I had become to the earth, the mountains, the rivers, the sky and snow, even the landsliding rocks. Although they had almost killed me, I didn't view the earth as menacing.

Not believing in an afterlife, I had no reason to fear death, that moment when I would no longer exist. Although I had fought with an animal's instinct to preserve my life, it was not so much a passionate wish to avoid death as to avoid the act of dying. These thoughts troubled me, for they seemed somehow negative, and because I now realized that death itself need hold no fear for me.

But if death meant little to me, what would it mean to the other people in my life? What effect would my death have on my parents? I remembered my father at the airport on the day I left. Not a man to shed tears, he felt an anguish that I now understood. My mother, so quietly accepting of whatever it was that I wanted to do—what would it mean to her? I was their only son, they would be devastated if they lost me. And Clara? What did I mean to her? How would the news of my death affect her?

I said nothing as I sat, breathing heavily, lost in my contemplation of death. Then I heard the voice of a stranger. Turning, I saw that we were not alone. Prem was talking to Lama Dorje and his son. Where had they come from? How did they get here? Not having seen them since the day before, I felt disconcerted at their sudden appearance, I listened to the conversation, catching bits and pieces of what was said.

After fifteen minutes, Prem came and sat with me. "Parker Sahib, Lama Dorje says we can stay with him. In his house in Tarengaon. It is three hours' walk."

"Can we trust him, Prem?"

"Yes, Parker Sahib. I think so."

"Good. Will he sell us food?"

"Yes. He will sell us food—and *chang*!"

"Then tell him we will stay at his house, Prem."

Lama Dorje smiled broadly when Prem relayed the news to him. As it was already three in the afternoon, we set off quickly. We crossed a new wooden bridge and headed up the north side of the Barbung Khola. Pulverized rock covered this slope and soon the dust caked our clothing and faces, clogged our noses. Before long, Lama Dorje veered onto a shortcut up and over a *lekh*, leaving the trail behind. Struggling up through the loose soil, with each step up we sank down again.

We passed two long *mani* walls, each containing hundreds of stones carved in Tibetan script with the mantra, "*Om mani padme hum*." Fifty yards away sat the ruins of buildings, almost invisible against the desert mountainside. Above them I could trace the faintest outline of abandoned terraced fields. Prem asked Lama Dorje about this deserted place.

"Lama Dorje says that it was a large *gompa* and village," Prem said. "He says that when he was a small boy, they had big festivals here. Many *lama*s came from Nepal and Tibet. But then they had a fire. And many of the *lama*s left. Then the Khampas came. They burned houses and stole food. And then there was no more water. Nothing would grow, the people left."

"How long ago did all this happen?"

"He does not know."

"What was the name of this village and *gompa*?"

"Sorry, Parker Sahib. He does not remember."

I looked again and made out the faint traces of more buildings above. An eerie feeling overcame me as I remembered the Mani Rimdu festival at Thyangboche Monastery in eastern Nepal last November. *Lama*s had gathered from Nepal, Bhutan, Sikkim and India. From their scattered villages, hundreds of Sherpas flowed into the monastery in long lines. Early in the morning I had been awakened by the sound of the horns, twelve-foot-long brass *thugchen*. They boomed across the valley and, joined by the beat of drums and the ringing of six-foot gongs, created a lilting sensation, transporting me backwards in time. The masked dances had been alternately stately and wild. *Lama*s wore painted masks of deities, wrathful devil-faced gods that Buddhists believed they would meet after their death. Dozens of dancers in brilliant multihued silk costumes appeared before the crowds, moving with the music of conch shells, reed oboes, horns, cymbals and bells. I asked but never found an answer to my question about the meaning of all I had seen, the sounds and sights of the elemental, timeless legends of all cultures. That was what it must have been like here thirty years ago or more, when Lama Dorje was a young boy. I thought that if I closed my eyes, I might hear the *thugchen*'s deep bass call.

The top of the *lekh* stood at 13,000 feet. While the loose ground had left us panting on the way up, going down was pure joy. In just ten minutes, great bounding steps cushioned by the soft soil brought us back to the main trail eight hundred feet below. We hit the trail and headed east towards Tarengaon, following the Barbung Khola again, this time six hundred feet above the rushing waters. Dusk approached, and the sky turned a darker gray as the previously intermittent cloud cover consolidated into a blanket of drab slate.

A forest of *chortens* appeared. Hundreds, more than I had ever seen in one place before, straddled and blocked the trail. The path meandered among them on its way to Tarengaon. Many arched over the trail and one particularly large one caught my eye. Several tiers rose one above the other, and as I stepped inside I saw the hollow vaulted interior. On the ceiling were sixteen panels, each a two-foot-square *thangka*, a religious painting on cloth. Of mediocre quality, they were nevertheless adorned with generous amounts of gold and silver paint. One of the corner panels was missing, the canvas crudely ripped from the ceiling. That disappointed me; vandalism—particularly of religious artifacts—should have been unknown in this remote backwater.

We rounded a bend and the village of Tarengaon came into view, nestled in a large hollow in the mountainside. At first glance I missed the village altogether. The squat stone structures huddled together along the upper third of the hollow and blended in with the drab tan and gray shades of the surrounding mountains.

Whereas Tarakot and Khakotgaon looked medieval, Tarengaon was biblical, a Jericho in miniature. A dozen fortresslike houses were scattered over a few acres of parched land. On each flat roof was piled carefully hoarded *daura* (firewood), which at this altitude was little more than dried scrub. Except for a few tattered and dirty prayer flags moving in the wind above the larger houses, there was no sign of life. Fallow terraced fields stretched for a hundred yards below the houses. Below the fields, the slope fell away sharply to the abyss of the Barbung Khola.

As we approached the village, our feet kicked up clouds of dust from the parched soil. It seemed impossible that the meager rains that would arrive in June and July could bring life to this dust, but the proof that they did was this village.

We followed Lama Dorje as he wound his way towards the top-most house, his place of distinction as the nominal head of Tarengaon and the local dispenser of justice. As we neared his house he bellowed a few words in Tibetan and two small children, barefoot and filthy, with runny noses and dressed in tattered homespun, appeared on the roof. Above and to the left of the door, a carved stone mask was embedded in the wall, a religious icon to ward off evil spirits. Directly above the door, suspended from a wooden peg, hung a slate *mani* stone, intricately chiseled with Tibetan script.

Lama Dorje led us through a low wood-framed doorway and we found ourselves groping in the dark for the hewn log ladder that led to the upper floor. The porters remained below, stowing the loads away safely while Prem and I climbed to the upper level. The darkened main floor received light only from a single small window and from the flickering fire at the hearth burning in the center of the far wall. We ducked low to avoid the choking smoke. Lama Dorje beckoned us to sit next to him on small Tibetan rugs near the hearth.

His wife appeared from a small side room with three silver-lined

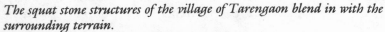

The squat stone structures of the village of Tarengaon blend in with the surrounding terrain.

wooden bowls and two bottles. A large metal ornament was perched on her head. Two pieces of flat brass, the ends rolled into thin cylinders, formed a peaked roof. Pieces of coral and turquoise dangled by sinew off the front and back. I had seen these strange headpieces only one other place, at Bodnath in the wintertime when Tibetans gathered from the far reaches of the Himalayas.

Lama Dorje poured us each a bowl of golden *chang*. Then, lighting a small piece of incense, he made an offering to the altar behind him. Using the smoking incense he traced a circle around a photograph of the Dalai Lama three times, then dipping two fingers into his bowl of *chang*, he flicked drops first to one side then the other. Turning back to us, he urged us to drink. Cool and refreshing, the *chang* reminded us of the drink we had found in Dalphu.

As soon as we drained our bowls and set them down, Lama Dorje's wife refilled them. Five minutes later, under their watchful eyes, we had downed our three polite bowlfuls.

Prem began bargaining for food. Quickly Lama Dorje agreed upon a price and summoned his wife. We were not sure what we had

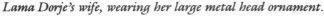

Lama Dorje's wife, wearing her large metal head ornament.

bargained for, but our entire group would be fed. To show our gratitude, Prem gave her a sizable chunk of our remaining petrified yak cheese, which she accepted with a great show of thanks.

Prem summoned the porters from below and together we sat around the fire. By now word had spread that a group of foreigners had arrived and villagers began to trickle in. An hour after we arrived I counted eighteen people in the room. Some sat but most stood, staring curiously at us. Our hostess served the food she had prepared, a hard *chapatti*-like flat bread and potatoes with fiery *achar* (chili). More *chang* appeared, and with the drink the villagers' tongues loosened.

As the center of attention, we had to submit to innumerable questions, asked through Lama Dorje. They were unable to distinguish my foreignness from that of Prem and the porters; to them we were all strangers from Kathmandu. Only a few of the men from the village—none of the women—had traveled as far as Kathmandu. Because the land was so barren, many men turned to trading for livelihood, traveling as far as Jumla in the west, Jomoson in the east and Tibet to the north. Lama Dorje indicated, though, that travel and trade into Tibet had decreased considerably in the last twenty years, making it more difficult for the villagers to turn a profit. Few traveled any further south than Jumla or Jomoson because they were afraid, and rightly so, of *aulo* (malaria), the lowland disease.

Suddenly Prem turned to me with a question from Lama Dorje. "Parker Sahib, Lama Dorje wants to know. Do you have any hashish?"

I stopped for a moment to think about how to answer this one. I *had* brought some hashish from Kathmandu which I was saving as a treat for the porters. "Yes. Tell him, Prem, that I have some hashish."

When Lama Dorje heard this he asked if we could smoke some. I found a small chunk and handed it to him. He looked at it closely, turning it over in his fingers, smelling it like a fine cigar. He commented that it was very fine hashish.

"It's from Afghanistan," I said. Prem translated but Lama Dorje had no idea where Afghanistan was.

He produced a *chillum*, a small pipe, which he loaded with hash and passed around the room. Within minutes everyone was high and, emboldened by the drug, many who had held back in the shadows moved forward, pressing questions on us.

Where were we from? Prem answered that he was a Nepalese, but not from Kathmandu, from further away. How many days walk was it from the sahib's village to Tarengaon? To these people the world was flat, or rather a series of mountains, and every distance was gauged by how many days it took to walk.

I thought, trying to calculate. "One thousand two hundred days' walk," I answered. "And many great lakes to cross."

This answer was met with exclamations of disbelief, but Prem insisted it was true. When the villagers tried to counter this bizarre answer, he still insisted, although I don't think anyone ever truly believed him.

Late in the evening our attention turned to barter. We needed food and these villagers wanted our belongings. The first topic, the most important to them, was our boots. We repeatedly insisted that our boots weren't for sale. Next they focused on our plastic containers, two empty, beat-up cooking oil jugs. A woman appeared from the crowd wanting to buy one, but refused to produce her barter. She indicated she wanted me to accompany her down the stairs.

I rose and followed her in the dark down to our loads stowed below. I picked through my pack and found a flashlight, the only one that still worked among the three we carried. She pointed to the battered green oil container that she wanted. Then, rummaging in her sleeve, she pulled out a rolled-up piece of canvas.

In the beam of my dim flashlight she carefully unrolled the object. It was a *thangka*. Startled, I looked closely at it, the lines of the figure lavishly illuminated in gold and silver. It was the missing panel from the chorten just outside the village. Taken aback, I untied the jug from Akaal Bahadur's basket and gave it to her.

She handed me the *thangka*, but I pushed it away. "No," I indicated to her, "keep it, I don't want it."

She scuttled out the door before I could change my mind and demand payment for the plastic container. How could she do such a thing? How could she desecrate the beautiful *chorten* for an old cooking oil jug? Perhaps the answer lay in a different way of looking at things. Perhaps the *chorten* was not beautiful or sacred to her, merely something she could use, or abuse, to ease her life a bit. This plundering and destruction of the indigenous culture and religion occurred throughout Nepal. Was it an inevitable effect of foreign influence? It was not only the villagers who destroyed the ancient monuments and relics to benefit from them. Profits had been known to line the pockets of some of the highest government officials.

My only solace that night was that the panel had been ripped from the *chorten* before my arrival. At least it was not the direct result of my being there. But if not to me, then to whom did she intend to sell or barter it?

We slept that night curled up on Tibetan rugs next to the hearth. As I drifted off to sleep, I recalled my close encounter with death earlier in the day. What would happen to me if I died here? They could hardly send my body home to be buried in a cemetery in Connecticut. Would I be given a Buddhist burial?

On the way from the Khumbu last December, I had witnessed a funeral that the Tibetans call a "sky burial." A long procession carried the body, flexed into a tight sitting position, from the village of Bhandar to the top of a nearby pass. The last two men in line carried axes. We watched them as they hacked the body to pieces, exposing it to the elements and to the vultures, which would pick the flesh from the bones.

Or perhaps they would burn my body. I thought of the *ghats* (crematory platforms) at Pashupatinath near Kathmandu which poured forth smoke every morning. Was there enough firewood here in Dolpo? The thought of my body burning, not feeling the flames as they consumed my flesh, left me strangely abstracted. Probably if I had been buried in the slide that day, my body would never have been found. A fitting way to go, if that was to be my fate—united with the earth.

CHAPTER
ELEVEN

F OOD . The first business of the day was that of procuring food. For an hour we canvassed the village houses and in the end bought potatoes and thirty-eight eggs, enough to last for four days at full rations. Somehow, within that time, we had to make our way across the mountainous barrier that formed the eastern boundary of Dolpo to the Kali Gandaki watershed. The Kali Gandaki river sliced between the towering peaks of Dhaulagiri and Annapurna, creating a gorge nearly four miles deep, the deepest on earth. For us it was our immediate destination, an inhabited region and a source of food and supplies.

We ate our first meal early before setting out, already dipping into our meager supplies. After packing the *dokos*, we sat with Lama Dorje and thanked him for his generous hospitality.

"Prem, yesterday he told us about a way to the Kali Gandaki that was shorter. Ask him to describe this route very carefully for us." I took out a notepad to write down his directions.

Prem, Akaal Bahadur and Jeet Bahadur sat listening carefully while Prem translated for me.

"We will go north for one day. Then east over two passes to the Kali

Gandaki River. It will be maybe four days. He says we could also take the Mukut baato, but this has much snow and is very high."

We stood and I pressed my hands together, thanking Lama Dorje one last time. His genuine friendliness and persistence in pursuing our acquaintance impressed me. He had been a beacon of hospitality, his house a place of refuge, his village a source of sustenance for our small band of wanderers. Although we had met him only three days before, he had assumed a place of importance far outweighing what he had actually done for us.

As the trail ascended out of Tarengaon, we could look down into the deep gorge to the point where the southward flowing Barbung Khola was forced by a 10,000-foot wall of the Dhaulagiri Himal to make an abrupt right turn and flow east to west. Below us we could see a tiny bridge spanning the river and on the far side a thin ribbon of trail heading east towards the Mukut Himal. In passing this trail junction we had forsaken that route in favor of one of two possible routes further north. Prem and I had decided that this evening we would take a hard look at the options and then settle on which of the northern routes to take.

For an hour, we headed east as the winds steadily increased in intensity. At the elbow, just where the river turned, the winds were funneled and deflected by the wall of the Dhaulagiri Himal looming to our right. The northern flanks of Dhaulagiri II, III and IV, each at over 25,000 feet, were only fleetingly visible through dense, snow-laden clouds, dazzling white jewels floating miles above us.

As the winds increased to forty miles per hour, our porters struggled to make headway. The constant roaring blast of air caught and pulled at their bulky loads. Prem and I forced our way ahead, dropped our packs in the lee of a side canyon and went back to help.

We found Akaal Bahadur in the lead, followed by Jeet Bahadur and Auri Bahadur, their eyes mere slits, their clothes pressed tightly against their bodies as they tried desperately to hold their own against the gale. Prem took the lead, I pushed from the rear. In tight single file, pressed against the man in front, we slowly made headway. When we rounded the bend, the wind abated and we stumbled gratefully down the trail. I dashed on ahead and, looking back, saw Prem and the porters, tiny specks silhouetted against the immense barrier of rock and ice to their backs.

Now in the lee of the elbow, we got our first look at the terrain

Rounding the great bend in the canyon of the Barbung Khola, the tiny figure of a porter is silhouetted against the immense rock and ice barrier of the Dhauligiri Himal.

ahead and to the east of the Barbung Khola. Bleak, awesomely rugged peaks lined up one after the other, monstrous hurdles stretching as far as we could see. As we looked at them, we all knew that somewhere up ahead the lack of food would force us to attempt a crossing of these formidable mountains.

Three times we emerged from side canyons to face the fierce winds on the promontories overlooking the river. Each time the porters became immobilized by the wind, unable to move without help from Prem and me. Each time, we lined up and forced our way around the point to the next side canyon. Slowly the path dropped towards the riverbed and the winds diminished. By midafternoon, we had reached the *khola*.

"Parker Sahib," Prem said. "We should go along the river. The trail above is too windy. The porters cannot walk."

"Okay," I said. "But the trail goes back up the mountainside just ahead. I wonder why it does that? Why doesn't it just follow the river?"

I got my answer an hour later when we came to a cliff rising directly out of the water on this west side of the river. We had no alternative but to cross the frigid waters. No doubt about it, trails went where they did in the Himalaya for a good reason. Generations had traveled on foot or horseback with yaks, sheep and goats. They had chosen routes along the path of least resistance. Our choice was to return and face the wind or stay and face the icy waters.

We chose the waters. We stripped off our shoes and socks, rolled up our pants legs as high as possible. The water looked no more than two feet deep, but moved swiftly over smooth rounded stones. And it was cold, as if just that morning it had been part of an icy glacier. We discussed and agreed on a plan of attack. For better balance, we would link arms and wade the river together.

We lined up, linked together and stepped into the water.

"Ahhhhhh," a collective gasp rose from the five of us. In a matter of seconds, our feet went from cold to numb.

We moved quickly, but being linked together made it difficult for us to go at our own pace; we were forced to adopt the timing of the slowest, the one who was currently having the most trouble. The bank was only twenty-five yards away but it seemed like miles as we agonizingly made our way towards it. Steadily, with gasps of pain, we progressed. As we neared the far side, I opened my mouth to express delight at the end of the torture.

Our first glimpse of the terrain east of the Barbung Khola; awesomely rugged peaks lined up one after the other, monstrous hurdles stretching as far as we could see.

"We're almost theeeeeeee . . ." I stepped down. Chilling tendrils of water reached up my legs. Over my thighs. Stopped at my waist. We had hit a depression. Caution and sure footing no longer mattered. With screeches of alarm, defiance and pain, we moved more quickly than I have ever seen five men move.

We crumpled as we hit the far bank, each falling to the ground, immersed in his own private agony. Although it took only a few minutes to cross the river, my feet had turned an ugly blotched purple. I heard gasps and whimpering around me as I sat hunched over my tortured feet, then realized it was myself I heard, crying out loud in pain. But the way to warmth lay in movement and we pulled our socks and shoes on quickly.

With soaked pants we continued along the river bank, hoping for no more river crossings. But just as my pants began to dry out a half hour later, we found ourselves again staring at a vertical wall of rock emerging from the water and blocking our way.

The river was shallower at this point, but, at seventy-five yards, twice as wide. With no questions asked, we sat down and took off our shoes and socks again.

"Parker Sahib," Prem said. "I don't like this. Maybe this time we should go faster."

"Right. Look, if we link arms like we did the last time, but go much faster, as fast as we can, I think we can make it. It's not as deep and if somebody slips, he will have the others to help him. What do you think?"

Prem consulted with the others and we all agreed with this strategy. We stood on the edge of the river, frigid water lapping the stones inches from our exposed feet. Prem counted down for us, "*Ek, dui, tin*!" ('One, two, three!')

"Arghhhhh!" we bellowed together, plunging into the freezing stream.

We splashed energetically, keeping up our momentum until halfway across. But the river exhausted us and then we slowed, agonizing over every step yet again. Although my feet were numb, every protruding rock, every sharp stone pierced through the unfeeling outer layers of flesh to the sensitive ones underneath.

Nearing the far bank, we broke ranks and each of us stumbled onto shore by himself. Just as I hit the bank, I heard a cry and turned. Jeet Bahadur had stumbled only a few feet from the edge, his bulky *doko* pulling him off balance. He floundered for only a few seconds as I watched, unable to even think of reaching out to him. Then he pulled himself to his feet and came to shore. I slumped down on the ground in agony.

I wanted nothing more than to curl up and cry. Involuntary whimpers once more escaped from my lips as I forced myself to reach for my shoes and socks. *They will make you warm, put them on now, Parker.*

Around me the others lay each absorbed in his own personal anguish. Akaal Bahadur lay on the ground, repeating an undecipherable Tamang phrase over and over. Prem hunched over his feet, crying out and clutching his toes in his hands. Jeet Bahadur sat miserably wet, shivering and moaning. While the first river crossing had been painful and a nuisance, this second one had broken us. For fifteen minutes we sat, saying nothing, each concentrating on warming his own frozen toes. Then the clouds parted and the welcome warmth of the sun spread over and around us, a gesture of mercy from the gods.

I looked ahead and spotted a flat sandy area slightly up from the river. "Prem," I called out. "Camp there?" I pointed to the spot.

Slowly Prem raised his head to look to where I pointed, then smiled. "Yes, Parker Sahib. We cannot go any farther today."

We set camp and ate potatoes, *tsampa* and tea. I had no stomach for any of it, but forced myself to swallow the tasteless food. After our meal, the temperature began to drop, so we crowded into one tent to discuss the route options that lay ahead.

Using one of the three remaining candles, I spread out the map and we all perused it. Suggestions and possibilities flew back and forth until we had narrowed them down to two.

The first we called the "long route." This route, which was marked on our map, would take us far to the north, along the Barbung Khola, past the village of Charkabhotgaon, then south, in a large arc, crossing either the Sangdak Pass or the Dhampus Pass to reach the Kali Gandaki. We estimated it would take six days. That would leave us short of rations and would mean that we had to find food in Charkabhotgaon.

The porters favored this option because the route was easy and we would cross only one high pass. But Prem and I hesitated for several reasons. First, we had heard that Charkabhotgaon was a sparsely inhabited village, and might even be deserted this time of year. Therefore, resupplying with food along this route seemed dubious. Also, we had heard that it was a Khampa stronghold, and that the villagers had in the past not taken kindly to strangers. Based on our past experiences, I was uncertain that we could reach the Sangdak Pass even in six days by this route. If we didn't find food somewhere along the way, we might come close to starving.

The second option was what we termed the "Dorje route," after Lama Dorje who had described it to us. By this route, we would continue north along the river until reaching the village of Daragaon. From there we would turn east, ascending past the village and over a pass. After this, we would descend to a river which flowed north, then follow this river upstream until we crossed either the Sangdak Pass or the Dhampus Pass, we weren't sure which. From our present position to this pass, according to Lama Dorje, would take us two days. The drawback to this plan was that no such trail was marked on our map and, although Lama Dorje was most sincere, experience told us that sincerity did not always mean accuracy. And even given the gross inaccuracies of the map, the distance seemed too great to cover in two days. Although shorter, this route would also take us over two high passes. Given our alternatives, I was more afraid of running out of food than ascending passes. As we all felt the effects of prolonged poor diet combined with a high exercise level, I could not imagine we would fare well at this altitude without food.

Prem and I favored this second option and ultimately won the porters over. Now we were unanimous in our choice of the "Dorje route" which, when translated, meant the Path of Lightning Bolts. A light to guide our way.

That night, lying in my sleeping bag, I felt a sense of relief, knowing which way we would go in the morning. I had worried about this crossing for a long time, how we would reach the Kali Gandaki. The choice seemed appropriate for us, given our food supplies, although I knew it would be far from easy.

The next morning, having abandoned the trail of the previous day, we continued along the riverbed. Within half an hour, we once again found ourselves facing a river crossing. This time we scouted the river, looking for the best place. We chose a twenty-five-yard-wide section with an even depth, and then crossed in silence. With the bright sun warming us, the chore seemed easier.

Crossing a 25-yard wide section of the Barbung Khola.

By late morning, the village of Daragaon came into view, three hundred feet above the river. Squat flat-roofed houses sat among a few scrubby conifers. We stopped for our first meal a mile before reaching the village.

After lunch, we passed young boys tending yaks that grazed near the river. There was no response to us, only unfriendly glares. After we had passed, I turned at the sound of stones hitting the earth behind me. An ominous reception from the first inhabitants of this remote village.

A line of *chortens*, overgrown with weeds, with peeling plaster and faded whitewash, heralded the approach to the village. A remarkable *gompa*, a stone fortress structure of white and red built directly into the cliff, greeted us. The cliff, made of sedimentary layers laid down by the ocean hundreds of millions of years ago, had buckled into a swirling vision of the cataclysmic forces of nature. An astonishing sight, the *gompa* represented a tiny intrusion of man into the overwhelming predominance of raw nature here in Dolpo.

A few yards further on, just before we reached the village, we passed a stream descending from the ridges far above us. A vision of frothing white water flowing over the rocks met our gaze, but no sound emanated from it. No gurgling, babbling, swishing rush of water met us. We walked closer, but the stream didn't move, the water didn't flow. Frozen solid, the water had been caught and trapped in the act of flowing downstream to meet the Barbung Khola. We stopped and looked, not quite believing this frozen apparition. Auri Bahadur poked and chipped at it with his ice axe, but did not find a single flowing drop. A stone causeway had been set on top of the ice and thus we crossed this bizarre frozen stream.

Coming up to the village we saw several people on their roofs. "Prem," I said. "Let's see if we can buy some food here."

Setting down his pack, Prem approached the first small house. Just as he called out, we heard the door slam shut with a heavy *thunk*. Prem knocked and called, but no one answered.

He went to the next house and received the same treatment. Looking up, I could see no one. They had all disappeared inside their houses. Two scraggly mongrels eyed us from atop a wall a few yards away. The entire village had shut its collective door to us.

Below we saw groups of women preparing the fields for planting. Their bent figures seemed to ignore us as surely as the people in the village.

"Parker Sahib, should I ask these women for food?"

"No, Prem. I don't think anyone wants to sell us food. I don't think anyone wants to talk to us. I don't think anyone wants us here at all. Let's go."

Hoisting our loads, we followed the faint trail leading upwards out of the village. As we climbed, we realized we would soon be above the tree line, above any vegetation at all. Having sold the kerosene for our stove to the mayor of Dalphu, we spread out across the slope and collected anything that might burn; twigs, sticks, dried yak dung.

We climbed for two hours. The late afternoon wind blew steadily at our backs as the temperature fell. Behind us the corrugated peaks of Dolpo turned earth shades of ocher, then ethereal shades of pink, orange and finally the night shade of purple as the sun descended.

A small grassy level area became our camping site, a summer yak

Approaching the village of Daragaon, we passed a stream that was frozen solid.

pasture at 15,600 feet. As we set the tents, a movement caught my eye a hundred yards above us on the slope. I turned to look, but saw nothing and returned to the task of setting camp. A few moments later, I saw it again, a subtle stirring among the rocks. I looked, staring for twenty long seconds at the spot that I thought had moved.

Then they materialized. One, then three, finally twenty sheeplike animals camouflaged against the rocky terrain. I pulled out my binoculars and picked out a male, his head weighed down with huge spiraling horns.

"Prem," I called. "Come and look. A herd of *bharal* (blue sheep)."

"The Tibetans call them *nah*," Prem informed me.

For ten minutes I stood watching as they slowly made their way up and across the slope away from us. With brown legs, dark chests and nearly white underbellies, they blended in well with their surroundings. If their slight movement hadn't caught my eye, I would have missed them, these magnificent wild animals of the Himalayas. In all the wilderness I had crossed in Nepal, I had seen so few wild creatures. The others—bears, wolves, leopards, wild yaks—had been hunted almost out of existence or their habitats destroyed by the pressures of human population. How long would this herd of blue sheep survive here on this mountain slope? Would my descendants be able to return here in twenty or thirty years to see theirs?

Reluctantly, I turned from the sheep and back to the camp chores. The temperature had plunged after the sun dipped below the Himalaya to the south and east. Using the circular cakes of dried yak dung scattered near the camp, Prem soon had a hot fire to cook the evening meal. Yak dung makes a particularly good fuel, burning hot with an even, reddish glow. Luckily, we had a ready fuel source in the pasture. I was not sure what we would do the next day if we were forced to camp still higher. The fuel we collected on the way up from Daragaon would last only through one more meal.

Akaal Bahadur and I went to the nearest frozen river and hacked off several large ice chunks for our evening water. Huddling around the fire we watched our miniature icebergs melt in our largest pot. Into it went two large potatoes and two eggs each, our evening ration. At our altitude of over 15,000 feet, it took more than an hour for the potatoes to soften sufficiently for us to force them down. Tea laced with salt and pepper was a favorite of the porters, and that night we each got a large mugful. I forced that down as well, even though I thought it tasted like the Pacific Ocean.

As soon as we had finished eating, we slipped off to our sleeping bags or, in the case of the porters, blankets. The temperature had fallen into the low teens.

I woke at three-thirty, my bladder aching. I tried to ignore the call of nature, but eventually extracted myself from my warm cocoon. Stumbling over a sleeping Prem's head, I unzipped the tent door and stepped out into the night.

Wind, blowing subzero air from the heights above, hit me with a chilling force. High in the sky, a blazingly white half moon flooded the earth with light. The entire length of the Dhaulagiri Himal spanned the southern horizon, ghostly frozen citadels. To the west in Dolpo, uncounted, unnamed peaks stretched into the distance, reflecting white under the light of the bleak, raw moon. As forbidding a land as I had ever seen, this stained moonscape looked uninhabitable, uncrossable, as cold and as hard as any earthly place. I shuddered against the piercing cold, then remembered my business. I finished quickly, sending my compliments in a great arc down the slope towards Daragaon.

I smiled as I remembered another nighttime foray, the previous November at Thyangboche. We had camped on the field just below the monastery, along with hundreds of other foreigners and locals who had come for the Mani Rimdu festival. There, when I also woke late one night and had to get up, I had witnessed another frozen spectacle. It had been fifteen degrees and a dusting of frost clung to the tents, the trees, the ground, even the yaks scattered in the one hundred acre grounds. The full moon of November, the harbinger of the festival, reflected brilliantly off the frost. To the northeast the summit of Everest rose behind the Nupste-Lhotse face; to the east, Ama Dablam, Kangtega and Tamserku; to the southwest, framing the famous Thyangboche Gompa itself were the twin peaks of Kwangde. To the west rose the sacred Khumbiyula. The full moon high in the sky, its resplendent light reflecting off the peaks, convinced me that this must be the most beautiful place on earth.

Awestruck by my surroundings, I had returned to my sleeping bag. Just as I had tucked myself in and stopped shivering, I realized that I had forgotten what I had gone out to do! Groaning in frustration, I pulled on my clothes, hat and boots and crawled out of the tent, refusing to look up until I had finished. Then I stood for another ten minutes with my mouth agape, not quite believing that anything could look quite like that, a 360-degree vision of glistening peaks conceived in an artist's eye. Suddenly, the deep bass rumble of the *thugchen*s resonated from within the monastery, announcing the beginning of another day of the festival.

The frigid winds brought me back to Dolpo. As I stepped back towards my tent, I heard a soft guttural sound. Walking closer to the porters' tent, I made out Jeet Bahadur's moaning voice. The cold had penetrated through his lightweight sleeping bag and the too-thin Jeet Bahadur could not withstand the intensely frigid temperatures. His discomfort followed me as I returned to my warm sleeping bag.

CHAPTER
TWELVE

ABOVE DARAGAON

Thursday, April 5, 1984

FOOLISHLY, I had left my water bottle out instead of putting it into the bottom of my sleeping bag along with my boots. In the morning, a solid block of ice was my reward. I looked at the thermometer. It had dropped to the minimum on the gauge, minus four degrees Fahrenheit.

That morning, we remained huddled in our bags until the sun began to wash our tents with warmth. As soon as I got up, I took all of my clothes and laid them out on my sleeping bag. Separating everything into two piles, I put aside only what I could wear at one time. Then, I took the other pile—a pair of pants, four pairs of socks, a pair of gloves, one flannel and one wool shirt, a light polypropylene top, a wool hat and a bunting jacket—and distributed them among the porters. They made a show of refusal, but I insisted.

"Please take them," I said. "They will keep you warm. Tonight it may be colder than last night."

At this the porters took the clothes and thanked me. Auri Bahadur, who up until now had seemed especially impervious to the cold, accepted a shirt, then a pair of socks which he immediately put over his hands and pulled up his arms as far as they would go. I knew I had parted with these things forever. At least I was now on a similar level in terms of clothing, if not in the way of sleeping gear. The haunting sounds of Jeet Bahadur's shivering would not allow me to act otherwise.

To take advantage of the available fuel, we decided to have our first meal of the day before starting out. Because there was no source of running water, we had to melt our drinking water for the day as well. It was well after ten before we got underway.

We followed the course of a frozen stream upwards through loose scree slopes. The stream became smaller, then just intermittent patches of white ice along a dry course. Finally it petered out altogether at over 17,000 feet, having sublimated into the dry desert atmosphere.

The mountains now appeared totally barren, devoid of any form of life. Not even lichen clung to the talus around us. The shifting loose slopes made our ascent arduous; with each step forward we slid backwards half the gain. A saddle several hundred feet above gave us hope of finding a pass and we pushed on towards this goal without stopping. Our breath wheezed in our chests as we struggled towards the pass. Close together, we came up onto the saddle, but stopped only briefly. Disappointed, we found it to be a false pass and I looked ahead to see yet another saddle still hundreds of feet higher.

"Damn," I said aloud.

"Yiss, Sahib," Akaal Bahadur answered, making it the consensus of us all.

An hour later fierce, cold winds greeted us as we neared the top. Any joy at reaching the pass soon evaporated, however, as we looked out on nothing but vast expanses of frozen rivers and lifeless mountains. Total desolation to the horizon. Our spirits plummeted.

With stiff, cold fingers, I extracted my altimeter from my pack. It read just over 19,000 feet. The porters started off the pass ahead of me; they had started to shiver with cold in the blasting winds despite their new clothes. Lingering, I hastily took a few photographs, then plunged down after them. We descended effortlessly with great bounding strides in the soft earth. Forty minutes and 1500 feet later brought us to another ribbon of ice which we followed down to its confluence with yet another larger frozen river. Auri Bahadur spotted a few yak patties and started a small fire. At 16,500 feet we had tea.

We had now followed the first part of Lama Dorje's instructions, we had crossed a pass high above Daragaon. The next step was to find a north-flowing tributary of the Barbung Khola.

"This must be the river that flows north that Lama Dorje told us about," Prem said.

"It looks like it flows north to me," I answered.

Akaal Bahadur countered this, insisting that the river flowed south. I looked again. The river was frozen solid. The barren, treeless terrain was disorienting. To our left the river appeared to flow towards us, yet in the distance to our right it also appeared to flow in our direction. My head ached, I had no desire to argue with the river. A deep gnawing hunger stretched to all parts of my body, making me tired, fatigued beyond words. But words there were. An argument quickly arose as to which direction the river actually flowed. Prem, Jeet Bahadur and I felt that it flowed to the north, as Lama Dorje had indicated to us. Akaal Bahadur and Auri Bahadur insisted that it went in the other direction. Words flew about, overheated in the thin, cold air.

Akaal Bahadur jumped up. Pacing back and forth in an imaginary cage, he shouted at us. Agitated, he shook his fist as foul Nepali curses spewed forth. We were fools if we thought that the river flowed north. Couldn't we see with our eyes that it had to flow south? Our brains were less intelligent than a demented yak's and our opinions as worthless as its excrement.

"Sit down and be quiet," Prem told him in Nepali.

"No, I won't. You are all fools."

Prem leapt to his feet and confronted Akaal Bahadur. Chest to chest they stood, arguing with rising voices. Auri Bahadur and I bounded up and placed ourselves between the antagonists, angry shouts ringing in our ears. *Stop this before anarchy breaks out. At all costs, we must stay together. Now, more than ever we cannot afford to degenerate into quarreling.*

Disgusted, Akaal Bahadur took his ice axe to the river. Stepping out onto the ice, he began chopping away at it, venting his anger on the white frozen froth.

"He's out of his mind," I said to Prem in English. "What does he think he can prove?"

"You're crazy, Akaal Bahadur," Prem yelled at him. "Parker Sahib thinks so, too. Breaking up the whole river won't do any good."

"Fuck off," Akaal Bahadur answered in Nepali. He threw more

curses at us as he continued to flail wildly at the ice, chipping away pieces that flew in the air along with his swearing.

Such erratic behavior unsettled me. This deep, brutal anger was intense, destructive and so out of character. Akaal Bahadur had a fine vocabulary of curses, but they usually accompanied laughter rather than anger. What had caused this radical change in behavior—lack of food, mental fatigue, altitude?

We turned our backs to him, gathering around the teapot, waiting for our water to boil. Twenty minutes later, we heard him.

"*Pani!*" he yelled, throwing his hands into the air. "Look, look," he commanded us.

He stood over a two-foot-deep hole in the ice, sweat standing out on his forehead despite the chill air. His face bore traces of anger, but it also showed triumph. At the bottom of the hole a tiny trickle of water, *pani*, flowed, dripping steadily through the ice. It flowed south.

He was right. This river ran south, not north. Akaal Bahadur gloated. Incongruously, now that we knew which way the river flowed, more confusion entered the picture.

"Maybe we are turned around," Jeet Bahadur suggested. "Maybe this is north and that is south. Maybe this river really does flow north."

"That's crazy," I groaned.

"What ever gave you such a stupid idea?" Prem asked him in Nepali.

"Maybe he's right," Akaal Bahadur joined in. "Everything here is turned around. There are no trees, the mountains all look the same. Maybe this river does flow north."

Auri Bahadur agreed with Akaal Bahadur. I shook my head.

"What's happening here?" I wailed. "Look, I'll get my compass out, that will prove it to you." I dug deep in my pack and produced my magic piece of western technology. We crowded around as the needle swung gently and stopped, pointing to the north, the direction opposite to that of the stream's flow.

"Why should we trust this?" Akaal Bahadur said. "What does this thing do that we cannot do? How do we know what it says is true? Foreigners' machines break, maybe it is broken."

Jeet Bahadur and Auri Bahadur seconded Akaal Bahadur's opinion. I sat stunned. They didn't believe the compass!

Angrily, I snapped at Akaal Bahadur in Nepali. "Now that you have so much ice, put it in the pot. We will have another cup of tea. No one will talk until the tea is ready."

Quietly we sat watching the pot until the bubbles rose and the water steamed, far below 212 degrees. With fresh mugs of tea, we sat close together, ready to voice our opinions. Prem suggested that every one be allowed to speak and that no one interrupt until that person was finished. We all nodded, in agreement at least about this point.

Prem went first. "I believe this river runs south. I know which way is north and Parker Sahib's compass points this way, too. Maybe Lama Dorje is wrong or maybe we have not yet come to his river. Maybe we need to cross another pass. This is what I think we should do. Follow this river north. When we find a good place, we should go up and over the next ridge. There we should find the river that flows north."

None of us had thought of this insightful suggestion, and I realized that it was a good plan.

Jeet Bahadur said he wanted to talk next. "I don't know which way is north or south. But I trust Prem and Sahib. Wherever they go, I will go with them."

Inwardly sighing a cautious breath of relief, I felt the tensions lessen. Now we had three on our side.

Auri Bahadur spoke next. In a quiet assured voice he spoke his mind. "I think we should stay together. It would be dangerous and foolish for us to go two ways. I, too, will go where Prem and Sahib go."

I turned to Akaal Bahadur. The still air held an expectant hush. He pursed his lips and stared at us. I could tell he weighed the consequences of heading off alone. There were no trails, no sign of humans anywhere. We had just had an hour's confrontation and discussion about which way was north and which way was south. How could he think he could find his way alone? Stubborn, angry, but not stupid. "I will go with you. *But,*" he growled, still angry, "I am right. We will be lost if we go the way Prem says to go. You will see. I will come with you and you will see."

With Akaal Bahadur's final words ringing in our ears, we finished our tea and quickly got underway. It was now late in the afternoon, the skies were overcast and slate gray. We hurried along the river valley, anxious to cover as much distance as possible before cold and darkness overtook us. Despite our consensus, we felt an uneasiness, an urgency to our journey. To say whether or not we were lost was only a matter of semantics.

We walked until dusk, then dropped our loads as we spread out along the river valley, searching for precious fuel. Isolated tufts of grass stuck out of the rocky soil, but not in sufficient kind and quantity to cook a meal. Although we still carried a few sticks, we needed something else, preferably yak dung.

Deepening twilight threatened to rob us of the necessary light when Jeet Bahadur called out to us from a third of a mile up the frozen river. We converged on the site, ultimately finding enough fuel for a sizable fire. Gathering as many yak patties as we could, we hurried back to the campsite. We worked with near-desperation in setting the tents and starting the fire. Sharp gusts blew down the river valley, and as the sun set the temperature plunged towards zero. We chopped our ration of potatoes into small pieces to speed the cooking, then added them to the boiling water along with one egg each. None of us had much appetite, and Jeet Bahadur complained of nausea and headache. He had not felt well since early afternoon, but now he groaned in misery. His symptoms resembled those of altitude sickness. This worried me because at 16,700 feet, our campsite was the lowest place for miles around. He asked for medicine but I had nothing for altitude sickness. I gave him some aspirin, but within a few minutes he vomited it up.

As night fell, the sky cleared, an ominous harbinger of a frigid night. Prem and I had heavy sleeping bags, though neither was rated below five degrees. The porters had only an assortment of light sleeping bags, bedrolls and blankets. Before we went to sleep, Prem and I emptied our packs, into which Jeet Bahadur and Auri Bahadur stuffed their feet as short bivvy sacks. They slept huddled together, body heat as important as blankets that night.

Just as I headed for my warm sleeping bag, I felt my bowels complain and quickly headed over a small ridge behind our tents. Before returning, I stopped and looked at the stars. In clarity and abundance, they were the most magnificent display I had ever seen. Hundreds of miles from the nearest city, there was no light, nothing to dilute their brilliance. The Milky Way spilled across the center of the sky, the accumulated glow from billions of stars. For the first time, I noticed the great spiraling arms of our galaxy. With our tents not visible, I felt truly alone, not a trace of human existence anywhere in sight. Now, here, in the remotest place I had ever been, my thoughts turned to my family, my parents, my friends back home. I wondered what they were doing at this moment, whether they thought of me. So incredibly far away in every respect, so many layers removed from me. Kathmandu. How distant that city seemed now! From where I stood, it seemed the center of civilization. Even to the Nepalese of Kathmandu, Dolpo represented a mysterious, far-off place few had ever visited. Huge mountains, a vast portion of the Himalayas, stood between us and Kathmandu.

I remembered that when I left the U.S., a friend had commented that his vision of Kathmandu was of a place at the very ends of the earth. New York City to a frozen river in Dolpo, how far must that be? Was it more than fortuitous that a person could not jump instantly from one to the other, that one had to approach in steps? Almost as if it could damage a person to make that leap too quickly; damaging to the psyche if not to the physical being.

During the months in eastern Nepal and especially here in western Nepal, I had sensed an awakening of a spirit that seemed new to me. Something that had been lying dormant in my life in the West, with its remarkable capacity to buffer our daily lives from the earth, struggled to the surface. I felt a new kinship with the mountains, the water, the wind; the daily cycle of day and night, the monthly cycle of the moon, the yearly cycle of the planet.

By coming halfway around the world, by removing myself in multiple cultural and physical layers from the West, the life, the culture, the view of the world that I had known, I began to see the earth and my relation to it in a new light. I sensed my spirit more closely tied to the earth than I had ever imagined.

Was this perhaps the reason for my coming here, for attempting this traverse of the Himalayas? Could this have been the real reason why I left my family, my job, my friends, my life at home? Was this longing to make a connection between myself and the earth as the cradle of human existence what lay at the root of my dissatisfaction?

I hurried back to my tent. Burying myself in my icy sleeping bag along with my boots and my water bottle, I shivered uncontrollably until my body heat warmed it. Prem lay beside me.

"Parker Sahib, I am worried."

"So am I, Prem. We don't really know where we are, our map may be inaccurate, but we're still farther from Jomoson than Lama Dorje said we should be in three days."

"We have only one day's food left."

"The question is, then, how far to the nearest village, and can we get food there?"

"The nearest village on our map is Sangdak. Lama Dorje said that we must go over two passes. But Parker Sahib, maybe it will take more than one day to reach there. Maybe almost two."

"So what will we do?"

"If we eat less, we can have three meals. Then maybe we can get to Sangdak."

"Cut rations? We haven't got enough to eat as it is. This is a Catch–22, Prem. That means that if we don't get enough to eat, we can't go far or fast enough to get to the village where we can find food. Whatever we do, we get screwed." I sighed in resignation. "Okay, cut rations. What else can we do?"

I fell asleep, thinking of the unsettling prospect of running out of food. I pondered the possibility of a yak steak or two, hot, sizzling. Would it be asking too much for them to be tender as well?

The night treated us brutally, reaching into our bedding with icy cold talons, causing us to shiver for long hours. As soon as the sun reached our tents, we got up and moved around. The porters looked tired, lines of fatigue creased their faces, their movements were slow and uncoordinated. We brewed large pots of tea, and once more ate our first meal before setting out. When Prem announced the rationing scheme, the porters nodded in agreement, taking it in stride, although I knew they were hungry. I was; we all were.

We broke camp after collecting what yak dung we could find and stuffing it into our packs. We headed upstream due north for a mile. Finding a small frozen tributary that entered from the mountains directly to the east, we decided to begin our ascent following this stream. Our climb seemed a carbon copy of our ascent of the day before. The same scree slope, the small river of ice dissipating above 18,000 feet, a false pass and more climb.

At 18,500 feet we rested for a time. Looking back we could clearly see the pass we had crossed the day before and our route along the frozen river. Looking upwards, we could not yet see the next pass.

With a mighty heave I righted myself and trudged upward on the endless slope. Soon I saw the porters stop and heft curious rocks, round and the size of grapefruit. Jeet Bahadur struck one on another rock, breaking it open. I peered over his shoulder to look at his treasure.

Crystals! The rock had a hollow interior lined with dazzling quartz and purple rhomboid crystals that I could not identify. Each porter stuffed several of these geodes into his load, exclaiming that they would fetch a high price in Kathmandu. My mind reeled with the thought of adding more weight to their *dokos* by loading up on rocks, of all things.

Here we were ascending to over 19,000 feet, half lost and almost without food somewhere in the most remote part of the Himalayas. No trails, our map so inaccurate as to be nearly useless, no sign of another human anywhere, and these men stuffed their loads with rocks! At least it was a sign of their faith. They had no thought of not reaching Kathmandu.

After more than three hours of slow climbing, the crest of what appeared to be a pass loomed above us. The altitude slowed us to a crawl and I locked into a regular rhythm. Step, inhale, step, exhale, for thirty steps. Then, when my pulse thumped alarmingly in my temples, I stopped for ten breaths before continuing. In the thin air we moved, each in his own oxygen-starved world, each at his own pace. Soon we were stretched out for half a mile as we climbed towards the broad saddle that we hoped was the pass. As we neared the top the wind increased and the temperature dropped. The weather pattern of the previous days held; clear morning skies, then increasing winds and overcast by midafternoon. In fact, it had not rained or snowed on us, and as we ascended towards 20,000 feet, even the frozen rivulets had evaporated into the atmosphere.

Ahead of me, I watched Prem and Akaal Bahadur struggle to reach the pass. I stopped, rested heavily on my ice axe and watched their progress. They climbed the loose scree slowly, almost painfully, the wind whipping their clothes. A steep headwall marked the last hundred feet. A nightmare for them, as a step forward was followed by a slide back almost as far. They neared the top, and as the slope leveled out, they sped up and made a final dash to the pass.

They leaned forward, almost doubled over into the fierce wind. Waiting for their reaction, I found myself holding my breath, watching to see what effect the view of the other side might have on them. Two small figures, so familiar to me, their loads resting easily on their backs as if they had grown there. I waited for a sign of what they saw ahead.

With a shake of his body, Akaal Bahadur swung his bulky load back and forth, as if he were saying, "No!" Prem dropped to one knee.

With heightened anxiety, I pushed on, reaching the pass ten minutes later alongside Jeet Bahadur. The wind tore at our clothes, roared in our ears. Desperate to descend but anxious to take a photo, I took off my pack. Checking my altimeter, I found it reading 20,200 feet. I now saw for myself the desolate and forbidding view to the east. More of the same, frozen rivers, snow-capped mountains, crumbling cliffs of burnt umber and gray as far as I could see.

With freezing fingers, I took two quick photos, then Jeet Bahadur and I followed Prem and Akaal Bahadur down the far side. They had stopped a mere hundred feet below the top where the wind had slackened considerably. Auri Bahadur soon arrived and we rested together. Closing my eyes, I sucked in deep draughts of the thin air. My rapid heartbeat pounded in my ears. A minute later, I opened my eyes, astonished at what I saw.

Prem sucked at a cigarette, then passed it on to the porters. At 20,000 feet, I was dizzy from the lack of oxygen, and I watched in amazement as the porters puffed at the dregs of this cigarette. I could not imagine smoking at this altitude, but these men had the capacity to smoke just about anything, anywhere. I remembered them in the forest just beyond Mandu, out of cigarettes, out of *beedies*, pulling oily birchbark off the trees to roll and smoke the foul marijuana I had bought for them. My head spun just looking at them now.

Once again, we made quick work of the descent on the vast open slopes, dropping four thousand feet to reach a valley floor within two hours. We found a river, frozen on top, but we could clearly hear the rush of flowing water underneath the top layer of ice. I approached it cautiously, fearful of what I would find. Which way did it flow? Was it north or south? Was this Lama Dorje's river? Or had we lost ourselves again?

It flowed north!

The weather closed in, thick clouds lowered around us, making it seem later than it was. A summer yak corral nearby with readily available fuel tempted us to camp for the night. I had hoped to

Prem and Akaal Bahadur reaching the 20,000-foot pass.

continue on towards early evening, our food supplies being so meager. But the route began ascending once more from here, and with the increased altitude came the cold. In the interest of the porters we elected to set camp in the shelter of the corral at 15,500 feet.

Once again we turned in with the setting sun. With more than ten hours until daylight, I lay awake in my sleeping bag. My thoughts turned to Clara.

She was an enigma in many ways. We had met almost every afternoon on the roof of the hotel where we perused the Kathmandu valley and watched the sun set over the majestic Himalayas.

Although she never said anything, I began to suspect that she was involved somehow with the hotel owner, Praven. I saw them leaving the hotel together in his car and, from his manner towards her, surmised the closeness of the relationship. One afternoon I made an oblique remark about it.

At 20,000 feet, I watched as Akaal Bahadur passed out the cigarettes.

Camping in the shelter of a summer yak corral at 15,500 feet.

She responded, "And what do you think my involvement with him is?"

I looked at her and spoke truthfully, "I think he is keeping you as a mistress."

She seemed pained by the suggestion, but did not answer. I knew it was true. Despite this revelation, every afternoon I waited for her on the roof, and she too kept the unspoken rendezvous. Our mutual attraction was evident to the other foreigners and to her friend Sera. One day Clara appeared late in the afternoon, visibly upset. We talked desultorily for a few minutes.

"Clara. What's wrong?"

Close to tears, she blurted it all out. "You were right, Parker. Praven is keeping me. But it was all right, he said he would marry me. You must understand, our family has obligations to his. His family has helped mine for many many years, even before I was born. He has always been very good to me. He has paid for many things. It is our families, you see.

"But now things are different. He has kept things from me. I didn't understand. Some of his family I never met. Now I have learned that he has betrayed me. The maid told me. She said that of course he could afford to keep three wives. Three wives! He has two wives already and he thought that he could marry me and I would be his third wife! The maid is right, he can afford it. He would just keep me in a separate house, away from the others. He was only waiting until I got pregnant, and then I would have to marry him."

I shook my head; this was a bizarre turn of events. "Clara, I don't understand."

"In Nepal it is okay to have more than one wife if you can provide for them. But how could he think I would do that? I am a Catholic, not a Hindu. How could I marry a man who is already married? How could I have not seen this? How could I be so blind?"

"Clara." I reached out for her. She looked at me through the tears in her eyes, and I sensed her yearning for me as well.

"For me, this is terrible news. I must go now." She rose and walked towards the stairs.

The next day Sera and Clara came to the fourth-floor balcony. Clara looked around anxiously, then whispered, "May we see you in your room?"

"Of course." Quickly the three of us slipped into my room and I closed the door. We talked for a few minutes, then Sera got up and left. As soon as the door closed we were in each other's arms, our lips met and for a long minute we kissed. Finally she gently pushed me back and spoke.

"Parker, I have something to tell you. I have decided to go back to Darjeeling."

Devastated by this news, I tightened my hold on her.

"I cannot stay here with him, he has betrayed me. It is the only thing I can do, go back and live with my parents. I'm so sorry."

We held each other, but every minute or so she looked towards the window, afraid someone was spying on us through the curtains. Finally she jumped up and headed for the door.

"This is too dangerous, I must go."

I stopped her just behind the door and we kissed again. "Please, Parker, they may be watching. I must go."

"How can I let you go when I may never see you again?"

"Oh, you will see me again." With that she walked out of my room.

The Asian ways of male-female relationships frustrated me. I couldn't understand how she could be kept by a Nepalese but couldn't be seen with me. Praven had two wives already and wanted her as a third. But if I were to take her to dinner, she would have been immediately branded as a prostitute. I didn't fully understand, but I was awakening to the vast chasms that existed between East and West.

Clara left later that afternoon on the night bus to Darjeeling.

Ten days later, I bounded up the stairs to the fourth floor, two at a time. Rounding one of the landings in the gloom with my head down, I plowed into someone coming down the stairs. She let out a quickly stifled scream as we collided. Instinctively I grabbed her to keep from falling and looked up into Clara's face, six inches from mine. She smiled at me and my heart raced. She let my arms linger for a moment around her, then gently she pried them loose, fearful that someone may have seen us.

"I came back," she said.

"So I see."

"I couldn't stay away."

"I'm glad."

Like a magnet I felt drawn to her. I reached out for her again. But she pushed me away and scooted down the stairs with a happy laugh, leaving me gasping for breath, with surprise, and hope. She paused and looked back. "I'll see you later on the roof."

A tantalizing sweet pain, to see her, to talk with her, but unable to be alone with her. I met her on the roof.

"I have come back to Praven. But we are not really together. I came back to see you."

Our clandestine meetings continued. We talked of her life in Darjeeling, going to Catholic schools, how she became involved with Praven. She told me then that his relatives who worked in the hotel had been telling her she should be happy with her lot in life. After all, she was twenty-five and an old maid, unlikely to get married to anyone else, why not just marry the man, be happy with a house and children, not worry about the other wives.

"That may be all right with them. But I don't want to share my husband with anyone. I cannot forgive him for what he has done." She burned with rage and the humiliation of what she saw as betrayal.

I suspected that Praven's relatives who worked at the hotel knew what was going on between us. I received long stares from many of them and I think they probably told Praven of their suspicions. Western friends warned me to leave Clara alone, that it was just bad news, nothing could come of it. I might even get hurt in more ways than one. But I couldn't leave her alone. For two weeks while I waited for our departure to western Nepal, I fell in love—for only the second time in my life.

On our last afternoon, we sat behind the short wall on the roof, saying nothing. She had decided to go back to Darjeeling as soon as I left and wait for me there. Our fingertips touched as we watched the late afternoon sun paint the glaciered peaks to the north golden, then pink. When the eastern sky turned purple she rose from our spot on the roof.

"Goodbye, Parker."

"Goodbye," I said, almost inaudibly.

She stepped quickly down the stairs. I waited for a few minutes, then slipped off the back of the roof onto the narrow rear balcony and crawled in the window to my room.

It had been all so confusing to me. I had just scratched the surface of the vast cultural differences that separated us, choking social customs that made it so difficult for us even to discover if we wanted to be together, let alone explore what we meant to one another. I loved her, of that I was sure. But what of the future?

Now in my sleeping bag in the mountains, the future muddied in my mind with the present. Fatigue overcame me. Lack of food, the altitude, our uncertain situation—could I think clearly about anything now?

CHAPTER
THIRTEEN

SOMEWHERE EAST OF THE BARBUNG KHOLA, DOLPO
Saturday, April 7, 1984

IT snowed during the night. Three inches of white powder covered the barren, lifeless terrain, transforming the landscape to a sparkling and brilliant white. The thermometer read zero, the air was still, with a clarity found only in the high mountains.

We did not wait until the sun hit the tents to get started that morning, so anxious were we to make good mileage. Our food supplies now consisted of a dozen potatoes, four eggs, chicken bouillon, tea, salt, pepper and one packet of dried soup that Prem found in the bottom of Jeet Bahadur's *doko*. The tea and bouillon would last for several days, but the other food would make only one meal. We decided to save the food for later in the day, and so had only a large mug of salt-and-pepper tea.

We headed upriver towards what we hoped was Lama Dorje's pass. Just around the first bend, the river forked into two streams, the larger continuing upstream to the left, the smaller remaining on a steady course. We discussed which to follow for several minutes without any of the arguments that had divided us two days earlier. The porters had defaulted, leaving the route choice to me and Prem.

Prem and I opted for the larger stream that headed left, more in the southeast direction that we imagined the pass might take. For two hours we followed as it meandered through rolling hills. Although we continued to gain elevation, the landscape changed from the barren rocky slopes to gently undulating hills covered with stubby brown grass. Abruptly the river bent far to the left, heading due north. For another half hour we followed the rapidly diminishing stream directly towards the Tibetan border. To continue further meant a steep ascent. We admitted our mistake in following it, and made the return trip to the river fork in an hour and a half. But the total time loss stood at four hours. Dejected, frustrated and hungry, we built a fire and cooked our last full meal.

As the potatoes boiled in water hacked from the frozen stream, I contemplated our predicament. The situation was deteriorating. *Critical* was the word that came to mind. Without food, we had to commit ourselves to move with all the speed we could muster until we found some sort of civilization. Sangdak, the only village on our map, lay somewhere ahead, over the pass. At that point, I did not even know which pass we were looking for, whether the Sangdak or the Dhampus. With all the jumbled information we had received, I now began to wonder if they might be one and the same.

If we found Sangdak or some other village, our four-hour delay would have only been an inconvenience. But if we couldn't find food, if we made another mistake in finding the route or encountered bad weather, we would rapidly find ourselves desperate. Until now, I had never considered that we might not make it through. Intellectually, I feared the high passes; emotionally, I dreaded the police. But not until this moment, looking ahead to the unknown, did I seriously consider that we could lose our way and starve.

I pulled Prem aside. "Prem, things are becoming very serious. We must move out of here—fast. Our mistake in following the wrong *khola* has cost us a half day. We can't afford to do that again."

"Yes, Parker Sahib. I know this. We should walk until dark, and maybe later. If we can find our way. We only have one torch left."

"And that's hardly any help, its batteries are almost dead. But we have two candles. And what about the moon?"

"Yes. Maybe the moon will light the way. It is almost full and it will be very bright."

"The moon. I never thought I would rely so much on the moon. But the weather pattern is against us. It's been clear in the mornings, then clouding up in the afternoon."

"Yes, Parker Sahib, but now it is two o'clock and still clear. Maybe today will be different."

Quickly we downed our meal, packed up and were back on the trail by three o'clock. We set out rapidly along the khola, hoping to regain some of the distance we had lost that morning. Two hours on, we rounded a bend in the river valley and saw dozens of dark forms on the hillside a mile away. Excited by what they might be, we hurried closer.

Yaks. A whole hillside full of grazing yaks. The sight made me want to cheer. For where yaks grazed, yak herders watched over them. Yak herders needed to eat, food would be available. Pressing forward rapidly, we approached the yak herd. An unearthly howling greeted us. Three hundred yards away and closing in, a black animal hurled himself in our direction. We stood transfixed, gripping our ice axes, not knowing what we would do if he reached us. The large black mastiff barked ferociously as he tore across the slope towards us. When he was a hundred and fifty yards away, the porters hastily dropped their loads.

At fifty yards he pulled up, just on the far side of the *khola*. A huge animal, more bear than dog, he had jet-black hair and a thick mane that stood straight out as he barked. As he guarded his domain, he set our teeth on edge with a cry that seemed to come from beyond the grave. So furious were his howls, so loud his bark, so unexpected his appearance before us that he seemed to me to be a dreaded reincarnation of the Hound of the Baskervilles.

We backed two hundred feet up the hillside and made our way along a ridge, following the contour of the river. The mastiff matched us move for move, remaining just on the far side of the *khola*. Barking incessantly, he forced us in a wide arc above the river. For a mile we walked like this.

A lone black tent beside a crude stone corral marked civilization. As we descended towards the river and approached to within two hundred feet, the dog raised his protests to a frenzied level. I estimated he weighed eighty pounds, all of that powerful body attached to snapping, lethal jaws. I couldn't imagine surviving an attack by such a ferocious animal.

A dilemma faced us; we did not dare approach any closer yet no one appeared out of the tent. Certainly the dog had done his duty and alerted his owner to our presence, but where was the yak herder? Perhaps he had gone up the hillside to tend the yaks or see to some other business. For fifteen minutes, we stood our ground, unsure of what to do as the dog's fervor remained undiminished. Suddenly the tent flap opened and a man stepped out. He whistled shrilly and the mastiff turned and headed towards his master at full tilt. Relieved, we slowly crossed the frozen stream while the yak herder tethered his animal to a stake driven into the ground. The black monster strained against his rope, snapping and growling.

We walked to within one hundred feet and stopped by the corral. The herder approached us and said a few words in a Tibetan dialect that none of us understood. Prem asked him a question in simple Nepali. The Tibetan replied with a shrug of his shoulders. Using a universal sign for food, Prem motioned to his mouth with his hand and showed the Tibetan a few rupees. Understanding dawned. He motioned us to enter the corral where Prem and I dropped our packs. Then the two of us followed him towards the tent.

The dog had continued his delirious howling and now, ten yards from the tent we hesitated. Eyeballing the length of the rope, it seemed to me that the dog could reach us even at the entrance. Seeing the fear on our faces, the Tibetan picked up a large piece of firewood and literally beat the mastiff into submission. The dog, pinned to the ground and impervious to the pain, strained to attack us. Once the dog lay on the ground underneath the short log, the Tibetan turned his head to us and, smiling, indicated we could go into the tent.

Stepping rapidly towards the entrance flap, Prem bent to enter. The Tibetan let the hound up. No sooner was he free than the monster once more leapt toward us but was yanked off his feet by the taut rope only inches from me. The Tibetan entered and smiled broadly. If I thought the village of Tarakot was medieval, Tarengaon biblical, this lonely yak herder's shelter was a holdover from the Stone Age. The tent itself was made of a thin black wool cloth, the weaving coarse enough to let sunlight through. Two of several colorful Tibetan rugs served as a bed. Knickknacks of the usual sort, old and new, useful and ornamental, traditional and modern lay heaped in a jumble in the corners. Our eyes roved over the assortment, seeking what might prove useful, lighting on an urn of fresh butter and a large burlap bag of *tsampa*.

Thinking that this man must have a large food cache, being so far from habitation, we immediately started bargaining for food. He grabbed the bag of *tsampa* and a sack of potatoes from behind him and indicated that he was willing to sell us some of these. We laid rupees in front of him and pointed to a measuring cup. By pointing first at the measuring cup or a potato, he indicated the price of each. We bargained in this silent manner for only a few minutes before we struck a deal. In the end we were able to buy one day's worth of food for the five of us.

Once the goods and money had changed hands, I stood and made a move towards the door. The renewal of fierce barking froze me. The black mastiff attempted once again to attack us, almost strangling himself on his tether. I shuddered at the thought that the frayed yak hair rope was the only thing keeping me alive at that moment. The Tibetan stepped outside, picked up the log and, with sev-

A lone black yurt beside a crude stone corral marked civilization. The yak herder tethered his dog and approached us.

eral thumping blows to the animal's head and shoulders, once again
beat the dog to the ground so we could leave. Meanwhile the porters
had collected yak dung from the corral and had a huge mountain of
it ready.

"Parker Sahib," Prem said. "We should camp here."

"Good idea. We have fuel, and now that we have food we don't
need to push on tonight."

Once we had set our tents in the corral and started to cook, the
Tibetan joined us for some tea. He crouched on his haunches near the
two-foot-high pile of red-hot yak coals and slurped his tea noisily.
Prem tried a few more Tibetan and Nepali phrases, but they found
only a few words in common, not enough to carry on any kind of
conversation.

We asked as best we could by gestures, about the route ahead. He
responded by pointing up the river, the direction in which we were
already heading. We sat in silence, smiling and drinking the salty tea.
Finally he put his hands together, bade us goodnight and returned to
his tent.

*A two-foot-high pile of dried yak dung used for cooking at the yak herder's
corral.*

When the sun went down behind a nearby ridge, we quickly huddled into our individual bedrolls for what we knew would be a long, cold night. My altimeter read 16,700 feet.

Luck had run with us that day, to have happened upon the lone yak herder in the midst of this vast desolate area. We had bought food and although we had already eaten half of it, we had some *tsampa* and potatoes left for whatever lay ahead.

Snow fell once again during the night, adding two inches to the three that already lay on the ground. But by morning, the sky had cleared and we emerged from our tents to another brilliant day. Everywhere a blazing white mantel was offset by a clear blue sky.

During breakfast, which once again consisted only of tea, I dug out the sunglasses and made sure everyone wore them. At this altitude, snow blindness, sunburn of the retina, was a genuine concern. It could be debilitating as well as painful.

We followed the stream for several miles. Ahead, rugged peaks stood directly in our path, blanketed with snow. I assumed we would make our way across them, perhaps that afternoon. We stopped and ate our remaining potatoes, which we had cooked the night before. We washed them down with a large mugful of *suchia*, Tibetan tea made with yak butter, a gift from the Tibetan.

Two miles further upstream, a wall of rock rose vertically out of the water and blocked our way. At this point the *khola* tumbled through a series of rock ledges, thus preventing it from freezing over altogether. Stopping to assess the situation, I shook my head. *Backtrack for a mile to the last safe crossing?*

"Parker Sahib, I think I can go this way." Prem pointed to a narrow band of snow abutting the cliff just at water's edge.

A five-inch-wide path, covered with frost, seemed to stretch from where we stood all along the base of the rock.

"All right, try it, Prem." I stood immediately behind him as he inched out over the rushing water.

Facing the rock, he spread his arms out along the wall for balance. The first few feet of the icy pathway wobbled ominously, but Prem rapidly covered them with two light-footed steps. Next, he took one long step with his right foot. Hesitating only momentarily, he carefully brought his left foot alongside his right. Now he stood with both

Snow fell during the night and we woke to a brilliant day; this was the view looking east towards the Sangdak Pass.

feet together and his arms outstretched on the rock. He turned back to look at me. From the corner of my eye I saw a subtle motion in the ice at his feet. His eyes grew large and his mouth formed into a small round "O!" So soft was the sound, I could barely hear it. A trapdoor opened and he disappeared.

The water and ice had swallowed him completely. Frantically, I shoved my ice axe as far underwater as I could. The swirling icy water made it difficult to see, but a hand reached out in desperation to grab the axe. I pulled. Heavy weight on the other end told me he had seized the proffered ice axe, but nothing moved. Plunging into the water up to my thighs, I braced myself and yanked on the ice axe again. *Hang on, Prem, just hang on.*

Tugging with frantic power against heavy, wet clothes and the pack on his back, I strained to bring him to the surface. Then the swift current caught him, moving him downstream past the cliff face and towards me. My hand closed on his wrist. Gritting my teeth, I hung on. Suddenly his face popped to the surface, red and contorted with his frenzied efforts. His mouth opened and he gasped desperately for air. He let go of the ice axe and grabbed for my legs. Reaching down, I pulled on his sodden clothes, bringing him into knee-deep water. Quickly we scrambled out.

The porters had not been far behind and now they raced to us. Taking Prem by the arms, they swiftly peeled off his clothes. Untying our loads, we searched for something extra for him to wear. Within a minute he wore dry clothing. But his teeth chattered and his body shook uncontrollably. Akaal Bahadur unpacked Prem's sleeping bag and, wrapping it around him, we sat and watched him closely as he slowly calmed down.

In the panic to find warm dry clothes for Prem, I had forgotten my own plunge in the river. I now realized that my boots, pants and long underwear had been soaked as well. I took them off, then remembered I had nothing dry to put on. Wringing my long underwear out as best I could, I put it back on. I did the same with my pants, but my boots were as heavy and sodden as Prem's. We drained the boots and laid them out in the sun to dry.

Taking stock of Prem's gear, we realized that several items had been lost. His pack had remained firmly on his back—indeed, had he lost it, he might have come to the surface sooner. But a precious ice axe had gone down as well as a small zippered pouch he had carried on the top of his pack.

Prem fell into the river but within one minute he wore dry clothing.

Ascending towards the Sangdak Pass.

Jeet Bahadur borrowed my ice axe and tried to snare the lost axe from the river. The rushing water had cut a trench, easily eight feet deep, just at the point where Prem fell. I thought his valiant attempt to retrieve the ice axe futile, but he persevered for fifteen minutes. When Jeet Bahadur's hands became frozen and unmoving, Akaal Bahadur took over the effort. After thirty minutes, they abandoned the search.

By now, Prem had rewarmed sufficiently to resume walking and we got underway once more, ascending with the stream for several hours. Gradually, the stream became smaller; then, at 17,000 feet it narrowed to just a trickle running down the center of a broad valley bounded by low rolling hills. The sun had melted all the snow from the south-facing slopes; wiry yellowish brown grasses and lichens covered the ground. Just up from the stream, we stopped in a cave to rest and have a cup of tea. Leaning against his pack, sipping his steaming mug, Prem turned to me with a smile.

"Parker Sahib, you saved my life. I must say, 'Thank you.' Now you are responsible for me."

Akaal Bahadur nodded vigorously at this remark and repeated it to me in Nepali.

I smiled and didn't say anything. I had heard of this way of looking at saving someone's life, but I thought it a joke. The water had been deep just where Prem fell in, but the current would have brought him to shallow water soon enough. I had pulled him out, but if I had not been there, I doubt if he would have drowned. Maybe not, possibly not. Anyway, now safe and dry, he walked in our company.

The stream we followed became nothing more than a narrow ribbon of ice, then it vanished completely. We climbed another two hundred feet of gentle rise and found ourselves on a broad, flat expanse running due east, perhaps half a mile wide and two or more long. Sloping ridges a thousand feet high bounded us to the north and south.

Dead ahead beyond the eastern edge of this broad plateau we saw the upper reaches of snowy peaks, great sedimentary layers tilted at sharp angles into the sky. From what we could see, their bases lay far below where we stood, as though, at the far end, the plateau fell precipitously away. A *chorten* appeared several hundred feet ahead, just where the slope leveled off.

We stopped to rest beside the *chorten*, dropping our loads and leaning against this lone man-made object in the midst of stark wilderness. Having expected a high and dangerous crossing of the mountains, I found myself surprised and relieved at having reached this remarkably gentle pass. Taking out my map, I turned it first one way, then another until I had succeeded in roughly orienting myself. Although it was obvious that the map contained glaring errors, I nevertheless convinced myself that we stood on the Sangdak Pass, at 17,600 feet above sea level.

From the western edge of the pass emerged a frozen stream which drained another broad valley to the south. I wondered if this was perhaps the northern terminus of the Hidden Valley described by the 1950 French Annapurna Expedition during their reconnaissance of Dhaulagiri. If so, the Dhampus Pass lay somewhere in that direction. To the southeast, lost in the rapidly building clouds, loomed the brooding north face of Dhaulagiri.

CHAPTER
FOURTEEN

SANGDAK PASS

Sunday, April 8, 1984

Two o'clock; time to move out. A mile ahead, I saw a faint ribbon of trail ascending the ridge to the north. It was the first trail we had seen since leaving the Barbung Khola at Daragaon, and I was determined to be on it. Even though that meant climbing another thousand feet, something the porters were sure not to like, I believed it the best route to take.

While I lingered at the *chorten* for ten minutes, taking some photos and changing a roll of film, Prem and the porters headed off along the broad expanse of the Sangdak Pass. Finished with my photos, I hurried to catch up with the others, already nearly half a mile ahead, moving slowly towards the jumble of snowy peaks. As I caught up with Prem, walking last in line, I saw that the porters had passed the point where the faint trail headed up the ridge to the north. Prem had stopped and was sitting on the ground.

"Prem," I demanded. "What in the hell is going on? I thought we decided to take the trail. Now the porters are heading straight."

"They don't want to climb any more, they want to go this way, straight to the edge, not up."

The porters head off along the broad expanse of the Sangdak Pass.

I looked angrily at the porters continuing onto the far side of the plateau.

"We agreed to head up the trail to the ridge. Who's in charge here anyway, us or the porters?"

"I don't know, Parker Sahib," Prem said, his normally assertive voice strangely faint and lethargic. "I just don't know."

"What the . . ." I started to shout, turning to look at him seated on the ground. The words stuck in my throat as I peered into his face. Something was wrong, *very* wrong.

Prem lay propped against his pack, eyes closed, hands pressing on either side of his head. He grimaced with pain.

"Prem, what's wrong?" I bent closer.

"I have a headache. And everything is dizzy."

"You've probably got altitude sickness. Come on, the best thing is to go down."

Gripping him firmly under his elbow, I helped him to his feet. He stood unsteadily, took a few steps and faltered. I grabbed his arm again, trying to keep him up and on a straight course.

Although I was still steamed up about the change of route, I could not manage to hold onto Prem and also run ahead to stop the porters. They had now reached the far end of the pass and I could see only the tops of their baskets as the ground slowly fell away. I had to accept the fact Prem was in no condition to climb anymore. The porters were beyond recall. Powerless to change our course, I let them go. Supporting Prem with one arm, I guided us slowly towards the far end of the plateau. The uplifted mass of the Himalaya drew closer, dwarfing us with its bulk. The glaciered flanks caught intermittent shafts of sunlight.

Two solitary beings, three miles above sea level, we trudged on across the vast, barren plateau. Hunger and fatigue gripped me; I felt mentally aloof, my mind oddly separated from my physical efforts as I focused on the mountains ahead. After two months on the trail, we were lost, lost on a trackless crest of the Himalaya, virtually without food. I felt beyond the point of rational thinking, as though my mind had gone through the wall. Yet the cathedral spires pushing upward through the broken clouds were inspiring beyond anything I could imagine.

In crossing the pass, we drew closer to one of the great faultlines of the Himalayas. The geological plate of India, in its timeless trek northeast, had slammed into Asia 25 million years ago. Continuing its thrust, the Indian subcontinent had crumpled and broken the earth's surface, forming the vertical landscape of the Himalayan range. Ahead of us, the ancient sea bed thrust skyward in a mass of unconsolidated rock.

At the eastern terminus of the pass, we began a gentle descent. Dull yellow lichens and short wiry grass covered the tundra. A trickle of water emerged from the ground, cutting a shallow depression in the soft soil. Rivulets from both sides soon merged with the trickle to form a small stream. Following this stream, we descended several hundred feet as the slope steepened.

Where the slope dropped off, the porters had stopped and set down their loads. They sat cross-legged, holding their knees, contemplating the terrain ahead. As Prem and I approached, they ignored us. They sat motionless, eyes fixed forward. I let Prem down gently next to Akaal Bahadur's *doko*, propping him against the basket, and started to join the porters. When I got my first glimpse of the route ahead, I froze.

Below us, the landscape changed abruptly. Geological mayhem, total destruction of earthly order faced us. Cascading precipitously into a rock-strewn chasm, the stream dropped over several rock shelves and then cut down amidst boulders and slide debris. Near-vertical walls rose on either side, rotten and crumbling, cut at frequent intervals by rock slides.

"Holy shit," I whispered to myself.

Removing my pack, I sat down next to the porters as we all stared silently into the gorge. Intermittently, rocks broke away from the sheer walls, falling, bouncing, tumbling to the stream bed before coming to rest. The smaller ones made short staccato cracks like rifle fire, the larger rocks rumbled like distant cannons. At that rate of erosion, it seemed not long before the whole mountainside would fall, piece by piece, to the stream bed. Perhaps the earthquake we had felt the week before had precipitated this bombardment of the canyon.

Climbing back to the pass seemed out of the question. It lay at least six hundred feet above us now, and I doubted that I could convince the porters to make the climb. I turned to Prem, who was half-lying against Akaal Bahadur's basket, his features twisted in pain, his eyes closed. I knelt beside him, asked where it hurt, touched his now-feverish forehead. Slowly, weakly, he described a severe headache, with pain extending down the back of his neck. The porters gathered around me, sensing serious trouble.

"Prem," I said gently. "Open your eyes, let me see them."

"No, Parker Sahib, no," he mumbled. "It hurts, the light hurts to see."

"Prem," I said. "It is very bad going ahead. Do you think you can make it?"

"Yes, I will try. But my head hurts so much. I can barely see. Something is not good, Parker Sahib."

"Something is not good," I echoed.

I ran the symptoms and possible implications through my mind. It didn't appear, as I first thought, to be classic altitude sickness. All signs pointed to a central nervous system infection. A word flashed into my head, and I tried immediately to oust it. But it crept back and I could not dislodge it. Endemic in the Himalayas, highly contagious, often fatal: meningitis. A flash of fear engulfed me. Meningitis, I knew, was no joke in well-equipped western hospitals. Now all of us had been exposed. Had we struggled across nature's wild and treacherous terrain only to succumb to an infection picked up from a fellow human? *What should we do now*?

We had only one choice, to continue on.

I helped Prem to his feet and started to distribute the contents of his pack among the rest of us.

"No, no, Parker Sahib. I can carry my pack."

"Prem, this is stupid. We can go faster, all of us, if you let us carry some weight for you."

"I can carry my own pack." He pulled the pack from my hands and struggled with it. I relented.

We hoisted our loads and started our descent. Just then, the clouds that had been building steadily all afternoon closed in around us. Large flakes began to fall.

Scrambling, sometimes slipping along the course of the stream, we followed it down the middle of the canyon, but after only two hundred yards we saw the folly of this plan. A barrage of rocks cascaded and crashed around us. It would be only a matter of time before one of them hit and injured someone seriously.

We switched to the north side of the slope, heading for the protection of an overhanging cliff face. Scrabbling through loose rock debris for a hundred feet, we stopped directly under the crumbling rock wall.

We studied our situation while partially protected. Finally, we made the decision to continue along the base of this cliff as far as we could rather than stay with the descending stream bed. While this gave us a more or less horizontal trail, it actually took us higher and higher above the stream that continued to fall away at the bottom of the gorge.

Prem slumped beside me and took little or no part in the decision-making, now done by Akaal Bahadur and me. During this short pause, he weakened still more.

"Parker Sahib. My arms, they are hurting here." He indicated the backs of his arms and then pointed to the front of his thighs. "And here, my legs. It is so difficult to walk."

Sympathetically, I grasped his shoulder. "We've got to keep going, Prem. We have no other choice."

Once more I helped him to his feet, and we started to wend our way along the rock face. Our trail was little more than a two-foot ledge, with a sheer cliff rising so high on our left we could not see the top and, falling off to the right, a steep drop to the winding stream. The porters, walking together in front of us, helped each other over the more difficult spots.

Prem moaned and groaned with every body movement, and I stayed close to him, keeping up a one-sided conversation, encouraging him at every tortured step he took. Then abruptly, the porters stopped and we all stared ahead at a fifty-foot section of nothing but crumbling rotten rock. The narrow ledge we had been following had disappeared.

Somehow we had to cross that gap.

Akaal Bahadur crossed first. He carried a less bulky load, and he was more agile than the others. With surprising quickness he picked his way across, finding the best hand- and footholds. Once across, he dropped his load and returned to help Jeet Bahadur and Auri Bahadur make the same precarious crossing. Once all three porters had crossed safely, Akaal Bahadur hoisted his doko and the three moved on around a bend in the cliff and out of sight, walking in a close single file. With their bulky loads, they could do little to help Prem cross. That task fell to me.

I took a step out onto the rock. My heart pounded, my mouth went dry with fear. Immediately I realized I had to put Prem in front of me and spot him across. It was a desperate maneuver I didn't want to

On the north side of the Cha Lungpa Gorge, scrabbling through loose rock and debris in the protection of an overhanging rock wall.

make, but I could think of nothing else. Without ropes, it was the best hope we had.

I backed off the rock. Behind me, Prem leaned against the wall, his eyes closed. Grabbing both shoulders, I shook him gently. Trying to penetrate the fog that surrounded him, I shouted, "Prem, you *must* pay attention here. This is *very* dangerous. You cannot fall. Do you understand?"

He made no response for several seconds, then, pulling in a deep breath and summoning will power to overcome his drained state, he whispered. "Yes, I hear. But you must help me, Parker Sahib."

Help him? How could I help him when fear filled my chest and my knees trembled? I was afraid of falling, but I couldn't tell him that. Fortunately, Prem took my silent nod as confidence in my ability to get us both safely across. Prem faced the cliff, easing himself out onto the steep rock, feeling his way tentatively, his eyes half-closed. I looked down at the gorge, a straight drop of three hundred feet, and I felt sure he would fall. I gripped the ice axe loop on the bottom of his pack and slowly pushed him out further along the gap. The gray-and-buff conglomerate rock wall looked and felt like a crumbling cookie, breaking off in small pieces at unexpected intervals. Faces pressed against the cliff, we shuffled along, inching our way across. I shouted encouragement at every step.

"Go, Prem. Good. One more step. You're doing it."

An interminable ten minutes brought us back onto the narrow ledge on the other side of the gap. Exhausted, we slumped against the wall, large wet flakes of snow hitting our faces. Drops of sweat rolled down my back and off my forehead, stinging as I wiped them out of my eyes. Peering across the chasm at the opposite wall, I saw that we had now worked our way three hundred feet above the stream bed.

Pzing. A small rock whizzed by, bouncing off the protecting rock above us. *Pink, pink, pzing.* Smaller ones followed, deflected by our shield. Groaning involuntarily with every breath, Prem lay precariously on the narrow ledge, his eyes closed. Watching the snow accumulate on his chest, I felt anew the urgency to keep going. It was already late afternoon, and darkness threatened. I pulled Prem to his feet and half dragged him along. Two more trailless traverses, shorter but even more precarious than the first, brought us to a corner. Rounding it, we found the porters stopped in a small cliff shelter.

Jeet Bahadur had untied the top of his load and fished out a few precious yak patties. He started a small fire and brewed some tea. Reaching deeper into his *doko*, he produced a cloth bag of dry, floury *tsampa*. We mixed this with our tea and ate greedily. It provided only a few mouthfuls each, but the heavy *tsampa* filled a portion of the emptiness in our stomachs.

We were now completely out of food.

During that break, Akaal Bahadur and I weighed the danger of continuing along the ledge part way up the cliff. As the stream dropped down towards the river, we were left higher and higher along the wall. I feared that by following our present route we might come to a dead end, leaving us trapped hundreds of feet up on a sheer face. Looking across and down the deep chasm, we saw that the gorge had vertical faces thousands of feet high. A half mile ahead, the gorge bent to the left. Akaal Bahadur shared my concern about being stranded, so we decided that he and I would go ahead to reconnoiter the route.

Free of our loads, we clambered swiftly onto the conglomerate, traversing along the ledge. Occasionally, we climbed a hundred or more feet up steep, loose rockfalls, then down again in our desperate attempt to find a passage. Akaal Bahadur was out in front, and as on that day several weeks earlier when we looked for my lost necklace near Hurikot, he set a blistering pace. Humbled once again by his stamina, I gasped for breath trying to keep up.

A half mile ahead, we found ourselves once more traversing near-vertical walls of dirt and loose rocks. But from our position, it appeared we could go on, although the last half mile we had just crossed would be treacherous with loads, and even more so with an ill Prem.

Quickly we returned to the others and immediately started on our way. Prem's legs had stiffened while he sat and now he hobbled, unable to extend his leg muscles fully. Once again I spotted him through the difficult parts, grabbing him by the back of his collar and by the ice axe loop on his pack, forcing his face against the rock.

He had particular trouble with the climbs up the loose rockfalls. At the worst places, I climbed just ahead of and above him, braced myself, then instructed him to hang onto my feet just over his head. I feared we might both go at any moment, that Prem would pull both of us into the void below. I didn't say anything about it. I was not being stoically macho; I simply saw no point in speaking about a situation that I couldn't change.

Akaal Bahadur led the group through slides and across crumbling walls. Being the most sure-footed, he went across each one first and, having done it once, dropped his load and returned to help the others. One especially bad section stretched one hundred and fifty feet, and it took an hour for the five of us to cross it. After the porters carefully inched across, Akaal Bahadur returned to help me with Prem. Akaal Bahadur grabbed Prem from the right side, I took him from the left. Between the two of us, we were able to maintain our balance as we pushed and pulled him across. After fifteen minutes, we had covered half the distance, but Prem begged us, "Stop, stop. I cannot go any more."

His legs shook uncontrollably and his eyes were clenched shut.

"Prem, you *must* go on! We will help you. But you cannot stop now," I urged him, agonizing over his predicament.

Akaal Bahadur spoke to him in Nepali, words of encouragement, admonishment, whatever would keep him going. Prem moaned and allowed us to push, pull and drag him across the rock, helping us as much as he was able. And finally, after another muscle-straining fifteen minutes, we got Prem to the opposite side.

Not far ahead the chasm turned left and headed almost due north. Here was evidence of a great faultline, which had formed along the interface of the Indian and Asian tectonic plates. On our left the cliffs rose up until they disappeared in clouds, the sedimentary layers horizontal. To our right, a hundred yards away on the opposite side of the gorge, great sections of the earth's crust had been forced upward, with the layers now vertical. They had been crumpled so violently that some soared almost straight up, then turned in tight spiraling arcs and dropped straight down.

The stream below merged with another emanating from an even narrower and deeper gorge to the south to become a tumbling river. At this point, we made our way down to the river, then followed its banks. Boulders and immense piles of debris often blocked our passage, testaments to powerful floods that swept through these desolate canyons. We wound our way around them. On level ground Prem could move faster, but his condition continued to worsen. I walked close behind him, guiding him along the riverbed.

Then, when it seemed that we would have easier going for at least a while, we hit a wall. Impenetrable. Or so it looked. Ahead of us we saw a two-hundred-foot-high rock wall that appeared to block the canyon completely. The *khola*, however, seemed to disappear into the base of the rock. Standing deep within the gorge, we searched the walls for a way to get through. Then Akaal Bahadur's sharp eyes found what seemed to be a solution.

"*Baato!*" he shouted, pointing to the faint remnants of a trail that climbed up through the scree slopes on the left side of the gorge.

"Let's go," I said, wanting to be on our way without losing any more daylight.

We lost the trail several times as it disappeared under rock slides and fallen debris. We knew it went through this section because we kept recovering faint traces of it, only to lose them again. Eventually we found ourselves once more at the river side, the rock wall closer but still blocking our way. Just ahead we saw the river disappear into a five-foot-wide fissure in the rock wall, leaving us with no more bank to follow. Our passage along the river was terminated. We huddled together with nowhere to go. Great blocks of ice which had fallen from the cliffs above littered the ground around us. From the overcast sky, more snow threatened. The grains of sand in the hourglass of this day were running low. We had to find a way out.

"Sahib," Jeet Bahadur pointed.

Lost in the swirling clouds and camouflaged by the same dun color as the surrounding rocks was a thin dark line more than two hundred feet above our heads.

A bridge! A bridge spanning the fissure through which the river flowed. By scrambling up the steep scree slope to our left, it appeared we might get over the massive rock wall that blocked the river and approach the bridge. As we climbed, we had to urge Prem on continually to make him keep up. His mind wandered. He stopped constantly, but we pushed him on again and again until we came upon the trail that lead up to the bridge.

Akaal Bahadur reached the bridge first, and when I arrived moments later, practically holding Prem upright, I found him standing still. Without his load, Akaal Bahadur stood on the edge of the bridge staring hypnotically down into the roiling waters deep in the chasm two hundred feet below. A quick glance to the other side of the bridge revealed why he stood so still.

Clearly a great deal of time and effort had gone into building the bridge. Starting fifty feet below the lip of the gorge, from stone shelves on the far side, forty-foot-high rock buttresses had been built

A tenuous bridge spanning a fissure in the rock wall that blocked our descent through the Cha Lungpa Gorge.

up. The next ten feet on both sides consisted of thick rough-hewn logs projecting towards each other, each layer extending further out than the one below. A ten-foot gap remained between the two sides.

Although at one time a sturdy bridge, now the gap was spanned by two aging pine logs six inches in diameter, a foot and a half apart. Neither old log gave much assurance. One seemed sure to roll if anyone stepped on it. The other had worked loose from its mooring on the opposite bank. Some flat stones balanced on the top of the logs for a walkway. But many were missing, leaving a space of about six feet with nothing but the unsteady logs and a terrifying view to the void below. Standing as close as I dared to the edge, I peered down two hundred feet to the churning river, which roared through a narrow fissure in the rock.

To cross this bridge with our loads would have meant taking a horrifying three or four steps balancing only on the two loosened logs. The thought made me shudder. We would have to repair that part of the bridge. But although flat stones of the proper size lay strewn about, very few were on our side. I saw plenty of good bridge stones on the opposite bank and thought anxiously about how to get at them. Akaal Bahadur obviously had the same thought.

Suddenly, Akaal Bahadur began to walk, carefully and slowly, out onto the bridge. Arms out from his body to help him balance, he stepped cautiously onto the first flat rock. It moved under his weight, so he quickly went down on his stomach, stretched full-length on the stones. Fearlessly, it seemed, he crawled towards the gap. There he stopped and looked down through the logs to the empty space below.

"Ayaaah!" he uttered balefully, then without hesitation crawled all the way across the bridge. On the other side, with a sheer release of nervous energy, he jumped up and ran towards a pile of stones.

Now, with Akaal Bahadur pushing stones out from his side, we worked for a good half hour, carefully rebuilding the center portion of the bridge, shoring up the loose spanner log and filling in the gap with flat rocks. When we had done all we could, it was still not as sturdy as we would have liked, but neither was it so terrifying. Akaal Bahadur tested our reconstruction project by crawling across towards us on his knees. Then he hoisted his load and nonchalantly walked back across to the far side. Jeet Bahadur and Auri Bahadur followed.

I went back to Prem, who had been lying propped up on a rock this whole time, unable to help. I got him to his feet. His legs had stiffened again and he walked stooped over with shuffling, unsteady steps. He still wore his pack.

"Prem, take off your pack and give it to me."

"No, Parker Sahib, I can carry it," he answered, slurring every word.

"Prem, it will be no disgrace. Don't be stubborn. Let me have your pack."

But an iron core of pride would not let him do it. "No, Parker Sahib. I can carry it."

Finally, I turned, exasperated, and waited for him to move.

As he neared the first large flat stone, Prem hesitated. He tried to lift his leg to place his boot onto the rock. But his foot, not raised high enough, snagged the lip of the rock and he crumpled, pitching forward towards the yawning chasm.

"No, Prem," I yelled, leaping forward.

His dark form sank, the top-heavy pack pulling him towards the edge of the precipice. I threw myself towards him, arms outstretched, and I pulled him back as we slammed together into the dirt.

We had cheated death again.

Still gripping Prem tightly, I twisted my head around and looked down. I could hear the river thundering and crashing wild, far below. I also could see it; my head hung over the edge of the first rock of the bridge.

"Prem, Prem."

"O Parker Sahib. I am sorry."

I pulled him to his feet and, carefully coaxing him back from the edge, made him sit down away from the bridge. Calling out for Akaal Bahadur to help me, I took off Prem's pack.

With as much authority as I could muster, I said, "Don't move, Prem. Akaal Bahadur and I will help you across the bridge."

With my own pack on my back, I slipped on the shoulder straps of Prem's pack so it rested on my chest. I turned towards the bridge and without looking down, held my breath and walked across to the other side. Once there, I shed both packs and returned.

With Akaal Bahadur's help, I again got Prem up to the edge of the bridge, this time on his knees. Akaal Bahadur got in front and I got behind, and we tried to coax him across as we had done on the crumbling conglomerate walls. But his cries of pain as he tried to crawl on all fours forced us to retreat.

Once more on the edge of the bridge, I racked my brains. *How were we going to get Prem across? Could we carry him?* I wished we had a rope. Finally, I visualized a way that might work.

"Akaal Bahadur," I instructed, "you stand here." I stood him in front of Prem, facing in the direction of the bridge. Sandwiching Prem between our bodies, I grabbed Akaal Bahadur's arms tightly, locking Prem between us, all facing forward. Slowly, we shuffled across the bridge.

Thankfully, the going turned easier on the other side of the bridge as the chasm opened up and the trail followed high above the river on relatively level ground. I continued to help Prem. Several times I urged him to stop for a rest, but each time he insisted that we move on. After two hours, we stopped in a small cave and brewed tea. We were all exhausted, and the small shelter beckoned us to spend the night there. But we had no food, and our only hope of finding any was to reach the village of Sangdak. By my reckoning, the village lay another twelve miles ahead on the other side of the river. Given Prem's condition and the state of the weather, it seemed important to keep moving as long as we could.

Now the trail climbed steadily away from the river. Prem kept up with us on what must have been sheer will power, grunting with each step, his legs no longer completely supporting his weight. I half carried, half led him along, talking to him constantly.

"Come on, Prem," I yelled. "We've got to make it."

"Yes, we must make it," he replied in a hoarse whisper, parroting my words. His legs moved mechanically though ineffectively beneath him.

After climbing a thousand feet, the trail slowly descended onto slightly easier terrain. Twilight was closing in. I heard Akaal Bahadur and Jeet Bahadur talking excitedly ahead. They stopped and I came up behind them, Prem supported by my arm. They pointed to a ridge a half mile ahead. Two *chorten*s stood side by side. *Chorten*s meant a village.

"We must find the village," I said to Akaal Bahadur.

There must be a village. I will believe in a god if there is.

But with Prem it was torturously slow going. I carried him on my back for about fifty yards, but then, panting with exhaustion, I put him down again. He took feeble steps, legs flailing, eyes closed, grunting with every effort. His inner strength, an iron resolve that had kept him moving all afternoon—even that seemed to dissipate. I could not rid myself of the thought that wherever our tiny caravan finally halted on this gray evening in April 1984, would be his burial place.

It was dusk, gray fading to black, when we finally reached the *chorten*s. From below, I could see that they were old, rounded by the elements into nondescript mounds. Akaal Bahadur and Jeet Bahadur stood silhouetted against the ridgeline, their large baskets clearly visible against the fading light. I watched intently as they slowly approached the ridge from where they would be able to see what lay ahead. Prem leaned against me, his breath heavy and labored. Step by step, the two porters struggled to reach the top. Then they stopped

Akaal Bahadur and Jeet Bahadur silhouetted at the chortens, their dokos visible against the fading light; no village lay beyond.

and stood still for fifteen seconds. I saw Akaal Bahadur's figure move. He shook the *doko* that was attached to his head back and forth in great sweeping motions. No. No village. No fields, no more *chortens*, no sign of man. A great sigh of anguish escaped from me. Drained, empty, all of my desire and power to move evaporated. *How could this be happening to us? We had come so far, endured so much, how could we lose now?*

No answers came. My only thought was to get to those *chortens* and collapse. Why struggle anymore? I didn't know. But somehow, reaching them meant not giving up.

"Come on, Prem," I said loudly to the form slumped against me. "Dammit, we have *got* to make it to those *chortens*."

"Uhhh," was his rasping reply.

One step, one more step. Then two steps. Another step. I thought only of reaching the *chortens*, forcing Prem to move his feeble legs one at a time. Finally, we reached them.

Standing on the crest of the ridge in the dwindling light, I looked out upon an open side canyon, gently sloping towards a vertical drop of undetermined depth into the black gorge of the Cha Lungpa Khola. I could just make out the porters resting in some trees a short way down the slope. Afraid that if we stopped here we wouldn't be able to go any farther, we continued without resting. After fifteen minutes, just as darkness fell, we reached the porters. The ground was covered with four inches of loose, dry dirt. Immediately this powder insinuated itself into everything, compounding our misery. I pulled a tent from a *doko*, spread it on the dirt and laid Prem out on it.

Because we had firewood, the porters soon had a roaring fire going. But we needed water. Akaal Bahadur and Auri Bahadur volunteered to find some. They hoped that a stream ran at the bottom of this side canyon somewhere below us. Within half an hour, they returned with water.

We drank it in great thirsty gulps. Too tired to set up the tents, we spread them out in the miserable dust and laid down on them. I helped Prem to take some codeine to ease his headache. Perhaps it wasn't the proper medication to give him if he did have meningitis, but his low cries of pain made any such concerns irrelevant. I spoke to him and his answer came back slurred, almost incoherent. Frightened, grieving over Prem's misery, I said goodnight and lay beside him. As I lay back, I saw that the sky was now clear and full of stars.

There was nothing more I could do, with us so far away from anywhere. I didn't know if he would still be with us in the morning. I tried not to think of his death, but the inescapable facts of his condition made me do so. Twice that day he had escaped, but would Death come this night to claim him?

Pain and sorrow overcame me and compounded my exhaustion. My companion for the last six months, Prem meant more to me than just a *sirdar*. He had been my guide to the mountains as well as to the people who lived there. He had loved the great towering white peaks as much as I, the blue sheep, the Tibetans in their wretched villages. Weariness—and hopelessness—overwhelmed me. My eyes closed and I drifted into a troubled sleep.

CHAPTER FIFTEEN

CHA LUNGPA GORGE
Monday, April 9, 1984

I WOKE just after two o'clock to find everything covered with two inches of heavy wet snow. I rolled over and looked at Prem. I could hardly see in the dim light, but I could tell it was not a gray, lifeless corpse lying there. It was Prem, still alive. Too exhausted to set up the tents, I woke the others and we crawled underneath the tents and tarps. Lying in the loose dirt, we fell back asleep.

Gray dawn light filtered through the snow that floated from the sky as I pushed back the tent that covered me. My watch said six o'clock. Eight inches lay on the ground and it was snowing heavily.

"Prem?" I said.

He opened his eyes and turned slightly towards me. "Parker Sahib."

"How do you feel?" I leaned close to hear his words.

"My head hurts and my legs." His slurred speech and continuing pain concerned me.

Great wet flakes drifted down, adding to our misery. Everything was soaked and because we hadn't set up the tents, only crawled under them, the moisture-laden snow mixed with the loose dirt to create a clinging, gooey mud that caked everything it touched.

228

We were reluctant to do anything, but our only option was to get up and move on. As best we could in the driving snow and sticky mud, we packed the baskets. Because he was still unsteady, I helped Prem to his feet. We had nothing to eat or drink.

Visibility extended no more than two hundred feet in any direction. We followed what we thought was a path as it contoured along the broad side canyon. When we reached the canyon's far side, the terrain once again became steep. The snow and mud made our progress slow and risky. To fall here was too easy to do, too dangerous to contemplate. The winds picked up and blew snow into our faces. Visibility dropped to one hundred feet. We hoped that the trail would descend to the river. The map showed the village of Sangdak on the opposite side, no villages at all on this side until the Kali Gandaki Gorge, still twenty miles away. But as we plodded along, the storm's fury increased and the trail contoured up and away from the khola, now far below us.

We came to a small stream. Akaal Bahadur and Jeet Bahadur dropped their loads and disappeared into the rock-strewn depression. If we could follow this stream down to the river, we thought, we might find a way across. But after a few minutes they returned with bad news. A short way below, the stream tumbled over a precipice into the Cha Lungpa Gorge. The porters had not been able to see beyond the edge of the stream's spray.

Exhausted, disheartened, I could not force my mind to hold more than one thought at a time. And my obsessive thought was *We must find Sangdak.* Somehow we must get to the other side of the river, we must find a way to do it. I could not imagine our condition getting any worse. We were lost, without food, a raging snowstorm blew around us. It seemed a miracle to me that Prem was still alive, but how much longer could his iron will carry his ailing body? I helped him walk, as he could no longer do so by himself. I had no way of diagnosing his condition; I knew only that he was not getting better.

Despairing utterly, I didn't know where to turn. We were abandoned in the fury of the wilderness that we had had the temerity to enter, to challenge. Man, nature, the gods—all had withdrawn their help; none offered us refuge or even hope. Alone now, just the five of us, how much longer could we struggle? The snow swirled white around me, but blackness possessed my soul.

A gust of wind blew stinging flakes of snow into my eyes. I stopped and Prem stumbled against me. We had to get to the other side of the river, we had to find the village of Sangdak. "Akaal Bahadur," I called out.

We talked. We would have to change our direction and head down towards the khola. Akaal Bahadur nodded and turned to lead us down the slope, intending to bushwhack a trail.

Then, Jeet Bahadur let out a yell. I looked up the slope and through the swirling snow flakes I saw the dark shape of his slender body and the bulky basket on his back. One arm, a gray, shadowy arrow, pointed upwards. I blinked twice through the blowing snow and the dim shape at which he pointed slowly focused into one I easily recognized.

A *chorten*!

"Prem." I grabbed his arm tightly. "There's a *chorten*. There must be a village here somewhere."

As we slowly drew closer, I could see that it was new and brightly painted. Pulling Prem's arm, I tried to walk faster, anxious to learn what lay beyond the *chorten*.

Fields, neatly terraced. They came into view slowly through the billows of snowflakes. A village—there must be a village nearby. I began to feel a hope that perhaps we had not been forsaken after all, maybe I could start to believe in a god, in *something*.

Through the driving snowstorm, we did not see the flat-roofed houses until we were only two hundred feet away. Then we saw a few figures on the rooftops as we staggered towards them. Giddy, elated with this seemingly miraculous appearance of a village that wasn't even on our map, I hobbled towards the nearest stone house.

Two women on the roof looked down as we stumbled into their view. With looks of fear, they quickly scrambled down into the house and we could hear the scrape of log bolts barring the entrance. I could imagine our appearance, covered with mud, looming suddenly out of the storm. But this was no way to react to strangers in need. Akaal Bahadur and Jeet Bahadur knocked on the door, calling to those within. In a stupor, too tired, cold and hungry to fight anymore, I slumped against a wall, leaning Prem against a basket. The snow fell and began to stick on our silent, still figures.

The porters returned, saying that no one would open their doors to us. Looking up at them, I blinked stupidly. *How could they leave us sitting outside in the snow? How could they ignore us?* I dug into my pack.

"Here," I said. "Here are two hundred rupees. Give it to them."

"Okay," Akaal Bahadur answered, taking the wad of bills from my hand.

"Tell them we will buy many things from them."

"Yes, Sahib."

I slumped back against the wall, then turned to look at Prem. His eyes were closed, his face lined with fatigue, his breathing shallow and uneven.

Ten minutes later we climbed a ladder to the entrance of the nearest house. As in Jumla when J.B. had needed a plane ticket, money talked.

The sound of oil crackling and the sweet smell of potato cutlets frying on the hearth just a few feet from my head woke me. My watch told me it was just after 6:00 P.M. Wrapped in homespun blankets, my feet inches from the fire, I felt truly warm for the first time in a week. Over my head I saw our gear; tents, sleeping bags, jackets, pants, socks, hung off the rough-hewn rafters to dry. The smell of the food caused me to salivate, to yearn for the salty, spicy taste of it, to feel it on my tongue, to fill my mouth.

Although this was the second meal we had had since arriving at eleven that morning, I saw the others gathered around the fire with the same anxious looks on their faces as mine.

We had been settled into the main floor of a sturdy stone house, just at the bottom of the entrance ladder. A six-foot square hole in the flat roof served as both door and chimney. The gray sky above gave notice that the storm still raged. Periodic gusts blew swirls of spindrift through the hole. Although lying directly below the door/chimney that opened to the sky, I felt warm and secure. Twenty-four hours before, our situation had been perilous; now in this warm enclave, everything seemed safe.

I turned to Prem. Propped up on one of the baskets, he sipped a constantly renewed cup of tea. His eyes shone brighter and were more alert than earlier in the day. *He will live.* If he survived the night and the desperate walk this morning, he would live.

The owner of the house had taken the 200 rupees from Akaal

Bahadur before letting us inside that morning. Whether he considered it prepayment for our food and fuel supplies or *baksheesh* was not immediately clear. At the moment, it didn't matter. But with the money in hand, he had become gracious and welcoming, placing us close to the fire, piling on oily pinewood that gave off acrid smoke. Normally this would have irritated us, but it made no difference; we were warm and out of the storm. Our hostess made a huge meal of rice and with it we downed glasses of *rakshi*. Then came blissfully dry and warm sleep.

With all our wandering, we had at last reached the village of Sangdak. If Jeet Bahadur had not noticed the *chorten*, we would have headed down the hill towards the river. If the *chorten* had been another two hundred yards further on, we would have missed it entirely. Just luck? The reward of men refusing to give up, pushing on, searching? Someone, it seems, had watched over us that day.

As we waited for our meal, four heads appeared in the hole above, backlit against the stormy sky. As my eyes adjusted, I made out the faces of four teenage girls, perhaps fifteen or sixteen years old. They peered down intently at us, their brilliant white teeth offsetting smudged dirty faces, black eyes and oily black hair.

Sangdak after the storm.

Akaal Bahadur saw them immediately. He nudged Jeet Bahadur, and the two porters began to flirt. While some villagers spoke Nepali, most spoke only an odd Tibetan dialect. The language barrier hindered verbal communication, but the porters managed nicely with the girls despite this.

Giggling enticingly, the girls grew braver and moved through the hole to sit on the steps hacked out of the log. We could see that although they were quite young, each carried a baby strapped to her back. Exquisitely beautiful, they captivated us with their strong Tibetan features, flashing smiles and youthful exuberance. The harshness of their precarious existence in the inhospitable Himalaya had yet to dull their love of life.

It seemed to me a long time since I had seen or even thought of beautiful young girls. During the last few weeks my mind had been too frequently occupied with simple survival to permit any room for such thoughts. Now I smiled and enjoyed their company as much as the porters did.

We ate heartily of fried potato cutlets and boiled potatoes washed down with *chang*. A feeling of contentment washed over me as I finished.

I turned to Prem. The food had revived him as well and a smile lit his face. In answer to my question, he indicated that his thighs and upper arms were still painful and swollen. I thought this most likely the result of myositis, involvement of the muscles in the infection. But his speech was no longer impaired, and he had a request for me.

"Parker Sahib, could we stay here one day? The porters would like to celebrate."

"No problem, we could all use the rest."

"They want to buy one goat, from their own money. We will have a feast."

"Good idea. I will buy *chang* and *rakshi*. And potatoes."

"*Very* good, Parker Sahib."

I glanced up at the hole in the roof, now dark and vacant. What other motives might the porters have in wanting an extra day and planning such a feast? *Who cares? We could use the rest and food—and entertainment.*

The heavy meal made me drowsy, and I curled up near the hearth. I had long since given up on the large, heavy-bound journal and now, in my small notebook, I made cryptic notes on the events of the last

two days. The last note for that day read, "First night below 14,000'
in a week."

I tucked the notebook back into my pack, curled up and fell soundly
asleep.

I woke late the next morning, still tired. Eating our morning meal of
rice and potato *tarkaari* took energy I didn't have. A combination of
queasy stomach and sixty days of the same diet permitted me to eat
only a few mouthfuls. I crawled back to the comfort of the fire and my
sleeping bag and drowsed the morning away. By midafternoon I
finally felt rested enough to think about exploring outside. From the
bottom of the ladder, I could see intensely clear blue sky overhead. I
climbed the log ladder to the roof but the brilliance of the sunlight
made me quickly duck back in. I searched for my sunglasses and then,
properly protected, I reemerged.

Looking back towards the Sangdak Pass I saw snow sparkling on the
peaks, receding as the mountains fell away to the black gash that
marked the Cha Lungpa River. In the pristine Himalayan air every
detail etched itself clearly. Sangdak perched 1,500 feet above the *khola*.
Just two hundred feet below the village, the canyon dropped away.

On the other side of the canyon, the sun had already melted the
snow on the south facing slope and I could now clearly see an
abandoned village. Directly across from where I stood lay "Old Sangdak." A desert now, its terraced fields had long ago slid into the
canyon, buildings had returned to the earth from which they had been
built. This was the Sangdak marked on my map. Prem had told me
what the villagers had said. "It was too hot and too dry there. There
was no more firewood for cooking. The soil would not grow any
more barley. So all the people left and they came here. They built new
houses and made new fields."

I cursed the map makers. Old Sangdak had been abandoned for
decades. I thought about what might have happened if we had crossed
the river and found that pile of rubble. And what if we had ended up
there? What would I be thinking now standing on the opposite side of
the canyon and looking at the new village of Sangdak? All those what-
ifs bothered me so much, I forced them from my mind.

Akaal Bahadur and Jeet Bahadur had spent much of the day bargaining. Finally, they arranged to buy a small goat for 200 rupees. A

runt, the goat was missing an eye and unable to forage for food as well as the others. The owner was pleased to be rid of it. Now came the time to slaughter it, and we brought the animal down into the house.

While the porters made preparations, I held the little animal. I wondered how this species had managed to survive. They seemed defenseless, with horns too short to gore anything. Perhaps they survived by running away from danger. Yet, when I stood him up and pushed against the front of his head, his knobby head pushed back. I repeated my push, he repeated his. I realized then that if I stood there for half an hour pushing, he would continue pushing back. Maybe they didn't run away. I smiled at his cute antics and his spunk, and then a twinge of remorse hit me. We were famished and he was to be our dinner.

Old Sangdak, long abandoned, on the opposite (south) facing slope of the Cha Lungpa Gorge.

While Jeet Bahadur carefully sharpened his *kukri*, Akaal Bahadur picked the goat up by its hind legs and suspended it over a wash basin. Jeet Bahadur motioned for me to hold the goat's mouth shut with the neck extended downwards. As soon as I did this, he took his *kukri* and sliced into the underside of the throat. Blood spurted from both carotid arteries and splashed into the wash basin. There was no noise but a sucking sound as Jeet Bahadur cut through the windpipe. The goat showed no sign of pain, nor did it struggle as we waited for it to lose consciousness. Soon its eye closed. Jeet Bahadur, with a few swift strokes, severed the head and it fell into my hands. The jaw and neck muscles twitched as I held the still-warm cranium. I felt a sudden queasiness, and I looked around for a clean place to put the thing down. Finding nowhere, I continued holding it upside down in the palm of my hand as I watched the rest of the butchering.

Jeet Bahadur stuck the knife in the underside and with one quick stroke sliced the goat up the belly, through the sternum and chest. Quickly locating the heart, he hacked it free and set it aside, waiting for the carcass to clear of blood. When the flow of blood eased, Akaal Bahadur lowered the body and the butchering began in earnest.

First the organs were removed, the lungs, liver, spleen, stomach, small intestine, kidneys, pancreas all placed in a large bowl. The only item discarded was the large intestine. Next Jeet Bahadur removed the limbs. He pulled the skin back from the joint, then with a few sharp blows severed the front and hind legs at hip and shoulder. The limbless carcass was laid on its back. As Akaal Bahadur grabbed the ribs and pried them open, Jeet Bahadur sliced them free from the skin from the inside. The skin remained attached to the rest of the body. The tenderloins were removed from just near the spine. Finally the rest of the carcass was hacked into small pieces with a few dozen rapid *kukri* blows. Total elapsed time: four minutes.

Akaal Bahadur now cut the lower spindly portion of the legs from the upper meaty portion. He relieved me of the head, which I still held, and with the legs, he placed it just above the hearth to smoke. I couldn't imagine what Akaal Bahadur thought he was going to do with a smoked head and the bony lower legs.

Auri Bahadur picked up the bowl of innards and disappeared up the ladder. He returned a half hour later with everything washed thoroughly. The small intestine had been sliced lengthwise and chopped into small pieces. The other organs also had been washed and hacked into chunks. Mixed together the pieces no longer were identifiable as heart, liver, intestine or other innards. Each part of the animal had been set aside, including the blood, for the upcoming feast.

The owner of the house came around to offer us some of his *rakshi*, much of which he obviously had imbibed already. I had tasted it the night before and now politely declined. It reeked of kerosene. I decided to hold out for more of his wife's tasty, thick *chang*. Earlier I had felt the rumblings that preceded the intestinal ailments to which I had become so prone in Nepal. Perhaps it would have been better to drink the *rakshi*; I knew that it was distilled, whereas they made the *chang* with whatever water they had available. I decided it didn't matter, I would drink the *chang* and worry about the consequences tomorrow.

Our host lurched from side to side as he meandered into the next room where he slumped down against a pile of old blankets. He would probably sleep the rest of the afternoon away, as he did most days. A tall man, apparently of pure Tibetan stock, he possessed one gold tooth which he showed us repeatedly with generous smiles. A great piece of coral dangled from one ear.

I felt it unkind to note that his wife, now off tending the goats and yaks, was homely as sin, with eyes that seemed painfully crossed. But what she lacked in beauty, she compensated for by a generous heart and boundless energy. At five o'clock when she returned, she scurried about tending the fire, making food, fetching water, blithely stepping around her drunken husband. I doubt she complained about her condition, as most of the village men appeared to be plastered by midafternoon every day. The women missed this dissipated lifestyle since they all left for the pastures early each morning.

As I watched the domestic comings and goings of the household, I heard giggling. Looking up, I saw six heads outlined against the sky through the hole. A smile creased my face and I felt warmed by the sight before me. Beside me, Prem stirred, and I saw him smiling too. I knew then that he was well on his way to recovery.

The girls sat around the chimney hole and on the ladder, whispering quietly to each other, multicolored homespun blankets wrapped around them like shawls. Their babies made no sound; we were aware of them only as bulges on each girl's back. Akaal Bahadur and Jeet Bahadur began to sing Tamang folk songs. The girls responded by singing two songs in Tibetan. As the porters launched into another song, Prem leaned over to me. "Parker Sahib. This is a marriage song. First the men sing and then the women sing."

The porters had finished the men's part and started to sing the women's part, when the Tibetan girls picked up the melody and sang with them. Astonished, Akaal Bahadur and Jeet Bahadur stopped. Pleased with themselves, the girls finished the female part with a flourish as the men picked up the next verse. Prem and I laughed with amazement as the Tamang porters sang their part in Tamang and the Tibetan women sang their part in Tibetan. The end of the song brought smiles and laughter from all.

After an hour, the Sangdak girls placed the palms of their hands together in front of their faces and drifted off without a word. Hastily, Akaal Bahadur, Jeet Bahadur and I clambered up the ladder and watched them disappear into their houses. They looked back at us several times, coyly laughing.

Wistfully, with bittersweet smiles, we watched them go. We had truly enjoyed their company. The women of Sangdak clearly were much more interesting and full of life than the men. Our judgment may have been prejudiced from being on the trail for two months, but the presence of these simple girls had certainly changed our demeanor. That day in Sangdak, they seemed to me the most enchanting women in the world.

The porters climbed back down into the house to prepare our feast. I stood on the rooftop in the twilight, the halo of happiness left by the singing girls still warm around me. I missed Clara. It would be only a few weeks now before I would see her again. Her shining black hair, those exquisitely shaped, expressive eyes. Her shy smile and her whispered words of goodbye when I had left. *Soon*.

Our feast began with a mixture of fiery chilies, garlic, liver, heart, kidney and lungs. Our hostess offered no *chang*, so we washed it down with the kerosene-flavored *rakshi* firewater. For the next course we had the small intestine fried in blood. Finally we ate the meat with fried potatoes. We ate until we nearly burst and drank *rakshi* until we passed out.

Dawn found me desperately searching for a "toilet." Every village had a spot—not too close, not too far and generally not easy to find. My guts rumbled as I hastily searched below the village, crossing terraced fields just above the drop-off into the gorge. I found the open-air spot

*A young
Sangdak girl
and child.*

The enchanting girls of Sangdak.

in a cul-de-sac only yards from where the cliffs began. Feeling lousy and hung over, I still couldn't help but notice the scenery. It was stunningly beautiful this morning, not a cloud obscured the sky. After I had taken care of my urgent problems, I fetched my camera and spent an hour photographing the village and its occupants.

Returning to the house, I found the rest of our band badly hung over and downing cup after cup of strong tea. As we slowly packed up the *doko*s, Prem and I turned our attention to a woman who told us about our route.

"Parker Sahib, she says we have one day to Jomoson."

"That's great, Prem. I'll be so glad to see the Kali Gandaki. We're going to have to forget about going over the Thorung La and through Manang. We'd never make it. Instead we can head down the Kali Gandaki and get to Pokhara in a few days. Ask her where the trail is."

Using hand signs and a few words of broken Nepali, Prem questioned her at length. He turned to me.

"There are two ways to go. This one is the Lekh Baato." He pointed up towards the 17,000-foot lekh behind us to the south. "It is shorter this way."

"I don't know, Prem. There's at least three feet of new snow up there. I don't like it at all. What's the other way?"

The woman used a snakelike hand motion to describe the other route.

"The Khola Baato. It is longer and we will follow the river," Prem interpreted.

I looked towards the black gorge of the Cha Lungpa Khola. Gently sloping hillsides, like the one on which Sangdak perched, stretched atop the steep cliffs that fell sharply to the river. Although deep snow covered the higher slopes, most had melted at this elevation. It looked passable. Our map showed a straightforward route to the Kali Gandaki.

"We'll take the Khola Baato, even though it's longer. You agree, Prem?"

"Yes, Parker Sahib. The snow would not be good for me."

By eight o'clock, we were ready to leave. Still sated by our feast on the goat the night before and immensely relieved at being so close to our destination, we said our goodbyes and left, turning many times to look back at the ocher-colored buildings of Sangdak.

CHAPTER
SIXTEEN

SANGDAK

Wednesday, April 11, 1984

W E left Sangdak, climbing up out of the village for several hundred feet, then headed for a low ridge that separated two drainage areas on the southern side of the canyon. Prem had recovered somewhat. His fever had lowered and his head ached less than during the previous three days. His thighs and upper arms, however, were still swollen, forcing him to walk in a stiff-legged shuffle, using his ice axe as a cane. We kept an eye on him, ready to help if he faltered.

Reaching the ridge, we looked northeast through the canyon and caught our first glimpse of the snow-covered Damodar Himal to the northeast on the far side of the Kali Gandaki. We were sobered, however, by the view of the terrain that lay between us and the Kali Gandaki. The Cha Lungpa Khola formed the most rugged canyon I had ever seen. The river had cut a narrow vertical notch through the steep, mountainous terrain. From where we stood, eight hundred feet of the vertical rock walls were visible, their upper ramparts in some places only a hundred yards apart. The river was easily another thousand feet below, lost in the depths of the canyon. Although the locals called the trail we were attempting to follow the Khola Baato, we

Looking east from Sangdak over the precipitous Cha Lungpa Gorge. The snow-covered Damodar Himal rises beyond the Kali Gandaki Valley.

could see that getting down to the waters of the Cha Lungpa would be out of the question.

Above the vertical walls, the mountains rose steeply several thousand feet and were cut into by numerous side canyons. Our intended route looked impassable. Several slide areas cut across what we could see of the trail ahead, wiping it out completely for long stretches. I feared that we would not see Jomoson that day.

We made our way along shifting scree slopes, contouring as best we could into a great side canyon above the gorge. A stream ran down its center. Because we had water here we stopped early for our first meal.

That's when I realized that we might once again run out of food. Because the villagers assured us that we could reach Jomoson in one day, and because we wanted to travel as light as possible, we had brought only a minimal supply of food from Sangdak. Akaal Bahadur and Jeet Bahadur had asked Prem how much food to bring and he had told them one day's supply. It had slipped my mind to check on how much we had before we left, and now I didn't know with whom I was more upset, them or myself.

Still, I ripped into Akaal Bahadur and Jeet Bahadur and then took my bowl of potatoes and *tsampa* off to eat in angry silence. They seemed surprised and offended by my raised voice, and a pall descended over the group. Soon I felt guilty about berating them after all we had been through. In exchange for a few rupees a day they had done everything asked of them and more. Nevertheless it seemed unthinkable to me that after all our food shortages we could be caught short once again. If I had known, I would have carried the damn food myself.

Despite my tinge of guilt, I sank deeper into a black mood. Looking at the terrain ahead, I felt we had been duped once again. Hadn't we learned yet that what people told us didn't always correspond to reality? Yes, maybe in the best weather, with the trails in excellent condition, with a light load and strong legs, someone had made it to Jomoson in a day. But that person's easy walk to Jomoson might be two or even three days for us. I felt incredibly weary, physically and mentally run down, having thought that the worst was over only to be confronted with additional trials.

As we sat among bushes next to the small stream, we could see across to the next slope. An almost constant bombardment of rocks crashed down, one after the other or several simultaneously, loosened from their frozen perches by the brilliant sun. A few landed in our midst and we scattered, clutching our food bowls. As we finished our meal, we contemplated the next slope, its thick ice covered with loose gravel.

Akaal Bahadur and I headed out to the slope with our ice axes and began cutting a trail for the others to follow. Auri Bahadur kept watch for falling rocks, whistling when he saw danger coming. Several times he whistled shrilly and we dove for cover, watching rocks bounce by. We were playing a deadly game, knowing that a rock the size of a baseball could kill when hurtling down from above.

Fortunately, one at a time, we all made it across that slope, a dangerous dash of more than three hundred feet, without being hit. Near the end, Prem's pace slowed to a crawl. His thighs, now badly swollen, froze up on him. He could hardly bend his legs. We took his pack from him despite his weak protests and that helped, but not much.

More side canyons snaked ahead, making this kind of travel terribly disheartening. We could see that from one side to the other was only a half mile, but frequently we had to travel two or more miles in a long descent followed by an arduous ascent to get to the other side. The canyons cut through hundreds of feet of rock and dirt conglomerate, and in places the trail disappeared, carried down into the deep gorge below by water, snow and earthquakes. At times we could see far into the gorge, a 2,000-foot vertical drop to the white, foaming waters.

We climbed down and up four more side canyons before meeting the dividing ridgeline of yet another canyon. Looking down, we saw the deepest and widest yet, and after just a few feet the trail simply ended. Water and wind had carved the compacted rock and dirt into free-standing spires and knife-edge ridges, a labyrinth through which we had no idea how to make our way. This couldn't possibly be the route. At least it wasn't any longer, if it ever was. But with nighttime approaching and our anxiety to make progress increasing, we didn't stop to think this through. We started down into the canyon, edging our way along, clinging with hands and feet to the conglomerate.

Two hundred feet along, we came to a small depression in the steep slope, a slanting ledge just large enough to support a lone pine tree. We stopped to rest and consider our next move. Once again Akaal Bahadur and I went ahead to scout while the others waited. Beyond the tree, we were relieved to see the semblance of a trail reappear just ahead and slightly above us. We climbed up and followed this track around a corner and further into the morass. I followed close behind Akaal Bahadur as we came to yet another corner. Here, the slope fell away in a sheer wall of dirt and rocks before merging with a steep slide a hundred feet below. The path appeared as little more than an indistinct strand, working its way along just above the drop-off.

Akaal Bahadur began to cross this area, but I held back. An oddly familiar feeling, centered somewhere between the butterflies in my stomach and the deep pounding throbs of my heartbeat, gave me pause. I broke into a cold, clammy sweat. Adrenaline pumped a what-am-I-doing-here queasy kind of feeling into my veins—a feeling I knew only too well from rock-climbing. The feeling you get on lead and forty feet out from the last protection, hand and foot placements tenuous at best, when your legs begin hammering up and down like synchronized sewing machines. As forearms cramp and hands start losing their clawlike grip on the rock, you dream of a flat piece of real estate and make a pact with the gods that you will gladly live in Iowa City for the rest of your life if you are just spared the ankle-breaking, skull-crushing fall that you feel sure is coming. I had been out on that "pointy" end of the rope enough times to heed the feeling before the nasty stuff began.

But Akaal Bahadur was already thirty feet along and now perched just above the vertical section. I didn't want to tell him the truth: that I was beginning to lose the mind game. That I was half paralyzed with the fear of falling off the slope, bouncing and scraping and thudding to the bottom of the canyon over two hundred feet below. So I asked him if maybe this wasn't the trail after all, but maybe just an animal path. *"O Akaal Bahadur, baato ho?"* I said weakly.

He looked first at what lay ahead, then took a furtive glance down-ward. For the first time since I had met him over six months before, I saw fear in his wide eyes. Finally he grasped the fragility of his position, with arms spread too wide and feet barely gripping the crumbling rocks. He remained frozen in place for half a minute, looking at the wall inches from his face, at his feet, at the drop below. Slowly he edged back towards me, one foot and one hand at a time, testing each placement gingerly before shifting his weight onto it. Reaching the rock where I stood, he let out a long, airy whistle and waited for his breath to return to normal.

"No good, Sahib." he finally gasped in English.

Then, in Nepali, *"Yo baato kahaaho?"* ('Where is the trail?')

"Musalai kaideo," ('The mouse ate it.') I replied.

Akaal Bahadur burst out laughing. He laughed until he could no longer breathe, and I laughed along with him, thinking that the joke had finally come full circle. *"Musalai kaideo,"* I repeated.

"Yiss, Sahib," Akaal Bahadur replied, chuckling again at the joke.

Satisfied that I had made the point about the trail ahead, we worked our way slowly back to the others waiting beside the tree. I talked with Prem. We agreed that we should return to the stream that cut through the previous canyon, the last place we had seen any semblance of a real trail. We would follow the stream uphill in hopes of getting above this series of side canyons blocking our way. First we had to retrace our steps back two hundred feet from our current position to the ridge that bisected the two canyons. Because we had consistently gone downhill while traversing, we were now faced with an uphill climb, a decidedly unpleasant prospect.

Akaal Bahadur took the lead, followed by Jeet Bahadur, Auri Bahadur, Prem and then me. Akaal Bahadur crossed the section rapidly, dropped his basket and then came back to help Jeet Bahadur, who was having trouble keeping his bulky load balanced. I helped Prem as best I could as he limped along. He groaned every time he had to stretch to reach the next foothold.

Fifteen feet before the ridgeline and safe ground came a particularly difficult section. We had to face the near-vertical slope, making three reaching steps onto three rocks protruding from the conglomerate. I went ahead of Prem, dropped my pack and returned. He made the first step with my help, then the second two with Akaal Bahadur's help. I followed directly behind him. In my hurry to cross back again I stepped onto the first rock facing away from the wall instead of towards it. My foot touched but did not hold on the sloping sand-covered rock, and slipped off into the void.

Instinctively I spun around as I fell, arresting my fall by bearhugging the rock from which I had slipped. My chest and chin slammed into the rock, knocking the wind out of me and driving my teeth into the side of my tongue. I sucked for breath that wouldn't come. My feet flailed in empty space. I started to slip. Frantically grabbing for a more secure hold, my hands met only grit, sliding across the uneven rocks. Sand trickled off the rock onto my face. I stopped slipping, my hands clutched something firm. My feet still dangled though, and I swung them around blindly, desperately searching for purchase on anything.

Realizing I had nothing below me, I pulled myself up until the side of my face pressed against the wall. With a contortionist's maneuver I pulled one foot up onto the rock. Slowly, taking shallow gulps of air, I pushed and pulled myself to my feet. Prem and the porters watched all of this in utter silence, their mouths agape. Auri Bahadur, who was closest to me, finally spoke. *"Bistaari, Sahib"* ('Go slowly, sir').

I stood until my breath returned and my forearms began to un-cramp. I couldn't bring myself to look down, I didn't even want to know what I had missed this time.

Half of my tongue was numb where I had bitten down on it and now I hacked great pink globs of blood and spit into the air. Along with the blood came a few bits from a front tooth. Finally, I brought myself to make my way cautiously back the remaining ten feet to where the others waited.

Silently we picked our way back a mile to the stream at the bottom of the preceding canyon. Although it remained the only logical place for the trail to be, we saw nothing but dense brush lining the stream. We pushed our way through, looking everywhere for any hint of a path. A third of a mile up the stream bank Jeet Bahadur let out a yell. *"Baato ho!"* His words were music to our ears.

We converged on him and found ourselves staring down at what might be called a major thoroughfare for this part of the world. It came in above us from the west and followed along the stream uphill in the direction we were going. Buoyed by our good fortune, we followed the trail upstream for more than an hour until it veered off to the east, heading up a scree slope in steep switchbacks.

Prem announced wearily, "Parker Sahib, I cannot go any further today." Even though we had less than one full meal left, we had no option but to set camp here near this source of water. Akaal Bahadur and I began our daily ritual of putting up the tents. As we did, he puzzled me by muttering beneath his breath. I could catch only a few words but knew they were derogatory and apparently aimed at the rest of us.

Quietly, I asked Prem about Akaal Bahadur's mumbling and he answered with a sigh, "Akaal Bahadur is calling us all fools. He swears at us and curses our relatives."

"But why should he do that?"

Prem shrugged. Perhaps Akaal Bahadur was upset because we had lost the trail that afternoon. More likely, it was just frustration and the friction caused by all of us being together for so many months. There had certainly been enough frustrations to cause anyone to curse; it just wasn't pleasant to be the object of his swearing.

Carefully, we ate our last meal of *rotis* and potatoes. My tongue was swollen and sore, making it impossible to enjoy my bit of food. After we were finished with our small meal, I searched out the last remaining piece of Afghan hash from the bottom of my pack. Taking Akaal Bahadur's last *beedie*, I carefully removed the tobacco. Breaking the hash into small pieces, I mixed it with the tobacco and refilled the dried leaf skin of the *beedie*. We smoked it in silence. When it was gone, I worked myself into my sleeping bag. My mouth still throbbed, but I no longer cared. In my hash-induced haze, I fell into a fitful sleep.

The next morning, the switchbacks led us up a small hill—steep, rocky going. With only tea and a small amount of chicken bouillon in our bellies, lack of food began to sap our strength. We stopped frequently, and I found myself drinking pint after pint of water trying to fill the void. This didn't do much to assuage the hunger pangs, however. It only contributed to the aching of my distended stomach.

But from the top of the hill we could see eastward and our first view of the waters of the Kali Gandaki. To the north and east across the vast desert of the upper Kali Gandaki stretched the barren region of Mustang. Far below and a few miles ahead we could see the Cha Lungpa Khola, its energy spent, now a gray ribbon on its final journey to join the Kali Gandaki River. At the confluence lay the village of Tangbe. Its irrigated fields formed a tiny green emerald in the sea of parched brown earth.

The trail was easier now, and our pace quickened. We walked downhill, down towards the Kali Gandaki, which had been our destination for the last two months. Prem increased his pace to a stiff-legged trot. He gouged parallel tracks in the sandy soil as he shuffled from side to side with the help of his ice axe. But an hour later, we rounded a promontory and looked down into yet another side canyon.

I felt utterly drained. With an almighty groan, I threw myself backwards onto a large flat rock. Dolpo, it seemed, would loosen its physical hold on us only with the greatest reluctance. Having wrung us dry, having squeezed from us the last drops of our physical, mental and spiritual strength, it now threw up one last obstacle to overcome, this final deep gorge between us and the Kali Gandaki.

But we *had* glimpsed our destination. To be certain that we chose the best way through this canyon, we paused to rest and discuss the route ahead. The side gorge was several hundred feet deep and the far slope, sheltered from the sun, lay blanketed in snow. Bypassing it completely by making our way down to the Cha Lungpa Khola looked possible from where we sat, but the khola ran east and a little north towards the Kali Gandaki and Tangbe. This would have added several miles at least to the route between here and the town of Jomoson. We decided to follow the trail as it contoured into this side canyon, betting that this would be the last such canyon before we found ourselves on the slopes heading down into the Kali Gandaki Valley.

Making our way to the stream that cut through the center of the canyon was straightforward, and within an hour we stopped along its banks. The opposite snow-covered slope revealed that an ascent of seven or eight hundred feet awaited us. Above the ridge crest shone a brilliant blue sky. Lack of food and the bright warm sun sucked the strength out of us.

To heat water for some chicken bouillon, we built a small fire from thorny scrub. We all watched intently as Prem unwrapped our last few bouillon cubes and threw them into the boiling water along with some salt, pepper and the last few chilies. Then he turned to Akaal Bahadur and said something quickly in Nepali.

Akaal Bahadur untied the length of yak rope that held the top of his load, removed a piece of plastic and laid it out on a flat rock. Then he reached further into his basket and extracted a small package wrapped in tattered bits of homespun. He put the bundle down on the plastic and slowly, teasingly untied the bit of wool yarn that held it together.

"Hungry, Sahib?" Akaal Bahadur asked in Nepali, showing a crooked little smile as he removed the cloth.

The goat's head! I had forgotten it, or rather more accurately, I had put it out of my mind, along with the goat's stringy lower legs, which Akaal Bahadur now held up. Grabbing his *kukri*, he hacked at the head with great swinging blows, crushing the skull and leg bones into dozens of pieces. He carefully picked up the plastic and slid the entire blackened mess—bones, skin, brains and feet—into the boiling chicken broth.

We gathered around the fire and sat on our haunches without speaking, staring at the mysterious dark chunks of goat rising and falling in the roiling liquid. I found myself not the least bit reluctant to down my share of this meal. I was literally starving, the hunger coming from deep within me, a primitive need for food that over-whelmed all my other sensibilities. Although we had gorged ourselves on the more palatable portions of this goat only two days before, that feast came nowhere near recouping the long-term food debt of the last few months. I would never again speak those empty words, "I'm starving," without a twinge of remembrance as to how starving really felt.

Waiting expectantly, we watched as Prem carefully ladled out each portion. I salivated—literally drooled—as a bowl was passed to me. I held the steaming bowl and looked at the dark fragments of skull and a few lighter chunks of what I took to be brain. How strange it was, how great and transforming my struggle had been, that I could at this moment relish the sight of a steaming bowl of goat's head soup. Life was stripped of any complexity except the simple overpowering need for food.

Taking my bowl a few feet away from the others, I ate my share as if it were a feast. I savored the still hairy skin, played with the small gobs of fatty brain with my tongue, chewed the bones until they were pulp, extracting every last bit of nutrient. All too soon I held an empty bowl; I stuck my face in it to lick it clean. The others also finished quickly, and Auri Bahadur collected the bowls to wash in the stream. Except for the large intestine, we had now eaten that entire goat. I wondered who had eaten the eyeball from the poor one-eyed creature. I was thankful that it had only had one and that I hadn't found it in my portion, because it was the only body part that still made me queasy.

Soon after leaving the stream we passed through a large stand of gnarled birch. It was now early afternoon, and the sun had finally found its way onto the snowy slope. The foot of snow that remained had turned to mush and the ground underneath it had melted into a slick layer of mud. The powerful reflection of the sun pushed the temperature into the eighties.

Because Prem had lost an ice axe in the accident at the stream on the other side of the Sangdak Pass, we were left with only two. So from the birch around us, Akaal Bahadur and Jeet Bahadur cut three additional staffs for the climb. Without them, it would have been nearly impossible to climb up the steep muddy slope. Even with the aid of ice axes and staffs, we all fell several times.

The trick of eventually making it up the hill, not losing any more than we gained, was to stop ourselves as quickly as possible after falling. We knew the best method was to try to lie completely prone and perform an ice axe arrest or dig a stick into the mud. Even so, twice Jeet Bahadur fell and wiped three of us out with him. Soon we were all soaked and covered with a freezing mixture of snow and mud.

But the sun warmed us, restoring at least some energy, and two hours after the first slippery step, Prem reached the top and turned a corner out of view. I followed five minutes behind him. Rounding the corner, I was confronted by a lone *chorten* and a breathtaking panorama of the land we had been seeking for so long. I stopped, almost with a foot in midair, transfixed by the view before me.

To the north lay an eroded desert landscape leading to Mustang and the Tibetan plateau. The Tibetan border stood clearly demarcated by the snowy peaks of the Damodar Himal. Directly across the vast basin of the Kali Gandaki, the dry barren plateau rose gently and then in a great rush to the snow-covered *V* of the Thorung La, gateway to Manang and the region north of the Annapurna Himalaya. Further south was the massive thrust of the Himalaya of central Nepal, with Tilicho and Niligiri forming a sheer 10,000-foot wall of rock and hanging glaciers. Unable to turn away from the sight, I dropped my pack and sank down next to Prem, who was leaning against the *chorten.*

The porters rounded the corner, one by one. Akaal Bahadur came first and I watched his expression as he approached me. The tumpline on his load kept his gaze downwards, permitting him to take only fleeting glances ahead. But each time he raised his eyes I could see his expression change as the beginnings of a broad smile creased his face. He jogged the last few steps before squatting down to drop his load. Then he stood with his hands on his hips, looking out across the great valley below.

"*O Akaal Bahadur, Kali Gandaki ho!*" ('This is the Kali Gandaki') I exclaimed.

Pointing to the scene he asked in an incredulous voice, *"Kali Gandaki?"*

"Ho, ho," I answered, beaming like an idiot.

"Ahhhhh," was his only reply.

Jeet Bahadur and Auri Bahadur arrived in close succession. Dropping their loads, they flopped down against the *chorten* beside us. We sat and gazed to the east for several minutes without speaking, all moved by the scene before us, relieved, happy beyond words to have finally reached this spot for which we had struggled so desperately for so many weeks.

I finally broke the silence with a half-whisper. "We made it, Prem, we made it through Dolpo."

Saying nothing in reply, he pursed his lips and nodded slowly, still looking straight ahead. After a while he looked at me with a crooked smile and I smiled back. We shook our heads in wonderment. I turned away to regain my composure.

By God, we had made it. Almost.

CHAPTER
SEVENTEEN

"*Jaau*," Prem called, our signal to be up and on our way.

We hoisted our loads and followed the long, contouring trail down towards the riverbed. We lost altitude in great gulps, as though unseen forces were sucking us deeper into the vast watershed of the Kali Gandaki. The land was a barren, treeless desert.

Late in the afternoon, we came to a lone yak herder's hut set amidst a series of stone corrals. A Tibetan man and his small boy emerged from the low doorway and motioned us inside. They offered us Tibetan tea and minutes later we gratefully accepted bowls of the salted, buttery broth. We bought some *tsampa* from the yak herder and mixed it into the steaming liquid.

Immensely tired and wanting to be alone, I stooped through the hut door and climbed a log ladder to the roof. I propped my dusty pack against stones that formed a low wall around the roof edge, sat down and leaned against it. I ate slowly, scooping the salty mixture of tea and *tsampa* out of the bowl with my fingers, savoring each mouthful. Absently, I scanned the same Kali Gandaki view we had seen earlier in the day, only now much closer at hand. Directly across from me was the Thorung La, framed to the north and south by 21,000-

foot snow-covered peaks. Nearer and far below the pass lay Muktinath, a holy pilgrimage site, an island in the sea of brown.

I scraped out the last of my simple meal, laid the bowl aside and
licked the remaining *tsampa* from my fingers. My hands were filthy,
still caked with mud from the slippery climb a few hours earlier. But it
didn't matter. After eating the blackened, smoked goat's head, a little
Himalayan dirt didn't seem so terrible. My tongue snatched up a bit
of cracking mud and I ground it gently between my teeth. Earth, no
doubt about it.

I sat quietly, staring at the scene before me, the raw and untouched
earth. Soon the bright rim of the moon appeared from the *V* of the
Thorung La. I watched, mesmerized as the first half appeared. Then,
with such surprising speed it seemed the earth had squeezed it forth,
the whole moon floated free, suspended in the sky. Almost full, a
barely perceptible yellow, so beautiful it made me think of my camera,
of taking a photo of this familiar companion. So often during the last
few weeks, I had struggled against exhaustion to record my journey
on film. Now, with all energy spent, a numbing weariness gripped me

*We came upon a lone yak herder's hut. Looking east across the vast Kali
Gandaki watershed towards the Thorung La.*

and my camera remained buried in my pack. No strength left to even lift it to my eye.

My mind wandered to other moons. I was at Thyangboche five months earlier at the Mani Rimdu festival, when the full moon had risen directly out of the summit pinnacle of Ama Dablam. I was in Surkhet in February, at the beginning of this journey, with all of us still fresh and strong. In Gum Gadhi, passing silently in the night. In Dolpo, where it was cold and hard, reflecting blue white off the Dhaulagiri Massif. This same moon had been my light through all those dark nights.

Kathmandu. She had risen as a yellow ball, impossibly large, out of the Khumbu Himalaya far to the northeast. Clara, our first words. *Your Full Moon*, she had called herself. I wanted desperately to be with her now, to hold her in my arms.

"Claaaarraaaah!" The cry rose in anguish from deep within my chest, the sound quickly dissipating in the vast open valley.

A few moments passed in silence, then Prem stuck his head above the roof. "Okay, Parker Sahib?"

"Okay," I answered softly, still gazing off towards the Thorung La. I felt him watch me for a long moment, then disappear into the hut below.

I continued to drift, my eyes open but only half conscious of what I saw. Now, with the Kali Gandaki so near, I felt a lifting of weight, a letting down of barriers, a dissolution of emotional control. The visceral emotions I had experienced on this journey emerged as tears that filled my eyes and flowed down my cheeks. Frustration, anger, pain, grief; an emotional maelstrom rose up from my subconscious. With a dirty sleeve I rubbed tears from my face.

Why had I come to the Himalayas? To conquer them? Had I been the quintessential American simply assuming a conquest of these storied peaks? Had I been *that* naive? Those magnificent and beautiful mountains had barely let me through alive. "There are no conquerors—only survivors." That phrase whispered through my mind, taunting me.

I recalled the vision of Akaal Bahadur, water streaming down his face as he dug a trench for my tent; felt the rain drops from his wet clothes when he came in smiling, satisfied in having done his job no matter what. Jeet Bahadur kneeling by the stream, washing my clothes in the freezing water, his hands purple with cold but his work dignified by his satisfaction. Had their culture given them a different view of life, one that saw not a need to conquer but rather a need to view all life as transitory, and that therefore found prizes of little value? And had I, in all my years of collecting awards, titles, degrees; and in my ambition for material success—had I "conquered" nothing of lasting importance? Had Akaal Bahadur, Jeet Bahadur and Prem begun to teach me that true satisfaction lay not in prizes won, but rather in the doing with competence and decorum life's daily work, whatever it might be?

Yet they had gone beyond a simple day's work, for we *had* defied these Himalayas, struggling through where natives feared to trek and warned us not to go. We *had* conquered. But perhaps here lay the meaningful difference; we now held no prize. Only a shared honoring of the indomitable human spirit, a bond that crossed our cultural differences and united us.

Asia. A kaleidoscope of images flashed through my mind. I saw a beggar child in Delhi, her withered stump of a hand pinned to her chest by her parent for a extra rupee or two of pity. I smelled the stench of feces, heard the buzzing of flies, saw the children of Mandu. Bloated bellies, thin reddish hair falling out in clumps, uncomprehending eyes, the handless child. Puraba's children, caked with dirt, minds dulled, destined for a life of toil in a forgotten canyon of western Nepal. Would they experience any joy in their lives? How long would they live? Would their short lives be filled only with pain, despair, affliction?

Death. Memories of my own confrontations with it. Warm salty blood from my tongue where I had bitten down on it; sand on the sloping rock grinding into my fingers as I slipped towards the void. The freight-train roar of the mountainside crashing down to the river and about to take me with it. The smell of dust filling my nose. My brain frantic, my head feeling light and dizzy.

I saw Prem, just a few days before, that night below the Sangdak Pass. I felt his weight on my arm as I half dragged him onwards. I had felt certain he was dying, that he wouldn't survive the night.

Those close calls had shaken me to the core. I had tried to suppress my fear then, tried to accept the possibility of dying. But those experiences had confronted me for the first time with the understanding, the internalization of the idea that someday I would die. The adolescent sense of immortality ended on that rock, in that landslide, on that bridge. And with it went the childish notion of self-importance, the idea of occupying the center of the universe, to be replaced by an acceptance of myself as a mere member in the family of all living creatures.

The tears slowed, I looked out once again at the magnificence of the scene before me. In the stillness of the early evening, in the absolute silence, my emotional turmoil ebbed. Then, as the background noises of my mind quieted, a peacefulness, a clarity emerged from deep within me. For a moment, I sensed an understanding, a harmony. As though the earth and my self were one, inextricably tied together, bound in the cycles of life and death.

With incredible clarity I felt this. My mind, with all its senses sharpened, went beyond weariness to a new level of awareness. Though I had prepared myself for physical hardship—plunging into the icy rivers, scaling crumbling canyon walls—I had not imagined how my experiences would twist and challenge my mind. I had taken a mental journey through frustration, exhilaration, fear, despair and hope to new perception. Facing the tenuousness of life and death, I had experienced the body as it confronts mortality, the mind as it confronts immortality.

The clear silence brought peace, a singular harmony to body and mind. And then, unexpectedly, a sense of sadness, a loss of something. A melancholic network of feelings, tenuous and vague, crept into my small clear silence. Would something be gone forever as I moved on?

Never having adequately answered for myself the question of why I had come to the Himalayas, I felt I had found something of an answer. At least a beginning of one. Yes, physical challenge had brought me here and spurred me on, but something much deeper had happened. My physical journey now almost over, I sensed I was embarking on another odyssey, a journey of the spirit.

I looked again at the rising moon, now glowing in the washed-out blue of the evening sky. From below, I heard the scrape of the hut door and the porters' voices speaking softly. The log ladder creaked a protest as someone climbed it.

"O Parker Sahib," Prem stuck his head above the rooftop. "It is time, we must go."

CHAPTER
EIGHTEEN

UPPER KALI GANDAKI

Thursday, April 12, 1984

DARKNESS enveloped us as we descended the final 2,000 feet into the Kali Gandaki Gorge. By the moon's light we saw the tightly clustered buildings of the village of Kagbeni across the river. A police checkpost guarded the restricted routes north to Mustang and west into Dolpo. We scanned the silvered moonlit buildings for any signs of activity, then cautiously descended to the river's edge. Reaching the second of two bridges that led to Kagbeni, the porters dropped their loads and we rested in the shadows.

As we sat quietly in the darkness, I thought of the long discussions back in Kathmandu in January about our trekking permits. Two major problems had arisen. First, our intended route and projected time on the trail would put us past our visas' three-month limit. This we could easily correct with judicious use of *baksheesh*. But the second problem had no such easy solution. The route we planned to follow would take us to both Jumla and Jomoson. "Not possible" the government officials told us. "One or the other."

We had opted for the route to Jumla. From the perspective of Kathmandu in January, Jomoson seemed lost in the distant future anyway and other obstacles loomed much closer. We had decided to worry about the Kali Gandaki if and when we ever reached it.

Now I held an expired visa and no permit for trekking in this region. One option was to pass by night all the checkposts between here and Tatopani, two days' travel to the south where the route from Jumla joined this trail. Jeet Bahadur had passed through here some years before, and Prem questioned him closely about the number and placements of the police *chaulki*s, but unfortunately he remembered little.

Now, on stiffened legs, Prem leaned against the bridge abutment and scanned the broad floodplain that formed the floor of the gorge. It extended far to the south, flat and strewn with rounded stones.

"Prem, what are you thinking?"

He replied without turning. "Ahead is a much-traveled trail, even at night, Parker Sahib. And maybe *chaulki*s before Jomoson. We should cross this bridge quickly and leave the trail. Walk on the riverbed."

"Sounds good to me. Let's do it."

In single file we wended our way across the river plain, lit blue-white by the brilliant moon. A steady warm breeze washed our faces, the air at only 9,000 feet syrupy-thick in our lungs. Although hungry, I felt alive, energized by my time spent on the roof of the shepherd's hut.

An hour later Prem stopped and pointed south to glimmering pinpoints of light, the electric lights of Jomoson. We now found ourselves on the most heavily trekked route in Nepal, from Pokhara to Muktinath. And where there were trekkers, there were teahouses ready to offer shelter and food.

Hunger consumed us, dominated our thoughts, and a mile further on we diverted towards the main trail to Jomoson. To find food, we would take our chances with the police. In making our way back up to the trail, now seventy feet above our heads, we climbed through a steep, boulder-filled gully. Jeet Bahadur, always so steady and strong, was now so weak he needed help with his load. And we had to hoist Prem up and over boulders to get him onto the trail. A mile on, we came to a teahouse.

I entered first, stepping into a large, open room lined on one side with a dozen single bunks. The fire from the sooty kitchen beyond cast grotesque, flickering shadows on the earthen walls. Round tables and chairs cluttered the remaining space. I sat in a blue aluminum chair with "Dhaulagiri 78" stenciled in now-faded black lettering on the back, an expedition relic. A shy adolescent girl with lovely almond eyes brought menus, a plastic yellow bucket of *chang*, a bottle of *rakshi* and five dirty water glasses. I scanned the menu.

"Toste," "nudels," dozens of other goodies. Unabashedly I ordered "pancaks, omlait and *momos*." Prem and the porters ordered their favorite meal, *daal bhaat*.

Apprehensively, I turned and looked at the two rows of bunks full of sleeping trekkers. Two, in bright orange bags, read by the light of a single candle. They eyed us curiously. I thought about what they saw; decrepit bodies, matted hair, smelly, blackened clothes. I had a momentary urge to charge over to their corner to say hello, to talk, to ask about the outside world, to speak English with someone besides Prem. But I held back.

Prem, Akaal Bahadur, Jeet Bahadur and Auri Bahadur chatted easily. As I watched them, I felt the bonds among us, bonds forged by months of putting one foot in front of the other, leading up and down trails unimagined by any of us a year before. Bonds that we would remember for the rest of our lives. Together we had endured privation and physical hardships, experienced frustration and soaring exhilaration, traversed a rugged land, survived on little food, traveled day and night, dodged bandits and soldiers alike.

As I contemplated the westerners asleep in their bunks only a few feet away, I sensed that contact with the outside world would pull us apart, splinter our tiny band, make us individuals again. I turned back to my Nepalese companions, warmed by our present kinship and content to remain with them for a while longer.

With our bellies full, we talked quietly. About the women of Sangdak, the frozen rivers, Lama Dorje, and of J.B. Despite our disagreements before Jumla, which I now attributed to nothing more than the stresses of trekking, I felt acutely his absence from our group.

After a lull, I turned and spoke to Prem in English. "Prem, you can hardly walk. I'm worried that you might become sick again. I want you to fly back to Pokhara. I will pay." I said this knowing that we didn't have enough rupees for the flight. I would borrow from other foreigners if necessary.

I could have predicted his response. "I will not fly back, Parker Sahib."

I opened my mouth to argue, then closed it. I knew he meant it. By the light of the flickering fire, I studied his profile and saw beyond the dirt, the grime, the thin, weakened body, to the man's soul—to his inner strength and dignity.

*　　*　　*

Just before 11:00 P.M., we hoisted our loads and continued south. Once on the trail, we stopped to discuss our plan for getting through the checkposts. Although I knew that the scheme we used for Dunai had worked, it still seemed farfetched to me. Yet we decided to try it again. Akaal Bahadur and I walked ahead, with Prem, Jeet Bahadur and Auri Bahadur a hundred yards behind us. Surprise would be our strategy.

Taking our positions, we approached the cluster of buildings that straddled the trail a few hundred yards ahead. The guttural bark of a dog sounded menacingly in the darkness ahead. As we drew closer, several dogs surrounded us. But after the mastiffs of Dolpo, these scrawny beasts seemed pathetically harmless, and Akaal Bahadur and I took a sort of revenge for our previous troubles with others of their species. Swinging bold, windmilling strokes with our ice axes, we broke their ranks, chasing one and then another as they backpedaled, whined and scattered in retreat. But the commotion awoke the occupants of one of the houses, where lights blinked on. Akaal Bahadur gave me a warning look, along with a big-jawed grin as we reluctantly ceased our attack and moved quickly on into the dark.

Ahead stood a brightly lit cable suspension bridge and, beyond that, a small enclosed booth with a bell, a *chaulki* for reviewing trekking permits. No one in sight. So I pulled my Chinese hat down low my brow and we stepped out onto the bridge. Swiftly and silently we crossed it, passed the *chaulki* and made our way up the hill past shuttered shops.

Ahead two figures appeared in the trail. They watched us approach, then spoke sharply to us. Ignoring them, I stepped in the shadow of Akaal Bahadur's basket and hurried on by, picking up the pace. After fifty yards I looked back, and with relief saw no one following. Fifteen minutes later, we came to the southern edge of town and yet another checkpost. A gate, a booth, a bell and under a single bright bulb, a police guard. I hid behind the *doko* once more, but just as we came abreast of the guard, I glanced up. For an instant our eyes met. Immediately my heart pounded with a rush of adrenaline. But the guard made no move to stop us and we sped on. For half a mile we walked, then stepped off the trail to rest.

As my heartbeat slowed, I wondered why the guard had done nothing to stop me. Perhaps he didn't recognize me as a foreigner, or maybe he had just been caught unawares, not expecting anyone past midnight. Twenty minutes later, several figures approached from Jom-oson. We recognized Prem's halting gait and went out to meet them. Prem bent over and rested his hands on his knees, sucking for breath.

"I think they are coming after us!" he said. "They stopped us three times. At the bridge, in town and just back at the government post. They questioned us. I told them I was a student in botany coming from Manang, walking all night because of a leg injury, after a rest in Muktinath. They did not believe me. They wanted to open our loads to check for the number of people with us. To search for stolen art objects. Finally they let us go. Each time I told them the same thing."

He looked back along the trail, pointing at half a dozen lights bobbing a hundred yards away. "See there. They're coming."

For several seconds, I stood rooted, staring back up the trail, not willing to believe that once again we would be chased by the police. But the bouncing lights were real and coming closer. I grabbed Prem's arm and we ran as best we could, stopping every hundred yards to look back and take a few breaths. But on they came. A mile later, at the small settlement of Syang, we stopped once again, waiting for the porters. A quick glance back told me our pursuers had not yet abandoned the chase.

"Quickly," I whispered. "Let's leave the trail and go behind those buildings. Get over by the river."

The porters joined us as we hurried down an embankment and over a dilapidated stone wall. We settled in close against the wall and waited in silence. No one came.

I awoke at daybreak, shivering, huddled against the cold stones, covered by our unrolled tents and sleeping bags. The others lay asleep, buried under gear and our makeshift cover. I looked towards a building thirty yards away and saw a young man squatting in the doorway, watching us. With daylight our secure hiding place had vanished. I woke the others. Hastily we packed our gear.

Less than an hour later I passed two trekkers on the trail. I had spotted them when they were still a quarter a mile away and had eagerly awaited my first contact with foreigners and some conversation about the outside world. I smiled as they approached, but they passed by without so much as a nod, eyes averted. To them, I supposed, foreigners were to be avoided as intrusions into their "Nepal experience." A few minutes later, we stopped at a teahouse in Marpha.

Three Americans sat at a nearby table, but now I felt out of sorts, hungry and in no mood to talk to anyone.

Another hour and a half brought us to Tukuche and another rest stop at a small lodge. I walked into the front room to find several trekkers sitting at a long table. I sat with Prem at the far end of the table as the porters continued through to the sunny interior courtyard.

I spotted them right away—several warm bottles of Golden Eagle on a shelf behind Prem, the first I had seen since Surkhet. A smiling woman in Sherpa dress approached and asked what we wanted. I greedily ordered two Golden Eagles while Prem ordered *chang* for himself and the porters. I popped the cap on the first large bottle of beer and almost drained it in a single draw. After a prolonged and satisfying belch, I looked over at the other foreigners, who watched us with a peculiar mix of curiosity and revulsion. They had the latest in equipment, bright multicolored packs of red, blue and green; new boots, fresh clothes, scrubbed faces. I had lived in my clothes for three weeks, my hair was uncombed, greasy and matted. I looked at Prem. That fastidious Nepalese was filthy and unkempt. When the porters came in and sat down, our stench filled the room.

After a meal of *daal bhaat* and more beer, the porters went outside to unpack our gear. I lingered at the table. Sated with food and drink, my eyelids closed.

I woke to find one of the foreigners sitting across from me. "Where have you come from?" He spoke with a Scandinavian accent.

It took several seconds for his query to penetrate my haze. "To the north and west."

"From behind Dhaulagiri?"

I paused, then nodded weakly.

"But I heard you cannot go there, that it is restricted. And dangerous."

After fifteen seconds of silence, he looked away. But he didn't leave. *This guy really wants to talk.* I asked him about the Olympics, about what was happening in the world. But he obviously wanted to talk about other things, and the conversation soon petered out.

Then I rose unsteadily and entered the white sunlight of the courtyard, finding Prem checking supplies and Akaal Bahadur washing clothes at a water tap. Rummaging through Jeet Bahadur's basket, I found a scrap of soap at the bottom and decided to wash. I stripped off my polypropylene shirt. White skin, brown forearms, *Bodhissatva* ribs. Removing my long underwear for the first time in weeks, I was shocked at the sight of my legs. So thin. I took my hands and completely encircled one thigh.

"Prem, what have you done to me?"

Prem studied me with his crooked smile, then grinned broadly. "Now you are Asia thin, Parker Sahib. Like the rest of us."

Moving to the tap, I sluiced my body with frigid water and washed head, arms, legs, toes, every inch several times over. While I scrubbed, Akaal Bahadur took my pile of clothes and washed them, then wrung them out as best he could. Having handed out my extra clothes weeks ago in Dolpo, I put the damp clothes back on and lay down in the midday sun.

An hour later swirling winds and dark clouds forced me inside, where I slept until Prem roused me.

Our plan was to hurry south and pass the checkpost at Lete under cover of darkness. Towards dusk, however, the clouds lowered and yellow flashes lit the sky. Large drops spattered on the rounded rocks of the floodplain. We dashed ahead, looking for shelter and finding it in a small lodge in Dhumpus.

At 4:00 A.M., Prem and I set off to pass the checkpost at Lete before dawn. The porters would catch up with us later in the day. Roosters announced the coming day as we moved silently past the checkpost, which sat ghostly in the predawn twilight. An hour later, we waited for the porters under the shady porch of a teahouse.

At eleven, the porters arrived, sweatsoaked in their mountain clothes. That day we would drop another 4,000 feet down through the twisting Kali Gandaki Gorge. From the cold windswept reaches of Dolpo to the sultry green subtropics in two days. I found myself still wearing my long underwear, wool shirt and jacket, my second skin for so many weeks. But before heading for Tatopani, I changed into shorts for the first time since Surkhet.

Prem, the porters and I lost sight of each other and I walked alone. Not alone, really—the trail was crowded with an odd assortment of locals, trekkers and Indians on pilgrimage to Muktinath. After the stark isolation of Dolpo, I found the stimuli of civilization disorienting. My eyes and thoughts darted to one exciting sight after another, so many villages, so much humanity. Within the spray of a waterfall a short distance off the trail a large group of trekkers bathed. White, blubbery paunches jiggled as they splashed in the tumbling waters, Germanic-accented shouts accosted the surrounding silent beauty.

Prem and the porters heading down the Kali Gandaki.

What species did these creatures belong to? Loud, gaudily clad, defiantly obese in a land of hunger.

The porters, I knew, had stopped somewhere for food and the lodges along the way tempted me with their signs. "Welcom! All you can Eat!" proclaimed one. "Tasty Western Snaks Served Here" said another.

I stopped at one and looked up and down the trail for Prem and the others. Not seeing them, I ducked inside. I sat at a table covered with a white linen tablecloth and holding salt and pepper shakers, an ashtray and pink rhododendron blooms in a earthenware vase. A menu of more than fifty items boasted Nepalese, Chinese, American and Japanese cuisine, right down to sukiyaki fritters. I ordered a double stack of apple "pancaks" with powdered sugar and coffee.

Around five o'clock I met Prem at the outdoor restaurant of the Namaste Lodge in Tatopani. I took off my pack and sat down. "Prem, where are the porters?"

"Don't worry, they are behind us. They will come later. The *chaulki* is at the edge of town. We can bypass it by going out the back door of the kitchen and heading to the river. We can follow the river to the hot springs. From there we can get back on the trail beyond the *chaulki*."

In celebration we ordered beer and *suggotti*. After the porters passed by, we left, going out the back door past two smelly outhouses and down to the river. A half mile later we came to an open-sided building and a small concrete pool filled with dirty tepid water, the hot water from whence Tatopani got its name. Earlier, we had thought of soaking in the hot water, but the sight of the pool now made us reconsider. We left the spring to two dreadlocked *saddhus* (holy men) and found the path back to the main trail. Congratulating ourselves on bypassing the checkpost, we cruised on up the trail. Stone walls lined the path as it wound between houses and small fields.

I rounded a bend to see a uniformed policeman sitting on a wall only thirty yards ahead! My mood sank immediately. Another checkpost. Prem saw him at the same moment I did and whispered, "Wait just a little, then come."

Prem went ahead. The policeman stopped and questioned him. As the policeman was thus occupied, I started to walk on by, hoping he wouldn't notice me.

"*Namaste*, this is a checkpost. Please show your permit." He pointed to a chair on the porch of the low building on the other side of the trail.

I sat down, took off my pack and rummaged through for my passport and permit, which I presented to another officer seated there.

"I am coming from Jumla." I assumed a false bravado.

"Jumla?"

"Yes, I came past here from the south last night looking for a place to stay in Tatopani. I was very tired."

He looked at my passport and inspected my permit carefully. "But your permit is expired by ten days, and your passport also."

"Yes." I kept up the false front. "We had a very difficult time coming over the Thakurji Lekh. Lots of snow and it delayed us for two weeks."

The policeman turned to Prem and spoke in Nepali. "Do you know this *bideshi* ('foreigner')?"

"No," Prem said. "I met him on the trail just last night. He was lost so I showed him the way to Tatopani. His porters are just ahead."

To my relief and surprise, the policeman stamped my permit and returned it. "Okay, but you must get a new visa in Kathmandu. It will cost you several hundred rupees."

"Yes, I know. I am just happy to have made it back from Jumla."

"Yes, a very bad place," the officer said. "I used to live in Jumla. And that Dhorpatan is a dangerous place, so many *dacoits* ('bandits')."

"Yes, the people were unfriendly," I said over my shoulder as I headed down the trail. I waved goodbye to Prem.

I waited a quarter of a mile down the trail, and shortly Prem followed.

"That's it Prem," I said with a big grin. "I'm legal! They stamped my permit."

"Yes, Parker Sahib, we're almost home."

For two days we walked with the other trekkers along the well-trodden paths, eating and drinking our way from teahouse to trekker's lodge. We went down 6,000 feet to Birethanti, 2,000 feet of it consisting of steep stone steps that left my legs aching, yearning for an up of any sort. After six hundred miles on the trail I surprised myself—I didn't know there was anything my legs couldn't handle easily. That night we celebrated with chicken and drank *chang* into the wee hours.

The next day's ascent through hot, muggy weather intensified my hangover, headache and queasy stomach. I hadn't discovered until long into the night that the *chang* had been made with water drawn directly from the Modi Khola. Hot, frustrated, reeling with fever, I left Prem and the porters and rushed on to Naudanda, where I planned to cash my last traveler's check at the bank.

At the Nepal Rastra Bank I found a long line snaking out into the street. For forty-five minutes I waited in the stifling sun, straining to keep my bowels from exploding. And when I finally handed a teller my traveler's check, he looked confused and referred me upstairs. Why, I didn't know and didn't care. All I wanted was my money and a toilet, maybe in reverse order. After another half hour, I emerged to find Prem waiting for me.

I opened my mouth to speak, then thought better of it and rushed off to the relative privacy of some nearby bushes. An hour's walk and a forty-five-minute jeep ride brought us to the edge of Pokhara, where we waited still another hour to board a packed local bus. Once aboard I scrunched into a window seat and concentrated on not soiling my shorts for the trip into town.

Soon we found ourselves stopped in the midst of the bazaar, caught in a gridlock of cows, cars, lorries, bicycles and *tongas*. Two arguing drivers traded fists as a swarming crowd surged around for a better view, shouting encouragement and groaning with each well-landed blow. Inside the bus, the hundred-degree heat made me claustro-phobic, and I leaned out the window for a fresh breath. Instead I got a lungful of noxious diesel fumes. Feverish and queasy, with the din of the crowd and honking horns, the polluted air, I leaned my aching head against the window frame wanting nothing more than to be back amidst the mountains of Dolpo.

When we reached the Himalayan Lodge, Prem and the porters made plans to hit the town. This outing had been planned for some time, but I was too sick to go with them. I asked Prem to buy me a bus ticket to Kathmandu for the next morning. The four of them would stay in Pokhara for a few days and meet me later.

I awoke before dawn to catch my bus. My head ached from only two hours' sleep and my stomach still felt queasy. I swallowed two codeine tablets and Prem fed me two large mugs of steamy sweet tea, then made sure I got on the bus.

At four that afternoon the bus crested the last switchback and the Kathmandu Valley stretched out before me, just as it had during my first approach from the plains of India seven months before. Back then I thought I had reached Nirvana. I laughed to myself. Was that only seven months ago? It seemed like seven lifetimes. The countryside, then cloaked in twenty shades of green, lush from the lifegiving monsoon rains, now lay brown and dormant, the terraced hillsides awaited the nourishment of summer rains.

As we rumbled down into the valley, two Tibetans in black *chubas* pushed their way into the aisle of the bus. Gesturing excitedly, they raised their arms overhead and bowed towards the great *stupa* of Swayambhunath atop an isolated hillock above the city. I, too, revived at the sight of the *stupa* and those great brooding Buddha eyes that had surveyed our departure two and a half months earlier.

I had come full circle. I closed my eyes against the dust billowing in through the open window and let my forehead rest against the window post. My thoughts wandered and I found myself once again lost in the mountains of Dolpo. Prem, Akaal Bahadur, Jeet Bahadur and I had literally stumbled there, not knowing where we had come from or exactly where we were heading. Lost within a massive geological backwater, isolated from the world by the crumpled crust of the earth. Was I ever really there? Or did I create that place in a warped dream?

I opened my eyes and looked down at my shrunken body, sinewy muscles, taut skin. It had been no dream. But even with its vision vivid in my mind, Dolpo remained somehow secretive and aloof. As though our circuitous passage through Jumla and Dalphu had been a necessary prelude, a hardening of the body, softening of the mind, a shedding of values and preconceptions to prepare us for those stark and mysterious mountains, the utter desolation, the awesome and frightening power of the earth.

I thought again of Tibrikot, Dunai, Tarakot, our brushes with the police and military. Lama Dorje, who had appeared from nowhere to tell us of a route through the mountains, our Dorje Route, the Path of Lightning Bolts. Sangdak, into which we stumbled in a raging blizzard, on the "wrong" side of the Cha Lungpa Gorge. All just happenstance? Perhaps. I thought so at the time, for I was no believer in Fate or God. But the time on the shepherd's roof, watching the moon, had challenged my beliefs. Now I knew nothing.

The bus crossed the bridge spanning the Bagmati River and entered Kathmandu. Left off at Ratna Park, I headed on foot through the crooked streets towards Asan Tole. In the sticky afternoon heat, rickshaw wallas approached and circled me, hungry for a few rupees.

But I was determined to walk the last mile by myself and told them to go away, perhaps more sternly than I should have. Turning the corner in Thamel, I spotted Pema at the same moment he spotted me.

"Parker, my God!" he said. "You are so thin!" Taking me inside his cramped shop, he pulled the dirty worn pack from my back and found a place for me to sit among the piles of ropes and sleeping bags. Summoning a boy from the street, Pema pressed a few rupees in his hand and sent him scurrying in search of *chang*.

"We were so worried. J.B. did not think you would make it. He was already planning how to look for you if you did not come back by May first."

"We were lucky many times, Pema. Many times."

The *chang* arrived and we ceremoniously drank three glasses in toast of my return.

"Where is J.B.?"

"At the same hotel. He went to pick up the extra supplies you left in India last year and returned only two days ago."

"I should go find him." I stood to leave. "Will you have dinner with us tonight?"

"Yes. Yes, of course."

I paused, the one question I really wanted to ask burning on my tongue. "Oh, Pema. Have you seen Clara?"

"She is in Darjeeling. Some letters came for you. They are at my home. I can give them to you tomorrow."

"Thanks," I desperately wanted to read her words, but persuaded myself tomorrow was soon enough.

I found J.B. in his second-floor room. I rattled the window. He looked up, startled, then his face softened and he jumped up to greet me. "Parker, good to see you."

He took my hand in both of his. The warmth of his greeting was a welcome relief. I felt guilty about the turn of events in western Nepal, and I knew that our differences on the trail were as much my fault as his. In my mind, these were events of the past, and I was relieved to sense that they were to him, too. We feasted that night on buffalo steak and apple pie. After dinner, I went back to our room and slept for fourteen hours.

Four days later, Prem and the porters showed up. Our gear—the cooking pots, kerosene stove, tents, tarp—was all neatly packed into two baskets. We sat on the balcony and talked for a time about our extraordinary trip together. But it surprised and disappointed me how soon the status of westerner and hired help returned, and the intense closeness faded. I thanked and paid them all, including large tips. Auri Bahadur had decided to take a bus back to Surkhet and walk home from there. Flying in the iron bird scared him too much. Prem planned to remain in Kathmandu and regain his health. Akaal Bahadur and Jeet Bahadur were to leave for their village the next morning. I found out later that Prem had gone to a doctor in Kathmandu who gave him some pills. Prem, as is the custom in Nepal and much of Asia, never bothered to question the doctor but took the pills and subsequently recovered his health. His symptoms resembled the symptoms of meningitis, but I never found out whether that was what he had. In any case, I'm grateful that he got better.

When the time came for them to leave, they walked down the stairs and crossed the open courtyard, Akaal Bahadur last. Before he disappeared from view, I called out to him.

"O Akaal Bahadur!"

He turned. I raised my hands, palms together over my head. "*Dhanyabaad*! ('Thank you.')"

For a moment he stood there. He was dressed once more in his lavender pantaloons, his long-sleeved shirt and blue sweater vest, and I took a mental picture I will never forget. "Yiss, Sahib, thank you. *Namaste.*" He bowed slightly, turned and moved into the street.

During the following days, J.B. and I discussed the possibilities of continuing our trans-Himalayan traverse through northern India in the summer. But they were futile discussions because J.B.'s ankle had been examined in Delhi, with a grim diagnosis. He faced the possibility of further damage and he still walked with a limp. We both knew his trekking days were over.

I could have gone alone, but the prospects looked poor. Sporadic news reports had reached Kathmandu about unrest in northern India. The Sikhs were agitating for an independent state and there was also trouble in Kashmir. Neither the Nepalese newspapers nor the Indian embassy could supply any reliable information. Our only hard sources were contacts within the British embassy. And they gave ominous news; Indira Gandhi's government and the Sikhs were headed for a showdown at the Golden Temple.

Beyond the political problems, I had personal doubts about continuing. My finances were low, and after months on the trail I felt physically and mentally drained. My journey through western Nepal had left me with a sustained glow, but it had also taken its toll.

A week after I returned, I ventured up to the fourth floor where we had stayed in December and January. Deserted now in the off-season, the place that had been so vital and alive only a few months before now seemed tired and disheveled. Those few weeks around New Year's had been a special time, a random union of unique personalities and circumstances. Americans, Swiss, Belgians, Canadians; trekkers, wanderers, seekers, smugglers. Through a concatenation of circumstances, we had all found ourselves in Kathmandu, and the result was a release of euphoric, synergistic energy. Now the others had scattered over the globe and only J.B. and I remained, a day late for the party. I felt their ghostly presence as I walked along the balcony, then sat briefly in a worn rattan chair.

I climbed the creaking steps to the roof and sat on the low wall that surrounded it, looking out over the rooftops of Kathmandu to the brown fields and hills beyond. It all appeared so different now. Back then, the January sun, lower in the sky, had cast a cool, exotic aura over the valley. Now in the brighter light, the city stood naked to my view, imperfections exposed. The bamboo scaffolding of new construction sprouted everywhere, especially in the tourist area of Thamel. The day before, during a conversation overheard in one of the new upscale bakery-restaurants, I had heard Thamel referred to as a "tourist ghetto." An apt label for a place fast becoming insulated from the people and culture of Nepal.

I remained on the roof for two hours as the sun set, a pocketful of chocolates and two letters from Clara my companions. More and more during the last weeks she had filled my thoughts. I relived the delicious sensual frustration of our time together in January. In my memory, I replayed bits of our conversations and actions. Slowly I began to see the essence of what had happened. And, as I did, I began to feel what I was not seeking: doubts about the vast cultural differences between us. Could we overcome them?

During our descent of the Kali Gandaki, I had tormented myself. I feared Clara had forgotten me, written me off as just another foreigner tramping through her country. By the time I reached Kathmandu, these doubts and fears had pitched me into a deep well of depression. But she *had* written, using Pema's address, and now I reread those letters. Through anguished pages she pleaded with me not to forget her, to visit her in Darjeeling as I had promised. As I watched the sun set to the west beyond Swayambhunath, her presence next to me was palpable.

On the first of May I said goodbye to J.B., who had decided to head for the northern Sahara and Morocco. We made plans to meet in the U.S. when we both returned. I boarded the overnight bus to Kakarvitta on the eastern border with India.

The next day I crossed the border and hitched a ride with a tea plantation manager in his Land Rover. We left the Indian plains and drove up along the twisting road into the lush Himalayan foothills. In the town of Darjeeling I wandered through the crazy winding hillside streets, and soon stood before the modest cottage Clara's parents rented not far from the Mall.

Nervously, I opened the gate and walked up to the door. As though expecting me, Clara opened it before I could knock. Our eyes met and a rush of emotion flushed my face. Then she smiled, black eyes sparkling, deep dimples piercing her cheeks, black hair brushed and glistening. Standing in the doorway, she looked the part of an English schoolgirl in a plaid pleated skirt, white blouse and knee socks. Her mother stood behind her in a traditional sari.

I smiled at her mother and put my hands together. She returned the greeting. She spoke no English, and although functional, my Nepali wasn't up to the subtleties of social conversation. Clara led me to the sitting room and we sat stiffly on a couch, knee to knee. When her mother left the room to get tea, I leaned towards her. She turned demurely and I gently kissed her cheek.

"Oh Parker, when I saw you at the door, it gave me such a start. I thought you had forgotten me." She spoke quietly in the Nepali British accent I found so appealing.

"And I was so afraid you had forgotten me," I said. This time she leaned towards me and I reached out for her. We embraced in a long, lingering kiss.

"No, I didn't forget," she whispered. "How could I forget?"

Clara's mother brought tea and cookies, then left us to our conversation.

"Just a few days ago, Praven's brother came here along with a friend, looking for a place to stay. I could not turn them away, so they are staying here with us. Just now they are out, but they may come back any time. Please, I will take you to my cousin's house. You can stay there until they leave."

More complications. For a week I stayed in her cousin's cottage, confined inside so as not to risk running into Praven's brother on the street. Once again I found myself near Clara but able to see her for only an hour a day, when she could slip away unnoticed. After a week, Praven's brother left for Kathmandu and I moved into the guest room at Clara's house.

There I spent two of the most peaceful weeks I have ever known. The monsoons had arrived, leaving the days overcast with intermittent afternoon showers, the foggy nights cool and damp. In the mornings I awoke from under heavy blankets to the delicious scent of steaming tea and warm flatbread. During the days, Clara and I spent long hours together talking about our childhoods, our backgrounds and our hopes for the future. I learned of her Catholic upbringing, attendance at the local schools run by nuns, the repressive atmosphere of the narrow-minded town of Darjeeling. She told rather ugly stories about nuns beating and tormenting students, instilling lifelong guilt for what seemed the smallest actions. Darjeeling society itself seemed a peculiar mix of the restrictive Catholic school atmosphere, the stifling British tradition and the timeless stratification of Indian culture.

This restrictive social system was particularly hard on women, most of whom had resigned themselves to its strict rules of behavior. But Clara had not yet totally given in. She longed for an escape from the guilt she felt about many things, including her attraction to me. More than anything else, our time together proved to both of us that Kathmandu in December and January had been more than just a brief interlude. Our mutual attraction seemed guided by forces outside either of us; in each other's presence we found ourselves uncontrollably drawn together.

Through the groundswell of emotional and physical longing, however, I sensed that different needs and desires motivated each of us, some embedded in the very cultural differences between us. I recognized that for Clara, I represented a chance to escape, a way out of this society. I knew that dealt me the upper hand in our relationship, but I saw that as a responsibility, a reason to be extra careful with Clara, not to mislead her—or myself.

Evenings I usually spent with Clara's brother, since it was expected of the men to socialize together. Invariably we would go to a friend's house for dinner, then drink glass after glass of warm scotch or rum. Our conversation ranged from politics early on, to drunken ramblings by men who also felt trapped, resigned to living boring lives in a repressive society.

Occasionally Clara and I took advantage of the late-night veil of darkness and fog to walk through the streets of Darjeeling. Just as in Kathmandu, for her to be seen with me would have raised eyebrows and sent vicious rumors scurrying through the streets of this small, provincial town.

After three weeks I had to leave, my special Darjeeling permit having been renewed twice already. On the last afternoon, Clara took me for a walk along the Mall, the promenade set on the ridge above town. She linked her arm with mine and we walked through town. Walking thus, the statement she made was an act of defiance for which I knew she would pay a stiff price in jealous comments from "friends."

That night she sneaked into my room for a time and we spoke quietly in the darkness. We made plans. I had been thinking seriously of staying in Asia; even if I couldn't continue my trek in northern India, I wasn't ready to go home. And now, with Clara so close, what other thoughts could I have but to stay? I knew a number of foreigners working in Nepal, and I thought I could find a job. Clara also thought she could find work in Kathmandu.

"We could live together," she said quietly after a long pause. "And if you go trekking in India, I will find a place to live and wait for you. I will write to Pema's mailbox at the post office to tell you when I arrive."

This suggestion both surprised and pleased me, because it would give me something I longed for—to be alone with her. For her it was a major step, perhaps an irrevocable shift in her social status. Maybe these plans came from the heart and not from the mind. But we were intoxicated with each other, and emotions easily overpowered logic. And that night, we truly believed in our plans.

In the morning, I packed my rucksack and headed off with Clara's brother for the taxi stand. As I reached the front gate, Clara and I parted with just a wave and goodbye. Without telephones, and with poor postal service, long separations with little or no means of communication were a way of life in Asia. I had grown accustomed to it. Besides, we had made our plans the night before.

Back in Kathmandu the monsoons had driven the tourists from Nepal. Landslides and leech-infested jungles do not lend themselves to comfortable trekking. By the first of June, events in India had degenerated into near-civil war. Gandhi had sent troops into the Golden Temple, hundreds had been killed, martial law and curfews had been ordered throughout northern India. Reports trickled into town of hijacked buses with all passengers killed. Such news dashed my hopes for continuing on to northern India.

So I looked for work. USAID had no openings for biologists, but the U.S. Embassy school needed a middle-grade science teacher, and I applied for the job.

Clara wrote that she was having trouble returning to Kathmandu. Forbidden to come alone, she waited until her friend Sera could leave Darjeeling. Finally, early in June, I received a letter saying she was now in Kathmandu, staying with her aunt in Dilli Bazaar. She did not give me an address.

"I want to see you so much," she wrote. "But certain circumstances beyond my control prevent me from doing so. Please to understand. Your Clara."

Please to understand? What was she talking about? I was desperate to see her and all she could ask of me was to understand some unexplained reasons for not being able to see her. I was puzzled, angry and hurt. But the best I could do was an exchange of letters via Poste Restante at the post office. She asked me to be patient. And I waited, though not patiently. Finally, two weeks later, we arranged a rendezvous. She would come to Pema's shop and I would wait for her in a nearby restaurant. She feared that Praven or his friends would see us together.

At the appointed time, I waited upstairs by the window in a second-floor restaurant. I watched the narrow, crowded street below. Pema stood in the doorway of his shop.

Then I saw her, walking with her friend Sera. My frustration and resentment disappeared, for Clara seemed the most beautiful woman I had ever seen. She found Pema, who pointed up at me. She turned and waved and then came up to the restaurant.

"Please," she whispered as she sat down. "Could we move away from the window?"

We moved to the other side of the table, which was crowded with my friends. We talked quietly but with constraint, unable to speak of what was most on our minds. I wanted so much to be alone with her. Still, we managed to communicate that our plan was still on. But her aunt was very strict, so she was trying to find a place to stay with Sera. First, she had to return to Darjeeling and hoped to return by mid-July. After fifteen minutes she said she had to go. I walked downstairs with her. Just inside the doorway, she turned and leaned back towards me.

"Do you have something to say to me, Parker?"

I whispered in her ear. "I love you."

"Thank you!" she smiled at the answer she wanted to hear and stepped out into the street. Then she was gone and I was left wondering when I would see her next.

Trekking in India was out of the question, but my impatience wouldn't let me sit in Kathmandu and wait. I decided to return to Khumbu and try to climb a couple of peaks I had missed the previous fall. I hoped that by the time I returned a month later, something would have happened. Wind and weather once again foiled my attempts, and after a long slog through mud and leeches, I arrived back in Kathmandu by the last week in July.

More letters awaited me. Clara had arrived in Kathmandu and was once again staying in Dilli Bazaar. Again she left no address. I left a letter at Poste Restante and waited impatiently. A week later she had not come to check for mail. I fumed. *What was going on? What kind of game was she playing?* I didn't know what she was doing, but I suspected I was being toyed with. Finally the letter was picked up. She wrote back saying she would meet me at a restaurant near Ratna Park. "Four o'clock, the day after tomorrow."

Two days later at three-thirty, the streets were jammed with people leaving work and heading home. In a downpour I walked through the crowd and arrived at the restaurant fifteen minutes early, excited at the thought of seeing her. At last we could talk again about our future.

I found a table near the door, ordered a beer and waited. By five she had not appeared. I went outside and stood across the street in the steady rain, watching the entrance to the restaurant, scanning faces on the street. At seven I walked back to my hotel, both furious and frightened that I would never see her again.

I left letters daily at the post office. No reply. One afternoon I rented a Chinese bicycle and rode under threatening skies through Dilli Bazaar, looking, searching. Mud splashed up at me from the wet street. Strangers' faces haunted and mocked me. A quixotic gesture, but I had to do something. Riding back to the hotel, my mind and stomach were in turmoil from the internal fight between my pride and my passion. To think I had once worried about not misleading *her*, not falsely raising *her* hopes. What was she doing to *me* now?

I arrived wet, discouraged, frustrated. I flung open the door to the extra room I had rented to store all our expedition gear. Searching once again, digging through the mounds of rucksacks and *doko*s, pulling out tents, sleeping bags, extra socks. Smelly kerosene stoves rubbed soot on my hands, plastic bowls tumbled around my feet. I *knew* it was there, it had to be there somewhere. But I could not find it. I had lost Clara's good-luck charm.

In a rage of frustration, I hurled a cooking pot against the wall, then slumped into a chair. *Stop and think. About yourself instead of her.* Was this a fantasy I created? To live and work here in Kathmandu, was that a realistic thing for me to even think of doing? What about my education, all those years in graduate school, training for highly specialized research? Being a teacher was an honest occupation, a needed service, especially in Nepal, but couldn't I put my knowledge to better use elsewhere?

What about Clara and me? Could we really live together in Kathmandu, or anywhere? Was the cultural chasm too deep and wide to bridge? With the way she left me hanging, did she really love me? She could not—or would not—tell me why she couldn't see me. I wanted to believe it wasn't because she didn't care, but what signs had I had lately that she did? She asked for understanding, but how long did it take for understanding to turn to foolish hope? I suspected she saw me as her savior, a way out of an unhappy situation in her life. And I was willing, in part, to play that role—but would I be satisfied with that for very long? I didn't know. I could no longer sort fantasy from reality.

Finally, I knew that I had to get out of Kathmandu, try to develop some sensible perspective on the situation. Our cultures clashed with a violence that had shattered my equilibrium. Hers was infinitely patient, willing to wait for events to happen, for years, for lifetimes. Mine was impatient, and I could not wait.

I bought a plane ticket and wrote her a letter saying my father was ill, that I had to return home immediately. I felt foolish lying, but I couldn't put into words the uncertainties, frustrations and doubts that were tearing me apart.

And so I boarded the plane—the hardest thing I have ever done.

EPILOGUE

DARIEN, CONNECTICUT

Late September, 1984

I ARRIVED in New York after detours to Thailand, New Zealand, Hawaii and San Francisco. Around the world in just over a year. For two weeks in Darien I cut grass, painted and chopped wood around my parents' home, readjusting to life back in the U.S. But I was broke and needed a job.

So on a crisp fall morning in early October, I took the three-hour train ride to Philadelphia. From the Thirtieth Street Station I trekked a mile and a half through urban streets to the University of Pennsylvania campus. The ivy-covered entrance to the medical school seemed as impressive as I remembered it, the colonial portraits of the school's founders and the huge Thomas Eakins painting still lined the marbled halls.

On the second floor of the Anatomy-Chemistry building I paused for a few moments to go over the list of reasons why I should be rehired for my old job. Then I walked in, unannounced, to the office of Howard Holtzer, my graduate school mentor. My rehearsed lines proved unnecessary. Although only three months earlier he had written a glowing letter of recommendation for the teaching job in Kathmandu, I discovered he had also, on a hunch, kept a position open for

279

me in his lab. I signed a few forms and slipped behind my old desk, surrounded by the same labeled bottles of chemicals and solutions I had abandoned fourteen months before.

In West Philly, I found a dirty, roach-infested apartment, and tried to continue my work as though I had never left. I glided through the first few weeks, trying to believe I was happy and that in coming back I had done the right thing.

The pretense proved shortlived. It ended the day the first thick envelopes, taped together to hold all the pages, arrived from Darjeeling. Long, anguished letters from Clara, crying out her shock and sorrow at my leaving, telling of how she had been helpless in the face of events she could not control, pleading again for understanding, saying what she did not say while I waited futilely in Kathmandu.

Clara's letters cracked my veneer of calm and brought roiling to the surface memories of painful and emotional experiences that had fundamentally altered my outlook on life. Once again I sat dirty, half starved and dead-tired on a shepherd's roof, staring at the Kali Gandaki. Physically and mentally extended by my ordeal, emotions laid bare, I had found myself torn by questions about pain and suffering and death—things I had never contemplated during my comfortable, cocooned life, but that so dominated the Third World.

All the questions I had pondered on that April day came back as on a page of a long-ago-written diary. Though I soon came to realize that over the millenia others had grappled with these same questions, that made them no less real to me. How could there be so much poverty, disease and ignorance on the same planet with the upper-middle-class postcard towns such as the one in which I grew up? Why had no one—my teachers, my parents—told me that other worlds existed beyond New England stone walls and freshly mown grass? Perhaps they had tried but I hadn't been ready to hear it. Not with soccer games to play and proms to attend.

But now I spent long, sleepless nights haunted by visions of hollow-eyed children with bloated bellies, of ghostly wisps of smoke from burning *ghat*s. I passed, in a predictable progression, from immense sorrow to searing guilt.

I had assumed that by leaving Asia, by returning to my old and familiar surroundings, I could regain some equilibrium, some perspective. But my experiences in the Himalayas had altered the framework in which I lived my life. And back in Philadelphia, the people, the sprawling ghettos and gritty streets seemed more alien than the desolate peaks of Dolpo. My old values and aspirations lay in tatters; new ones had yet to emerge.

And even my closest friends, who lacked an experiential framework for understanding my point of view, sat stone-faced while I ranted anxiously about our distorted values, our selfish lives. It was as if I were speaking in tongues.

I needed to do something. I found the pace of my biomedical research work maddeningly slow and the results abstract. I longed to do something tangible, where results could be seen now rather than through some obscure ripple-down effect generations hence. I wanted to save the world, or at least work at it until I exhausted the guilt inside of me.

And I missed Clara. The frustrations of not being able to see her during those mysterious months in Kathmandu had begun to fade from my memory, replaced by guilt at having left her. How could I not have made a last bold attempt to see her just one more time? To talk with her, to ask her why. Should I have stayed? With her? This question troubled me most of all. I dwelt on it at length, and with despair. For finally I came to accept the truth that leaving Kathmandu had been the best thing for both of us. The cultural differences were, at least for me, insurmountable. My expectations of relationships between men and women, between husband and wife, between individual and society were too different from hers. In August in Kathmandu my emotions had swallowed my rational thoughts. Now I began to see that this relationship needed more than emotions to survive.

We drew some comfort from each other's letters, hers anguished, mine sorrowful. But with pen and paper, I could not adequately tell her what I felt.

I had to return. To see Clara once more and tell her how I felt. I needed to see Kathmandu again. To somehow reconcile with my life the immense guilt and sorrow I felt for the suffering I had witnessed. To find a reason for my medical research and to validate my choice of career. I also had to retrieve a part of me that had not come back with my body, a piece of my spirit without which I felt I could not go forward with my life.

On September 15, 1985, I arrived in Kathmandu. A group of friends, including J.B., who had taken a job a few months earlier as the

Nepalese judo coach, met me at the airport and drove me into town. It was great to see them all again.

The next afternoon I sat talking with Pema in his shop, surrounded by the dusty paraphernalia of trekking. With no warning, she appeared in the doorway. I jumped up to greet her and Clara's eyes smiled their welcome as her lips said hello to me.

Pema had rented the top room of an old Edwardian house on the edge of Kathmandu. For three weeks Clara and I met every afternoon in his apartment. We listened to music and talked. She explained how her spinster aunt had prevented her from coming to meet me that day at the restaurant, how desperate she had been to see me. Hearing this, feeling the depth of emotion in her words, I knew that the rift between us had simply been our inability to communicate during those summer months. I couldn't help but wonder, with some despair, how different our lives might have been had she kept that one rendezvous.

We also talked of little things. I told her of life in Philadelphia; she spoke of events of the last year, a protracted illness and how difficult it was to be an old maid at twenty-six.

One afternoon we sat on the balcony and watched dozens of brightly colored kites play tag over the lush green rice fields. The last of the monsoon clouds had wet the valley an hour earlier, and now the slanting rays of the sun set the emerald paddies aglow. We talked for a time about nothing in particular.

For more than two weeks we had carefully sidestepped the major issues between us. So happy were we to have even these few weeks together, we pretended that I was not going to board a plane soon and fly back to another world. I had come halfway around the world to tell her that I could not spend the rest of my life with her. That the cultural chasm was too deep. We had to talk, I needed to explain, to make her understand. I wanted to make it all right. I summoned my courage and turned to her.

"Clara, we need to talk about what is going to happen between us. You know that I . . ." She put her hand over my mouth to stop me.

"Please, Parker, I know what is in your mind. Please don't say anything. Let's just watch the kites. There are so many beautiful colors."

I held her hand and she leaned against my shoulder. It was another example of the gulf between us. For me, explanations were necessary, we had to talk it out, to make neat, wrapped ends. For Clara, her culture gave her the patience and wisdom to know that we cannot control our destiny, to accept what life gives.

I watched the kites through tears until the colors blended, red, yellow, green against the blue sky. Never before I had I felt such helplessness. Wanting desperately to take her away, to remake her life, but knowing that I could not. Within the week I would escape. But she would remain, born into the confines of her culture, someday to die within them.

My last night in Kathmandu we had a private party in K.C.'s restaurant. At nine o'clock, I found a cab and rode with Clara to her aunt's house. The taxi halted at the end of a rutted dirt road and I walked with her the fifty yards to the house. Stopping in front of the gate, we turned towards one another and fell into a final embrace.

"No, don't, Parker. Others may see." She unwrapped my arms from around her.

I started back towards the taxi. Knowing that I would never see her again, several times I stopped and turned to capture the memory of her brilliant white jacket shining in the beam of the taxi's headlights. At the taxi door I stopped and held up my hand. She raised hers for several seconds, then disappeared behind the gate.

Distraught, I returned to K.C.'s. My friends tried to buoy my spirits and kept me up all night, ending with a dawn rickshaw ride through the awakening streets of Kathmandu. At seven in the morning I stumbled to bed. My flight left at six that evening.

In the early afternoon, I woke and packed my belongings. Fighting a cold and nursing a hangover, I stumbled around my room, trying not to think of having to leave.

Suddenly she was there, climbing the stairs in a brilliant white dress, a red ribbon in her hair. She had never looked so beautiful. I had not expected to see her again and this extra time together was like a gift. Having accepted the sorrow of our parting, expressed all we could, given her way and mine, we were at last at peace. For two hours we talked and watched the clouds build over the Himalaya to the north.

When it was time to go, Pema performed the traditional Buddhist ceremony. He placed a white scarf around my neck, and dipping into the small bowl of *chang*, flicked droplets first one direction, then another. I downed three quick glasses of the milky *chang*. We piled into two taxis and headed for the airport.

We sat in the large, open visitors' pavilion set up across the road from the terminal entrance. For a while I talked with my friends, and then it was time to go. I moved down the line of chairs, saying my goodbyes to Pema, J.B., my Peace Corps friends, Bob and Sean. And last of all, to Clara.

I wanted to express all I felt for her, the joy she had given me. But now the final moment had come and I couldn't speak. I leaned down and kissed her on the cheek, then turned towards the terminal.

She stood, grasped my hand and walked with me across the road, right to the entrance.

I climbed the first two steps, then turned towards her. Our eyes met, she tilted her head and smiled. I tried to return her smile, but couldn't. We moved apart, her hand slid from my grasp, but I paused. For a moment we touched by just an outstretched fingertip.

I turned and left.

GLOSSARY

Note: Tibetan terms are indicated with a "T."

A

achar	chili sauce
alu	potatoes
aulo	malaria
ausadhi	medicine

B

baato	trail
baksheesh	tip, a gratuity given for service, or a bribe
beedies	small, cheap cigarettes that are hand-rolled from tobacco leaves with no paper
bhaat	rice that has been cooked as opposed to uncooked rice
bharal	blue sheep (pseudois nayaur), sheep-like in appearance but exhibiting the behavior of a goat; found north of the main Himalayan range
bideshi	foreigner
bistaari	slowly

285

Bodhissatva	an enlightened being, one who, on the verge of reaching Nirvana, chooses instead to be reincarnated and returns to the world to help all other sentient beings achieve enlightenment

C

chang	homemade beer, found throughout the Himalayas, it is made from whatever grain is available, rice, wheat, barley, millet
chapattis	unleavened flatbread made from flour and water and cooked on a flat metal pan or plate
chaulki	checkpost for checking trekking permits and to control outsiders
Chetri	a caste
chha	there is, it is
chhainna	negative, not, no, none
chillum	pipe
chitto	hurry
chorten (T)	Buddhist funerary monument, the same as the Sanscrit "stupa"; built with a square base and dome shaped upper portion, they are repositories of relics of *lamas* or other important personages; found on the approaches to villages and *gompas,* one should always pass on the left
chu (T)	water or river
chuba (T)	Tibetan overcoat; nomads wear chubas of sheepskin with the wool on the inside; country-dwellers have ones made of homespun, townsfolk from black machine-made cloth, the wealthy from silk; the sleeves are long, the garment loose-fitting with a sash around the waist, the extra room is used as storage for personal items; traditionally worn off the right shoulder to free the arm for work or warfare

D

daal	thick lentil soup, a staple in the Indian subcontinent, nutritious when combined with rice
dacoits	bandits
dahi	yogurt
daura	firewood, logs, branches or sticks
dhanyabaad	thank you, used to communicate sincere gratitude
dhauliya	protective spirit figures found in the area around Jumla; generally seen in pairs, a male and a female, they guard the fields, houses and especially bridges; believed to be holdovers from pre-Buddhist, pre-Hindu religious practices, they are generally carved from wood; because they are often unclothed and sexually explicit, they are frequently referred to as "pornographic" or "erotic."
dinos	give me
doko	funnel-shaped bamboo basket carried by a rope around the forehead called a tumpline
dorje (T)	lightening bolt, also a religious object symbolizing lightning
Drokpas (T)	nomads
dui	two
dzong (T)	fort, built on hillsides, usually with a commanding view of the approaches

E

ek	one

G

ganja	marijuana, grows wild in the hill country of the Himalayas

ghat	platform by the river used for washing and for cremating bodies
gompa (T)	Buddhist monastery, literally "high place," frequently built on top of or into the side of a mountain
Gurkha	caste, ethnic group known for being mercenary soldiers

H

himal	mountain or range of mountains
ho	there is, it is

J

jaanasakchha	possible
jaau	let's go (colloquial)
jane	go
jodhpurs	cotton trousers loose in the waist and hips, narrow around the ankles

K

kahaa	where
Khampa (T)	Tibetan from Kham, eastern Tibet, known as fierce warriors and nomadic traders
khola	stream or river; also the canyon formed by a river
korsani	chilies
kukri	traditional Nepalese knife, generally with a wide flat blade that is curved

L

la (T)	pass; in thanksgiving for going over a pass, Tibetans build *cairns* or *chortens* and string prayer

flags; travelers traditionally add a stone or prayer flag as they pass.

lama (T)	Buddhist monk
lekh	hill or mountain; long winding ridges under 20,000 ft. found across Nepal south of the main Himalayan peaks.
linos	take it

M

maanchhe	man
Magar	a caste
Manangi	villager from Manang, an isolated village behind the Annapurna range
manna	unit of measurement, about one pound
mate	high
momos (T)	potstickers, Tibetan raviolis, filled with meat or vegetables and boiled or steamed
musalai kaideo	"The mouse ate it!"

N

na	no, not, negative
nah (T)	blue sheep (see bharal)
namaskar	formal greeting to an important person
Namaste	greeting, literally "I greet the god within you"
Newari	ethnic caste from the Kathmandu Valley
Nirvana	a state beyond suffering, free from reincarnation

O

Om mani padme hum	Hail to the Jewel in the Lotus

P

paathis	a measure, about five pounds
pani	water
pradhan panch	mayor or village headman responsible to outside authorities and consulted by the villagers

R

rakshi	distilled spirits made throughout the Himalayas in homemade stills with whatever grain, vegetable or fruit is available
ramro	good
rotis	flatbread
rupee	unit of money, approximately Nepalese Rs17 to U.S.$1 in 1984

S

saddhu	Hindu holy man who has frequently taken vows of poverty and therefore begs for all his worldly possessions
sahib	sir, form of address used for all foreigners as well as high-ranking Nepalese
sakdaaina	not possible
Sherpa	Tibetan from the Khumbu region of Nepal, known for being Himalayan climbers, guides and high altitude porters
sirdar	guide, head of the trekking group, liaison with the locals, translator
sisnu	a dish made from cooked stinging nettles
stupa	funerary monument, see *chorten*
suchia (T)	Tibetan butter tea made by churning together hot tea, butter and salt or baking soda
suggotti	dried buffalo or yak meat

T

tarkaari	curried vegetables
Tamang	caste from eastern Nepal
tapaai	you are
terai	plains of the Indian subcontinent
Thakuri	a caste
thangka (T)	Buddhist religious painting
thugchen (T)	long brass horns with a deep, bass sound, blown on ceremonial occasions by Buddhist monks, frequently from the *gompa* roof
tin	three
tonga	two-wheeled horse-drawn carriage
topee	Nepalese brimless cloth hat
tsampa (T)	roasted barley flour, a staple for Tibetans, made into flat bread or mixed directly into butter tea
tulo	big

V

Vishnu	Hindu god, the Preserver

W

wallas	workman, e.g., the worker who peddles a bicycle rickshaw is a rickshaw walla

Y

yak (T)	member of the cow family adapted to high altitudes, cross-bred by the Tibetans with cows; the milk has a high butterfat content and is used for cheese, in making tea and for butter lamps

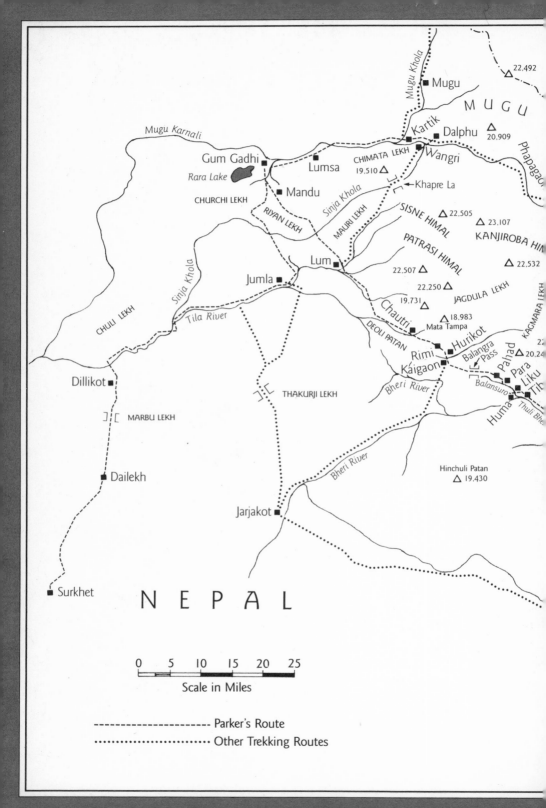

22,492

Mugu Khola

Mugu

MUGU

Mugu Karnali

Kartik Dalphu
20,909

Gum Gadhi

Rara Lake

Lumsa CHIMATA LEKH Wangri

Phapagaon

CHURCHI LEKH Mandu

19,510 ← Khapre La

RIYAN LEKH

MAURI LEKH

Sinja Khola

SISNE HIMAL 22,505 23,107

PATRASI HIMAL KANJIROBA HIM

Lum

22,507 22,532

Jumla

22,250

CHULI LEKH Sinja Khola

19,731 JAGDULA LEKH

Tila River

Chautri 18,983
Mata Tampa

DEOLI PATAN

KAGMARA LEKH

Rimi Hurikot Balangra Pahad
Kaigaon Pass 22
Para 20,24
Liku

THAKURJI LEKH

Bheri River Balansuro Tib

Dillikot

MARBU LEKH

Huma Thuli Bhe

Dailekh

Bheri River

Hinchuli Patan
19,430

Jarjakot

Surkhet N E P A L

0   5   10   15   20   25

Scale in Miles

- - - - - - - - - - - - Parker's Route

· · · · · · · · · · · · Other Trekking Routes